FOURTH EDITION

THE MACMILLAN READER

Judith Nadell

John Langan
Atlantic Community College

Linda McMeniman
Rowan College of New Jersey

Allyn and Bacon
Boston   London   Toronto   Sydney   Tokyo   Singapore

Editor: Eben W. Ludlow
Production Administrator: Marjorie Payne
Executive Marketing Manager: Lisa Kimball
Text and Cover Designer: Studio Nine
Composition/Prepress Buyer: Linda Cox
Manufacturing Buyer: Megan Cochran

Library of Congress Cataloging-in-Publication Data
Nadell, Judith
    The MacMillan reader / Judith Nadell, John Langan, Linda
McMeniman. — 4th ed.
    p. cm.
    Includes bibliographical references and index.
    ISBN 0-02-385890-7 (pbk)
    1. College readers. 2. English language—Rhetoric. I. Langan,
John, . II. McMeniman, Linda. III. Title.
PE1417.N33 195
808'.0427—dc20   95-10133
                                             CIP

PRINTED IN THE UNITED STATES OF AMERICA
10 9 8 7 6 5   00 99 98 97

ABOUT THE AUTHORS

Judith Nadell was until recently an Associate Professor of Communication at Rowan College of New Jersey. During her eighteen years at Rowan, she coordinated the introductory course in the Freshman Writing Sequence and served as Director of the Writing Lab. A Phi Beta Kappa graduate of Tufts University, she received a doctorate from Columbia University. She is the founder of the consulting firm Communication Training Associates and coauthor of *Doing Well in College* (McGraw-Hill) and *The Macmillan Writer.* The recipient of a New Jersey award for excellence in the teaching of writing, Judith Nadell lives with her coauthor husband, John Langan, near Philadelphia.

John Langan has taught reading and writing courses at Atlantic Community College near the New Jersey shore for the past twenty-three years. He earned advanced degrees in reading at Glassboro State College and in writing at Rutgers University. Coauthor of *The Macmillan Writer* and author of a series of college textbooks on both reading and writing, he has published widely with McGraw-Hill Book Company, Townsend Press, and Macmillan

Publishing Company. His books include *English Skills, Reading and Study Skills,* and *College Writing Skills.*

Linda McMeniman has been a member of the Communication Department at Rowan College of New Jersey for seventeen years. At Rowan, she teaches composition, public speaking, the research process, business writing, and semantics. She also has played a significant role in guiding the college's Freshman Writing Sequence. A Phi Beta Kappa graduate of New York University, she holds a Ph.D. from the University of Pennsylvania. Coauthor of *The Macmillan Writer,* she has also been a free-lance writer and an editorial consultant to several arts and corporate publications. Linda McMeniman lives in Pennsylvania with her husband and family.

CONTENTS

3   WRITING ON A WORD PROCESSOR   81

4   DESCRIPTION   89

Gordon Parks   FLAVIO'S HOME   104

Having battled poverty and prejudice himself, writer-photographer Gordon Parks visits a Brazilian slum and finds, among the wretched thousands forgotten by the outside world, a dying yet smiling boy.

Russell Baker   IN MY DAY   114

The author visits his elderly mother in the hospital and muses on the entwining of lives within a family.

Annie Dillard   IN THE JUNGLE   122

White egrets and piranhas, deer and tarantulas are all part of the eternal beauty of the Ecuadorian jungle.

5 NARRATION   149

7 DIVISION-CLASSIFICATION   271

If you have a neighborhood friend, an on-the-job friend, a child-hood friend, and a best friend, you'll enjoy Viorst's essay on degrees of intimacy.

According to Zinsser, many students concentrate almost exclu-sively on the practical—and miss some of the most important parts of college life.

Worker or warrior: these were the two roles open to men during the author's childhood. Men killed themselves laboring with their bodies or they died on the battlefield preparing to kill others.

Propaganda is not just a tool of totalitarian states. American advertisers also use propaganda to get us to buy their products.

In our feverish attempts to save time, could we be missing the point of living?

8 PROCESS ANALYSIS   333

9 COMPARISON-CONTRAST   395

11   DEFINITION   509

12 ARGUMENTATION-PERSUASION   557

Pro-Con Pair: Legalizing Drugs

13   FOR FURTHER READING   685

14   A CONCISE GUIDE TO DOCUMENTATION   721

Glossary   731

Index   753

THEMATIC CONTENTS

COMMUNICATION AND LANGUAGE

EDUCATION AND WORK

ETHICS AND MORALITY

FAMILY AND CHILDREN

GOVERNMENT AND LAW

HEALTH AND MEDICINE

HUMAN GROUPS AND SOCIETY

HUMOR AND SATIRE

MEANING IN LIFE

MEMORIES AND AUTOBIOGRAPHY

MEN AND WOMEN

NATURE AND SCIENCE

PREFACE

Our bookshelves, and perhaps yours, sag under the weight of all the readers published over the years. Semester after semester, we used to switch texts until we finally realized that we wanted more than was offered. For one thing, we found that many of the readers contained an all-too-predictable blend of selections, with the same pieces cropping up from one book to the next. We also discovered that the books provided students with little guidance on ways to read, think, and write about the selections. And so, when we first began working on *The Macmillan Reader*, we aimed for a different kind of text—one that would offer fresh examples of professional prose, one that would take a more active role in helping students become stronger readers, thinkers, and writers.

As in the first three editions, our primary goal in the fourth edition has been to enliven the mix of selections commonly appearing in readers. Although *The Macmillan Reader* includes widely read and classic essays, a number of our selections have not yet appeared in other anthologies. Among these are Susan Jacoby's

"Common Decency," Gordon Parks's "Flavio's Home," Art Carey's "Things Fall Apart," Caroline Rego's "The Fine Art of Complaining," and Janet Mendell Goldstein's "The Quick Fix Society." We've been careful to choose selections that range widely in subject matter and approach, from the humorous to the informative, from personal meditation to polemic. We've also made sure that each selection captures students' interest and clearly illustrates a specific pattern of development or combination of patterns.

Our second concern has remained the quality of instruction in the book. As before, our objective has been to help students bridge the gap between the product and process approaches to reading and writing. Throughout, we describe possible sequences and structures but emphasize that such steps and formats are not meant to be viewed as rigid prescriptions; rather, they are strategies for helping students discover what works best in a particular situation. Buoyed by compliments about the previous editions' teachability, we haven't tinkered with the book's underlying format. Such a structure, we've been told, does indeed help students read more critically, think more logically, and write more skillfully. Although a new chapter (Chapter 3, "Writing on a Word Processor") has been added, the book's basic format remains the same:

- **Chapter 1, "The Reading Process,"** is designed to reflect current theories about the interaction of reading, thinking, and writing. The chapter provides guided practice in a three-part process for reading with close attention and a high level of interpretive skill. This step-by-step process sharpens students' understanding of the book's selections and promotes the rigorous thinking needed to write effective essays. An activity at the end of the chapter gives students a chance to use the three-step process. First, they read an essay by journalist Phyllis Theroux. The essay has been annotated both to show students the reading process in action and to illustrate how close critical reading can pave the way to promising writing topics. Then they respond to sample questions and writing assignments, all similar to those accompanying each of the book's selections. The chapter thus does more than just tell students how to sharpen their reading abilities; it guides them through a clearly sequenced plan for developing critical reading skills.

- **Chapter 2, "The Writing Process,"** introduces students to essay writing. To make the composing process easier for students to grasp, we provide a separate section for each of the following stages: prewriting, identifying a thesis, supporting the thesis with evidence, organizing the evidence, writing the first draft, and revising. From the start, we point out that the stages are fluid. Indeed, the case history of an evolving student paper illustrates just how recursive and individualized the writing process can be. Guided activities at the end of each section give students practice taking their essays through successive stages in the composing process.

    To illustrate the link between reading and writing, the writing chapter presents the progressive stages of a student paper written in response to Phyllis Theroux's "The Worry Factor," the selection presented in Chapter 1. Commentary following the student paper highlights the essay's strengths and points out spots that could use additional work. In short, by the end of the second chapter, the entire reading-writing process has been illustrated, from reading a selection to writing about it.

- **Chapter 3, "Writing on a Word Processor,"** new to this edition, shows students how to use a computer during each phase of the composing sequence.

- **Chapters 4–12** of *The Macmillan Reader* contain selections grouped according to **nine patterns of development:** description, narration, exemplification, division-classification, process analysis, comparison-contrast, cause-effect, definition, and argumentation-persuasion. The sequence progresses from the more personal and expressive patterns to the more public and analytic. However, because each chapter is self-contained, the patterns may be covered in any order. Instructors preferring a thematic approach will find the Thematic Contents list helpful.

    The Macmillan Reader treats the patterns separately because such an approach helps students grasp the distinctive characteristics of each pattern. At the same time, the book continually shows the way writers usually combine patterns in their work. We also encourage students to view the patterns as strategies for generating and organizing ideas. Writers, we explain, rarely set out to compose an essay in a specific pattern. Rather, they choose a pattern or combination of patterns because it suits their purpose, audience, and subject.

Each of the nine pattern-of-development chapters follows this format:

1. **A detailed explanation of the pattern** begins the chapter. The explanation includes (a) a definition of the pattern, (b) a description of the way the pattern helps a writer accommodate his or her purpose and audience, and (c) step-by-step guidelines for using the pattern.
2. Next, we present **an annotated student essay** using the pattern. Written in response to one of the professional selections in the chapter, each essay illustrates the characteristic features of the pattern discussed in the chapter.
3. **Commentary** after each student essay points out the blend of patterns in the piece, identifies the paper's strengths, and locates areas needing improvement. "First draft" and "revised" versions of one section of the essay reveal how the student writer went about revising, thus illustrating the relationship between the final draft and the steps taken to produce it.
4. The **professional selections** in the pattern-of-development chapters are accompanied by these items:
   - *A biographical note and preview* give students a perspective on the author and create interest in the piece.
   - *Questions for Close Reading* help students dig into and interpret the selection. The first question asks them to identify the selection's thesis; the last provides work on vocabulary development.
   - *Questions About the Writer's Craft* deal with such matters as purpose, audience, tone, organization, sentence structure, diction, and figures of speech. The first question in the series (labeled "The Pattern") focuses on the distinctive features of the pattern used in the selection. And often there's another question (labeled "Other Patterns") that asks students to analyze the writer's use of additional patterns in the piece.
   - *Questions for Further Thought* inspire lively classroom discussion and help students refine their thoughts before beginning to write.

- *Writing Assignments,* four in all, follow each selection. Packed with suggestions on how to proceed, the assignments use the selection as a springboard. The first two assignments ask students to write an essay using the same pattern as the one in the selection; the last two encourage students to discover for themselves which combination of patterns would be most appropriate for an essay. Frequently, the assignments are preceded by the symbol ∞, indicating a cross-reference to at least one other professional selection in the book. By encouraging students to make connections among readings, such assignments broaden students' perspective and give them additional material to draw on when they write. These "paired assignments" will be especially welcome to instructors stressing recurring ideas and themes.

5. At the end of each pattern-of-development chapter are two sets of **Additional Writing Assignments:** "General Assignments" and "Assignments With a Specific Purpose and Audience." The first set provides open-ended topics that prompt students to discover the best way to use a specific pattern; the second set develops their sensitivity to rhetorical context by asking them to apply the pattern in a real-world situation.

- **Chapter 13, "For Further Reading,"** offers two essays each by three very different prose stylists. Annotations on one of the selections show how writers often blend patterns of development in their work. The chapter also provides guidelines to help students analyze this fusing of patterns.
- **Chapter 14, "A Concise Guide to Documentation,"** explains how to use and document outside sources in a paper.

The Macmillan Reader also includes a glossary that lists all the key terms presented in the text. In addition, a comprehensive *Instructor's Manual* contains the following: in-depth answers to the "Questions for Close Reading" and "Questions About the Writer's Craft"; suggested activities; pointers about using the book; a detailed syllabus; a list of the book's "paired" writing assignments; and an analysis of the blend of patterns in the selections in the "For Further Reading" chapter.

WHAT'S NEW IN THE FOURTH EDITION

In preparing the fourth edition of *The Macmillan Reader,* we looked closely at scores of questionnaires completed by instructors using the book. Their comments helped us identify additional directions the book might take. Here, then, are the most important new features of this edition of *The Macmillan Reader:*

- *Roughly one-fifth of the selections are new.* Many of these new readings were suggested by instructors across the country; others were chosen after a lengthy search through magazines, nonfiction collections, newspapers, autobiographies, and the like. Whether written by a well-known figure like Martin Luther King, Jr. ("The World House"), or a relative newcomer like Caroline Rego ("The Fine Art of Complaining"), the new selections are bound to stimulate strong writing on a variety of topics—altruism, prejudice, gender identity, family life, ethnic roots, and animal rights, to name just a few. When selecting new readings, we took special care to include several *longer, more sustained pieces,* written from the *third-person point of view.*
- *There are many more guided composition activities in Chapter 2, "The Writing Process."* These exercises take students through each successive step in the composing process and get them working on paragraphs and first drafts right away.
- *New textual explanations help students follow with greater ease the development of an evolving student paper.* Students come to appreciate more fully how a paper is continually reshaped as it moves through the composing process.
- *Chapter 2, "The Writing Process," and Chapter 6, "Exemplification," illustrate additional strategies for making paragraphs specific and coherent.*
- *Chapter 3, "Writing on a Word Processor," is new to this edition.* It includes concise, practical suggestions for using a computer in each step of the composing sequence.

- *An increased number of paired assignments (indicated by the symbol ∞) are included.* These broaden students' outlook by encouraging them to examine recurrent themes in the book's selections.
- *The value of collaborative learning is underscored.* Besides calling for peer review, many assignments ask students to brainstorm with classmates, question friends, speak with family members, or interview "experts" on an issue. Such assignments prompt students to investigate various sides of an issue and to check the soundness of their opinions.
- *Chapter 12, "Argumentation-Persuasion," already more comprehensive than any other reader's, now includes helpful coverage of Rogerian argument and Toulmin logic, along with full discussions of logic, audience analysis, refutation, bias, and objectivity.*
- *Explicit emphasis is placed on the way writers blend patterns and use them as strategies to generate and organize material.* An expanded Chapter 13, "For Further Reading," now features a professional selection, accompanied by annotations and comments, to show how a writer draws upon several patterns to achieve a specific rhetorical purpose. This new material reinforces earlier explanations, examples, questions, and assignments showing how writers often use a combination of patterns to develop and structure their essays.

ACKNOWLEDGMENTS

At Allyn and Bacon, our thanks go to Eben Ludlow for his perceptive editorial guidance and continued enthusiasm for *The Macmillan Reader*. We're also indebted to Linda Stern for her scrupulous copyediting and to Pat Smythe for giving the book such a clear, crisp design. And Marjorie Payne deserves our thanks for her skillful handling of the never-ending complexities of the production process.

Over the years, many writing instructors have reviewed *The Macmillan Reader* and responded to detailed questionnaires about its selections and pedagogy. Their comments have guided our work every step of the way. To the following reviewers we are indeed grateful: Donald W. Adams, Chipola Junior College; James C. Addison, Jr., Western Carolina University; Rebecca L. Allen, Louisburg College; Ken Anania, Massasoit Community College; Chris Anson,

University of Minnesota; Bruce J. Ardinger, Columbus State Community College; Constantina Rhodes Bailly, Hillsborough Community College; A. M. Belmont, Southern Arkansas University; Wilson C. Boynton, Holyoke Community College; John S. Capps, Virginia Western Community College; Barbara Carr, Stephen F. Austin State University; Bruce Coad, Mountain View College; David Cole, Quinnipiac College; Howard J. Coughlin, Jr., Eastern Connecticut University; Michael Cross, Tulsa Junior College; F. Marino D'Amato, Manchester Community College; Betty Keating Dietz, Ohlone College; Benjamin B. Edwards, Tulsa Junior College; Mary Faraci, Florida Atlantic University; Benjamin Fiester, Wilkes College; Raymond W. Foster, Scottsdale Community College; Sister Pauline Fox, Mt. Mercy College; Margaret Franson, Valparaiso University; Lois Friesen, Butler County Community College; Loris D. Galford, McNeese State University; Anita Gandolfo, West Virginia University; Michael G. Gessner, Central Arizona College; Patricia Graves, Georgia State University; Gary Griswold, California State University, Long Beach; Mary M. Hatcher, Burlington County College; Betty Boyd Heard, Averett College; Patricia Hummel, Albright College; Ginger A. Hurajt, Northern Essex Community College; Eleanor D. James, Montgomery County Community College; Wanda L. Jared, Tennessee Technological University; Shakuntala Jayswal, University of New Haven; Kellie Jones, University of Tennessee at Martin; Sue V. Lape, Columbus State Community College; Stephen Larson, Wake Technical Community College; Robert Lesman, Northern Virginia Community College; Barry Maid, University of Arkansas at Little Rock; Paul Marx, University of New Haven; Catherine Mau, Leeward Community College; Brian McRea, University of Florida; Elizabeth Metzger, University of South Florida; Teresa Miller, Rogers State University; Kathy Mincey, Morehead State University; R. H. Moody, Madison Area Tech College; Steve Odden, University of Wisconsin at Stevens Point; Michael G. O'Hara, Muscatine Community College; M. Cathleen Raymond, Florida Atlantic University; Marcia Bundy Seabury, University of Hartford; Marie Secor, Pennsylvania State University; Carl Singleton, Fort Hays State University; Carolyn Smith, University of Florida; Eric R. Smith, SUNY College at Cortland; James Gregory Smith, Lamar University; Margo Smith, Rogers State College; Cynthia Somin, Long Beach City College;

Charles Staats, Broward Community College–North; Judith Stanford, Merrimack College; Jacqueline Stark, Los Angeles Valley College; Virginia Stein, Community College of Allegheny County; George Stoll, Broward Community College–North; Ralph Sturm, Edinboro University of Pennsylvania; John W. Taylor, South Dakota State University; Robert Thompson, Macomb County Community College; Vivian Tortorici, Hudson Valley Community College; Larry K. Uffelman, Mansfield University; Cyrilla M. Vessey, Northern Virginia Community College; Anna Villegas, San Joaquin Delta College; Cheryl L. Ware, McNeese State University; Samuel W. Whyte, Montgomery County Community College; David Wickham, Mountain View College; Dorena Allen Wright, Loyola Marymount University; and Wei-hsiung Kitty Wu, Bowie State University.

We also thank these respondents to a questionnaire on the third edition: Constantina Bailly, Hillsborough Community College; Mary Beth Bamforth, Wake Technical Community College; B. G. Bardin, Rogers State College; Viralene J. Coleman, U. of Arkansas, Pine Bluff; Charles R. Croghan, Jr., Indian River Community College; Benjamin B. Edwards, Tulsa Junior College; Raymond Foster, Scottsdale Community College; Casey Gilson, Broward Community College-North; Chrysanthy M. Grieco, Seton Hall University; Angela Hilterbrand, Ashland Community College; Jean Hodgin, North Shore Community College; Eleanor James, Montgomery County Community College; Paul Marx, University of New Haven; Joseph F. McCadden, Burlington County College; Mary Ann McCandless, Butler County Community College; Thomas B. O'Grady, U. of Massachusetts, Boston; Barbara J. Porter, Canisius College; John Rogers, Vincennes University; Susan Schmeling, Vincennes University; Suzanne St. Laurent, Broward Community College; George Stoll, Broward Community College-North; John W. Taylor, South Dakota State University; Merle Thompson, North Virginia Community College; Cheryl L. Ware, McNeese State University; and Mildred J. White, Ohlone College.

For help in preparing the fourth edition of *The Macmillan Reader*, we owe thanks to the insightful comments of these reviewers: Raymond Foster, Scottsdale Community College; Casey Gilson, Broward Community College-North; Michael Gress, Vincennes University; Eleanor James, Montgomery County Community College; Paul Marx, University of New Haven; Joseph McCadden, Burlington County College; Susan Schmeling, Vincennes University; and George Stoll, Broward Community College-North.

Our work on this edition was influenced too by the many students who took advantage of the questionnaire at the back of the third edition to tell us which selections they preferred.

Special thanks go to Dorothy Carroll in our at-home office. For nearly fifteen years, we've come to depend increasingly on her friendship as well as on her research skills, word-processing abilities, and organizational talents. Finally, we're thankful to our students. Their reaction to various drafts of material sharpened our thinking and helped focus our work. And we are especially indebted to the ten students whose essays are included in the book. Their thoughtful, carefully revised papers dramatize the potential of student writing and the power of the composing process.

Judith Nadell
John Langan
Linda McMeniman

1

THE READING PROCESS

More than two hundred years ago, essayist Joseph Addison commented, "Of all the diversions of life, there is none so proper to fill up its empty spaces as the reading of useful and entertaining authors." Addison might have added that reading also challenges our beliefs, deepens our awareness, and stimulates our imagination.

Why, then, don't more people delight in reading? After all, most children feel great pleasure and pride when they first learn to read. As children grow older, though, the initially magical world of books is more and more associated with homework, tests, and grades. Reading turns into an anxiety-producing chore. Also, as demands on a person's time accumulate throughout adolescence and adulthood, reading often gets pushed aside in favor of something that takes less effort. It's easier simply to switch on the television and passively view the ready-made images that flash across the screen. In contrast, it's almost impossible to remain passive while reading. Even a slick best-seller requires that the reader decode, visualize, and interpret what's on the page. The more challenging the material, the more actively involved the reader must be.

1

The essays we selected for this book call for active reading. Representing a broad mix of styles and subjects, the essays range from the classic to the contemporary. They contain language that will move you, images that will enlarge your understanding of other people, ideas that will transform your views on complex issues.

The selections serve other purposes as well. For one thing, they'll help you develop a repertoire of reading skills—abilities that will benefit you throughout life. Second, as you become a better reader, your own writing style will become more insightful and polished. Increasingly, you'll be able to draw on the ideas presented in the selections and employ the techniques that professional writers use to express such ideas. As novelist Saul Bellow has observed, "A writer is a reader moved to emulation."

In the pages ahead, we outline a three-stage approach for getting the most out of this book's selections. Our suggestions will enhance your understanding of the book's essays, as well as help you read other material with greater ease and assurance.

STAGE 1: GET AN OVERVIEW OF THE SELECTION

Ideally, you should get settled in a quiet place that encourages concentration. If you can focus your attention while sprawled on a bed or curled up in a chair, that's fine. But if you find that being very comfortable is more conducive to daydreaming and dozing off than it is to studying, avoid getting too relaxed.

Once you're settled, it's time to read the selection. To ensure a good first reading, try the following hints:

- Get an overview of the essay and its author. Start by reading the biographical note and preview that precede the selection. By providing background information about the author, the biographical note helps you evaluate the writer's credibility as well as his or her slant on the subject. For example, if you know that George Gallup, Jr., is president of a well-known research firm that measures public opinion, you can better assess whether he is a credible source for the analysis he presents in his essay "The Faltering Family" (page 467). The preview introduces you to the essay's subject and often raises questions to consider as you read.

- Consider the selection's title. A good title often expresses the essay's main idea, giving you insight into the selection even before you read it. For example, the title of Marie Winn's essay, "TV Addiction" (page 541), suggests that the piece will focus on television's negative effects. A title may also hint at a selection's tone. Paul Roberts's "How to Say Nothing in 500 Words" (page 369) points to an essay that's light in spirit, whereas George Orwell's "Shooting an Elephant" (page 172) suggests a piece with a serious mood.
- Read the selection straight through purely for pleasure. Allow yourself to be drawn into the world the author has created. Just as you first see a painting from the doorway of a room and form an overall impression without perceiving the details, you can have a preliminary, subjective feeling about a reading selection. Moreover, because you bring your own experiences and viewpoints to the piece, your reading will be unique. As Ralph Waldo Emerson said, "Take the book, my friend, and read your eyes out; you will never find there what I find."
- After this initial reading of the selection, focus your first impressions by asking yourself whether you like the selection. In your own words, briefly describe the piece and your reaction to it.

STAGE 2: DEEPEN YOUR SENSE OF THE SELECTION

At this point, you're ready to move further into the selection. A second reading will help you identify the specific features that triggered your initial reaction. Here are some suggestions on how to proceed:

- Mark off the selection's main idea, or thesis, often found near the beginning or end. If the thesis isn't stated explicitly, write down your own version of the selection's main idea.
- Locate the main supporting evidence used to develop the thesis. You may even want to number in the margin each key supporting point.
- Take a minute to write "Yes" or "No" beside points with which you strongly agree or disagree. Your reaction to these points often explains your feelings about the aptness of the selection's ideas.

- Return to any unclear passages you encountered during the first reading. The feeling you now have for the piece as a whole will probably help you make sense of initially confusing spots. However, this second reading may also reveal that, in places, the writer's thinking isn't as clear as it could be.
- Use your dictionary to check the meanings of any unfamiliar words.
- Ask yourself if your initial impression of the selection has changed in any way as a result of this second reading. If your feelings *have* changed, try to determine why you reacted differently on this reading.

STAGE 3: EVALUATE THE SELECTION

Now that you have a good grasp of the selection, you may want to read it a third time, especially if the piece is long or complex. This time, your goal is to make judgments about the essay's effectiveness. Keep in mind, though, that you shouldn't evaluate the selection until after you have a strong hold on it. A negative, even a positive reaction is valid only if it's based on an accurate reading.

At first, you may feel uncomfortable about evaluating the work of a professional writer. But remember: Written material set in type only *seems* perfect; all writing can be fine-tuned. By identifying what does and doesn't work in others' writing, you're taking an important first step toward developing your own power as a writer. You might find it helpful at this point to get together with other students to discuss the selection. Comparing viewpoints often opens up a piece, enabling you to gain a clearer perspective on the selection and the author's approach.

To evaluate the essay, ask yourself the following questions:

1. *Where does support for the selection's thesis seem logical and sufficient? Where does support seem weak?* Which of the author's supporting facts, arguments, and examples seem pertinent and convincing? Which don't?
2. *Is the selection unified? If not, why not?* Where does something in the selection not seem relevant? Where are there any unnecessary digressions or detours?
3. *How does the writer make the selection move smoothly from beginning to end?* How does the writer create an easy flow

between ideas? Are any parts of the essay abrupt and jarring? Which ones?

4. *Which stylistic devices are used to good effect in the selection?* Which pattern of development or combination of patterns does the writer use to develop the piece? Why do you think those patterns were selected? How do paragraph development, sentence structure, and word choice contribute to the piece's overall effect? What tone does the writer adopt? Where does the writer use figures of speech effectively? (The next chapter and the glossary explain these terms.)

5. *How does the selection encourage further thought?* What new perspective on an issue does the writer provide? What ideas has the selection prompted you to explore in an essay of your own?

It takes some work to follow the three-step approach just described, but the selections in *The Macmillan Reader* are worth the effort. Bear in mind that none of the selections sprang full-blown from the pen of its author. Rather, each essay is the result of hours of work—hours of thinking, writing, rethinking, and revising. As a reader, you should show the same willingness to work with the selections, to read them carefully and thoughtfully. Henry David Thoreau, an avid reader and prolific writer, emphasized the importance of this kind of attentive reading when he advised that "books must be read as deliberately and unreservedly as they were written."

To illustrate the multi-stage reading process just described, we've annotated the professional essay that follows: "The Worry Factor" by Phyllis Theroux. Note that annotations are provided in the margin of the essay as well as at the end of the essay. As you read Theroux's essay, try applying the three-stage sequence. You can measure your ability to dig into the selection by making your own annotations on Theroux's essay and then comparing them to ours. You can also see how well you evaluated the piece by answering the preceding five questions and then comparing your responses to ours on pages **9–11**.

Phyllis Theroux

A frequent contributor to the *Washington Post, McCall's,* and *Reader's Digest,* Phyllis Theroux (1939–   ) won special recognition for a series of pieces she wrote for the *New York Times'* "Hers" column. Theroux's essays, often about the complex relationship between child and parent, combine wry humor with keen insight. Theroux has collected her work in three books: *California and Other States of Grace: A Memoir* (1980), *Peripheral Visions* (1982), and *Night Lights* (1987), from which the following selection is taken.

The Worry Factor

Worrying kills joy and saps energy. Yet the tendency to obsess about real and imagined problems is something most of us cling to—almost as though it were a precious, life-affirming right. As Phyllis Theroux points out in the following essay, rarely is the destructive nature of worrying more apparent than when the worrier is a much-loved child.

Marginal annotations

Relevant?

Drops this idea.

Means "ineffective"

Awkward transition (like "And" in ¶1)

Theroux also a worrier

It is commonly acknowledged that the organ   1
that gives us the most pain in life is our brain—or
somebody else's in close proximity. And, according
to the "EST" training[1] I have so far managed to
avoid, a great many heads are badly "wired" and
can electrocute us with worries that the human being is not rubberized to withstand.

Why we like to worry is another question, as is the   2
difference between feckless and fertile worrying, which
can produce ulcers or symphonies. But once, while
moving half-witted with worry around the kitchen, I
stopped, mentally pushed everything that I couldn't
do anything about at that moment out of my head,
and then, regrounded, looked around to see who was
sharing that moment with me. My eyes fell upon my
eleven-year-old daughter. Her eyes were full of tears.

[1]A self-help program, especially popular during the 1970s.

Narrative to support thesis starts here.

Smoother transitions

Paragraph gives examples of the daughter's worries.

Sounds like a child talking; essay has chatty tone.

Figure of speech shows that Theroux realizes her efforts are probably futile. (See ¶s 8, 10, 11.)

Advice doesn't help.

Touching image Like "Red Cross worker" in ¶5

3 She needed to talk. We went into the living room and sat down. She felt terrible, she said. It became clear, as she explained herself, that she had a lot of worries on her mind.

4 For one thing, she was not very pretty. For another, she was not very smart. She was not rich, didn't have clothes as nice as everyone else's, her brother was oftentimes mean to her, and her best friend, to quote her exactly, "totally hates my guts."

5 There were other deprivations, deeper and therefore deserving of a curtain of privacy that I will now draw across the rods. But it was a fairly devastating list of liabilities, many of them not of her own making, and I let her spread them all out in their full horror without jumping in like some kind of Red Cross worker to tell her that her worries were only in her mind. Of course, that's where they were!

6 Without necessarily agreeing with her on every point, I talked about people who had more than she did, and people who had less. Some rich girls are ugly. Some pretty girls are poor. I felt compelled to add that, inexplicably, some rich girls are also pretty, which is a mystery and nothing we can truly understand. But it seemed to me, I said, that one could look at the world in a couple of ways: as an imperfect place that makes us miserable or as a place that is imperfect and gives us something positive to do.

7 "You know," I explained, "like when you see a little boy crying in the playground. You can either say, 'How awful, he is so sad,' or go up and ask him what's the matter and try to fix it up."

8 My daughter of the heart-shaped face didn't quite understand this friendly-carpenter approach to existence. In her mind, at that moment, she was the kid crying on the playground and her chief worry was who (or Who) would *fix her up*.

"I used to ask God to please, please give me a   9
nice day. But it never worked, so I stopped asking."

Feels daughter's   "Maybe," I suggested (telling my heart to stop   10
pain   twitching), "you could turn the question around
and ask God to please let you give the day something nice."

Again, advice   Maybe yes, but maybe no. Maybe I hadn't   11
doesn't work.   heard her the first time when she listed her prob-

"As" shows time   lems, and as we walked upstairs to her bedroom she
passing.   repeated them for me again. As I watched her climb
into bed I observed, "You know, if all you were
were your worries, you wouldn't even exist. You'd
be a minus."

Hiding under the quilt that all too soon she   12
would be forced to throw off the next morning, my
daughter tried to understand this.

Part of implied   "You can wreck the day you're still in," I con-   13
thesis   tinued, "worrying about the day that hasn't even
arrived."

What many   "But you *have* to worry!" she exclaimed, and   14
people think!   the look on her face poking over the quilt was in-
credulous that someone my age did not know that
this was one of the first facts and obligations of life.

Part of implied   "You do?" I answered. "But doesn't worry-   15
thesis   ing just make you more tense by the time tomorrow
finally comes?"

A small but hopeful expression flickered across   16
her features. Perhaps, she conceded, there was
something to this line of thinking. She smiled, nodded her head and yawned.

"Why don't you take all your worries," I said,   17
bending down to kiss her goodnight, "and shove
them right out the window where they belong."

Then, in a final bit of dialogue that reminded   18
me that two heads in close proximity can produce
something a great deal more significant than pain,

Dialogue here   she changed the subject.
and earlier
conveys mother-   "This doesn't have anything to do with what   19
daughter   we're talking about," she said, "but why is it that
relationship.   when I cry my nose gets stuffy?"

"I don't know," I answered. "Maybe there are   20
just too many tears to fit in your eyes."

"My tears are salty."   21

"That's because you have salt in your body."   22

"Mom," she asked, "can you taste my fore-   23
head and tell me if it's salty?"

I gave it a taste and said, "No, actually it isn't."   24

Surrise end-   "Oh, good!" she exclaimed, her face break-   25
ing—the girl has   ing into a wide, relieved smile. "That means I don't
been worrying   have cystic fibrosis."
about this, too.

Annotations at End of Selection

Thesis (implied): We know that worrying is a waste of time, but that doesn't
keep us from worrying.

First reading: Humorous and fun to read but also touching. Easy to relate to.
Nicely captures what worry warts we can be.

Second and third readings:
1. Uses narration and examples of the daughter's worries to show the negative
   effect of worrying (thesis).
2. Not everything works (awkward transitions and reference to EST), but
   overall the essay succeeds.
3. Unexpected ending holds up even after additional readings. Shows how
   endless and groundless our worries can be. Creates sympathy for the young
   girl but also pokes gentle fun at her.
4. Possible essay topics: A humorous paper on how to avoid worrying about
   something (school, social life) or a serious paper on the positive aspects of
   worrying (it encourages action, we can anticipate and avoid problems, and
   so on).

The following answers to the questions on pages 4–5 will help
crystallize your reactions to Theroux's essay.

1. *Where does support for the selection's thesis seem logical and sufficient?
   Where does support seem weak?*

   The most explicit statement of Theroux's thesis lies in her comments to her daughter: "You can wreck the day you're still in worrying
   about the day that hasn't even arrived" (paragraph 13), and "But
   doesn't worrying just make you more tense by the time tomorrow
   finally comes?" (paragraph 15). But these two remarks aren't the most
   complete statement of Theroux's main idea: They don't mention the

essay's central paradox—that although Theroux tries to allay her daughter's anxieties, she herself is also a worrier. Stating the thesis in your own words may be best: Worrying is a painful waste of energy, yet knowing this does not necessarily help us resist it.

Theroux dramatizes her thesis with a single, strong example—a conversation in which she attempts to allay her daughter's numerous worries. The author provides several examples of what a parent might say to reduce a child's anxiety. Although these reassurances don't entirely console her daughter, they do offer some relief.

2. *Is the selection unified? If not, why not?*

The introductory paragraph contains a somewhat distracting reference to "EST" training, and the second paragraph raises an issue—"Why we like to worry"—that is then dropped. From the end of the second paragraph on, however, the essay focuses tightly on a single conversation between Theroux and her daughter. While some of Theroux's suggestions fail to help her daughter (for example, the suggestion in paragraph 10 that her daughter do something positive), these unsuccessful efforts belong in the essay because they illustrate how hard it is to make someone else's worries go away. The concluding bit of conversation turns out to be anything but a change of subject: It reveals that the daughter has been worrying about cystic fibrosis, as well as about her looks, her clothes, her popularity, and almost everything else.

3. *How does the writer make the selection move smoothly from beginning to end?*

Theroux's first two paragraphs aren't as smooth as one might like. The second sentence begins with the word "And" even though the point Theroux makes in the sentence isn't a continuation of the first sentence. Similarly, in the second paragraph, the phrase "But once" that she uses to lead into the conversation doesn't contrast (as the "But" implies) with the idea expressed in the preceding paragraph. From this point on, however, Theroux writes sharply focused paragraphs and provides clear signals that guide the reader through the conversation with her daughter. For example, she signals her daughter's worries using "For one thing" and "For another" (paragraph 4). She also supplies cues indicating the passage of time: "*as* we walked," "*As* I watched" (paragraph 11), and "*Then*" (paragraph 18).

4. *Which stylistic devices are used to good effect in the selection?*

Theroux uses several patterns of development in her essay. The selection as a whole shows the *effect* of useless worry; paragraphs 2 and 7–25 are developed through *narration;* paragraphs 4, 6, and 7 use *examples. Short dramatic sentences* highlight her daughter's strong emotions ("She needed to talk") and punctuate Theroux's own ideas ("Some rich girls are ugly," "Some pretty girls are poor"). The first-person point of view contributes to Theroux's *informal tone* ("I talked about," "I explained," "I felt compelled"). Lively dialogue, including colloquial language ("totally hates my guts," "You'd be a minus"), as well as a fragment ("Maybe yes, but maybe no") add to the essay's conversational feeling. *Figurative language* in paragraphs 1 ("a great many heads are badly 'wired'"), 5 ("some kind of Red Cross worker"), and 8 ("friendly-carpenter approach to existence") further enliven the essay. Finally, although Theroux is concerned about the corrosive effect of worrying, she leavens her essay with dashes of humor. Certainly, her decision to include the final bit of conversation ("That means I don't have cystic fibrosis") shows how laughable our self-imposed anxieties can be.

5. *How does the selection encourage further thought?*

Theroux's essay treats a broad issue that affects all of us—the tendency to worry and thus cause ourselves pain. Her specific concern is the difficulties that parents face trying to divert children from needless fretting. Although Theroux offers no solutions, her personal account sharpens our awareness and prompts us to reexamine what is and is not worth worrying about.

If, for each essay you read in this book, you consider the preceding questions, you'll be able to respond thoughtfully to the *Questions for Close Reading, Questions About the Writer's Craft,* and *Questions for Further Thought* presented after each selection. Your responses will, in turn, prepare you for the writing assignments that follow the questions. Interesting and varied, the assignments invite you to examine issues raised by the selections and encourage you to experiment with various writing styles and organizational patterns.

Following are some sample questions and writing assignments based on the Theroux essay; all are similar to the sort that appear later in this book. Note that the final writing assignment paves the way for a student essay, the stages of which are illustrated in Chapter 2.

Questions for Close Reading

1. How do you know that Theroux is herself a worrier? How does she handle her anxieties?

2. Why do you suppose Theroux's daughter restates her problems as she goes up to bed? What kind of response does she most likely want from her mother?

Questions About the Writer's Craft

1. The last sentence in paragraph 4 tumbles along in a somewhat rambling fashion. Why might Theroux have decided to write the sentence this way?
2. Why do you think Theroux ends the essay with her daughter's comment, rather than with her own response to that comment?

Questions for Further Thought

1. What specifically can parents do to minimize the everyday anxieties that children feel?
2. Do you think that television contributes in any way to children's anxieties? Discuss the kinds of shows that you think might disturb or confuse children.

Writing Assignments

1. Theroux has difficulty allaying her daughter's worries. Write an essay explaining the steps that you think parents and/or schools should take to minimize children's anxieties about a specific present-day danger—perhaps AIDS, sexual abuse, or divorce.
2. Because the contemporary world is a difficult, even dangerous place, parents understandably worry about their children. Write an essay supporting the idea that today's world is, in many ways, hostile—particularly to children.

The benefits of active reading are many. Books in general and the selections in *The Macmillan Reader* in particular will bring you face to face with issues that concern all of us. If you study the selections and the questions that follow them, you'll be on the way to discovering ideas for your own papers. Chapter 2, "The Writing Process," offers practical suggestions for turning those ideas into well-organized, thoughtful essays.

2
THE WRITING PROCESS

Not many people retire at age thirty-eight. But Michel Montaigne, a sixteenth-century French attorney, did exactly that. Montaigne retired at a young age because he wanted to read, think, and write about all the subjects that interested him. After spending years getting his ideas down on paper, Montaigne finally published his short prose pieces. He called them *essais*—French for "trials" or "attempts."

In fact, all writing is an attempt to transform ideas into words, thus giving order and meaning to life. By using the term *essais,* Montaigne acknowledged that a written piece is never really finished. Of course, writers have to stop at some point, especially if they have deadlines to meet. But, as all experienced writers know, even after they dot the final *i,* cross the final *t,* and say "That's it," there's always something that could have been explored further or expressed a little better.

Because writing is a process, shaky starts and changes in direction aren't uncommon. Although there's no way to eliminate the work needed to write effectively, certain approaches can make the process more manageable and rewarding. This chapter describes a sequence of steps for writing essays. Familiarity with a specific sequence develops your awareness of strategies and choices, making you feel more confident when it comes time to write. You're less likely to look at a blank piece of paper and think, "Help! Now what do I do?" During the sequence, you do the following:

1. Prewrite
2. Identify the thesis
3. Support the thesis with evidence
4. Organize the evidence
5. Write the first draft
6. Revise the essay

We present the sequence as a series of stages, but we urge you not to view it as a rigid formula that must be followed step by unchanging step. Most people develop personalized approaches to the writing process. Some writers mull over a topic in their heads, then move quickly into a promising first draft; others outline their essays in detail before beginning to write. Between these two extremes are any number of effective approaches. The sequence here can be streamlined, juggled around, or otherwise altered to fit individual writing styles as well as the requirements of specific assignments. (Pages 81–87 present practical suggestions for using a word processor in every stage of the writing process.)

STAGE 1: PREWRITE

Prewriting refers to strategies you can use to generate ideas *before* starting the first draft of a paper. Prewriting techniques are like the warm-ups you do before going out to jog—they loosen you up, get you moving, and help you to develop a sense of well-being and confidence. Since prewriting techniques encourage imaginative exploration, they also help you discover what interests you most about your subject. Having such a focus early in the writing process keeps you from plunging into your initial draft without first giving some thought to what you want to say.

Prewriting can help in other ways, too. When we write, we often sabotage our ability to generate material because we continually critique what we put down on paper. During prewriting, you deliberately ignore your internal critic. Your purpose is simply to get ideas down on paper *without evaluating* their effectiveness. Writing without immediately judging what you produce can be liberating. Once you feel less pressure, you'll probably find that you can generate a good deal of material. And that can make your confidence soar.

Keep a Journal

Of all the prewriting techniques, keeping a journal (daily or almost daily) is the one most likely to make writing a part of your life. Some journal entries focus on a single theme; others wander from topic to topic. Your starting point may be a dream, a snippet of overheard conversation, a video on MTV, a political cartoon, an issue raised in class or in your reading—anything that surprises, interests, angers, depresses, confuses, or amuses you. You may also use a journal to experiment with your writing style—say, to vary your sentence structure if you tend to use predictable patterns.

Here is a fairly focused excerpt from a student's journal:

Today I had to show Paul around school. He and Mom got here by 9. I didn't let on that this was the earliest I've gotten up all semester! He got out of the car looking kind of nervous. Maybe he thought his big brother would be different after a couple of months of college. I walked him around part of the campus and then he went with me to Am. Civ. and then to lunch. He met Greg and some other guys. Everyone seemed to like him. He's got a nice, quiet sense of humor. When I went to Bio., I told him that he could walk around on his own since he wasn't crazy about sitting in on a science class. But he said "I'd rather stick with you." Was he flattering me or was he just scared? Anyway it made me feel good. Later when he was leaving, he told me he's definitely going to apply. I guess that'd be kind of nice, having him here. Mom thinks it's great and she's pushing it. I don't know. I feel kind of like it would invade my privacy. I found this school and have made a life for myself here. Let him find his own school! But it could be great having my kid brother here. I guess this is a classic case of what my psych teacher calls ambivalence. Part of me wants him to come, and part of me doesn't! (November 10)

Although some instructors collect students' journals, you needn't be overly concerned with spelling, grammar, sentence structure, or organization. While journal writing is typically more structured than freewriting (see page 23), you don't have to strive for entries that read like mini-essays. The important thing is to let your journal writing prompt reflection and new insights, providing you with material to draw upon in your writing. It is, then, a good idea to reread each week's entries to identify recurring themes and concerns. Keep a list of these issues at the back of your journal, under a heading like "Possible Essay Subjects." Here, for instance, are a few topics suggested by the preceding journal entry: deciding which college to attend, leaving home, sibling rivalry. Each of these topics could be developed in a full-length essay.

Journal writing stimulates thinking in a loose, unstructured way. But when you have a specific piece to write, you should approach prewriting in a purposeful, focused manner. You need to:

- Understand the boundaries of the assignment.
- Determine your purpose, audience, and tone.
- Discover your essay's limited subject.
- Generate raw material about your limited subject.
- Organize the raw material.

We'll discuss each of these steps in turn. But first, here's a practical tip: If you don't use a word processor during the prewriting stage, try using a pencil and scrap paper. They're less intimidating than pen, typewriter, and "official" paper; they also reinforce the notion that prewriting is tentative and exploratory. If you *do* use a word processor when prewriting, you'll find the hints on pages 83–84 helpful.

Understand the Boundaries of the Assignment

You shouldn't start writing a paper until you know what's expected. First, clarify the *kind of paper* the instructor has in mind. Assume the instructor asks you to discuss the key ideas in an assigned reading. What does the instructor want you to do? Should you include a brief summary of the selection? Should you compare the author's ideas with your own view of the subject? Should you determine if the author's view is supported by valid evidence?

If you're not sure about an assignment, ask your instructor—not the student next to you, who may be as confused as you—to make the requirements clear. Most instructors are more than willing to provide an explanation. They would rather take a few minutes of class time to explain the assignment than spend hours reading dozens of student essays that miss the mark.

Second, find out *how long* the paper is expected to be. Many instructors will indicate the approximate length of the papers they assign. If no length requirements are provided, discuss with the instructor what you plan to cover and indicate how long you think your paper will be. The instructor will either give you the go-ahead or help you refine the direction and scope of your work.

Determine Your Purpose, Audience, and Tone

Once you understand the requirements for a writing assignment, you're ready to begin thinking about the essay. What is its *purpose?* For what *audience* will it be written? What *tone* will you use? Later on, you may modify your decisions about these issues. That's fine. But you need to understand the way these considerations influence your work in the early phases of the writing process.

Purpose. The papers you write in college are usually meant to *inform* or *explain,* to *convince* or *persuade,* and sometimes to *entertain.* In practice, writing often combines purposes. You might, for example, write an essay trying to *convince* people to support a new trash recycling program in your community. But before you win readers over, you most likely would have to *explain* something about current waste-disposal technology.

When purposes blend this way, the predominant one determines the essay's content, organization, emphasis, and choice of words. Assume you're writing about a political campaign. If your primary goal is to *entertain,* to take a gentle poke at two candidates, you might start with several accounts of one candidate's "foot-in-mouth" disease and then describe the attempts of the other candidate, a multi-millionaire, to portray himself as an average Joe. Your language, full of exaggeration, would reflect your objective. But if your primary purpose is to *persuade* readers that the candidates are incompetent and shouldn't be elected, you might adopt a serious, straightforward style. Rather than poke fun at one candidate's gaffes, you would use them to illustrate her insensitivity to important issues. Similarly, the other candidate's posturing would be presented, not as a foolish pretension, but as evidence of his lack of judgment.

Audience.   To write effectively, you need to identify who your readers are and to take their expectations and needs into account. An essay about the artificial preservatives in the food served by the campus cafeteria would take one form if submitted to your chemistry professor and a very different one if written for the college newspaper. The chemistry paper would probably be formal and technical, complete with chemical formulations and scientific data: "Distillation revealed sodium benzoate particles suspended in a gelatinous medium." But such technical material would be inappropriate in a newspaper column intended for general readers. In this case, you might provide specific examples of cafeteria foods loaded with additives—"Those deliciously smoky cold cuts are loaded with nitrates and nitrites, both known to cause cancer in laboratory animals"— and suggest ways to eat more healthfully—"Pass by the deli counter and fill up instead on vegetarian pizza and fruit juices."

Ask yourself the following questions when analyzing your audience:

- What are my readers' age, sex, and educational level?
- What are their political, religious, and other beliefs?
- What interests and needs motivate my audience?
- How much do my readers already know about my subject?
- Do they have any misconceptions?
- What biases do they have about me, my subject, my opinion?
- How do my readers expect me to relate to them?
- What values do I share with my readers that will help me communicate with them?

Tone.   Just as your voice may project a range of feelings, your writing can convey one or more *tones,* or emotional states: enthusiasm, anger, resignation, and so on. Tone is integral to meaning; it permeates writing and reflects your attitude toward yourself, your purpose, your subject, and your readers. How do you project tone? You pay close attention to sentence structure and word choice.

Sentence structure refers to the way sentences are shaped. Although the two paragraphs that follow deal with exactly the same subject, note how differences in sentence structure create sharply dissimilar tones:

During the 1960s, many inner-city minorities considered the police an occupying force and an oppressive agent of control. As a result, violence against police grew in poorer neighborhoods, as did the number of residents killed by police.

An occupying force. An agent of control. An oppressor. That's how many inner-city minorities in the '60s viewed the police. Violence against police soared. Police killings of residents mounted.

Informative in its approach, the first paragraph projects a neutral, almost dispassionate tone. The sentences are fairly long, and clear transitions ("During the 1960s"; "As a result") mark the progression of thought. But the second paragraph, with its dramatic, almost alarmist tone, seems intended to elicit a strong emotional response; its short sentences, fragments, and abrupt transitions reflect the turbulence of earlier times.

Word choice also plays a role in establishing the tone of an essay. Words have *denotations,* neutral dictionary meanings, as well as *connotations,* emotional associations that go beyond the literal meaning. The word *beach,* for instance, is defined in the dictionary as "a nearly level stretch of pebbles and sand beside a body of water." This definition, however, doesn't capture individual responses to the word. For some, *beach* suggests warmth and relaxation; for others, it calls up images of hospital waste and sewage washed up on a once-clean stretch of shoreline.

Since tone and meaning are tightly bound, you must be sensitive to the emotional nuances of words. In a respectful essay about police officers, you wouldn't refer to *cops, narcs,* or *flatfoots;* such terms convey a contempt inconsistent with the tone intended. Your words must also convey tone clearly. Suppose you're writing a satirical piece criticizing a local beauty pageant. Dubbing the participants "livestock on view" leaves no question about your tone. But if you simply referred to the participants as "attractive young women," readers might be unsure of your attitude. Remember, readers can't read your mind, only your paper.

Discover Your Essay's Limited Subject

Once you have a firm grasp of the assignment's boundaries and have determined your purpose, audience, and tone, you're ready to focus on a limited aspect of the general assignment. Because too broad a subject can result in a diffuse, rambling essay, be sure to restrict your general subject before starting to write.

The following examples show the difference between general subjects that are too broad for an essay and limited subjects that are appropriate and workable. The examples, of course, represent only a few among many possibilities.

General Subject	Less General	Limited
Education	Computers in education	Computers in elementary school arithmetic classes
	High school education	High school electives
Transportation	Low-cost travel	Hitchhiking
	Getting around a metropolitan area	The transit system in a nearby city
Work	Planning for a career	College internships
	Women in the work force	Women's success as managers

How do you move from a general to a narrow subject? Imagine that you're asked to prepare a straightforward, informative essay for your writing class. The assignment, prompted by Phyllis Theroux's essay "The Worry Factor" (page 6), is as follows:

Because the contemporary world is a difficult, even dangerous place, parents understandably worry about their children. Write an essay supporting the idea that today's world is, in many ways, hostile—particularly to children.

You might feel unsure about how to proceed. But two techniques can help you limit such a general assignment. Keeping your purpose, audience, and tone in mind, you may *question* or *brainstorm* the general subject. These two techniques have a paradoxical effect. Although they encourage you to roam freely over a subject, they also help restrict the discussion by revealing which aspects of the subject interest you most.

1. Question the general subject.   One way to narrow a subject is to ask a series of *who, how, why, where, when,* and *what* questions. The following example shows how one student, Harriet Davids, used this technique to limit the Theroux assignment. A thirty-eight-year-old college student and mother of two teenagers, Harriet was understandably intrigued by the assignment. She started by asking a number of pointed questions about the general topic. As she proceeded, she was aware that the same questions could have led to different limited subjects—just as other questions would have.

General Subject: We live in a world that is difficult, even dangerous for children.

Question	Limited Subject
Who is to blame for the difficult conditions under which children grow up?	Parents' casual attitude toward childrearing
How have schools contributed to the problems children face?	Not enough counseling programs for kids in distress
Why do children feel frightened?	Divorce
Where do kids go to escape?	Television, which makes the world seem even more dangerous
When are children most vulnerable?	The special problems of adolescents
What dangers or fears should parents discuss with their children?	AIDS, drugs, alcohol, war, terrorism

2. Brainstorm the general subject. Another way to focus on a limited subject is to list quickly everything about the general topic that pops into your mind. Working vertically down the page, jot down brief words, phrases, and abbreviations to capture your free-floating thoughts. Writing in complete sentences will slow you down. Don't try to organize or censor your ideas. Even the most fleeting, random, or seemingly outrageous thoughts can be productive.

Here's an example of the brainstorming that Harriet Davids decided to do in an effort to gather even more material on the Theroux assignment:

General Subject: We live in a world that is difficult, even dangerous for children.

- Too many divorces
- Parents squabbling over material goods in settlements
- Kids feel unimportant
- Families move a lot
- I moved in fourth grade--hated it
- Nobody graduates from high school in the same district they went to kindergarten in
- Drug abuse all over, in little kids' schools
- Pop music glorifies drugs
- Kids not innocent--know too much
- TV shows depict corrupt politicians, sex, pollution, violence
- Kids babysat by TV
- Kids raise selves
- Single-parent homes
- Day-care problems
- TV coverage of day-care abuse frightens kids
- Perfect families on TV make kids feel inadequate

As you can see, questioning and brainstorming suggest many possible limited subjects. To identify especially promising ones, reread your material. What arouses your interest, anger, or curiosity? What themes seem to dominate and cut to the heart of the matter? Star or circle ideas with potential.

After marking the material, write several phrases or sentences summarizing the most promising limited subjects. These, for example, are just a few that emerged from Harriet Davids's questioning and brainstorming the Theroux assignment:

- TV partly to blame for children having such a hard time
- Relocation stressful to children
- Schools also at fault
- The special problems that parents face raising children today

Harriet decided to write on the last of these limited subjects—the special problems that parents face raising children today. This topic, in turn, is the focus of our discussion in the pages ahead.

Generate Raw Material About Your Limited Subject

When a limited subject strikes you as having possibilities, your next step is to see if you have enough interesting and insightful things to say about the subject to write an effective essay. To find out if you do, you may use any or all of the following techniques:

1. Freewrite on your limited subject. *Freewriting* means jotting down in rough sentences or phrases everything that comes to mind. To capture this continuous stream of thought, write nonstop for ten minutes or more. Don't censor anything; put down whatever pops into your head. Don't reread, edit, or pay attention to organization, spelling, or grammar. If your mind goes blank, repeat words until another thought emerges.

Here is part of the freewriting that Harriet Davids generated about her limited subject, "The special problems that parents face raising children today":

> Parents today have tough problems to face. Lots of dangers. Drugs and alcohol for one thing. Also crimes of violence against kids. Parents also have to keep up with cost of living, everything costs more, kids want and expect more. Television? Another thing is <u>Playboy,</u> <u>Penthouse.</u> Sexy ads on TV, movies deal with sex. Kids grow up too fast, too fast. Drugs. Little kids can't handle knowing too much at an early age. Both parents at work much of the day. Finding good day care a real problem. Lots of latchkey kids. Another problem is getting kids to do homework, lots of other things to do. Especially like going to the mall! When I was young, we did homework after dinner, no excuses accepted by my parents.

2. Brainstorm your limited subject. Let your mind wander freely, as you did when using brainstorming to narrow your subject.

This time, though, list every idea, fact, and example that occurs to you about your limited subject. Use brief words and phrases, so you don't get bogged down writing full sentences. For now, don't worry whether ideas fit together or whether the points listed make sense.

To gather additional material on her limited subject for the Theroux assignment ("The special problems that parents face raising children today"), Harriet Davids brainstormed the following list:

- Trying to raise kids when both parents work
- Day care not always the answer--cases of abuse
- Day care very expensive
- Prices of everything outrageous
- Commercials make kids want <u>more</u> of everything
- Clothes so important
- Sexy clothes on little kids. Absurd!
- Sex everywhere--TV, movies, magazines
- Sexual abuse of kids
- Violence against kids when parents abuse drugs
- Cocaine, crack, AIDS
- Schools have to teach kids about these things
- Schools doing too much--not as good as they used to be
- Not enough homework assigned--kids unprepared
- Distractions from homework--malls, TV, phones, stereos, MTV

3. Use group brainstorming.   Brainstorming can also be conducted as a group activity. Thrashing out ideas with other people stretches the imagination, revealing possibilities you may not have considered on your own. Group brainstorming doesn't have to be conducted in a formal classroom situation. You can bounce ideas around with friends and family anywhere—over lunch, at the student center, and so on.

4. Map out the limited subject.   If you're the kind of person who doodles while thinking, you may want to try *mapping*, sometimes called *diagramming* or *clustering*. Like other prewriting techniques, mapping proceeds rapidly and encourages the free flow of ideas. Begin by expressing your limited subject in a crisp phrase and placing it in the center of a blank sheet of paper. As ideas come to you, put them along lines or in boxes or circles around the limited subject. Draw arrows and lines to show the relationships among ideas. Don't stop there, however. Focus on each idea; as subpoints and details come to you, connect them to their source idea, again using boxes, lines, circles, or arrows to clarify how everything relates.

5. Use the patterns of development. Throughout this book, we show how writers use various patterns of development (narration, process analysis, definition, and so on), singly or in combination, to develop and organize their ideas. Because each pattern has its own distinctive logic, the patterns encourage you, when you prewrite, to think about a subject in different ways, causing insights to surface that might otherwise remain submerged.

The various patterns of development are discussed in detail in Chapters 4–12. At this point, though, you should find the following chart helpful. It not only summarizes the broad purpose of each pattern but also shows the way each pattern can generate different raw material for the limited subject of Harriet Davids's essay:

Limited Subject: The special problems that parents face raising children today.

Pattern	Purpose	Raw Material
Description	To detail what a person, place or object is like	Detail the sights and sounds of a glitzy mall that attracts kids
Narration	To relate an event	Recount what happened when neighbors tried to forbid their kids from going to a rock concert
Exemplification	To provide specific instances or examples	Offer examples of family arguments. Can a friend known to use drugs visit? Can a child go to a party where alcohol will be served? Can parents outlaw MTV?
Division-classification	To divide something into parts or to group related things in categories	Identify components of a TV commercial that distorts kids' values

Pattern	Purpose	Raw Material
		Classify the kinds of commercials that make it difficult to teach kids values
Process analysis	To explain how something happens or how something is done	Explain step by step how family life can disintegrate when parents have to work all the time to make ends meet
Comparison-contrast	To point out similarities and/or dissimilarities	Contrast families today with those of a generation ago
Cause-effect	To analyze reasons and consequences	Explain why parents are not around to be with their kids: Industry's failure to provide day care and inflexibility about granting time off for parents with sick kids
		Explain the consequences of absentee parents: Kids feel unloved; they're undisciplined; they take on adult responsibility too early
Definition	To explain the meaning of a term or concept	What is meant by "tough love"?
Argumentation-persuasion	To win people over to a point of view	Convince parents to work with schools to develop programs that make kids feel more safe and secure

(For more on ways to use the patterns of development in different phases of the writing process, see pages 36–37, 45–46, and 685–87.)

6. Conduct research. Depending on your topic, you may find it helpful to visit the library and look for books and articles about your limited subject in the card catalog, the *Readers' Guide to Periodical Literature,* or a computerized reference system. At this point, you don't need to read closely the material you find. Just skim and perhaps take a few brief notes on ideas and points that could be useful.

If researching the Theroux assignment, for instance, Harriet Davids could look under headings and subheadings like the following:

> Day care
> Drug abuse
> Family
> Parent-child relationship
> > Child abuse
> > Children of divorced parents
> > Children of working mothers
> School and home

Organize the Raw Material

Once you generate the raw material for your limited subject, you're ready to shape your rough, preliminary ideas. Preparing a *scratch outline* or *scratch list* is an effective strategy. On pages 48–52, we talk about the more formal outline you may need later on in the writing process. Here we show how a rough outline or scratch list can impose order on the tentative ideas generated during prewriting.

Reread your exploratory thoughts about the limited subject. Cross out anything not appropriate for your purpose, audience, and tone; add points that didn't originally occur to you. Star or circle compelling items that warrant further development. Then draw arrows between related items, your goal being to group such material under a common heading. Finally, determine what seems to be the best order for those headings.

By giving you a sense of the way your free-form material might fit together, a scratch outline makes the writing process more manageable. You're less likely to feel overwhelmed once you actually start writing because you'll already have some idea about how to shape your material into a meaningful statement. Remember, though, the scratch outline can, and most likely will, be modified along the way.

The following scratch outline shows how Harriet Davids began to shape her brainstorming (page 24) into a more organized format. Note the way she eliminated some items (for example, the point about outrageous prices), added others (for example, the point about video arcades), and grouped the brainstormed items under four main headings, with the appropriate details listed underneath. (If you'd like to see Harriet's more formal outline and her first draft, turn to pages 51 and 66–67.)

Limited Subject: The special problems that parents face raising children today.

1. Day care for two-career families
   • Expensive
   • Cases of abuse

2. Distractions from homework
   • Stereos, televisions in room at home
   • Places to go—malls, video arcades, fast-food restaurants, rock concerts

3. Sexually explicit materials
   • Magazines and books
   • Television shows
   • MTV
   • Movies
   • Rock posters

4. Life-threatening dangers
   • AIDS
   • Drugs
   • Drinking
   • Violence against children

The prewriting strategies just described provide a solid foundation for the next stages of your work. But invention and imaginative exploration don't end when prewriting is completed. As you'll see, remaining open to new ideas is crucial during all phases of the writing process.

Activities: Prewrite

1. Number the items in each set from 1 (*broadest subject*) to 5 (*most limited subject*):

Set A	Set B
Abortion	Business majors
Controversial social issue	Students' majors
Cutting state abortion funds	College students
Federal funding of abortions	Kinds of students on campus
Social issues	Why many students major in business

2. Which of the following topics are too broad for an essay of two to five typewritten pages: soap operas' appeal to college students; day care; trying to "kick" the junk-food habit; male and female relationships; international terrorism?

3. Use the techniques indicated in parentheses to limit each general topic listed below. Then, identify a specific purpose, audience, and tone for the one limited subject you consider most interesting. Next, with the help of the patterns of development, generate raw material about that limited subject. (You may find it helpful to work with others when developing this material.) Finally, shape your raw material into a scratch outline—crossing out, combining, and adding ideas as needed. (Save your scratch outline so you can work with it further after reading about the next stage in the writing process.)

> Friendship (*journal writing*)
> Malls (*mapping*)
> Leisure (*freewriting*)
> Television (*brainstorming*)
> Required courses (*group brainstorming*)
> Manners (*questioning*)

STAGE 2: IDENTIFY THE THESIS

The process of prewriting—discovering a limited subject and generating ideas about it—prepares you for the next stage in writing an essay: identifying the paper's *thesis*, or controlling idea. Presenting your opinion on a subject, the thesis should focus on an interesting and significant issue, one that engages your energies and merits your consideration. You may think of the thesis as the essay's hub—the central point around which all the other material revolves. Your thesis determines what does and does not belong in the essay. The thesis, especially when it occurs early in an essay, also helps focus the reader on the piece's central point.

Sometimes the thesis emerges early in the prewriting stage, particularly if a special angle on your limited topic sparks your interest or becomes readily apparent. Often, though, you'll need to do some work to determine your thesis. For some topics, you may need to do some library research. For others, the best way to identify a promising thesis is to look through your prewriting and ask yourself questions like these: "What statement does all this prewriting support? What aspect of the limited subject is covered in most detail? What is the focus of the most provocative material?" (For hints about using a word processor to find a thesis, see page 84.)

For a look at the process of finding the thesis within prewriting material, glance back at the scratch outline (page 28) that Harriet Davids prepared for the limited subject "The special problems that parents face raising children today." Harriet devised the following thesis to capture the focus of this prewriting: "Being a parent today is much more difficult than it was a generation ago." (The full outline for Harriet's paper appears on page 51; the first draft on pages 66–67; the final draft on pages 74–75.)

Writing an Effective Thesis

What makes a thesis effective? Generally expressed in one or two sentences, a thesis statement often has two parts. One part presents your paper's *limited subject;* the other presents your *point of view,* or *attitude,* about that subject. Here are some examples of the way you might move from general subject to limited subject to thesis statement. In each thesis statement, the limited subject is underlined once and the attitude twice.

General Subject	Limited Subject	Thesis
Education	Computers in elementary school arithmetic classes	Computer programs in arithmetic can individualize

General Subject	Limited Subject	Thesis
		instruction more effectively than the average elementary school teacher can.
Transportation	A metropolitan transit system	Although the city's transit system still has problems, it has become safer and more efficient in the last two years.
Work	College internships	College internships provide valuable opportunities to students uncertain about what to do after graduation.
Our anti-child world	Special problems that parents face raising children today	Being a parent today is much more difficult than it was a generation ago.

(*Reminder:* The last of these thesis statements is the one that Harriet Davids devised for the essay she planned to write in response to the assignment on page 12. Harriet's prewriting appears on pages 24 and 28. You can find her first draft on pages 66–67.)

Because identifying your thesis statement is an important step in writing a sharply focused essay, you need to avoid three common problems that lead to an ineffective thesis.

Don't make an announcement. Some writers use the thesis statement merely to announce the limited subject of their paper and forget to indicate their attitude toward the subject. Such statements are announcements of intent, not thesis statements.

Compare the following three announcements with the thesis statements beside them.

Announcements	Thesis Statements
My essay will discuss whether a student pub should exist on campus.	This college should not allow a student pub on campus.
Handgun legislation is the subject of this paper.	Banning handguns is the first step toward controlling crime in America.
I want to discuss cable television.	Cable television has not delivered on its promise to provide an alternative to network programming.

Don't make a factual statement.   Your thesis and thus your essay should focus on an issue capable of being developed. If a fact is used as a thesis, you have no place to go; a fact generally doesn't invite much discussion.

Notice the difference between these factual statements and thesis statements:

Factual Statements	Thesis Statements
Many businesses pollute the environment.	Tax penalties should be levied against businesses that pollute the environment.
Many movies today are violent.	Movie violence provides a healthy outlet for aggression.
America's population is growing older.	The aging of the American population will eventually create a crisis in the delivery of health-care services.

Don't make a broad statement.   Avoid stating your thesis in vague, general, or sweeping terms. Broad statements make it difficult for readers to grasp your essay's point. Moreover, if you start with a broad thesis, you're saddled with the impossible task of trying to develop a book-length idea in an essay that runs only several pages.

The following examples contrast statements that are too broad with thesis statements that are focused effectively:

Broad Statements	Thesis Statements
Nowadays, high school education is often meaningless.	High school diplomas have been devalued by grade inflation.
Newspapers cater to the taste of the American public.	The success of *USA Today* indicates that people want newspapers that are easy to read and entertaining.
The computer revolution is not all that we have been led to believe it is.	Home computers are still an impractical purchase for many people.

You have considerable freedom regarding the placement of the thesis in an essay. The thesis is often stated near the beginning, but it may be delayed, especially if you need to provide background information before it can be understood. Sometimes the thesis is reiterated—using fresh words—in the essay's conclusion or elsewhere. You may even leave the thesis unstated, relying on strong evidence to convey the essay's central idea.

One final point: Once you start writing your first draft, some feelings, thoughts, and examples may emerge that qualify, even contradict, your initial thesis. Don't resist these new ideas; they frequently move you toward a clearer statement of your main point. Remember, though, your essay must have a thesis. Without this central concept, you have no reason for writing.

Activities: Identify the Thesis

1. For each of the following limited subjects, four possible thesis statements are given. Indicate whether each is an announcement (*A*), a factual statement (*FS*), too broad a statement (*TB*), or an effective thesis (*OK*). Then, for each effective thesis, identify a possible purpose, audience, and tone.

   Limited Subject: The ethics of treating severely handicapped infants

   Some babies born with severe handicaps have been allowed to die.

There are many serious issues involved in the treatment of handicapped newborns.

The government should pass legislation requiring medical treatment for handicapped newborns.

This essay will analyze the controversy surrounding the treatment of severely handicapped babies who would die without medical care.

Limited Subject: Privacy and computerized records

Computers raise some significant and crucial questions for all of us.

Computerized records keep track of consumer spending habits, credit records, travel patterns, and other personal information.

Computerized records have turned our private lives into public property.

In this paper, the relationship between computerized records and the right to privacy will be discussed.

2. Each of the following sets lists the key points in an essay. Based on the information provided, prepare a possible thesis for each essay.

Set A

- One evidence of this growing conservatism is the reemerging popularity of fraternities and sororities.
- Beauty contests, ROTC training, and corporate recruiting—once rejected by students on many campuses—are again popular.
- Most important, many students no longer choose risky careers that enable them to contribute to society but select, instead, safe fields with money-making potential.

Set B

- We do not know how engineering new forms of life might affect the earth's delicate ecological balance.
- Another danger of genetic research is its potential for unleashing new forms of disease.
- Even beneficial attempts to eliminate genetic defects could contribute to the dangerous idea that only perfect individuals are entitled to live.

3. Following are four pairs of general and limited subjects. Generate an appropriate thesis statement for each pair. Select one thesis, and determine which pattern of development would support it most effectively. Use that pattern to draft a paragraph developing the thesis. (Save the paragraph so you can work with it further after reading about the next stage in the writing process.)

General Subject	Limited Subject
Psychology	The power struggles in a classroom
Health	Doctors' attitudes toward patients
American politics	Television's coverage of presidential campaigns
Work	Minimum-wage jobs for young people

4. Return to the scratch outline you prepared for activity 3 on page 29. After examining the outline, identify a thesis that conveys the central idea behind most of the raw material. Then, ask others to evaluate your thesis in light of the material in the outline. Finally, keeping the thesis— as well as your purpose, audience, and tone—in mind, refine the scratch outline by deleting inappropriate items, adding relevant ones, and indicating where more material is needed. (Save your refined scratch outline and thesis so you can work with them further after reading about the next stage in the writing process.)

STAGE 3: SUPPORT THE THESIS WITH EVIDENCE

After identifying a preliminary thesis, you should develop the evidence needed to support the central idea. Such supporting material grounds your essay, showing readers you have good reason for feeling as you do about your subject. Your evidence also adds interest and color to your writing. In college essays of five hundred to fifteen hundred words, you usually need at least three major points of evidence to develop your thesis. These major points—each focusing on related but separate aspects of the thesis—eventually become the supporting paragraphs in the body of the essay.

What Is Evidence?

By *evidence*, we mean a number of different kinds of support. *Examples* are just one option. To develop your thesis, you might also include *reasons, facts, details, statistics, anecdotes,* and *quotations from experts.* Imagine you're writing an essay with the thesis, "People normally unconcerned about the environment can be galvanized to constructive action if they feel personally affected by an environmental problem." You could support this thesis with any combination of the following types of evidence:

- *Examples* of successful recycling efforts in several neighborhoods.
- *Reasons* why people got involved in a neighborhood recycling effort.
- *Facts* about other residents' efforts to preserve the quality of their well water.
- *Details* about the steps that people can take to get involved in environmental issues.
- *Statistics* showing the number of Americans concerned about the environment.
- An *anecdote* about your involvement in environmental efforts.
- A *quotation* from a well-known scientist about the impact that citizens can have on environmental legislation.

Where Do You Find Evidence?

Where do you find the examples, anecdotes, details, and other types of evidence needed to support your thesis? As you saw when you followed Harriet Davids's strategies for gathering material for an essay (pages 21–28), a good deal of evidence is generated during the prewriting stage. In this phase of the writing process, you tap into your personal experiences, draw upon other people's observations, perhaps interview a person with special knowledge about your subject. The library, with its abundant material, is another rich source of supporting evidence. In addition, the various patterns of development are a valuable source of evidence.

How the Patterns of Development Help Generate Evidence

On pages 25–26, we discussed the way patterns of development help generate material about a limited subject. The same patterns also help develop support for a thesis. Consider the way they generate evidence for this thesis: "To those who haven't done it, babysitting looks easy. In practice, though, babysitting can be difficult, frightening, even dangerous."

Pattern	Evidence Generated
Description	Details about a child who, while being babysat, was badly hurt.

Pattern	Evidence Generated
Narration	Story about the time a friend babysat an ill child whose condition was worsened by the babysitter's actions.
Exemplification	Examples of potential babysitting problems: an infant rolls off a changing table; a toddler sticks objects in an electric outlet; a school-age child is bitten by a neighborhood dog.
Division-classification	A typical babysitting evening divided into stages: playing with the kids; putting them to bed; dealing with their nighttime fears once they're in bed.
	Classify kids' nighttime fears: of monsters under their beds; of bad dreams; of being abandoned by their parents.
Process analysis	Step-by-step account of what a babysitter should do if a child becomes ill or injured.
Comparision-contrast	Contrast between two babysitters: one well-prepared, the other unprepared.
Cause-effect	Why children have temper tantrums; the effect of such tantrums on an unskilled babysitter.
Definition	What is meant by a *skilled* babysitter?
Argumentation-persuasion	A proposal for a babysitting training program.

(For more on ways to use the patterns of development in different phases of the writing process, see pages 25–26, 45–46, 56–57, and 685–87.)

Characteristics of Evidence

No matter how it is generated, all types of supporting evidence share the characteristics described in the following sections. You should keep these characteristics in mind as you review your thesis and scratch outline. That way, you can make the changes needed to strengthen the evidence gathered earlier. As you'll see shortly, Harriet Davids focused on many of these issues as she worked with the evidence she collected during the prewriting phase.

The evidence is relevant and unified. All the evidence in an essay must clearly support the thesis. It makes no difference how riveting material might be; if the evidence doesn't *relate directly* to the essay's central point, it should be eliminated. Irrelevant material can weaken your position by implying that no relevant support exists. It also distracts readers from your controlling idea, thus disrupting the paper's overall unity.

The following paragraph, taken from an essay illustrating recent changes in Americans' television-viewing habits, demonstrates the importance of unified evidence. The paragraph focuses on people's reasons for switching from network to cable television. As you'll see, the paragraph lacks unity because it contains points (underlined) unrelated to its main idea. Specifically, the comments about cable's foul language should be deleted. Although these observations bring up interesting points, they shift the paragraph's focus. If the writer wants to present a balanced view of the pros and cons of cable and network television, these points *should* be covered, but in *another paragraph*.

Nonunified Support

Many people consider cable TV an improvement over network television. For one thing, viewers usually prefer the movies on cable. Unlike network films, cable movies are often only months old, they have not been edited by censors, and they are not interrupted by commercials. Growing numbers of people also feel that cable specials are superior to the ones the networks grind out. Cable viewers may enjoy such pop stars as Bruce Springsteen, Tina Turner, or Eddie Murphy in concert, whereas the networks continue to broadcast tired Bob Hope variety shows and boring awards ceremonies. <u>There is, however, one problem with cable comedians. The foul language many of them use</u>

makes it hard to watch these cable specials with children. The networks, in contrast, generally present "clean" shows that parents and children can watch together. Then, too, cable TV offers viewers more flexibility since it schedules shows at various times over the month. People working night shifts or attending evening classes can see movies in the afternoon, and viewers missing the first twenty minutes of a show can always catch them later. It's not surprising that cable viewership is growing while network ratings have taken a plunge.

Early in the writing process, Harriet Davids was aware of the importance of relevant evidence. Take a moment to compare Harriet's brainstorming (page 22) and her scratch outline (page 28). Even though Harriet hadn't identified her thesis when she prepared the scratch outline, she realized she should delete a number of items on the reshaped version of her brainstorming—for example, the fourth item and third-to-last item ("prices of everything outrageous" and "schools doing too much"). Harriet eliminated these points because they weren't consistent with the focus of her limited subject.

The evidence is specific.   When evidence is vague and general, readers lose interest in what you're saying, become skeptical of your ideas' validity, and feel puzzled about your meaning. In contrast, *specific, concrete evidence* provides sharp *word pictures* that engage your readers, persuade them that your thinking is sound, and clarify meaning.

Consider, for example, the differences between the following two sentences: "The young man had trouble lifting the box out of an old car" and "Joe, only twenty years old but more than fifty pounds overweight, struggled to lift the heavy wooden crate out of the rusty, dented Chevrolet." The first sentence, filled with generalities, is fuzzy and imprecise while the second sentence, filled with specifics, is crisp and clear.

As the preceding sentences illustrate, three strategies can be used, singly or in combination, to make writing specific. First, you can provide answers to *who, which, what,* and similar *questions.* (The question "How does the car look?" prompts a change in which "an old car" becomes "a rusty, dented Chevrolet"). Second, you can use *vigorous verbs* ("had trouble lifting" becomes "struggled to lift"). Finally, you can replace vague abstract *nouns* with *vivid, concrete* nouns or phrases ("the young man" becomes "Joe, only twenty years old but more than fifty pounds overweight").

Following are two versions of a paragraph from an essay about trends in the business community. Although both paragraphs focus on one such trend—flexible working hours—note how the first version's bland language fails to engage the reader and how its vague generalities leave meaning unclear. What, for example, is meant by the term "flex-time scheduling"? The second paragraph answers this question (as well as several others) with clear specifics; it also uses strong, energetic language. As a result, the second paragraph is more informative and more interesting than the first.

Nonspecific Support

More and more companies have begun to realize that flex-time scheduling offers advantages. Several companies outside Boston have tried flex-time scheduling and are pleased with the way the system reduces the difficulties their employees face getting to work. Studies show that flex-time scheduling also increases productivity, reduces on-the-job conflict, and minimizes work-related accidents.

Specific Support

More and more companies have begun to realize that flex-time scheduling offers advantages over a rigid 9-to-5 routine. Along suburban Boston's Route 128, such companies as Compugraphics and Consolidated Paper now permit employees to schedule their arrival any time between 6 a.m. and 11 a.m. The corporations report that the number of rush-hour jams and accidents has fallen dramatically. As a result, employees no longer arrive at work weighed down by tension induced by choking clouds of exhaust fumes and the blaring horns of gridlocked drivers. Studies sponsored by the journal *Business Quarterly* show that this more mellow state of mind benefits corporations. Traffic-stressed employees begin their workday anxious and exasperated, still grinding their teeth at their fellow commuters, their frustration often spilling over into their performance at work. By contrast, stress-free employees work more productively and take fewer days off. They are more tolerant of coworkers and customers, and less likely to balloon minor irritations into major confrontations. Perhaps most importantly, employees arriving at work relatively free of stress can focus their attention on working safely. They rack up significantly fewer on-the-job accidents, such as falls and injuries resulting from careless handling of dangerous equipment. Flex-time improves employee well-being, and as well-being rises, so do company profits.

At this point, it will be helpful to compare once again Harriet Davids's brainstorming (page 24) and her scratch outline (page 28). Note the way she added new details to make her brainstorming more specific. For example, to the item "Distractions from homework," she added the new examples "video arcades," "fast-food restaurants," and "rock concerts." And, as you'll see when you read Harriet's first and final drafts (pages 66–67 and 74–75), she added many more vigorous specifics during later stages of the writing process.

The evidence is adequate.   Readers won't automatically accept your thesis; you need to provide *enough specific evidence* to support your viewpoint. On occasion, a single extended example will suffice. Generally, though, you'll need a variety of evidence: facts, examples, reasons, personal observations, expert opinion, and so on.

Following are two versions of a paragraph from a paper showing how difficult it is to get personal, attentive service nowadays at gas stations, supermarkets, and department stores. Both paragraphs focus on the problem at gas stations, but one paragraph is much more effective. As you'll see, the first paragraph starts with good specific support, yet fails to provide enough of it. The second paragraph offers additional examples, descriptive details, and dialogue—all of which make the writing stronger and more convincing.

Inadequate Support

Gas stations are a good example of this impersonal attitude. At many stations, attendants have even stopped pumping gas. Motorists pull up to a combination convenience store and gas island where an attendant is enclosed in a glass booth with a tray for taking money. The driver must get out of the car, pump the gas, and walk over to the booth to pay. That's a real inconvenience, especially when compared with the way service stations used to be run.

Adequate Support

Gas stations are a good example of this impersonal attitude. At many stations, attendants have even stopped pumping gas. Motorists pull up to a combination convenience store and gas island where an attendant is enclosed in a glass booth with a tray for taking money. The driver must get out of the car, pump the gas, and walk over to the booth to pay. Even at stations that still have "pump jockeys," employees seldom ask, "Check your oil?" or wash windshields, although they may grudgingly point out the location of the bucket and squeegee. And customers with a balky engine or a nonfunctioning heater are usually out of luck. Why? Many gas stations have eliminated on-duty mechanics. The skillful mechanic who could replace a belt or fix a tire in a few minutes has been replaced by a teenager in a jumpsuit who doesn't know a carburetor from a charge card and couldn't care less.

Now take a final look at Harriet Davids's scratch outline (page 28). You'll see that Harriet realized she needed more than one block of supporting material to develop her limited subject; that's why she identified four separate blocks of evidence (day care, homework distractions, sexual material, and dangers). When Harriet prepared her first and final drafts (pages 66–67 and 74–75), she decided to eliminate the material about day care. But she added so many more specific and dramatic details that her evidence was more than sufficient.

The evidence is accurate.   When you have a strong belief and want readers to see things your way, you may be tempted to overstate or downplay facts, disregard information, misquote, or make up details. Suppose you plan to write an essay making the point that dormitory security is lax. You begin supporting your thesis by narrating the time you were nearly mugged in your dorm hallway. Realizing the essay would be more persuasive if you also mentioned other episodes, you decide to invent some material. Perhaps you describe several supposed burglaries on your dorm floor or exaggerate the amount of time it took campus security to respond to an emergency call from a residence hall. Yes, you've supported your point—but at the expense of truth.

The evidence is representative.   Using representative evidence means that you rely on the typical, the usual, to show that your point is valid. Contrary to the maxim, exceptions don't prove the rule. Perhaps you plan to write an essay contending that the value of seat belts has been exaggerated. To support your position, you mention a friend who survived a head-on collision without wearing a seat belt. Such an example isn't representative because the facts and figures on accidents suggest your friend's survival was a fluke.

Borrowed evidence is documented.   If you include evidence from outside sources (books, articles, interviews), you need to acknowledge where that information comes from. If you don't, readers may consider your evidence nothing more than your point of view, or they may regard as dishonest your failure to cite your indebtedness to others for ideas that obviously aren't your own.

For help in documenting sources in brief, informal papers, turn to page 566. For information on acknowledging sources in longer, more formal papers, refer to Chapter 14.

Strong supporting evidence is at the heart of effective writing. Without it, essays lack energy and fail to convey the writer's perspective. Such lifeless writing is more apt to put readers to sleep than to engage their interest and convince them that the points being made are valid. Taking the time to accumulate solid supporting material is, then, a critical step in the writing process.

Activities: Support the Thesis With Evidence

1. Each of the following sets includes a thesis statement and four points of support. In each set, identify the one point that is off target.

   ### Set A

   Thesis: Colleges should put less emphasis on sports.

   Encourages grade fixing
   Creates a strong following among former graduates
   Distracts from real goals of education
   Causes extensive and expensive injuries

   ### Set B

   Thesis: America is becoming a homogenized country.

   Regional accents vanishing
   Chain stores blanket country
   Americans proud of their ethnic identities
   Metropolitan areas almost indistinguishable from one another

2. For each of the following thesis statements, develop three points of relevant support. Then use the patterns of development to generate evidence for each point of support.

   Thesis: The trend toward disposable, throw-away products has gone too far.

   Thesis: The local (or college) library fails to meet the needs of those it is supposed to serve.

   Thesis: Television portrays men as incompetent creatures.

3. Choose one of the following thesis statements. Then identify an appropriate purpose, audience, and tone for an essay with this thesis. Using

freewriting, mapping, or the questioning technique, generate at least three supporting points for the thesis. Last, write a paragraph about one of the points, making sure your evidence reflects the characteristics discussed in these pages. Alternatively, you may go ahead and prepare the first draft of an essay having the selected thesis. (If you choose the second option, you may want to turn to page 65 to see a diagram showing how to organize a first draft.) Save whatever you prepare so you can work with it further after reading about the next stage in the writing process.

- Winning the lottery may not always be a blessing.
- All of us can take steps to reduce the country's trash crisis.
- Drug education programs in public schools are (or are not) effective.

4. Select one of the following thesis statements. Then determine your purpose, audience, and tone for an essay with this thesis. Next, use the patterns of development to generate at least three supporting points for the thesis. Finally, write a paragraph about one of the points, making sure that your evidence demonstrates the characteristics discussed in these pages. Alternatively, you may go ahead and prepare a first draft of an essay having the thesis selected. (If you choose the latter option, you may want to turn to page 65 to see a diagram showing how to organize a first draft.) Save whatever you prepare so you can work with it further after reading about the next stage in the writing process.

- Teenagers should (or should not) be able to obtain birth-control devices without their parents' permission.
- The college's system for awarding student loans needs to be over-hauled.
- VCRs have changed for the worse (or the better) the way Americans entertain themselves.

5. Retrieve the paragraph you wrote in response to activity 3 on pages 34–35. Keeping in mind the characteristics of effective evidence discussed in these pages, make whatever changes are needed to strengthen the paragraph. (Save the paragraph so you can work with it further after reading about the next stage in the writing process.)

6. Look at the thesis and refined scratch outline you prepared in response to activity 4 on page 35. Where do you see gaps in the support for your thesis? By brainstorming with others, generate material to fill these gaps. If some of the new points generated suggest that you should modify your thesis, make the appropriate changes now. (Save this material so you can work with it further after reading about the next stage in the writing process.)

STAGE 4: ORGANIZE THE EVIDENCE

After you've generated supporting evidence, you're ready to *organize* that material. Even highly compelling evidence won't illustrate the validity of your thesis or achieve your purpose if readers have to plow through a maze of chaotic evidence. Some writers can move quickly from generating support to writing a clearly structured first draft. (They usually say they have sequenced their ideas in their heads.) Most, however, need to spend some time sorting out their thoughts on paper before starting the first draft; otherwise, they tend to lose their way in a tangle of ideas.

When moving to the organizing stage, you should have in front of you your scratch outline (see page 28) and thesis plus any supporting material you've accumulated since you did your prewriting. To find a logical framework for all this material, you'll need to (1) determine which pattern of development is implied in your evidence, (2) select one of four basic approaches for organizing your evidence, and (3) outline your evidence. These issues are discussed in the pages ahead.

Use the Patterns of Development

As you saw on pages 25–26 and 36–37 the patterns of development (definition, narration, process analysis, and others) can help you develop prewriting material and generate evidence for a thesis. In the organizing stage, the patterns provide frameworks for presenting evidence in an orderly, accessible way. Here's how.

Each pattern of development has its own internal logic that makes it appropriate for some writing purposes but not others. (You may find it helpful at this point to turn to pages 25–26 so you can review the broad purpose of each pattern.) Once you see which pattern (or combination of patterns) is implied by your purpose, you can block out your paper's general structure. Imagine that you're writing an essay *explaining why* some students drop out of college during the first semester. You might organize the essay around a three-part discussion of the key *causes* contributing to the difficulty that students have adjusting to college: (1) they miss friends and family, (2) they take inappropriate courses, and (3) they experience conflicts with roommates. As you can see, your choice of pattern of development significantly influences your essay's content and organization.

Some essays follow a single pattern, but most blend them, with a predominant pattern providing the piece's organizational framework. In our example essay, you might include a brief *description* of an overwhelmed first-year college student; you might *define* the psychological term "separation anxiety"; you might end the paper by briefly explaining a *process* for making students' adjustment to college easier. Still, the essay's overall organizational pattern would be *cause-effect* since the paper's primary purpose is to explain why students drop out of college. (For more information on the way patterns often blend in writing, see Chapter 13, "For Further Reading.")

Although writers often combine the patterns of development, your composition instructor may ask you to write an essay organized according to a single pattern. Such an assignment helps you understand a particular pattern's unique demands. Keep in mind, though, that most writing begins not with a specific pattern but with a specific *purpose*. The pattern or combination of patterns used to develop and organize an essay evolves out of that purpose.

Select an Organizational Approach

No matter which pattern(s) of development you select, you need to know four general approaches for organizing supporting evidence. These are explained below.

Chronological approach.   When an essay is organized *chronologically*, supporting material is arranged in a clear time sequence, usually starting with what happened first and ending with what happened last. Occasionally, chronological sequences can be rearranged to create flashback or flashforward effects, two techniques discussed in Chapter 5 on narration. Essays using narration (for example, an experience with prejudice) or process analysis (for instance, how to deliver an effective speech) are most likely to be organized chronologically. The paper on public speaking might use a time sequence to present its points: how to prepare a few days before the presentation is due; what to do right before the speech; what to concentrate on during the speech itself. (For examples of chronologically arranged student essays, turn to pages 158 and 342.)

Spatial approach.   When you arrange supporting evidence spatially, you discuss details as they occur in space, or from certain locations. This strategy is particularly appropriate for description. Imagine that you plan to write an essay describing the joyous times you spent as a child playing by a towering old oak tree in the neighborhood park. Using spatial organization, you start by describing the rich animal life (the plump earthworms, swarming anthills, and numerous animal tracks) you observed while hunkered down *at the base* of the tree. Next, you re-create the contented feeling you experienced sitting on a branch *in the middle* of the tree. Finally, you end by describing the glorious view of the world you had *from the top* of the tree.

Although spatial arrangement is flexible (you could, for instance, start with a description from the top of the tree), you should always proceed systematically. And once you select a particular spatial order, you should usually maintain that sequence throughout the essay; otherwise, readers may get lost along the way. (A spatially arranged student essay appears on page 97.)

Emphatic approach.   In *emphatic* order, the most compelling evidence is saved for last. This arrangement is based on the psychological principle that people remember best what they experience last. Emphatic order has built-in momentum because it starts with the least important point and builds to the most significant. This method is especially effective in argumentation-persuasion essays, in papers developed through examples, and in pieces involving comparison-contrast, division-classification, or causal analysis.

Consider an essay analyzing the negative effect that workaholic parents can have on their children. The paper might start with a brief discussion of relatively minor effects like the family's eating mostly frozen or take-out foods. Paragraphs on more serious effects might follow: children get no parental help with homework; they try to resolve personal problems without parental advice. Finally, the essay might close with a detailed discussion of the most significant effect—children's lack of self-esteem because they feel unimportant in their parents' lives. (The student essays on pages 24, 404, and 517 all use an emphatic arrangement.)

Simple-to-complex approach.   A final way to organize an essay is to proceed from relatively *simple* concepts to more *complex* ones. By starting with easy-to-grasp, generally accepted evidence, you establish rapport with your readers and assure them that the essay is firmly grounded in shared experience. In contrast, if you open with difficult or highly technical material, you risk confusing and alienating your audience.

Assume you plan to write a paper arguing that your college has endangered students' health by not making an all-out effort to remove asbestos from dormitories and classroom buildings. It probably wouldn't be a good idea to begin with a medically sophisticated explanation of precisely how asbestos damages lung tissue. Instead, you might start with an observation that is likely to be familiar to your readers—one that is part of their everyday experience. You could, for example, open with a description of asbestos—as readers might see it—wrapped around air ducts and furnaces or used as electrical insulation and fireproofing material. Having provided a basic, easy-to-visualize description, you could then go on to explain the complicated process by which asbestos can cause chronic lung inflammation. (See page 460 for an example of a student essay using the simple-to-complex arrangement.)

Depending on your purpose, any one of these four organizational approaches might be appropriate. For example, assume that you want to develop this thesis: "Being a parent today is much more difficult than it was a generation ago." To emphasize that the various stages in children's lives present parents with different difficulties, you'd probably select a *chronological* sequence. To show that the challenges that parents face vary depending on whether children are at home, at school, or in the world at large, you'd probably choose a *spatial* sequence. To stress the range of problems that parents face (from less to more serious), you'd probably use an *emphatic* sequence. To illustrate today's confusing array of theories for raising children, you might take a *simple-to-complex* approach, moving from the basic to the most sophisticated theories.

Prepare an Outline

Do you, if asked to submit an outline, prepare it *after* you've written the essay? If you do, we hope to convince you that having an outline—a skeletal version of your paper—*before* you begin the first draft makes the writing process much more manageable. The outline helps you organize your thoughts beforehand, and it guides your writing as you work on the draft. Even though ideas continue to evolve during the draft, an outline clarifies how ideas fit together, which points are major, which should come first, and so on. An outline may also reveal places where evidence is weak, underscoring the need, perhaps, for more prewriting.

Like previous stages in the writing process, outlining is individualized. Some people prepare highly structured outlines; others make only a few informal jottings. Sometimes outlining will go quickly, with points falling easily into place; at other times you'll have to work hard to figure out how points are related. If that happens, be glad you caught the problem while outlining, rather than while writing the first draft.

To prepare an effective outline, you should reread and evaluate your scratch outline and thesis as well as any other evidence you've generated since the prewriting stage. Then decide which pattern of development (description, cause-effect, and so on) seems to be suggested by your evidence. Also determine whether your evidence lends itself to a chronological, a spatial, an emphatic, or a simple-to-complex order. Having done all that, you're ready to identify and sequence your main and supporting points.

The amount of detail in an outline will vary according to the paper's length and the instructor's requirements. A scratch outline (like the one on page 28) is often sufficient, but for longer papers, you'll probably need a more detailed and formal outline. In such cases, the suggestions in the accompanying checklist will help you develop a sound plan. Feel free to modify these guidelines to suit your needs.

Outlining Checklist

- Write your purpose, audience, tone, and thesis at the top of the outlining page.
- Below the thesis, enter the pattern of development that seems to be implied by the evidence you've accumulated.
- Also record which of the four organizational approaches would be most effective in sequencing your evidence.
- Reevaluate your supporting material. Delete anything that doesn't develop the thesis or that isn't appropriate for your purpose, audience, and tone.

- Add any new points or material. Group related items together. Give each group a heading that represents a main topic in support of your thesis.
- Label these main topics with roman numerals (I, II, III, and so on). Let the order of the numerals indicate the best sequence.
- Identify subtopics and group them under the appropriate main topics. Indent and label these subtopics with capital letters (A, B, C, and so on). Let the order of the letters indicate the best sequence.
- Identify supporting points (often, reasons and examples) and group them under the appropriate subtopics. Indent and label these supporting points with arabic numbers (1, 2, 3, and so on). Let the numbers indicate the best sequence.
- Identify specific details (secondary examples, facts, statistics, expert opinions, quotations) and group them under the appropriate supporting points. Indent and label these specific details with lowercase letters (a, b, c, and so on). Let the letters indicate the best sequence.
- Examine your outline, looking for places where evidence is weak. Where appropriate, add new evidence.
- Double-check that all main topics, subtopics, supporting points, and specific details develop some aspect of the thesis. Also confirm that all items are arranged in the most logical order.

(For suggestions on using a word processor to ease the preparation of an outline, see page 85.)

The following sample outline develops the thesis "Being a parent today is much more difficult than it was a generation ago." You may remember that this is the thesis that Harriet Davids devised for the essay she planned to write in response to the assignment on page 12. Harriet's scratch list appears on page 28. When you compare Harriet's scratch list and outline, you'll find some differences. On the whole, the outline contains more specifics, but it doesn't include all the material in the scratch list. For example, after reconsidering her purpose, audience, tone, point of view, and thesis, Harriet decided to omit from her outline the section on day care and the points about rock concerts, MTV, rock posters, and AIDS.

The plan shown below is called a *topic outline* because it uses phrases, or topics, for each entry. For a lengthier or more complex paper, a *sentence outline* would be more appropriate.

Purpose: To inform

Audience: Instructor as well as class members, most of whom are 18–20 years old

Tone: Serious and straightforward

Thesis: Being a parent today is much more difficult than it was a generation ago.

Pattern of development: Exemplification

Organizational approach: Emphatic order

  I. Distractions from homework
    A. At home
      1. Stereos, radios, tapes
      2. Television
    B. Outside home
      1. Malls
      2. Video arcades
      3. Fast-food restaurants

  II. Sexually explicit materials
    A. In print
      1. Sex magazines
        a. <u>Playboy</u>
        b. <u>Penthouse</u>
      2. Pornographic books
    B. In movies
      1. Seduction scenes
      2. Casual sex
    C. On television
      1. Soap operas
      2. R-rated comedians
      3. R-rated movies on cable

  III. Increased dangers
    A. Drugs
    B. Alcohol
    C. Violent crimes against children

(If you'd like to see the first draft that resulted from Harriet's outline, turn to pages 66–67. Hints for moving from an outline to a first draft appear on page 54.)

Before starting to write your first draft, show your outline to several people (your instructor, friends, classmates). Their reactions will indicate whether your proposed organization is appropriate for your thesis, purpose, audience, and tone. Their comments can also highlight areas needing additional work. After making whatever changes are needed, you're in a good position to go ahead and write the first draft of your essay.

Activities: Organize the Evidence

1. The thesis statement below is followed by a scrambled list of supporting points. Prepare an outline for a potential essay, being sure to distinguish between major and secondary points.

   Thesis: Our schools, now in crisis, could be improved in several ways.

   Certification requirements for teachers
   Schedules
   Teachers
   Longer school year
   Merit pay for outstanding teachers
   Curriculum
   Better textbooks for classroom use
   Longer school days
   More challenging content in courses

2. Assume you plan to write an essay based on the following brief outline, which consists of a thesis and several points of support. Determine which pattern of development (pages 45–46) you would probably use for the essay's overall framework. Also identify which organizational approach (pages 46–48) you would most likely adopt to sequence the points of support listed. Then, use one or more patterns of development to generate material to support those points. Having done that, review the material generated, deleting, adding, combining, and arranging ideas in logical order. Finally, make an outline for the body of the essay. (Save your outline so you can work with it further after reading about the next stage in the writing process.)

   Thesis: Friends of the opposite sex fall into one of several categories: the pal, the confidant, or the pest.

- Frequently, an opposite-sex friend is simply a "pal."
- Sometimes, though, a pal turns, step by step, into a confidant.
- If a confidant begins to have romantic thoughts, he or she may become a pest, thus disrupting the friendship.

3. Retrieve the writing you prepared in response to activity 3, 4, or 5 on pages 43–44. As needed, reshape that material, applying the organizational principles discussed in these pages. Be sure, for example, that you select the approach (chronological, spatial, emphatic, or simple-to-complex) that would be most appropriate, given your main idea, purpose, audience, and tone. (Save whatever you prepare so you can work with it further after reading about the next stage in the writing process.)

4. Look again at the thesis and scratch outline you refined and elaborated in response to activity 6 on page 44. Reevaluate this material by deleting, adding, combining, and rearranging ideas as needed. Also, keeping your purpose, audience, and tone in mind, consider whether a chronological, a spatial, an emphatic, or a simple-to-complex approach will be most appropriate. Now prepare an outline of your ideas. Finally, ask at least one person to evaluate your organizational plan. (Save your outline. After reading about the next stage in the writing process, you can use it to write the essay's first draft.)

STAGE 5: WRITE THE FIRST DRAFT

After prewriting, deciding on a thesis, and developing and organizing evidence, you're ready to write a *first draft*—a rough, provisional version of your essay. Because of your work in the preceding stages, the first draft may flow quite smoothly. But don't be discouraged if it doesn't. You may find that your thesis has to be reshaped, that a point no longer fits, that you need to return to a prewriting activity to generate additional material. Such stopping and starting is to be expected. Writing the first draft is a process of discovery, involving the continual clarification and refining of ideas.

How to Proceed

There's no single right way to prepare a first draft. Some writers rely on their scratch lists or outlines heavily; others glance at them only occasionally. Some people write the first draft in longhand; others use a typewriter or a computer. (For hints on using a computer during the preparation of a first draft, see pages 85–86.)

However you choose to proceed, consider the following suggestions when moving from an outline or scratch list to a first draft:

- Make the outline's *main topics* (I, II, III) the *topic sentences* of the essay's supporting paragraphs. (Topic sentences are discussed later on pages 55–56.)
- Make the outline's *subtopics* (A, B, C) the *subpoints* in each paragraph.
- Make the outline's *supporting points* (1, 2, 3) the key *examples* and *reasons* in each paragraph.
- Make the outline's *specific details* (a, b, c) the *secondary examples, facts, statistics, expert opinion,* and *quotations* in each paragraph.

(To see how one student, Harriet Davids, moved from outline to first draft, turn to pages 66–67.)

Although outlines and lists are valuable for guiding your work, don't be so dependent on them that you shy away from new ideas that surface during your writing of the first draft. If promising new thoughts pop up, jot them down in the margin. Then, at the appropriate point, go back and evaluate them: Do they support your thesis? Are they appropriate for your essay's purpose, audience, and tone? If so, go ahead and include the material in your draft.

It's easy to get bogged down while preparing the first draft if you try to edit as you write. Remember: A draft isn't intended to be perfect. For the time being, adopt a relaxed, noncritical attitude. Working as quickly as you can, don't stop to check spelling, correct grammar, or refine sentence structure. Save these tasks for later. One good way to help remind you that the first draft is tentative is to use scrap paper and pencil. Writing on alternate lines also underscores your intention to revise later on, when the extra space will make it easier to add and delete material. Similarly, writing on only one side of the paper can prove helpful if, during revision, you decide to move a section to another part of the paper.

What should you do if you get stuck while writing your first draft? Stay calm and try to write something—no matter how awkward or imprecise it may seem. Just jot a reminder to yourself in the margin ("Fix this," "Redo," or "Ugh!") to fine-tune the section later. Or leave a blank space to hold a spot for the right words when they finally break loose. It may also help to reread—out loud is best—what you've already written. Regaining a sense of the larger context is often enough to get you moving again. You might also try talking your way through a troublesome section. By speaking aloud, you tap your natural oral fluency and put it to work in your writing.

If a section of the essay strikes you as particularly difficult, don't spend time struggling with it. Move on to an easier section, write that, and then return to the challenging part. If you're still getting nowhere, take a break. Watch television, listen to music, talk with friends. While you're relaxing, your thoughts may loosen up and untangle the knotty section.

Because you read essays from beginning to end, you may assume that writers work the same way, starting with the introduction and going straight through to the conclusion. Often, however, this isn't the case. In fact, since an introduction depends so heavily on everything that follows, it's usually best to write the introduction *after* the essay's body.

When preparing your first draft, you may find it helpful to follow this sequence:

1. Write the supporting paragraphs.
2. Connect ideas in the supporting paragraphs.
3. Write the introduction.
4. Write the conclusion.
5. Write the title.

Write the Supporting Paragraphs

Drawn from the main sections in your outline or scratch list, each *supporting paragraph* should develop an aspect of your essay's thesis. Besides containing relevant, concrete, and sufficient evidence (see pages 38–43), a strong supporting paragraph is (1) often focused by a topic sentence and (2) organized around one or more patterns of development. We'll focus on both features in the pages ahead. As you read our discussion, though, keep in mind that you shouldn't expect your draft paragraphs to be perfect; you'll have a chance to revise them later on.

Use topic sentences.   Frequently, each supporting paragraph in an essay is focused by a *topic sentence* that functions as a kind of minithesis for the paragraph. Generally one or two sentences in length, the topic sentence usually appears at or near the beginning of the paragraph. However, it may also appear at the end, in the middle, or—with varied wording—several times within the paragraph.

Regardless of its length or location, the topic sentence states the paragraph's main idea. The other sentences in the paragraph provide support for this central point in the form of examples, facts, expert opinion, and so on. Like a thesis statement, the topic sentence *signals the paragraph's subject* and frequently *indicates the writer's attitude* toward that subject. In the topic sentences that follow, the subject of the paragraph is underlined once and the attitude toward that subject is underlined twice:

> Some students select a particular field of study for the wrong reasons.
> The ocean dumping of radioactive waste is a ticking time bomb.
> Several contemporary rock groups show unexpected sensitivity to social issues.
> Political candidates are sold like slickly packaged products.

As you work on the first draft, you may find yourself writing paragraphs without paying too much attention to topic sentences. That's fine, as long as you evaluate the paragraphs later on. When revising, you can provide a topic sentence for a paragraph that needs a sharper focus, recast a topic sentence for a paragraph that ended up taking an unexpected turn, even eliminate a topic sentence altogether if a paragraph's content is sufficiently unified to imply its point.

Use the patterns of development.   As you saw on pages 45–46, an entire essay can be organized around one or more patterns of development (narration, process analysis, definition, and so forth). These patterns can also provide the organizational framework for an essay's supporting paragraphs. Assume you're writing an article for your town newspaper with the thesis "Year-round residents of an ocean community must take an active role in safeguarding the seashore environment." Your supporting paragraphs could develop this thesis through a variety of patterns, with each paragraph's topic sentence suggesting a specific pattern or combination of patterns. For example, one paragraph might start with the topic sentence "In a nearby ocean community, signs of environmental danger are every-where" and go on to *describe* a seaside town with polluted waters, blighted trees, and diseased marine life. The next paragraph might have the topic sentence "Fortunately, not all seaside towns are plagued by such environmental problems" and continue by *con-trasting* the troubled community with another, more ecologically sound shore town. A later paragraph, focused by the topic sentence "Residents can get involved in a variety of pro-environment activi-ties," might use *division-classification* to elaborate on activities at the neighborhood, town, and municipal levels.

Connect Ideas in the Supporting Paragraphs

While writing the supporting paragraphs, you can try to smooth out the progression of ideas within and between para-graphs. In a *coherent* essay, the relationship between points is clear; readers can easily follow the development of your thoughts. (Some-times, working on coherence causes a first draft to get bogged down; if this happens, move on, and wait until the revision stage to focus on such matters.)

The following paragraph lacks coherence for two main reasons. First, it sequences ideas improperly. (The idea about the toll atten-dants' being cut off from coworkers is introduced, dropped, then picked up again. References to motorists are similarly scattered throughout the paragraph.) Second, it doesn't indicate how individ-ual ideas are related. (What, for example, is the connection between drivers who pass by without saying anything and attendants who have to work at night?)

Incoherent Support

Collecting tolls on the turnpike must be one of the loneliest jobs in the world. Each toll attendant sits in his or her booth, cut off from other attendants. Many drivers pass by each booth. None stays long enough for a brief "hello." Most don't acknowledge the attendant at all. Many toll attendants work at night, pushing them "out of synch" with the rest of the world. And sometimes the attendants have to deal with rude drivers who treat them like non-people, swearing at them for the long lines at the tollgate. Attendants also dislike how cut off they feel from their coworkers. Except for infrequent breaks, they have little chance to chat with each other and swap horror stories—small pleasures that would make their otherwise routine jobs bearable.

Coherent Support

Collecting tolls on the turnpike must be one of the loneliest jobs in the world. First of all, although many drivers pass by the attendants, none stays long enough for more than a brief "hello." Most drivers, in fact, don't acknowledge the toll collectors at all, with the exception of those rude drivers who treat the attendants like non-people, swearing at them for the long lines at the tollgate. Then, too, many toll attendants work at night, pushing them further "out of synch" with the rest of the world. Worst of all, attendants say, is how isolated they feel from their coworkers. Each attendant sits in his or her booth, cut off from other attendants. Except for infrequent breaks, they have little chance to chat with each other and swap horror stories—small pleasures that would make their otherwise routine jobs bearable.

To avoid the kinds of problems found in the incoherent paragraph, use—as the revised version does—two key strategies: (1) a clearly *chronological, spatial, emphatic* ("*Worst of all,* the attendants say...*"*), or *simple-to-complex* approach and (2) *signal devices* ("*First of all,* although many drivers pass by...") to show how ideas are connected. For a discussion of the four organizational approaches, see pages 46–48. The following paragraphs describe signal devices.

Once you determine a logical approach for presenting your points, you need to make sure readers can follow the progression of those points. Signal devices provide readers with cues, reminding them where they have been and indicating where they are going.

Aim to include some signals—however awkward or temporary—in your first draft. If you find you *can't,* that's probably a warning that your ideas may not be arranged logically. A light touch should be your goal with such signals. Too many call attention to themselves, making the essay mechanical and plodding. In any case, here are some signaling devices to consider:

1. Transitions.   Words and phrases that ease readers from one idea to another are called *transitions.* Among such signals are the following:

Time	Space	Addition	Examples
first	above	moreover	for instance
next	below	also	for example
now	next to	furthermore	to illustrate
finally	behind	in addition	specifically

Contrast	Comparison	Summary
but	similarly	therefore
however	also	thus
otherwise	likewise	in short
on the one/other hand	too	in conclusion

Here's an earlier paragraph from this chapter. Note how the italicized transitions show readers how ideas fit together.

> *After* you've generated supporting evidence, you're ready to organize that material. Even highly compelling evidence won't illustrate the validity of your thesis or achieve your purpose if the readers have to plow through a maze of chaotic evidence. Some writers can move quickly from generating support to writing a clearly structured first draft. (They usually say they have sequenced their ideas in their heads.) Most, *however,* need to spend some time sorting out their thoughts on paper before starting the first draft; *otherwise,* they tend to lose their way in a tangle of ideas.

2. Bridging sentences. Although bridging sentences may be used within a paragraph, they are more often used to move readers from one paragraph to the next. Look again at the first sentence in the preceding paragraph. Note that the sentence consists of two parts: The first part reminds readers that the previous discussion focused on techniques for generating evidence; the second part tells readers that the focus will now be the organization of such evidence.

3. Repeated words, synonyms, and pronouns. The repetition of important words maintains continuity, reassures readers that they are on the right track, and highlights key ideas. Synonyms—words similar in meaning to key words or phrases—also provide coherence, while making it possible to avoid unimaginative and tedious repetitions. Finally, pronouns (*he, she, it, they, this, that*) enhance coherence by causing readers to think back to the original word (antecedent) the pronoun replaces. When using pronouns, however, be sure there is no ambiguity about antecedents.

Reprinted here is another paragraph from this chapter. Repeated words have been underlined once, synonyms underlined twice, and pronouns printed in italic type to illustrate how these techniques were used to integrate the paragraph's ideas.

> The process of prewriting—discovering a limited subject and generating ideas about *it*—prepares you for the next stage in writing an essay: identifying the paper's <u>thesis</u> or <u>controlling idea.</u> Presenting your opinion on a subject, the <u>thesis</u> should focus on an interesting and significant issue, *one* that engages your energies and merits your consideration. You may think of the <u>thesis</u> as the essay's <u>hub</u>—the <u>central point</u> around which all the other material revolves. Your <u>thesis</u> determines what does and does not belong in the essay. The <u>thesis,</u> especially when *it* occurs early in an essay, also helps focus the reader on the piece's central point.

Write the Introduction

Many writers don't prepare an introduction until they have started to revise; others feel more comfortable if their first draft includes in basic form all parts of the final essay. If that's how you feel, you'll probably write the introduction as you complete your first draft. No matter when you prepare it, keep in mind how crucial the introduction is to your essay's success. Specifically, the introduction serves three distinct functions: It arouses readers' interest, introduces your subject, and presents your thesis.

The length of your introduction will vary according to your paper's scope and purpose. Most essays you write, however, will be served best by a one- or two-paragraph beginning. To write an effective introduction, use any of the following methods, singly or in combination. The thesis statement in each sample introduction is underlined.

Broad Statement Narrowing to a Limited Subject

For generations, morality has been molded primarily by parents, religion, and schools. Children traditionally acquired their ideas about what is right and wrong, which goals are important in life, and how other people should be treated from these three sources. But now there is another powerful force influencing youngsters. <u>Television is implanting in children negative values about sex, work, and family life.</u>

Brief Anecdote

At a local high school recently, students in a psychology course were given a hint of what it is like to be the parents of a newborn. Each "parent" had to carry a raw egg around at all times to symbolize the responsibilities of parenthood. The egg could not be left alone; it limited the "parents'" activities; it placed a full-time emotional burden on "Mom" and "Dad." This class exercise illustrates a common problem facing the majority of new mothers and fathers. <u>Most people receive little preparation for the job of being parents.</u>

Ideas That Are the Opposite of the One Developed

We hear a great deal about divorce's disastrous impact on children. We are deluged with advice on ways to make divorce as painless as possible for youngsters; we listen to heartbreaking stories about the confused, grieving children of divorced parents. Little attention has been paid, however, to a different kind of effect that divorce may have on children. <u>Children from divorced families may become skilled manipulators, playing off one parent against the other, worsening an already painful situation.</u>

Series of Short Questions

What happens if a child is caught vandalizing school property? What happens if a child goes for a joyride in a stolen car and accidentally hits a pedestrian? Should parents be liable for their children's mistakes? Should parents have to pay what might be hundreds of thousands of dollars in damages? Adults have begun to think seriously about such questions because the laws concerning the limits of parental responsibility are changing rapidly. <u>With unfortunate frequency, courts have begun to hold parents legally and financially accountable for their children's misdeeds.</u>

Quotation

Educator Neil Postman believes that television has blurred the line between childhood and adulthood. According to Postman, "All the secrets that a print culture kept from children...are revealed all at once by media that do not, and cannot, exclude any audience." <u>This media barrage of information, once intended only for adults, has changed childhood for the worse.</u>

Refutation of a Common Belief

Adolescents care only about material things; their lives revolve around brand-name sneakers, designer jeans, the latest fad in stereo equipment. They resist education, don't read, barely know who is president, mainline rock 'n' roll, experiment with drugs, and exist on a steady diet of Ring-Dings, nachos, and beer. This is what many adults, including parents, seem to believe about the young. <u>The reality is, however, that young people today show more maturity and common sense than most adults give them credit for.</u>

Dramatic Fact or Statistic

Seventy percent of the respondents in a poll conducted by columnist Ann Landers stated that if they could live their lives over, they would choose not to have children. This startling statistic makes one wonder what these people believed parenthood would be like. <u>Most parents, it seems, have unrealistic expectations about their children.</u> Parents want their children to accept their values, follow their paths, and succeed where they failed.

Introductory paragraphs sometimes end with a *plan of development:* a quick preview of the essay's major points in the order in which those points will be discussed. The plan of development may be part of the thesis (as in the first sample introduction) or it may immediately follow the thesis (as in the last sample introduction). Because the plan of development outlines the essay's organizational structure, it helps prepare the reader for the essay's progression of ideas. In a brief essay, readers can often keep track of the ideas without this extra help. In a longer paper, though, a plan of development can be an effective unifying device since it highlights the main ideas the essay will develop.

Write the Conclusion

You may have come across essays that ended with jarring abruptness because they had no conclusions at all. Other papers may have had conclusions, but they sputtered to a weak close, a sure sign that the writers had run out of steam and wanted to finish as quickly as possible. Just as satisfying closes are an important part of everyday life (we feel cheated if dinner doesn't end with dessert or if a friend leaves without saying goodbye), a strong conclusion is an important part of an effective essay. Generally one or two paragraphs in length, the conclusion should give the reader a feeling of completeness and finality. One way to achieve this sense of "rounding off" is to return to an image, idea, or anecdote from the introduction. Because people tend to remember most clearly the points they read last, the conclusion is also a good place to remind readers of your thesis. You may also use the conclusion to make a final point about your subject. Be careful, though, not to open an entirely new line of thought at the essay's close.

Illustrated briefly here are several strategies for writing sound conclusions. These techniques may be used singly or in combination. The first strategy, the summary conclusion, can be especially helpful in long, complex essays since readers may appreciate a review of your points. Tacked onto a short essay, though, a summary conclusion often seems boring and mechanical.

Summary

Contrary to what many adults think, most adolescents are not only aware of the important issues of the times but also deeply concerned about them. They are sensitive to the plight of the homeless, the destruction of the environment, and the pitfalls of rampant materialism. Indeed, today's young people are not less mature and sensible than their parents were. If anything, they are more so.

Prediction

The growing tendency on the part of the judicial system to hold parents responsible for the actions of their wayward children can have a disturbing impact on all of us. Parents will feel bitter toward their own children and cynical about a system that holds them accountable for the actions of minors. Children, continuing to escape the consequences of their actions, will become even more lawless and destructive. Society cannot afford two such possibilities.

Quotation

The comic W. C. Fields is reputed to have said, "Anyone who hates children and dogs can't be all bad." Most people do not share

Fields's cynicism. Viewing childhood as a time of purity, they are alarmed at the way television exposes children to the seamy side of life, stripping youngsters of their innocence and giving them a glib sophistication that is a poor substitute for wisdom.

Statistic

Granted, divorce may, in some cases, be the best thing for families torn apart by parents who battle one another. However, in longitudinal studies of children from divorced families, psychologist Judith Wallerstein found that only 10 percent of the youngsters felt relief at their parents' divorce; the remaining 90 percent felt devastated. Such statistics surely call into question parents' claims that they are divorcing for their children's sake.

Recommendation or Call for Action

It is a mistake to leave parenting to instinct. Instead, we should make parenting skills a required course in schools. In addition, a nationwide hotline should be established to help parents deal with crises. Such training and continuing support would help adults deal more effectively with many of the problems they face as parents.

Write the Title

Some writers say that they began a certain piece with only a title in mind. But for most people, writing a title is a finishing touch. Although creating a title for your paper is usually one of the last steps in writing an essay, it shouldn't be done haphazardly. It may take time to write an effective title—one that hints at the essay's thesis and snares the reader's interest.

Good titles may make use of the following techniques: repetition of sounds ("Why I Want a Wife"); questions ("Are the Homeless Crazy?"), and humor ("How to Say Nothing in 500 Words"). More often, though, titles are straightforward phrases derived from the essay's subject or thesis: "Shooting an Elephant" and "TV Addiction," for example.

Pulling It All Together

Now that you know how to prepare a first draft, you might find it helpful to examine the accompanying illustration to see how the different parts of a draft can fit together. Keep in mind that not every essay you write will take this shape. As your purpose, audience, and tone change, so will your essay's structure. An introduction or conclusion, for instance, may be developed in more than one paragraph; the thesis statement may be implied or delayed until the essay's middle or end; not all paragraphs may have topic sentences; and several supporting paragraphs may be needed to develop a single topic sentence. Even so, the basic format presented here offers a strategy for organizing a variety of writing assignments—from term papers to lab reports. Once you feel comfortable with the structure, you have a foundation on which to base your variations. (This book's student and professional essays illustrate some possibilities.) Even when using a specific format, you always have room to give your spirit and imagination free play. The language you use, the details you select, the perspective you offer are uniquely yours. They are what make your essay different from everyone else's.

Introductory Paragraph(s)	Opening comments Thesis statement Plan of development (optional)
Supporting Paragraphs	Topic sentence 1 Specific details
	Topic sentence 2 Specific details
	Topic sentence 3 Specific details
Concluding Paragraph(s)	Closing comments

Sample First Draft

Here is the first draft of Harriet Davids's essay. (The assignment and prewriting for the essay appear on pages 24 and 28.) Harriet wrote the draft in one sitting. Working at a computer, she started by typing her thesis at the top of the first page. Then, following the guidelines on page 54, she moved the material in her outline (page 54) to her draft. Harriet worked rapidly; she started with the first body paragraph and wrote straight through to the last supporting paragraph.

By moving quickly, Harriet got down her essay's basic text rather easily. Once she felt she had captured in rough form what she wanted to say, she reread her draft to get a sense of how she might open and close the essay. Then she drafted her introduction and conclusion; both appear here, together with the body of the essay. The commentary following the draft will give you a clearer sense of how Harriet proceeded.

Challenges for Today's Parents
by Harriet Davids

Thesis: Being a parent today is much more difficult than it was a generation ago.

Raising children used to be much simpler in the '50s and '60s. I remember TV images from that era showing that parenting involved simply teaching kids to clean their rooms, do their homework, and _____(ADD SPECIFICS). But being a parent today is much more difficult because nowadays parents have to shield/protect kids from lots of things, like distractions from schoolwork, from sexual material, from dangerous situations.

Parents have to control all the new distractions/temptations that turn kids away from schoolwork. These days many kids have stereos and televisions in their rooms. Certainly, my girls can't resist the urge to listen to MTV, especially if it's time to do homework. Unfortunately, though, kids aren't assigned much homework and what is assigned too often is busywork. And there are even more distractions outside the home. Teens no longer hang out/congregate on the corner where Dad and Mom can yell to them to come home and do homework. Instead they hang out at the mall, in video arcades, and fast-food restaurants. Obviously, parents and school can't compete with all this.

Also (WEAK TRANS.) parents have to help kids develop responsible sexual values even though sex is everywhere. Kids see sex magazines and dirty paperbacks in the corner store where they used to get candy and comic books. And instead of the artsy nude shots of the past, kids see ronchey (SP?), explicit shots in <u>Playboy</u> and <u>Penthouse</u>. And movies have sexy stuff in them today. Teachers seduce students and people treat sex casually/as a sport. Not exactly traditional values. Even worse is what's on TV. Kids see soap-opera characters in bed and cable shows full of nudity by just flipping the dial (FIX). The situation has gotten so out of hand that maybe the government should establish guidelines on what's permissible.

Worst of all are the life-threatening dangers that parents must help children fend off over the years. With older kids, drugs fall into place as a main concern (AWK). Peer pressure to try drugs is bigger (WRONG WORD) to kids than their parents' warnings. Other kinds of warnings are common when children are small. Then parents fear violence since news shows constantly report stories of little children being abused (ADD SPECIFICS). And when kids aren't much older, they have to resist the pressure to drink. Alcohol has always attracted kids, but nowadays they are drinking more and this can be deadly, especially when drinking is combined with driving (REDO).

Most adults love their children and want to be good parents. But it's difficult because the world seems stacked against young people. Even Holden Caufield (SP?) had trouble dealing with society's confusing pressures. Parents must give their children some freedom but not so much that the kids lose sight of what's important.

Commentary

As you can see, Harriet's draft is rough. Because she knew she would revise later on (page 68), she "zapped out" the draft in an informal, colloquial style. For example, she occasionally expressed her thoughts in fragments ("Not exactly traditional values"), relied heavily on "and" as a transition, and used slangy expressions like "kids," "dirty paperbacks," and "lots of things." Similarly, rather than fine-tuning, Harriet simply used capital letters to type parenthetic notes to herself: "REDO" or "FIX" to signal awkward sentences; "ADD SPECIFICS" to mark overly general statements; "WRONG WORD" after an imprecise word; "SP?" to remind herself to check spelling in the dictionary; "WEAK TRANS." to indicate where a stronger signaling device was needed. Note, too, that she used slashes between alternative word choices and left a blank space when wording just wouldn't come. (Harriet's final draft appears on pages 74–75.)

Writing a first draft may seem like quite a challenge, but the tips offered in these pages should help you proceed with confidence. Indeed, as you work on the draft, you may be surprised how much you enjoy writing. After all, this is your chance to get down on paper something you want to say.

Activities: Write the First Draft

1. Retrieve the writing you prepared in response to activity 3 on page 53. Applying the principles just presented, rework that material. If you wrote a single paragraph earlier, expand the material into a full essay draft. If you prepared an essay, strengthen what you wrote. In both cases, remember to consider your purpose, audience, and tone as you write the body of the essay as well as its introduction and conclusion. (Save your draft so you can rework it even further after reading about the next stage in the writing process.)

2. Referring to the outline you prepared in response to activity 2 or activity 4 on pages 52–53, draft the body of your essay, making your evidence as strong as possible. As you work, keep your purpose, audience, and tone in mind. After reading what you've prepared, go ahead and draft a rough introduction, conclusion, and title. Finally, ask at least one other person to react to your draft by listing its strengths and weaknesses. (Save the draft so you can work with it further after reading about the next stage in the writing process.)

STAGE 6: REVISE THE ESSAY

By now, you've probably abandoned any preconceptions you might have had about good writers sitting down and creating a finished product in one easy step. Alexander Pope's comment that "true ease in writing comes from art, not chance" is as true today as it was more than two hundred years ago. Writing that seems effortlessly clear is often the result of sustained work, not of good luck or even inborn talent. And much of this work takes place during the final stage of the writing process when ideas, paragraphs, sentences, and words are refined and reshaped.

Professional writers—novelists, journalists, textbook authors— seldom submit a piece of writing that hasn't been revised. They recognize that rough, unpolished work doesn't do them justice.

What's more, they often look forward to revising. Columnist Ellen Goodman puts it this way: "What makes me happy is rewriting.... It's like cleaning house, getting rid of all the junk, getting things in the right order, tightening up."

In a sense, revision occurs throughout the writing process: At some earlier stage, you may have dropped an idea, overhauled your thesis, or shifted paragraph order. What, then, is different about the rewriting that occurs in the revision stage? The answer has to do with the literal meaning of the word *revision*—to resee, or to see again. Genuine revision involves casting clear eyes on your work, viewing it as though you're a reader rather than the writer. Revision means that you go through your paper looking for trouble, ready to pick a fight with your own writing. And then you must be willing to sit down and make the changes needed for your writing to be as effective as possible.

Revision is not, as some believe, simply touch-up work— changing a sentence here or a word there, eliminating spelling errors, typing a neat final copy. Revision means cutting deadwood, rearranging paragraphs, substituting new words for old ones, recasting sentences, improving coherence, even generating new material when appropriate. Because such work is challenging, you may resist revision or feel shaky about how to proceed.

Strategies to Make Revision Easier

The following pointers should help get you going if you balk at or feel overwhelmed by revising.

- *Set your draft aside for a while* before revising. When you pick up your paper again, you'll have a fresh, more objective point of view.
- *Work from typed material* whenever possible. Having your essay in neutral typed letters instead of in your own familiar writing helps you see the paper impartially, as if someone else had written it. Each time you make major changes, try to retype that section so that you can see it anew. (For hints on using a word processor to revise, see pages 86–87.)
- *Read your draft aloud* as often as you can. Hearing how your writing sounds helps you pick up problems that passed you by before: places where sentences are awkward, meaning is

ambiguous, words are imprecise. Even better, have another person read aloud to you what you have written. If the reader slows to a crawl over a murky paragraph or trips over a convoluted sentence, you know where you have to do some rewriting.

- *Ask for feedback.* Many instructors include feedback sessions as a regular part of a composition course. If your instructor does not, you can set up feedback sessions on your own, adapting the suggestions here to fit your needs. Start by selecting readers who are critical (not a love-struck admirer or doting grandparent) and who are skilled enough to provide useful commentary. To ensure that you leave feedback sessions with specific observations about what does and doesn't work in your writing, give your readers a clear sense of what you want from them. If you simply ask, "How's this?" you may receive a vague comment like "It's not very effective." What you want are concrete observations and suggestions: "I'm confused because what you say in the fifth sentence contradicts what you say in the second."

  To promote such specific responses, ask your readers targeted questions like "I'm having trouble moving from my second to my third point. How can I make the transition smoother?" Such questions require more than "yes" or "no" responses; they encourage readers to dig into your writing where you sense it needs work. You may develop your own questions or adapt the revision checklist on pages 72–73.

- *Listen with an open mind* to those giving you feedback. Take notes on their observations, and when everyone is finished commenting, reread your notes. Which remarks seem valid? Which don't? Try using a *feedback chart* or a system of *marginal annotations* to help you evaluate and remedy any perceived weaknesses in your draft.

  Here's how to use a three-column feedback chart. In the first column, list the major problems you and your readers see in the draft. Next, rank the problems, designating the most critical as 1. Then, in the second column, jot down possible solutions—your own as well as your readers'. Finally, in the third column, briefly describe what action you'll take to correct each problem.

  If you don't use a feedback chart, be sure to enter marginal annotations on your draft before revising it. In the margins, jot down any major problems, numbered in order of importance, along with possible remedies. Marking your draft this way, much as an instructor might, helps you view your paper as though it were written by someone else. Then, keeping the draft's problems in mind, start revising. You may make changes directly above the appropriate line or, when necessary, rework sections on a separate sheet of paper.

The feedback chart and marginal annotations will also help you evaluate your instructor's comments on your paper. Like many students, you may be tempted to look only briefly at your instructor's comments. Perhaps you've "had it" with the essay and don't want to think about preparing a revised version that reflects the instructor's remarks. And if there's a grade on the essay, you may think that's the only thing that counts. But remember: Although grades are important, comments are even more so. They can help you *improve* your writing—if not in this paper, then in the next one. If you don't understand or agree with the instructor's observations, don't hesitate to request a conference. Getting together gives both you and the instructor a chance to clarify your respective points of view.

- *View revision as a series of steps.* Don't try to tackle all of a draft's problems at once; instead, proceed step by step. (The feedback chart and annotation system described above will help you do just that.) Whenever possible, read your draft several times, each time focusing on different issues and asking yourself different questions. Move from a broad view of the draft to an up-close look at its mechanics.

The following checklist describes a number of questions you and your readers can ask when moving through the various steps in the revising process. (To see how one student, Harriet Davids, used the checklist when revising, turn to pages 78–79.) Keep in mind, though, that there are no hard-and-fast rules about the revision steps outlined here. Everyone approaches revision differently. There are bound to be occasions when you have time for only one quick pass over a draft. And with experience, you'll learn how to streamline the process so you can focus on the most critical issues for a particular piece of writing. Feel free, then, to adapt our suggestions to your individual needs.

Revision Checklist

First Step: Revise Overall Meaning and Structure

- Considering the essay's purpose, audience, and tone (pages 17–21), in what ways does or doesn't the paper accomplish what was intended?
- What is the essay's thesis (pages 29–33)? Is it stated explicitly, or is it implied? If the perceived thesis isn't what was intended, what changes need to be made?
- What are the essay's main points of support (pages 35–36)? If any of these stray from or contradict the thesis (pages 38–39), what changes need to be made?
- Are the main points arranged in a chronological, spatial, emphatic, or simple-to-complex sequence (pages 46–48)? How does this organizational format reinforce the thesis?
- Which patterns of development (pages 45–46) provide the essay's organizational framework? How do these patterns reinforce the thesis?

Second Step: Revise Paragraph Development

- Where in each paragraph does support seem irrelevant, vague, insufficient, inaccurate, or nonrepresentative (pages 38–43)? What could be done to remedy these problems?
- By what organizational principles (pages 45–48) are the ideas in each paragraph arranged? Why is this the most effective arrangement?
- What signal devices (pages 58–60) are used to connect ideas within and between paragraphs? Where are there too few signals or too many?
- What strategies are used to open (pages 60–62) and close (pages 62–64) the essay? How could the introduction and conclusion be made more effective?

Third Step: Revise Sentences and Words

- Which sentences seem inconsistent with the essay's intended tone (pages 18–20)? How could the problem be corrected?
- Where does sentence structure become monotonous and predictable (pages 96 and 156–157)? How could a different sentence pattern add variety?
- Which words are vague and overly general (pages 95–96 and 156–157)? How could the language be made more vigorous and concrete?

- Where does gender-biased language (pages 738–39) appear? How could the problem be eliminated?

Fourth Step: Proofread for Grammar, Punctuation, and Typing Errors

- A note about proofreading: Although proofing seems to involve relatively minor matters, an accumulation of small errors—misspellings, typos, misplaced commas—can distract readers and sabotage an otherwise strong essay. So before handing in the final draft of your essay, proofread it closely, keeping a dictionary and English handbook nearby. When proofing, people tend to see what they think is on the page rather than what really is there. Reading the essay out loud and backwards, starting with the last word first, can highlight errors that otherwise might slip by.

STUDENT ESSAY

In this chapter, we've taken you through the various stages in the writing process. You've seen how Harriet Davids used prewriting (pages 21–24 and 28) and outlining (page 51) to arrive at her first draft (pages 66–67). In the following pages, you'll look at Harriet's final draft—the paper she submitted to her instructor.

Harriet, a thirty-eight-year-old college student and mother of two teenagers, wanted to write an informative paper with a straightforward, serious tone. While preparing her essay, she kept in mind that her audience would include her course instructor as well as her classmates, most of them considerably younger than she. This is the assignment that prompted Harriet's essay:

Because the world these days is a difficult, even dangerous place, parents understandably worry about their children. Write an essay supporting the idea that today's world is, in many ways, hostile—particularly to children.

Harriet's essay is annotated so you can see how it illustrates the essay format described on page 65. As you read her essay, try to determine how well it reflects the principles of effective writing. The commentary following the paper will help you look at the essay more closely and give you some sense of the way Harriet went about revising her first draft.

Challenges for Today's Parents
by Harriet Davids

Introduction

Reruns of situation comedies from the 1950s and   1
early 1960s dramatize the kinds of problems that parents used to have with their children. The Cleavers
scold Beaver for not washing his hands before dinner;
the Andersons ground Bud for not doing his homework; the Nelsons dock little Ricky's allowance

Thesis

because he keeps forgetting to clean his room. But
times have changed dramatically. Being a parent
today is much more difficult than it was a generation

Plan of
development

ago. Parents nowadays must protect their children
from a growing number of distractions, from sexually
explicit material, and from life-threatening situations.

First supporting
paragraph

Today's parents must try, first of all, to control all   2
the new distractions that tempt children away from
schoolwork. At home, a child may have a room fur-

Topic sentence

nished with a stereo and television. Not many young
people can resist the urge to listen to an album or
watch MTV--especially if it is time to do schoolwork.
Outside the home, the distractions are even more
alluring. Children no longer "hang out" on a neighborhood corner within earshot of Mom or Dad's reminder
to come in and do homework. Instead, they congregate in vast shopping malls, buzzing video arcades,
and gleaming fast-food restaurants. Parents and
school assignments have obvious difficulty competing with such enticing alternatives.

Second
supporting
paragraph

Besides dealing with these distractions, par-   3
ents have to shield their children from a flood of sexually explicit materials. Today, children can find sex

Topic sentence
with link to
previous
paragraph

magazines and pornographic paperbacks in the
same corner store that once offered only comics and
candy. Children will not see the fuzzily photo-
graphed nudes that a previous generation did but
will encounter the hard-core raunchiness of <u>Playboy</u>
or <u>Penthouse</u>. Moreover, the movies young people
attend often focus on highly sexual situations. It is
difficult to teach children traditional values when
films show teachers seducing students and young
people treating sex as a casual sport. An even more
difficult matter for parents is the heavily sexual

content of programs on television. With just a flick of the dial, children can see soap-opera stars cavorting in bed or watch cable programs where nudity is common.

Third supporting paragraph

Topic sentence with emphasis signal

Most disturbing to parents today, however, is   4
the increase in life-threatening dangers that face young people. When children are small, parents fear that their youngsters may be victims of violence. Every news program seems to carry a report about a mass murderer who preys on young girls, a deviant who has buried six boys in his cellar, or an organized child pornography ring that molests preschoolers. When children are older, parents begin to worry about their kids' use of drugs. Peer pressure to experiment with drugs is often stronger than parents' warnings. This pressure to experiment can be fatal. Finally, even if young people escape the hazards associated with drugs, they must still resist the pressure to drink. Although alcohol has always held an attraction for teenagers, reports indicate that they are drinking more than ever before. As many parents know, the consequences of this attraction can be deadly--especially when drinking is combined with driving.

Conclusion

References to TV shows recall introduction

Within one generation, the world as a place to   5
raise children has changed dramatically. One wonders how yesterday's parents would have dealt with today's problems. Could the Andersons have kept Bud away from MTV? Could the Nelsons have shielded little Ricky from sexually explicit material? Could the Cleavers have protected Beaver from drugs and alcohol? Parents must be aware of all these distractions and dangers yet be willing to give their children the freedom they need to become responsible adults. It is not an easy task.

COMMENTARY

Introduction and thesis.   The opening paragraph attracts readers' interest by recalling several vintage television shows that have almost become part of our cultural heritage. Harriet begins with these examples from the past because they offer such a sharp contrast to the present, thus underscoring the idea expressed in her *thesis:* "Being a parent today is much more difficult than it was a generation ago." Opening in this way, with material that serves as a striking contrast to what follows, is a common and effective strategy. Note, too, that Harriet's thesis states the paper's subject (being a parent) as well as her attitude toward the subject (the job is more demanding than it was years ago).

Plan of development.   Harriet follows her thesis with a *plan of development* that anticipates the three major points to be covered in the essay's supporting paragraphs. Unfortunately, this particular plan of development is somewhat mechanical, with the major points being trotted past the reader in one long, awkward sentence. To deal with the problem, Harriet could have rewritten the sentence or eliminated the plan of development altogether, ending the introduction with her thesis.

Patterns of development.   Although Harriet develops her thesis primarily through *examples,* she also draws on two other patterns of development. The whole paper implies a *contrast* between the way life is now and the way it used to be. The essay also contains an element of *causal analysis* since all the factors that Harriet cites affect children and the way they are raised.

Purpose, audience, and tone.   Given the essay's *purpose* and *audience,* Harriet adopts a serious *tone,* providing no-nonsense evidence to support her thesis. But assume she had been asked by her daughters' school newspaper to write a humorous column about the trials and tribulations that parents face raising children. Aiming for a different tone, purpose, and audience, Harriet would have taken another approach. Drawing on her experience as a mother of two teenage daughters, she might have confessed how she survives MTV's flash and dazzle, as well as the din of stereos blasting rock music at all hours: she stuffs her ears with cotton, hides her daughters' tapes, and cuts off the electricity. This material—with its personalized perspective, exaggeration, and light tone—would be appropriate.

Organization.   Structuring the essay around a series of *relevant* and *specific examples,* Harriet uses *emphatic order* to sequence the paper's three main points: that a growing number of distractions, sexually explicit materials, and life-threatening situations make parenting difficult nowadays. The third supporting paragraph begins with the words "Most disturbing to parents today...," signaling that Harriet feels particular concern about the physical dangers children face. Moreover, she uses basic organizational strategies to sequence the supporting examples within each paragraph. The details in the first supporting paragraph are organized *spatially,* starting with distractions at home and moving to those outside the home. The second supporting paragraph arranges examples *emphatically.* Harriet starts with sexually explicit publications and ends with the "even more difficult matter" of sexuality on television. The third and final supporting paragraph is organized *chronologically;* it begins by discussing dangers to small children and concludes by talking about teenagers.

The essay also displays Harriet's familiarity with other kinds of organizational strategies. Each supporting paragraph opens with a *topic sentence.* Further, *signal devices* are used throughout the paper to show how ideas are related to one another: *transitions* ("Instead, they congregate in vast shopping malls"; "Moreover, the movies young people attend often focus on highly sexual situations"); *repetition* ("sexual situations" and "sexual content"); *synonyms* ("distractions...enticing alternatives" and "life-threatening...fatal"); *pronouns* ("young people...they"); and *bridging sentences* ("Besides dealing with these distractions, parents have to shield their children from a flood of sexually explicit material").

Two minor problems.   Harriet's efforts to write a well-organized essay result in a somewhat predictable structure. It might have been better had she rewritten one of the paragraphs, perhaps embedding the topic sentence in the middle of the paragraph or saving it for the end. Similarly, Harriet's signal devices are a little heavy-handed. Even so, an essay with a sharp focus and clear signals is preferable to one with a confusing or inaccessible structure. As she gains more experience, Harriet can work on making the structure of her essays more subtle.

Conclusion.   Harriet brings the essay to a satisfying *close* by reminding readers of the paper's central idea and three main points. The final paragraph also extends the essay's scope by introducing a new but related issue: that parents have to strike a balance between their need to provide limitations and their children's need for freedom.

Revising the first draft.   With the help of several classmates, Harriet reworked her essay a number of times. Using the checklist on pages 72–73 to focus their feedback, Harriet's revising team offered various suggestions to strengthen the paper. To get a sense of Harriet's revising process, compare the final version of her conclusion (page 75) with the original version reprinted here.

Original Version of Conclusion

Most adults love their children and want to be good parents. But it's difficult because the world seems stacked against young people. Even Holden Caulfield had trouble dealing with society's pressures. Parents must give their children some freedom but not so much that kids lose sight of what's important.

As soon as Harriet heard her paper read aloud during a group session, she realized the conclusion didn't work at all, but she wisely waited to rework the conclusion until after she had fine-tuned the rest of the essay. At that point, she made marginal annotations summarizing the problems that she and her editing group detected in the conclusion. Together, they identified three problems, numbered in order of importance. First, the conclusion seemed tacked on, rather like a tired afterthought. Second, the allusion to *The Catcher in the Rye* misrepresented the essay's focus since Harriet discusses children of all ages, not just teens. Third, the first sentence in the conclusion was bland and boring.

Keeping these points in mind, Harriet decided to scrap her original conclusion. Working at a word processor, she prepared a much stronger concluding paragraph. Besides eliminating the distracting reference to Holden Caulfield, she replaced the shopworn opening sentence ("Most adults love their children...") with three interesting and rhythmical questions ("Could the Andersons...? Could the Nelsons...? Could the Cleavers...?"). Because these questions recall the essay's main points and echo the introduction's reference to vintage television shows, they help unify Harriet's paper and bring it to a satisfying close.

These are just a few of the changes Harriet made when reworking her essay. Realizing that writing is a process, she left herself enough time to revise. She was gratified by her classmates' responses to what she had written and pleased by the lively discussion her essay provoked. Early in her composition course, Harriet learned that attention to the various stages in the writing process yields satisfying results, for writer and reader alike.

Activity: Revise the Essay

Return to the draft you wrote in response to either activity 1 or activity 2 on page 68. Also look at any written feedback you received on the draft. To identify any further problems in the draft, get together with several people (classmates, friends, or family members) and request that one of them read the draft aloud to you. Then ask your audience focused questions about the areas you sense need work, or use the checklist on pages 72–73 to focus the feedback. In either case, summarize and rank the comments on a feedback chart or in marginal annotations. Then, using the comments as a guide, go ahead and revise the draft. Either type a new version or do your revising by hand, perhaps on a photocopy of the draft. Don't forget to proofread closely before submitting the paper to your instructor.

3

WRITING ON A WORD PROCESSOR

Even if you've never gone within ten feet of a computer, you'll probably have the chance to use one in college for word processing—that is, for writing, editing, and printing texts (or *documents*, in computer talk). These days, most computers are easy to use. Text can be rearranged with only a few keystrokes; commands tend to be easy to remember; and instruction manuals are usually accurate and readable.

At your college, there's probably at least one room of computers for student use, if not several computer centers. Often, students can arrange for free computer instruction or get on-the-spot assistance as they work.

Many colleges have arrangements with computer manufacturers allowing students to buy computers at a discount. If you decide to purchase one, don't be shy about asking any computer-savvy folks you know for advice. Most computer buffs like to share their enthusiasm and their knowledge. They can recommend the kind of computer (*hardware*) and programs (*software*) best suited to your needs. Basic word-processing software (available on *floppy disks*) allows you to insert, delete, and move words, phrases, sentences, even entire sections of text. It also formats your text for margins, spacing, page numbering, and the like. In addition, many word-processing programs include spelling checks, ready-to-fill-in outline forms, and automatic footnoting options.

SOME OBSERVATIONS AND HINTS

There's no single way to use a word processor. Some people use one in all phases of the writing process; others save the computer for revising and editing. As you become increasingly comfortable with a word processor, you'll probably use it more and more in all stages.

Word processing is wonderfully fluid. The ease with which you can move text around helps you capture the often helter-skelter nature of the thinking process. After a while, writing in longhand or on a typewriter may seem slow and confining.

Here are some general tips for using a word processor to write a college essay:

- Be sure to save your work at frequent intervals. Otherwise, you risk losing a hefty chunk of text—or even your entire file—through a keystroke error, power failure, or system glitch.
- Always keep a backup disk of work in progress—a spare disk with a copy of your work to date.
- If you use a computer in your college's computer center, don't go to the center an hour before a paper is due expecting to produce a final draft. You may wind up with nothing to hand in but an excuse like "The computers were all taken" or "I accidentally deleted two pages." To avoid these problems, you need to plan your time wisely.
- At the end of each computer session, print out the work you have done, and move to the end of the file any material you plan to work on in the next phase.
- Before making significant on-screen changes, print out a copy of the original material. It's also a good idea each time to leave the original file intact and work on a copy of the file. Be sure to give each copy a different file name—for instance, "essay 2," "essay 3," and so forth. Once you have an intact version, you're free to make whatever on-screen modifica-

tions you wish; if the changes don't work out, you can still retrieve whatever you need from the original.

- Use a *single-spaced format* when typing so you get the maximum amount on screen. Similarly, prepare a single-spaced printout of your work (especially an outline or draft) to get a general impression of your material's overall effectiveness.

- Before asking friends or classmates to respond to your work, use the computer's spell check and grammar check functions so readers won't be distracted by mechanical errors.

- When asking readers to respond to what you've prepared, provide them with a *double-spaced* printout with wide margins. The extra space gives readers plenty of room to record their comments.

- Until you have the absolutely final draft of your paper, keep all the versions on your backup disk. After considering your readers' responses, you may decide to include material from an earlier version.

- Even after you hand in a paper, keep the final version on your disk—just in case you'd like to produce another copy at a later date.

The following sections discuss ways to use a word processor in successive stages of the writing process.

PREWRITE

In the prewriting stage, a computer's speed can help you capture even the most fleeting thoughts generated by, say, brainstorming, freewriting, or journal writing. For example, you might want to record your journal entries on a computer disk. Simply get down all your thoughts as fast as you can, filing the entries by date. If you work in a computer lab, save your entries on your own disk and, then, for privacy's sake, delete the entries from the lab's start-up disk or hard drive.

Generating material about a subject also moves along quickly when you use a word processor. Here's how you can proceed. Take a moment to type and then print out your purpose, audience, and tone. Having that material in front of you will keep you focused as you freewrite, brainstorm, use the mapping technique, and so on. To encourage a free and uncensored flow of ideas, try not to look at your words as you type your rough, preliminary thoughts. Instead, stare into space or turn down the screen's brightness.

Once you're ready to pull together a scratch list or scratch outline of your raw material, you may find that adding, grouping, and deleting points proceed most smoothly when you work directly on screen. Indeed, you might want to experiment with any split-screen function that your software provides. Put your raw material in one window and your scratch outline in the other. With the two documents in view, you can jump from one to the other, editing either or both.

Rather than working directly on the screen, you may decide to shape your prewriting by working on a printed version of your raw material. Such an approach allows you to see everything all at once, not just a screen's worth at a time. If you work from a printout, reread your rough ideas, marking points that seem workable, crossing out those that don't, and so on. Then, with your marked-up printout beside you, type your scratch outline into the computer.

IDENTIFY THE THESIS

The ease of computing means that you can play out all your hunches about a possible thesis. Simply type in as many versions of the thesis as you can generate. Then, if your software has a split-screen function, you can view your scratch outline in one window and the alternative thesis statements in the other. This simultaneous view of the scratch outline and alternative thesis statements helps clarify which thesis best fits the material in the scratch outline. Be sure, though, to save the alternative thesis statements; later on, you may decide that a previously rejected thesis is the most effective after all.

SUPPORT THE THESIS WITH EVIDENCE

When you're ready to generate evidence for your thesis, call up all your working material so far: your purpose, audience, tone, and point of view; your scratch outline; and your thesis. Start by moving all these items to one location at the top of the screen. Then add space between the points in your scratch outline. As you move among points, locate spots where additional evidence is needed. At such places, return to a prewriting technique to collect more facts, examples, reasons, and details. If you're using material from outside sources, key in that information, and begin a file of bibliographic information on the sources; later on, you can retrieve this data when you're ready to document borrowed material. Finally, evaluate all the evidence by printing out the material or by scrolling through it on screen. Make whatever modifications are needed.

ORGANIZE THE EVIDENCE

When moving evidence into an outline format, you'll find that the computer's flexibility helps you identify which sequence of ideas is most effective. To start, move your purpose, audience, tone, and thesis to the top of an empty screen. Underneath, place the latest version of your scratch outline, including any newly generated evidence. Next, review all the material, and decide which organizational approach (chronological, spatial, emphatic, or simple-to-complex) and which pattern of development (cause-effect, comparison-contrast, and so on) you'll use to structure the evidence. Then start moving the material around to reflect your concept of how different parts of the evidence should fit together. Finally, use tab stops or your software's outlining mode to create indentations for different levels of support. (Some software programs have a function that provides a ready-to-fill-in skeleton outline.)

WRITE THE FIRST DRAFT

Although some people write the first draft in longhand and then type it into the computer for revising, others write the first draft directly on screen. If you feel comfortable with the latter approach, you might begin by typing your purpose, audience, tone, and thesis at the top of the screen. With these considerations firmly in mind, review your outline; either print out the outline or place it in a split-screen window so you can look at it while you type your first draft in the other window.

As you draft the body paragraphs, don't waste time retyping supporting facts, statistics, anecdotes, and so forth from your outline; instead, use the computer's cut-and-paste functions to move such material into your draft. At this point, there's no need to blend in the transferred material seamlessly; you can smooth out any rough edges later. When writing the body paragraphs, you may find yourself creating several versions of the paragraphs. That's fine. If you're typing, say, the third paragraph and decide the first part of the paragraph belongs at the end of the previous paragraph, just select the material to be moved, tap the appropriate keys, and relocate the sentences in question.

When you're ready to write the introductory and concluding paragraphs, scroll back through your prewriting and rough supporting evidence to see if there are striking examples or facts that you didn't include in the body paragraphs. Some of these "leftovers" might provide an effective opening or closing. Remember, though, that the material you use to open and close the essay must fit the paper's purpose, audience, tone, and thesis. So, before typing in the introduction and conclusion, scroll through the body paragraphs to reinforce your sense of the whole essay. Then key in the essay's opening and closing paragraphs.

REVISE THE ESSAY

It is during revision that word processors reveal their full glory. With only a few keystrokes, for example, you can add, move, or delete words, sentences, or whole sections of text. You can recast a paragraph with ease and—if you dislike the result—make the revisions disappear.

When reworking meaning, structure, and paragraph development, you may feel most comfortable combining longhand revision with on-screen modification. In such a case, it's a good idea to print out your draft for another look. Ask some classmates or friends to react to the draft; then synthesize their comments in a feedback chart or in marginal annotations. That done, enter by hand any changes in your draft. Finally, key in your changes and make a printout of the revised version, leaving extra space for you and others to continue revising.

Instead of working in longhand, you may feel most comfortable revising almost exclusively at the computer. If that's your preference, scroll through your entire first draft, making notes on a sheet of paper about overall meaning, structure, and paragraph development. (On another piece of paper, note any word or sentence problems you want to tackle later on.) Then, moving from paragraph to paragraph, type in your changes.

Now you're ready to have readers respond to the essay's sentences and words. Show them the latest version of your essay, and record their observations and suggestions. Also, dig out any notes you made earlier about areas needing work and scroll through the essay once again, this time identifying other spots where sentences and words aren't as effective as they could be. If you're unsure which word or which version of a sentence works best in a paragraph, print out just the paragraph, including alternative options, and ask someone to help you decide. Having taken these steps, you're ready to type in your changes.

It's difficult to detect problems in grammar and spelling by looking at a computer screen. So, for best results, work from a printout when editing and proofreading. There is, though, some risk in seeing your draft neatly printed out; you might feel so pleased with your material's professional look that you fail to read it closely. Be sure not to shortchange this vital final stage in the writing process.

Work from a double-spaced printout that uses correct manuscript form. Be on the lookout for the most common errors in computer copy—a missing word or line, a misplaced paragraph, a repeated word. Also, don't forget to take advantage of any spell check and grammar check functions your computer might have. But remember: A spell check can't tell you that you should have used *affect* instead of *effect* or *whose* instead of *who's*. It can only flag a spelling that doesn't match *any* word in its dictionary. Similarly, grammar checks identify only certain kinds of errors; it's your responsibility to track down and correct those errors the grammar check misses. You may find that you can detect previously hidden mechanical errors if you "de-familiarize" your essay by adjusting its margins so that the text appears as if it were a newspaper column. Type in any needed changes; read through the on-screen text one more time to catch any remaining problems; then restore the appropriate format and print out your final version.

The time you spend learning how to use a word processor will be well worth it. Once you have the knack of thinking at the keyboard, you may never go back to writing in longhand or using a typewriter. However, if you find that writing in longhand or on a typewriter provides better results, then you should do what works for you. As we emphasize throughout this book, professional and student writers alike must find their own best ways for approaching the writing process.

4

DESCRIPTION

WHAT IS DESCRIPTION?

All of us respond in a strong way to sensory stimulation. The sweet perfume of a candy shop takes us back to childhood; the blank white walls of the campus infirmary remind us of long vigils at a hospital where a grandmother lay dying; the screech of a subway car sets our nerves on edge.

Without any sensory stimulation, we sink into a less-than-human state. Neglected babies, left alone with no human touch, no colors, no lullabies, become withdrawn and unresponsive. And prisoners dread solitary confinement, knowing that the sensory deprivation can be unbearable, even to the point of madness.

Because sensory impressions are so potent, descriptive writing has a unique power and appeal. *Description* can be defined as the expression, in vivid language, of what the five senses experience. A richly rendered description freezes a subject in time, evoking sights, smells, sounds, textures, and tastes in such a way that readers become one with the writer's world.

HOW DESCRIPTION FITS YOUR PURPOSE AND AUDIENCE

Description can be a supportive technique that develops part of an essay, or it can be the dominant technique used throughout an essay. Here are some examples of the way description can help you meet the objective of an essay developed chiefly through another pattern of development:

- In a *causal analysis* showing the *consequences* of pet overpopulation, you might describe the desperate appearance of a pack of starving stray dogs.
- In an *argumentation-persuasion* essay urging more rigorous handgun control, you might start with a description of a violent family confrontation that ended in murder.
- In a *process analysis* explaining the pleasure of making ice cream at home, you might describe the beauty of an old-fashioned, hand-cranked ice cream maker.
- In a *narrative essay* recounting a day in the life of a street musician, you might describe the musician's energy and the joyous appreciation of passersby.

In each case, the essay's overall purpose would affect the amount of description needed.

Your readers also influence how much description to include. As you write, ask yourself, "What do my particular readers need to know to understand and experience keenly what I'm describing? What descriptive details will they enjoy most?" Your answers to these and similar questions will help you tailor your description to specific readers. Consider an article intended for professional horticulturists; its purpose is to explain a new technique for controlling spider mites. Because of readers' expertise, there would be little need for a lengthy description of the insects. Written for a college newspaper, however, the article would probably provide a detailed description of the mites so student gardeners could distinguish between the pesky parasites and flecks of dust.

While your purpose and audience define *how much* to describe, you have great freedom deciding *what* to describe. Description is especially suited to objects (your car or desk, for example), but you can also describe a person, an animal, a place, a time, and a phenomenon or concept. You might write an effective description about a friend who runs marathons (person), a pair of ducks who return each year to a neighbor's pond (animals), the kitchen of a fast-food restaurant (place), a period when you were unemployed (time), the "fight or flight" response to danger (phenomenon or concept).

Description can be divided into two types: *objective* and *subjective*. In an objective description, you describe the subject in a straightforward and literal way, without revealing your attitude or feelings. Reporters, as well as technical and scientific writers, specialize in objective description; their jobs depend on their ability to detail experiences without emotional bias. For example, a reporter may write an unemotional account of a township meeting that ended in a fistfight. Or a marine biologist may write a factual report describing the way sea mammals are killed by the plastic refuse (sandwich wrappings, straws, fishing lines) that humans throw into the ocean.

In contrast, when writing a subjective description, you convey a highly personal view of your subject and seek to elicit a strong emotional response from your readers. Such subjective descriptions often take the form of reflective pieces or character studies. For example, in an essay describing the rich plant life in an inner-city garden, you might reflect on people's longing to connect with the soil and express admiration for the gardeners' hard work—an admiration you'd like readers to share. Or, in a character study of your grandfather, you might describe his stern appearance and gentle behavior, hoping that the contradiction will move readers as much as it moves you.

The *tone* of a subjective description is determined by your purpose, your attitude toward the subject, and the reader response you wish to evoke. Consider an essay about a dynamic woman who runs a center for disturbed children. If your goal is to make readers admire the woman, your tone will be serious and appreciative. But if you want to criticize the woman's high-pressure tactics and create distaste for her management style, your tone will be disapproving and severe.

The language of a descriptive piece also depends, to a great extent, on whether your purpose is primarily objective or subjective. If the description is objective, the language is straightforward, precise, and factual. Such *denotative* language consists of neutral dictionary meanings. If you want to describe as dispassionately as possible fans' violent behavior at a football game, you might write about the "large crowd" and its "mass movement onto the field." But if you are shocked by the fans' behavior and want to write a subjective piece that inspires similar outrage in readers, then you might write about the "swelling mob" and its "rowdy stampede onto the field." In the latter case, the language used would be *connotative* and emotionally charged so that readers would share your feelings.

Subjective and objective descriptions often overlap. Sometimes a single sentence contains both objective and subjective elements: "Although his hands were large and misshapen by arthritis, they were gentle to the touch, inspiring confidence and trust." Other times, part of an essay may provide a factual description (the physical appearance of a summer cabin your family rented), while another part of the essay may be highly subjective (how you felt in the cabin, sitting in front of a fire on a rainy day).

SUGGESTIONS FOR USING DESCRIPTION IN AN ESSAY

The following suggestions will be helpful whether you use description as a dominant or supportive pattern of development.

1. Focus a descriptive essay around a dominant impression. Like other kinds of writing, a descriptive essay must have a thesis, or main point. In a descriptive essay with a subjective slant, the thesis usually centers on the *dominant impression* you have about your subject. Suppose you decide to write an essay on your ninth-grade history teacher, Ms. Hazzard. You want the paper to convey how unconventional and flamboyant she was. The essay could, of course, focus on a different dominant impression—how insensitive she could be to students, for example. What's important is that you establish—early in the paper—the dominant impression you intend to convey. Although descriptive essays often imply, rather than explicitly state, the dominant impression, that impression should be unmistakable.

2. Select the details to include. The power of description hinges on your ability to select from all possible details only those that support the dominant impression. All others, no matter how vivid or interesting, must be left out. If you're describing how flamboyant

Ms. Hazzard could be, the details in the following paragraph would be appropriate.

> A large-boned woman, Ms. Hazzard wore her bright red hair piled on top of her head, where it perched precariously. By the end of class, wayward strands of hair tumbled down and fell into eyes fringed by spiky false eyelashes. Ms. Hazzard's nails, filed into crisp points, were painted either bloody burgundy or neon pink. Plastic bangle bracelets, also either burgundy or pink, clattered up and down her ample arms as she scrawled on the board the historical dates that had, she claimed, "changed the world."

Such details—the heavy eye makeup, stiletto nails, gaudy bracelets—contribute to the impression of a flamboyant, unusual person. Even if you remembered times that Ms. Hazzard seemed perfectly conventional and understated, most likely you wouldn't describe those times since they contradict the dominant impression.

You must also be selective in the *number of details* you include. Having a dominant impression helps you eliminate many details gathered during prewriting, but there still will be choices to make. For example, it would be inappropriate to describe in exhaustive detail everything in a messy room:

> The brown desk, made of a grained plastic laminate, is directly under a small window covered by a torn yellow-and-gold plaid curtain. In the left corner of the desk are four crumbled balls of blue-lined yellow paper, three red markers, two fine-point blue pens, an ink eraser, and four letters, two bearing special wildlife stamps. A green down-filled vest and a red cable-knit sweater are thrown over the back of the bright blue metal bridge chair pushed under the desk. Under the chair is an oval braided rug, its once brilliant blues and greens spotted by old coffee stains.

Readers will be reluctant to wade through such undifferentiated specifics. Even more important, such excessive detailing dilutes the focus of the essay. You end up with a seemingly endless list of specifics, rather than with a carefully crafted picture in words. In this regard, sculptors and writers are similar—what they take away is as important as what they leave in.

Perhaps you're wondering how to generate the details that support your dominant impression. As you can imagine, you have to develop heightened powers of observation and recall. To sharpen these key faculties, it can be helpful to make up a chart with separate columns for each of the five senses. If you can observe your subject directly, enter in the appropriate columns what you see, hear, taste, and so on. If you're attempting to remember something from the past, try to recollect details under each of these sense headings. Ask yourself questions ("How did it smell? What did I hear?") and list each memory recaptured. You'll be surprised how this simple technique can tune you in to your experiences and help uncover the specific details needed to develop your dominant impression.

3. Organize the descriptive details.   Select the organizational pattern (or combination of patterns) that best supports your dominant impression. The paragraphs in a descriptive essay are usually sequenced *spatially* (from top to bottom, interior to exterior, near to far) or *chronologically* (as the subject is experienced in time). But the paragraphs can also be ordered *emphatically* (ending with your subject's most striking elements) or by *sensory impression* (first smell, then taste, then touch, and so on).

You might, for instance, use a *spatial* pattern to organize a description of a large city as you viewed it from the air, a taxi, and a subway car. A description of your first day on a new job might move *chronologically*, starting with how you felt the first hour on the job and proceeding through the rest of the day. In a paper describing a bout with the flu, you might arrange details *emphatically*, beginning with a description of your low-level aches and pains and concluding with an account of your raging fever. An essay about a neighborhood garbage dump, euphemistically called an "ecology landfill" by its owners, could be organized by *sensory impressions:* the sights of the dump, its smells, its sounds. Regardless of the organizational pattern you use, provide enough *signal devices* (for example, *about, next, worst of all*) so that readers can follow the description easily.

Finally, although descriptive essays don't always have conventional topic sentences, each descriptive paragraph should have a clear focus. Often this focus is indicated by a sentence early in the paragraph that names the scene, object, or individual to be described. Such a sentence functions as a kind of *informal topic sentence;* the paragraph's descriptive details then develop that topic sentence.

4. Use vivid sensory language and varied sentence structure.
The connotative language typical of subjective description should be richly evocative. The words you select must etch in readers' minds the same picture that you have in yours. For this reason, rather than relying on vague generalities, you must use language that involves readers' senses. Consider the difference between the following paired descriptions:

Vague	Vivid
The food was unappetizing.	The stew congealed into an oval pool of milky-brown fat.
The toothpaste was refreshing.	The toothpaste, tasting minty sweet, felt good against slippery teeth, free finally from braces.
Filled with passengers and baggage, the car moved slowly down the road.	Burdened with its load of clamoring children and well-worn suitcases, the car labored down the interstate on bald tires and worn shocks, emitting puffs of blue exhaust and an occasional backfire.

Unlike the *concrete, sensory-packed* sentences on the right, the sentences on the left fail to create vivid word pictures that engage readers. While all good writing blends abstract and concrete language, descriptive writing demands an abundance of specific sensory language.

Keep in mind, too, that *verbs pack more of a wallop* than adverbs. The following sentence has to rely on adverbs (italicized) because its verbs are so weak: "She walked *casually* into the room and *deliberately* tried not to pay much attention to their stares." Rewritten, so that verbs (italicized), not adverbs, do the bulk of the work, the sentence becomes more powerful: "She *strolled* into the room and *ignored* their stares."

Figures of speech—nonliteral, imaginative comparisons between two basically dissimilar things—are another way to enliven descriptive writing. *Similes* use the words *like* or *as* when comparing; *metaphors* state or imply that two things being compared are alike; and *personification* attributes human characteristics to inanimate things.

The examples that follow show how effective figurative language can be in descriptive writing.

Moving as jerkily as a marionette on strings, the old man picked himself up off the sidewalk and staggered down the street. (*simile*)

Stalking their prey, the hall monitors remained hidden in the corridors, motionless and ready to spring on any unsuspecting student who dared to sneak into class late. (*metaphor*)

The scoop of vanilla ice cream, plain and unadorned, cried out for hot fudge sauce and a sprinkling of sliced pecans. (*personification*)

Finally, when writing descriptive passages, you need to *vary sentence structure*. Don't use the same subject-verb pattern in all sentences. The second example above, for instance, could have been written as follows: "The hall monitors stalked their prey. They hid in the corridors. They remained motionless and ready to spring on any unsuspecting student who tried to sneak into class late." But the sentence is richer and more interesting when the descriptive elements are embedded, eliminating what would otherwise have been a clipped and predictable subject-verb pattern.

Henry James, American novelist and master of description, gave this advice to beginning writers: "Try to be one of the people on whom nothing is lost." If you work to become the kind of writer "on whom nothing is lost," you will find you have a rich mine of sensory impressions to explore and transmute into written form. To develop your descriptive powers, you must be alert to your inner and outer worlds. And you must develop sensitivity to the nuances of language, finding just the right words to convey the essence of your experiences. It is no wonder that descriptive writing can be a source of such pleasure for writer and reader alike.

STUDENT ESSAY

The following student essay was written by Marie Martinez in response to this assignment:

> The essay "Once More to the Lake" is an evocative piece about a spot that had special meaning in E. B. White's life. Write an essay about a place that holds rich significance for you, centering the description on a dominant impression.

While reading Marie's paper, try to determine how well it applies the principles of description. The annotations on Marie's paper and the commentary following it will help you look at the essay more closely.

Salt Marsh
by Marie Martinez

Introduction

In one of his journals, Thoreau told of the difficulty he had escaping the obligations and cares of society: "It sometimes happens that I cannot easily shake off the village. The thought of some work will run in my head and I am not where my body is--I am out of my senses. In my walks I...return to my senses." All of us feel out of our senses at times. Overwhelmed by problems or everyday annoyances, we lose touch with sensory pleasures as we spend our days in noisy cities and stuffy classrooms. Just as Thoreau walked in the woods to return to his senses, I have a special place where I return to mine: the salt marsh behind my grandparents' house.

Dominant impression (thesis)

Informal topic sentence: Definition paragraph

My grandparents live on the East Coast, a mile or so inland from the sea. Between the ocean and the mainland is a wide fringe of salt marsh. A salt marsh is not a swamp, but an expanse of dark, spongy soil threaded with saltwater creeks and clothed in a kind of grass called salt meadow hay. All the water in the marsh rises and falls daily with the ocean tides, an

1

2

endless cycle that changes the look of the marsh--
partly flooded or mostly dry--as the day progresses.

Informal topic sentence: First paragraph in a four-part spatial sequence →

Heading out to the marsh from my grandpar- 3
ents' house, I follow a short path through the woods.
As I walk along, a sharp smell of salt mixed with the
rich aroma of peaty soil fills my nostrils. I am always
amazed by the way the path changes with the seasons. Sometimes I walk in the brilliant green of
spring, sometimes in the tawny gold of autumn,
sometimes in the grayish-tan of winter. No matter
the season, the grass flanking the trail is often flat-

Simile ———

tened into swirls, like thick Van Gogh brush strokes
that curve and recurve in circular patterns. No people
come here. The peacefulness heals me like a sooth-

Informal topic sentence: Second paragraph in the spatial sequence →

ing drug.

After a few minutes, the trail suddenly opens up 4
to a view that calms me no matter how upset or discouraged I might be: a line of tall waving reeds bordering and nearly hiding the salt marsh creek. To get
to the creek, I part the reeds.

Informal topic sentence: Third paragraph in the spatial sequence →

The creek is a narrow body of water no more 5
than fifteen feet wide, and it ebbs and flows as the
ocean currents sweep toward the land or rush back
toward the sea. The creek winds in a sinuous pattern
so that I cannot see its beginning or end, the places
where it trickles into the marsh or spills into the open
ocean. Little brown birds dip in and out of the reeds
on the far shore of the creek, making a special
"tweep-tweep" sound peculiar to the marsh. When I
stand at low tide on the shore of the creek, I am on a
miniature cliff, for the bank of the creek falls abruptly
and steeply into the water. Below me, green grasses
wave and shimmer under the water while tiny minnows flash their silvery sides as they dart through the
underwater tangles.

Informal topic sentence: Last paragraph in the spatial sequence →

The creek water is often much warmer than the 6
ocean, so I can swim there in three seasons. Sitting
on the edge of the creek, I scoop some water into my
hand, rub my face and neck, then ease into the water.
Where the creek is shallow, my feet sink into a foot of

Simile ———

muck that feels like mashed potatoes mixed with
motor oil. But once I become accustomed to it, I enjoy
squishing the slimy mud through my toes. Some-

times I feel brushing past my legs the blue crabs that live in the creek. Other times, I hear the splash of a turtle or otter as it slips from the shore into the water. Otherwise, it is silent. The salty water is buoyant and lifts my spirits as I stroke through it to reach the middle of the creek. There in the center, I float weightlessly, surrounded by tall reeds that reduce the world to water and sky. I am at peace.

Conclusion

The salt marsh is not the kind of dramatic landscape found on picture postcards. There are no soaring mountains, sandy beaches, or lush valleys. The marsh is a flat world that some consider dull and uninviting. I am glad most people do not respond to the marsh's subtle beauty because that means I can be alone there. Just as the rising tide sweeps over the marsh, floating debris out to the ocean, the marsh washes away my concerns and restores me to my senses.

Echo of idea in introduction

7

COMMENTARY

The dominant impression.   Marie responded to the assignment by writing a moving tribute to a place having special meaning for her—the salt marsh near her grandparents' home. Like most descriptive pieces, Marie's essay is organized around a *dominant impression:* the marsh's peaceful solitude and gentle, natural beauty. The essay's introduction provides a context for the dominant impression by comparing the pleasure Marie experiences in the marsh to the happiness Thoreau felt in his walks around Walden Pond.

Other patterns of development.   Before developing the essay's dominant impression, Marie uses the second paragraph to *define* a salt marsh. An *objective description,* the definition clarifies that a salt marsh—with its spongy soil, haylike grass, and ebbing tides—is not to be confused with a swamp. Because Marie offers such a factual definition, readers have the background needed to enjoy the personalized view that follows.

Besides the definition paragraph and the comparison in the opening paragraph, the essay contains a strong element of *causal analysis:* Throughout, Marie describes the marsh's effect on her.

Sensory language.   At times, Marie develops the essay's dominant impression explicitly, as when she writes "No people come here" (paragraph 3) and "I am at peace" (6). But Marie generally uses the more subtle techniques characteristic of *subjective description* to convey the dominant impression. First of all, she fills the essay with strong *connotative language,* rich with *sensory images.* The third paragraph describes what she smells (the "sharp smell of salt mixed with the rich aroma of peaty soil") and what she sees ("brilliant green," "tawny gold," and "grayish-tan"). In the fifth paragraph, she tells us that she hears the chirping sounds of small birds. And the sixth paragraph includes vigorous descriptions of how the marsh feels to Marie's touch. She splashes water on her face and neck; she digs her toes into the mud at the bottom of the creek; she delights in the delicate brushing of crabs against her legs.

Figurative language, vigorous verbs, and varied sentence structure.   You might also have noted that *figurative language, energetic verbs,* and *varied sentence patterns* contribute to the essay's descriptive power. Marie develops a *simile* in the third paragraph when she compares the flattened swirls of swamp grass to the brush strokes in a painting by Van Gogh. Later she uses another simile when she writes that the creek's thick mud feels "like mashed potatoes mixed with motor oil." Moreover, throughout the essay, she uses lively verbs ("shimmer," "flash") to capture the marsh's magical quality. Similarly, Marie enhances descriptive passages by varying the length of her sentences. Long, fairly elaborate sentences are interspersed with short, dramatic statements. In the third paragraph, for example, the long sentence describing the circular swirls of swamp grass is followed by the brief statement "No people come here." And the sixth paragraph uses two short sentences ("Otherwise, it is silent" and "I am at peace") to punctuate the paragraph's longer sentences.

Organization.   We can follow Marie's journey through the marsh because she uses an easy-to-follow combination of *spatial, chronological,* and *emphatic* patterns to sequence her experience. The essay relies primarily on a spatial arrangement since the four body paragraphs focus on the different spots that Marie reaches: first, the path behind her grandparents' house (paragraph 3); then the area bordering the creek (4); next, her view of the creek (5); last, the creek itself (6). Each stage of her walk is signaled by an *informal topic sentence* near the start of each paragraph. Furthermore, *signal devices* (marked by italics here) indicate not only her location but also the chronological passage of time: "*As* I walk along, a sharp smell...fills my nostrils" (3); "*After* a few minutes, the trail suddenly opens up..." (4); "*Below* me, green grasses wave..." (5). And to call attention to the creek's serene beauty, Marie saves for last the description of the peace she feels while floating in the creek.

An inappropriate figure of speech.   Although the four body paragraphs focus on the distinctive qualities of each location, Marie runs into a minor problem in the third paragraph. Take a moment to reread that paragraph's last sentence. Comparing the peace of the marsh to the effect of a "soothing drug" is jarring. The effectiveness of Marie's essay hinges on her ability to create a picture of a pure, natural world. A reference to drugs is inappropriate. Now, reread the paragraph aloud, stopping after "No people come here." Note how much more in keeping with the essay's dominant impression the paragraph is when the reference to drugs is omitted.

Conclusion.   The concluding paragraph brings the essay to a graceful close. The powerful *simile* found in the last sentence contains an implied reference to Thoreau and to Marie's earlier statement about the joy to be found in special places having restorative powers. Such an allusion echoes, with good effect, the paper's opening comments.

Revising the first draft.   When Marie met with some classmates during a group feedback session, the students agreed that Marie's first draft was strong and moving. But they also said that they had difficulty following her route through the marsh; they found her third paragraph especially confusing. Marie kept track of her classmates' comments on a separate piece of paper and then entered them, numbered in order of importance, in the margin of her first draft. Reprinted here is the original version of Marie's third paragraph.

Original Version of the Third Paragraph

As I head out to the marsh from the house, I follow a short trail through the woods. A smell of salt mixed with the aroma of soil fills my nostrils. The end of the trail suddenly opens up to a view that calms me no matter how upset or discouraged I might be: a line of tall waving reeds bordering the salt marsh creek. Civilization seems far away as I walk the path of flattened grass and finally reach my goal, the salt marsh creek hidden behind the tall waving reeds. The path changes with the seasons; sometimes I walk in the brilliant green of spring, sometimes in the tawny gold of autumn, sometimes in the quiet grayish-tan of winter. In some areas, the grass is flattened into swirls that make the marsh resemble one of those paintings by Van Gogh. No people come here. The peacefulness heals me like a soothing drug. The path stops at the line of tall waving reeds, standing upright at the border of the creek. I part the reeds to get to the creek.

When Marie looked more carefully at the paragraph, she agreed it was confusing. For one thing, the paragraph's third and fourth sentences indicated that she had come to the path's end and had reached the reeds bordering the creek. In the following sentences, however, she was on the path again. Then, at the end, she was back at the creek, as if she had just arrived there. Marie resolved this confusion by breaking the single paragraph into two separate ones—the first describing the walk along the path, the second describing her arrival at the creek. This restructuring, especially when combined with clearer transitions, eliminated the confusion.

While revising her essay, Marie also intensified the sensory images in her original paragraph. She changed the "smell of salt and soil" to the "sharp smell of salt mixed with the rich aroma of peaty soil." And when she added the phrase "thick Van Gogh brush strokes that curve and recurve in circular patterns," she made the comparison between the marsh grass and a Van Gogh painting more vivid.

These are just some of the changes Marie made while rewriting her paper. Her skillful revisions provided the polish needed to make an already strong essay even more evocative.

All the selections ahead use description to make their subjects come alive and to provide supporting evidence for a controlling idea or impression. Gordon Parks's "Flavio's Home" assaults the reader with the sights, sounds, and smells of the Brazilian slum that is home to one sickly boy. Russell Baker's "In My Day" is a wistful memoir of the author's aging mother. Annie Dillard's "In the Jungle" depicts the timeless quality of primeval places. In "Once More to the Lake," E. B. White recalls his youth when visiting a childhood vacation spot with his son. Finally, in "A Partial Remembrance of a Puerto Rican Childhood," Judith Ortiz Cofer presents a vivid portrait of family life.

Gordon Parks

The son of deeply religious tenant farmers, Gordon Parks
(1912–   ) grew up in Kansas knowing both the comforts of familial love and the torments of poverty and racism. Sent as a
teenager to live with his sister in Minnesota after his mother's
death, Parks was thrown out on his own in a frigid winter by his
brother-in-law. To support himself, Parks worked as a janitor in
a flophouse and as a piano player in a bordello. These and other
odd jobs gave Parks the means to buy his first camera. Fascinated
by photographic images, Parks studied the masters and eventually developed his own powers as a photographer. So evocative
were his photographic studies that both *Life* and *Vogue* brought
him on staff, the first black photographer to be hired by the two
magazines. Parks's prodigious creativity has found expression in
filmmaking (*Shaft*), musical composition (both classical and
jazz), fiction, nonfiction, and poetry (titles include *The Learning
Tree, A Choice of Weapons, To Smile in Autumn,* and *Arias in Silence,* published, respectively, in 1986, 1987, 1988, and 1994).
But it is Parks's photographic essays, covering five decades of
American life, that have brought him the most acclaim. In the
following essay, taken from his 1990 autobiography, *Voices in
the Mirror,* Parks tells the story behind one of his most memorable photographic works.

Flavio's Home

On the outskirts of Rio de Janeiro, Brazil, seven hundred thousand people live in the slums known as *favelas*. Sent to one *favela*
by *Life* magazine, photographer Gordon Parks found a twelve-
year-old boy, Flavio da Silva, whose story spoke volumes about
the horrors of poverty. Parks's photo-essay on Flavio generated an
unprecedented response from *Life* readers. Indeed, they sent so
much money to the da Silvas that the family was able to leave the
favela for better living conditions. Parks brought Flavio to the
United States for medical treatment, and the boy's health was restored. However, Flavio's story didn't have an unqualifiedly happy ending. Although he overcame his illness and later married and

had a family, Flavio continuously fantasized about returning to
the United States, convinced that only by returning to America
could he improve his life. His obsession eventually eroded the
promise of his life in Brazil.

I've never lost my fierce grudge against poverty. It is the most   1
savage of all human afflictions, claiming victims who can't mobilize
their efforts against it, who often lack strength to digest what little
food they scrounge up to survive. It keeps growing, multiplying,
spreading like a cancer. In my wanderings I attack it wherever I can—
in barrios, slums and favelas.

Catacumba was the name of the favela where I found Flavio da   2
Silva. It was wickedly hot. The noon sun baked the mud-rot of the
wet mountainside. Garbage and human excrement clogged the open
sewers snaking down the slopes. José Gallo, a *Life* reporter, and I
rested in the shade of a jacaranda tree halfway up Rio de Janeiro's
most infamous deathtrap. Below and above us were a maze of shacks,
but in the distance alongside the beach stood the gleaming white
homes of the rich.

Breathing hard, balancing a tin of water on his head, a small boy   3
climbed toward us. He was miserably thin, naked but for filthy denim
shorts. His legs resembled sticks covered with skin and screwed into
his feet. Death was all over him, in his sunken eyes, cheeks and jaundiced coloring. He stopped for breath, coughing, his chest heaving
as water slopped over his bony shoulders. Then jerking sideways like
a mechanical toy, he smiled a smile I will never forget. Turning, he
went on up the mountainside.

The detailed *Life* assignment in my back pocket was to find an   4
impoverished father with a family, to examine his earnings, political
leanings, religion, friends, dreams and frustrations. I had been sent
to do an essay on poverty. This frail boy bent under his load said
more to me about poverty than a dozen poor fathers. I touched Gallo, and we got up and followed the boy to where he entered a shack
near the top of the mountainside. It was a leaning crumpled place of
old plankings with a rusted tin roof. From inside we heard the bab-
blings of several children. José knocked. The door opened and the
boy stood smiling with a bawling naked baby in his arms.

Still smiling, he whacked the baby's rump, invited us in and of-   5
fered us a box to sit on. The only other recognizable furniture was a
sagging bed and a broken baby's crib. Flavio was twelve, and with
Gallo acting as interpreter, he introduced his younger brothers and
sisters: "Mario, the bad one; Baptista, the good one; Albia, Isabel
and the baby Zacarias." Two other girls burst into the shack, screaming and pounding on one another. Flavio jumped in and parted
them. "Shut up, you two." He pointed at the older girl. "That's
Maria, the nasty one." She spit in his face. He smacked her and
pointed to the smaller sister. "That's Luzia. She thinks she's pretty."

Having finished the introductions, he went to build a fire under the   6
stove—a rusted, bent top of an old gas range resting on several bricks. Beneath it was a piece of tin that caught the hot coals. The shack was about
six by ten feet. Its grimy walls were a patchwork of misshapen boards with
large gaps between them, revealing other shacks below stilted against the
slopes. The floor, rotting under layers of grease and dirt, caught shafts
of light slanting down through spaces in the roof. A large hole in the
far corner served as a toilet. Beneath that hole was the sloping mountainside. Pockets of poverty in New York's Harlem, on Chicago's south
side, in Puerto Rico's infamous El Fungito seemed pale by comparison.
None of them had prepared me for this one in the favela of Catacumba.

Flavio washed rice in a large dishpan, then washed Zacarias's feet   7
in the same water. But even that dirty water wasn't to be wasted. He
tossed in a chunk of lye soap and ordered each child to wash up. When
they were finished he splashed the water over the dirty floor, and, dropping to his knees, he scrubbed the planks until the black suds sank in.
Just before sundown he put beans on the stove to warm, then left, saying he would be back shortly. "Don't let them burn," he cautioned
Maria. "If they do and Poppa beats me, you'll get it later." Maria, happy to get at the licking spoon, switched over and began to stir the
beans. Then slyly she dipped out a spoonful and swallowed them. Luzia
eyed her. "I see you. I'm going to tell on you for stealing our supper."

Maria's eyes flashed anger. "You do and I'll beat you, you little   8
bitch." Luzia threw a stick at Maria and fled out the door. Zacarias
dropped off to sleep. Mario, the bad one, slouched in a corner and
sucked his thumb. Isabel and Albia sat on the floor clinging to each
other with a strange tenderness. Isabel held onto Albia's hair and Albia clutched at Isabel's neck. They appeared frozen in an act of quiet
violence.

Flavio returned with wood, dumped it beside the stove and sat 9
down to rest for a few minutes, then went down the mountain for
more water. It was dark when he finally came back, his body sagging
from exhaustion. No longer smiling, he suddenly had the look of an
old man and by now we could see that he kept the family going. In
the closed torment of that pitiful shack, he was waging a hopeless
battle against starvation. The da Silva children were living in a coffin.

When at last the parents came in, Gallo and I seemed to be part of 10
the family. Flavio had already told them we were there. "Gordunn
Americano!" Luzia said, pointing at me. José, the father, viewed us
with skepticism. Nair, his pregnant wife, seemed tired beyond speaking.
Hardly acknowledging our presence, she picked up Zacarias, placed
him on her shoulder and gently patted his behind. Flavio scurried about
like a frightened rat, his silence plainly expressing the fear he held of his
father. Impatiently, José da Silva waited for Flavio to serve dinner. He
sat in the center of the bed with his legs crossed beneath him, frowning,
waiting. There were only three tin plates. Flavio filled them with black
beans and rice, then placed them before his father. José da Silva tasted
them, chewed for several moments, then nodded his approval for the
others to start. Only he and Nair had spoons; the children ate with their
fingers. Flavio ate off the top of a coffee can. Afraid to offer us food, he
edged his rice and beans toward us, gesturing for us to take some. We
refused. He smiled, knowing we understood.

Later, when we got down to the difficult business of obtaining per- 11
mission from José da Silva to photograph his family, he hemmed and
hawed, wallowing in the pleasant authority of the decision maker. He finally gave in, but his manner told us that he expected something in return. As we were saying good night Flavio began to cough violently. For
a few moments his lungs seemed to be tearing apart. I wanted to get away
as quickly as possible. It was cowardly of me, but the bluish cast of his skin
beneath the sweat, the choking and spitting were suddenly unbearable.

Gallo and I moved cautiously down through the darkness trying 12
not to appear as strangers. The Catacumba was no place for strangers after sundown. Desperate criminals hid out there. To hunt them out, the
police came in packs, but only in daylight. Gallo cautioned me. "If you
get caught up here after dark it's best to stay at the da Silvas' until morning." As we drove toward the city the large white buildings of the rich
loomed up. The world behind us seemed like a bad dream. I had already
decided to get the boy Flavio to a doctor, and as quickly as possible.

The plush lobby of my hotel on the Copacabana waterfront was   13
crammed with people in formal attire. With the stink of the favela in
my clothes, I hurried to the elevator hoping no passengers would be
aboard. But as the door was closing a beautiful girl in a white lace
gown stepped in. I moved as far away as possible. Her escort entered
behind her, swept her into his arms and they indulged in a kiss that
lasted until they exited on the next floor. Neither of them seemed to
realize that I was there. The room I returned to seemed to be over-
sized; the da Silva shack would have fitted into one corner of it. The
steak dinner I had would have fed the da Silvas for three days.

Billowing clouds blanketed Mount Corcovado as we ap-   14
proached the favela the following morning. Suddenly the sun burst
through, silhouetting Cristo Redentor, the towering sculpture of
Christ with arms extended, its back turned against the slopes of Catacumba. The square at the entrance to the favela bustled with hundreds of favelados. Long lines waited at the sole water spigot. Others
waited at the only toilet on the entire mountainside. Women, unable
to pay for soap, beat dirt from their wash at laundry tubs. Men, bur-
dened with lumber, picks and shovels and tools important to their
existence threaded their way through the noisy throngs. Dogs
snarled, barked and fought. Woodsmoke mixed with the stench of
rotting things. In the mist curling over the higher paths, columns of
favelados climbed like ants with wood and water cans on their heads.

We came upon Nair bent over her tub of wash. She wiped away   15
sweat with her apron and managed a smile. We asked for her husband
and she pointed to a tiny shack off to her right. This was José's store,
where he sold kerosene and bleach. He was sitting on a box, dozing.
Sensing our presence, he awoke and commenced complaining about
his back. "It kills me. The doctors don't help because I have no money. Always talk and a little pink pill that does no good. Ah, what is to
become of me?" A woman came to buy bleach. He filled her bottle.
She dropped a few coins and as she walked away his eyes stayed on
her backside until she was out of sight. Then he was complaining
about his back again.

"How much do you earn a day?" Gallo asked.   16
"Seventy-five cents. On a good day maybe a dollar."   17
"Why aren't the kids in school?"   18
"I don't have money for the clothes they need to go to school."   19
"Has Flavio seen a doctor?"   20

He pointed to a one-story wooden building. "That's the clinic 21
right there. They're mad because I built my store in front of their
place. I won't tear it down so they won't help my kids. Talk, talk, talk
and pink pills." We bid him good-bye and started climbing, following mud trails, jutting rock, slime-filled holes and shack after shack
propped against the slopes on shaky pilings. We sidestepped a dead
cat covered with maggots. I held my breath for an instant, only to in-
hale the stench of human excrement and garbage. Bare feet and legs
with open sores climbed above us—evils of the terrible soil they trod
every day, and there were seven hundred thousand or more afflicted
people in favelas around Rio alone. Touching me, Gallo pointed to
Flavio climbing ahead of us carrying firewood. He stopped to glance
at a man descending with a small coffin on his shoulder. A woman
and a small child followed him. When I lifted my camera, grumbling
erupted from a group of men sharing beer beneath a tree.

"They're threatening," Gallo said. "Keep moving. They fear 22
cameras. Think they're evil eyes bringing bad luck." Turning to
watch the funeral procession, Flavio caught sight of us and waited.
When we took the wood from him he protested, saying he was used
to carrying it. He gave in when I hung my camera around his neck.
Then, beaming, he climbed on ahead of us.

The fog had lifted and in the crisp morning light the shack 23
looked more squalid. Inside the kids seemed even noisier. Flavio
smiled and spoke above their racket. "Someday I want to live in a real
house on a real street with good pots and pans and a bed with
sheets." He lit the fire to warm leftovers from the night before. Stale
rice and beans—for breakfast and supper. No lunch; midday eating
was out of the question. Smoke rose and curled up through the ceiling's cracks. An air current forced it back, filling the place and Flavio's lungs with fumes. A coughing spasm doubled him up, turned his
skin blue under viscous sweat. I handed him a cup of water, but he
waved it away. His stomach tightened as he dropped to his knees.
His veins throbbed as if they would burst. Frustrated, we could only
watch; there was nothing we could do to help. Strangely, none of his
brothers or sisters appeared to notice. None of them stopped doing
whatever they were doing. Perhaps they had seen it too often. After
five interminable minutes it was over, and he got to his feet, smiling
as though it had all been a joke. "Maria, it's time for Zacarias to be
washed!"

"But there's rice in the pan!" 24

"Dump it in another pan—and don't spill water!"   25

Maria picked up Zacarias, who screamed, not wanting to be   26
washed. Irritated, Maria gave him a solid smack on his bare bottom. Flavio stepped over and gave her the same, then a free-for-all
started with Flavio, Maria and Mario slinging fists at one another.
Mario got one in the eye and fled the shack calling Flavio a dirty
son-of-a-bitch. Zacarias wound up on the floor sucking his thumb
and escaping his washing. The black bean and rice breakfast helped
to get things back to normal. Now it was time to get Flavio to the
doctor.

The clinic was crowded with patients—mothers and children   27
covered with open sores, a paralytic teenager, a man with an ear in a
state of decay, an aged blind couple holding hands in doubled darkness. Throughout the place came wailings of hunger and hurt. Flavio
sat nervously between Gallo and me. "What will the doctor do to
me?" he kept asking.

"We'll see. We'll wait and see."   28

In all, there were over fifty people. Finally, after two hours, it   29
was Flavio's turn and he broke out in a sweat, though he smiled at
the nurse as he passed through the door to the doctor's office. The
nurse ignored it; in this place of misery, smiles were unexpected.

The doctor, a large, beady-eyed man with a crew cut, had an air   30
of impatience. Hardly acknowledging our presence, he began to examine the frightened Flavio. "Open your mouth. Say 'Ah.' Jump up
and down. Breathe out. Take off those pants. Bend over. Stand up.
Cough. Cough louder. Louder." He did it all with such cold efficien-
cy. Then he spoke to us in English so Flavio wouldn't understand.
"This little chap has just about had it." My heart sank. Flavio was
smiling, happy to be over with the examination. He was handed a
bottle of cough medicine and a small box of pink pills, then asked to
step outside and wait.

"This the da Silva kid?"   31

"Yes."   32

"What's your interest in him?"   33

"We want to help in some way."   34

"I'm afraid you're too late. He's wasted with bronchial asthma,   35
malnutrition and, I suspect, tuberculosis. His heart, lungs and teeth
are all bad." He paused and wearily rubbed his forehead. "All that at
the ripe old age of twelve. And these hills are packed with other kids

just as bad off. Last year ten thousand died from dysentery alone. But what can we do? You saw what's waiting outside. It's like this every day. There's hardly enough money to buy aspirin. A few wealthy people who care help keep us going." He was quiet for a moment. "Maybe the right climate, the right diet, and constant medical care might...." He stopped and shook his head. "Naw. That poor lad's finished. He might last another year—maybe not." We thanked him and left.

"What did he say?" Flavio asked as we scaled the hill.   36

"Everything's going to be all right, Flav. There's nothing to worry about."   37

It had clouded over again by the time we reached the top. The rain swept in, clearing the mountain of Corcovado. The huge Christ figure loomed up again with clouds swirling around it. And to it I said a quick prayer for the boy walking beside us. He smiled as if he had read my thoughts. "Papa says 'El Cristo' has turned his back on the favela."   38

"You're going to be all right, Flavio."   39

"I'm not scared of death. It's my brothers and sisters I worry about. What would they do?"   40

"You'll be all right, Flavio."   41

Questions for Close Reading

1. What is the selection's thesis (or dominant impression)? Locate the sentence(s) in which Parks states his main idea. If he doesn't state the thesis explicitly, express it in your own words.
2. What is Flavio's family like? Why does Flavio have so much responsibility in the household?
3. What are some of the distinctive characteristics of Flavio's neighborhood and home?
4. What seems to be the basis of Flavio's fear of giving food to Parks and Gallo? What did Parks and Gallo understand that led them to refuse?
5. Refer to your dictionary as needed to define the following words used in the selection: *barrios* (paragraph 1), *jacaranda* (2), *jaundiced* (3), and *spigot* (14).

Questions About the Writer's Craft

1. **The Pattern.** Without stating it explicitly, Parks conveys a dominant impression about Flavio. What is that impression? What details create it?

2. **Other Patterns.**   When relating how Flavio performs numerous house-hold tasks, Parks describes several processes. How do these step-by-step explanations reinforce Parks's dominant impression of Flavio?

3. Parks provides numerous sensory specifics to depict Flavio's home. Look closely, for example, at the description in paragraph 6. Which words and phrases convey strong sensory images? How does Parks use transitions to help the reader move from one sensory image to another?

4. Paragraph 13 includes a scene that occurs in Parks's hotel. What's the effect of this scene? What does it contribute to the essay that the most detailed description of the *favela* could not?

Questions for Further Thought

1. Examine the scene in which Flavio's parents return to the shack (paragraph 10). Why do you think the da Silva parents treat their children as they do? How do you feel about the way the parents interact with their children?

2. Parks feels it was cowardly of him to want "to get away as quickly as possible" when Flavio was seized by a coughing spell. Do you agree with Parks's self-assessment? Why or why not?

3. The *favela*, which isn't far from the "gleaming white homes of the rich," is on the outskirts of a major city, Rio de Janeiro. Do you think there's something about large cities that desensitizes affluent people to the plight of the poverty-stricken? Would people in small towns be more sensitive? Why or why not?

4. Flavio's family, already suffering terrible deprivation, can hardly afford another child, yet Flavio's mother is once again pregnant. Some people argue that one way to help break the poverty cycle is to pay financial incentives to poor women to use birth control. Why do you think such a policy is controversial? What are your views on this approach to the problem of poverty?

Writing Assignments Using Description as a Pattern of Development

∞ 1. Parks paints a wrenching portrait of a person who remains vibrant and hopeful even though he is suffering greatly—from physical illness, poverty, overwork, and worry. Write a description about someone you know who has shown courage or other positive qualities during a time of personal trouble. Include, as Parks does, plentiful details about the person's appearance and behavior so that you don't have to state directly what you admire about the person. Maya Angelou's "Grandmother's Victory" (page 164) shows how one writer conveys the special quality of an admirable individual.

2. Parks presents an unforgettable description of the *favela* and the living conditions there. Write an essay about a region, city, neighborhood, or building that also projects an overwhelming negative feeling. Include only those details that convey your dominant impression, and provide—as Parks does—vivid sensory language to convey your attitude toward your subject.

Writing Assignments Using Other Patterns of Development

∞ 3. The doctor reports that a few wealthy people contribute to the clinic, but the reader can tell from the scene in Parks's hotel that most people are insensitive to those less fortunate. Write an essay describing a specific situation that you feel reflects people's tendency to ignore the difficulties of others. Analyze why people distance themselves from the problem; then present specific steps that could be taken to sensitize them to the situation. Jonathan Kozol's "Are the Homeless Crazy?" (page 500), Gloria Naylor's "Mommy, What Does 'Nigger' Mean?" (page 535), and Mark Twain's "The Damned Human Race" (page 609) will provide some perspective on the way people harden themselves to the pain of others.

4. Although Parks celebrates Flavio's generosity of spirit, the writer also illustrates the brutalizing effect of an impoverished environment. Prepare an essay in which you also show that setting, architecture, even furnishings can influence mood and behavior. You may, as Parks does, focus on the corrosive effect of a negative environment, or you may write about the nurturing effect of a positive environment. Possible subjects include a park in the middle of a city, a bus terminal, and a college library.

Russell Baker

Currently the host of the popular PBS series *Masterpiece Theatre,*
Baker writes a column "The Observer" for the *New York Times.*
In the column, he applies his unique brand of humor to social
commentary. Born in Virginia in 1925, Baker received his B. A.
from Johns Hopkins University and spent several years working as
a reporter for the *Baltimore Sun* before joining the *Times* in the
mid-1950s. In 1979, Baker won a Pulitzer Prize, journalism's
highest honor. Baker's columns have been collected in several
books, including *No Cause for Panic* (1969), *Poor Russell's Alma-
nac* (1972), *So This Is Depravity* (1980), and *There's a Country in
My Cellar* (1990). He also edited the book *Russell Baker's Book of
American Humor.* Baker has written a widely read and critically
acclaimed two-volume autobiography, *Growing Up* (1982),
which was awarded a Pulitzer Prize, and *The Good Times* (1989).
The following selection is taken from *Growing Up.*

In My Day

We often expect the most from—and are most intolerant of—the
people we depended on when we were young. In the following selection, Russell Baker describes his aging mother and the tangled
feelings she arouses in him as she takes refuge in her memories.
Her mental deterioration leads Baker to ponder the weaving of
past and present that flows through all families.

At the age of eighty my mother had her last bad fall, and after   1
that her mind wandered free through time. Some days she went to
weddings and funerals that had taken place half a century earlier. On
others she presided over family dinners cooked on Sunday afternoons
for children who were now gray with age. Through all this she lay in
bed but moved across time, traveling among the dead decades with
a speed and ease beyond the gift of physical science.

"Where's Russell?" she asked one day when I came to visit at the   2
nursing home.

"I'm Russell," I said.   3

She gazed at this improbably overgrown figure out of an incon- 4
ceivable future and promptly dismissed it.

"Russell's only this big," she said, holding her hand, palm 5
down, two feet from the floor. That day she was a young country
wife with chickens in the backyard and a view of hazy blue Virginia
mountains behind the apple orchard, and I was a stranger old
enough to be her father.

Early one morning she phoned me in New York. "Are you com- 6
ing to my funeral today?" she asked.

It was an awkward question with which to be awakened. "What 7
are you talking about, for God's sake?" was the best reply I could
manage.

"I'm being buried today," she declared briskly, as though an- 8
nouncing an important social event.

"I'll phone you back," I said and hung up, and when I did 9
phone back she was all right, although she wasn't all right, of course,
and we all knew she wasn't.

She had always been a small woman—short, light-boned, deli- 10
cately structured—but now, under the white hospital sheet, she was
becoming tiny. I thought of a doll with huge, fierce eyes. There had
always been a fierceness in her. It showed in that angry, challenging
thrust of the chin when she issued an opinion, and a great one she
had always been for issuing opinions.

"I tell people exactly what's on my mind," she had been 11
fond of boasting. "I tell them what I think, whether they like it
or not." Often they had not liked it. She could be sarcastic to
people in whom she detected evidence of the ignoramus or the
fool.

"It's not always good policy to tell people exactly what's on your 12
mind," I used to caution her.

"If they don't like it, that's too bad," was her customary reply, 13
"because that's the way I am."

And so she was. A formidable woman. Determined to speak 14
her mind, determined to have her way, determined to bend those
who opposed her. In that time when I had known her best,
my mother had hurled herself at life with chin thrust forward,
eyes blazing, and an energy that made her seem always on the
run.

She ran after squawking chickens, an axe in her hand, deter-   15
mined on a beheading that would put dinner in the pot. She ran
when she made the beds, ran when she set the table. One Thanksgiv-
ing she burned herself badly when, running up from the cellar oven
with the ceremonial turkey, she tripped on the stairs and tumbled
back down, ending at the bottom in the debris of giblets, hot gravy,
and battered turkey. Life was combat, and victory was not to the lazy,
the timid, the slugabed, the drugstore cowboy, the libertine, the
mushmouth afraid to tell people exactly what was on his mind
whether people liked it or not. She ran.

But now the running was over. For a time I could not accept the   16
inevitable. As I sat by her bed, my impulse was to argue her back to
reality. On my first visit to the hospital in Baltimore, she asked who
I was.

"Russell," I said.   17
"Russell's way out west," she advised me.   18
"No, I'm right here."   19
"Guess where I came from today?" was her response.   20
"Where?"   21
"All the way from New Jersey."   22
"When?"   23
"Tonight."   24
"No. You've been in the hospital for three days," I insisted.   25
"I suggest the thing to do is calm down a little bit," she replied.   26
"Go over to the house and shut the door."

Now she was years deep into the past, living in the neighbor-   27
hood where she had settled forty years earlier, and she had just been
talking with Mrs. Hoffman, a neighbor across the street.

"It's like Mrs. Hoffman said today: The children always wander   28
back to where they come from," she remarked.

"Mrs. Hoffman has been dead for fifteen years."   29
"Russ got married today," she replied.   30
"I got married in 1950," I said, which was the fact.   31
"The house is unlocked," she said.   32

So it went until a doctor came by to give one of those oral quiz-   33
zes that medical men apply in such cases. She failed catastrophically,
giving wrong answers or none at all to "What day is this?" "Do
you know where you are?" "How old are you?" and so on. Then, a
surprise.

"When is your birthday?" he asked. 34
"November 5, 1897," she said. Correct. Absolutely correct. 35
"How do you remember that?" the doctor asked. 36
"Because I was born on Guy Fawkes Day," she said. 37
"Guy Fawkes?" asked the doctor. "Who is Guy Fawkes?" 38
   She replied with a rhyme I had heard her recite time and again 39
over the years when the subject of her birth date arose:

> *"Please to remember the Fifth of November,*
> *Gunpowder treason and plot.*
> *I see no reason why gunpowder treason*
> *Should ever be forgot."*

Then she glared at this young doctor so ill informed about Guy
Fawkes' failed scheme to blow King James off his throne with barrels
of gunpowder in 1605. She had been a schoolteacher, after all, and
knew how to glare at a dolt. "You may know a lot about medicine,
but you obviously don't know any history," she said. Having told
him exactly what was on her mind, she left us again.
   The doctors diagnosed a hopeless senility. Not unusual, they 40
said. "Hardening of the arteries" was the explanation for laymen. I
thought it was more complicated than that. For ten years or more the
ferocity with which she had once attacked life had been turning to a
rage against the weakness, the boredom, and the absence of love that
too much age had brought her. Now, after the last bad fall, she
seemed to have broken chains that imprisoned her in a life she had
come to hate and to return to a time inhabited by people who loved
her, a time in which she was needed. Gradually I understood. It was
the first time in years I had seen her happy.
   She had written a letter three years earlier which explained more 41
than "hardening of the arteries." I had gone down from New York to
Baltimore, where she lived, for one of my infrequent visits and, afterwards, had written her with some banal advice to look for the silver lin-
ing, to count her blessings instead of burdening others with her
miseries. I suppose what it really amounted to was a threat that if she
was not more cheerful during my visits I would not come to see her
very often. Sons are capable of such letters. This one was written out
of a childish faith in the eternal strength of parents, a naive belief that
age and wear could be overcome by an effort of will, that all she needed

was a good pep talk to recharge a flagging spirit. It was such a foolish, innocent idea, but one thinks of parents differently from other people. Other people can become frail and break, but not parents.

She wrote back in an unusually cheery vein intended to demon-   42
strate, I suppose, that she was mending her ways. She was never a woman to apologize, but for one moment with the pen in her hand she came very close. Referring to my visit, she wrote: "If I seemed unhappy to you at times—" Here she drew back, reconsidered, and said something quite different:

"If I seemed unhappy to you at times, I am, but there's really   43
nothing anyone can do about it, because I'm just so very tired and lonely that I'll just go to sleep and forget it." She was then seventy-eight.

Now, three years later, after the last bad fall, she had managed   44
to forget the fatigue and loneliness and, in these free-wheeling excursions back through time, to recapture happiness. I soon stopped trying to wrest her back to what I considered the real world and tried to travel along with her on those fantastic swoops into the past. One day when I arrived at her bedside she was radiant.

"Feeling good today," I said.   45
"Why shouldn't I feel good?" she asked. "Papa's going to take   46
me up to Baltimore on the boat today."

At that moment she was a young girl standing on a wharf at   47
Merry Point, Virginia, waiting for the Chesapeake Bay steamer with her father, who had been dead sixty-one years. William Howard Taft was in the White House, Europe still drowsed in the dusk of the great century of peace, America was a young country, and the future stretched before it in beams of crystal sunlight. "The greatest country on God's green earth," her father might have said, if I had been able to step into my mother's time machine and join him on the wharf with the satchels packed for Baltimore.

I could imagine her there quite clearly. She was wearing a blue   48
dress with big puffy sleeves and long black stockings. There was a ribbon in her hair and a big bow tied on the side of her head. There had been a childhood photograph in her bedroom which showed all this, although the colors of course had been added years later by a restorer who tinted the picture.

About her father, my grandfather, I could only guess, and in-   49
deed, about the girl on the wharf with the bow in her hair, I was merely sentimentalizing. Of my mother's childhood and her people, of their time and place, I knew very little. A world had lived and died,

and though it was part of my blood and bone I knew little more about it than I knew of the world of the pharaohs. It was useless now to ask for help from my mother. The orbits of her mind rarely touched present interrogators for more than a moment.

Sitting at her bedside, forever out of touch with her, I wondered 50 about my own children, and their children, and children in general, and about the disconnections between children and parents that prevent them from knowing each other. Children rarely want to know who their parents were before they were parents, and when age finally stirs their curiosity there is no parent left to tell them. If a parent does lift the curtain a bit, it is often only to stun the young with some exemplary tale of how much harder life was in the old days.

I had been guilty of this when my children were small in the ear- 51 ly 1960s and living the affluent life. It galled me that their childhoods should be, as I thought, so easy when my own had been, as I thought, so hard. I had developed the habit, when they complained about the steak being overcooked or the television being cut off, of lecturing them on the harshness of life in my day.

"In my day all we got for dinner was macaroni and cheese, and 52 we were glad to get it."

"In my day we didn't have any television." 53

"In my day . . ." 54

"In my day . . ." 55

At dinner one evening a son had offended me with an inade- 56 quate report card, and as I leaned back and cleared my throat to lecture, he gazed at me with an expression of unutterable resignation and said, "Tell me how it was in your days, Dad."

I was angry with him for that, but angrier with myself for having 57 become one of those ancient bores whose highly selective memories of the past become transparently dishonest even to small children. I tried to break the habit, but must have failed. A few years later my son was referring to me when I was out of earshot as "the old-timer." Between us there was a dispute about time. He looked upon the time that had been my future in a disturbing way. My future was his past, and being young, he was indifferent to the past.

As I hovered over my mother's bed listening for muffled signals 58 from her childhood, I realized that this same dispute had existed between her and me. When she was young, with life ahead of her, I had been her future and resented it. Instinctively, I wanted to break free, cease being a creature defined by her time, consign her future to the past, and create my own. Well, I had finally done that, and then with my own children I had seen my exciting future become their boring past.

These hopeless end-of-the-line visits with my mother made me   59
wish I had not thrown off my own past so carelessly. We all come from the past, and children ought to know what it was that went into their making, to know that life is a braided cord of humanity stretching up from time long gone, and that it cannot be defined by the span of a single journey from diaper to shroud.

Questions for Close Reading

1. What is the selection's thesis (or dominant impression)? Locate the sentence(s) in which Baker states his main idea. If he doesn't state the thesis explicitly, express it in your own words.
2. What was Mrs. Baker's philosophy of life? How did it change in her old age?
3. Why does Baker feel "forever out of touch" with his mother? Does he feel equally out of touch with his children?
4. Why does Baker stop trying to get his eighty-year-old mother to return to the real world? Is he being kind or unkind?
5. Refer to your dictionary as needed to define the following words used in the selection: *inconceivable* (paragraph 4), *libertine* (15), *banal* (41), *wrest* (44), *exemplary* (50), *galled* (51), and *consign* (58).

Questions About the Writer's Craft

1. **The pattern.**   How does the series of scenes in "In My Day" develop the essay's dominant impression?
2. Baker describes his mother by using details about her actions and her appearance, as well as by quoting things she said. Both are typical techniques for revealing character in a descriptive piece. Which technique is more effective in conveying Mrs. Baker's personality?
3. In paragraph 15, Baker repeats the word *ran* when describing his mother's energy. He also speaks several times of her *falls*. What do you think might have been Baker's purpose for repeating these words? What do they suggest about the pattern of his mother's life?
4. If something is *ironic,* there is a discrepancy between what is said and what is known. In paragraph 28, Mrs. Baker says, "The children always wander back to where they come from." How is this comment by Baker's mother ironic? Find some other examples of irony in the essay.

Questions for Further Thought

1. Baker writes, "Other people can become frail and break, but not parents" (paragraph 41). What does he mean? What illusions do we have about our parents?

2. On the whole, would you say Russell Baker has been a good son? A good father? What do you think he would do differently if he had another chance? Will reading this essay affect your behavior toward your parents or children?

3. Baker feels that there is no way for parents and children truly to know each other. Do you agree or not—and why?

4. Is it inevitable that children will reject their parents' values and their parents' lives? What forms might this rejection take?

Writing Assignments Using Description as a Pattern of Development

1. Write a description of a parent or relative at a certain age, for example, "My Brother at Fourteen" or "My Mother at Fifty-five." Your description should create a dominant impression by conveying the person's characteristic approach to life. Be sure to select lively details that support this dominant impression. Before planning your paper, you might want to read Judith Ortiz Cofer's "A Partial Remembrance of a Puerto Rican Childhood" (page 138), and Maya Angelou's "Grandmother's Victory" (page 164), two essays that pay loving tribute to indomitable figures.

2. Describe one or more active, vital older people who have not retreated into the past to find happiness. Your examples could be people you know, people you have heard about, or people in the public eye. Choose vivid details that show how such people's actions and attitudes keep them "young." Draw some conclusions about what older people can do to stay involved with life.

Writing Assignments Using Other Patterns of Development

3. Russell Baker's essay concerns a crisis in his family. Write an essay about a crisis situation in a family—your own or someone else's. The crisis might be a divorce, serious or chronic illness, loss of a job, financial difficulties, or some other serious problem. Your essay might explore the causes and/or effects of the crisis; it might outline the steps the family has taken to deal with the crisis; it might be a narrative that points to some conclusion about how people deal with crises.

4. In the past, most elderly parents lived in an extended family—children, grandchildren, and other relatives were all part of a single household. Today, though, many old people are isolated from families. In addition, many people feel our society—unlike some others—doesn't seem to revere older people; indeed, we often disregard their experience, wisdom, and traditions. Write an essay showing how society's attitude toward older people affects the lives of both the old and the young.

Annie Dillard

Pilgrim at Tinker Creek (1974) is probably Annie Dillard's best-known work. A collection of lyrical observations and reflections about the natural world, Pilgrim was awarded a Pulitzer Prize for general nonfiction. Born in 1945, Dillard is currently Adjunct Professor at Wesleyan University in Connecticut and a contributing editor at Harper's. Over the years, she has published a variety of books: Tickets for a Prayer Wheel (1974), a book of poetry; Holy the Firm (1978), Teaching a Stone to Talk (1982), and The Annie Dillard Reader (1994), collections of essays; Living by Fiction (1982), literary criticism; Encounters With Chinese Writers (1984), narrative nonfiction; An American Childhood (1987), an autobiography; and The Writing Life (1989), miscellaneous reflections on writing. Her first novel, The Living, was published to critical acclaim in 1992. "In the Jungle" is taken from Teaching a Stone to Talk.

In the Jungle

In the world inhabited by most North Americans, the quality of life is often defined in terms of possessions: cars, stereos, apartments. But in the Ecuadorian jungle, Annie Dillard discovers that such items have no meaning. Indeed, the richness of the rain forest underscores how impoverished contemporary life may be.

Like any out-of-the-way place, the Napo River in the Ecuadorian 1
jungle seems real enough when you are there, even central. Out of the
way of *what*? I was sitting on a stump at the edge of a bankside palm-
thatch village, in the middle of the night, on the headwaters of the Amazon. Out of the way of human life, tenderness, or the glance of heaven?

A nightjar in a deep-leaved shadow called three long notes, and 2
hushed. The men with me talked softly in clumps: three North Americans, four Ecuadorians who were showing us the jungle. We were
holding cool drinks and idly watching a hand-sized tarantula seize
moths that came to the lone bulb on the generator shed beside us.

It was February, the middle of summer. Green fireflies spattered   3
lights across the air and illumined for seconds, now here, now there,
the pale trunks of enormous, solitary trees. Beneath us the brown
Napo River was rising, in all silence; it coiled up the sandy bank and
tangled its foam in vines that trailed from the forest and roots that
looped the shore.

Each breath of night smelled sweet, more moistened and sweet   4
than any kitchen, or garden, or cradle. Each star in Orion seemed to
tremble and stir with my breath. All at once, in the thatch house
across the clearing behind us, one of the village's Jesuit priests began
playing an alto recorder, playing a wordless song, lyric, in a minor
key, that twined over the village clearing, that caught in the big trees'
canopies, muted our talk on the bankside, and wandered over the river, dissolving downstream.

This will do, I thought. This will do, for a weekend, or a season,   5
or a home.

Later that night I loosed my hair from its braids and combed it   6
smooth—not for myself, but so the village girls could play with it in
the morning.

We had disembarked at the village that afternoon, and I had   7
slumped on some shaded steps, wishing I knew some Spanish or
some Quechua so I could speak with the ring of little girls who were
alternately staring at me and smiling at their toes. I spoke anyway,
and fooled with my hair, which they were obviously dying to get
their hands on, and laughed, and soon they were all braiding my hair,
all five of them, all fifty fingers, all my hair, even my bangs. And then
they took it apart and did it again, laughing, and teaching me Spanish
nouns, and meeting my eyes and each other's with open delight,
while their small brothers in blue jeans climbed down from the trees
and began kicking a volleyball around with one of the North American men.

Now, as I combed my hair in the little tent, another of the men,   8
a free-lance writer from Manhattan, was talking quietly. He was telling us the tale of his life, describing his work in Hollywood, his apartment in Manhattan, his house in Paris. . . . "It makes me wonder," he
said, "what I'm doing in a tent under a tree in the village of
Pompeya, on the Napo River, in the jungle of Ecuador." After a
pause he added, "It makes me wonder why I'm going *back*."

The point of going somewhere like the Napo River in Ecuador   9
is not to see the most spectacular anything. It is simply to see what is
there. We are here on the planet only once, and might as well get a
feel for the place. We might as well get a feel for the fringes and hollows in which life is lived, for the Amazon basin, which covers half a
continent, and for the life that—there, like anywhere else—is always
and necessarily lived in detail: on the tributaries, in the riverside villages, sucking this particular white-fleshed guava in this particular
pattern of shade.

What is there is interesting. The Napo River itself is wide (I mean   10
wider than the Mississippi at Davenport) and brown, opaque, and
smeared with floating foam and logs and branches from the jungle.
White egrets hunch on shoreline deadfalls and parrots in flocks dart in
and out of the light. Under the water in the river, unseen, are anacondas—which are reputed to take a few village toddlers every year—and
water boas, stingrays, crocodiles, manatees, and sweet-meated fish.

Low water bares gray strips of sandbar on which the natives   11
build tiny palm-thatch shelters, arched, the size of pup tents, for
overnight fishing trips. You see these extraordinarily clean people
(who bathe twice a day in the river, and whose straight black hair is
always freshly washed) paddling down the river in dugout canoes,
hugging the banks.

Some of the Indians of this region, earlier in the century, used   12
to sleep naked in hammocks. The nights are cold. Gordon Mac-
Creach, an American explorer in these Amazon tributaries, reported
that he was startled to hear the Indians get up at three in the morning. He was even more startled, night after night, to hear them walk
down to the river slowly, half asleep, and bathe in the water. Only
later did he learn what they were doing: they were getting warm. The
cold woke them; they warmed their skins in the river, which was always ninety degrees; then they returned to their hammocks and slept
through the rest of the night.

The riverbanks are low, and from the river you see an unbroken   13
wall of dark forest in every direction, from the Andes to the Atlantic.
You get a taste for looking at trees: trees hung with the swinging
nests of yellow troupials, trees from which ant nests the size of grain
sacks hang like black goiters, trees from which seven-colored tana-
gers flutter, coral trees, teak, balsa and breadfruit, enormous emer-
gent silk-cotton trees, and the pale-barked *samona* palms.

When you are inside the jungle, away from the river, the trees   14
vault out of sight. It is hard to remember to look up the long trunks
and see the fans, strips, fronds, and sprays of glossy leaves. Inside the
jungle you are more likely to notice the snarl of climbers and creepers
round the trees' boles, the flowering bromeliads and epiphytes in every bough's crook, and the fantastic silk-cotton tree trunks thirty or
forty feet across, trunks buttressed in flanges of wood whose curves
can make three high walls of a room—a shady, loamy-aired room
where you would gladly live, or die. Butterflies, iridescent blue,
striped, or clear-winged, thread the jungle paths at eye level. And at
your feet is a swath of ants bearing triangular bits of green leaf. The
ants with their leaves look like a wide fleet of sailing dinghies—but
they don't quit. In either direction they wobble over the jungle floor
as far as the eye can see. I followed them off the path as far as I dared,
and never saw an end to ants or to those luffing chips of green they
bore.

Unseen in the jungle, but present, are tapirs, jaguars, many spe-   15
cies of snake and lizard, ocelots, armadillos, marmosets, howler monkeys, toucans and macaws and a hundred other birds, deer, bats,
peccaries, capybaras, agoutis, and sloths. Also present in this jungle,
but variously distant, are Texaco derricks and pipelines, and some of
the wildest Indians in the world, blowgun-using Indians, who killed
missionaries in 1956 and ate them.

Long lakes shine in the jungle. We traveled one of these in dug-   16
out canoes, canoes with two inches of freeboard, canoes paddled
with machete-hewn oars chopped from buttresses of silk-cotton
trees, or poled in the shallows with peeled cane or bamboo. Our
part-Indian guide had cleared the path to the lake the day before;
when we walked the path we saw where he had impaled the lopped
head of a boa, open-mouthed, on a pointed stick by the canoes, for
decoration.

The lake was wonderful. Herons, egrets, and ibises plodded the   17
sawgrass shores, kingfishers and cuckoos clattered from sunlight to
shade, great turkeylike birds fussed in dead branches, and hawks
lolled overhead. There was all the time in the world. A turtle slid into
the water. The boy in the bow of my canoe slapped stones at birds
with a simple sling, a rubber throng and leather pad. He aimed brilliantly at moving targets, always, and always missed; the birds were
out of range. He stuffed his sling back in his shirt. I looked around.

The lake and river waters are as opaque as rain-forest leaves; they   18
are veils, blinds, painted screens. You see things only by their effects.
I saw the shoreline water roil and the sawgrass heave above a thrashing *paichi,* an enormous black fish of these waters; one had been
caught the previous week weighing 430 pounds. Piranha fish live in
the lakes, and electric eels. I dangled my fingers in the water, figuring
it would be worth it.

We would eat chicken that night in the village, and rice, yucca,   19
onions, beets, and heaps of fruit. The sun would ring down, pulling
darkness after it like a curtain. Twilight is short, and the unseen birds
of twilight wistful, uncanny, catching the heart. The two nuns in
their dazzling white habits—the beautiful-boned young nun and the
warm-faced old—would glide to the open cane-and-thatch school-
room in darkness, and start the children singing. The children would
sing in piping Spanish, highpitched and pure; they would sing
"Nearer My God to Thee" in Quechua, very fast. (To reciprocate, we
sang for them "Old MacDonald Had a Farm"; I thought they might
recognize the animal sounds. Of course they thought we were out of
our minds.) As the children became excited by their own singing,
they left their log benches and swarmed around the nuns, hopping,
smiling at us, everyone smiling, the nuns' faces bursting in their
cowls, and the clear-voiced children still singing, and the palm-leafed
roofing stirred.

The Napo River: it is not out of the way. It is *in* the way, catch-   20
ing sunlight the way a cup catches poured water; it is a bowl of sweet
air, a basin of greenness, and of grace, and, it would seem, of peace.

Questions for Close Reading

1. What is the selection's thesis (or dominant impression)? Locate the sen-
tence(s) in which Dillard states her main idea. If she doesn't state the thesis explicitly, express it in your own words.
2. To what extent do the non-natives of the Ecuadorian jungle—the North
Americans, priests, and nuns—harmonize with the place and its Indian
inhabitants? Are there any times the non-natives seem out of place or ludicrous? When?
3. What can we infer about Dillard's attitude toward the natives who display
severed snake heads, sling stones at birds, and eat other human beings?
4. Although Dillard writes that the Napo River is a place "of peace" (paragraph 20), an undercurrent of menace runs throughout her essay. Where

does she mention threatening possibilities? What do these dangers suggest about the jungle? About life?

5. Refer to your dictionary as needed to define the following words used in the selection: *tributary* (paragraphs 9 and 12), *opaque* (10, 18), *bole* (14), *buttressed* (14), *derrick* (15), and *impaled* (16).

Questions About the Writer's Craft

1. **The pattern.**   In descriptive essays, writers often use a fairly straightforward organizational structure. Why doesn't Dillard use strict chronological, sensory, spatial, or emphatic order to structure her essay? Why, for example, does she delay the account of her arrival until paragraph 7?

2. Dillard is a master of rich sensory detail. For instance, she writes that the Napo River "coiled up the sandy bank and tangled its foam in vines" (paragraph 3). Find additional examples of words and phrases that appeal powerfully to the senses. How do these word choices support Dillard's thesis?

3. **Other patterns.**   Dillard contrasts descriptions of the sweet and peaceful directly with descriptions of the sinister and violent. In one sentence, for example, she matter-of-factly mentions refreshing drinks and a tarantula attacking its prey. Find other instances of such startling juxtapositions. What do they suggest about the jungle? About life?

4. Although Dillard relies heavily on visual details, she also refers repeatedly to the invisibly present (paragraphs 10, 14, 15, 18). What is her purpose in reminding readers of what is unseen?

Questions for Further Thought

1. Dillard seems to accept all creatures and behaviors as a natural part of life. Do you have the same attitude, or are you more judgmental? What are the dangers of being either too judgmental or too accepting?

2. What effect does Dillard's not understanding Spanish or Quechua have on her experience with the natives? Were you ever in a region where you didn't understand the language? What effect did this have on your impression of the place?

3. Were you disturbed when you read about the moths being eaten by the tarantula? Were you more disturbed when you read about the boy attempting to pelt the birds with stones? Or perhaps only the references to cannibalism and human-eating animals upset you. What might your reactions reveal about your attitude toward living things?

4. Dillard depicts a continuous cycle of life and death in which chronological time is of little importance. Do you feel society is too conscious of schedules and deadlines? If you think it is, what do we lose by such regimentation? What do we gain?

Writing Assignments Using Description as a Pattern of Development

1. Dillard suggests that many of us feel frazzled by our everyday lives. Where do you go when you want to get away from it all? Do you shut yourself in your room and turn on the music? Do you go to a gym? Write an essay describing where you feel most at peace. Like Dillard, use vivid sensory details and figurative language to convey your paper's dominant impression.

∞ 2. Write a description of a place that seems ugly, harmful, or otherwise offensive—cigarette stubs and debris on the beach, tipped-over trash cans and cracked sidewalks in a nearby neighborhood. Organized around a clear dominant impression, your description should capture the look, smell, sound, and feel of this unpleasant place. Use the description to make a point about humans' interaction with their environment. Gordon Parks's "Flavio's Home" (page 104) might give you some good ideas for your essay.

Writing Assignments Using Other Patterns of Development

3. Write an essay arguing that living in what Dillard calls "out of the way places" is superior to city living. Or take the opposing stance and argue that urban living is preferable. Support your contention through vivid examples of the inconvenience, danger, and unhappiness experienced by those dwelling in the area you find unpleasant. The essay's tone may be serious or playful. One part of the paper, perhaps the introduction, should recognize the opposing viewpoint.

4. Dillard seems to suffer little or no culture shock in the Ecuadorian jungle. Narrate a time you felt out of place—in a new school, a foreign country, another region of the country, a stranger's home. To show what happened, focus on the experience's humorous, embarrassing, or threatening elements. What did the experience teach you about yourself and your ability to adapt?

E. B. White

Elwyn Brooks White (1899–1985) is considered one of America's finest essayists. For many years, White was a member of the *New Yorker* magazine staff and wrote the magazine's popular column, "The Talk of the Town." He also wrote children's books, including the classic *Charlotte's Web* (1952), and was the coauthor with William Strunk, Jr., of the renowned guide for writers, *The Elements of Style* (1959). But most memorable are the essays White produced during his life—gems of clarity, wit, and heartfelt expression. White's contribution to literature earned him many awards, including the Presidential Medal of Freedom and the National Medal for Literature. The classic essay reprinted here is taken from *The Essays of E. B. White* (1977).

Once More to the Lake

In this celebrated essay, E. B. White describes his return to a vacation spot he had known intimately in his childhood, a cabin on a lake in Maine. This time White is accompanied by his son. In many ways the lake, the cabin, and the surrounding fields and woods are the same, but in other respects they are different. With great skill, White describes his past and present experiences at the lake, exploring the nature of life cycles and of change itself.

One summer, along about 1904, my father rented a camp on a 1 lake in Maine and took us all there for the month of August. We all got ringworm from some kittens and had to rub Pond's Extract on our arms and legs night and morning, and my father rolled over in a canoe with all his clothes on; but outside of that the vacation was a success and from then on none of us ever thought there was any place in the world like that lake in Maine. We returned summer after summer—always on August 1 for one month. I have since become a salt-water man, but sometimes in summer there are days when the restlessness of the tides and the fearful cold of the sea water and the incessant wind that blows across the afternoon and into the evening make me wish for the placidity of a lake in the woods. A few weeks ago this feeling got so strong I bought myself a couple of bass hooks and a spinner and returned to the lake where we used to go, for a week's fishing and to revisit old haunts.

I took along my son, who had never had any fresh water up his   2
nose and who had seen lily pads only from train windows. On the journey over to the lake I began to wonder what it would be like. I wondered how time would have marred this unique, this holy spot— the coves and streams, the hills that the sun set behind, the camps and the paths behind the camps. I was sure that the tarred road would have found it out, and I wondered in what other ways it would be desolated. It is strange how much you can remember about places like that once you allow your mind to return into the grooves that lead back. You remember one thing, and that suddenly reminds you of another thing. I guess I remembered clearest of all the early morn- ings, when the lake was cool and motionless, remembered how the bedroom smelled of the lumber it was made of and of the wet woods whose scent entered through the screen. The partitions in the camp were thin and did not extend clear to the top of the rooms, and as I was always the first up I would dress softly so as not to wake the oth- ers, and sneak out into the sweet outdoors and start out in the canoe, keeping close along the shore in the long shadows of the pines. I re- membered being very careful never to rub my paddle against the gunwale for fear of disturbing the stillness of the cathedral.

The lake had never been what you would call a wild lake. There   3
were cottages sprinkled around the shores, and it was in farming country although the shores of the lake were quite heavily wooded. Some of the cottages were owned by nearby farmers, and you would live at the shore and eat your meals at the farmhouse. That's what our family did. But although it wasn't wild, it was a fairly large and un- disturbed lake and there were places in it that, to a child at least, seemed infinitely remote and primeval.

I was right about the tar: it led to within half a mile of the shore.   4
But when I got back there, with my boy, and we settled into a camp near a farmhouse and into the kind of summertime I had known, I could tell that it was going to be pretty much the same as it had been before—I knew it, lying in bed the first morning, smelling the bedroom and hearing the boy sneak quietly out and go off along the shore in a boat. I began to sustain the illusion that he was I, and therefore, by sim- ple transposition, that I was my father. This sensation persisted, kept cropping up all the time we were there. It was not an entirely new feel- ing, but in this setting it grew much stronger. I seemed to be living a

dual existence. I would be in the middle of some simple act, I would be picking up a bait box or laying down a table fork, or I would be saying something, and suddenly it would be not I but my father who was saying the words or making the gesture. It gave me a creepy sensation.

We went fishing the first morning. I felt the same damp moss covering the worms in the bait can, and saw the dragonfly alight on the tip of my rod as it hovered a few inches from the surface of the water. It was the arrival of this fly that convinced me beyond any doubt that everything was as it always had been, that the years were a mirage and that there had been no years. The small waves were the same, chucking the rowboat under the chin as we fished at anchor, and the boat was the same boat, the same color green and the ribs broken in the same places, and under the floorboards the same fresh-water leavings and débris—the dead helgramite, the wisps of moss, the rusty discarded fishhook, the dried blood from yesterday's catch. We stared silently at the tips of our rods, at the dragonflies that came and went. I lowered the tip of mine into the water, tentatively, pensively dislodging the fly, which darted two feet away, poised, darted two feet back, and came to rest again a little farther up the rod. There had been no years between the ducking of this dragonfly and the other one—the one that was part of memory. I looked at the boy, who was silently watching his fly, and it was my hands that held his rod, my eyes watching. I felt dizzy and didn't know which rod I was at the end of. 5

We caught two bass, hauling them in briskly as though they were mackerel, pulling them over the side of the boat in a businesslike manner without any landing net, and stunning them with a blow on the back of the head. When we got back for a swim before lunch, the lake was exactly where we had left it, the same number of inches from the dock, and there was only the merest suggestion of a breeze. This seemed an utterly enchanted sea, this lake you could leave to its own devices for a few hours and come back to, and find that it had not stirred, this constant and trustworthy body of water. In the shallows, the dark, water-soaked sticks and twigs, smooth and old, were undulating in clusters on the bottom against the clean ribbed sand, and the track of the mussel was plain. A school of minnows swam by, each minnow with its small individual shadow, doubling the attendance, so clear and sharp in the sunlight. Some of the other campers were in swimming, along the shore, one of them with a cake of soap, and the water felt thin and clear and unsubstantial. Over the years 6 there had been this person with the cake of soap, this cultist, and here he was. There had been no years.

Up to the farmhouse to dinner through the teeming, dusty field, the road under our sneakers was only a two-track road. The middle track was missing, the one with the marks of the hooves and the splotches of dried, flaky manure. There had always been three tracks to choose from in choosing which track to walk in; now the choice was narrowed down to two. For a moment I missed terribly the middle alternative. But the way led past the tennis court, and something about the way it lay there in the sun reassured me; the tape had loosened along the backline, the alleys were green with plantains and other weeds, and the net (installed in June and removed in September) sagged in the dry noon, and the whole place steamed with midday heat and hunger and emptiness. There was a choice of pie for dessert, and one was blueberry and one was apple, and the waitresses were the same country girls, there having been no passage of time, only the illusion of it as in a dropped curtain—the waitresses were still fifteen; their hair had been washed, that was the only difference—they had been to the movies and seen the pretty girls with the clean hair.

Summertime, oh, summertime, pattern of life indelible, the fade-proof lake, the woods unshatterable, the pasture with the sweet-fern and the juniper forever and ever, summer without end; this was the background, and the life along the shore was the design, the cottagers with their innocent and tranquil design, their tiny docks with the flagpole and the American flag floating against the white clouds in the blue sky, the little paths over the roots of the trees leading from camp to camp and the paths leading back to the outhouses and the can of lime for sprinkling, and at the souvenir counters at the store the miniature birch-bark canoes and the postcards that showed things looking a little better than they looked. This was the American family at play, escaping the city heat, wondering whether the newcomers in the camp at the head of the cove were "common" or "nice," wondering whether it was true that the people who drove up for Sunday dinner at the farmhouse were turned away because there wasn't enough chicken.

It seemed to me, as I kept remembering all this, that those times and those summers had been infinitely precious and worth saving. There had been jollity and peace and goodness. The arriving (at the beginning of August) had been so big a business in itself, at the railway station the farm wagon drawn up, the first smell of the pine-laden air, the first glimpse of the smiling farmer, and the great importance of the trunks and your father's enormous authority in such matters, and the feel of the wagon under you for the long ten-mile haul, and at the top of the last long hill catching the first view of the lake after eleven months of not seeing this cherished body of water. The shouts and cries of the other campers when they saw you, and the trunks to be unpacked, to give up their rich burden. (Arriving was less exciting nowadays, when you sneaked up in your car and parked it under a tree near the camp and took out the bags and in five minutes it was all over, no fuss, no loud wonderful fuss about trunks.)

Peace and goodness and jollity. The only thing that was wrong   10
now, really, was the sound of the place, an unfamiliar nervous sound of the outboard motors. This was the note that jarred, the one thing that would sometimes break the illusion and set the years moving. In those other summertimes all motors were inboard; and when they were at a little distance, the noise they made was a sedative, an ingredient of summer sleep. They were one-cylinder and two-cylinder engines, and some were make-and-break and some were jump-spark, but they all made a sleepy sound across the lake. The one-lungers throbbed and fluttered, and the twin-cylinder ones purred and purred, and that was a quiet sound, too. But now the campers all had outboards. In the daytime, in the hot mornings, these motors made a petulant, irritable sound; at night, in the still evening when the afterglow lit the water, they whined about one's ears like mosquitoes. My boy loved our rented outboard, and his great desire was to achieve single-handed mastery over it, and authority, and he soon learned the trick of choking it a little (but not too much), and the adjustment of the needle valve. Watching him I would remember the things you could do with the old one-cylinder engine with the heavy flywheel, how you could have it eating out of your hand if you got really close to it spiritually. Motorboats in those days didn't have clutches, and you would make a landing by shutting off the motor at the proper time and coasting in with a dead rudder. But there was a way of reversing them, if you learned the trick, by cutting the switch and putting it on again exactly on the final dying revolution of the flywheel, so that it would kick back against compression and begin reversing. Approaching a dock in a strong following breeze, it was difficult to slow up sufficiently by the ordinary coasting method, and if a boy felt he had complete mastery over his motor, he was tempted

to keep it running beyond its time and then reverse it a few feet from the dock. It took a cool nerve, because if you threw the switch a twentieth of a second too soon you would catch the flywheel when it still had speed enough to go up past center, and the boat would leap ahead, charging bullfashion at the dock.

We had a good week at the camp. The bass were biting well and 11 the sun shone endlessly, day after day. We would be tired at night and lie down in the accumulated heat of the little bedrooms after the long hot day and the breeze would stir almost imperceptibly outside and the smell of the swamp drift in through the rusty screens. Sleep would come easily and in the morning the red squirrel would be on the roof, tapping out his gay routine. I kept remembering everything, lying in bed in the mornings—the small steamboat that had a long rounded stern like the lip of a Ubangi, and how quietly she ran on the moonlight sails, when the older boys played their mandolins and the girls sang and we ate doughnuts dipped in sugar, and how sweet the music was on the water in the shining night, and what it had felt like to think about girls then. After breakfast we would go up to the store and the things were in the same place—the minnows in a bottle, the plugs and spinners disarranged and pawed over by the youngsters from the boys' camp, the Fig Newtons and the Beeman's gum. Outside, the road was tarred and cars stood in front of the store. Inside, all was just as it had always been, except there was more Coca-Cola and not so much Moxie and root beer and birch beer and sarsaparilla. We would walk out with the bottle of pop apiece and sometimes the pop would backfire up our noses and hurt. We explored the streams, quietly, where the turtles slid off the sunny logs and dug their way into the soft bottom; and we lay on the town wharf and fed worms to the tame bass. Everywhere we went I had trouble making out which was I, the one walking at my side, the one walking in my pants.

One afternoon while we were there at the lake a thunderstorm 12 came up. It was like the revival of an old melodrama that I had seen long ago with childish awe. The second-act climax of the drama of the electrical disturbance over a lake in America had not changed in any important respect. This was the big scene, still the big scene. The whole thing was so familiar, the first feeling of oppression and heat and a general air around camp of not wanting to go very far away. In midafternoon (it was all the same) a curious darkening of the sky, and a lull in everything that had made life tick; and then the way the boats suddenly swung the other way at their moorings with the coming of a breeze out of the new quarter, and premonitory rumble. Then the kettle drum, then the snare, then the bass drum and cymbals, then cackling light against the dark, and the gods grinning and licking their chops in the hills. Afterward the calm, the rain steadily rustling in the calm lake, the return of light and hope and spirits, and the campers running out in joy and relief to go swimming in the rain, their bright cries perpetuating the deathless joke about how they were getting simply drenched, and the children screaming with delight at the new sensation of bathing in the rain, and the joke about getting drenched linking the generations in a strong indestructible chain. And the comedian who waded in carrying an umbrella.

When the others went swimming, my son said he was going in, too. He pulled his dripping trunks from the line where they had hung all through the shower and wrung them out. Languidly, and with no thought of going in, I watched him, his hard little body, skinny and bare, saw him wince slightly as he pulled up around his vitals the small, soggy, icy garment. As he buckled the swollen belt, suddenly my groin felt the chill of death.   13

Questions for Close Reading

1. What is the selection's thesis (or dominant impression)? Locate the sentence(s) in which White states his main idea. If he doesn't state the thesis explicitly, express it in your own words.
2. Why does White return to the lake in Maine he had visited as a child? Why do you think he has waited to revisit it until he has a young son to bring along?
3. Several times in the essay, White notes that he felt as if he were his own father—and that his son became his childhood self. What event first prompts this sensation? What actions and thoughts cause it to recur?
4. How is the latest visit to the lake similar to White's childhood summers? What differences does White notice? What effects do the differences have on him?
5. Refer to your dictionary as needed to define the following words used in the selection: *incessant* (paragraph 1), *placidity* (1), *primeval* (3), *transposition* (4), *undulating* (6), *indelible* (8), *petulant* (10), and *languidly* (13).

Questions About the Writer's Craft

1. **The pattern.** Through vivid language, descriptive writing evokes sensory experiences. In "Once More to the Lake," White overlays two sets of sensory details: those of the present-day lake and those of the lake as it was in his boyhood. Which set of details is more objective? Which seems sharper and more powerful? Why?
2. To describe the lake, White chooses many words and phrases with religious connotations. Give some examples. What might have been his purpose in using such language?
3. **Other patterns.** In paragraph 12, White uses a metaphor to describe a thunderstorm. To what does he compare a thunderstorm? Why does he make this comparison?
4. White refers to "the chill of death" in the final paragraph. What brings on this feeling? Why does he feel it "in his groin"? Where has this idea been hinted at previously in the essay?

Questions for Further Thought

1. In paragraph 9, White says about his boyhood visits to the lake that "those times and those summers had been infinitely precious and worth saving." From your own perspective, what makes an experience worth savoring and storing in the memory?
2. When White refers to his son, he never uses the boy's first name (he calls him "the boy" or "my boy"); only in the last scene does he call him "my son." Why do you think White uses this impersonal form of reference? Would this essay have been different if the author's child had been a girl?
3. In your opinion, was the visit to the lake a good experience for White— or a bad one? In general, is it or is it not a good idea to try to relive the past?
4. This essay touches on a universal human feeling—the sensation that time is slipping by, that our lives are spinning out their allotted spans. When do people first become aware of their own mortality? What events or phases of life heighten this feeling?

Writing Assignments Using Description as a Pattern of Development

1. Write an essay describing a special place in your life. The place need not be a natural setting like White's lake; it could be a city or building that has meant a great deal to you. Use sensory details and figurative language, as White does, to enliven your description and convey the place's significance for you.
∞ 2. White was fortunate that his lake had remained virtually unchanged. But many other special spots have been destroyed or are threatened with

destruction. Write an essay describing a place (a park, a school, an old-fashioned ice cream parlor) that is "infinitely precious and worth saving." For your dominant theme, show which aspects of your subject make it worthy of being preserved for future generations. Before writing your essay, you might want to read Rachel Carson's "A Fable for Tomorrow" (page 410), an essay that laments the loss of a special place.

Writing Assignments Using Other Patterns of Development

3. Sometimes, we, like White, are suddenly reminded of the nearness of death: a crushed animal lies in the road, a politician is assassinated, a classmate is killed in a car crash. Write an essay about a time you were forced to think about mortality. Explain what happened and describe your thoughts and feelings afterwards.

∞ 4. Have your older relatives attempted to share with you some special experiences of their younger years? Have you done the same thing with your own children, nephews, or nieces? You may have taken loved ones to a special place, as White did, or listened to stories or looked at photographs. Write an essay recounting such an experience. Explain the motivations of the older generation and the effects on the younger one. Judith Ortiz Cofer's "A Partial Remembrance of a Puerto Rican Childhood" (page 138) will spark some thoughts about special family times.

Judith Ortiz Cofer

Born in Puerto Rico, raised both on her native island and in the United States, and educated in sites that included Oxford University in England, Judith Ortiz Cofer (1952–) knows what it is to move between cultures, absorbing from each while keeping mindful of her own heritage. Cofer earned a master's degree in English from the University of Florida before spending a year in graduate study at Oxford. Following a stint as a bilingual teacher, Cofer taught English at several colleges and universities. She has published collections of poetry, including *Peregrine* (1986) and *Terms of Survival* (1987); a novel, *The Line of the Sun* (1989); and a book of essays, *Silent Dancing: A Partial Remembrance of a Puerto Rican Childhood* (1990). The following essay is taken from *Silent Dancing*.

A Partial Remembrance of a Puerto Rican Childhood

In a Puerto Rican parlor, a Minnesota kitchen, a Kenyan hut, a Bedouin tent—wherever they are, the women of a family often draw together to tell their tales, to talk of their disappointments and dreams. For those few moments, the world of men briefly fades away as the women share the timeless stories that bind them together and shape their lives. In her affectionate reminiscence, Judith Ortiz Cofer describes such a gathering, her details evoking the texture of this special time and the messages it conveyed.

At three or four o'clock in the afternoon, the hour of *café con leche*,[1]   1
the women of my family gathered in Mamá's living room to speak of important things and retell familiar stories meant to be overheard by us young girls, their daughters. In Mamá's house (everyone called my grandmother Mamá) was a large parlor built by my grandfather to his wife's exact specifications so that it was always cool, facing away from the sun. The doorway was on the side of the house so no one could walk directly into her living room. First they had to take a little stroll through and around her beautiful garden where prize-winning orchids grew in the trunk of an ancient tree she had hollowed out for that purpose. This room was furnished with several mahogany rocking chairs, ac-

[1]Spanish for "coffee with milk."

quired at the births of her children, and one intricately carved rocker that had passed down to Mamá at the death of her own mother.

It was on these rockers that my mother, her sisters, and my grand-   2
mother sat on these afternoons of my childhood to tell their stories, teaching each other, and my cousin and me, what it was like to be a woman, more specifically, a Puerto Rican woman. They talked about life on the island, and life in *Los Nueva Yores,* their way of referring to the United States from New York City to California: the other place, not home, all the same. They told real-life stories though, as I later learned, always embellishing them with a little or a lot of dramatic detail. And they told *cuentos,* the morality and cautionary tales told by the women in our family for generations: stories that became a part of my subconscious as I grew up in two worlds, the tropical island and the cold city, and that would later surface in my dreams and in my poetry.

One of these tales was about the woman who was left at the al-   3
tar. Mamá liked to tell that one with histrionic intensity. I remember the rise and fall of her voice, the sighs, and her constantly gesturing hands, like two birds swooping through her words. This particular story usually would come up in a conversation as a result of someone mentioning a forthcoming engagement or wedding. The first time I remember hearing it, I was sitting on the floor at Mamá's feet, pretending to read a comic book. I may have been eleven or twelve years old, at that difficult age when a girl was no longer a child who could be ordered to leave the room if the women wanted freedom to take their talk into forbidden zones, nor really old enough to be considered a part of their conclave. I could only sit quietly, pretending to be in another world, while absorbing it all in a sort of unspoken agreement of my status as silent auditor. On this day, Mamá had taken my long, tangled mane of hair into her ever-busy hands. Without looking down at me and with no interruption of her flow of words, she began braiding my hair, working at it with the quickness and determination that characterized all her actions. My mother was watching us impassively from her rocker across the room. On her lips played a little ironic smile. I would never sit still for *her* ministrations, but even then, I instinctively knew that she did not possess Mamá's matriarchal power to command and keep everyone's attention. This was never more evident than in the spell she cast when telling a story.

"It is not like it used to be when I was a girl," Mamá announced.   4
"Then, a man could leave a girl standing at the church altar with a bouquet of fresh flowers in her hands and disappear off the face of the

earth. No way to track him down if he was from another town. He could be a married man, with maybe even two or three families all over the island. There was no way to know. And there were men who did this. Hombres[2] with the devil in their flesh who would come to a pueblo,[3] like this one, take a job at one of the haciendas,[4] never meaning to stay, only to have a good time and to seduce the women."

The whole time she was speaking, Mamá would be weaving my   5
hair into a flat plait that required pulling apart the two sections of hair with little jerks that made my eyes water; but knowing how grandmother detested whining and *boba* (sissy) tears, as she called them, I just sat up as straight and stiff as I did at La Escuela San Jose, where the nuns enforced good posture with a flexible plastic ruler they bounced off of slumped shoulders and heads. As Mamá's story progressed, I noticed how my young Aunt Laura lowered her eyes, refusing to meet Mamá's meaningful gaze. Laura was seventeen, in her last year of high school, and already engaged to a boy from another town who had staked his claim with a tiny diamond ring, then left for Los Nueva Yores to make his fortune. They were planning to get married in a year. Mamá had expressed serious doubts that the wedding would ever take place. In Mamá's eyes, a man set free without a legal contract was a man lost. She believed that marriage was not something men desired, but simply the price they had to pay for the privilege of children and, of course, for what no decent (synonymous with "smart") woman would give away for free.

"María La Loca was only seventeen when *it* happened to her." I lis-   6
tened closely at the mention of this name. María was a town character, a fat middle-aged woman who lived with her old mother on the outskirts of town. She was to be seen around the pueblo delivering the meat pies the two women made for a living. The most peculiar thing about María, in my eyes, was that she walked and moved like a little girl though she had the thick body and wrinkled face of an old woman. She would swing her hips in an exaggerated, clownish way, and sometimes even hop and skip up to someone's house. She spoke to no one. Even if you asked her a question, she would just look at you and smile, showing her yellow teeth. But I had heard that if you got close enough, you could hear her humming a tune without words. The kids yelled out nasty things at her, calling her *La Loca*,[5] and the men who hung out at the bodega[6] playing domi-

[2]Spanish for "men."
[3]Spanish for "community."
[4]Spanish for "large estate" or "ranch."
[5]Spanish for "crazy one."
[6]Spanish for a neighborhood grocery store.

noes sometimes whistled mockingly as she passed by with her funny, outlandish walk. But María seemed impervious to it all, carrying her basket of *pasteles*[7] like a grotesque Little Red Riding Hood through the forest.

María La Loca interested me, as did all the eccentrics and crazies of our pueblo. Their weirdness was a measuring stick I used in my serious quest for a definition of normal. As a Navy brat shuttling between New Jersey and the pueblo, I was constantly made to feel like an oddball by my peers, who made fun of my two-way accent: a Spanish accent when I spoke English, and when I spoke Spanish I was told that I sounded like a *Gringa*.[8] Being the outsider had already turned my brother and me into cultural chameleons. We developed early on the ability to blend into a crowd, to sit and read quietly in a fifth story apartment building for days and days when it was too bitterly cold to play outside, or, set free, to run wild in Mamá's realm, where she took charge of our lives, releasing Mother for a while from the intense fear for our safety that our father's absences instilled in her. In order to keep us from harm when Father was away, Mother kept us under strict surveillance. She even walked us to and from Public School No. 11, which we attended during the months we lived in Paterson, New Jersey, our home base in the States. Mamá freed all three of us like pigeons from a cage. I saw her as my liberator and my model. Her stories were parables from which to glean the *Truth*.

"María La Loca was once a beautiful girl. Everyone thought she would marry the Méndez boy." As everyone knew, Rogelio Méndez was the richest man in town. "But," Mamá continued, knitting my hair with the same intensity she was putting into her story, "this *macho* made a fool out of her and ruined her life." She paused for the effect of her use of the word "macho," which at that time had not yet become a popular epithet for an unliberated man. This word had for us the crude and comical connotation of "male of the species," stud; a *macho* was what you put in a pen to increase your stock.

I peeked over my comic book at my mother. She too was under Mamá's spell, smiling conspiratorially at this little swipe at men. She was safe from Mamá's contempt in this area. Married at an early age, an unspotted lamb, she had been accepted by a good family of strict Spaniards whose name was old and respected, though their

7

8

9

---

[7]Spanish for "pastries."
[8]A negatively charged Latin American slang expression for a female foreigner.

fortune had been lost long before my birth. In a rocker Papá had painted sky blue sat Mamá's oldest child, Aunt Nena. Mother of three children, stepmother of two more, she was a quiet woman who liked books but had married an ignorant and abusive widower whose main interest in life was accumulating wealth. He too was in the mainland working on his dream of returning home rich and triumphant to buy the *finca*[9] of his dreams. She was waiting for him to send for her. She would leave her children with Mamá for several years while the two of them slaved away in factories. He would one day be a rich man, and she a sadder woman. Even now her life-light was dimming. She spoke little, an aberration in Mamá's house, and she read avidly, as if storing up spiritual food for the long winters that awaited her in Los Nueva Yores without her family. But even Aunt Nena came alive to Mamá's words, rocking gently, her hands over a thick book in her lap.

Her daughter, my cousin Sara, played jacks by herself on the tile   10
porch outside the room where we sat. She was a year older than I. We shared a bed and all our family's secrets. Collaborators in search of answers, Sara and I discussed everything we heard the women say, trying to fit it all together like a puzzle that, once assembled, would reveal life's mysteries to us. Though she and I still enjoyed taking part in boys' games—chase, volleyball, and even *vaqueros,* the island version of cowboys and Indians involving cap-gun battles and violent shoot-outs under the mango tree in Mamá's backyard—we loved best the quiet hours in the afternoon when the men were still at work, and the boys had gone to play serious baseball at the park. Then Mamá's house belonged only to us women. The aroma of coffee perking in the kitchen, the mesmerizing creaks and groans of the rockers, and the women telling their lives in *cuentos* are forever woven into the fabric of my imagination, braided like my hair that day I felt my grandmother's hands teaching me about strength, her voice convincing me of the power of storytelling.

That day Mamá told how the beautiful María had fallen prey to   11
a man whose name was never the same in subsequent versions of the story; it was Juan one time, José, Rafael, Diego, another. We understood that neither the name or any of the *facts* were important, only that a woman had allowed love to defeat her. Mamá put each of us in María's place by describing her wedding dress in loving detail: how

[9]Spanish for "farm" or "ranch."

she looked like a princess in her lace as she waited at the altar. Then, as Mamá approached the tragic denouement of her story, I was distracted by the sound of my Aunt Laura's violent rocking. She seemed on the verge of tears. She knew the fable was intended for her. That week she was going to have her wedding gown fitted, though no firm date had been set for the marriage. Mamá ignored Laura's obvious discomfort, digging out a ribbon from the sewing basket she kept by her rocker while describing María's long illness, "a fever that would not break for days." She spoke of a mother's despair: "that woman climbed the church steps on her knees every morning, wore only black as a *promesa* to the Holy Virgin in exchange for her daughter's health." By the time María returned from her honeymoon with death, she was ravished, no longer young or sane. "As you can see, she is almost as old as her mother already," Mamá lamented while tying the ribbon to the ends of my hair, pulling it back with such force that I just knew I would never be able to close my eyes completely again.

"That María's getting crazier every day." Mamá's voice would   12
take a lighter tone now, expressing satisfaction, either for the perfection of my braid, or for a story well told—it was hard to tell. "You know that tune María is always humming?" Carried away by her enthusiasm, I tried to nod, but Mamá still had me pinned between her knees.

"Well, that's the wedding march." Surprising us all, Mamá sang   13
out, "Da, da, dara...da, da, dara." Then lifting me off the floor by my skinny shoulders, she would lead me around the room in an impromptu waltz—another session ending with the laughter of women, all of us caught up in the infectious joke of our lives.

Questions for Close Reading

1. What is the selection's thesis (or dominant impression)? Locate the sentence(s) in which Cofer states her main idea. If she doesn't state the thesis explicitly, express it in your own words.
2. Who are the women who participate in the storytelling sessions? Why is Cofer allowed to join them? Why aren't men or boys part of the group?
3. What lessons about men and women does Mamá intend the story of María La Loca to teach?
4. What information does Cofer provide about her aunts and her mother? What similarities and/or differences are there between each of their lives and the story of María La Loca?
5. Refer to your dictionary as needed to define the following words used in the selection: *intricately* (paragraph 1), *embellishing* (2), *cautionary* (2),

histrionic (3), *conclave* (3), *auditor* (3), *impassively* (3), *ministrations* (3), *matriarchal* (3), *quest* (7), *chameleons* (7), *surveillance* (7), *conspiratorially* (9), *aberration* (9), *mesmerizing* (10), *denouement* (11), *ravished* (11), and *impromptu* (13).

Questions About the Writer's Craft

1. **The pattern.** Of all the women mentioned in the essay, only María La Loca is described in detail. What descriptive details does Cofer offer about her? Why do you suppose Cofer provides so much description about this particular woman?

2. In paragraph 7, Cofer provides some specifics about her childhood as a "Navy brat." What would have been lost if Cofer hadn't included this material?

3. **Other patterns.** Reread paragraphs 4, 6, 8, and 11–13, where Cofer recounts her grandmother's story. Why do you think Cofer doesn't tell the story straight through, without interruptions? What purpose do the interruptions serve? How does Cofer signal when she is moving away from the story or back to it?

4. Why might Cofer have mentioned in several spots the braiding of her hair, which goes on the whole time Mamá tells María's story? What similarities are there between the braiding and the storytelling session? What similarities are there between the braiding and Cofer's descriptive style (consider especially the last sentence of paragraph 10)?

Questions for Further Thought

1. Did you listen to family stories when you were growing up? If so, did any special circumstances or occasion inspire the telling of stories? Were the stories simply entertaining yarns, or were they—like Mamá's—meant to teach important lessons? Explain.

2. At the time she heard the story of María La Loca, Cofer was considered too old to be sent out to play, yet too young to be invited to listen. Should children be allowed to know about complex or delicate family matters? Until what age should they be protected from such stories?

3. Feeling like an outsider in the two cultures she inhabited, Cofer adapted by becoming a "cultural chameleon." Do you believe that "blending in" is the best strategy for someone who feels like an outsider? Why or why not?

4. Because of economic reasons, Cofer's mother and Aunt Nena have marriages that involve long separations, either from their husbands or from their children. Do you think that it is legitimate for family members to live apart for financial or professional reasons? How damaging are such

separations to partners and children? What can people do to maintain family cohesiveness in spite of these separations?

Writing Assignments Using Description as a Pattern of Development

1. Cofer paints a vivid picture of a childhood ritual: the telling of stories among the women in her family. Think of a specific scene, event, or ritual from your own childhood or youth that has special meaning for you. Then write a descriptive essay conveying the distinctive flavor of that occasion. Draw upon vivid sensory language to capture your dominant impression of that time. Consider using dialogue, as Cofer does, to texturize your description and to reveal character.

∞ 2. To Cofer, Mamá was a "liberator" and a "model." Think of a person in your life who served as a role model or opened doors for you, and write an essay describing that person. Like Cofer, place the person in a characteristic setting and supply vigorous details about the person's actions, speech, looks, and so forth. Make sure that all the descriptive details reinforce your dominant impression of the individual. You may want to read Maya Angelou's "Grandmother's Victory" (page 164) to see how one especially skilled writer describes a powerful, influential person.

Writing Assignments Using Other Patterns of Development

3. Cofer's family is close-knit, but family life nowadays is more likely to be fragmented, with everyone going separate ways. Write an essay explaining what steps families could take to offset this tendency toward fragmentation. You might want to focus on a particular area of family life, such as mealtimes, after-supper hours, or vacations. Be sure to spend some time discussing the expected outcomes of the steps you propose.

∞ 4. The stories Cofer heard taught her "what it was like to be a woman." What information and experiences shaped your understanding of your gender? Write an essay showing how your perception of your gender identity was influenced by what you heard, witnessed, and experienced as a child. Before writing your paper, you may wish to read Scott Russell Sanders's "The Men We Carry in Our Minds" (page 308), which explores how early experiences affect the sex roles we adopt. Other essays providing insight into gender expectations include Barbara Ehrenreich's "What I've Learned From Men" (page 261), Deborah Tannen's "Sex, Lies, and Conversation" (page 428), Judy Brady's "Why I Want a Wife" (page 530), Camille Paglia's "Rape: A Bigger Danger than Feminists Know" (page 638), and Susan Jacoby's "Common Decency" (page 645).

Additional Writing Topics

DESCRIPTION

General Assignments

Write an essay using description to develop any of the following topics. Remember that an effective description focuses on a dominant impression and arranges details in a way that best supports that impression. Your details—vivid and appealing to the senses—should be carefully chosen so that the essay isn't overburdened with material of secondary importance. When writing, keep in mind that varied sentence structure and imaginative figures of speech are ways to make a descriptive piece compelling.

1. A favorite item of clothing
2. A school as a young child might see it
3. A hospital room you visited or stayed in
4. An individualist's appearance
5. A coffee shop, a bus shelter, a newsstand, or some other small place
6. A parade or victory celebration
7. A banana, a squash, or another fruit or vegetable
8. A particular drawer in a desk or bureau
9. A houseplant
10. A "media event"
11. A dorm room
12. An elderly person
13. An attractive man or woman
14. A prosthetic device or wheelchair
15. A TV, film, or music celebrity
16. A student lounge
17. A once-in-a-lifetime event
18. The inside of something, such as a cave, boat, car, shed, or machine
19. A friend, a roommate, or another person you know well
20. An essential gadget or a useless gadget

Assignments With a Specific Purpose and Audience

1. For an audience of incoming first-year students, prepare a speech describing registration day at your college. Use specific details to help prepare students for the actual event. Choose an adjective that represents your dominant impression of the experience, and keep that word in mind as you write.

2. As a subscriber to a dating service, you've been asked to submit a description of the kind of person you'd like to meet. Describe your ideal date.

Focus on specifics about physical appearance, personal habits, character traits, and interests.

3. Your college has decided to replace an old campus structure (for example, a dorm or dining hall) with a new version. Write a letter of protest to the administration, describing the place so vividly and appealingly that its value and need for preservation are unquestionable.

4. As a staff member of the campus newspaper, you have been asked to write a weekly column of social news and gossip. For your first column, you plan to describe a recent campus event—a dance, party, concert, or other social activity. With a straightforward or tongue-in-cheek tone, describe where the event was held, the appearance of the people who attended, and so on.

5. Students at your college have complained that the course catalog is inaccurate. Its course descriptions are often brief, misleading, or just plain incorrect. You're part of a student-faculty group responsible for revising the catalog. Write a full and accurate description of a course with which you're familiar. Tell exactly what the course is about, who teaches it, and how it is run.

6. As a resident of a particular town, you're angered by the appearance of a certain spot and by the activities that take place there. Write a letter to the town council, describing in detail the undesirable nature of this place (a video arcade, an adult bookstore, a bar, a bus station, a neglected park or beach). End with some suggestions about ways to improve the situation.

5

NARRATION

WHAT IS NARRATION?

Human beings are instinctively storytellers. In prehistoric times, our ancestors huddled around campfires to hear tales of hunting and magic. In ancient times, warriors gathered in halls to listen to bards praise in song the exploits of epic heroes. Things are no different today. Boisterous children invariably settle down to listen when their parents read to them; millions of people tune in day after day to the ongoing drama of their favorite soap operas; vacationers sit motionless on the beach, caught up in the latest best-sellers; and all of us enjoy saying, "Just listen to what happened to me today." Our hunger for storytelling is a basic part of us.

Narration means telling a single story or several related stories. The story can be a means to an end, a way to support a main idea or thesis. For instance, to demonstrate that television has become the constant companion of many children, you might narrate a typical child's day in front of the television—starting with frantic cartoons in the morning and ending with dizzy situation comedies at night. Or to support the point that the college registration process should be reformed, you could tell the tale of a chaotic morning spent trying to enroll in classes.

Narration is powerful. Every public speaker, from politician to classroom teacher, knows that stories capture the attention of listeners as nothing else can. Narration speaks to us strongly because it is about us; we want to know what happened to others, not simply because we're curious, but because their experiences shed light on the nature of our own lives. Narration lends force to opinions, triggers the flow of memory, and evokes places and times in ways that are compelling and affecting.

HOW NARRATION FITS YOUR PURPOSE AND AUDIENCE

Since narratives tell a story, you may think they are found only in novels or short stories. But narration can also appear in essays, sometimes as a supplemental pattern of development. For example, if your purpose in a paper is to *persuade* apathetic readers that airport security regulations must be followed strictly, you might lead off with a brief account of an armed terrorist who easily boarded a plane. In a paper *defining* good teaching, you might keep readers engaged by including satirical anecdotes about one hapless instructor, the antithesis of an effective teacher. An essay on the *effects* of an overburdened judicial system might provide—in an attempt to involve readers—a dramatic account of the way one clearly guilty murderer plea-bargained his way to freedom.

In addition to providing effective support in one section of your paper, narration can also serve as an essay's dominant pattern of development. In fact, most of this chapter shows you how to use a single extended narrative to convey a central point and share with readers your view of what happened. You might choose to narrate the events of a day spent with your three-year-old nephew as a way of revealing how you rediscovered the importance of family life. Or you might relate the story of your roommate's mugging, evoking the powerlessness and terror of being a victim. Any story can form the basis for a narrative essay as long as you convey the essence of the experience and evoke its meaning.

SUGGESTIONS FOR USING NARRATION IN AN ESSAY

The following suggestions will be helpful whether you use narration as a dominant or supportive pattern of development.

1. Identify the conflict in the event. The power of many narratives is rooted in a special kind of tension that "hooks" readers and makes them want to follow the story to its end. This narrative tension is often a by-product of some form of *conflict* within the story. Many narratives revolve around an internal dilemma experienced by a key person in the story. Or the conflict may be between people in the story or between a pivotal character and some social institution or natural phenomenon.

2. Identify the point of the narrative. In *The Adventures of Huckleberry Finn*, Mark Twain warned: "Persons attempting to find a motive in this narrative will be prosecuted; persons attempting to find a moral in it will be banished; persons attempting to find a plot in it will be shot." Twain was, of course, being ironic; his novel's richness lies in its "motives" and "morals." Similarly, when you recount a narrative, it's your responsibility to convey the event's *significance* or *meaning*. In other words, be sure readers are clear about your *narrative point*, or thesis.

Suppose you decide to write about the time you got locked in a mall late at night. Your narrative might focus on the way the mall looked after hours and the way you struggled with mounting terror. But you would also use the narrative to make a point. Perhaps you want to emphasize that fear can be instructive. Or your point might be that malls have a disturbing, surreal underside. You could state this thesis explicitly. ("After hours, the mall shed its cheerful daytime demeanor and took on a more sinister quality.") Or you could refrain from stating the thesis directly, relying on your details and language to convey the point of the narrative: "The mannequins stared at me with glazed eyes and frozen smiles" and "The steel grates pulled over each store glinted in the cold light, making each shop look like a prison cell."

3. Develop only those details that advance the narrative point. You know from experience that nothing is more boring than a story-teller who gets sidetracked and drags out a story with nonessential details. If a friend started to tell about the time his car broke down in the middle of an expressway—but interrupted his story to complain at length about the slipshod work done by his auto repair shop—you might clench your teeth in annoyance, wishing your friend would hurry up and get back to the interesting part of the story.

Brainstorming ("What happened? When? Where? Who was involved? Why did it happen?") can be valuable for helping you amass narrative details. Then, after generating the specifics, you cull out the nonessential and devote your energies to the key specifics needed to advance your narrative point. When telling a story, you maintain an effective narrative pace by focusing on that point and eliminating details that don't support it. A good narrative depends not only on what is included, but also on what has been left out.

But how do you determine which specifics to omit, which to treat briefly, and which to emphasize? Having a clear sense of your narrative point and knowing your audience are crucial. Assume you're writing a narrative about a disastrous get-acquainted dance sponsored by your college the first week of the academic year. In addition to telling what happened, you want to make a point; perhaps you want to emphasize that, despite the college's good intentions, such "official" events actually make it difficult to meet people. With this purpose in mind, you might write about how stiff and unnatural students seemed, all dressed up in their best clothes; you might narrate snatches of strained conversation you overheard; you might describe the way males gathered on one side of the room, females on the other—reverting to behaviors supposedly abandoned in fifth grade. All these details would support your narrative point.

Because you don't want to get waylaid by detours that lead away from that point, you would leave out details about the top-notch band and the appetizing refreshments at the dance. The music and food may have been surprisingly good, but since these details don't advance the point you want to make, they should be omitted.

You also need to keep your audience in mind when selecting narrative details. If the audience consists of your instructor and other students—all of them familiar with the new student center where the dance was held—specific details about the center probably wouldn't have to be provided. But imagine that the essay is going to appear in the quarterly magazine published by the college's community relations office. Many of the magazine's readers are former graduates who haven't been on campus for several years. They may need some additional specifics about the student center: its location, how many people it holds, how it is furnished.

As you write, keep asking yourself, "Is this detail or character or snippet of conversation essential? Does my audience need this detail to understand the conflict in the situation? Does this detail advance or intensify the narrative action?" Summarize details that have some importance but do not deserve lengthy treatment ("Two hours went by...."). And try to limit *narrative commentary*—statements that tell rather than show what happened—since such remarks interrupt the narrative flow. Focus instead on the specifics that propel action forward in a vigorous way.

Sometimes, especially if the narrative re-creates an event from the past, you won't be able to remember what happened detail for detail. In such a case, you should take advantage of what is called *dramatic license*. Using as a guide your powers of recall as well as the perspective you now have of that particular time, feel free to reshape events to suit your narrative point.

4. Organize the narrative sequence. All of us know the traditional beginning of fairy tales: "Once upon a time...." Every narrative begins somewhere, presents a span of time, and ends at a certain point. Frequently, you'll want to use a straightforward time order, following the event *chronologically* from beginning to end: first this happened, next this happened, finally this happened.

But sometimes a strict chronological recounting may not be effective—especially if the high point of the narrative gets lost somewhere in the middle of the time sequence. To avoid that possibility, you may want to disrupt chronology, plunge the reader into the middle of the story, and then return in a *flashback* to the beginning of the tale. You're probably familiar with the way flashback is used on television and in film. You see someone appealing to the main character for financial help, then return to an earlier time when both were students in the same class, before learning how the rest of the story unfolds. Narratives can also use *flashforward*. You give readers a glimpse of the future (the main character being jailed) before the story continues in the present (the events leading to the arrest). These techniques shift the story onto several planes and keep it from becoming a step-by-step, predictable account. Reserve flashfor-wards and flashbacks, however, for crucial incidents only, since breaking out of chronological order acts as emphasis. Here are examples of how flashback and flashforward can be used in narrative writing:

Flashback

Standing behind the wooden counter, Greg wielded his knife expertly as he shucked clams--one every ten seconds--with practiced ease. The scene contrasted sharply with his first day on the job, when his hands broke out in blisters and when splitting each shell was like prying open a safe.

Flashforward

Rushing to move my car from the no-parking zone, I waved a quick good-bye to Karen as she climbed the steps to the bus. I didn't know then that by the time I picked her up at the bus station later that day, she had made a decision that would affect both our lives.

Whether or not you choose to include flashbacks or flashfor-wards in an essay, remember to limit the time span covered by the narrative. Otherwise, you will have trouble generating the details needed to give the story depth and meaning. Also, regardless of the time sequence you select, organize the tale so it drives toward a strong finish. Be careful that your story doesn't trail off into minor, anticlimactic details.

5. Make the narrative easy to follow. Describing each distinct action in a separate paragraph helps readers grasp the flow of events. Although narrative essays don't always have conventional topic sen-tences, each narrative paragraph should have a clear focus. Often this focus is indicated by a sentence early in the paragraph that directs attention to the action taking place. Such a sentence functions as a kind of *informal topic sentence*; the rest of the paragraph then devel-ops that topic sentence. You should also be sure to use time signals when narrating a story. Words like *now, then, next, after,* and *later* ensure that your reader won't get lost as the story progresses.

6. Make the narrative vigorous and immediate. A compelling narrative provides an abundance of specific details, making readers feel as if they're experiencing the story being told. Readers must be able to see, hear, touch, smell, and taste the event you're narrating. *Vivid sensory description* is, therefore, an essential part of an effective narrative. Not only do specific sensory details make writing a pleasure to read—we all enjoy learning the particulars about people, places, and things—but they also give the narrative the stamp of reality. The specifics convince the reader that the event being described actually did, or could, occur.

Compare the following excerpts from a narrative essay. The first version is lifeless and dull; the revised version, packed with sensory images, grabs readers with its sense of foreboding:

> That eventful day started out like every other summer day. My sister Tricia and I made several elaborate mud pies, which we decorated with care. A little later on, as we were spraying each other with the garden hose, we heard my father walk up the path.

> That sad summer day started out uneventfully enough. My sister Tricia and I spent a few hours mixing and decorating mud pies. Our hands caked with dry mud, we sprinkled each lopsided pie with alternating rows of dandelion and clover petals. Later when the sun got hotter, we tossed our white T-shirts over the red picket fence--forgetting my grandmother's frequent warnings to be more ladylike. Our sweaty backs bared to the sun, we doused each other with icy sprays from the garden hose. Caught up in the primitive pleasure of it all, we barely heard my father as he walked up the garden path, the gravel crunching under his heavy work boots.

A caution: Sensory language enlivens narration, but it also slows the pace. Be sure that the slower pace suits your purpose. For example, a lengthy description fits an account of a leisurely summer vacation but is inappropriate in a tale about a frantic search for a misplaced wallet.

Another way to create an aura of narrative immediacy is to use *dialogue* while telling a story. Our sense of other people comes, in part, from what they say and from the way they sound. Conversational exchanges allow the reader to experience characters directly. Compare the following fragments of a narrative, one with dialogue and one without, noting how much more energetic the second version is.

> When I finally found my way back to the campsite, the trail guide commented on my disheveled appearance.

When I finally found my way back to the campsite, the trail guide took one look at me and drawled, "What on earth happened to you, Daniel Boone? You look as though you've been dragged through a haystack backwards."

"I'd look a lot worse if I hadn't run back here. When a bullet whizzes by me, I don't stick around to see who's doing the shooting."

Note that, when using dialogue, you generally begin a new paragraph to indicate a shift from one person's speech to another's (as in the second example above).

Using *varied sentence structure* is another strategy for making narratives lively and vigorous. Sentences that plod along predictably (subject-verb, subject-verb) put readers to sleep. Experiment with your sentences by juggling length and sentence type; mix long and short sentences, simple and complex. Compare the following original and revised versions to get an idea of how effective varied sentence rhythm can be in narrative writing.

Original

The store manager went to the walk-in refrigerator every day. The heavy metal door clanged shut behind her. I had visions of her freezing to death among the hanging carcasses. The shiny door finally swung open. She waddled out.

Revised

Each time the store manager went to the walk-in refrigerator, the heavy metal door clanged shut behind her. Visions of her freezing to death among the hanging carcasses crept into my mind until the shiny door finally swung open and she waddled out.

Original

The yellow-and-blue-striped fish struggled on the line. Its scales shimmered in the sunlight. Its tail waved frantically. I saw its desire to live. I decided to let it go.

Revised

Scales shimmering in the sunlight, tail waving frantically, the yellow-and-blue-striped fish struggled on the line. Seeing its desire to live, I let it go.

Finally, *vigorous verbs* lend energy to narratives. Use active verb forms ("The boss *yelled at* him") rather than passive ones ("He *was yelled at* by the boss"), and try to replace anemic *to be* verbs ("She *was* a good basketball player") with more dynamic constructions ("She *played* basketball well").

7. Keep your point of view and verb tense consistent. All stories have a *narrator*, the person who tells the story. If you, as narrator, tell a story as you experienced it, the story is written in the *first-person point of view* ("*I* saw the dog pull loose"). But if you observed the event (or heard about it from others) and want to tell how someone else experienced the incident, you would use the *third-person point of view* ("*Anne* saw the dog pull loose"). Each point of view has advantages and limitations. First person allows you to express ordinarily private thoughts and to re-create an event as you actually experienced it. This point of view is limited, though, in its ability to depict the inner thoughts of other people involved in the event. By way of contrast, third person makes it easier to provide insight into the thoughts of all the participants. However, its objective, broad perspective may undercut some of the subjective immediacy typical of the "I was there" point of view. No matter which point of view you select, stay with that vantage point throughout the entire narrative.

Knowing whether to use the *past* or *present tense* ("I *strolled* into the room" as opposed to "I *stroll* into the room") is important. In most narrations, the past tense predominates, enabling the writer to span a considerable period of time. Although more rarely used, the present tense can be powerful for events of short duration—a wrestling match or a medical emergency, for instance. A narrative in the present tense prolongs each moment, intensifying the reader's sense of participation. Be careful, though; unless the event is intense and fast-paced, the present tense can seem contrived. Whichever tense you choose, avoid shifting midstream—starting, let's say, in the past tense ("she skated") and switching to present ("she runs").

Effective narratives may be exciting or charming or moving; writing them can be great fun and devilishly difficult at the same time. It's no mean feat to re-create an event, drawing on your powers of recall as well as your skill with language to make the narrative action come alive.

Although some narratives relate unusual experiences, most tread familiar ground, telling tales of joy, love, loss, frustration, fear—all common emotions experienced during a life. Don't think, however, that writing about the familiar makes your story predictable. On the contrary. All of us feel an energizing shock of recognition whenever the human condition is written about with grace and power. Narratives can take the ordinary and transmute it into something significant, even extraordinary. As Willa Cather, the American novelist, wrote: "There are only two or three human stories and they go on repeating themselves as fiercely as if they had never happened before." The challenge lies in applying your own vision to a tale, thereby making it unique.

STUDENT ESSAY

The following student essay was written by Paul Monahan in response to this assignment.

> In "Shooting an Elephant," George Orwell tells about an incident that forced him to act in a manner that ran counter to his better instincts. Write a narrative about a time when you faced a disturbing conflict and ended up doing something you later regretted.

While reading Paul's paper, try to determine how well it applies the principles of narration. The annotations on Paul's paper and the commentary following it will help you look at the essay more closely.

If Only
by Paul Monahan

Introduction	Having worked at a 7-Eleven store for two years, 1 I thought I had become successful at what our manager calls "customer relations." I firmly believed that a friendly smile and an automatic "sir," "ma'am," and "thank you" would see me through any situation that might arise, from soothing impatient or unpleasant people to apologizing for giving out the wrong

Narrative Point (thesis) — change. But the other night an old woman shattered my belief that a glib response could smooth over the rough spots of dealing with other human beings.

Informal topic sentence → The moment she entered, the woman presented 2 a sharp contrast to our shiny store with its bright lighting and neatly arranged shelves. Walking as if each step were painful, she slowly pushed open the glass door and hobbled down the nearest aisle. She

Sensory details — coughed dryly, wheezing with each breath. On a forty-degree night, she was wearing only a faded print dress, a thin, light-beige sweater too small to button, and black vinyl slippers with the backs cut out to expose calloused heels. There were no stockings or socks on her splotchy, blue-veined legs.

After strolling around the store for several min- 3 utes, the old woman stopped in front of the rows of canned vegetables. She picked up some corn niblets

Informal topic sentence — and stared with a strange intensity at the label. At that point, I decided to be a good, courteous employee and asked her if she needed help. As I stood close to her, my smile became harder to main-

Sensory details — tain; her red-rimmed eyes were partially closed by yellowish crusts; her hands were covered with layer upon layer of grime, and the stale smell of sweat rose in a thick vaporous cloud from her clothes.

Start of dialogue → "I need some food," she muttered in reply to my 4 bright "Can I help you?"

"Are you looking for corn, ma'am?" 5

"I need some food," she repeated. "Any kind." 6

"Well, the corn is ninety-five cents," I said in my 7 most helpful voice. "Or, if you like, we have a special on bologna today."

"I can't pay," she said. 8

Conflict established → For a second, I was tempted to say, "Take the 9 corn." But the employee rules flooded into my mind: Remain polite, but do not let customers get the best of you. Let them know that you are in control. For a moment, I even entertained the idea that this was some sort of test, and that this woman was someone from the head office, testing my loyalty. I responded dutifully, "I'm sorry, ma'am, but I can't give away anything free."

Informal topic ──────▶ The old woman's face collapsed a bit more, if   10
sentence   that were possible, and her hands trembled as she
                          put the can back on the shelf. She shuffled past me
                          toward the door, her torn and dirty clothing barely
                          covering her bent back.

Conclusion   Moments after she left, I rushed out the door   11
                          with the can of corn, but she was nowhere in sight.
                          For the rest of my shift, the image of the woman
Echoing of   haunted me. I had been young, healthy, and smug.
narrative point   She had been old, sick, and desperate. Wishing with
in the   all my heart that I had acted like a human being
introduction   rather than a robot, I was saddened to realize how
                          fragile a hold we have on our better instincts.

COMMENTARY

Point of view, tense, and conflict.   Paul chose to write "If Only"
from the *first-person point of view*, a logical choice because he
appears as a main character in his own story. Using the *past tense*,
Paul recounts an incident filled with *conflicts*—between him and the
woman and between his fear of breaking the rules and his human
instinct to help someone in need.

Narrative point.   It isn't always necessary to state the *narrative
point* of an essay; it can be implied. But Paul decided to express the
controlling idea of his narrative in two places—in the introduction
("But the other night an old woman shattered my belief that a glib
response could smooth over the rough spots of dealing with other
human beings") and again in the conclusion, where he expands his
idea about rote responses overriding impulses of independent judgment and compassion. All of the essay's *narrative details* contribute
to the point of the piece; Paul does not include any extraneous
information that would detract from the central idea he wants to
convey.

Organization and other patterns of development.   The narrative
is *organized chronologically*, from the moment the woman enters the
store to Paul's reaction after she leaves. Paul limits the narrative's
time span. The entire incident probably occurs in under ten minutes, yet the introduction serves as a kind of *flashback* by providing

some necessary background about Paul's past experiences. To help the reader follow the course of the narrative, Paul uses *time signals*: "*The moment* she entered, the woman presented a sharp contrast" (paragraph 2); "*At that point,* I decided to be a good, courteous employee" (3); "*For the rest of my shift,* the image of the woman haunted me" (11).

The paragraphs (except for those consisting solely of dialogue) also contain *informal topic sentences* that direct attention to the specific stage of action being narrated. Indeed, each paragraph focuses on a distinct event: the elderly woman's actions when she first enters the store, the encounter between Paul and the woman, Paul's resulting inner conflict, the woman's subsequent response, and Paul's delayed reaction.

This chain of events, with one action leading to another, illustrates that the *cause-effect* pattern underlies the essay's basic structure. And another pattern—*description*—gives dramatic immediacy to the events being recounted. Throughout, rich sensory details engage the reader's interest. For instance, the sentence "her red-rimmed eyes were partially closed by yellowish crusts" (3) vividly re-creates the woman's appearance while also suggesting Paul's inner reaction to the woman.

Dialogue and sentence structure.   Paul uses other techniques to add energy and interest to his narrative. For one thing, he dramatizes his conflict with the woman through *dialogue* that crackles with tension. And he achieves a vigorous narrative pace by *varying the length and structure of his sentences.* In the second paragraph, a short sentence ("There were no stockings or socks on her splotchy, blue-veined legs") alternates with a longer one ("On a forty-degree night, she was wearing only a faded print dress, a thin, light-beige sweater too small to button, and black vinyl slippers with the backs cut out to expose calloused heels"). Some sentences in the essay open with a subject and verb ("She coughed dryly"), while others start with dependent clauses or participial phrases ("As I stood close to her, my smile became harder to maintain"; "Walking as if each step were painful, she slowly pushed open the glass door") or with a prepositional phrase ("For a second, I was tempted").

Revising the first draft.   Comparing the final version of the essay's third paragraph, shown above, with the preliminary version reprinted below reveals some of the changes Paul made while revising the essay.

Original Version of the Third Paragraph

After sneezing and hacking her way around the store, the old woman stopped in front of the vegetable shelves. She picked up a can of corn and stared at the label. She stayed like this for several minutes. Then I walked over to her and asked if I could be of help.

After putting the original draft aside for a while, Paul reread his paper aloud and realized the third paragraph especially lacked power. So he decided to add compelling descriptive details about the woman ("the stale smell of sweat," for example). When revising, he also worked to reduce the paragraph's choppiness. By expanding and combining sentences, he gave the paragraph an easier, more graceful rhythm. Much of the time, revision involves paring down excess material. In this case, though, Paul made the right decision to elaborate his sentences. Furthermore, he added the following comment to the third paragraph: "I decided to be a good, courteous employee." These few words introduce an appropriate note of irony and serve to echo the essay's controlling idea.

Finally, Paul decided to omit the words "sneezing and hacking" because he realized they were too comic or light for his subject. Still, the first sentence in the revised paragraph is somewhat jarring. The word *strolling* isn't quite appropriate since it implies a leisurely grace inconsistent with the impression he wants to convey. Replacing *strolling* with, say, *shuffling* would bring the image more into line with the essay's overall mood.

Despite this slight problem, Paul's revisions are right on the mark. The changes he made strengthened his essay, turning it into a more evocative, more polished piece of narrative writing.

The following selections are examples of skillfully written narratives, each with vivid characters, compelling scenes, dramatic conflicts, and vigorous language. In "Grandmother's Victory," Maya Angelou recalls the day neighborhood girls did their best to humiliate her beloved grandmother. George Orwell's classic "Shooting an Elephant" recounts a man's encounter with an unruly crowd, a rampaging animal, and his own conscience. In "Little Deaths," T. H. Watkins joins a professional trapper on his rounds and learns something important about the complexity of life. Langston Hughes in "Salvation" narrates the wrenching loss of his innocence. Last, in "So Tsi-Fai," Sophronia Liu recalls her sixth-grade classroom and the tragedy that unfolded there.

Maya Angelou

Born Marguerite Johnson in 1928, Maya Angelou spent her childhood in Stamps, Arkansas, with her brother, Bailey, and her grandmother, "Momma." Although her youth was difficult—she was raped at age eight and a mother at sixteen—Angelou somehow managed to thrive. Multi-talented, she later worked as a professional dancer, starred in an off-Broadway play, appeared in the television miniseries *Roots*, served as a coordinator for the Southern Christian Leadership Conference, and wrote several well-received volumes of poetry—among them *Oh Pray My Wings Are Gonna Fit Me Well* (1975) and *And Still I Rise* (1978). She has also written a children's book about South African customs, *My Painted House, My Friendly Chicken, and Me*. A professor at Wake Forest University since 1991, Angelou delivered at the 1993 presidential inauguration a stirring poem written for the occasion. The recipient of numerous honorary doctorates, Angelou is best known for her series of five autobiographical books, starting with *I Know Why the Caged Bird Sings* (1970) and concluding with *All God's Children Need Traveling Shoes* (1986). The following essay is taken from *I Know Why the Caged Bird Sings*.

Grandmother's Victory

Maya Angelou's proper, deeply religious grandmother created a loving yet strictly ordered environment for her grandchildren. But that orderly world was surrounded by a larger and far more chaotic world, one in which hatred and racism reigned supreme. In this account from her childhood, Angelou tells about her grandmother's reaction to a painful encounter with that other reality.

"Thou shalt not be dirty" and "Thou shall not be impudent" 1
were the two commandments of Grandmother Henderson upon which hung our total salvation.

Each night in the bitterest winter we were forced to wash faces, 2
arms, necks, legs and feet before going to bed. She used to add, with

a smirk that unprofane people can't control when venturing into profanity, "and wash as far as possible, then wash possible."

We would go to the well and wash in the ice-cold, clear water, 3 grease our legs with the equally cold stiff Vaseline, then tiptoe into the house. We wiped the dust from our toes and settled down for schoolwork, cornbread, clabbered milk, prayers and bed, always in that order. Momma was famous for pulling the quilts off after we had fallen asleep to examine our feet. If they weren't clean enough for her, she took the switch (she kept one behind the bedroom door for emergencies) and woke up the offender with a few aptly placed burning reminders.

The area around the well at night was dark and slick, and boys 4 told about how snakes love water, so that anyone who had to draw water at night and then stand there alone and wash knew that moccasins and rattlers, puff adders and boa constrictors were winding their way to the well and would arrive just as the person washing got soap in her eyes. But Momma convinced us that not only was cleanliness next to Godliness, dirtiness was the inventor of misery.

The impudent child was detested by God and a shame to its parents and could bring destruction to its house and line. All adults had to be addressed as Mister, Missus, Miss, Auntie, Cousin, Unk, Uncle, Buhbah, Sister, Brother and a thousand other appellations indicating familial relationship and the lowliness of the addressor. 5

Everyone I knew respected these customary laws, except for the 6 powhitetrash children.

Some families of powhitetrash lived on Momma's farm land behind the school. Sometimes a gaggle of them came to the Store, filling the whole room, chasing out the air and even changing the well-known scents. The children crawled over the shelves and into the potato and onion bins, twanging all the time in their sharp voices like cigar-box guitars. They took liberties in my Store that I would never dare. Since Momma told us that the less you say to white-folks (or even powhitetrash) the better, Bailey and I would stand, solemn, quiet, in the displaced air. But if one of the playful apparitions got close to us, I pinched it. Partly out of angry frustration and partly because I didn't believe in its flesh reality. 7

They called my uncle by his first name and ordered him around 8 the Store. He, to my crying shame, obeyed them in his limping dip-straight-dip fashion.

My grandmother, too, followed their orders, except that she   9
didn't seem to be servile because she anticipated their needs.

"Here's sugar, Miz Potter, and here's baking powder. You   10
didn't buy soda last month, you'll probably be needing some."

Momma always directed her statements to the adults, but some-   11
times, Oh painful sometimes, the grimy, snotty-nosed girls would
answer her.

"Naw, Annie..."—to Momma? Who owned the land they lived   12
on? Who forgot more than they would ever learn? If there was any
justice in the world, God should strike them dumb at once!— "Just
give us some extra sody crackers, and some more mackerel."

At least they never looked in her face, or I never caught them   13
doing so. Nobody with a smidgen of training, not even the worst
roustabout, would look right in a grown person's face. It meant the
person was trying to take the words out before they were formed.
The dirty little children didn't do that, but they threw their orders
around the Store like lashes from a cat-o'-nine-tails.

When I was around ten years old, those scruffy children caused   14
me the most painful and confusing experience I had ever had with
my grandmother.

One summer morning, after I had swept the dirt yard of leaves,   15
spearmint-gum wrappers and Vienna-sausage labels, I raked the yel-
low-red dirt, and made half-moons carefully, so that the design stood
out clearly and mask-like. I put the rake behind the Store and came
through the back of the house to find Grandmother on the front
porch in her big, wide white apron. The apron was so stiff by virtue
of the starch that it could have stood alone. Momma was admiring
the yard, so I joined her. It truly looked like a flat redhead that had
been raked with a big-toothed comb. Momma didn't say anything
but I knew she liked it. She looked over toward the school principal's
house and to the right at Mr. McElroy's. She was hoping one of
those community pillars would see the design before the day's business wiped it out. Then she looked upward to the school. My head
had swung with hers, so at just about the same time we saw a troop
of the powhitetrash kids marching over the hill and down by the side
of the school.

I looked to Momma for direction. She did an excellent job of   16
sagging from her waist down, but from the waist up she seemed to
be pulling for the top of the oak tree across the road. Then she began

to moan a hymn. Maybe not to moan, but the tune was so slow and the meter so strange that she could have been moaning. She didn't look at me again. When the children reached halfway down the hill, halfway to the Store, she said without turning, "Sister, go on inside."

I wanted to beg her, "Momma, don't wait for them. Come on inside with me. If they come in the Store, you go to the bedroom and let me wait on them. They only frighten me if you're around. Alone I know how to handle them." But of course I couldn't say anything, so I went in and stood behind the screen door. 17

Before the girls got to the porch I heard their laughter crackling and popping like pine logs in a cooking stove. I suppose my lifelong paranoia was born in those cold, molasses-slow minutes. They came finally to stand on the ground in front of Momma. At first they pretended seriousness. Then one of them wrapped her right arm in the crook of her left, pushed out her mouth and started to hum. I realized that she was aping my grandmother. Another said, "Naw, Helen, you ain't standing like her. This here's it." Then she lifted her chest, folded her arms and mocked that strange carriage that was Annie Henderson. Another laughed, "Naw, you can't do it. Your mouth ain't pooched out enough. It's like this." 18

I thought about the rifle behind the door, but I knew I'd never be able to hold it straight, and the .410, our sawed-off shotgun, which stayed loaded and was fired every New Year's night, was locked in the trunk and Uncle Willie had the key on his chain. Through the fly-specked screen-door, I could see that the arms of Momma's apron jiggled from the vibrations of her humming. But her knees seemed to have locked as if they would never bend again. 19

She sang on. No louder than before, but no softer either. No slower or faster. 20

The dirt of the girls' cotton dresses continued on their legs, feet, arms and faces to make them all of a piece. Their greasy uncolored hair hung down, uncombed, with a grim finality. I knelt to see them better, to remember them for all time. The tears that had slipped down my dress left unsurprising dark spots, and made the front yard blurry and even more unreal. The world had taken a deep breath and was having doubts about continuing to revolve. 21

The girls had tired of mocking Momma and turned to other means of agitation. One crossed her eyes, stuck her thumbs in both sides of her mouth and said, "Look here, Annie." Grandmother 22 hummed on and the apron strings trembled. I wanted to throw a handful of black pepper in their faces, to throw lye on them, to scream that they were dirty, scummy peckerwoods, but I knew I was as clearly imprisoned behind the scene as the actors outside were confined to their roles.

One of the smaller girls did a kind of puppet dance while her fel-   23
low clowns laughed at her. But the tall one, who was almost a woman, said something very quietly, which I couldn't hear. They all moved backward from the porch, still watching Momma. For an awful second I thought they were going to throw a rock at Momma, who seemed (except for the apron strings) to have turned into stone herself. But the big girl turned her back, bent down and put her hands flat on the ground—she didn't pick up anything. She simply shifted her weight and did a hand stand.

Her dirty bare feet and long legs went straight for the sky. Her   24
dress fell down around her shoulders, and she had on no drawers. The slick pubic hair made a brown triangle where her legs came together. She hung in the vacuum of that lifeless morning for only a few seconds, then wavered and tumbled. The other girls clapped her on the back and slapped their hands.

Momma changed her song to "Bread of Heaven, bread of   25
Heaven, feed me till I want no more."

I found that I was praying too. How long could Momma hold   26
out? What new indignity would they think of to subject her to? Would I be able to stay out of it? What would Momma really like me to do?

Then they were moving out of the yard, on their way to town.   27
They bobbed their heads and shook their slack behinds and turned, one at a time:

"'Bye, Annie."   28
"'Bye, Annie."   29
"'Bye, Annie."   30

Momma never turned her head or unfolded her arms, but she   31
stopped singing and said, "'Bye, Miz Helen, 'bye, Miz Ruth, 'bye, Miz Eloise."

I burst. A firecracker July-the-Fourth burst. How could Mom-   32
ma call them Miz? The mean nasty things. Why couldn't she have come inside the sweet, cool store when we saw them breasting the hill? What did she prove? And then if they were dirty, mean and impudent, why did Momma have to call them Miz?

She stood another whole song through and then opened the 33
screen door to look down on me crying in rage. She looked until I
looked up. Her face was a brown moon that shone on me. She was
beautiful. Something had happened out there, which I couldn't
completely understand, but I could see that she was happy. Then she
bent down and touched me as mothers of the church "lay hands on
the sick and afflicted" and I quieted.

"Go wash your face, Sister." And she went behind the candy 34
counter and hummed, "Glory, glory, hallelujah, when I lay my burden down."

I threw the well water on my face and used the weekday hand- 35
kerchief to blow my nose. Whatever the contest had been out front,
I knew Momma had won.

I took the rake back to the front yard. The smudged footprints 36
were easy to erase. I worked for a long time on my new design and laid
the rake behind the wash pot. When I came back in the Store, I took
Momma's hand and we both walked outside to look at the pattern.

It was a large heart with lots of hearts growing smaller inside, 37
and piercing from the outside rim to the smallest heart was an arrow.
Momma said, "Sister, that's right pretty." Then she turned back to
the Store and resumed, "Glory, glory, hallelujah, when I lay my burden down."

Questions for Close Reading

1. What is the selection's thesis (or narrative point)? Locate the sentence(s)
   in which Angelou states her main idea. If she doesn't state the thesis explicitly, express it in your own words.
2. What standing does Grandmother Henderson have in the community?
   What are her values and standards?
3. Who are the "powhitetrash" children? In what ways do the "powhitetrash"
   children violate Grandmother Henderson's standards? What might have
   been some of the reasons for the children's impudence and mockery?
4. How does Mrs. Henderson behave during the girls' mockery of her? Why
   is Grandmother Henderson's behavior a "victory"?
5. Refer to your dictionary as needed to define the following words used in
   the selection: *appellations* (paragraph 5), *familial* (5), *gaggle* (7), *twanging* (7), *apparitions* (7), *smidgen* (13), *roustabout* (13), *paranoia* (18), *finality* (21), *agitation* (22), and *indignity* (26).

Questions About the Writer's Craft

1. The pattern. The main conflict in the narrative occurs between Momma and the "powhitetrash" children. What additional conflicts make the story suspenseful?

2. Other patterns. Angelou's introductory paragraphs about Momma's philosophy of child-rearing serve to contrast the children in Momma's care with the "powhitetrash" children. How does this contrast prepare the reader for the selection's narrative point?

3. Angelou uses the slang term "powhitetrash" even though it isn't in the dictionary. Why do you think she uses this term instead of a more standard or "official" expression? What effect might she hope the term will have on readers?

4. Angelou provides an explicit description of Momma—her values, her philosophy of child-rearing, her appearance, her behavior—all of which helps the reader understand Grandmother Henderson. Angelou doesn't offer a comparably explicit description of herself, yet the reader learns a good deal about her. How does Angelou go about creating a portrait of herself as a young girl?

Questions for Further Thought

1. How good a child-rearer do you think Momma was? Do you agree with her two "commandments"? Or do you believe there are other more important values that should be stressed when raising children? What would these values be?

2. "Nobody with a smidgen of training...would look right in a grown person's face," Angelou writes. What types of behaviors were considered impudent by the adults who raised you? Are these still considered disrespectful today? Why or why not?

3. Momma advises that "the less you say to white-folks...the better." Do you agree that distancing yourself from those who treat you disrespectfully is the best policy? Explain.

4. The term "powhitetrash" is a label with numerous negative connotations. What other stereotyped terms have you heard to describe people? Consider, for example, language that describes women, college athletes, people having specific religious, ethnic, or racial backgrounds. What's the effect of these labels?

Writing Assignments Using Narration as a Pattern of Development

∞ **1.** Angelou's narrative explains a mystery—the fact that her all-powerful grandmother accepted ill-treatment and impudence. Children often are mystified by the responses of the adults around them. Write a narrative about an incident in which a respected adult behaved in a manner that confused you or that caused you to change your views of the adult, the situation, or life. Before planning your paper, you might read Langston Hughes's "Salvation" (page 191), another narrative about the different ways that adults and children view the world.

2. Angelou writes that she was "mad enough to kill" during the incident at her grandmother's store. Write a narrative about a time when a strong emotion overwhelmed you or another person, creating conflict about whether to act on the emotion or to suppress it. Tell how the conflict was resolved, and indicate whether the resolution was satisfying to the person involved. The emotion you focus on may be negative, like rage and envy, or positive, like pride and affection.

Writing Assignments Using Other Patterns of Development

3. The "powhitetrash" children attempt to irritate Grandmother Henderson in a variety of ways. In truth, most children have a repertoire of tricks they can draw upon to irritate adults or otherwise get attention. Write an essay classifying the various techniques that children (including yourself when younger) deliberately use to annoy parents, teachers, or each other. Your essay may be serious or light in tone.

∞ 4. Momma's power to resist insult seems based partly on her ability to stand still as stone and partly on her value system, in which politeness and forbearance rank high. Determine what you believe is the best way to respond when confronted by hostility. Then explain the process that you would recommend to someone being attacked. Barbara Ehrenreich's "What I've Learned From Men" (page 261), Caroline Rego's "The Fine Art of Complaining" (page 385), and Gloria Naylor's "Mommy, What Does 'Nigger' Mean?" (page 535) will help you think about strategies for dealing with insulting behavior.

George Orwell

Born Eric Blair in the British colony of India, George Orwell (1903–50) is probably best known for his two novels, *Animal Farm* (1946) and *1984* (1949), both searing depictions of totalitarian societies. Orwell was also the author of numerous books and essays, many based on his diverse life experiences. He served with the Indian imperial police in Burma, worked at various jobs in London and Paris, and fought in the Spanish Civil War. His experiences in Burma provide the basis for the following essay, which is taken from his collection, *Shooting an Elephant and Other Essays* (1950).

Shooting an Elephant

At one time or another, most of us have done something just so people wouldn't laugh at or think badly of us. In this essay, George Orwell describes how he felt pressured into taking an action against his better judgment—killing an elephant that had strayed into the center of a town in Burma. Beside offering powerful insights into human behavior, Orwell's essay presents a vivid and horrifying picture of an animal's death.

In Moulmein, in Lower Burma, I was hated by large numbers 1 of people—the only time in my life that I have been important enough for this to happen to me. I was sub-divisional police officer of the town, and in an aimless, petty kind of way anti-European feeling was very bitter. No one had the guts to raise a riot, but if a European woman went through the bazaars alone somebody would probably spit betel juice over her dress. As a police officer I was an obvious target and was baited whenever it seemed safe to do so. When a nimble Burman tripped me up on the football field and the referee (another Burman) looked the other way, the crowd yelled with hideous laughter. This happened more than once. In the end the sneering yellow faces of young men that met me everywhere, the insults hooted after me when I was at a safe distance, got badly on my nerves. The young Buddhist priests were the worst of all. There were several thousand of them in the town and none of them seemed to have anything to do except stand on street corners and jeer at Europeans.

All this was perplexing and upsetting. For at that time I had already made up my mind that imperialism was an evil thing and the sooner I chucked up my job and got out of it the better. Theoretically—and secretly, of course—I was all for the Burmese and all against their oppressors, the British. As for the job I was doing, I hated it more bitterly than I can perhaps make clear. In a job like that you see the dirty work of Empire at close quarters. The wretched prisoners huddling in the stinking cages of the lock-ups, the grey, cowed faces of the long-term convicts, the scarred buttocks of the men who had been flogged with bamboos—all these oppressed me with an intolerable sense of guilt. But I could get nothing into perspective. I was young and ill-educated and I had had to think out my problems in the utter silence that is imposed on every Englishman in the East. I did not even know that the British Empire is dying, still less did I know that it is a great deal better than the younger empires that are going to supplant it. All I knew was that I was stuck between my hatred of the empire I served and my rage against the evil-spirited little beasts who tried to make my job impossible. With one part of my mind I thought of the British Raj as an unbreakable tyranny, as something clamped down, in *saecula saeculorum*,[1] upon the will of prostrate peoples; with another part I thought that the greatest joy in the world would be to drive a bayonet into a Buddhist priest's guts. Feelings like these are the normal by-products of imperialism; ask any Anglo-Indian official, if you can catch him off duty.

One day something happened which in a roundabout way was enlightening. It was a tiny incident in itself, but it gave me a better glimpse than I had had before of the real nature of imperialism—the real motives for which despotic governments act. Early one morning the sub-inspector at a police station at the other end of the town rang me up on the 'phone and said that an elephant was ravaging the bazaar. Would I please come and do something about it? I did not know what I could do, but I wanted to see what was happening and I got onto a pony and started out. I took my rifle, an old .44 Winchester and much too small to kill an elephant, but I thought the

[1]For ever and ever.

noise might be useful *in terrorem*.[2] Various Burmans stopped me on the way and told me about the elephant's doings. It was not, of course, a wild elephant, but a tame one which had gone "must." It had been chained up, as tame elephants always are when their attack of "must" is due, but on the previous night it had broken its chain and escaped. Its mahout, the only person who could manage it when it was in that state, had set out in pursuit, but had taken the wrong direction and was now twelve hours' journey away, and in the morning the elephant had suddenly reappeared in the town. The Burmese population had no weapons and were quite helpless against it. It had already destroyed somebody's bamboo hut, killed a cow and raided some fruit-stalls and devoured the stock; also it had met the municipal rubbish van and, when the driver jumped out and took to his heels, had turned the van over and inflicted violence upon it.

The Burmese sub-inspector and some Indian constables were waiting for me in the quarter where the elephant had been seen. It was a very poor quarter, a labyrinth of squalid bamboo huts, thatched with palm-leaf, winding all over a steep hillside. I remember that it was a cloudy, stuffy morning at the beginning of the rains. We began questioning the people as to where the elephant had gone and, as usual, failed to get any definite information. That is invariably the case in the East; a story always sounds clear enough at a distance, but the nearer you get to the scene of events the vaguer it becomes. Some of the people said that the elephant had gone in one direction, some said that he had gone in another, some professed not even to have heard of any elephant. I had almost made up my mind that the whole story was a pack of lies, when we heard yells a little distance away. There was a loud, scandalized cry of "Go away, child! Go away this instant!" and an old woman with a switch in her hand came round the corner of a hut, violently shooing away a crowd of naked children. Some more women followed, clicking their tongues and exclaiming; evidently there was something that the children ought not to have seen. I rounded the hut and saw a man's dead body sprawling in the mud. He was an Indian, a black Dravidian coolie, almost naked, and he could not have been dead many minutes. The people said that the elephant had come suddenly upon him round the corner of the hut, caught him with its trunk, put its foot on his back and ground him into the earth. This was the rainy season and the ground was soft, and his face had scored a trench a foot deep and a couple of

4

---

[2]As a warning.

yards long. He was lying on his belly with arms crucified and head sharply twisted to one side. His face was coated with mud, the eyes wide open, the teeth bared and grinning with an expression of unendurable agony. (Never tell me, by the way, that the dead look peaceful. Most of the corpses I have seen looked devilish.) The friction of the great beast's foot had stripped the skin from his back as neatly as one skins a rabbit. As soon as I saw the dead man I sent an orderly to a friend's house nearby to borrow an elephant rifle. I had already sent back the pony, not wanting it to go mad with fright and throw me if it smelt the elephant.

The orderly came back in a few minutes with a rifle and five cartridges, and meanwhile some Burmans had arrived and told us that the elephant was in the paddy fields below, only a few hundred yards away. As I started forward practically the whole population of the quarter flocked out of the houses and followed me. They had seen the rifle and were all shouting excitedly that I was going to shoot the elephant. They had not shown much interest in the elephant when he was merely ravaging their homes, but it was different now that he was going to be shot. It was a bit of fun to them, as it would be to an English crowd; besides they wanted the meat. It made me vaguely uneasy. I had no intention of shooting the elephant—I had merely sent for the rifle to defend myself if necessary—and it is always unnerving to have a crowd following you. I marched down the hill, looking and feeling a fool, with the rifle over my shoulder and an ever-growing army of people jostling at my heels. At the bottom, when you got away from the huts, there was a metalled road and beyond that a miry waste of paddy fields a thousand yards across, not yet ploughed but soggy from the first rains and dotted with coarse grass. The elephant was standing eight yards from the road, his left side towards us. He took not the slightest notice of the crowd's approach. He was tearing up bunches of grass, beating them against his knees to clean them and stuffing them into his mouth.

I had halted on the road. As soon as I saw the elephant I knew with perfect certainty that I ought not to shoot him. It is a serious matter to shoot a working elephant—it is comparable to destroying a huge and costly piece of machinery—and obviously one ought not to do it if it can possibly be avoided. And at that distance, peacefully eating, the elephant looked no more dangerous than a cow. I thought then and I think now that his attack of "must" was already passing off; in which case he would merely wander harmlessly about until the mahout came back and caught him. Moreover, I did not in the least want to shoot

5

6

him. I decided that I would watch him for a little while to make sure that he did not turn savage again, and then go home.

But at that moment I glanced round at the crowd that had fol- 7 lowed me. It was an immense crowd, two thousand at the least and growing every minute. It blocked the road for a long distance on either side. I looked at the sea of yellow faces above the garish clothes—faces all happy and excited over this bit of fun, all certain that the elephant was going to be shot. They were watching me as they would watch a conjurer about to perform a trick. They did not like me, but with the magical rifle in my hands I was momentarily worth watching. And suddenly I realized that I should have to shoot the elephant after all. The people expected it of me and I had got to do it; I could feel their two thousand wills pressing me forward, irresistibly. And it was at this moment, as I stood there with the rifle in my hands, that I first grasped the hollowness, the futility of the white man's dominion in the East. Here was I, the white man with his gun, standing in front of the unarmed native crowd—seemingly the leading actor of the piece; but in reality I was only an absurd puppet pushed to and fro by the will of those yellow faces behind. I perceived in this moment that when the white man turns tyrant it is his own freedom that he destroys. He becomes a sort of hollow, posing dummy, the conventionalized figure of a sahib. For it is the condition of his rule that he shall spend his life in trying to impress the "natives," and so in every crisis he has got to do what the "natives" expect of him. He wears a mask, and his face grows to fit it. I had got to shoot the elephant. I had committed myself to doing it when I sent for the rifle. A sahib has got to act like a sahib; he has got to appear resolute, to know his own mind and do definite things. To come all that way, rifle in hand, with two thousand people marching at my heels, and then to trail feebly away, having done nothing—no, that was impossible. The crowd would laugh at me. And my whole life, every white man's life in the East, was one long struggle not be laughed at.

But I did not want to shoot the elephant. I watched him beating 8 his bunch of grass against his knees, with that preoccupied grandmotherly air that elephants have. It seemed to me that it would be murder to shoot him. At that age I was not squeamish about killing animals, but I had never shot an elephant and never wanted to. (Somehow it always seems worse to kill a *large* animal.) Besides, there was the beast's owner to be considered. Alive, the elephant was worth at least a hundred pounds; dead, he would only be worth the value of his tusks, five pounds, possibly. But I had got to act quickly. I turned to some experienced-looking Burmans who had been there when we arrived, and asked them how the elephant had been behaving. They all said the same thing: he took no notice of you if you left him alone, but he might charge if you went too close to him.

It was perfectly clear to me what I ought to do. I ought to walk 9 up to within, say, twenty-five yards of the elephant and test his behavior. If he charged, I could shoot; if he took no notice of me, it would be safe to leave him until the mahout came back. But also I knew that I was going to do no such thing. I was a poor shot with a rifle and the ground was soft mud into which one would sink at every step. If the elephant charged and I missed him, I should have about as much chance as a toad under a steam-roller. But even then I was not thinking particularly of my own skin, only of the watchful yellow faces behind. For at that moment, with the crowd watching me, I was not afraid in the ordinary sense, as I would have been if I had been alone. A white man mustn't be frightened in front of "natives"; and so, in general, he isn't frightened. The sole thought in my mind was that if anything went wrong those two thousand Burmans would see me pursued, caught, trampled on and reduced to a grinning corpse like that Indian up the hill. And if that happened it was quite probable that some of them would laugh. That would never do. There was only one alternative. I shoved the cartridges into the magazine and lay down on the road to get a better aim.

The crowd grew very still, and a deep, low, happy sigh, as of people 10 who see the theatre curtain go up at last, breathed from innumerable throats. They were going to have their bit of fun after all. The rifle was a beautiful German thing with cross-hair sights. I did not then know that in shooting an elephant one would shoot to cut an imaginary bar running from ear-hole to ear-hole. I ought, therefore, as the elephant was sideway on, to have aimed straight at his ear-hole; actually I aimed several inches in front of this, thinking the brain would be further forward.

When I pulled the trigger I did not hear the bang or feel the 11 kick—one never does when a shot goes home—but I heard the devilish roar of glee that went up from the crowd. In that instant, in too short a time, one would have thought, even for the bullet to get there, a mysterious, terrible change had come over the elephant. He neither stirred nor fell, but every line of his body had altered. He looked suddenly stricken, shrunken, immensely old, as though the frightful impact of the bullet had paralyzed him without knocking him down. At last, after what seemed a long time—it might have been five seconds, I dare say—he sagged flabbily to his knees. His mouth slobbered. An enormous senility seemed to have settled upon him. One could have imagined him thousands of years old. I fired again into the same spot. At the second shot he did not collapse but climbed with desperate slowness to his feet and stood weakly upright, with legs sagging and head drooping. I fired a third time. That was the shot that did for him. You could see the agony of it jolt his whole body and knock the last remnant of strength from his legs. But in falling he seemed for a moment to rise, for as his hind legs collapsed beneath him he seemed to tower upward like a huge rock toppling, his trunk reaching skywards like a tree. He trumpeted, for the first and only time. And then down he came, his belly towards me, with a crash that seemed to shake the ground even where I lay.

I got up. The Burmans were already racing past me across the   12
mud. It was obvious that the elephant would never rise again, but he was not dead. He was breathing very rhythmically with long rattling gasps, his great mound of a side painfully rising and falling. His mouth was wide open—I could see far down into caverns of pale pink throat. I waited a long time for him to die, but his breathing did not weaken. Finally I fired my two remaining shots into the spot where I thought his heart must be. The thick blood welled out of him like red velvet, but still he did not die. His body did not even jerk when the shots hit him, the tortured breathing continued without a pause. He was dying, very slowly and in great agony, but in some world remote from me where not even a bullet could damage him further. I felt that I had got to put an end to that dreadful noise. It seemed dreadful to see the great beast lying there, powerless to move and yet powerless to die, and not even to be able to finish him. I sent back for my small rifle and poured shot after shot into his heart and down his throat. They seemed to make no impression. The tortured gasps continued as steadily as the ticking of a clock.

In the end I could not stand it any longer and went away. I   13
heard later that it took him half an hour to die. Burmans were bringing dahs and baskets even before I left, and I was told they had stripped the body almost to the bones by the afternoon.

Afterwards, of course, there were endless discussions about the   14
shooting of the elephant. The owner was furious, but he was only an Indian and could do nothing. Besides, legally I had done the right thing, for a mad elephant has to be killed, like a mad dog, if its owner fails to control it. Among the Europeans opinion was divided. The older men said I was right, the younger men said it was a damn shame to shoot an elephant for killing a coolie, because an elephant

was worth more than any damn Coringhee coolie. And afterwards I was very glad that the coolie had been killed; it put me legally in the right and it gave me a sufficient pretext for shooting the elephant. I often wondered whether any of the others grasped that I had done it solely to avoid looking a fool.

Questions for Close Reading

1. What is the selection's thesis (or narrative point)? Locate the sentence(s) in which Orwell states his main idea. If he doesn't state the thesis explicitly, express it in your own words.
2. How does Orwell feel about the Burmans? What words does he use to describe them?
3. What reasons does Orwell give for shooting the elephant?
4. In paragraph 3, Orwell says that the elephant incident gave him a better understanding of "the real motives for which despotic governments act." What do you think he means? Before you answer, reread paragraph 7 carefully.
5. Refer to your dictionary as needed to define the following words used in the selection: *imperialism* (paragraph 2), *prostrate* (2), *despotic* (3), *mahout* (3), *miry* (5), *conjurer* (7), *futility* (7), and *sahib* (7).

Questions About the Writer's Craft

1. **The pattern.** Most effective narratives encompass a restricted time span. How much time elapses from the moment Orwell gets his gun to the death of the elephant? What time signals does Orwell provide to help the reader follow the sequence of events in this limited time span?
2. Orwell doesn't actually begin his narrative until the third paragraph. What purposes do the first two paragraphs serve?
3. **Other patterns.** In paragraph 6, Orwell says that shooting a working elephant "is comparable to destroying a huge and costly piece of machinery." This kind of comparison is called an *analogy*—describing something unfamiliar, often abstract, in terms of something more familiar and concrete. Find at least three additional analogies in Orwell's essay. What effect do they have?
4. **Other patterns.** Much of the power of Orwell's narrative comes from his ability to convey sensory impressions—what he saw, heard, smelled. Orwell's description becomes most vivid when he writes about the death of the elephant in paragraphs 11 and 12. Find some evocative words and phrases that give the description its power.

Questions for Further Thought

1. In the first paragraph of "Shooting an Elephant," Orwell tells us he was "hated by large numbers of people—the only time in my life that I have been important enough for this to happen to me." What is Orwell implying about people's attitudes toward authority? Do you think Orwell has a valid point? To decide, think about the people who have power over you and how you feel about their authority.

2. The Burmese population was eager to see Orwell shoot the elephant. Why do you believe this incident held such significance for them?

3. In paragraph 7, Orwell comments that "when the white man turns tyrant it is his own freedom that he destroys." This is a *paradox*—a statement that seems to contradict itself. Explain the meaning of this paradox.

4. At the end of his essay, Orwell says he is glad the elephant had killed someone because it put him "legally in the right" for shooting the animal. What actions today are considered legally right that you, or others, feel are morally wrong?

Writing Assignments Using Narration as a Pattern of Development

∞ 1. Orwell recounts a time he acted under great pressure. Write a narrative about an action you once took simply because you felt pressured. Perhaps you were attempting to avoid ridicule or to fulfill someone else's expectations. Like Orwell, use vivid details to bring the incident to life and to convey its effect on you. Langston Hughes's "Salvation" (page 191) may lead you to some insights about the way stress influences behavior.

2. Write a narrative essay about an experience that gave you, like Orwell, a deeper insight into your own nature. You may have discovered, for instance, that you can be surprisingly naive, compassionate, petty, brave, rebellious, or good at something.

Writing Assignments Using Other Patterns of Development

3. Was Orwell justified in shooting the elephant? Write an essay arguing that Orwell was either justified *or* not justified. To develop your thesis, cite several specific reasons, each supported by details drawn from the essay. Here are some points you might consider: The legality of Orwell's act, the elephant's temperament, the crowd's presence, the aftermath of the elephant's death, the death itself.

4. Orwell's essay concerns, in part, the tendency to conceal indecision and confusion behind a facade of authority. Focusing on one or two groups of people (parents, teachers, doctors, politicians, and so on), write an essay about the way people in authority sometimes *pretend* to know what they are doing so that subordinates won't suspect their insecurity or incompetence. Part of your essay should focus on the consequences of such behaviors.

T. H. Watkins

Historian and environmentalist, T. H. Watkins has been editor of
Wilderness, the Wilderness Society's magazine, since 1982. He is
the author of more than twenty books, among them *Righteous
Pilgrim: The Life and Times of Harold L. Ickes* (1990), winner of
the *Los Angeles Times* Book Award; *The Great Depression* (1993);
and *Stone Time: Southern Utah, a Portrait and a Meditation*
(1994). Watkins's numerous articles have appeared in many publications, including *American Heritage, Smithsonian, Audubon,*
and the *Sierra Club Bulletin*, in which the following selection was
published in 1974.

Little Deaths

We Americans coddle our pets; yet every year, thousands of cats
and dogs are abandoned by their owners. We take our children to
zoos to see the beauty of wild animals, but we wear furs fashioned
from the pelts of nearly extinct species. In this selection, T. H.
Watkins describes an expedition he took with his cousin, a professional trapper whose job is to "clear the varmints" from the land.
As Watkins accompanies his cousin, he experiences some conflicting emotions.

It has been more than ten years since the day my cousin let me   1
walk his traplines with him. We never see each other now. Our
worlds, never very close, have grown even farther apart. He left California several years ago to become a trapping supervisor somewhere
in Nevada, while I have joined the ranks of those who would cheerfully eliminate his way of life. He would, rightly enough, consider me
one of his natural enemies, and it is not likely that we would have
much to say if we did meet. Still, I am grateful to him for giving me
a glimpse into the reality of a world normally hidden from us, a dark
little world where death is the only commonplace.

At the time, my cousin was a lowly field trapper at the beck and   2
call of any rancher or farmer who made an official complaint to the
trapping service about varmint troubles—coyotes or wildcats getting
after newborn lambs, foxes sneaking into chicken coops, that sort of
thing. His current assignment was to trap out the varmint population
of some ranchland high in the Diablo Hills southeast of Oakland, a
country of rolling grassland, scrub oak, and chaparral dominated by
the 3,000-foot upthrust of Mount Diablo. His base was a house trailer planted on the edge of one of the ranches he was servicing near
Livermore, although he got into Oakland quite a lot for weekend visits to a lady of his acquaintance. I lived in Oakland at the time, and
he usually made a point of stopping by to see my children, of whom
he was particularly fond.

I was then a practicing student of western history and thorough-   3
ly intrigued by the glittering adventure that pervaded my reading—
especially in the stories of the mountain men, those grizzled, anarchic beings with a lust for far places and far things, stubborn individ-
ualists who had lived freer than any Indian and had followed their
quest for beaver pelts into nearly all the mysterious blanks of the
American West, from Taos, New Mexico, to Puget Sound, from the
Marys River of the northern Rockies to the Colorado River of the
Southwest; hopelessly romantic creatures with a predilection for Indian women, a talent for profanity, and a thirst for liquor profound
enough to melt rivets. And here was my cousin, the literary—if not
lineal—descendant of the mountain man. True, he was neither grizzled nor given much to profanity, nor had he, so far as I knew, ever
offered his blanket to an Indian woman. Still, he was a *trapper*, by
God, and when on one of his visits he invited me to accompany him
on his rounds, I was entranced with the notion.

Late one spring afternoon I bundled wife and children into the   4
car and drove down to Livermore and out to the ranch where he was
staying. After a dinner cooked in the trailer's tiny kitchen, my wife
and the children bedded down in the trailer's two little bunks.
"When we get back tomorrow afternoon," my cousin told the children, "I'll take you out and show you some spring lambs. You'd like
that, right?" he added, giving them a pinch and tickle that set them
to giggling in delight. He and I bundled up in sleeping bags on the
ground outside.

It was pitch black when he woke me that next morning at five   5
o'clock. After shocking ourselves out of sleep by bathing our faces in

water from the outside faucet, we got into his pickup and drove off for breakfast at an all-night diner on the road. Dawn was insinuating itself over the dark hills by the time we finished breakfast, and had laid a neon streak across the sky when we finally turned off the highway and began climbing a rutted dirt road that led to the first trapline (we would be walking two traplines, my cousin explained, one on the western side of the hills, one on the eastern; these were two of the six he had scattered over the whole range, each of them containing between 15 and 20 traps and each checked out and reset or moved to a new location every ten days or so). As we bumped and rattled up the road, daylight slowly illuminated the hills. For two or three months in the spring, before the summer sun turns them warm and brown, these hills look as if they had been transplanted whole from Ireland or Wales. They are a celebration of green, all shades of green, from the black-green of manzanita leaves to the bright, pool-table green of the grasses. Isolated bunches of cows and sheep stood almost motionless, like ornaments added for the effect of contrast, and morning mist crept around the base of trees and shrouded dark hollows with the ghost of its presence. Through all this, the exposed earth of the road cut like a red scar, and the sounds of the pickup's engine and the country-western music yammering out of its radio intruded themselves on the earth's silence gracelessly.

    We talked of my cousin's father, whom he worshipped and emulated. My cousin was, in fact, almost literally following in his father's footsteps, for "the old man" had been a state trapper himself and was now a trapping supervisor. Before that, back in the deep of the Depression, he had been a lion hunter for the state, when a mountain lion's ears were good as money, and before that he had "cowboyed some," as he put it; at one time, according to family tradition, his grandfather's ranch had encompassed much of what became the town of San Bernardino in Southern California. At one point in his life, he had led jaguar-hunting trips to the jungles of northwestern Mexico, and he was still a noteworthy hunter, though now he confined himself principally to an occasional deer, antelope, or bear. My cousin had grown up in a house where skins of various types served as rugs and couchthrows, where stuffed heads glared unblinkingly from the walls, where sleek hounds were always in-and-out, where hunting magazines dominated the tables, hunting talk dominated the conversations, and everywhere was the peculiarly masculine smell of newly oiled guns, all kinds of guns—pistols

  6

(including an old Colt once used by my cousin's great-grandfather, legend had it, to kill a man), rifles, shotguns. It was a family that had been killing things for a long time, sometimes for meat, sometimes for a living, sometimes for what was called the sport of it, and one of my cousin's consuming ambitions was to bag a bighorn sheep, something his father had never managed to do.

I had never killed anything in my life except fish, and since fish   7
neither scream, grunt, squeal, nor moan when done in, it had never seemed like killing at all. In any case, I was by no means prepared for the first sight of what my cousin did to earn his bread. I don't know what I had expected with my romantic notions of the trapper's life, but surely it was something other than what I learned when we crawled up the road through increasingly heavy underbrush and stopped to check out the first of my cousin's traps.

We got out of the truck and beat our way through the brush to   8
a spot perhaps 30 feet from the road. I did not see the animal until we were nearly on top of it. It was a raccoon, the first raccoon I had ever seen in person, and at that moment I wished that I never had seen one. It was dead, had been dead for several days, my cousin informed me. "Hunger, thirst, and shock is what kills them, mostly," he said in response to my question. "That, and exhaustion, I reckon." The animal seemed ridiculously tiny in death. It lay on its side, its small mouth, crawling with ants, open in a bared-tooth grin, and its right rear leg in the clutch of the steel trap. It was easy to see how the animal had exhausted itself; it had been at its leg. A strip of flesh perhaps three inches in width had been gnawed away, leaving the white bone and a length of tendon exposed. Tiny flies sang about the ragged wound and over the pool of dried blood beneath the leg. There was a stink in the air, and it suddenly seemed very, very warm to me there in the morning shadows of the brush.

"Once in a while," my cousin said, prying open the curved jaws   9
of the trap, "one of them will chew his way loose, and if he doesn't lose too much blood he can live. I caught a three-legged coyote once. Too stupid to learn, I guess."

"Do you ever find one of them still alive?" I asked.   10

"Sometimes."   11

"What do you do with them?"   12

He looked up at me. "Do with them? I shoot them," he said,   13
patting the holstered pistol at his waist. He lifted the freed raccoon by the hind legs and swung it off into the brush. "Buzzard meat," he

said. He then grabbed the steel stake to which the trap was attached by a chain and worked it out of the ground. "I've had this line going for over a month, now. The area's just about trapped out." He carried the trap back to the road, threw it in the back of the pickup, and we drove up the increasingly rough road to the next trap. It was empty, as was the one after it. I was beginning to hope they would all be empty, but the fourth one contained a small skunk, a black-and-white pussycat of a creature that had managed to get three of its feet in the trap at once and lay huddled in death like a child's stuffed toy. It, too, was disengaged and tossed into the brush. A little further up the ridge, and we found a fox, to my cousin's visible relief. "Great," he said. "That has to be the mate to the one I got a couple of weeks ago. Pregnant, too. There won't be any little foxes running around this year." Into the brush the animal went.

By the time we reached the top of the long ridge on which my cousin had set his traps, the morning had slipped toward noon and our count had risen to seven animals: three raccoons, three skunks, and the pregnant fox. There was only one trap left now, but it was occupied by the prize of the morning, a bobcat. "I'll be damned," my cousin said, "I've been after that bugger all month. Just about give up hope." The bobcat had not died well, but in anger. The marks of its rage and anguish were laid out in a torn circle of earth described by the length of the chain that had linked the animal to its death. Even the brush had been ripped and clawed at, leaves and twigs stripped from branches, leaving sweeping scars. Yellow tufts of the animal's fur lay scattered on the ground, as if the bobcat had torn at its own body for betraying it, and its death-mask was a silent howl of outrage. My cousin took it out of the trap and heaved it down the side of the hill. Buzzard meat.

We had to go back down the hills and around the range in order to come up the eastern slopes and check out the second trapline, and on the way we stopped at a small roadhouse in Clayton for a hamburger and a beer. I found I could eat, which surprised me a little, and I certainly had a thirst for the beer. We sat side-by-side at the bar, not saying much. Something Wallace Stegner had once written kept flashing through my mind. "Like most of my contemporaries," he had said, "I grew up careless. I grew up killing things." I wondered if my cousin would know what Stegner had been talking about, and decided it would be best not to bring it up. I could have cancelled out right there, I suppose, asking him to take me back to his camp,

14

15

explaining that I had seen enough, too much, of the trapper's life. I could always plead exhaustion. After all, the day's hiking had been more real exercise than I had had in months, and I was, in fact, tired. A stubborn kernel of pride would not let me do it. I would see the day through to the end.

So the ritual continued. We climbed back up into the hills on   16
the east side of the range in the oven-heat of a strong spring sun. The day's count rose even more as the pickup bounced its way up the ragged weedgrown road: two more skunks, another fox, two more raccoons. The work went more slowly than the morning's run, for this was a new line, and each trap had to be reset. My cousin performed this task with an efficient swiftness and the kind of quiet pride any craftsman takes in his skill, snapping and locking the jaws of the traps, covering them with a thin scattering of earth and twigs, sprinkling the ground about with dog urine from a plastic squeeze bottle to cover up the man-smell. By the time we were ready to approach the last three traps of the line, it was well after three o'clock. We were very high by then, well up on the slopes of Mount Diablo itself, and we had to abandon the pickup to hike the rest of the way on foot. We broke out of the brush and walked along a spur of the hills. About 1,500 feet below us and some miles to the east, we could see the towns of Pittsburgh and Martinez sending an urban haze into the air. Ahead of me, my cousin suddenly stopped.

"Wait a minute. Listen," he said.   17

A distant thrashing and rattling sound came from the slope be-   18
low us. "That's where the trap is," he said. "Might be a bobcat, but I didn't expect to get him so soon. Come on."

The slope was very steep, and we slid much of the way down to   19
the trap on our bottoms, slapped at and tangled by brush. The animal was not a bobcat. It was a dog, a large, dirty-white mongrel whose foreleg was gripped in the trap. The dog snarled at us as we approached it. Saliva had gathered at its lips and there was a wildness in its eyes.

"*Dammit*," my cousin said. He had owned dogs all his life. "A   20
wild dog. Probably abandoned by somebody. They do it all the time. Dogs turn wild and start running in packs. Some people ought to be shot."

I didn't know what he wanted to do. He hadn't pulled out his   21
gun. "Can we turn him loose? Maybe he isn't wild. Maybe he just wandered up here on his own."

My cousin looked at me. "Maybe. There's a noose-pole in the back of the truck—a kind of a long stick with a loop of rope at the end. Why don't you get it?"   22

I scrambled back up the slope and made my way back to the pickup, where I found the noose-pole. As thick as a broomhandle and about five feet in length, it looked like a primitive fishing pole. When I got back down to the trap, the dog was still snarling viciously. My cousin took the pole from me, opened the loop at the end, and extended it toward the dog. "If I can hook him," he said, "I'll hold his head down while you open the trap. You've seen how I do it."   23

It was useless. The dog fought at the loop frantically in a madness of pain and fear. After perhaps 15 minutes, my cousin laid the pole down. "He just isn't going to take it."   24

"What'll we do?" I asked, though I'm sure I knew.   25

He shrugged. "Can't just leave him here to die." He unsnapped his holster and pulled out the gun. He duck-walked to within a couple of feet of the animal, which watched him suspiciously. "I'll try to do it with one shot," he said. The gun's discharge slammed into the silence of the mountain. The dog howled once, a long, penetrating song of despair that ran in echoes down the hill. My cousin nudged the animal with his boot. It was dead. He opened the trap, freed the leg, and heaved the body down the slope. The crashing of its fall seemed to go on for a long time. My cousin reset the trap. "Come on," he said. "It's getting late."   26

The last trap of the day held a dead raccoon.   27

My cousin was pleased with the day's work. "If it keeps up like this," he said as we rattled down the highway toward his trailer, "I could be out of here in a month."   28

"What's the hurry?"   29

He indicated a small housing development by the side of the road. "Too much civilization around here for me. Too many people. I need to get back up into the mountains."   30

There was plenty of light left when we got back, and true to his promise, my cousin took the children out into the fields to see a newborn lamb. While its mother bleated in protest, he ran one down and brought it to my children so they could pet it. I watched his face as he held the little creature. There was no hint in it of all the death we had harvested that day, no hint of the half-eaten legs we had seen, no hint of the fearful thrashing agony the animals had endured before   31 dying. No hint, even, of the death-howl of the dirty white dog that may or may not have been wild. There was neither irony nor cynicism in him. He held the lamb with open, honest delight at the wonder my children found in touching this small, warm, live thing.

My cousin is not an evil man. We are none of us evil men.   32

Questions for Close Reading

1. What is the selection's thesis (or narrative point)? Locate the sentence(s) in which Watkins states his main idea. If he does not state the thesis explicitly, express it in your own words.

2. Watkins explains that even ten years ago, he and his cousin weren't close or much alike. Why, then, was Watkins so eager to accompany his cousin on a trapping expedition? What fascination did trapping hold for Watkins?

3. Although Watkins doesn't approve of what his cousin does for a living, he is fair to him. Find places in the essay where Watkins points out (a) his cousin's good qualities and (b) his cousin's reasons for trapping.

4. What is the difference between the incident of the trapped dog and the other trapping incidents described in the essay? Why do you think Watkins described the episode with the dog at such length?

5. Refer to your dictionary as needed to define the following words used in the selection: *chaparral* (paragraph 2), *anarchic* (3), *predilection* (3), *lineal* (3), *emulated* (6), and *encompassed* (6).

Questions About the Writer's Craft

1. **The pattern.**   Narratives rely on vivid description for much of their impact. As a narrator, Watkins is a master of sensory detail, particularly when he wants us to see the death agonies of the trapped animals. Locate two paragraphs in which his descriptions of death are especially vivid. Which words and phrases make you understand the pain and horror of the animals' deaths?

2. What are some of the time signals that Watkins uses to indicate the sequence of events in his essay?

3. Watkins skillfully employs simile, a technique that uses the word *like* or *as* to highlight the similarities between two seemingly unlike objects. One example of simile can be found in paragraph 13, where Watkins describes the dead skunk as looking "like a child's stuffed toy." Find two more examples of similes in "Little Deaths."

4. How does Watkins use dialogue to reveal his cousin's attitudes toward animals? How do these comments help us understand Watkins's thesis?

Questions for Further Thought

1. In what ways are the animals' deaths "little" deaths? In what ways are they significant deaths? What else might have "died" during Watkins's experience?

2. The last paragraph of the selection reads, "My cousin is not an evil man. We are none of us evil men." Do you think Watkins is correct about his cousin? About humanity in general?

3. How might Watkins's cousin, so gentle with young children and a new-born lamb, justify to himself what he does for a living? Is there necessarily a conflict between the two sides of his character?

4. The essay raises the question of justifiable killing. Was the trapper justified in killing the animals because they were "varmints"? Should human needs and desires take precedence over an animal's right to live?

Writing Assignments Using Narration as a Pattern of Development

∞ 1. As Watkins has done, write a narrative about a moment of harsh discovery in your life. Describe how someone or something you had idealized turned out to be sharply different from what you had expected. Be sure you describe briefly, perhaps in the introduction, your original expectations. Langston Hughes's "Salvation" (page 191) may spark some insight into the all-too-common discrepancy between expectation and reality.

2. Undoubtedly, Watkins feels that his cousin treats life too casually. Write a narrative about a time when you treated life too lightly. The life could be an animal's, another person's, even your own. Use specific details to tell what happened.

Writing Assignments Using Other Patterns of Development

∞ 3. Write an essay on either the pros or the cons of hunting. To identify helpful articles, look up "Hunting" or "Wildlife Management" in the *Readers' Guide to Periodical Literature* or in your library's computerized database. In addition, you might talk to people you know about their attitudes toward hunting. Then take a position. Direct your essay to a confirmed nonhunter and show that hunting is beneficial. Or, conversely, direct the essay to an enthusiastic hunter and support the nonhunting position. Ron Kline's "A Scientist: 'I Am the Enemy'" (page 651) and Patricia Curtis's "The Argument Against Animal Experimentation" (page 657) will help sensitize you to animal rights issues.

∞ 4. The philosopher Hannah Arendt refers in her writings to "the banality of evil." Evil may at times be part of the most ordinary, most normal people or activities. Write an essay about one commonly accepted activity that you believe is evil—or at least immoral. Offer detailed support showing how or why this activity is wrong. You might consider one of the following: killing animals for fur or food; our treatment of old people or children; our neglect or abuse of our environment. The scathing indictment of human nature that Mark Twain presents in "The Damned Human Race" (page 609) may give you some ideas for your essay.

Langston Hughes

One of the foremost members of the 1920s literary movement known as the Harlem Renaissance, Langston Hughes (1902–67) committed himself to portraying the richness of black life in America. A poet and a writer of short stories, Hughes was greatly influenced by the rhythms of blues and jazz. In his later years, he published two autobiographical works, *The Big Sea* (1940) and *I Wonder as I Wander* (1956), and he wrote a history of the National Association for the Advancement of Colored People (NAACP). The following selection is from *The Big Sea*.

Salvation

Disillusionment is part of growing up. As children, we start out expecting the best from people and from life. But as we grow older, experiences tend to chip away our cherished beliefs and trusting expectations. In "Salvation," Langston Hughes uses humor and poignancy to recount a time in his own childhood when he faced such a moment of disillusionment.

I was saved from sin when I was going on thirteen. But not really 1 saved. It happened like this. There was a big revival at my Auntie Reed's church. Every night for weeks there had been much preaching, singing, praying, and shouting, and some very hardened sinners had been brought to Christ, and the membership of the church had grown by leaps and bounds. Then just before the revival ended, they held a special meeting for children, "to bring the young lambs to the fold." My aunt spoke of it for days ahead. That night I was escorted to the front row and placed on the mourners' bench with all the other young sinners, who had not yet been brought to Jesus.

My aunt told me that when you were saved you saw a light, and 2 something happened to you inside! And Jesus came into your life! And God was with you from then on! She said you could see and hear and feel Jesus in your soul. I believed her. I had heard a great many old people say the same thing and it seemed to me they ought to know. So I sat there calmly in the hot, crowded church, waiting for Jesus to come to me.

The preacher preached a wonderful rhythmical sermon, all   3
moans and shouts and lonely cries and dire pictures of hell, and then he sang a song about the ninety and nine safe in the fold, but one little lamb was left out in the cold. Then he said: "Won't you come? Won't you come to Jesus? Young lambs, won't you come?" And he held out his arms to all us young sinners there on the mourners' bench. And the little girls cried. And some of them jumped up and went to Jesus right away. But most of us just sat there.

A great many older people came and knelt around us and   4
prayed, old women with jet-black faces and braided hair, old men with work-gnarled hands. And the church sang a song about the lower lights are burning, some poor sinners to be saved. And the whole building rocked with prayer and song.

Still I kept waiting to *see* Jesus.   5

Finally all the young people had gone to the altar and were   6
saved, but one boy and me. He was a rounder's son named Westley. Westley and I were surrounded by sisters and deacons praying. It was very hot in the church, and getting late now. Finally Westley said to me in a whisper: "God damn! I'm tired o' sitting here. Let's get up and be saved." So he got up and was saved.

Then I was left all alone on the mourners' bench. My aunt came   7
and knelt at my knees and cried, while prayers and songs swirled all around me in the little church. The whole congregation prayed for me alone, in a mighty wail of moans and voices. And I kept waiting serenely for Jesus, waiting, waiting—but he didn't come. I wanted to see him, but nothing happened to me. Nothing! I wanted something to happen to me, but nothing happened.

I heard the songs and the minister saying: "Why don't you   8
come? My dear child, why don't you come to Jesus? Jesus is waiting for you. He wants you. Why don't you come? Sister Reed, what is this child's name?"

"Langston," my aunt sobbed.   9

"Langston, why don't you come? Why don't you come and be   10
saved? Oh, Lamb of God! Why don't you come?"

Now it was really getting late. I began to be ashamed of myself,   11
holding everything up so long. I began to wonder what God thought

about Westley, who certainly hadn't seen Jesus either, but who was now sitting proudly on the platform, swinging his knickerbockered legs and grinning down at me, surrounded by deacons and old women on their knees praying. God had not struck Westley dead for taking his name in vain or for lying in the temple. So I decided that maybe to save further trouble, I'd better lie, too, and say that Jesus had come, and get up and be saved.

So I got up. 12

Suddenly the whole room broke into a sea of shouting, as they 13 saw me rise. Waves of rejoicing swept the place. Women leaped in the air. My aunt threw her arms around me. The minister took me by the hand and led me to the platform.

When things quieted down, in a hushed silence, punctuated by 14 a few ecstatic "Amens," all the new young lambs were blessed in the name of God. Then joyous singing filled the room.

That night, for the last time in my life but one—for I was a big 15 boy twelve years old—I cried. I cried, in bed alone, and couldn't stop. I buried my head under the quilts, but my aunt heard me. She woke up and told my uncle I was crying because the Holy Ghost had come into my life, and because I had seen Jesus. But I was really crying because I couldn't bear to tell her that I had lied, that I had deceived everybody in the church, and I hadn't seen Jesus, and that now I didn't believe there was a Jesus any more, since he didn't come to help me.

Questions for Close Reading

1. What is the selection's thesis (or narrative point)? Locate the sentence(s) in which Hughes states his main idea. If Hughes doesn't state the thesis explicitly, express it in your own words.
2. During the revival meeting, what pressures are put on the young Langston to get up and be saved?
3. How does Westley's attitude differ from Hughes's?
4. Does the narrator's Auntie Reed really understand him? Why can't he tell her the truth about his experience in the church?
5. Refer to your dictionary as needed to define the following words used in the selection: *revival* (paragraph 1), *knickerbockered* (11), *punctuated* (14), and *ecstatic* (14).

Questions About the Writer's Craft

1. **The pattern.** A narrative's power can often be traced to a conflict within the event being recounted. What conflict does the narrator of "Salvation" experience? How does Hughes create tension about this conflict?
2. What key role does Westley serve in the resolution of the narrator's dilemma? How does Hughes's inclusion of Westley in the story help us to understand the narrator better?
3. The thirteenth paragraph presents a metaphor of the church as an ocean. What images develop this metaphor? What does the metaphor tell us about Hughes's feelings and those of the church people?
4. The singing of hymns is a major part of this religious service. Why do you think Hughes has the narrator reveal the subjects and even the lyrics of some of the hymns?

Questions for Further Thought

1. What did Hughes expect to happen when he was "saved"? Was he led to have unrealistic expectations about this religious moment? Do you think children understand religious ideas differently from the way adults do? Explain.
2. Given the circumstances, do you think young Langston Hughes did the right thing? Why or why not?
3. Young people often feel pressured by family and community to adopt certain values, beliefs, or traditions. What are some of the pressures that you've experienced? Should young people presume that the older generation knows more about what to believe and do?
4. Is disillusionment with adults and with society's institutions an inevitable part of growing up? Why or why not?

Writing Assignments Using Narration as a Pattern of Development

1. Like Hughes, we sometimes believe that deception is our best alternative. Write a narrative about a time you felt deception was the best way either to protect those you care about or to maintain the respect of those important to you.
2. Write a narrative essay about a chain of events that caused you to become disillusioned about a person or institution you had previously regarded highly. Begin as Hughes does by presenting your initial beliefs. Relate the sequence of events that changed your evaluation of the person or organization. In the conclusion, explain the short- and long-term effects of the incident.

Writing Assignments Using Other Patterns of Development

3. Hughes writes, "My aunt told me that when you were saved, you saw a light, and something happened to you inside! And Jesus came into your life!" What causes people to change their beliefs? Do such changes come from waiting calmly, as Hughes tried to do in church, or must they come from a more active process? Write an essay explaining your viewpoint. You may use process analysis, causal analysis, or some other organizational pattern to develop your thesis. Be sure to include specific examples to support your understanding of the way beliefs change.

∞ 4. Write a persuasive essay arguing either that lying is sometimes right or that lying is always wrong. Apply your thesis to particular situations and show how lying is or is not the right course of action. Remember to acknowledge the opposing viewpoint. Lewis Thomas's "The Lie Detector" (page 495) may help you define your position. You might even mention Thomas's perspective in your essay.

Sophronia Liu

In 1973, at the age of twenty, Sophronia Liu came to the United States from her native Hong Kong. She earned a bachelor's degree in English and French and a master's degree in English from the University of South Dakota. She now makes her home in the Minneapolis-St. Paul area, where she is active as an organizer and educational consultant within the Asian-American community. An actress as well as a writer, Liu is a founding member of The Asian American Renaissance, a grassroots organization dedicated to building the Asian-American community through the arts. Initially written in response to a class assignment, the selection below was published in the feminist journal *Hurricane Alice* in 1986.

So Tsi-Fai

Grimy, profane, defiant: Fourteen-year-old So Tsi-fai is nothing but trouble to the missionary sisters in his Hong Kong school. Clearly, they conclude, he isn't cut out for education, so why waste time on him? From her vantage point as a star pupil, Sophronia Liu watches with increasing horror as So Tsi-fai's fate is tragically sealed.

Voices, images, scenes from the past—twenty-three years ago, 1 when I was in sixth grade:

"Let us bow our heads in silent prayer for the soul of So Tsi-fai. 2 Let us pray for God's forgiveness for this boy's rash taking of his own life..." Sister Marie (Mung Gu-liang). My sixth-grade English teacher. Missionary nun from Paris. Principal of The Little Flower's School. Disciplinarian, perfectionist, authority figure: awesome and awful in my ten-year-old eyes.

"I don't need any supper. I have drunk enough insecticide." So 3 Tsi-fai. My fourteen-year-old classmate. Daredevil; good-for-nothing lazybones (according to Mung Gu-liang). Bright black eyes, disheveled hair, defiant sneer, creased and greasy uniform, dirty hands, careless walk, shuffling feet. Standing in the corner for being late, for forgetting his homework, for talking in class, for using foul language. ("Shame on you! Go wash your mouth with soap!" Mung Gu-liang's sharp command. He did, and came back with a grin.) So Tsi-fai: Sticking his tongue out behind Mung Gu-liang's back, passing secret notes to his friends, kept behind after school, sent to the Principal's office for repeated offenses. So Tsi-fai: incorrigible, hopeless, and without hope.

It was a Monday in late November when we heard of his death, returning to school after the weekend with our parents' signatures on our midterm reports. So Tsi-fai also showed his report to his father, we were told later. He flunked three out of the fourteen subjects: English Grammar, Arithmetic, and Chinese Dictation. He missed each one by one to three marks. That wasn't so bad. But he was a hopeless case. Overaged, stubborn, and uncooperative; a repeated offender of school rules, scourge of all teachers; who was going to give him a lenient passing grade? Besides, being a few months over the maximum age—fourteen—for sixth graders, he wasn't even allowed to sit for the Secondary School Entrance Exam.

All sixth graders in Hong Kong had to pass the SSE before they could obtain a seat in secondary school. In 1964 when I took the exam, there were more than twenty thousand candidates. About seven thousand of us passed: four thousand were sent to government and subsidized schools, the other three thousand to private and grant-in-aid schools. I came in around no. 2000; I was lucky. Without the public exam, there would be no secondary school for So Tsi-fai. His future was sealed.

Looking at the report card with three red marks on it, his father was furious. So Tsi-fai was the oldest son. There were three younger children. His father was a vegetable farmer with a few plots of land in Wong Juk-hang, by the sea. His mother worked in a local factory. So Tsi-fai helped in the fields, cooked for the family, and washed his own clothes. ("Filthy, dirty boy!" gasped Mung Gu-liang. "Grime behind the ears, black rims on the fingernails, dirty collar, crumpled shirt. Why doesn't your mother iron your shirt?") Both his parents were illiterate. So Tsi-fai was their biggest hope: He made it to the sixth grade.

Who woke him up for school every morning and had breakfast waiting for him? Nobody. ("Time for school! Get up! Eat your rice!" Ma nagged and screamed. The aroma of steamed rice and Chinese sausages spread all over the house. "Drink your tea! Eat your oranges! Wash your face! And remember to wash behind your ears!") And who helped So Tsi-fai do his homework? Nobody. Did he have older brothers like mine who knew all about the arithmetic of rowing a boat against the currents or with the currents, how to count the feet of chickens and rabbits in the same cage, the present perfect continuous tense of "to live" and the future perfect tense of "to succeed"? None. Nil. So Tsi-fai was a lost cause.

I came in first in both terms that year, the star pupil. So Tsi-fai   8 was one of the last in the class: He was lazy; he didn't care. Or did he?

When his father scolded him, So Tsi-fai left the house. When he   9 showed up again, late for supper, he announced, "I don't need any supper. I have drunk enough insecticide." Just like another one of his practical jokes. The insecticide was stored in the field for his father's vegetables. He was rushed to the hospital; dead upon arrival.

"He gulped for a last breath and was gone," an uncle told us at   10 the funeral. "But his eyes wouldn't shut. So I said in his ear, 'You go now and rest in peace.' And I smoothed my hand over his eyelids. His face was all purple."

His face was still purple when we saw him in his coffin. Eyes shut   11 tight, nostrils dilated and white as if fire and anger might shoot out, any minute.

In class that Monday morning, Sister Marie led us in prayer.   12 "Let us pray that God will forgive him for his sins." We said the Lord's Prayer and the Hail Mary. We bowed our heads. I sat in my chair, frozen and dazed, thinking of the deadly chill in the morgue, the smell of disinfectant, ether, and dead flesh.

"Bang!" went a gust of wind, forcing open a leaf of the double   13 door leading to the back balcony. "Flap, flap, flap." The door swung in the wind. We could see the treetops by the hillside rustling to and fro against a pale blue sky. An imperceptible presence had drifted in with the wind. The same careless walk and shuffling feet, the same daredevil air—except that the eyes were lusterless, dripping blood; the tongue hanging out, gasping for air. As usual, he was late. But he had come back to claim his place.

"I died a tragic death," his voice said. "I have as much right as   14 you to be here. This is my seat." We heard him; we knew he was back.

. . .So Tsi-fai: Standing in the corner for being late, for forget-   15 ting his homework, for talking in class, for using foul language. So

Tsi-fai: Palm outstretched, chest sticking out, holding his breath: "Tat. Tat. Tat." Down came the teacher's wooden ruler, twenty times on each hand. Never batting an eyelash: then back to facing the wall in the corner by the door. So Tsi-fai: grimy shirt, disheveled hair, defiant sneer. So Tsi-fai. Incorrigible, hopeless, and without hope.

The girls in front gasped and shrank back in their chairs. Mung   16
Gu-liang went to the door, held the doorknob in one hand, poked her head out, and peered into the empty balcony. Then, with a determined jerk, she pulled the door shut. Quickly crossing herself, she returned to the teacher's desk. Her black cross swung upon the front of her gray habit as she hurried across the room. "Don't be silly!" she scolded the frightened girls in the front row.

What really happened? After all these years, my mind is still   17
haunted by this scene. What happened to So Tsi-fai? What happened to me? What happened to all of us that year in sixth grade, when we were green and young and ready to fling our arms out for the world? All of a sudden, death claimed one of us and he was gone.

Who arbitrates between life and death? Who decides which life   18
is worth preserving and prospering, and which to nip in its bud? How did it happen that I, at ten, turned out to be the star pupil, the lucky one, while my friend, a peasant's son, was shoveled under the heap and lost forever? How could it happen that this world would close off a young boy's life at fourteen just because he was poor, undisciplined, and lacked the training and support to pass his exams? What really happened?

Today, twenty-three years later, So Tsi-fai's ghost still haunts   19
me. "I died a tragic death. I have as much right as you to be here. This is my seat." The voice I heard twenty-three years ago in my sixth-grade classroom follows me in my dreams. Is there anything I can do to lay it to rest?

Questions for Close Reading

1. What is the selection's thesis (or narrative point)? Locate the sentence(s) in which Liu states her main idea. If she doesn't state the narrative point explicitly, express it in your own words.

2. What is the immediate cause of So Tsi-fai's suicide? What other factors also come into play? Why might he have chosen the method to kill himself that he did?

3. How did Liu's home life compare to that of So Tsi-fai? What connections do you see between each one's family life and academic progress?

4. What does So Tsi-fai say when he returns as a ghost? What do his words indicate about his perception of the educational system—and of his place in it?

5. Refer to your dictionary as needed to define the following words used in the selection: *defiant* (paragraph 3), *incorrigible* (3), *scourge* (4), *subsidized* (5), *dilated* (11), *ether* (12), *imperceptible* (13), *lusterless* (13), and *arbitrates* (18).

Questions About the Writer's Craft

1. **The pattern.** Most narratives usually establish a conflict and then move to its resolution. In "So Tsi-Fai," however, the reader knows by paragraph 2 that the boy will commit suicide; flashbacks and flashforwards comprise the rest of the essay. Locate these flashbacks and flashforwards. How does Liu signal these time shifts?

2. Liu describes a number of relationships filled with conflict. Identify as many of these conflicted relationships as you can. How do they heighten the essay's narrative tension?

3. In paragraphs 3, 6, and 7, Liu calls attention to certain conversations by placing quotations in parentheses. How do these parenthetical quotations reinforce the contrast between the different ways the author and So Tsi-fai were treated?

4. Throughout the essay, Liu repeats significant material. For example, she repeats the boy's last words twice (3 and 9) as well as whole passages of description (3 and 15). What effect do you think Liu intended these repetitions to have? How do they support her narrative point?

Questions for Further Thought

1. The educational system in Hong Kong weeds out students deemed unsuitable for secondary school as soon as they complete the sixth grade. Do you think this system is fair? Why or why not?

2. So Tsi-fai didn't do well at school, but Liu doesn't indicate that he was unintelligent. What factors besides intelligence might be involved when a student does or does not get good grades? To what extent do good grades measure what a student has learned?

3. Liu mentions several kinds of punishment in the essay: washing the child's mouth out with soap, standing the child in the corner, rapping the child's hand with a ruler. Think back to your own childhood. What kinds of punishment—if any—do you remember? How effective were they?

4. Liu questions the assumption that So Tsi-fai "didn't care" about his schoolwork. Can you think of situations in which a person acted as if he or she "didn't care" when the opposite was actually true? Why might someone respond in this paradoxical way?

Writing Assignments Using Narration as a Pattern of Development

∞ 1. The death of So Tsi-fai marks the end of the author's childhood, the end of the time when she was "green and young and ready to fling [her] arms out for the world." Write an essay about a time when you were forced to grow up suddenly or were faced with a sobering reality. Your moment of lost innocence might have occurred when you were a child: perhaps you had to cope with illness or divorce. Or your moment of loss may have come when you were an adult: maybe you learned about a relative's unsavory business practices or a respected boss's discriminating hiring practices. Use vivid description and revealing dialogue to convey the tension and conflict you felt in the moment of discovery. Remember, though, to include only those details that reinforce your narrative point. Before writing, you may want to read Langston Hughes's "Salvation" (page 191) for its powerful depiction of lost innocence.

2. Liu depicts the unfairness of an educational system that penalizes children simply because they are disadvantaged. Brainstorm with others to identify injustices that exist in our educational system. You might, for example, decide that teachers single out males for discipline, that students with learning disabilities get a second-rate education, that student athletes receive preferential treatment at grading time. Focusing on a specific educational level, select *one* such type of unfairness, and write an essay recounting two or three dramatic incidents of this inequity. To depict each incident fully, you'll need to reconstruct conversations and provide vivid narrative details, always keeping in mind the narrative point you want to make.

Writing Assignments Using Other Patterns of Development

3. Liu writes, "After all these years, my mind is still haunted by this scene." All of us have witnessed dramatic events that continue to exert power over us even though they occurred in the past. Write an essay showing the effects of such an event on your life, behavior, attitudes, and values. Begin with a brief account of the event; then explain its consequences for you, making sure your discussion honors the inevitable complexity of cause-effect relationships.

∞ **4.** Liu's teacher clearly has no concern for her student's self-esteem, a factor that many consider crucial to children's well-being and success. Brainstorm with others to identify as many strategies as possible that elementary school teachers could use to strengthen students' self-image. Select what you consider to be the most compelling strategies, and categorize them into types, such as "group work," "independent study," "leadership experiences," "teacher-student conferences," and so on. Then write an essay explaining the techniques and their value. Be sure to illustrate the strategies with specific examples drawn from your own and other people's experiences. Alice Walker's "Beauty: When the Other Dancer Is the Self" (page 485) and Joan Didion's "On Self-Respect" (page 715) will provide insight into the development of a healthy self-esteem.

Additional Writing Topics

NARRATION

General Assignments

Prepare an essay on any of the following topics, using narration as the paper's dominant method of development. Be sure to select details that advance the essay's narrative purpose; you may even want to experiment with flashback or flashforward. In any case, keep the sequence of events clear by using transitional cues. Within the limited time span covered, use vigorous details and varied sentence structure to enliven the narrative. Tell the story from a consistent point of view.

1. An emergency that brought out the best or worst in you
2. The hazards of taking children out to eat
3. An incident that made you believe in fate
4. Your best or worst day at school or work
5. A major decision
6. An encounter with a machine
7. An important learning experience
8. A narrow escape
9. Your first date, first day on the job, or first anything
10. A memorable childhood experience
11. A fairy tale the way you would like to hear it told
12. A painful moment
13. An incredible but true story
14. A significant family event
15. An experience in which a certain emotion (pride, anger, regret, or some other) was dominant

Assignments With a Specific Purpose and Audience

1. As the fund-raiser for a particular organization (for example, Red Cross, SPCA, Big Brothers/Big Sisters), you're sending a newsletter to contributors. Support your cause by telling the story of a time when your organization made all the difference—the blood donation that saved a life, the animal that was rescued from abuse, and so on.
2. A friend of yours has seen someone cheat on a test, shoplift, or violate an employer's trust. In a letter, convince this friend to inform the instructor, store owner, or employer by narrating an incident in which a witness did (or did not) speak up in such a situation. Tell what happened as a result.
3. You have had a disturbing encounter with one of the people who seem to have "fallen through the cracks" of society—a street person, an unwanted child, or anyone else who is alone and abandoned. Write a letter

to the local newspaper describing this encounter. Your purpose is to arouse people's indignation and compassion and to get help for such unfortunates.

4. Write an article for your old high school newspaper. The article will be read primarily by seniors who are planning to go away to college next year. In the article, narrate a story that points to some truth about the "breaking away" stage of life.

5. A close friend has written a letter to you telling about a bad experience that he or she had with a teacher, employer, doctor, repair person, or some other professional. On the basis of that single experience, your friend now negatively stereotypes the entire profession. Write a letter to your friend balancing his or her cynical picture by narrating a story that shows the "flip side" of this profession—someone who made every effort to help.

6. Your younger brother, sister, relative, or neighborhood friend can't wait to be your age. By narrating an appropriate story, show the young person that your age isn't as wonderful as he or she thinks. Be sure to select a story that the person can understand and appreciate.

6

EXEMPLIFICATION

WHAT IS EXEMPLIFICATION?

If someone asked you, "Have you been to any good restaurants lately?" you probably wouldn't answer "Yes" and then immediately change the subject. Most likely, you would go on to illustrate with *examples.* Perhaps you'd give the names of restaurants you've enjoyed and talk briefly about the specific things you liked: the attractive prices, the tasty main courses, the pleasant service, the tempting desserts. Such examples and details are needed to convince others that your opinion—in this or any matter—is valid. Similarly, when you talk about larger and more important issues, people won't pay much attention to your opinion if all you do is string together vague generalizations: "We have to do something about acid rain. It's had disastrous consequences for the environment. Its negative effects increase every year. Action must be taken to control the problem." To be taken seriously and to convince others that your point is well-founded, you must provide specific supporting examples: "the forests in the Adirondacks are dying"; "yesterday's rainfall was fifty times more acidic than normal"; "Pine Lake, in the northern part of the state, was once a great fishing spot but now has no fish population."

Examples are equally important when you write an essay. It's not fuzzy generalities and highfalutin abstractions that make writing impressive. Just the opposite is true. Facts, anecdotes, statistics, details, opinions, and observations are at the heart of effective writing, giving your work substance and solidity.

HOW EXEMPLIFICATION FITS YOUR PURPOSE AND AUDIENCE

The wording of assignments and essay exam questions may signal the need for specific examples:

> Soap operas, whether shown during the day or in the evening, are among the most popular television programs. Why do you think this is so? Provide specific examples to support your position.

> Some observers claim that college students are less interested in learning than in getting ahead in their careers. Cite evidence to support or refute this claim.

> A growing number of people feel that parents should not allow young children to participate in highly competitive team sports. Basing your conclusion on your own experiences and observations, indicate whether you think this point of view is reasonable.

Such phrases as "Provide specific examples," "Cite evidence," and "Basing your conclusion on your own experiences and observations" signal that each essay would be developed through examples.

Usually, though, you won't be told so explicitly to provide examples. Instead, as you think about the best way to achieve your essay's purpose, you'll see the need for illustrative details—no matter which patterns of development you use. For instance, to *persuade* skeptical readers that the country needs a national health system, you might mention specific cases to dramatize the inadequacy of our current health-care system: a family bankrupted by medical bills; an uninsured accident victim turned away by a hospital; a chronically ill person rapidly deteriorating because he didn't have enough money to visit a doctor. Or imagine a lightly satiric piece that pokes fun at cat lovers. Insisting that "cat people" are pretty strange creatures, you might make your point—and make readers chuckle—with a series of examples *contrasting* cat lovers and dog lovers: the qualities admired by each group (loyalty in dogs versus independence in cats) and the different expectations each group has for its pets (dog lovers want Fido to be obedient and lovable, whereas cat lovers are satisfied with Felix's occasional spurts of docility and affection). Similarly, you would supply examples in a *causal analysis* speculating on the likely impact of a proposed tuition hike at your college. To convince the college administration of the probable negative effects of such a hike, you might cite the following examples: articles reporting a nationwide upswing in student transfers to less expensive schools; statistics indicating a significant drop in grades among already employed students forced to work more hours to pay increased tuition costs; interviews with students too financially strapped to continue their college education.

Whether you use examples as the primary or supplemental method of development, they serve a number of important purposes. For one thing, examples make writing *interesting*. Assume you're writing an essay about sexism in television commercials. Your essay would be lifeless and boring if all it did was repeat, in a general way, that commercials present stereotyped views of men and women:

> Sexism is rampant in television commercials. It is very much alive, yet most viewers seem to take it all in stride. Few people protest the obviously sexist characters and statements on such commercials. Surely, these commercials misrepresent the way most of us live.

Without interesting particulars, readers may respond, "Who cares?" But if you provide specific examples, you'll attract your readers' attention:

> Sexism is rampant in television commercials. Although millions of women hold responsible jobs outside the home, commercials continue to portray women as simple creatures who spend most of their time thinking about wax buildup, cottony-soft bathroom tissue, and static-free clothes. Men, apparently, have better things to do than fret over

such mundane household matters. How many commercials can you recall that depict men proclaiming the virtues of squeaky-clean dishes or sparkling bathrooms? Not many.

Examples also make writing *persuasive*. Most writing conveys a point, but many readers are reluctant to accept someone else's point of view unless evidence demonstrates its validity. Imagine you're writing an essay showing that latchkey children are more self-sufficient and emotionally secure than children who return from school to a home where a parent awaits them. Your thesis is obviously controversial. Without specific examples—from your own experience, personal observations, or research studies—your readers would undoubtedly question your position's validity.

Further, examples *help explain* difficult, abstract, or unusual ideas. Suppose you're assigned an essay on a complex subject such as inflation, zero population growth, or radiation exposure. As a writer, you have a responsibility to your readers to make these difficult concepts concrete and understandable. If writing an essay on radiation exposure in everyday life, you might start by providing specific examples of home appliances that emit radiation—color televisions, computers, and microwave ovens—and tell exactly how much radiation we absorb in a typical day from such equipment. To illustrate further the extent of our radiation exposure, you could also provide specifics about unavoidable sources of natural radiation (the sun, for instance) and details about the widespread use of radiation in medicine (X rays, radiation therapy). These examples would ground your discussion, making it immediate and concrete, preventing it from flying off into the vague and theoretical.

Finally, examples *help prevent unintended ambiguity*. All of us have experienced the frustration of having someone misinterpret what we say. In face-to-face communication, we can provide on-the-spot clarification. In writing, however, instantaneous feedback isn't available, so it's crucial that meaning be as unambiguous as possible. Examples will help.

Assume you're writing an essay asserting that ineffective teaching is on the rise in today's high schools. To clarify what you mean by "ineffective," you provide examples: the instructor who spends so much time disciplining unruly students that he never gets around to teaching; the moonlighting teacher who is so tired in class that she regularly takes naps during tests; and the teacher who accepts obviously plagiarized reports because he's grateful that students hand in something. Without such concrete examples, your readers will supply their own ideas—and these may not be what you had in mind. Readers might imagine "ineffective" to mean harsh and puni-tive, whereas your concrete examples would show that you intend it to mean out of control and irresponsible. Such specifics help pre-vent misunderstanding.

SUGGESTIONS FOR USING EXEMPLIFICATION IN AN ESSAY

The following suggestions will be helpful whether you use examples as a dominant or supportive pattern of development.

1. Generate examples.   Where do you get the examples to develop your essay? The first batch of examples is generated during the prewriting stage. With your purpose and thesis in mind, you make a broad sweep for examples, using brainstorming, freewriting, the mapping technique—whichever prewriting technique you pre-fer. During this preliminary search for examples, you may also read through your journal for relevant specifics, interview other people, or conduct library research.

Examples can take several forms, including specific names (of people, places, products, and so on), anecdotes, personal observa-tions, expert opinion, as well as facts, statistics, and case studies gathered through research. While prewriting, try to generate more examples than you think you'll need. Starting with abundance—and then picking out the strongest examples—will give you a firm base on which to build the essay. If you have a great deal of trouble find-ing examples to support your thesis, you may need to revise the the-sis; you may be trying to support an idea that has little validity. On the other hand, while prewriting, you may unearth numerous exam-ples but find that many of them contradict the point you started out to support. If that happens, don't hesitate to recast your central point, always remembering that your thesis and examples must fit.

2. Select the examples to include.   Once you've used prewriting to generate as many examples as possible, you're ready to limit your examples to the strongest ones. Keeping your purpose, thesis, and audience in mind, ask yourself several key questions: "Which examples support my thesis? Which do not? Which are most convincing? Which are most likely to interest readers and clarify meaning?"

You may include several brief examples within a single sentence:

> The French people's fascination with some American literary figures, such as Poe and Hawthorne, is understandable, but their great respect for "artists" like comedian Jerry Lewis is a mystery.

Or you may develop a paragraph with a number of "for instances":

> A uniquely American style of movie-acting reached its peak in the 1950s. Certain charismatic actors completely abandoned the stage techniques and tradition that had been the foundation of acting up to that time. Instead of articulating their lines clearly, the actors mumbled; instead of making firm eye contact with their colleagues, they hung their heads, shifted their eyes, even talked with their eyes closed. Marlon Brando, Montgomery Clift, and then James Dean were three actors who exemplified this new trend.

As the preceding paragraph shows, *several examples* are usually needed to make a point. An essay with the thesis "Rock videos are dangerously violent" wouldn't be convincing if you gave only one example of a violent rock video. Several strong examples would be needed for readers to feel you had illustrated your point sufficiently.

As a general rule, you should strive for variety in the kinds of examples you include. For instance, you might choose a *personal-experience example* drawn from your own life or from the life of someone you know. Such examples pack the wallop of personal authority and lend drama to writing. Or you might include a *typical-case example,* an actual event or situation that did occur—but not to you or to anyone you know. (Perhaps you learned about the event through a magazine article, newspaper account, or television report.) The objective nature of such cases makes them especially convincing. You might also include a speculative or *hypothetical example* ("Imagine how difficult it must be for an elderly person to carry bags of groceries from the market to a bus stop several blocks away"). You'll find that hypothetical cases are effective for clarifying and dramatizing key points, but be sure to acknowledge that the example is indeed invented ("*Suppose* that..." or "Let's for a moment *assume* that..."). Make certain, too, that the invented situation is easily imagined and could conceivably happen. Finally, you might create a *generalized example*—one that is a composite of the typical or usual. Such generalized examples are often signaled by words that involve the reader (*"All of us,* at one time or another, have been driven to distraction by a trivial annoyance like the buzzing of a fly or the sting of a paper cut"), or they may refer to humanity in general ("When *most people* get a compliment, they perk up, preen, and think the praise-giver is blessed with astute powers of observation").

Occasionally, *one extended example,* fully developed with many details, can support an essay. It might be possible, for instance, to support the thesis "Federal legislation should raise the legal drinking age to twenty-one" with a single compelling, highly detailed example of the effects of one teenager's drunken-driving spree.

The examples you choose must also be *relevant;* that is, they must have direct bearing on the point you want to make. You would have a hard time convincing readers that Americans have callous attitudes toward the elderly if you described the wide range of new programs, all staffed by volunteers, at a well-financed center for senior citizens. Because these examples *contradict,* rather than support, your thesis, readers are apt to dismiss what you have to say.

Make certain, too, that your examples are *accurate.* Exercise special caution when using statistics. An old saying warns that there are lies, damned lies, and statistics—meaning that statistics can be misleading. A commercial may claim, "In a taste test, 80 percent of those questioned indicated that they preferred Fizzy Cola." Impressed? Don't be—at least, not until you find out how the test was conducted. Perhaps the subjects had to choose between Fizzy Cola and battery acid, or perhaps there were only five subjects, all Fizzy Cola vice presidents.

Finally, select *representative* examples. Picking the oddball, one-in-a-million example to support a point—and passing it off as typical—is dishonest. Consider an essay with the thesis "Part-time jobs contribute to academic success." Citing only one example of a student who works at a job twenty-five hours a week while earning straight As isn't playing fair. Why not? You've made a *sweeping generalization* based on only one case. To be convincing, you need to show how holding down a job affects *most* students' academic performance. (For more on sweeping generalizations, see pages 573–576.)

3. Develop your examples sufficiently. To ensure that you get your ideas across, your examples must be *specific*. An essay on the types of heroes in American movies wouldn't succeed if you simply strung together a series of undeveloped examples in paragraphs like this one:

> Heroes in American movies usually fall into types. One kind of hero is the tight-lipped loner, men like Clint Eastwood and Humphrey Bogart. Another movie hero is the quiet, shy, or fumbling type who has appeared in movies since the beginning. The main characteristic of this hero is lovableness, as seen in actors like Jimmy Stewart. Perhaps the most one-dimensional and predictable hero is the superman who battles tough odds. This kind of hero is best illustrated by Sylvester Stallone as Rocky and Rambo.

If you developed the essay in this way—if you moved from one undeveloped example to another—you would be doing little more than making a list. To be effective, key examples must be expanded in sufficient detail. The examples in the preceding paragraph could be developed in paragraphs of their own. You could, for instance, develop the first example this way:

> Heroes can be tight-lipped loners who appear out of nowhere, form no permanent attachments, and walk, drive, or ride off into the sunset. In many of his Westerns, from the low-budget "spaghetti Westerns" of the 1960s to Unforgiven in 1992, Clint Eastwood personifies this kind of hero. He is remote, mysterious, and untalkative. Yet he guns down an evil sheriff, runs other villains out of town, and helps a handicapped girl--acts that cement his heroic status. The loner might also be Sam Spade as played by Humphrey Bogart. Spade solves the crime and sends the guilty off to jail, yet he holds his emotions in check and has no permanent ties beyond his faithful secretary and shabby office. One gets the feeling that he could walk away from these, too, if necessary. Even in The Right Stuff, an account of America's early astronauts, the scriptwriters mold Chuck Yeager, the man who broke the sound barrier, into a classic loner. Yeager, portrayed by the aloof Sam Shepard, has a wife, but he is nevertheless insular. Taking mute pride in his ability to distance himself from politicians, bureaucrats, even colleagues, he soars into space, dignified and detached.

(For hints on ways to make writing specific, see pages 39–40.)

4. Organize the examples. If, as is usually the case, several examples support your point, be sure that you present the examples in an *organized* manner. Often you'll find that other patterns of development (cause-effect, comparison-contrast, definition, and so on) suggest ways to sequence examples. Let's say you're writing an essay showing that stay-at-home vacations offer numerous opportunities to relax. You might begin the essay with examples that *contrast* stay-at-home and get-away vacations. Then you might move to a *process analysis* that illustrates different techniques for unwinding at home. The essay might end with examples showing the *effect* of such leisurely at-home breaks.

Finally, you need to select an *organizational approach consistent* with your *purpose* and *thesis.* Imagine you're writing an essay about students' adjustment during the first months of college. The supporting examples could be arranged *chronologically.* You might start by illustrating the ambivalence many students feel the first day of college when their parents leave for home; you might then offer an anecdote or two about students' frequent calls to Mom and Dad during the opening weeks of the semester; the essay might close with an account of students' reluctance to leave campus at the mid-year break.

Similarly, an essay demonstrating that a room often reflects the character of its occupant might be organized *spatially:* from the empty soda cans on the floor to the spitballs on the ceiling. In an essay illustrating the kinds of skills taught in a composition course, you might move from *simple* to *complex* examples: starting with relatively matter-of-fact skills like spelling and punctuation and ending with more conceptually difficult skills like formulating a thesis and organizing an essay. Last, the *emphatic sequence*—in which you lead from your first example to your final, most significant one—is another effective way to organize an essay with many examples. A paper about Americans' characteristic impatience might progress from minor examples (dependence on fast food, obsession with ever-faster mail delivery) to more disturbing manifestations of impatience (using drugs as quick solutions to problems, advocating simple answers to complex international problems: "Bomb them!").

5. Choose a point of view. Many essays developed by illustration place the subject in the foreground and the writer in the background. Such an approach calls for the *third-person point of view.* For example, even if you draw examples from your own personal experience, you can present them without using the *first-person* "I." You might convert such personal material into generalized examples (see page 211), or you might describe the personal experience as if it happened to someone else. Of course, you may use the first person if the use of "I" will make the example more believable and dramatic. But remember: Just because an event happened to you personally doesn't mean you have to use the first-person point of view.

Without appropriate and dynamic examples, an essay is a dry, bloodless thing. Even provocative and intriguing ideas lose their power—or may be misunderstood—if writers don't provide the specific details needed to explain and develop their central points. Remember that most readers will not take seriously a writer who has been too lazy to do anything but spout a series of vague generalities. If you examine a stirring speech, a riveting newspaper article, an informative book, you're sure to find clear, well-developed examples. These specifics engage the reader and provide the writing with its distinctive energy.

STUDENT ESSAY

The following student essay was written by Michael Pagano in response to this assignment:

> In "Things Fall Apart," Art Carey contends that the United States has become a nation of incompetents. In an essay of your own, critique another aspect of American society, using—as Carey does—numerous compelling examples to support your viewpoint.

While reading Michael's paper, try to determine how effectively it applies the principles of exemplification. The annotations on Michael's paper and the commentary following it will help you look at the essay more closely.

Pursuit of Possessions
by Michael Pagano

Introduction   Anne Morrow Lindbergh, a well-known novelist,   1
essayist, and poet, once wrote that Americans "who

could choose simplicity, choose complication." Lindbergh herself was a prime example of this phenomenon. Often in the spotlight as the wife of the famed aviation pioneer Charles Lindbergh, she also negotiated the demands of being a mother as well as a writer. Not surprisingly, Lindbergh sought to simplify her life. In one of her best-known essays, "Channelled Whelk," she describes her escape to a beach cottage, bare except for driftwood and seashells. There she was happy. But few

Thesis of us Americans would be willing to simplify our lives as Lindbergh did. Instead, we choose to clutter our lives

Plan of development with a stream of material possessions. And what is the result of this mania for possessions? Much of our time goes to buying new things, dealing with the complications they create, and working madly to buy more things or pay for the things we already have.

Topic sentence We devote a great deal of our lives to acquiring   2

The first of three paragraphs in a chronological sequence the material goods we imagine are essential to our well-being. Hours are spent planning and thinking about our future purchases. We window-shop for designer jogging shoes; we leaf through magazines looking at ads for elaborate stereo equipment; we research back issues of <u>Consumer Reports</u> to find out about recent developments in exercise equipment. Moreover, once we find what we are looking for, more time is taken up when we decide to actually buy the items. How do we find this time? That's easy. We turn evenings, weekends, and holidays--time that used to be set aside for family and friends--into shopping expeditions. No wonder family life is deteriorating and children spend so much time in front of television sets. Their parents are seldom around.

Topic sentence As soon as we take our new purchases home, they   3

The second paragraph in the chronological sequence begin to complicate our lives. A sleek new sports car has to be washed, waxed, and vacuumed. A fashionable pair of skintight jeans can't be thrown in the washing machine but has to be taken to the dry cleaner. New stereo equipment has to be connected with a tangled network of cables to the TV, radio, and cassette deck.

A paragraph with many specific examples Eventually, of course, the inevitable happens. Our indispensable possessions break down and need to be repaired. The home computer starts to lose data, the microwave has to have its temperature controls adjusted, and the videotape recorder has to be serviced when a cassette becomes jammed in the machine.

Topic sentence ──────▶ After more time has gone by, we sometimes dis-   4
cover that our purchases don't suit us anymore, and
The third so we decide to replace them. Before making our
paragraph in replacement purchases, though, we have to find
the ways to get rid of the old items. If we want to replace
chronological our black-and-white 19-inch television set with a 25-
sequence inch color set, we have to find time to put an ad in
the classified section of the paper. Then we have to
handle phone calls and set up times people can come
to look at the TV. We could store the set in the base-
ment--if we are lucky enough to find a spot that isn't
already filled with other discarded purchases.

Topic sentence ──────▶ Worst of all, this mania for possessions often   5
with emphasis influences our approach to work. It is not unusual for
signal people to take a second or even a third job to pay off
the debt they fall into because they have overbought.
After paying for food, clothing, and shelter, many
people see the rest of their paycheck go to Visa, MasterCard, department store charge accounts, and time
payments. Panic sets in when they realize there simply is not enough money to cover all their expenses.
Just to stay afloat, people may have to work overtime
or take on additional jobs.

Conclusion   It is clear that many of us have allowed the pursuit   6
of possessions to dominate our lives. We are so busy
buying, maintaining, and paying for our worldly goods
that we do not have much time to think about what is
really important. We should try to step back from our
compulsive need for more of everything and get in touch
with the basic values that are the real point of our lives.

COMMENTARY

**Thesis, other patterns of development, and plan of develop-
ment.** In "Pursuit of Possessions," Michael analyzes the American
mania for acquiring material goods. He begins with a quotation
from Anne Morrow Lindbergh and briefly explains Lindbergh's
strategy for simplifying her life. The reference to Lindbergh gives
Michael a chance to *contrast* the way she tried to lead her life with
the acquisitive and frenzied way many Americans lead theirs. This

contrast leads logically to the essay's *thesis:* "We choose to clutter our lives with a stream of material possessions."

Besides introducing the basic contrast at the heart of the essay, Michael's opening paragraph helps readers see that the essay contains an element of *causal analysis.* Michael asks, "What is the result of this mania for possessions?" and then answers that question in the next sentence. This sentence also serves as the essay's *plan of development* and reveals that Michael feels the pursuit of possessions negatively affects our lives in three key ways.

Essays of this length often don't need a plan of development. But since Michael's paper is filled with many *examples,* the plan of development helps readers see how all the details relate to the essay's central point.

Evidence.   Support for the thesis consists of numerous examples presented in the *first-person-plural point of view* ("*We* choose to clutter our lives...," "*We* devote a great deal of our lives..." and so on). Many of these examples seem drawn from Michael's, his friends', or his family's experiences; however, to emphasize the events' universality, Michael converts these essentially personal examples into generalized ones that "we" all experience.

These examples, in turn, are organized around the three major points signaled by the plan of development. Michael uses one paragraph to develop his first and third points and two paragraphs to develop his second point. Each of the four supporting paragraphs is focused by a *topic sentence* that appears at the start of the paragraph. The transitional phrase "Worst of all" (paragraph 5) signals that Michael has sequenced his major points *emphatically,* saving for last the issue he considers most significant: how the "mania for possessions...influences our approach to work."

Organizational strategies.   Emphatic order isn't Michael's only organizational technique. When reading the paper, you probably felt that there was an easy flow from one supporting paragraph to the next. How does Michael achieve such *coherence between paragraphs?* For one thing, he sequences paragraphs 2–4 *chronologically:* what happens before a purchase is made; what happens afterward. Secondly, topic sentences in paragraphs 3 and 4 include *signal devices* that indicate this passage of time. The topic sentences also strengthen coherence by *linking back* to the preceding paragraph:

"*As soon as we take our new purchases home,* they...complicate our lives" and "*After more time has gone by,* we...discover that our purchases don't suit us anymore."

The same organizing strategies are used *within paragraphs* to make the essay coherent. Details in paragraphs 2 through 4 are sequenced chronologically, and to help readers follow the chronology, Michael uses *signal devices:* "*Moreover, once* we find what we are looking for, more time is taken up..." (2); "Eventually, of course, the inevitable happens" (3); "*Then* we have to handle phone calls..." (4).

Problems with paragraph development. You probably recall that an essay developed primarily through exemplification must include examples that are *relevant, interesting, convincing, representative, accurate,* and *specific.* On the whole, Michael's examples meet these requirements. The third and fourth paragraphs, especially, include vigorous details that show how our mania for buying things can govern our lives. We may even laugh with self-recognition when reading about "skintight jeans that can't be thrown in the washing machine" or a basement "filled with discarded purchases."

The fifth paragraph, however, is underdeveloped. We know that this paragraph presents what Michael considers his most significant point, but the paragraph's examples are rather *flat* and *unconvincing.* To make this final section more compelling, Michael could mention specific people who overspend, revealing how much they are in debt and how much they have to work to become solvent again. Or he could cite a television documentary or magazine article dealing with the issue of consumer debt. Such specifics would give the paragraph the solidity it now lacks.

Shift in tone. The fifth paragraph has a second, more subtle problem; *a shift in tone.* Although Michael has, up to this point, been critical of our possession-mad culture, he has poked fun at our obsession and kept his tone conversational and gently satiric. In this paragraph, though, he adopts a serious tone and, in the next paragraph, his tone becomes even weightier, almost preachy. It is, of course, legitimate to have a serious message in a lightly satiric piece. In fact, most satiric writing has such an additional layer of meaning. But because Michael has trouble blending these two moods, there's a jarring shift in the essay.

Shift in focus. The second paragraph shows another kind of shift—in *focus*. The paragraph's controlling idea is that too much time is spent acquiring possessions. However, starting with "No wonder family life is deteriorating," Michael includes two sentences that introduce a complex issue beyond the scope of the essay. Since these last two sentences disrupt the paragraph's unity, they should be deleted.

Revising the first draft. Although the final version of the essay needs work in spots, it's much stronger than Michael's first draft. To see how Michael went about revising the draft, compare his paper's second and third supporting paragraphs with his draft version reprinted here.

Original Version of the Second Paragraph

  Our lives are spent not only buying things but in dealing with the inevitable complications that are created by our newly acquired possessions. First, we have to find places to put all the objects we bring home. More clothes demand more closets; a second car demands more garage space; a home entertainment center requires elaborate shelving. We shouldn't be surprised that the average American family moves once every three years. A good many families move simply because they need more space to store all the things they buy. In addition, our possessions demand maintenance time. A person who gets a new car will spend hours washing it, waxing it, and vacuuming it. A new pair of jeans has to go to the dry cleaners. New stereo systems have to be connected to already existing equipment. Eventually, of course, the inevitable happens. Our new items need to be repaired. Or we get sick of them and decide to replace them. Before making our replacement purchases, though, we have to get rid of the old items. That can be a real inconvenience.

  When Michael looked more closely at this paragraph, he realized it rambled and lacked energy. He started to revise the paragraph by tightening the first sentence, making it more focused and less awkward. Certainly, the revised sentence ("As soon as we take our new purchases home, they begin to complicate our lives") is crisper than the original. Next, he decided to omit the discussion about finding places to put new possessions; these sentences about inadequate closet, garage, and shelf space were so exaggerated that they undercut the valid point he wanted to make. He also chose to eliminate the sentences about the mobility of American families.

This was, he felt, an interesting point, but it introduced an issue too complex to be included in the paragraph.

Michael strengthened the rest of the paragraph by making his examples more specific. A "new car" became a "sleek new sports car," and a "pair of jeans" became a "fashionable pair of skintight jeans." Michael also realized he had to do more than merely write, "Eventually,...our new items need to be repaired." This point had to be dramatized by sharp, convincing details. Therefore, Michael added lively examples to describe how high-tech possessions—microwaves, home computers, VCRs—break down. Similarly, Michael realized it wasn't enough simply to say, as he had in the original, that we run into problems when we try to replace out-of-favor purchases. Vigorous details were again needed to illustrate the point. Michael thus used a typical "replaceable" (an old black-and-white TV) as his key example and showed the annoyance involved in handling phone calls and setting up appointments so people could see the TV.

After adding these specifics, Michael realized he had enough material to devote a separate paragraph to the problems associated with replacing old purchases. By dividing his original paragraph, Michael ended up with two well-focused paragraphs, neither of which has the rambling quality found in the original.

In short, Michael strengthened his essay through substantial revision. Another round of rewriting would have made the essay stronger still. Even without this additional work, Michael's essay provides an interesting perspective on an American preoccupation.

The selections that follow use abundant examples to make their points. In "Things Fall Apart," Art Carey provides one compelling example after another to illustrate the wave of incompetence that he feels threatens to engulf America. "Sexism and Language," by Alleen Pace Nilsen, presents numerous instances of the way our language discriminates against women. Hilarious examples of college misadventures make James Thurber's "University Days" a long-standing favorite. Neil Postman cites evidence from numerous sources to make his point that America is eagerly embracing a culture of "Future Shlock." Finally, in "What I've Learned From Men," Barbara Ehrenreich uses an event from her own life to discuss the conditioning that women receive to be pleasant and lady-like—no matter the cost to their personal well-being.

Art Carey

Art Carey is a staff writer and columnist for *The Philadelphia Inquirer*. Born in 1950, Carey did his undergraduate work at Princeton University, where he graduated with honors in English, and his graduate work at Columbia University, where he was awarded the Robert E. Sherwood Traveling Fellowship for excellence in the study and reporting of national affairs. Carey joined the staff of the *Inquirer* in 1977. He is the author of two books: *In Defense of Marriage* (1984) and *The United States of Incompetence* (1991). Both works grew out of articles he wrote for the *Inquirer*'s Sunday magazine. Carey writes that he enjoys "pursuing competence, and occasionally excellence, as a runner, weight lifter, carpenter, and restorer of old jeeps." The following piece is taken from *The United States of Incompetence.*

Things Fall Apart

There was a time, not so long ago, that the words "Made in America" were a proud boast, right up there with "Yankee ingenuity." The United States led the world in productivity, technological progress, and educational achievement. What about today? Art Carey points to an infuriating example of bungling in his neighborhood, believing that this local instance of incompetence is symptomatic of a widespread malaise afflicting the country.

It is just a bridge, a simple two-lane bridge. 1

Until recently, it carried a busy road—Bowman Avenue—over 2 the railroad tracks that give the Main Line, the swank, leafy suburbs west of Philadelphia, its name.

There is nothing special about this bridge, except that my 3 neighbors and I depend on it to travel from one side of the community to the other. There is nothing special about this bridge, except that the Pennsylvania Department of Transportation allowed it to deteriorate so badly that not long ago inspectors declared it unsafe and suddenly closed it. There is nothing special about this bridge, except that because of bureaucratic wrangling it won't be replaced, at the earliest, for another three years. As a commissioner in the township where the bridge is located griped, "The bridge over the River Kwai was built in less time."[1]

There is nothing special about this bridge, except that every 4 time I want to use it, and can't, my blood starts to boil, especially since, in all that time, during many inconvenient months, no matter what the hour or day, I've never seen a single person working on it.

What the hell is going on here?   5

Why is it that in one of the richest townships in one of the rich- 6 est counties in one of the richest nations in the world—a country that once gloried in its engineering derring-do—we can't rebuild a simple two-laned bridge in under three years?

Where is Teddy Roosevelt[2] when we need him? Where's the 7 can-do, take-charge, full-speed-ahead spirit that once defined the American character? What's happened to our political will and civic enterprise, our vision and moral fortitude, our Yankee know-how and ingenuity, our ability and desire to tackle any problem, to take on any challenge, to do what needs to be done—with dispatch and care and pride?

There's nothing special about the Bowman Avenue Bridge— 8 and that's the problem. This bridge is just another dismal example of a disease that's consuming the soul of America. For me, it's a maddening symbol, right in my own back yard, of the incompetence that is turning the United States into a second-rate nation and a Third World country.

- *In New Jersey, the State Commission of Investigation calls for drastic reforms to protect patients from drug-addicted, senile, mentally ill, or incompetent doctors. One case cited: an anesthesiologist who left a patient's side during an operation to have sex with a nurse in a closet. The patient died on the operating table.*

---

[1]In the 1957 movie *The Bridge on the River Kwai*, British soldiers in a Japanese prison camp endure a physical and psychological ordeal when ordered by their captors to build a bridge.

[2]Twenty-sixth president of the United States, known for his energy and never-say-die attitude.

- *New York Telephone has to test 57,000 people before it can find 2100 qualified enough to become operators and repair technicians.*

- *Because of inadequate soil testing, a new interchange for the Schuylkill Expressway in Philadelphia begins to sink so badly that it must be torn down, redesigned, and rebuilt—a monumental bungle that may cost taxpayers $50 million.*

- *A Piedmont jetliner, with a hundred people on board, makes an emergency landing in Greensboro, North Carolina, when its left landing gear cannot be lowered because it is jammed by a rubber wheel chock left behind by mechanics.*

- *Because of a mistake made by a printing contractor, all 990 diplomas awarded to the midshipmen who graduated from the U.S. Naval Academy at Annapolis in 1990 include the line "The Seal of the Navel Academy is hereunto affixed."*

- *Encouraged by the Pentagon's lax oversight, military suppliers pad their bills by outrageous amounts, charging taxpayers $117 each for soap dish covers, $120 each for cup dispensers, $436 each for hammers, $641 each for porcelain urinals, $999 each for pliers, and $1868 each for toilet seat covers.*

What do I mean by incompetence? Strictly speaking, it refers to a lack of ability, but today, for many Americans, *incompetence* has become a catchword for a larger malaise. Simply stated, we have lost our purpose, our moral ambition, our sense of social obligation. In this broader light, incompetence is the failure to do what you ought to do, either because you can't or because you won't.

Incompetents come in two varieties: those who don't do what they should because they don't have the skill or training, and those who don't do what they should because they're lazy, sloppy, careless, and, frankly, don't give a damn. The United States has plenty of both types, at every level of society, among all kinds of people, in all sorts of vocations and professions.

Incompetence is the *Exxon Valdez* (cost: at least $2 billion for cleanup, incalculable damage to the environment), and mismanagement of the Energy Department's nuclear weapons plants (cost: $150 billion), and a nation that continues to ring up tremendous

budget deficits (an estimated $318 billion for fiscal 1991) and for-
eign trade imbalances (about $100 billion for 1990).

Incompetence is the Philadelphia Police Department destroying   12
a neighborhood by dropping a bomb on an occupied row house to
evict a bunch of obnoxious revolutionaries (cost: eleven lives, sixty-
one houses, at least $22.6 million), and a doped-up Conrail engineer
running a string of locomotives into the path of an Amtrak passenger
train (cost: 16 lives, 175 persons injured, millions of dollars in equipment and property damage).

Incompetence is the high school graduate who can't read or   13
write or do simple arithmetic, the U.S. citizen who believes that the
Congress is appointed by the President, and the ninety-four million
Americans who don't know that their own planet orbits the sun once
a year.

Incompetence is the plumber who never shows, the mail-order   14
house that sends you the wrong merchandise, the hospital accounting department that keeps badgering you with computerized dun-
ning notices for a bill you paid a year ago, the sulky department store
clerk who acts as if she's doing you a favor by waiting on you, the
empty-headed operator who transfers your call to the wrong party,
and the gum-popping secretary who can't be bothered to help because she's too busy chatting on the phone or carrying on with her
cronies.

Incompetence is professors who plagiarize and scientists who   15
fudge data. It's arrogant doctors who are too self-important to return an anxious patient's telephone calls, and greedy lawyers who
make disputes so acrimonious that they cost a fortune to settle.

Incompetence is too many college grads chasing MBAs and   16
BMWs, specializing in M&As and arranging LBOs, peddling junk
bonds, shuffling paper assets, gutting companies, creating nothing of
value—but scoring high on their MBOs.[3] It's the self-promoting go-
go biz whiz who runs the company into the ground and then brassily
bails out with a million-dollar "golden parachute."

Incompetence is the Peter Principle and the art of failing up-   17
ward. It's corporate facemen and hustlers and nice-guy managers
who avoid conflict, straight talk, and tough decisions. It's insecure

[3]Abbreviations for *master's of business administration, mergers and acquisitions, lever-
aged buy outs,* and *management by objectives.*

company despots who filter reality through obeisant yes men. It's myopic, risk-averse CEOs[4] who starve R&D[5] to fatten quarterly profits, and timid, passive boards of directors who rubber-stamp spectacular raises for top executives despite unspectacular, often paltry, accomplishment.

Incompetence is arrogant reporters who mangle the facts. It's 18 *New Yorker* journalists who fabricate quotes and invent scenes to portray a "higher truth." It's newspapers that are so "reader friendly" and "customer driven" they've become glorified TV guides encapsulated in puff and fluff, trivia and ephemera. It's video hype and glitz and "infotainment" and TV news actors who know more about grooming their hair than reporting a story.

Incompetence is unsafe automobiles that have to be recalled, 19 houses with warped floors and flimsy walls, particle-board furniture that's stapled together, and plastic components that break before the product's out of the box.

Incompetence is corporate and political leaders who, after a ca- 20 lamity, piously proclaim, "I take full responsibility"—and then don't. It's workers who say, "It's not my job"; "Why knock yourself out?"; "It's good enough"; "Nobody will see it"; "Just pack it and ship it." It's the *mañana* mentality and the urge, in the face of a difficult task, to whistle, along with Bobby McFerrin, "Don't Worry, Be Happy."

Incompetence is vanity and PR and people who talk about 21 "massaging" or "positioning" or "spin control." It's a society that celebrates style over substance, image over reality, credentials over experience; a society that embraces the credo of the Philadelphia sheriff John Green—"Fake it till you make it"; a society devoted to consuming and acquiring, to self-fulfillment and self-indulgence; a society infatuated with money, power, sex, and drugs; a narcissistic, solipsistic, materialistic society saturated with advertising, dominated by entertainment, and living only for the here and now....

Every day, I see...glaring evidence of America's decline. In fact, 22 I'm confronted with it nearly every time I try to run an errand or drive into the city. For there, blocking my way, is the Bowman Avenue Bridge, overgrown with weeds, still barricaded. It is more than just a pain in the neck. It is more than just a construction project that seems

---

[4]Abbreviation for *chief executive officers.*
[5]Abbreviation for *research and development.*

forever on hold. It is a monument to bureaucratic bungling, to paralysis through analysis, to an effete technocracy more skillful at meeting and dealing than making and doing. As such, the Bowman Avenue Bridge is also a warning sign: that we've lost our grit and resolve, that we've become sluggish and diffident in the face of problems and challenges, that we aren't working as hard as we must and the work we're producing is too often slipshod and unacceptable, that indeed our greatness is in jeopardy because we've become—far faster than many of us realize and would like to admit—the United States of Incompetence.

Questions for Close Reading

1. What is the selection's thesis? Locate the sentences in which Carey states his main idea. If he doesn't state the thesis explicitly, express it in your own words.
2. What, according to Carey, are the two types of incompetent people? Does one type predominate? Explain.
3. What examples does Carey provide of incompetence in education? In the business and the corporate worlds?
4. Reread paragraphs 16–17 and 20–21. How, according to Carey, does public relations contribute to incompetence?
5. Refer to your dictionary as needed to define the following words used in the selection: *derring-do* (paragraph 6), *fortitude* (7), *dispatch* (7), *malaise* (9), *acrimonious* (15), *obeisant* (17), *myopic* (17), *averse* (17), *fabricate* (18), *encapsulated* (18), *ephemera* (18), *narcissistic* (21), *solipsistic* (21), *effete* (22), *technocracy* (22), and *diffident* (22).

Questions About the Writer's Craft

1. **The pattern.** Although Carey presents one compelling example after another, there is an overall logic to the way he sequences these examples. Reread paragraphs 11–20. What is the focus, or organizing principle, of each paragraph?
2. **Other patterns.** Why might Carey have delayed offering a definition of incompetence until paragraph 9? How does moving beyond the "strict" definition of the word to a broader interpretation help Carey achieve his purpose?
3. Why do you suppose Carey opens and closes his piece with the example of the Bowman Avenue Bridge? In particular, why does he keep saying "there is nothing special about this bridge"? What effect do you think Carey wanted this repetition to have on his readers?
4. How would you describe Carey's tone? Consider the way his sentence length, use of questions, and word choice create this tone. How does this tone help Carey make his point?

Questions for Further Thought

1. Do you agree with Carey that our country has become "the United States of Incompetence"? What examples of incompetence have you encountered in your own daily life—on campus and off?
2. Carey cites examples of incompetence from every walk of life. Is there one area of life that you would single out as exemplifying incompetence? Explain.
3. How do you react when you encounter incompetence? Do you expect it? Do you accept it? Explain.
4. What might cause people to not "give a damn" about their work? What steps might employers take to elicit more positive attitudes?

Writing Assignments Using Exemplification as a Pattern of Development

∞ 1. According to Carey, incompetents come in two varieties: people who lack skill and people who have poor attitudes. Focus on *one* of these types, and write an essay providing numerous examples that show how widespread this brand of incompetence can be. To generate examples for your paper, consider your own experiences and those of classmates, friends, and family members. You might follow Carey's lead by using one particularly dramatic example in your opening and closing. No matter how you proceed, remember to organize your examples so they flow logically from the beginning to the end of the essay. You might want to read Janet Mendell Goldstein's "The Quick Fix Society" (page 324) and Alleen Pace Nilsen's "Sexism and Language" (page 229); both essays illustrate strategies for organizing essays that have plentiful examples.

∞ 2. Carey claims that our society has lost its "grit and resolve." Perhaps he is too pessimistic. Write an essay in which you take issue with Carey's point, drawing upon your own and other people's experiences to provide abundant examples. Begin by briefly summarizing Carey's idea in the introduction, and then provide vivid examples that encourage readers to see that we are not, as Carey claims, "sluggish and diffident in the face of problems and challenges." Like Carey, you might catalogue a series of relatively brief examples or, instead, offer a few extended illustrations. In either case, be sure to present your examples in a logical sequence. Geoffrey Cowley's "Why a Disaster Brings Out the Best in People" (page 478) should spark some thoughts about the more positive aspects of human nature.

Writing Assignments Using Other Patterns of Development

3. Carey says that the Bowman Avenue Bridge closure makes his blood boil. Write an essay about a situation that you find intensely annoying. Perhaps you're frustrated by the careless maintenance of a nearby park, by your

college's system for airing student grievances, or by children's easy access to the 900 telephone-toll line. Start with a vivid illustration of the problem, and then present a clear explanation of the steps that could be taken to correct or minimize the situation. Be sure to explain who would be responsible for each step. End your essay on an optimistic note, predicting improvement if your step-by-step process is followed.

4. Carey shows the dangers inherent in the "it's good enough" approach to life. But perfectionism—the obsessive need to be the best and do the best—can be equally unproductive. Write an essay about a time that your perfectionism or someone else's created a conflict that had unfortunate consequences. Provide vivid sensory details and revealing dialogue to make the tensions in the event come alive for readers. At the end, reach some conclusions about the value and the limits of perfectionism.

Alleen Pace Nilsen

A specialist in sexist language and children's literature, Alleen Pace Nilsen (1936–   ) teaches at Arizona State University. Nilsen's doctoral dissertation concerned linguistic sexism in books written for children. Coauthor of the text *Literature for Today's Young Adults* (1993), she has written several books on language, including *Language Play: An Introduction to Language* (1983) and *The Language of Humor/The Humor of Language* (1985). The following selection is from *Sexism and Language* (1977), a collection of essays published by the National Council of Teachers of English.

Sexism and Language

Is there anything wrong in calling a woman a "fox" or a "chick"? Why is it embarrassing for a man to perform a job labeled "women's work," while it's a compliment for a woman to do "a man's job"? Would you rather be a female named "Sam" or a male called "Carroll"? Your response to these questions most likely results from the attitudes you've acquired as a speaker of American English. In the following selection, Alleen Pace Nilsen will help you look more closely at the language you use, showing how seemingly innocent words and phrases reflect society's attitudes toward the roles—and worth—of men and women.[1]

Over the last hundred years, American anthropologists have   1
travelled to the corners of the earth to study primitive cultures. They either became linguists themselves or they took linguists with them to help in learning and analyzing languages. Even if the culture was one that no longer existed, they were interested in learning its language because besides being tools of communication, the vocabulary and structure of a language tell much about the values held by its speakers.

---

[1] *Note:* If you'd like some advice on ways to avoid sexist language in your writing, turn to the entry "gender-biased language" in the Glossary.

However, the culture need not be primitive, nor do the people   2
making observations need to be anthropologists and linguists. Anyone living in the United States who listens with a keen ear or reads
with a perceptive eye can come up with startling new insights about
the way American English reflects our values.

Animal Terms for People—Mirrors of the Double Standard

If we look at just one semantic area of English, that of animal   3
terms in relation to people, we can uncover some interesting insights
into how our culture views males and females. References to identical
animals can have negative connotations when related to a female, but
positive or neutral connotations when related to a male. For example, a *shrew* has come to mean "a scolding, nagging, evil-tempered
woman," while *shrewd* means "keen-witted, clever, or sharp in practical affairs; astute...businessman, etc." (*Webster's New World Dictionary of the American Language,* 1964).

A *lucky dog* or a *gay dog* may be a very interesting fellow, but   4
when a woman is a *dog,* she is unattractive, and when she's a *bitch*
she's the personification of whatever is undesirable in the mind of the
speaker. When a man is self-confident, he may be described as *cock-
sure* or even *cocky,* but in a woman this same self-confidence is likely
to result in her being called a *cocky bitch,* which is not only a mixed
metaphor, but also probably the most insulting animal metaphor we
have. *Bitch* has taken on such negative connotations—children are
taught it is a swear word—that in everyday American English, speakers are hesitant to call a female dog a *bitch.* Most of us feel that we
would be insulting the dog. When we want to insult a man by comparing him to a dog, we call him a *son of a bitch,* which quite literally
is an insult to his mother rather than to him.

If the female is called a *vixen* (a female fox), the dictionary says   5
this means she is "an ill-tempered, shrewish, or malicious woman."
The female seems both to attract and to hold on longer to animal
metaphors with negative connotations. A *vampire* was originally a
corpse that came alive to suck the blood of living persons. The word
acquired the general meaning of an unscrupulous person such as a
blackmailer and then, the specialized meaning of "a beautiful but unscrupulous woman who seduces men and leads them to their ruin."
From this latter meaning we get the word *vamp.* The popularity of

this term and of the name *vampire bat* may contribute to the idea that a female being is referred to in a phrase such as *the old bat.*

Other animal metaphors do not have definitely derogatory con-   6
notations for the female, but they do seem to indicate frivolity or un-importance, as in *social butterfly* and *flapper.* Look at the differences between the connotations of participating in a *hen party* and in a *bull session.* Male metaphors, even when they are negative in connotation, still relate to strength and conquest. Metaphors related to aggressive sex roles, for example, *buck, stag, wolf,* and *stud,* will undoubtedly remain attached to males. Perhaps one of the reasons that in the late sixties it was so shocking to hear policemen called *pigs* was that the connotations of *pig* are very different from the other animal metaphors we usually apply to males.

When I was living in Afghanistan, I was surprised at the cruelty   7
and unfairness of a proverb that said, "When you see an old man, sit down and take a lesson; when you see an old woman, throw a stone." In looking at Afghan folk literature, I found that young girls were pictured as delightful and enticing, middle-aged women were sometimes interesting but more often just tolerable, while old women were always grotesque and villainous. Probably the reason for the negative connotation of old age in women is that women are valued for their bodies while men are valued for their accomplishments and their wisdom. Bodies deteriorate with age but wisdom and accomplishments grow greater.

When we returned home from Afghanistan, I was shocked to   8
discover that we have remnants of this same attitude in America. We see it in our animal metaphors. If both the animal and the woman are young, the connotation is positive, but if the animal and the woman are old, the connotation is negative. Hugh Hefner might never have made it to the big time if he had called his girls *rabbits* instead of *bunnies.* He probably chose *bunny* because he wanted something close to, but not quite so obvious as *kitten* or *cat*—the all-time winners for connoting female sexuality. Also *bunny,* as in the skiers' *snow bunny,* already had some of the connotations Hefner wanted. Compare the connotations of *filly* to *old nag; bird* to *old crow* or *old bat;* and *lamb* to *crone* (apparently related to the early modern Dutch *kronje, old ewe* but now *withered old woman*).

Probably the most striking examples of the contrast between   9
young and old women are animal metaphors relating to cats and chickens. A young girl is encouraged to be *kittenish,* but not *catty.*

And though most of us wouldn't mind living next door to a *sex kitten,* we wouldn't want to live next door to a *cat house.* Parents might name their daughter *Kitty* but not *Puss* or *Pussy,* which used to be a fairly common nickname for girls. It has now developed such sexual connotations that it is used mostly for humor, as in the James Bond movie featuring Pussy Galore and her flying felines.

In the chicken metaphors, a young girl is a *chick.* When she gets old enough she marries and soon begins feeling *cooped up.* To relieve the boredom she goes to *hen parties* and *cackles* with her friends. Eventually she has her *brood,* begins to *henpeck* her husband, and finally turns into an *old biddy.* 10

How English Glorifies Maleness

Throughout the ages physical strength has been very important, and because men are physically stronger than women, they have been valued more. Only now in the machine age, when the difference in strength between males and females pales into insignificance in comparison to the strength of earth-moving machinery, airplanes, and guns, males no longer have such an inherent advantage. Today a man of intellect is more valued than a physical laborer, and since women can compete intellectually with men, their value is on the rise. But language lags far behind cultural changes, so the language still reflects this emphasis on the importance of being male. For example, when we want to compliment a male, all we need to do is stress the fact that he is male by saying he is a *he-man,* or he is *manly,* or he is *virile.* Both *virile* and *virtuous* come from the Latin *vir,* meaning *man.* 11

The command or encouragement that males receive in sentences like "Be a man!" implies that *to be a man* is to be honorable, strong, righteous, and whatever else the speaker thinks desirable. But in contrast to this, a girl is never told to be a *woman.* And when she is told to be a *lady,* she is simply being encouraged to "act feminine," which means sitting with her knees together, walking gracefully, and talking softly. 12

The armed forces, particularly the Marines, use the positive masculine connotation as part of their recruitment psychology. They promote the idea that to join the Marines (or the Army, Navy, or Air Force) guarantees that you will become a man. But this brings up a problem, because much of the work that is necessary to keep a large 13 organization running is what is traditionally thought of as *women's work*. Now, how can the Marines ask someone who has signed up for a *man-sized job* to do *women's work?* Since they can't, they euphemize and give the jobs titles that either are more prestigious or, at least, don't make people think of females. Waitresses are called *orderlies,* secretaries are called *clerk-typists,* nurses are called *medics,* assistants are called *adjutants,* and cleaning up an area is called *policing* the area. The same kind of word glorification is used in civilian life to bolster a man's ego when he is doing such tasks as cooking and sewing. For example, a *chef* has higher prestige than a *cook* and a *tailor* has higher prestige than a *seamstress.*

Little girls learn early in life that the boy's role is one to be envied and emulated. Child psychologists have pointed out that experimenting with the role of the opposite sex is much more acceptable for little girls than it is for little boys. For example, girls are free to dress in boys' clothes, but certainly not the other way around. Most parents are amused if they have a daughter who is a *tomboy,* but they are genuinely distressed if they have a son who is a *sissy.* The names we give to young children reflect this same attitude. It is all right for girls to have boys' names, but pity the boy who has a girl's name! Because parents keep giving boys' names to girls, the number of acceptable boys' names keeps shrinking. Currently popular names for girls include *Jo, Kelly, Teri, Chris, Pat, Shawn, Toni,* and *Sam* (short for *Samantha*). *Evelyn, Carroll, Gayle, Hazel, Lynn, Beverley, Marion, Francis,* and *Shirley* once were acceptable names for males. But as they were given to females, they became less and less acceptable. Today, men who are stuck with them self-consciously go by their initials or by abbreviated forms such as *Haze, Shirl, Frank,* or *Ev.* And they seldom pass these names on to their sons.

Many common words have come into the language from people's names. These lexical items again show the importance of maleness compared to the triviality of the feminine activities being described. Words derived from the names of women include *Melba toast,* named for the Australian singer Dame Nellie Melba; *Sally Lunn cakes,* named after an eighteenth-century woman who first made them; *pompadour,* a hair style named after Madame Pompadour; and the word *maudlin,* as in *maudlin sentiment,* from Mary Magdalene, who was often portrayed by artists as displaying exaggerated sorrow.

There are trivial items named after men—*teddy bear* after The-   16
odore Roosevelt and *sideburns* after General Burnside—but most
words that come from men's names relate to significant inventions
or developments. These include *pasteurization* after Louis Pasteur,
sousaphone after John Philip Sousa, *mason jar* after John L. Mason,
boysenberry after Rudolph Boysen, *pullman car* after George M. Pullman, *braille* after Louis Braille, *franklin stove* after Benjamin Franklin, *diesel engine* after Rudolf Diesel, *ferris wheel* after George W. G.
Ferris, and the verb *to lynch* after William Lynch, who was a vigilante
captain in Virginia in 1780.

The latter is an example of a whole set of English words dealing   17
with violence. These words have strongly negative connotations.
From research using free association and semantic differentials, with
university students as subjects, James Ney concluded that English reflects both an anti-male and an anti-female bias because these biases
exist in the culture (*Etc.: A Review of General Semantics,* March
1976, pp. 67–76). The students consistently marked as masculine
such words as *killer, murderer, robber, attacker, fighter, stabber, rapist, assassin, gang, hood, arsonist, criminal, hijacker, villain,* and *bully,*
even though most of these words contain nothing to specify that
they are masculine. An example of bias against males, Ney observed,
is the absence in English of a pejorative term for women equivalent
to *rapist.* Outcomes of his free association test indicated that if "English speakers want to call a man something bad, there seems to be a
large vocabulary available to them but if they want to use a term
which is good to describe a male, there is a small vocabulary available.
The reverse is true for women."

Certainly we do not always think positively about males; witness   18
such words as *jerk, creep, crumb, slob, fink,* and *jackass.* But much of
what determines our positive and negative feelings relates to the roles
people play. We have very negative feelings toward someone who is
hurting us or threatening us or in some way making our lives miserable. To be able to do this, the person has to have power over us and
this power usually belongs to males.

On the other hand, when someone helps us or makes our life   19
more pleasant, we have positive feelings toward that person or that
role. *Mother* is one of the positive female terms in English, and we see
such extensions of it as *Mother Nature, Mother Earth, mother lode,
mother superior,* etc. But even though a word like *mother* is positive,
it is still not a word of power. In the minds of English speakers being

female and being powerless or passive are so closely related that we use the terms *feminine* and *lady* either to mean female or to describe a certain kind of quiet and unobtrusive behavior.

Words Labelling Women as Things

Because of our expectations of passivity, we like to compare females to items that people acquire for their pleasure. For example, in a...commercial for the television show "Happy Days," one of the characters announced that in the coming season they were going to have not only "cars, motorcycles, and girls," but also a band. Another example of this kind of thinking is the comparison of females to food since food is something we all enjoy, even though it is extremely passive. We describe females as such delectable morsels as a *dish*, a *cookie*, a *tart, cheesecake, sugar and spice*, a *cute tomato, honey*, a *sharp cookie*, and *sweetie pie*. We say a particular girl has a *peaches and cream complexion* or "she looks good enough to eat." And parents give their daughters such names as *Candy* and *Cherry*.

Other pleasurable items that we compare females to are toys. Young girls are called *little dolls* or *China dolls*, while older girls—if they are attractive—are simply called *dolls*. We might say about a woman, "She's pretty as a picture," or "She's a fashion plate." And we might compare a girl to a plant by saying she is a *clinging vine*, a *shrinking violet*, or a *wallflower*. And we might name our daughters after plants such as *Rose, Lily, Ivy, Daisy, Iris*, and *Petunia*. Compare these names to boys' names such as *Martin* which means warlike, *Ernest* which means resolute fighter, *Nicholas* which means victory, *Val* which means strong or valiant, and *Leo* which means lion. We would be very hesitant to give a boy the name of something as passive as a flower although we might say about a man that he is a *late-bloomer*. This is making a comparison between a man and the most active thing a plant can do, which is to bloom. The only other familiar plant metaphor used for a man is the insulting *pansy*, implying that he is like a woman.

Questions for Close Reading

1. What is the selection's thesis? Locate the sentence(s) in which Nilsen states her main idea. If she doesn't state the thesis explicitly, express it in your own words.

2. According to Nilsen, what do animal metaphors usually imply when used to describe women? What do male animal metaphors imply?

3. Why, according to Nilsen, do some professions have different names depending on whether the job is performed by a male or female? What is suggested by the existence of two different terms for the same occupation?

4. When positive terms are used for women, what personality characteristics do such terms suggest? Why are words connoting violence most often applied to men?

5. Refer to your dictionary as needed to define the following words used in the selection: *unscrupulous* (paragraph 5), *enticing* (7), *connotation* (8), *virile* (11), *lexical* (15), *maudlin* (15), and *vigilante* (16).

Questions About the Writer's Craft

1. **The pattern.** Why does Nilsen use so many examples to illustrate each type of sexism in the English language? What point of view is she trying to anticipate and counteract?

2. What three main sexist motifs in English does Nilsen examine? How does she signal her movement from one to the next?

3. Why do you think Nilsen begins by discussing animal terms for humans? What effect does placing this section first have on the reader?

4. What is Nilsen's tone? What terms and expressions reveal her personal viewpoint on sexism in our language?

Questions for Further Thought

1. Do you think most users of English are aware of the sexism in many everyday expressions? Were you surprised by any of Nilsen's examples? Why or why not?

2. Nilsen writes that "American English reflects our values." Do you agree that phrases like "man-sized jobs," "women's work," and "old biddy" indicate that Americans are sexist? Should we guard against gender-biased terms, or is such watchfulness being overly sensitive?

3. The names for many professions and occupations are gender-identified: Consider, for example, *policeman, chairman, actor/actress, foreman,* and *journeyman.* Should these terms be changed to gender-neutral ones, such as *police officer, chairperson, actor, supervisor,* and so on? Do gender-identified terms affect our thinking about people's worth? Do they influence the decisions young people make about their futures? Explain.

4. Can our language ever be made completely nonsexist? Should it be? Why or why not?

Writing Assignments Using Exemplification as a Pattern of Development

∞ 1. Nilsen claims that our language glorifies maleness and denigrates female-ness. Are there other areas of our lives where typical male behavior and attitudes are valued more than typical female roles or characteristics? Consider such areas as dating, marriage, sports, clothing, and occupa-tions. Focusing on a single area, write an essay showing that our culture glorifies one sex over the other. Try to include in your paper points made in one of the following essays: Barbara Ehrenreich's "What I've Learned From Men" (page 261), Deborah Tannen's "Sex, Lies, and Conversa-tion" (page 428), Judy Brady's "Why I Want a Wife" (page 530), or Vir-ginia Woolf's "Professions for Women" (page 695).

∞ 2. The English language embodies many prejudices besides sexism. Many words and expressions, for example, reflect prejudice against skin color, old age, youth, left-handedness, shortness, fatness, and so on. Focusing on one such area, write an essay using specific examples of prejudicial lan-guage to show how the words we use reflect our stereotypes and biases. Gloria Naylor's "Mommy, What Does 'Nigger' Mean?" (page 535) and William Raspberry's "The Handicap of Definition" (page 548) will develop further your understanding of the way language influences attitudes.

Writing Assignments Using Other Patterns of Development

∞ 3. Would your life have been different if you had been born the opposite sex? Would you have been treated differently by your parents, teachers, and friends? Are there any specific experiences or events that would have turned out differently had you been a different sex? Write an essay per-suading readers that your life would have been essentially the same *or* very different had you been born exactly as you were except for your sex. Scott Russell Sanders's "The Men We Carry in Our Minds" (page 308) and Virginia Woolf's "Professions for Women" (page 695) should spark some interesting ideas worth exploring in your paper.

∞ 4. Gender-based stereotyping exists in many areas of our culture besides language. Imagine you're a visitor to the United States and know noth-ing about the culture—perhaps you're a visitor from Mars. You observe people, watch television for a week, and study several issues of a popular general interest magazine, like *People, Time,* or *Newsweek.* Then you send a report to your home about the differences between males and females in the United States. Providing numerous examples to explain the dissim-ilarities, cover one or two of the following in your analysis: occupations, recreational activities, friendships, and so forth. Barbara Ehrenreich's "What I've Learned From Men" (page 261), Scott Russell Sanders's "The Men We Carry in Our Minds" (page 308), Deborah Tannen's "Sex, Lies, and Conversation" (page 428), and Judy Brady's "Why I Want a Wife" (page 530) highlight some issues to consider.

James Thurber

American humorist James Thurber (1894–1961) is perhaps best known as the author of "The Secret Life of Walter Mitty." Thurber often wrote about people's longings, using his skill as a satirist to portray the humor and poignancy of the human condition. He was able to give his wit—which often bordered on the acerbic—full play during his long career at the *New Yorker,* where he wrote satiric essays and drew cartoons. He also wrote several humorous books, including *Is Sex Necessary?* (1929), which he coauthored with E. B. White; *Fables for Our Time* (1940); *My World and Welcome to It* (1942); and *Thurber Country* (1953). The following selection first appeared in *My Life and Hard Times* (1933).

University Days

College and university catalogs depict higher education as one of life's loftier experiences, with confident undergrads strolling eagerly toward ivy-covered lecture halls. But in this hilarious essay, James Thurber takes the pomp and circumstance out of higher education. He reveals the bumbling, the incompetence, and the embarrassment that frequently beset him and his fellow students at Ohio State University. He shows professors with gritted teeth trying to educate the ineducable and coach the uncoachable. Even back in the early days of the twentieth century, college life was far from the idealized image depicted in the catalogs.

I passed all the other courses that I took at my university, but I 1
could never pass botany. This was because all botany students had to spend several hours a week in a laboratory looking through a microscope at plant cells, and I could never see through a microscope. I never once saw a cell through a microscope. This used to enrage my instructor. He would wander around the laboratory pleased with the progress all the students were making in drawing the involved and, so I am told, interesting structure of flower cells, until he came to

me. I would just be standing there. "I can't see anything," I would say. He would begin patiently enough, explaining how anybody can see through a microscope, but he would always end up in a fury, claiming that I could *too* see through a microscope but just pretended that I couldn't. "It takes away from the beauty of flowers anyway," I used to tell him. "We are not concerned with beauty in this course," he would say. "We are concerned solely with what I may call the *mechanics* of flars." "Well," I'd say, "I can't see anything." "Try it just once again," he'd say, and I would put my eye to the microscope and see nothing at all, except now and again a nebulous milky substance—a phenomenon of maladjustment. You were supposed to see a vivid, restless clockwork of sharply defined plant cells. "I see what looks like a lot of milk," I would tell him. This, he claimed, was the result of my not having adjusted the microscope properly, so he would readjust it for me, or rather, for himself. And I would look again and see milk.

I finally took a deferred pass, as they called it, and waited a year   2
and tried again. (You had to pass one of the biological sciences or you couldn't graduate.) The professor had come back from vacation brown as a berry, bright-eyed, and eager to explain cell-structure again to his classes. "Well," he said to me, cheerily, when we met in the first laboratory hour of the semester, "we're going to see cells this time, aren't we?" "Yes, sir," I said. Students to right of me and to left of me and in front of me were seeing cells; what's more, they were quietly drawing pictures of them in their notebooks. Of course, I didn't see anything.

"We'll try it," the professor said to me, grimly, "with every ad-   3
justment of the microscope known to man. As God is my witness, I'll arrange this glass so that you see cells through it or I'll give up teaching. In twenty-two years of botany, I—" He cut off abruptly for he was beginning to quiver all over, like Lionel Barrymore, and he genuinely wished to hold onto his temper; his scenes with me had taken a great deal out of him.

So we tried it with every adjustment of the microscope known   4
to man. With only one of them did I see anything but blackness or the familiar lacteal opacity, and that time I saw, to my pleasure and amazement, a variegated constellation of flecks, specks, and dots. These I hastily drew. The instructor, noting my activity, came back from an adjoining desk, a smile on his lips and his eyebrows high in hope. He looked at my cell drawing. "What's that?" he demanded,

with a hint of a squeal in his voice. "That's what I saw," I said. "You didn't, you didn't, you *didn't!*" he screamed, losing control of his temper instantly, and he bent over and squinted into the microscope. His head snapped up. "That's your eye!" he shouted. "You've fixed the lens so that it reflects! You've drawn your eye!"

Another course that I didn't like, but somehow managed to 5 pass, was economics. I went to that class straight from the botany class, which didn't help me any in understanding either subject. I used to get them mixed up. But not as mixed up as another student in my economics class who came there direct from a physics laboratory. He was a tackle on the football team, named Bolenciecwcz. At that time Ohio State University had one of the best football teams in the country, and Bolenciecwcz was one of its outstanding stars. In order to be eligible to play it was necessary for him to keep up in his studies, a very difficult matter, for while he was not dumber than an ox he was not any smarter. Most of his professors were lenient and helped him along. None gave him more hints in answering questions or asked him simpler ones than the economics professor, a thin, timid man named Bassum. One day when we were on the subject of transportation and distribution, it came Bolenciecwcz's turn to answer a question. "Name one means of transportation," the professor said to him. No light came into the big tackle's eyes. "Just any means of transportation," said the professor. Bolenciecwcz sat staring at him. "That is," pursued the professor, "any medium, agency, or method of going from one place to another." Bolenciecwcz had the look of a man who is being led into a trap. "You may choose among steam, horse-drawn, or electrically propelled vehicles," said the instructor. "I might suggest the one which we commonly take in making long journeys across land." There was a profound silence in which everybody stirred uneasily, including Bolenciecwcz and Mr. Bassum. Mr. Bassum abruptly broke this silence in an amazing manner. "Choo-choo-choo," he said, in a low voice, and turned instantly scarlet. He glanced appealingly around the room. All of us, of course, shared Mr. Bassum's desire that Bolenciecwcz should stay abreast of the class in economics, for the Illinois game, one of the hardest and most important of the season, was only a week off. "Toot, toot, too-toooooooot!" some student with a deep voice moaned, and we all looked encouragingly at Bolenciecwcz. Somebody else gave a fine imitation of a locomotive letting off steam. Mr. Bassum himself rounded off the little show. "Ding, dong, ding, dong," he said, hopefully. Bolenciecwcz was staring at the floor now, trying to think, his great brow furrowed, his huge hands rubbing together, his face red.

"How did you come to college this year, Mr. Bolenciecwcz?" 6
asked the professor. "*Chuffa* chuffa, *chuffa* chuffa."

"M'father sent me," said the football player. 7

"What on?" asked Bassum. 8

"I git an 'lowance," said the tackle, in a low, husky voice, obvi- 9
ously embarrassed.

"No, no," said Bassum. "Name a means of transportation. What 10
did you *ride* here on?"

"Train," said Bolenciecwcz. 11

"Quite right," said the professor. "Now, Mr. Nugent, will you 12
tell us—"

If I went through anguish in botany and economics—for differ- 13
ent reasons—gymnasium work was even worse. I don't even like to
think about it. They wouldn't let you play games or join in the exercises with your glasses on and I couldn't see with mine off. I bumped
into professors, horizontal bars, agricultural students, and swinging
iron rings. Not being able to see, I could take it but I couldn't dish
it out. Also, in order to pass gymnasium (and you had to pass it to
graduate) you had to learn to swim if you didn't know how. I didn't
like the swimming pool, I didn't like swimming, and I didn't like the
swimming instructor, and after all these years I still don't. I never
swam but I passed my gym work anyway, by having another student
give my gymnasium number (978) and swim across the pool in my
place. He was a quiet, amiable blond youth, number 473, and he
would have seen through a microscope for me if we could have got
away with it, but we couldn't get away with it. Another thing I didn't
like about gymnasium work was that they made you strip the day you
registered. It is impossible for me to be happy when I am stripped
and being asked a lot of questions. Still, I did better than a lanky agricultural student who was cross-examined just before I was. They
asked each student what college he was in—that is, whether Arts, Engineering, Commerce, or Agriculture. "What college are you in?"
the instructor snapped at the youth in front of me. "Ohio State University," he said promptly.

It wasn't that agricultural student but it was another a whole lot 14
like him who decided to take up journalism, possibly on the ground
that when farming went to hell he could fall back on newspaper

work. He didn't realize, of course, that that would be very much like falling back full-length on a kit of carpenter's tools. Haskins didn't seem cut out for journalism, being too embarrassed to talk to anybody and unable to use a typewriter, but the editor of the college paper assigned him to the cow barns, the sheep house, the horse pavilion, and the animal husbandry department generally. This was a genuinely big "beat," for it took up five times as much ground and got ten times as great a legislative appropriation as the College of Liberal Arts. The agricultural student knew animals, but nevertheless his stories were dull and colorlessly written. He took all afternoon on each of them, on account of having to hunt for each letter on the typewriter. Once in a while he had to ask somebody to help him hunt. "C" and "L," in particular, were hard letters for him to find. His editor finally got pretty much annoyed at the farmer-journalist because his pieces were so uninteresting. "See here, Haskins," he snapped at him one day, "why is it we never have anything hot from you on the horse pavilion? Here we have two hundred head of horses on this campus—more than any other university in the Western Conference except Purdue—and yet you never get any real lowdown on them. Now shoot over to the horse barns and dig up something lively." Haskins shambled out and came back in about an hour; he said he had something. "Well, start it off snappily," said the editor. "Something people will read." Haskins set to work and in a couple of hours brought a sheet of typewritten paper to the desk; it was a two-hundred-word story about some disease that had broken out among the horses. Its opening sentence was simple but arresting. It read: "Who has noticed the sores on the tops of the horses in the animal husbandry building?"

Ohio State was a land grant university and therefore two years [15] of military drill was compulsory. We drilled with old Springfield rifles and studied the tactics of the Civil War even though the World War was going on at the time. At 11 o'clock each morning thousands of freshmen and sophomores used to deploy over the campus, moodily creeping up on the old chemistry building. It was good training for the kind of warfare that was waged at Shiloh but it had no connection with what was going on in Europe. Some people used to think there was German money behind it, but they didn't dare say so or they would have been thrown in jail as German spies. It was a period of muddy thought and marked, I believe, the decline of higher education in the Middle West.

As a soldier I was never any good at all. Most of the cadets were   16
glumly indifferent soldiers, but I was no good at all. Once General
Littlefield, who was commandant of the cadet corps, popped up in
front of me during regimental drill and snapped, "You are the main
trouble with this university!" I think he meant that my type was the
main trouble with the university but he may have meant me individ-
ually. I was mediocre at drill, certainly—that is, until my senior year.
By that time I had drilled longer than anybody else in the Western
Conference, having failed at military at the end of each preceding
year so that I had to do it all over again. I was the only senior still in
uniform. The uniform which, when new, had made me look like an
interurban railway conductor, now that it had become faded and too
tight made me look like Bert Williams in his bellboy act. This had a
definitely bad effect on my morale. Even so, I had become by sheer
practice little short of wonderful at squad maneuvers.

One day General Littlefield picked our company out of the   17
whole regiment and tried to get it mixed up by putting it through
one movement after another as fast as we could execute them: squads
right, squads left, squads on right into line, squads right about,
squads left front into line, etc. In about three minutes one hundred
and nine men were marching in one direction and I was marching
away from them at an angle of forty degrees, all alone. "Company,
halt!" shouted General Littlefield. "That man is the only man who
has it right!" I was made a corporal for my achievement.

The next day General Littlefield summoned me to his office. He   18
was swatting flies when I went in. I was silent and he was silent too,
for a long time. I don't think he remembered me or why he had sent
for me, but he didn't want to admit it. He swatted some more flies,
keeping his eyes on them narrowly before he let go with the swatter.
"Button up your coat!" he snapped. Looking back on it now I can
see that he meant me although he was looking at a fly, but I just
stood there. Another fly came to rest on a paper in front of the general and began rubbing its hind legs together. The general lifted the
swatter cautiously. I moved restlessly and the fly flew away. "You
startled him!" barked General Littlefield, looking at me severely. I
said I was sorry. "That won't help the situation!" snapped the
General, with cold military logic. I didn't see what I could do except
offer to chase some more flies toward his desk, but I didn't say anything. He stared out the window at the faraway figures of co-eds

crossing the campus toward the library. Finally, he told me I could go. So I went. He either didn't know which cadet I was or else he forgot what he wanted to see me about. It may have been that he wished to apologize for having called me the main trouble with the university; or maybe he had decided to compliment me on my brilliant drilling of the day before and then at the last minute decided not to. I don't know. I don't think about it much any more.

Questions for Close Reading

1. What is the selection's thesis? Locate the sentence(s) in which Thurber states his main idea. If he doesn't state the thesis explicitly, express it in your own words.
2. In his writings and cartoons, Thurber reveals a distaste for authority. Find evidence of such an attitude in this selection.
3. Thurber passes gym class by having another student assume his identification number. What does this fact indicate about his gym class in particular and about his university in general?
4. Thurber sets up a comparison between himself and the fly in General Littlefield's office. How is this comparison related to Thurber's thesis?
5. Refer to your dictionary as needed to define the following words used in the selection: *nebulous* (paragraph 1), *lacteal* (4), *opacity* (4), *variegated* (4), *husbandry* (14), and *appropriation* (14).

Questions About the Writer's Craft

1. **The pattern.**   Thurber develops his piece through a series of examples, each in the form of a brief anecdote. Which two anecdotes does Thurber develop in most detail? What might have been his reason for proceeding in this way?
2. *Satire* uses humor to criticize a situation and create awareness of the need for change. One satiric technique is *caricature:* an oversimplified description in which one quality of an individual is exaggerated, resulting in a distorted stereotype. Where in "University Days" does Thurber employ caricature? What is he satirizing?
3. Thurber often uses dialogue rather than commentary to convey humor. Find several places in the essay where dialogue is especially effective in enhancing the essay's humor.
4. The inability to see is a recurrent theme in Thurber's essay. Locate instances of such difficulty. What might this inability symbolize?

Questions for Further Thought

1. Thurber shows an entire class struggling to help a slow-witted athlete. Do you think colleges and universities should make special concessions to athletes who may not be doing well academically? Why or why not?
2. Did Thurber act dishonorably in having another student pass his swimming test for him? Do you view this as cheating or as a way of getting around an unreasonable school requirement?
3. Thurber shows teachers having difficulty explaining concepts to students. Who is at fault when learning grinds to a halt? Teachers? Students? Both? What should teachers and students realistically expect from each other?
4. With great wit, Thurber looks under the surface to disclose some of the inadequacies of the education he received at Ohio State University. What shortcomings do you perceive with the education you received in the past? What were its merits?

Writing Assignments Using Exemplification as a Pattern of Development

∞ 1. Read William Zinsser's "College Pressures" (page 297). Zinsser sees college students as overly ambitious, driven to achieve credentials that will lead to financial success. But Thurber shows students too dull or apathetic to make much effort to move in any direction. Which view of students is more accurate? Using concrete examples of students you know or have observed, write an essay developing the point that college students are either too competitive or too lackadaisical. Save for last your most convincing example.
2. With great relish, Thurber illustrates ineptitude, showing people unable to master even the simplest of tasks. Write an essay illustrating excellence. Give several vivid examples of skill, even virtuosity, by depicting individuals engaged in tasks they have fully mastered. You might recall a rock musician you heard in concert, an Olympic gymnast you saw on television, a mechanic you watched repair a car. The people cited, though at first glance possibly quite dissimilar, should share one common trait: their basic excellence.

Writing Assignments Using Other Patterns of Development

3. Thurber and his instructors have different views about what's important. Write an essay recounting one or more occasions when your sense of what was important clashed with someone else's. How was the disagreement resolved? You might want to conclude with some generalization about the type of individual with whom you tend to come into conflict.
4. Thurber's instructors show varying degrees of patience, empathy, and success in dealing with their recalcitrant students. In a serious or playful

essay, contrast a teacher you consider excellent with one you consider inferior. Address the same aspects of each teacher's style—for example, patience, command of subject matter, ability to create and maintain interest. No matter which tone you select, the essay should make clear those traits you consider most essential to excellent teaching.

Neil Postman

Born in Brooklyn in 1931, Neil Postman became known as a lead-ing advocate of educational reform with the publication of the books *Teaching as a Subversive Activity* (1969) and *The Soft Rev-olution* (1971), both coauthored with Charles Weingartner. Post-man continues to write extensively about education, publishing articles in major periodicals such as the *Atlantic* and the *Nation*. He has also written and lectured widely on the effect of mass me-dia on American culture and politics. Postman's more recent books include *The Disappearance of Childhood* (1982) and *Amus-ing Ourselves to Death: Public Discourse in the Age of Show Business* (1985). A professor of media ecology at New York University, Postman numbers among the teaching and writing awards he has received the George Orwell Award for Clarity in Language. "Fu-ture Shlock" is taken from Postman's 1988 book *Conscientious Objections: Stirring Up Trouble About Language, Technology, and Education.*

Future Shlock[1]

Politicians conduct their campaigns in thirty-second "sound bites"; television commentaries on political upheavals abroad are punctuated by jingles for fast-food restaurants; televangelists, us-ing the talk-show format, gaze soulfully into the camera and pre-tend to wrestle with weighty moral issues. We are becoming a trivial people, says Neil Postman, unwilling to think about com-plex subject matter unless it's packaged as entertainment.

Human intelligence is among the most fragile things in nature.   1
It doesn't take much to distract it, suppress it, or even annihilate it.
In this century, we have had some lethal examples of how easily and
quickly intelligence can be defeated by any one of its several nemeses:
ignorance, superstition, moral fervor, cruelty, cowardice, neglect. In
the late 1920s, for example, Germany was, by any measure, the most

---

[1]Postman's title is a twist on Alvin Toffler's *Future Shock,* the 1970 best-seller detail-ing the adverse effects of rapid change on American society.

literate, cultured nation in the world. Its legendary seats of learning attracted scholars from every corner. Its philosophers, social critics, and scientists were of the first rank; its humane traditions an inspiration to less favored nations. But by the mid-1930s—that is, in less than ten years—this cathedral of human reason had been transformed into a cesspool of barbaric irrationality. Many of the most intelligent products of German culture were forced to flee—for example, Einstein, Freud, Karl Jaspers, Thomas Mann, and Stefan Zweig. Even worse, those who remained were either forced to submit their minds to the sovereignty of primitive superstition, or—worse still—willingly did so: Konrad Lorenz, Werner Heisenberg, Martin Heidegger, Gerhardt Hauptmann. On May 10, 1933, a huge bonfire was kindled in Berlin and the books of Marcel Proust, André Gide, Emile Zola, Jack London, Upton Sinclair, and a hundred others were committed to the flames, amid shouts of idiot delight. By 1936, Joseph Paul Goebbels, Germany's Minister of Propaganda, was issuing a proclamation which began with the following words: "Because this year has not brought an improvement in art criticism, I forbid once and for all the continuance of art criticism in its past form, effective as of today." By 1936, there was no one left in Germany who had the brains or courage to object.

Exactly why the Germans banished intelligence is a vast and largely unanswered question. I have never been persuaded that the desperate economic depression that afflicted Germany in the 1920s adequately explains what happened. To quote Aristotle: Men do not become tyrants in order to keep warm. Neither do they become stupid—at least not *that* stupid. But the matter need not trouble us here. I offer the German case only as the most striking example of the fragility of human intelligence. My focus here is the United States in our own time, and I wish to worry you about the rapid erosion of our own intelligence. If you are confident that such a thing cannot happen, your confidence is misplaced, I believe, but it is understandable. 2

After all, the United States is one of the few countries in the world founded by intellectuals—men of wide learning, of extraordinary rhetorical powers, of deep faith in reason. And although we have had our moods of anti-intellectualism, few people have been more generous in support of intelligence and learning than Americans. It was the United States that initiated the experiment in mass education that is, even today, the envy of the world. It was America's churches that laid the foundation of our admirable system of higher education; 3

it was the Land-Grant Act of 1862 that made possible our great state universities; and it is to America that scholars and writers have fled when freedom of the intellect became impossible in their own nations. This is why the great historian of American civilization Henry Steele Commager called America "the Empire of Reason." But Commager was referring to the United States of the eighteenth and nineteenth centuries. What term he would use for America today, I cannot say. Yet he has observed, as others have, a change, a precipitous decline in our valuation of intelligence, in our uses of language, in the disciplines of logic and reason, in our capacity to attend to complexity. Perhaps he would agree with me that the Empire of Reason is, in fact, gone, and that the most apt term for America today is the Empire of Shlock.

In any case, this is what I wish to call to your notice: the fright- 4 ening displacement of serious, intelligent public discourse in American culture by the imagery and triviality of what may be called show business. I do not see the decline of intelligent discourse in America leading to the barbarisms that flourished in Germany, of course. No scholars, I believe, will ever need to flee America. There will be no bonfires to burn books. And I cannot imagine any proclamations forbidding once and for all art criticism, or any other kind of criticism. But this is not a cause for complacency, let alone celebration. A culture does not have to force scholars to flee to render them impotent. A culture does not have to burn books to assure that they will not be read. And a culture does not need a Minister of Propaganda issuing proclamations to silence criticism. There are other ways to achieve stupidity, and it appears that, as in so many other things, there is a distinctly American way.

To explain what I am getting at, I find it helpful to refer to two 5 films, which taken together embody the main lines of my argument. The first film is of recent vintage and is called *The Gods Must Be Crazy*. It is about a tribal people who live in the Kalahari Desert plains of southern Africa, and what happens to their culture when it is invaded by an empty Coca-Cola bottle tossed from the window of a small plane passing overhead. The bottle lands in the middle of the village and is construed by these gentle people to be a gift from the gods, for they not only have never seen a bottle before but have never seen glass either. The people are almost immediately charmed by the gift, and not only because of its novelty. The bottle, it turns out, has multiple uses, chief among them the intriguing music it makes when one blows into it.

But gradually a change takes place in the tribe. The bottle be- 6 comes an irresistible preoccupation. Looking at it, holding it, thinking of things to do with it displace other activities once thought essential. But more than this, the Coke bottle is the only thing these people have ever seen of which there is only one of its kind. And so those who do not have it try to get it from the one who does. And the one who does refuses to give it up. Jealousy, greed, and even violence enter the scene, and come very close to destroying the harmony that has characterized their culture for a thousand years. The people begin to love their bottle more than they love themselves, and are saved only when the leader of the tribe, convinced that the gods must be crazy, returns the bottle to the gods by throwing it off the top of a mountain.

The film is great fun and it is also wise, mainly because it is about 7 a subject as relevant to people in Chicago or Los Angeles or New York as it is to those of the Kalahari Desert. It raises two questions of extreme importance to our situation: How does a culture change when new technologies are introduced to it? And is it always desirable for a culture to accommodate itself to the demands of new technologies? The leader of the Kalahari tribe is forced to confront these questions in a way that Americans have refused to do. And because his vision is not obstructed by a belief in what Americans call "technological progress," he is able with minimal discomfort to decide that the songs of the Coke bottle are not so alluring that they are worth admitting envy, egotism, and greed to a serene culture.

The second film relevant to my argument was made in 1967. It 8 is Mel Brooks's first film, *The Producers. The Producers* is a rather raucous comedy that has at its center a painful joke: An unscrupulous theatrical producer has figured out that it is relatively easy to turn a buck by producing a play that fails. All one has to do is induce dozens of backers to invest in the play by promising them exorbitant percentages of its profits. When the play fails, there being no profits to disperse, the producer walks away with thousands of dollars that can never be claimed. Of course, the central problem he must solve is to make sure that his play is a disastrous failure. And so he hits upon an excellent idea: he will take the most tragic and grotesque story of our century—the rise of Adolf Hitler—and make it into a musical.

Because the producer is only a crook and not a fool, he assumes   9
that the stupidity of making a musical on this theme will be immediately grasped by audiences and that they will leave the theater in
dumbfounded rage. So he calls his play *Springtime for Hitler,* which
is also the name of its most important song. The song begins with
the words:

> *Springtime for Hitler and Germany;*
> *Winter for Poland and France.*

The melody is catchy, and when the song is sung it is accompa-   10
nied by a happy chorus line. (One must understand, of course, that
Springtime for Hitler is no spoof of Hitler, as was, for example, Char-
lie Chaplin's *The Great Dictator.* The play is instead a kind of denial
of Hitler in song and dance; as if to say, it was all in fun.)

The ending of the movie is predictable. The audience loves the   11
play and leaves the theater humming *Springtime for Hitler.* The musical becomes a great hit. The producer ends up in jail, his joke having turned back on him. But Brooks's point is that the joke is on us.
Although the film was made years before a movie actor became President of the United States, Brooks was making a kind of prophecy
about that—namely, that the producers of American culture will increasingly turn our history, politics, religion, commerce, and education into forms of entertainment, and that we will become as a result
a trivial people, incapable of coping with complexity, ambiguity, uncertainty, perhaps even reality. We will become, in a phrase, a people
amused into stupidity.

For those readers who are not inclined to take Mel Brooks as   12
seriously as I do, let me remind you that the prophecy I attribute
here to Brooks was, in fact, made many years before by a more
formidable social critic than he. I refer to Aldous Huxley, who
wrote *Brave New World*[2] at the time that the modern monuments
to intellectual stupidity were taking shape: Nazism in Germany, fascism in Italy, communism in Russia. But Huxley was not concerned
in his book with such naked and crude forms of intellectual suicide.
He saw beyond them, and mostly, I must add, he saw America. To
be more specific, he foresaw that the greatest threat to the intelligence and humane creativity of our culture would not come from

---

[2]In *Brave New World* (1932), British novelist Aldous Huxley depicts a frightening
futuristic world—one that conditions people to relinquish, happily and without reservation, their individual freedom to an all-controlling central government.

Big Brother and Ministries of Propaganda, or gulags and concentration camps. He prophesied, if I may put it this way, that there is tyranny lurking in a Coca-Cola bottle; that we could be ruined not by
what we fear and hate but by what we welcome and love, by what we
construe to be a gift from the gods.

And in case anyone missed his point in 1932, Huxley wrote   13
Brave New World Revisited twenty years later. By then, George Orwell's *1984* had been published, and it was inevitable that Huxley
would compare Orwell's book with his own. The difference, he said,
is that in Orwell's book people are controlled by inflicting pain. In
Brave New World, they are controlled by inflicting pleasure.

The Coke bottle that has fallen in our midst is a corporation of   14
dazzling technologies whose forms turn all serious public business
into a kind of *Springtime for Hitler* musical. Television is the principal instrument of this disaster, in part because it is the medium Americans most dearly love, and in part because it has become the
command center of our culture. Americans turn to television not
only for their light entertainment but for their news, their weather,
their politics, their religion, their history—all of which may be said to
be their serious entertainment. The light entertainment is not the
problem. The least dangerous things on television are its junk. What
I am talking about is television's preemption of our culture's most serious business. It would be merely banal to say that television presents us with entertaining subject matter. It is quite another thing to
say that on television all subject matter is presented as entertaining.
And that is how television brings ruin to any intelligent understanding of public affairs.

Political campaigns, for example, are now conducted largely in   15
the form of television commercials. Candidates forgo precision, complexity, substance—in some cases, language itself—for the arts of
show business: music, imagery, celebrities, theatrics. Indeed, political
figures have become so good at this, and so accustomed to it, that
they do television commercials even when they are not campaigning,
as, for example, Geraldine Ferraro for Diet Pepsi and former vice-
presidential candidate William Miller and the late Senator Sam Ervin
for American Express. Even worse, political figures appear on variety
shows, soap operas, and sitcoms. George McGovern, Ralph Nader,
Ed Koch, and Jesse Jackson have all hosted "Saturday Night Live."
Henry Kissinger and former President Gerald Ford have done cameo
roles on "Dynasty." Tip O'Neill and Governor Michael Dukakis
have appeared on "Cheers." Richard Nixon did a short stint on

"Laugh-In." The late Senator from Illinois, Everett Dirksen,[3] was on "What's My Line?" a prophetic question if ever there was one. What *is* the line of these people? Or, more precisely, *where* is the line that one ought to be able to draw between politics and entertainment? I would suggest that television has annihilated it.

It is significant, I think, that although our current President,[4] a   16 former Hollywood movie actor, rarely speaks accurately and never precisely, he is known as the Great Communicator; his telegenic charm appears to be his major asset, and that seems to be quite good enough in an entertainment-oriented politics. But lest you think his election to two terms is a mere aberration, I must remind you that, as I write [1988], Charlton Heston is being mentioned as a possible candidate for the Republican nomination in 1988. Should this happen, what alternative would the Democrats have but to nominate Gregory Peck? Two idols of the silver screen going one on one. Could even the fertile imagination of Mel Brooks have foreseen this? Heston giving us intimations of Moses as he accepts the nomination; Peck re-creating the courage of his biblical David as he accepts the challenge of running against a modern Goliath. Heston going on the stump as Michelangelo; Peck countering with Douglas MacArthur. Heston accusing Peck of insanity because of *The Boys From Brazil*. Peck replying with the charge that Heston blew the world up in *Return to Planet of the Apes*. *Springtime for Hitler* could be closer than you think.

But politics is only one arena in which serious language has been   17 displaced by the arts of show business. We have all seen how religion is packaged on television, as a kind of Las Vegas stage show, devoid

---

[3]Geraldine Ferraro was the Democrats' choice in 1984 for vice president, the first woman to be nominated for that office; William Miller was the Republican candidate for vice president in 1984; Sam Ervin, a U.S. Senator for many years, chaired the Senate Watergate Investigation Committee; George McGovern was the Democratic presidential nominee in 1972 at the height of the protest against the Vietnam War; Ralph Nader is a prominent consumer advocate; Ed Koch served as mayor of New York City for twelve years; Jesse Jackson, a minister and civil rights activist, ran for the presidency in 1988; Henry Kissinger was Secretary of State during the Nixon years; Gerald Ford was president from 1974 to 1977; Tip O'Neill served as Speaker of the House between 1977 and 1987; Michael Dukakis, a Democrat, ran for the presidency in 1988; Richard Nixon was president from 1969 to 1974, when he was forced to resign; and Everett Dirksen served in the Senate for many years.

[4]Postman is referring to Ronald Reagan here.

of ritual, sacrality, and tradition. Today's electronic preachers are in no way like America's evangelicals of the past. Men like Jonathan Edwards, Charles Finney, and George Whitefield were preachers of theological depth, authentic learning, and great expository power. Electronic preachers such as Jimmy Swaggart, Jim Bakker, and Jerry Falwell[5] are merely performers who exploit television's visual power and their own charisma for the greater glory of themselves.

We have also seen "Sesame Street" and other educational shows   18
in which the demands of entertainment take precedence over the rigors of learning. And we well know how American businessmen, working under the assumption that potential customers require amusement rather than facts, use music, dance, comedy, cartoons, and celebrities to sell their products.

Even our daily news, which for most Americans means television   19
news, is packaged as a kind of show, featuring handsome news readers, exciting music, and dynamic film footage. Most especially, film footage. When there is no film footage, there is no story. Stranger still, commercials may appear anywhere in a news story—before, after, or in the middle. This reduces all events to trivialities, sources of public entertainment and little more. After all, how serious can a bombing in Lebanon be if it is shown to us prefaced by a happy United Airlines commercial and summarized by a Calvin Klein jeans commercial? Indeed, television newscasters have added to our grammar a new part of speech—what may be called the "Now. . .this" conjunction, a conjunction that does not connect two things, but disconnects them. When newscasters say, "Now. . .this," they mean to indicate that what you have just heard or seen has no relevance to what you are about to hear or see. There is no murder so brutal, no political blunder so costly, no bombing so devastating that it cannot be erased from our minds by a newscaster saying, "Now. . .this." He means that you have thought long enough on the matter (let us say, for forty seconds) and you must now give your attention to a commercial. Such a situation is not "the news." It is merely a daily version of *Springtime for Hitler,* and in my opinion accounts for the fact that Americans are among the most ill-informed people in the world. To be sure, we know *of* many things; but we know *about* very little.

[5]Jonathan Edwards, Charles Finney, and George Whitefield were respected members of the American clergy in the eighteenth century, whereas today's television evangelists Jimmy Swaggart, Jim Bakker, and Jerry Falwell have tended to invite controversy, even scandal.

To provide some verification of this, I conducted a survey a few   20
years back on the subject of the Iranian hostage crisis. I chose this
subject because it was alluded to on television *every day for more than
a year.* I did not ask my subjects for their opinions about the hostage
situation. I am not interested in opinion polls; I am interested in
knowledge polls. The questions I asked were simple and did not require deep knowledge. For example, Where is Iran? What language
do the Iranians speak? Where did the Shah come from? What religion
do the Iranians practice, and what are its basic tenets? What does
"Ayatollah" mean? I found that almost everybody knew practically
nothing about Iran. And those who did know something said they
had learned it from *Newsweek* or *Time* or the *New York Times.* Television, in other words, is not the great information machine. It is the
great disinformation machine. A most nerve-wracking confirmation
of this came some time ago during an interview with the producer
and the writer of the TV mini-series *Peter the Great.* Defending the
historical inaccuracies in the drama—which included a fabricated
meeting between Peter and Sir Isaac Newton[6]—the producer said
that no one would watch a dry, historically faithful biography. The
writer added that it is better for audiences to learn something that is
untrue, if it is entertaining, than not to learn anything at all. And just
to put some icing on the cake, the actor who played Peter, Maximil-
ian Schell, remarked that he does not believe in historical truth and
therefore sees no reason to pursue it.

I do not mean to say that the trivialization of American public   21
discourse is all accomplished on television. Rather, television is the
paradigm for all our attempts at public communication. It conditions
our minds to apprehend the world through fragmented pictures and
forces other media to orient themselves in that direction. You know
the standard question we put to people who have difficulty understanding even simple language: we ask them impatiently, "Do I have
to draw a picture for you?" Well, it appears that, like it or not, our
culture will draw pictures for us, will explain the world to us in pictures. As a medium for conducting public business, language has re-
ceded in importance; it has been moved to the periphery of culture
and has been replaced at the center by the entertaining visual image.

---

[6]Peter the Great was the despotic czar of Russia from 1682 to 1725. English mathe-
matician and philosopher Sir Isaac Newton (1642–1727) formulated the laws of gravity and motion.

Please understand that I am making no criticism of the visual   22
arts in general. That criticism is made by God, not by me. You will
remember that in His Second Commandment, God explicitly states
that "Thou shalt not make unto thee any graven image, nor any like-
ness of anything that is in Heaven above, or that is in the earth beneath, or the waters beneath the earth." I have always felt that God
was taking a rather extreme position on this, as is His way. As for myself, I am arguing from the standpoint of a symbolic relativist. Forms
of communication are neither good nor bad in themselves. They become good or bad depending on their relationship to other symbols
and on the functions they are made to serve within a social order.
When a culture becomes overloaded with pictures; when logic and
rhetoric lose their binding authority; when historical truth becomes
irrelevant; when the spoken or written word is distrusted or makes
demands on our attention that we are incapable of giving; when our
politics, history, education, religion, public information, and commerce are expressed largely in visual imagery rather than words, then
a culture is in serious jeopardy.

Neither do I make a complaint against entertainment. As an old   23
song has it, life is not a highway strewn with flowers. The sight of a
few blossoms here and there may make our journey a trifle more en-
durable. But in America, the least amusing people are our professional entertainers. In our present situation, our preachers, entre-
preneurs, politicians, teachers, and journalists are committed to entertaining us through media that do not lend themselves to serious,
complex discourse. But these producers of our culture are not to be
blamed. They, like the rest of us, believe in the supremacy of technological progress. It has never occurred to us that the gods might be
crazy. And even if it did, there is no mountaintop from which we can
return what is dangerous to us.

We would do well to keep in mind that there are two ways in   24
which the spirit of a culture may be degraded. In the first—the Or-
wellian—culture becomes a prison. This was the way of the Nazis,
and it appears to be the way of the Russians. In the second—the
Huxleyan—culture becomes a burlesque. This appears to be the way
of the Americans. What Huxley teaches is that in the Age of Advanced Technology, spiritual devastation is more likely to come from
an enemy with a smiling countenance than from one whose face exudes suspicion and hate. In the Huxleyan prophecy, Big Brother
does not watch us, by his choice; we watch him, by ours. When a

culture becomes distracted by trivia; when political and social life are redefined as a perpetual round of entertainments; when public conversation becomes a form of baby talk; when a people become, in short, an audience and their public business a vaudeville act, then— Huxley argued—a nation finds itself at risk and culture-death is a clear possibility. I agree.

Questions for Close Reading

1. What is the selection's thesis? Locate the sentence(s) in which Postman states his main idea. If he doesn't state the thesis explicitly, express it in your own words.
2. In paragraphs 11 and 12, Postman says that Mel Brooks, director of *The Producers,* made "a kind of prophecy" about America. What did Brooks predict? To what extent did his prediction come true?
3. Why does Postman blame television for the trivialization of American culture? According to the author, which aspects of contemporary life have been affected by television?
4. What does Postman find so telling about the newscasters' phrase "Now...this"? What does the phrase say about television's attitude toward the events it depicts? How, according to Postman, does this attitude contribute to the decline of serious thought?
5. Refer to your dictionary as needed to define the following words used in the selection: *shlock* (title and paragraph 3), *lethal* (1), *nemeses* (1), *fervor* (1), *rhetorical* (3), *precipitous* (3), *apt* (3), *ambiguity* (11), *Nazism* (12), *fascism* (12), *gulags* (12), *preemption* (14), *banal* (14), *forgo* (15), *cameo* (15), *telegenic* (16), *sacrality* (17), *expository* (17), *conjunction* (19), *paradigm* (21), *periphery* (21), *relativist* (22), *rhetoric* (22), *burlesque* (24), *countenance* (24), and *exudes* (24).

Questions About the Writer's Craft

1. **The pattern.** Look again at the extended examples of the two movies that Postman provides in paragraphs 5 to 7 and 8 to 11. How do these examples help the author clarify what he believes is wrong with American culture?
2. **Other patterns.** Postman compares and contrasts the cultural situation in the United States with that in Germany (paragraphs 1–4) and Russia (24). Why might he have chosen these comparison-contrasts to begin and end the essay? What other contrasting examples does Postman supply?

3. Examine the sentences in paragraph 4 and at the end of paragraphs 22 and 24. What technique does Postman use to make these sentences striking? Why might he have put special effort into the style of these paragraphs?

4. Locate places where Postman uses the personal pronouns *I, we, us, our,* and *you.* What effect do these references have on the essay's tone? What do they suggest about Postman's assumptions about his audience?

Questions for Further Thought

1. According to Postman, television's emphasis on "show business" hinders our ability to deal with serious and complex issues. Do you find this to be so in your own life? Do you, for example, expect television news to be entertaining? Are there other areas of your life that you expect to be entertaining? Consider your classes, the newspapers you read, and so forth.

2. In your opinion, is the United States becoming—as Postman claims in paragraph 11—a nation of "trivial people, incapable of coping with complexity, ambiguity, uncertainty, perhaps even reality"? What signs do you notice in our society that support or disprove his statement?

3. In paragraph 14, Postman writes that "the least dangerous things on television are its junk." Do you agree that the light entertainment on television is harmless? Can you think of some light entertainment that might contribute to our becoming—as Postman states in paragraph 11—"a people amused into stupidity"?

4. Reflecting on the situation depicted in *The Gods Must Be Crazy,* Postman asks whether it's always desirable for cultures to accommodate to new technologies. Do you think there are new technologies or inventions that we as a society should reject? If so, what are they? Why should we reject them?

Writing Assignments Using Exemplification as a Pattern of Development

∞ 1. Postman suggests that the line between entertainment and politics has been blurred, citing among other things the fact that the American public elected a Hollywood actor, Ronald Reagan, as president. Would you agree that our leaders are fairly "shlocky"? Express your opinion in an essay by examining the quality of leadership in one or two areas of American life (for example, education; religion; business; campus, local, state, or national politics). Provide numerous specific examples to support your thesis. Before planning the paper, you may want to read Art Carey's "Things Fall Apart" (page 221) for its cynical insights into American culture.

2. Postman feels that *The Gods Must Be Crazy* and *The Producers* are two films that reveal much about our lives. What film or films have you seen

that reflect a belief or attitude held by society today? Supplying examples of scenes or incidents from two or more films, write an essay showing that such a belief or attitude does indeed prevail in our contemporary culture.

Writing Assignments Using Other Patterns of Development

∞ 3. According to Postman, television has had a destructive effect on contemporary society. Another writer, Marie Winn, argues a similar point in "TV Addiction" (page 541). Is television-viewing (and the mind-set it creates) a major problem in our society? Write an essay arguing either that television *is* at the root of most of our social ills or that some other force is weakening society. Before writing your essay, take some time to brainstorm with friends about possible contributing factors. Then select the *one* factor you feel creates the most problems, and defend your position by illustrating its negative effects. If you focus on television, you may cite some of Postman's points, but be sure to provide your own examples as well.

4. While Postman explores the effects of television on modern life, other innovations—computers, car phones, answering machines, video games, VCRs—also influence the way we live today. Write an essay showing the effects—positive, negative, or neutral—that you see flowing from one or more of these new inventions. You may write a serious analysis or use a comic tone to explore the pitfalls caused by the new product.

Barbara Ehrenreich

Barbara Ehrenreich (1941–) has been a college professor, investigative reporter, magazine editor, and social activist. A graduate of Reed College, Ehrenreich received her Ph.D. in biology from Rockefeller University. She has cowritten several books, including *For Her Own Good: 150 Years of the Experts' Advice to Women* (1978) and *Remaking Love: The Feminization of Sex* (1986). Her more recent books include *Fear of Falling: The Inner Life of the Middle Class* (1989), *The Worst Years of Our Lives* (1990), and the novel *Kipper's Game* (1993). A regular columnist for *Time,* Ehrenreich has published articles in many other magazines, such as *Esquire, Vogue,* and the *New Republic.* "What I've Learned From Men" first appeared in *Ms.* in 1985.

What I've Learned From Men

"Smile. Be perky. Keep the conversation going. Ask him questions about himself. But don't ask him anything that might threaten his masculinity." From their earliest days on, Barbara Ehrenreich contends, advice like this is drummed into young girls. And what, according to Ehrenreich, is the effect of such advice? Women end up acting like wimps and ninnies.

For many years I believed that women had only one thing to   1
learn from men: how to get the attention of a waiter by some means short of kicking over the table and shrieking. Never in my life have I gotten the attention of a waiter, unless it was an off-duty waiter whose car I'd accidentally scraped in a parking lot somewhere. Men, however, can summon a maître d' just by thinking the word "coffee," and this is a power women would be well-advised to study. What else would we possibly want to learn from them? How to interrupt someone in mid-sentence as if you were performing an act of conversational euthanasia? How to drop a pair of socks three feet from an open hamper and keep right on walking? How to make those weird guttural gargling sounds in the bathroom?

But now, at mid-life, I am willing to admit that there are some   2
real and useful things to learn from men. Not from all men—in fact,
we may have the most to learn from some of the men we like the
least. This realization does not mean that my feminist principles have
gone soft with age: what I think women could learn from men is how
to get *tough*. After more than a decade of consciousness-raising, as-
sertiveness training, and hand-to-hand combat in the battle of the
sexes, we're still too ladylike. Let me try that again—we're just too
damn ladylike.

Here is an example from my own experience, a story that I blush   3
to recount. A few years ago, at an international conference held in an
exotic and luxurious setting, a prestigious professor invited me to his
room for what he said would be an intellectual discussion on matters
of theoretical importance. So far, so good. I showed up promptly.
But only minutes into the conversation—held in all-too-adjacent
chairs—it emerged that he was interested in something more substantial than a meeting of minds. I was disgusted, but not enough to
overcome 30-odd years of programming in ladylikeness. Every time
his comments took a lecherous turn, I chattered distractingly; every
time his hand found its way to my knee, I returned it as if it were
something he had misplaced. This went on for an unconscionable
period (as much as 20 minutes); then there was a minor scuffle, a
dash for the door, and I was out—with nothing violated but my self-
esteem. I, a full-grown feminist, conversant with such matters as rape
crisis counseling and sexual harassment at the workplace, had behaved like a ninny—or, as I now understand it, like a lady.

The essence of ladylikeness is a persistent servility masked as   4
"niceness." For example, we (women) tend to assume that it is our
responsibility to keep everything "nice" even when the person we are
with is rude, aggressive, or emotionally AWOL. (In the above example, I was so busy taking responsibility for preserving the veneer of
"niceness" that I almost forgot to take responsibility for myself.) In
conversations with men, we do almost all the work: sociologists have
observed that in male-female social interactions it's the woman who
throws out leading questions and verbal encouragements ("So how
did you *feel* about that?" and so on) while the man, typically, says
"Hmmmm." Wherever we go, we're perpetually smiling—the on-
cue smile, like the now-outmoded curtsy, being one of our culture's
little rituals of submission. We're trained to feel embarrassed if we're
praised, but if we see a criticism coming at us from miles down the

road, we rush to acknowledge it. And when we're feeling aggressive or angry or resentful, we just tighten up our smiles or turn them into rueful little moues. In short, we spend a great deal of time acting like wimps.

For contrast, think of the macho stars we love to watch. Think, 5 for example, of Mel Gibson facing down punk marauders in "The Road Warrior"...John Travolta swaggering his way through the early scenes of "Saturday Night Fever"...or Marlon Brando shrugging off the local law in "The Wild One." Would they simper their way through tight spots? Chatter aimlessly to keep the conversation going? Get all clutched up whenever they think they might—just might—have hurt someone's feelings? No, of course not, and therein, I think, lies their fascination for us.

The attraction of the "tough guy" is that he has—or at least 6 seems to have—what most of us lack, and that is an aura of power and control. In an article, feminist psychiatrist Jean Baker Miller writes that "a woman's using self-determined power for herself is equivalent to selfishness [and] destructiveness"—an equation that makes us want to avoid even the appearance of power. Miller cites cases of women who get depressed just when they're on the verge of success—and of women who do succeed and then bury their achievement in self-deprecation. As an example, she describes one company's periodic meetings to recognize outstanding salespeople: when a woman is asked to say a few words about her achievement, she tends to say something like, "Well, I really don't know how it happened. I guess I was just lucky this time." In contrast, the men will cheerfully own up to the hard work, intelligence, and so on, to which they owe their success. By putting herself down, a woman avoids feeling brazenly powerful and potentially "selfish"; she also does the traditional lady's work of trying to make everyone else feel better ("She's not really so smart, after all, just lucky").

So we might as well get a little tougher. And a good place to 7 start is by cutting back on the small acts of deference that we've been programmed to perform since girlhood. Like unnecessary smiling. For many women—waitresses, flight attendants, receptionists—smiling is an occupational requirement, but there's no reason for anyone to go around grinning when she's not being paid for it. I'd suggest that we save our off-duty smiles for when we truly feel like sharing them, and if you're not sure what to do with your face in the meantime, study Clint Eastwood's expressions—both of them.

Along the same lines, I think women should stop taking respon- 8
sibility for every human interaction we engage in. In a social encounter with a woman, the average man can go 25 minutes saying nothing
more than "You don't say?" "Izzat so?" and, of course, "Hmmmm."
Why should we do all the work? By taking so much responsibility for
making conversations go well, we act as if we had much more at stake
in the encounter than the other party—and that gives him (or her)
the power advantage. Every now and then, we deserve to get more
out of a conversation than we put into it: I'd suggest not offering information you'd rather not share ("I'm really terrified that my sales
plan won't work") and not, out of sheer politeness, soliciting information you don't really want ("Wherever did you get that lovely
tie?"). There will be pauses, but they don't have to be awkward for
you.

It is true that some, perhaps most, men will interpret any de- 9
crease in female deference as a deliberate act of hostility. Omit the
free smiles and perky conversation-boosters and someone is bound
to ask, "Well, what's come over *you* today?" For most of us, the first
impulse is to stare at our feet and make vague references to a termi-
nally ill aunt in Atlanta, but we should have as much right to be taciturn as the average (male) taxi driver. If you're taking a vacation
from smiles and small talk and some fellow is moved to inquire about
what's "bothering" you, just stare back levelly and say, the international debt crisis, the arms race, or the death of God.

There are all kinds of ways to toughen up—and potentially 10
move up—at work, and I leave the details to the purveyors of asser-
tiveness training. But Jean Baker Miller's study underscores a fundamental principle that anyone can master on her own. We can stop
acting less capable than we actually are. For example, in the matter
of taking credit when credit is due, there's a key difference between
saying "I was just lucky" and saying "I had a plan and it worked." If
you take the credit you deserve, you're letting people know that you
were confident you'd succeed all along, and that you fully intend to
do so again.

Finally, we may be able to learn something from men about 11
what to do with anger. As a general rule, women get irritated: men
get *mad*. We make tight little smiles of ladylike exasperation; they
pound on desks and roar. I wouldn't recommend emulating the full
basso profundo male tantrum, but women do need ways of expressing justified anger clearly, colorfully, and, when necessary, crudely. If
you're not just irritated, but *pissed off*, it might help to say so.

I, for example, have rerun the scene with the prestigious profes-   12
sor many times in my mind. And in my mind, I play it like Bogart. I
start by moving my chair over to where I can look the professor full
in the face. I let him do the chattering, and when it becomes evident
that he has nothing serious to say, I lean back and cross my arms, just
to let him know that he's wasting my time. I do not smile, neither do
I nod encouragement. Nor, of course, do I respond to his blandish-
ments with apologetic shrugs and blushes. Then, at the first flicker of
lechery, I stand up and announce coolly, "All right, I've had enough
of this crap." Then I walk out—slowly, deliberately, confidently. Just
like a man.

Or—now that I think of it—just like a woman.   13

Questions for Close Reading

1. What is the selection's thesis? Locate the sentence(s) in which Ehrenreich
   states her main idea. If she doesn't state the thesis explicitly, express it in
   your own words.
2. Why did Ehrenreich handle the lecherous professor as she did? In retro-
   spect, how does she wish she had dealt with the situation? How does her
   current perspective of the way she should have behaved reinforce her thesis in the essay?
3. What does "behaving like a lady" mean, according to Ehrenreich? What
   is her opinion of "ladylike" behavior?
4. Why, in Ehrenreich's view, do we like "macho stars" (paragraph 5)?
   What can we learn from them?
5. Refer to your dictionary as needed to define the following words used in
   the selection: *euthanasia* (paragraph 1), *guttural* (1), *lecherous* (3), *distractingly* (3), *unconscionable* (3), *ninny* (3), *servility* (4), *veneer* (4),
   moues (4), *marauders* (5), *aura* (6), *brazenly* (6), *deference* (9), *taciturn*
   (9), *purveyors* (10), *emulating* (11), *basso profundo* (11), and *blandish-
   ments* (12).

Questions About the Writer's Craft

1. **The pattern.**   In paragraphs 3 and 12, Ehrenreich uses her own personal
   experience as a key example. Why do you think she chooses to include
   this example? Why do you suppose she presents it so early in the essay and
   then returns to it at the end?
2. **Other patterns.**   Locate places in the essay where Ehrenreich uses examples to contrast the different responses and behaviors of males and females. How do these contrasts help the writer develop her main idea?
3. Do you think that Ehrenreich is speaking primarily to a male or to a female audience? What in the essay makes you feel this way? Do you think

that the author expects her audience to be positive, hostile, or neutral toward her ideas? What in the essay leads you to this conclusion?

4. In her attack on "ladylikeness," Ehrenreich deliberately avoids using a "ladylike" or "nice" tone. Which of her phrases or expressions seem to defy stereotypes about the way "ladies" should express themselves?

Questions for Further Thought

1. In paragraph 10, Ehrenreich says she'll leave to others the details of how women should "toughen up." Do you agree that women need to "toughen up"? Why or why not? If they do, in what ways do you think women should be tougher? How do you think others might respond to this toughness?

2. Ehrenreich states that women—much more than men—are conditioned to disregard praise but almost welcome criticism. Do you agree that this is a basic difference between the sexes? Explain.

3. In paragraphs 4 and 8, Ehrenreich states that women usually "do all the work" in male-female relationships. Do you feel that Ehrenreich's observation is valid? Why or why not?

4. Psychiatrist Jean Baker Miller claims that women who use their power for themselves are considered selfish and destructive, "an equation," Ehrenreich says, "that makes...[women] want to avoid even the appearance of power." Do you agree that having "an aura of power and control" has been a negative for women, but a positive for men? If so, how could women change the way their power is perceived?

Writing Assignments Using Exemplification as a Pattern of Development

∞ 1. If, as Ehrenreich suggests, women have much to learn from men, is it also true that men could learn from women? Write an essay illustrating your belief that men would indeed be better off if they acquired some attitudes and behaviors traditionally associated with women. Be sure to provide numerous examples from your own experience and observations. You may take a humorous or serious approach when showing that men should—in some respects—become more like women. Deborah Tannen's "Sex, Lies, and Conversation" (page 428) may spark some insight into characteristically male and female behavioral patterns.

2. Ehrenreich points to the popularity of several "macho stars": Mel Gibson in *The Road Warrior,* John Travolta in *Saturday Night Fever,* Marlon Brando in *The Wild One,* and Clint Eastwood in anything. Choose several female characters from film or television who you feel provide positive role models for both males and females. Write an essay in which you use these characters as examples of the way that men and women should conduct their lives.

Writing Assignments Using Other Patterns of Development

∞ **3.** Ehrenreich suggests that some of the problems women experience in relationships and careers are of their own making—they smile too much, are too deferential, and fail to claim their own achievements. Pick one or two areas in which women tend to experience difficulty and write an essay arguing either that women sabotage themselves or that they are sabotaged by society's attitudes and expectations. Brainstorm with others to gather ideas for your paper. For other perspectives, you may want to read one or more of the following essays: Alleen Pace Nilsen's "Sexism and Language" (page 229), Deborah Tannen's "Sex, Lies, and Conversation" (page 428), Judy Brady's "Why I Want a Wife" (page 530), Camille Paglia's "Rape: A Bigger Danger Than Feminists Know" (page 638), Susan Jacoby's "Common Decency" (page 645), and Virginia Woolf's "Professions for Women" (page 695).

∞ **4.** Like Ehrenreich, most of us have been subjected at one time or another to the inappropriate or unpleasant behavior of others: slurs on our abilities, interests, or appearance; derision about our sex or sexual preference; taunts about our race, religion, or ethnic background. Focus on *one* kind of insult, and brainstorm with others to identify ways for dealing with such an affront. Then write an essay describing different strategies for coping with the offensive behavior. Reach some conclusions about which approach is most effective. Maya Angelou's "Grandmother's Victory" (page 164) and Caroline Rego's "The Fine Art of Complaining" (page 385) may spark some ideas worth exploring.

Additional Writing Topics

EXEMPLIFICATION

General Assignments

Use examples to develop any one of the following topics into a well-organized essay. When writing the paper, choose enough relevant examples to support your thesis. Organize the material into a sequence that most effectively illustrates the thesis, keeping in mind that emphatic order is often the most compelling way to present specifics.

1. Many of today's drivers have dangerous habits.
2. Drug and alcohol abuse is (or is not) a serious problem among many young people.
3. One rule of restaurant dining is, "Management often seems oblivious to problems that are perfectly obvious to customers."
4. Children today are not encouraged to use their imaginations.
5. The worst kind of hypocrite is a religious hypocrite.
6. The best things in life are definitely not free.
7. A part-time job is an important experience that every college student should have.
8. Many TV and magazine ads use sexual allusions to sell their products.
9. _____ (name someone you know well) is a _____ (use a quality: open-minded, dishonest, compulsive, reliable, gentle, and so on) person.
10. Television commercials stereotype the elderly (or another minority group).
11. Today, salespeople act as if they're doing you a favor by taking your money.
12. Most people behave decently in their daily interactions with each other.
13. Pettiness, jealousy, and selfishness abound in our daily interactions with each other.
14. You can tell a lot about people by observing what they wear and eat.
15. Too many Americans are overly concerned with being physically fit.
16. There are several study techniques that will help a student learn more efficiently.
17. Some teachers seem to enjoy turning tests into ordeals.
18. "How to avoid bad eating habits" is one course all college students should take.
19. More needs to be done to eliminate obstacles faced by the physically handicapped.
20. Some of the best presents are those that cost the least.

Assignments With a Specific Purpose and Audience

1. A friend of yours has taken a job in a big city or moved to a small town. To prepare your friend for this new environment, write a letter giving examples of what life in a big city or small town is like. You might focus on the benefits or dangers with which your friend is unlikely to be familiar.

2. Shopping for a new car, you become annoyed at how many safety features are available only as expensive options. Write a letter of complaint to the auto manufacturer, citing at least three examples of such options. Avoid sounding hostile.

3. Lately, many people at your college or workplace have been experiencing stress. As a member of the Campus (or Company) Committee on Morale, you've been asked to prepare a pamphlet illustrating different strategies for reducing stress. Decide what strategies you'll discuss and explain them with helpful examples.

4. Assume that you're an elementary school principal planning to give a speech in which you'll try to convince parents that television distorts children's perceptions of reality. Write the speech, illustrating your point with vivid examples.

5. A pet food company is having an annual contest to choose a new animal to feature in its advertising. To win the contest, you must convince the company that your pet is personable, playful, unique. Write an essay giving examples of your pet's special qualities.

6. For your college humor magazine, write an article on what you consider to be the "three best consumer products of the past twenty-five years." Support your opinion with lively, engaging specifics that are consistent with the magazine's offbeat and slightly ironic tone.

7
DIVISION-
CLASSIFICATION

WHAT IS
DIVISION-CLASSIFICATION?

Imagine what life would be like if this is how an average day unfolded:

> You plan to stop at the supermarket for only five items, but your marketing takes over an hour because all the items in the store are jumbled together. Clerks put new shipments anywhere they please; the milk might be with the vegetables on Monday but with laundry detergent on Thursday. Next, you go to the drugstore to pick up some photos you left to be developed. You don't have time, though, to wait while the cashier roots through the large carton into which all the pickup envelopes have been thrown. You return to your car and decide to stop at the town hall to pay a parking ticket. But the town hall baffles you. The offices are unmarked, and there's not even a

directory to tell you on which floor the Violations Bureau can be found. Annoyed, you get back into your car and, minutes later, end up colliding with another car, which is driving toward you in your lane. When you wake up in the hospital, you find there are three other patients in your room: a middle-aged man with a heart problem, a young boy ready to have his tonsils removed, and a woman about to go into labor.

Such a muddled world, lacking the most basic forms of organization, would make daily life chaotic. All of us instinctively look for ways to order our environment. Without systems, categories, or sorting mechanisms, we'd be overwhelmed by life's complexity. An organization like a college or university, for example, is made manageable by being divided into various schools (Liberal Arts, Performing Arts, Engineering, and so on). The schools are then separated into departments (English, History, Political Science), and each department's offerings are grouped into distinct categories—English, for instance, into Literature and Composition—before being further divided into specific courses.

The kind of ordering system we've been discussing is called *division-classification,* a logical way of thinking that allows us to make sense of a complex world. Division and classification, though separate processes, are often used together as complementary techniques. *Division* involves taking a single unit or concept, breaking the unit down into its parts, and then analyzing the connections among the parts and between the parts and the whole. For instance, if we wanted to organize the chaotic hospital described at the start of the chapter, we might think about how the single concept "a hospital" could be broken down into its components. We might come up with the following breakdown: pediatric wing, cardiac wing, maternity wing, and so on.

What we have just done involves division: We've taken a single entity (a hospital) and divided it into some of its component parts (wings), each with its own facilities and patients.

In contrast, *classification* brings two or more related items together and categorizes them according to type or kind. If the disorganized supermarket described earlier were to be restructured, the clerks would have to classify the separate items arriving at the loading dock. Cartons of lettuce, tomatoes, cucumbers, butter, yogurt, milk, shampoo, conditioner, and setting lotion would be assigned to the appropriate categories:

Lettuce	Butter	Shampoo
Tomatoes	Yogurt	Conditioner
Cucumbers	Milk	Setting Lotion
↓	↓	↓
Produce	Dairy	Hair Products

HOW DIVISION-CLASSIFICATION
FITS YOUR PURPOSE AND AUDIENCE

The reorganized hospital and supermarket show the way division and classification work in everyday life. But division and classification also come into play during the writing process. Because division involves breaking a subject into parts, it can be a helpful strategy during prewriting, especially if you're analyzing a broad, complex subject: the structure of a film; the motivation of a character in a novel; the problem your community has with vandalism; the controversy surrounding school prayer. An editorial examining a recent hostage crisis, for example, might divide the crisis into three areas: how the hostages were treated by (1) their captors, (2) the governments negotiating their release, and (3) the media. The purpose of the editorial might be to show readers that the governments' treatment of the hostages was particularly exploitative.

Classification can be useful for imposing order on the hodge-podge of ideas generated during prewriting. You examine that material to see which of your rough ideas are alike and which are dissimilar, so that you can cluster related items in the same category. Classification would, then, be a helpful strategy in analyzing topics like these: techniques for impressing teachers; comic styles of talk-show hosts; views on abortion; reasons for the current rise in volunteerism. You might, for instance, use classification in a paper showing that Americans are undermining their health through their obsessive pursuit of various diets. Perhaps you begin by brainstorming all the diets that have gained popularity in recent years (Weight Watchers', Slim-Fast, Jenny Craig, whatever). Then you categorize the diets according to type: high-fiber, low-protein, high-carbohydrate, and so on. Once the diets are grouped, you can discuss the problems within each category, demonstrating to readers that none of the diets is safe or effective.

Division-classification can be crucial when responding to college assignments like the following:

Based on your observations, what kinds of appeals do television advertisers use when selling automobiles? In your view, are any of these appeals morally irresponsible?

Analyze the components that go into being an effective parent. Indicate those you consider most vital for raising confident, well-adjusted children.

Describe the hierarchy of the typical high school clique, identifying the various parts of the hierarchy. Use your analysis to support or refute the view that adolescence is a period of rigid conformity.

Many social commentators have observed that discourtesy is on the rise. Indicate whether you think this is a valid observation by characterizing the types of everyday encounters you have with people.

These assignments suggest division-classification through the use of such words as *kinds, components, parts,* and *types.* Generally, though, you won't receive such clear signals to use division-classification. Instead, the broad purpose of the essay—and the point you want to make—will lead you to the analytical thinking characteristic of division-classification.

Sometimes division-classification will be the dominant technique for structuring an essay; other times it will be used as a supplemental pattern in an essay organized primarily according to another pattern of development. Let's look at some examples. Say you want to write a paper *explaining a process* (surviving divorce; creating a hit record; shepherding a bill through Congress; using the Heimlich maneuver on people who are choking). You could *divide* the process into parts or stages, showing, for instance, that the Heimlich maneuver is an easily mastered skill that readers should acquire. Or perhaps you plan to write a light-spirited essay analyzing the *effect* that increased awareness of sexual stereotypes has had on college students' social lives. In such a case, you might use *classification*. To show readers that shifting gender roles make young men and women comically self-conscious, you could categorize the places where students scout each other out: in class, at the library, at parties, in dorms. You could then show how students—not wishing to be macho or coyly feminine—approach each other with laughable tentativeness in these four environments.

Now imagine that you're writing an *argumentation-persuasion* essay urging that the federal government prohibit the use of growth-inducing antibiotics in livestock feed. The paper could begin by *dividing* the antibiotics cycle into stages: the effects of antibiotics on livestock; the short-term effects on humans who consume the animals; the possible long-term effects of consuming antibiotic-tainted meat. To increase readers' understanding of the problem, you might also discuss the antibiotics controversy in terms of an even larger issue: the dangerous ways food is treated before being consumed. In this case, you would consider the various procedures (use of additives, preservatives, artificial colors, and so on), *classifying* these treatments into several types—from least harmful (some additives or artificial colors, perhaps) to most harmful (you might slot the antibiotics here). Such an essay would be developed using both division *and* classification: first, the division of the antibiotics cycle and then the classification of the various food treatments. Frequently, this interdependence will be reversed, and classification will precede rather than follow division.

SUGGESTIONS FOR USING DIVISION-CLASSIFICATION IN AN ESSAY

The following suggestions will be helpful whether you use division-classification as a dominant or supportive pattern of development.

1. Select a principle of division-classification consistent with your purpose. Most subjects can be divided or classified according to a *number of different principles.* For example, when writing about an ideal vacation, you could divide your subject according to any of these principles: location, cost, recreation available. Similarly, when analyzing students at your college, you could base your classification on a variety of principles: students' majors, their racial or ethnic background, whether they belong to a fraternity or sorority. In all cases, though, the principle of division-classification you select must meet one stringent requirement: it must help you meet your overall purpose and reinforce your central point.

Sometimes a principle of division-classification seems so attractive that you latch on to it without examining whether it's consistent with your purpose. Suppose you want to write a paper asserting that several episodes of a new television comedy are destined to become classics. Here's how you might go wrong.

You begin by doing some brainstorming about the episodes. Then, as you start to organize the prewriting material, you hit upon a possible principle of classification: grouping the characters in the show according to the frequency with which they appear (main characters appearing in every show, supporting characters appearing in most shows, and guest characters appearing once or twice). You name the characters and explain which characters fit where. But is this principle of classification significant? Has it anything to do with why the shows will become classics? No, it hasn't. Such an essay would be little more than a meaningless exercise in classifying things just to classify them.

In contrast, a significant principle of classification might involve categorizing a number of shows according to the easily recognized human types portrayed: the Pompous Know-It-All, the Boss Who's Out of Control, the Lovable Grouch, the Surprisingly Savvy Innocent. You might illustrate the way certain episodes offer delightful twists on these stock figures, making such shows models of comic plotting and humor.

When you write an essay that uses division-classification as its primary method of development, a *single principle* of division-classification provides the foundation for each major section of the paper. Imagine you're writing an essay showing that the success of contemporary music groups has less to do with musical talent than with the groups' ability to market themselves to a distinct segment of the listening audience. To develop your point, you might categorize several performers according to the age ranges they appeal to (preteens, adolescents, people in their late twenties) and then analyze the marketing strategies the musicians use to gain their fans' support. The essay's logic would be undermined if you switched, in the middle of your analysis, to another principle of classification—say, the influence of earlier groups on today's music scene.

Don't, however, take this caution to mean that essays can never use more than one principle of division-classification as they unfold. They can—as long as the *shift from one principle to another* occurs in *different parts* of the paper. Imagine you want to write about widespread disillusionment with student government leaders at your college. You could develop this point by breaking down the dissatisfaction into the following: disappointment with the students' qualifications for office; disenchantment with their campaign tactics; frustration with their performance once elected. That section of the essay completed, you might move to a second principle of division—how students can get involved in campus government. Perhaps you break the proposed involvement into the following possibilities: serving on nominating committees; helping to run candidates' campaigns; attending open sessions of the student government.

2. Apply the principle of division-classification logically.   In an essay using division-classification, you need to demonstrate to readers that your analysis is the result of careful thought. First of all, your division-classification should be as *complete* as possible. Your analysis should include—within reason—all the parts into which you can divide your subject, or all the types into which you can categorize your subjects. Let's say you're writing an essay showing that where college students live is an important factor in determining how satisfied they are with college life. Keeping your purpose in mind, you classify students according to where they live: with parents, in dorms, in fraternity and sorority houses. But what about all the students who live in rented apartments, houses, or rooms off campus? If these places of residence are ignored, your classification won't be complete; you will lose credibility with your readers because they'll probably realize that you have overlooked several important considerations.

Your division-classification should also be *consistent:* the parts into which you break your subject or the groups into which you place your subjects should be as mutually exclusive as possible. The parts or categories should not be mixed, nor should they overlap. Assume you're writing an essay describing the animals at the zoo in a nearby city. You decide to describe the zoo's mammals, reptiles, birds, and endangered species. But such a classification is inconsistent. You begin by categorizing the animals according to scientific class (mammals, birds, reptiles), then switch to another principle when you classify some animals according to whether they are endangered. Because you drift over to a different principle of classification, your categories are no longer mutually exclusive: endangered species could overlap with any of the other categories. In which section of the paper, for instance, would you describe an exotic parrot that is obviously a bird but is also nearly extinct? And how would you categorize the zoo's rare mountain gorilla? This impressive creature is a mammal, but it is also an endangered species. Such overlapping categories undercut the logic that gives an essay its integrity.

A helpful tip: A solid outline is invaluable when you use division-classification. The outline encourages you to do the rigorous thinking needed to arrive at divisions and classifications that are logical, complete, and consistent.

3. Prepare an effective thesis. If your essay uses division-classification as its dominant method of development, it might be helpful to prepare a thesis that does more than signal the paper's subject and suggest your attitude toward that general subject. You might also want the thesis to state the principle of division-classification at the heart of the essay. Furthermore, you might want the thesis to reveal which part or category you regard as most important.

Consider the two thesis statements that follow:

As the observant beachcomber moves from the tidal area to the upper beach to the sandy dunes, rich variations in marine life become apparent.

> Although most people focus on the dangers associated with the disposal of toxic waste in the land and ocean, the incineration of toxic matter may pose an even more serious threat to human life.

The first thesis statement makes clear that the writer will organize the paper by classifying forms of marine life according to location. Since the purpose of the essay is to inform as objectively as possible, the thesis doesn't suggest the writer's opinion about which category is most significant.

The second thesis signals that the essay will evolve by dividing the issue of toxic waste according to methods of disposal. Moreover, because the paper takes a stance on a controversial subject, the thesis is worded to reveal which aspect of the topic the writer considers most important. Such a clear statement of the writer's position is an effective strategy in an essay of this kind.

You may have noted that each thesis statement also signals the paper's plan of development. The first essay, for example, will use specific facts, examples, and details to describe the kinds of marine life found in the tidal area, upper beach, and dunes. However, thesis statements in papers developed primarily through division-classification don't have to be so structured. If a paper is well written, your principle of division-classification, your opinion about which part or category is most important, and the essay's plan of development will become apparent as the essay unfolds.

4. Organize the paper logically.   Whether your paper is developed wholly or in part by division-classification, it should have a logical structure. As much as possible, you should try to discuss *comparable points* in each section of the paper. In the essay on seashore life, for example, you might describe life in the tidal area by discussing the mollusks, crustaceans, birds, and amphibians that live or feed there. You would then follow through, as much as you could, with this arrangement in the paper's other sections (upper beach and dune). Forgetting to describe the birdlife thriving in the dunes, especially when you had discussed birdlife in the tidal and upper-beach areas, would compromise the paper's structure. Of course, perfect parallelism is not always possible—there are no mollusks in the dunes, for instance. You should also use *signal devices* to connect various parts of the paper: "*Another* characteristic of marine life battered by the tides"; "A *final* important trait of both tidal and upper-beach crustaceans"; "*Unlike* the creatures of the tidal area and the upper beach." Such signals clarify the connections among the essay's ideas.

5. State any conclusions or recommendations in the paper's final section. The analytic thinking that occurs during division-classification often leads to surprising insights. Such insights may be introduced early on, or they may be reserved for the end, where they are stated as conclusions or recommendations. A paper might categorize different kinds of coaches—from inspiring to incompetent—and make the point that athletes learn a great deal about human relations simply by having to get along with their coaches, regardless of the coaches' skills. Such a paper might conclude that participation in a team sport teaches more about human nature than several courses in psychology. Or the essay might end with a proposal: Rookies and seasoned team members should be paired, so that novice players can get advice on dealing with coaching eccentricities.

As products of Western culture, we consider order and exactness virtues, finding satisfaction in the process of dividing and classifying. Does our urge to divide and classify make us intolerant of that which can't be pigeonholed? Do we lose sight of the whole by focusing on types and parts? Some cultures and philosophers believe we do and criticize our mania for dissecting and segregating. Yet dividing and classifying can be a way to understand the whole. Our achievements in science and technology are based on such analytic thinking. We use division-classification to understand everything from plants to animals, from the geologic history of earth to the mysteries of human evolution. Division-classification can, in short, be a powerful strategy for making sense of the complexities around us.

STUDENT ESSAY

The following student essay was written by Gail Oremland in response to this assignment:

In "Propaganda Techniques in Today's Advertising," Ann McClintock describes the flaws in many of the persuasive strategies used by advertisers. Choose another group of people whose job is also to communicate—for example, parents, bosses, teachers. Then, in an essay of your own, divide the group into types according to the flaws they make when communicating.

While reading Gail's paper, try to determine how effectively it applies the principles of division-classification. The annotations on Gail's paper and the commentary following it will help you look at the essay more closely.

The Truth About College Teachers
by Gail Oremland

Introduction   A recent TV news story told about a group of college professors from a nearby university who were hired by a local school system to help upgrade the teaching in the community's public schools. The professors were to visit classrooms, analyze teachers' skills, and then conduct workshops to help the teachers become more effective at their jobs. But after the first round of workshops, the superintendent of schools decided to cancel the whole project. He fired the learned professors and sent them back to their ivory tower. Why did the project fall apart? There was a simple reason. The college professors, who were supposedly going to show the public school teachers how to be more effective, were themselves poor teachers. Many college students could have predicted such a disastrous outcome. They know, first-hand, that college teachers are strange. They know that professors often exhibit bizarre behaviors, relating to students in ways that make it difficult for students to stay awake, or--if awake--to learn.

Thesis

     One type of professor assumes, legitimately enough, that her function is to pass on to students the vast store of knowledge she has acquired. But because the "Knowledgeable One" regards herself as an expert

Topic sentence

1

2

The first of three paragraphs on the first category of teacher

The first paragraph in a three-part chronological sequence: What happens *before* class

and her students as the ignorant masses, she adopts an elitist approach that sabotages learning. The Knowledgeable One enters a lecture hall with a self-important air, walks to the podium, places her yellowed-with-age notes on the stand, and begins her lecture at the exact second the class is officially scheduled to begin. There can be a blizzard or hurricane raging outside the lecture hall; students can be running through freezing sleet and howling winds to get to class on time. Will the Knowledgeable One wait for them to arrive before beginning her lecture? Probably not. The Knowledgeable One's time is precious. She's there, set to begin, and that's what matters.

Topic sentence ⟶   Once the monologue begins, the Knowledgeable   3

The second paragraph on the first category of teacher

The second paragraph in the chronological sequence: What happens *during* class

One drones on and on. The Knowledgeable One is a fact person. She may be the history prof who knows the death toll of every Civil War battle, the biology prof who can diagram all the common biological molecules, the accounting prof who enumerates every clause of the federal tax form. Oblivious to students' glazed eyes and stifled yawns, the Knowledgeable One delivers her monologue, dispensing one dry fact after another. The only advantage to being on the receiving end of this boring monologue is that students do not have to worry about being called on to question a point or provide an opinion; the Knowledgeable One is not willing to relinquish one minute of her time by giving students a voice. Assume for one improbable moment that a student actually manages to stay awake during the monologue and is brave enough to ask a question. In such a case, the Knowledgeable One will address the questioning student as "Mr." or "Miss." This formality does not, as some students mistakenly suppose, indicate respect for the student as a fledgling member of the academic community. Not at all. This impersonality represents the Knowledgeable One's desire to keep as wide a distance as possible between her and her students.

Topic sentence ⟶   The Knowledgeable One's monologue always   4 comes to a close at the precise second the class is scheduled to end. No sooner has she delivered her last forgettable word than the Knowledgeable One

The third paragraph on the first category of teacher

The final paragraph in the chronological sequence: What happens *after* class

packs up her notes and shoots out the door, heading back to the privacy of her office, where she can pursue her specialized academic interests--free of any possible interruption from students. The Knowledgeable One's hasty departure from the lecture hall makes it clear she has no desire to talk with students. In her eyes, she has met her obligations; she has taken time away from her research to transmit to students what she knows. Any closer contact might mean she would risk contagion from students, that great unwashed mass. Such a danger is to be avoided at all costs.

Unlike the Knowledgeable One, the "Leader of Intellectual Discussion" seems to respect students. Emphasizing class discussion, the Leader encourages students to confront ideas ("What is Twain's view of morality?" "Was our intervention in Vietnam

Topic sentence

Paragraph on the second category of teacher

justified?" "Should big business be given tax breaks?") and discover their own truths. Then, about three weeks into the semester, it becomes clear that the Leader wants students to discover his version of the truth. Behind the Leader's democratic guise lurks a dictator. When a student voices an opinion that the Leader accepts, the student is rewarded by hearty nods of approval and "Good point, good point." But if a student is rash enough to advance a conflicting viewpoint, the Leader responds with killing politeness: "Well, yes, that's an interesting perspective. But don't you think that...?" Grade-conscious students soon learn not to chime in with their viewpoint. They know that when the Leader, with seeming honesty, says, "I'd be interested in hearing what you think. Let's open this up for discussion," they had better figure out what the Leader wants to hear before advancing their own theories. "Me-tooism" rather than independent thinking, they discover, guarantees good grades in the Leader's class.

Topic sentence

Paragraph on the third category of teacher

Then there is the professor who comes across as the students' "Buddy." This kind of professor does not see himself as an imparter of knowledge or a leader of discussion but as a pal, just one in a community of equals. The Buddy may start his course this way. "All of us know that this college stuff--grades, degrees,

5

6

exams, required reading--is a game. So let's not play it, okay?" Dressed in jeans, sweatshirt, and scuffed sneakers, the Buddy projects a relaxed, casual attitude. He arranges the class seats in a circle (he would never take a position in front of the room) and insists that students call him by his first name. He uses no syllabus and gives few tests, believing that such constraints keep students from directing their own learning. A free spirit, the Buddy often teaches courses like "The Psychology of Interpersonal Relations" or "The Social Dynamics of the Family." If students choose to use class time to discuss the course material, that's fine. If they want to discuss something else, that's fine, too. It's the self-expression, the honest dialogue, that counts. In fact, the Buddy seems especially fond of digressions from academic subjects. By talking about his political views, his marital problems, his tendency to drink one too many beers, the Buddy lets students see that he is a regular guy--just like them. At first, students look forward to classes with the Buddy. They enjoy the informality, the chitchat, the lack of pressure. But after a while, they wonder why they are paying for a course where they learn nothing. They might as well stay home and watch the soaps.

Conclusion

Echoes opening anecdote

Obviously, some college professors are excellent.   7
They are learned, hardworking, and imaginative; they enjoy their work and like being with students. On the whole, though, college professors are a strange lot. Despite their advanced degrees and their own exposure to many different kinds of teachers, they do not seem to understand how to relate to students. Rather than being hired as consultants to help others upgrade their teaching skills, college professors should themselves hire consultants to tell them what they are doing wrong and how they can improve. Who should these consultants be? That's easy: the people who know them best--their students.

COMMENTARY

Introduction and thesis.   After years of being graded by teachers, Gail took special pleasure in writing an essay that gave her a chance to evaluate her teachers—in this case, her college professors. Even the essay's title, "The Truth About College Teachers," implies that Gail is going to have fun knocking profs down from their ivory towers. To introduce her subject, she uses a timely news story. This brief anecdote leads directly to the essay's *thesis:* "Professors often exhibit bizarre behaviors, relating to students in ways that make it difficult for students to stay awake, or—if awake—to learn." Note that Gail's thesis isn't highly structured; it doesn't, for example, name the specific categories to be discussed. Still, her thesis suggests that the essay is going to *categorize* a range of teaching behaviors, using as a *principle of classification* the strange ways that college profs relate to students.

Purpose. As with all good papers developed through division-classification, Gail's essay doesn't use classification as an end in itself. Gail uses classification because it helps her achieve a broader *purpose.* She wants to *convince* readers—without moralizing or abandoning her humorous tone—that such teaching styles inhibit learning. In other words, there's a serious underside to her essay. This additional layer of meaning is characteristic of satiric writing.

Categories and topic sentences. The essay's body, consisting of five paragraphs, presents the three categories that make up Gail's analysis. According to Gail, college teachers can be categorized as the Knowledgeable One (paragraphs 2–4), the Leader of Intellectual Discussion (5), or the Buddy (6). Obviously, there are other ways professors might be classified. But given Gail's purpose, audience, tone, and point of view, her categories are appropriate; they are reasonably *complete, consistent,* and *mutually exclusive.* Note, too, that Gail uses *topic sentences* near the beginning of each category to help readers see which professorial type she's discussing.

Overall organization and paragraph structure. Gail is able to shift smoothly and easily from one category to the next. How does she achieve such graceful transitions? Take a moment to reread the sentences that introduce her second and third categories (paragraphs 5 and 6). Look at the way each sentence's beginning (in italics here) links back to the preceding category or categories: "*Unlike the Knowledgeable One,* the 'Leader of Intellectual Discussion' seems to respect students"; and "[the Buddy]...*does not see himself as an imparter of knowledge or a leader of discussion* but as a pal...."

Gail is equally careful about providing an easy-to-follow structure within each section. She uses a *chronological sequence* to organize her three-paragraph discussion of the Knowledgeable One. The first paragraph deals with the beginning of the Knowledgeable One's lecture; the second, with the lecture itself; the third, with the end of the lecture. And the paragraphs' *topic sentences* clearly indicate this passage of time. Similarly, *transitions* are used in the paragraphs on the Leader of Intellectual Discussion and the Buddy to ensure a logical progression of points: "*Then,* about three weeks into the semester, it becomes clear that the Leader wants students to discover *his* version of the truth" (5) and "*At first,* students look forward to classes with the Buddy....But *after a while,* they wonder why they are paying for a course where they learn nothing" (6).

Tone.   The essay's unity can also be traced to Gail's skill in sustaining her satiric tone. Throughout the essay, Gail selects details that fit her gently mocking attitude. She depicts the Knowledgeable One lecturing from "yellowed-with-age notes..., oblivious to students' glazed eyes and stifled yawns," unwilling to wait for students who "run...through freezing sleet and howling winds to get to class on time." Then she presents another tongue-in-cheek description, this one focusing on the way the Leader of Intellectual Discussion conducts class: "Good point, good point....Well, yes, that's an interesting perspective. But don't you think that...?" Finally, with similar killing accuracy, Gail portrays the Buddy, democratically garbed in "jeans, sweatshirt, and scuffed sneakers."

Other patterns of development.   Gail's satiric depiction of her three professorial types employs a number of techniques associated with *narrative* and *descriptive writing:* vigorous images, highly connotative language, and dialogue. *Definition, exemplification, causal analysis,* and *comparison-contrast* also come into play. Gail defines the characteristics of each type of professor; she provides numerous examples to support her categories; she explains the effects of the different teaching styles on students; and, in her description of the Leader of Intellectual Discussion, she contrasts the appearance of democracy with the dictatorial reality.

Unequal development of categories.   Although Gail's essay is unified, organized, and well-developed, you may have felt that the first category outweighs the other two. There is, of course, no need to balance the categories exactly. But Gail's extended treatment of the first category sets up an expectation that the others will be treated as fully. One way to remedy this problem would be to delete some material from the discussion of the Knowledgeable One. Gail might, for instance, omit the first five sentences in the third paragraph (about the professor's habit of addressing students as "Mr." or "Miss"). Such a change could be made without taking the bite out of her portrayal. Even better, Gail could simply switch the order of her sections, putting the portrait of the Knowledgeable One at the essay's end. Here, the extended discussion wouldn't seem out of proportion. Instead, the sections would appear in *emphatic order*, with the most detailed category saved for last.

Revising the first draft.   It's apparent that an essay as engaging as Gail's must have undergone a good deal of revising. That was in fact the case. Gail made many changes in the body of the essay, but it's particularly interesting to review what happened to the introduction as she revised the paper. Reprinted here is Gail's original introduction.

Original Version of the Introduction

Despite their high IQs, advanced degrees, and published papers, some college professors just don't know how to teach. Found in almost any department, in tenured and untenured positions, they prompt student apathy. They fail to convey ideas effectively and to challenge or inspire students. Students thus finish their courses having learned very little. Contrary to popular opinion, these professors' ineptitude is not simply a matter of delivering boring lectures or not caring about students. Many of them care a great deal. Their failure actually stems from their unrealistic perceptions of what a teacher should be. Specifically, they adopt teaching styles or roles that alienate students and undermine learning. Three of the most common ones are "The Knowledgeable One," "The Leader of Intellectual Discussion," and "The Buddy."

When Gail showed the first draft of the essay to her composition instructor, he laughed—and occasionally squirmed—as he read what she had prepared. He was enthusiastic about the paper but felt that there was a problem with the introduction's tone; it was too serious when compared to the playful, lightly satiric mood of the rest of the essay. When Gail reread the paragraph, she agreed, but she was uncertain about the best way to remedy the problem. After revising other sections of the essay, she decided to let the paper sit for a while before going back to rewrite the introduction.

In the meantime, Gail switched on the TV. The timing couldn't have been better; she tuned into a news story about several supposedly learned professors who had been fired from a consulting job because they had turned out to know so little about teaching. This was exactly the kind of item Gail needed to start her essay. Now she was able to prepare a completely new introduction, making it consistent in spirit with the rest of the paper.

With this stronger introduction and the rest of the essay well in hand, Gail was ready to write a conclusion. Now, as she worked on the concluding paragraph, she deliberately shaped it to recall the story about the fired consultants. By echoing the opening anecdote in her conclusion, Gail was able to end the paper with another poke at professors—a perfect way to close her clever and insightful essay.

The selections in this chapter show how division and classification can be used to explore a variety of subjects. Judith Viorst divides acquaintances into categories that include "Friends, Good Friends—and Such Good Friends." William Zinsser describes the sorts of "College Pressures" that students typically encounter, while Scott Russell Sanders, in "The Men We Carry in Our Minds," shows how he categorized the men he knew during his childhood. Classifying "Propaganda Techniques in Today's Advertising" is the method Ann McClintock uses to demonstrate how pervasive and effective such techniques can be. Finally, in "The Quick Fix Society," Janet Mendell Goldstein examines three different kinds of instant gratification and shows us the harm each causes.

Judith Viorst

A contributing editor at *Redbook,* Judith Viorst (1936–   ) is perhaps best known for her column in that magazine. She has also written several children's books, including *Alexander and the Terrible, Horrible, No Good, Very Bad Day* (1982) and *Sad Underwear and Other Complications* (1995); a number of volumes of light verse, including *It's Hard to Be Hip Over Thirty and Other Tragedies of Modern Life* (1970) and *How Did I Get to Be Forty and Other Atrocities* (1984); a novel, *Murdering Mr. Monti: A Merry Little Tale of Sex and Violence* (1994); and *Necessary Losses* (1986), a serious look at the process by which adults deal with change. Viorst's writing style, which often combines deeply felt emotion and wry humor, has made her works popular and widely read. The following selection first appeared in *Redbook* in 1977.

Friends, Good Friends— and Such Good Friends

There are people to whom we bare our souls; there are individuals we enjoy talking to whenever we see them in class or at work; there are those we look forward to seeing every few years when we visit our old high schools or hometowns. The degree of intimacy we share with these people varies greatly; yet all of them, says Judith Viorst, deserve to be called friends.

Women are friends, I once would have said, when they totally   1
love and support and trust each other, and bare to each other the secrets of their souls, and run—no questions asked—to help each other, and tell harsh truths to each other (no, you can't wear that dress unless you lose ten pounds first) when harsh truths must be told.

Women are friends, I once would have said, when they share the   2
same affection for Ingmar Bergman, plus train rides, cats, warm rain,

charades, Camus, and hate with equal ardor Newark and Brussels sprouts and Lawrence Welk[1] and camping.

In other words, I once would have said that a friend is a friend all the way, but now I believe that's a narrow point of view. For the friendships I have and the friendships I see are conducted at many levels of intensity, serve many different functions, meet different needs and range from those as all-the-way as the friendship of the soul sisters mentioned above to that of the most nonchalant and casual playmates.

Consider these varieties of friendship:

1. Convenience friends.   These are women with whom, if our paths weren't crossing all the time, we'd have no particular reason to be friends: a next-door neighbor, a woman in our car pool, the mother of one of our children's closest friends or maybe some mommy with whom we serve juice and cookies each week at the Glenwood Co-op Nursery.

Convenience friends are convenient indeed. They'll lend us their cups and silverware for a party. They'll drive our kids to soccer when we're sick. They'll take us to pick up our car when we need a lift to the garage. They'll even take our cats when we go on vacation. As we will for them.

But we don't, with convenience friends, ever come too close or tell too much; we maintain our public face and emotional distance. "Which means," says Elaine, "that I'll talk about being overweight but not about being depressed. Which means I'll admit being mad but not blind with rage. Which means that I might say that we're pinched this month but never that I'm worried sick over money."

But which doesn't mean that there isn't sufficient value to be found in these friendships of mutual aid, in convenience friends.

2. Special-interest friends.   These friendships aren't intimate, and they needn't involve kids or silverware or cats. Their value lies in some interest jointly shared. And so we may have an office friend or a yoga friend or a tennis friend or a friend from the Women's Democratic Club.

[1]Ingmar Bergman, a Swedish filmmaker noted for his deep probings into the darkness of the human soul; Albert Camus, a French writer whose essays and novels depict the human capacity for moral and responsible action in an otherwise pointless world; Lawrence Welk, a television band leader whose bubbly "champagne" music was often criticized as being bland and homogenized.

"I've got one woman friend," says Joyce, "who likes, as I do, to   10
take psychology courses. Which makes it nice for me—and nice for
her. It's fun to go with someone you know and it's fun to discuss
what you've learned, driving back from the classes." And for the
most part, she says, that's all they discuss.

"I'd say that what we're doing is *doing* together, not being to-   11
gether," Suzanne says of her Tuesday-doubles friends. "It's mainly a
tennis relationship, but we play together well. And I guess we all
need to have a couple of playmates."

I agree.   12

My playmate is a shopping friend, a woman of marvelous taste,   13
a woman who knows exactly *where* to buy *what*, and furthermore is
a woman who always knows beyond a doubt what one ought to be
buying. I don't have the time to keep up with what's new in eyeshadow, hemlines and shoes and whether the smock look is in or finished
already. But since (oh, shame!) I care a lot about eyeshadow, hemlines and shoes, and since I don't *want* to wear smocks if the smock
look is finished, I'm very glad to have a shopping friend.

3. Historical friends. We all have a friend who knew us   14
when...maybe way back in Miss Meltzer's second grade, when our
family lived in that three-room flat in Brooklyn, when our dad was
out of work for seven months, when our brother Allie got in that
fight where they had to call the police, when our sister married the
endodontist from Yonkers and when, the morning after we lost our
virginity, she was the first, the only, friend we told.

The years have gone by and we've gone separate ways and we've   15
little in common now, but we're still an intimate part of each other's
past. And so whenever we go to Detroit we always go to visit this
friend of our girlhood. Who knows how we looked before our teeth
were straightened. Who knows how we talked before our voice got
un-Brooklyned. Who knows what we ate before we learned about ar-
tichokes. And who, by her presence, puts us in touch with an earlier
part of ourself, a part of ourself it's important never to lose.

"What this friend means to me and what I mean to her," says   16
Grace, "is having a sister without sibling rivalry. We know the texture
of each other's lives. She remembers my grandmother's cabbage
soup. I remember the way her uncle played the piano. There's simply
no other friend who remembers those things."

4. Crossroads friends. Like historical friends, our crossroads   17
friends are important for *what was*—for the friendship we shared at a

crucial, now past, time of life. A time, perhaps, when we roomed in college together; or worked as eager young singles in the Big City together; or went together, as my friend Elizabeth and I did, through pregnancy, birth and that scary first year of new motherhood.

Crossroads friends forge powerful links, links strong enough to 18 endure with not much more contact than once-a-year letters at Christmas. And out of respect for those crossroads years, for those dramas and dreams we once shared, we will always be friends.

5. Cross-generational friends. Historical friends and cross- 19 roads friends seem to maintain a special kind of intimacy—dormant but always ready to be revived—and though we may rarely meet, whenever we do connect, it's personal and intense. Another kind of intimacy exists in the friendships that form across generations in what one woman calls her daughter-mother and her mother-daughter relationships.

Evelyn's friend is her mother's age—"but I share so much more 20 than I ever could with my mother"—a woman she talks to of music, of books and of life. "What I get from her is the benefit of her experience. What she gets—and enjoys—from me is a youthful perspective. It's a pleasure for both of us."

I have in my own life a precious friend, a woman of 65 who has 21 lived very hard, who is wise, who listens well; who has been where I am and can help me understand it; and who represents not only an ultimate ideal mother to me but also the person I'd like to be when I grow up.

In our daughter role we tend to do more than our share of self- 22 revelation; in our mother role we tend to receive what's revealed. It's another kind of pleasure—playing wise mother to a questing younger person. It's another very lovely kind of friendship.

6. Part-of-a-couple friends. Some of the women we call our 23 friends we never see alone—we see them as part of a couple at couples' parties. And though we share interests in many things and respect each other's views, we aren't moved to deepen the relationship. Whatever the reason, a lack of time or—and this is more likely—a lack of chemistry, our friendship remains in the context of a group. But the fact that our feeling on seeing each other is always, "I'm *so* glad she's here" and the fact that we spend half the evening talking together says that this too, in its own way, counts as a friendship.

(Other part-of-a-couple friends are the friends that came with 24 the marriage, and some of these are friends we could live without.

But sometimes, alas, she married our husband's best friend; and sometimes, alas, she *is* our husband's best friend. And so we find ourself dealing with her, somewhat against our will, in a spirit of what I'll call *reluctant* friendship.)

7. Men who are friends. I wanted to write just of women friends, but the women I've talked to won't let me—they say I must mention man-woman friendships too. For these friendships can be just as close and as dear as those that we form with women. Listen to Lucy's description of one such friendship:

"We've found we have things to talk about that are different from what he talks about with my husband and different from what I talk about with his wife. So sometimes we call on the phone or meet for lunch. There are similar intellectual interests—we always pass on to each other the books that we love—but there's also something tender and caring too."

In a couple of crises, Lucy says, "he offered himself for talking and for helping. And when someone died in his family he wanted me there. The sexual, flirty part of our friendship is very small, but *some*—just enough to make it fun and different." She thinks—and I agree—that the sexual part, though small, is always *some,* is always there when a man and a woman are friends.

It's only in the past few years that I've made friends with men, in the sense of a friendship that's *mine,* not just part of two couples. And achieving with them the ease and the trust I've found with women friends has value indeed. Under the dryer at home last week, putting on mascara and rouge, I comfortably sat and talked with a fellow named Peter. Peter, I finally decided, could handle the shock of me minus mascara under the dryer. Because we care for each other. Because we're friends.

8. There are medium friends, and pretty good friends, and very good friends indeed, and these friendships are defined by their level of intimacy. And what we'll reveal at each of these levels of intimacy is calibrated with care. We might tell a medium friend, for example, that yesterday we had a fight with our husband. And we might tell a pretty good friend that this fight with our husband made us so mad that we slept on the couch. And we might tell a very good friend that the reason we got so mad in that fight that we slept on the couch had something to do with that girl who works in his office. But it's only to our very best friends that we're willing to tell all, to tell what's going on with that girl in his office.

25

26

27

28

29

The best of friends, I still believe, totally love and support and   30
trust each other, and bare to each other the secrets of their souls, and
run—no questions asked—to help each other, and tell harsh truths
to each other when they must be told.

But we needn't agree about everything (only 12-year-old girl   31
friends agree about *everything*) to tolerate each other's point of view.
To accept without judgment. To give and to take without ever keeping score. And to *be* there, as I am for them and as they are for me,
to comfort our sorrows, to celebrate our joys.

Questions for Close Reading

1. What is the selection's thesis? Locate the sentence(s) in which Viorst
   states her main idea. If she doesn't state the thesis explicitly, express it in
   your own words.
2. Viorst's view of what constitutes a friendship has changed over time.
   What did she once believe was the essence of friendship? How and why
   has her definition of friendship changed?
3. According to Viorst, what do historical and crossroads friends have in
   common? How are they different?
4. What does Viorst mean when she writes that the intimacy level of our relationships is "calibrated with care" (paragraph 29)?
5. Refer to your dictionary as needed to define the following words used in
   the selection: *ardor* (paragraph 2), *nonchalant* (3), *sibling* (16), *calibrated* (29).

Questions About the Writer's Craft

1. **The pattern.**   What principle of division-classification does Viorst use
   to sequence the "varieties of friendship"?
2. **Other patterns.**   What is Viorst's purpose in this essay? What other patterns of development besides division-classification does she use to
   achieve this purpose?
3. Examine the essay's introduction and conclusion. What idea appears in
   both sections? What idea appears only in the conclusion? Why do you
   think Viorst ends with this idea?
4. How would you describe Viorst's tone in this essay? What words and
   phrases help create this tone? What effect do you think Viorst intends this
   tone to have on her readers?

Questions for Further Thought

1. Viorst discusses numerous types of friendships. Do you find that your life
   includes so many types of friends? Which of Viorst's friendship types have

you *not* experienced? Do you expect to encounter these other types of friends later in life?

2. Why do some crossroads and historical friendships endure, even though the people no longer live nearby or share similar lives? In your experience, have such friendships survived separation and the passage of time, or have they faded into the past?

3. Viorst writes that women's friendships with men can be "as close and as dear" as women's friendships with women. What is your experience with opposite-sex friendships? Do you agree that they can be as open and trusting as same-sex friendships? Why or why not?

4. In paragraph 31, Viorst says that friends "needn't agree about everything...to tolerate each other's point of view." Do you have friends with whom you disagree on some matter of significance, such as music preference, political affiliation, or religious belief? How difficult is it to maintain such friendships?

Writing Assignments Using Division-Classification as a Pattern of Development

∞ 1. Enlarge upon Viorst's analysis by interviewing some males about the types of friendships they typically form. Describe men's friendships in an essay, pointing out in the introduction or conclusion any differences you've discovered in the way males and females approach friendship. Before writing the paper, you may want to read what Deborah Tannen says in "Sex, Lies, and Conversation" (page 428) about the dissimilarities in men's and women's interpersonal styles.

2. Viorst writes about various kinds of friends. Following Viorst's lead, choose another group of people (for example, bosses, salespeople, or parents) and write an essay about the different types of individuals within that broad category. Your tone may be light or serious, but you should, as Viorst does, reach some conclusions about the types of people you describe.

Writing Assignments Using Other Patterns of Development

∞ 3. As Viorst indicates, friends survive disagreements by being tolerant and accepting of each other "without judgment." Sometimes, though, friendships erupt into conflict. Write an essay describing a process by which friends who are having a significant disagreement can restore the harmony of their relationship. Caroline Rego's "The Fine Art of Complaining" (page 385) and Deborah Tannen's "Sex, Lies, and Conversation" (page 428) offer some suggestions for resolving conflict.

4. Viorst suggests that women and men can be friends without there being a distracting sexual element. Think about the opposite-sex friendships you have had, and talk about such friendships with some people you know well. Then decide whether you believe that nonromantic opposite-

sex friendship is possible. Write an essay arguing either that all such friendships are tinged with significant sexual overtones or that pure friendship can occur between males and females. Remember to acknowledge the opposing viewpoint, and include plentiful examples from your own and others' experience to support your position.

William Zinsser

Currently executive editor of the Book-of-the-Month Club, William Zinsser has written news journalism, drama criticism, magazine columns, and several books on American culture. Born in 1922 in New York, Zinsser attended Princeton University and worked for the *New York Herald Tribune, Life,* and *Look.* In 1970, Zinsser designed a course in nonfiction writing for Yale University. Based on what he learned at Yale about the way college students approach the writing process, Zinsser wrote the popular guide *On Writing Well* (1976). His other books include *The City Dwellers* (1962), *Pop Goes America* (1966), *The Lunacy Boom* (1970), *Writing With a Word Processor* (1982), and *American Places: A Writer's Pilgrimage to 15 of This Country's Most Visited and Cherished Sites* (1992). The following essay first appeared in the magazine *Country Journal* in 1979.

College Pressures

Campuses today are flooded with business majors and budding computer scientists. Many students' primary goal is to go where the money is—to transform themselves into marketable commodities who will, by the age of thirty, have luxurious homes, expensive cars, and profitable investment portfolios. William Zinsser sympathizes with the pressures that lead to students' obsession with material success, yet he doubts that such a single-minded concern with a lucrative career is the surest route to happiness.

Dear Carlos: I desperately need a dean's excuse for my chem midterm which will begin in about 1 hour. All I can say is that I totally blew it this week. I've fallen incredibly, inconceivably behind.

Carlos: Help! I'm anxious to hear from you. I'll be in my room and won't leave it until I hear from you. Tomorrow is the last day for . . .

Carlos: I left town because I started bugging out again. I stayed up all night to finish a take-home make-up exam & am typing it to hand in on the 10th. It was due on the 5th. P.S. I'm going to the dentist. Pain is pretty bad.

Carlos: Probably by Friday I'll be able to get back to my studies. Right now I'm going to take a long walk. This whole thing has taken a lot out of me.

Carlos: I'm really up the proverbial creek. The problem is I really *bombed* the history final. Since I need that course for my major I...

Carlos: Here follows a tale of woe. I went home this weekend, had to help my Mom, & caught a fever so didn't have much time to study. My professor...

Carlos: Aargh! Trouble. Nothing original but everything's piling up at once. To be brief, my job interview...

Hey Carlos, good news! I've got mononucleosis.

Who are these wretched supplicants, scribbling notes so laden 1 with anxiety, seeking such miracles of postponement and balm? They are men and women who belong to Branford College, one of the twelve residential colleges at Yale University, and the messages are just a few of the hundreds that they left for their dean, Carlos Hortas—often slipped under his door at 4 A.M.—last year.

But students like the ones who wrote those notes can also be 2 found on campuses from coast to coast—especially in New England and at many other private colleges across the country that have high academic standards and highly motivated students. Nobody could doubt that the notes are real. In their urgency and their gallows humor they are authentic voices of a generation that is panicky to succeed.

My own connection with the message writers is that I am master 3 of Branford College. I live in its Gothic quadrangle and know the students well. (We have 485 of them.) I am privy to their hopes and fears—and also to their stereo music and their piercing cries in the dead of the night ("Does anybody *ca-a-are?*"). If they went to Carlos

to ask how to get through tomorrow, they come to me to ask how
to get through the rest of their lives.

Mainly I try to remind them that the road ahead is a long one 4
and that it will have more unexpected turns than they think. There
will be plenty of time to change jobs, change careers, change whole
attitudes and approaches. They don't want to hear such liberating
news. They want a map—right now—that they can follow unswervingly to career security, financial security, Social Security and, presumably, a prepaid grave.

What I wish for all students is some release from the clammy 5
grip of the future. I wish them a chance to savor each segment of
their education as an experience in itself and not as a grim preparation for the next step. I wish them the right to experiment, to trip
and fall, to learn that defeat is as instructive as victory and is not the
end of the world.

My wish, of course, is naïve. One of the few rights that America 6
does not proclaim is the right to fail. Achievement is the national
god, venerated in our media—the million-dollar athlete, the wealthy
executive—and glorified in our praise of possessions. In the presence
of such a potent state religion, the young are growing up old.

I see four kinds of pressure working on college students today: 7
economic pressure, parental pressure, peer pressure, and self-induced
pressure. It is easy to look around for villains—to blame the colleges
for charging too much money, the professors for assigning too much
work, the parents for pushing their children too far, the students for
driving themselves too hard. But there are no villains; only victims.

"In the late 1960s," one dean told me, "the typical question 8
that I got from students was 'Why is there so much suffering in the
world?' or 'How can I make a contribution?' Today it's 'Do you
think it would look better for getting into law school if I did a double
major in history and political science, or just majored in one of
them?'" Many other deans confirmed this pattern. One said:
"They're trying to find an edge—the intangible something that will
look better on paper if two students are about equal."

Note the emphasis on looking better. The transcript has become 9
a sacred document, the passport to security. How one appears on paper is more important than how one appears in person. *A* is for Admirable and *B* is for Borderline, even though, in Yale's official system

of grading, *A* means "excellent" and *B* means "very good." Today, looking very good is no longer good enough, especially for students who hope to go on to law school or medical school. They know that entrance into the better schools will be an entrance into the better law firms and better medical practices where they will make a lot of money. They also know that the odds are harsh. Yale Law School, for instance, matriculates 170 students from an applicant pool of 3,700; Harvard enrolls 550 from a pool of 7,000.

It's all very well for those of us who write letters of recommen-   10 dation for our students to stress the qualities of humanity that will make them good lawyers or doctors. And it's nice to think that admission officers are really reading our letters and looking for the extra dimension of commitment or concern. Still, it would be hard for a student not to visualize these officers shuffling so many transcripts studded with *A*s that they regard a *B* as positively shameful.

The pressure is almost as heavy on students who just want to   11 graduate and get a job. Long gone are the days of the "gentleman's *C*," when students journeyed through college with a certain relaxation, sampling a wide variety of courses—music, art, philosophy, classics, anthropology, poetry, religion—that would send them out as liberally educated men and women. If I were an employer I would rather employ graduates who have this range and curiosity than those who narrowly pursued safe subjects and high grades. I know countless students whose inquiring minds exhilarate me. I like to hear the play of their ideas. I don't know if they are getting *A*s or *C*s, and I don't care. I also like them as people. The country needs them, and they will find satisfying jobs. I tell them to relax. They can't.

Nor can I blame them. They live in a brutal economy. Tuition,   12 room, and board at most private colleges now comes to at least $7,000 [in 1979], not counting books and fees. This might seem to suggest that the colleges are getting rich. But they are equally battered by inflation. Tuition covers only 60 percent of what it costs to educate a student, and ordinarily the remainder comes from what colleges receive in endowments, grants, and gifts. Now the remainder keeps being swallowed by the cruel costs—higher every year—of just opening the doors. Heating oil is up. Insurance is up. Postage is up. Health-premium costs are up. Everything is up. Deficits are up. We are witnessing in America the creation of a brotherhood of paupers—colleges, parents, and students, joined by the common bond of debt.

Today it is not unusual for a student, even if he works part time   13
at college and full time during the summer, to accrue $5,000 in loans
after four years—loans that he must start to repay within one year after graduation. Exhorted at commencement to go forth into the
world, he is already behind as he goes forth. How could he not feel
under pressure throughout college to prepare for this day of reckoning? I have used "he," incidentally, only for brevity. Women at Yale
are under no less pressure to justify their expensive education to
themselves, their parents, and society. In fact, they are probably under more pressure. For although they leave college superbly
equipped to bring fresh leadership to traditionally male jobs, society
hasn't yet caught up with this fact.

Along with economic pressure goes parental pressure. Inevita-   14
bly, the two are deeply intertwined.

I see many students taking pre-medical courses with joyless te-   15
nacity. They go off to their labs as if they were going to the dentist.
It saddens me because I know them in other corners of their life as
cheerful people.

"Do you want to go to medical school?" I ask them.   16

"I guess so," they say, without conviction, or "Not really."   17

"Then why are you going?"   18

"Well, my parents want me to be a doctor. They're paying all   19
this money and..."

Poor students, poor parents. They are caught in one of the oldest   20
webs of love and duty and guilt. The parents mean well; they are trying to steer their sons and daughters toward a secure future. But the
sons and daughters want to major in history or classics or philosophy—subjects with no "practical" value. Where's the payoff on the
humanities? It's not easy to persuade such loving parents that the humanities do indeed pay off. The intellectual faculties developed by
studying subjects like history and classics—an ability to synthesize and
relate, to weigh cause and effect, to see events in perspective—are just
the faculties that make creative leaders in business or almost any general field. Still, many fathers would rather put their money on courses
that point toward a specific profession—courses that are pre-law, pre-
medical, pre-business, or, as I sometimes heard it put, "pre-rich."

But the pressure on students is severe. They are truly torn. One   21
part of them feels obligated to fulfill their parents' expectations; after
all, their parents are older and presumably wiser. Another part tells

them that the expectations that are right for their parents are not right for them.

I know a student who wants to be an artist. She is very obviously   22
an artist and will be a good one—she has already had several modest local exhibits. Meanwhile she is growing as a well-rounded person and taking humanistic subjects that will enrich the inner resources out of which her art will grow. But her father is strongly opposed. He thinks that an artist is a "dumb" thing to be. The student vacillates and tries to please everybody. She keeps up with her art somewhat furtively and takes some of the "dumb" courses her father wants her to take—at least they are dumb courses for her. She is a free spirit on a campus of tense students—no small achievement in itself—and she deserves to follow her muse.

Peer pressure and self-induced pressure are also intertwined, and   23
they begin almost at the beginning of freshman year.

"I had a freshman student I'll call Linda," one dean told me,   24
"who came in and said she was under terrible pressure because her roommate, Barbara, was much brighter and studied all the time. I couldn't tell her that Barbara had come in two hours earlier to say the same thing about Linda."

The story is almost funny—except that it's not. It's symptomatic   25
of all the pressures put together. When every student thinks every other student is working harder and doing better, the only solution is to study harder still. I see students going off to the library every night after dinner and coming back when it closes at midnight. I wish they would sometimes forget about their peers and go to a movie. I hear the clacking of typewriters in the hours before dawn. I see the tension in their eyes when exams are approaching and papers are due: *"Will I get everything done?"*

Probably they won't. They will get sick. They will get   26
"blocked." They will sleep. They will oversleep. They will bug out. *Hey, Carlos, help!*

Part of the problem is that they do more than they are expected   27
to do. A professor will assign five-page papers. Several students will start writing ten-page papers to impress him. Then more students will write ten-page papers, and a few will raise the ante to fifteen. Pity the poor student who is still just doing the assignment.

"Once you have twenty or thirty percent of the student popula-   28
tion deliberately overexerting," one dean points out, "it's bad for

everybody. When a teacher gets more and more effort from his class, the student who is doing normal work can be perceived as not doing well. The tactic works, psychologically."

Why can't the professor just cut back and not accept longer papers? He can, and he probably will. But by then the term will be half over and the damage done. Grade fever is highly contagious and not easily reversed. Besides, the professor's main concern is with his course. He knows his students only in relation to the course and doesn't know that they are also overexerting in their other courses. Nor is it really his business. He didn't sign up for dealing with the student as a whole person and with all the emotional baggage the student brought along from home. That's what deans, masters, chaplains, and psychiatrists are for.

To some extent this is nothing new: a certain number of professors have always been self-contained islands of scholarship and shyness, more comfortable with books than with people. But the new pauperism has widened the gap still further, for professors who actually like to spend time with students don't have as much time to spend. They are also overexerting. If they are young, they are busy trying to publish in order not to perish, hanging by their fingernails onto a shrinking profession. If they are old and tenured, they are buried under the duties of administering departments—as departmental chairmen or members of committees—that have been thinned out by the budgetary axe.

Ultimately it will be the students' own business to break the circles in which they are trapped. They are too young to be prisoners of their parents' dreams and their classmates' fears. They must be jolted into believing in themselves as unique men and women who have the power to shape their own future.

"Violence is being done to the undergraduate experience," says Carlos Hortas. "College should be open-ended: at the end it should open many, many roads. Instead, students are choosing their goal in advance, and their choices narrow as they go along. It's almost as if they think that the country has been codified in the type of jobs that exist—that they've got to fit into certain slots. Therefore, fit into the best-paying slot.

"They ought to take chances. Not taking chances will lead to a life of colorless mediocrity. They'll be comfortable. But something in the spirit will be missing."

I have painted too drab a portrait of today's students, making   34
them seem a solemn lot. That is only half of their story; if they were
so dreary I wouldn't so thoroughly enjoy their company. The other
half is that they are easy to like. They are quick to laugh and to offer
friendship. They are not introverts. They are unusually kind and are
more considerate of one another than any student generation I have
known.

Nor are they so obsessed with their studies that they avoid sports   35
and extracurricular activities. On the contrary, they juggle their
crowded hours to play on a variety of teams, perform with musical and
dramatic groups, and write for campus publications. But this in turn
is one more cause of anxiety. There are too many choices. Academically, they have 1,300 courses to select from; outside class they have
to decide how much spare time they can spare and how to spend it.

This means that they engage in fewer extracurricular pursuits   36
than their predecessors did. If they want to row on the crew and play
in the symphony they will eliminate one; in the '60s they would have
done both. They also tend to choose activities that are self-limiting.
Drama, for instance, is flourishing in all twelve of Yale's residential
colleges as it never has before. Students hurl themselves into these
productions—as actors, directors, carpenters, and technicians—with
a dedication to create the best possible play, knowing that the day will
come when the run will end and they can get back to their studies.

They also can't afford to be the willing slave of organizations   37
like the *Yale Daily News*. Last spring at the one-hundredth anniver-
sary banquet of that paper—whose past chairmen include such once
and future kings as Potter Stewart, Kingman Brewster, and William
F. Buckley, Jr.—much was made of the fact that the editorial staff
used to be small and totally committed and that "newsies" routinely
worked fifty hours a week. In effect they belonged to a club; Newsies
is how they defined themselves at Yale. Today's student will write
one or two articles a week, when he can, and he defines himself as a
student. I've never heard the word Newsie except at the banquet.

If I have described the modern undergraduate primarily as a   38
driven creature who is largely ignoring the blithe spirit inside who
keeps trying to come out and play, it's because that's where the
crunch is, not only at Yale but throughout American education. It's
why I think we should all be worried about the values that are nur-

turing a generation so fearful of risk and so goal-obsessed at such an early age.

I tell students that there is no one "right" way to get ahead— that each of them is a different person, starting from a different point and bound for a different destination. I tell them that change is a tonic and that all the slots are not codified nor the frontiers closed. One of my ways of telling them is to invite men and women who have achieved success outside the academic world to come and talk informally with my students during the year. They are heads of companies or ad agencies, editors of magazines, politicians, public officials, television magnates, labor leaders, business executives, Broadway producers, artists, writers, economists, photographers, scientists, historians—a mixed bag of achievers.

39

I ask them to say a few words about how they got started. The students assume that they started in their present profession and knew all along that it was what they wanted to do. Luckily for me, most of them got into their field by a circuitous route, to their surprise, after many detours. The students are startled. They can hardly conceive of a career that was not pre-planned. They can hardly imagine allowing the hand of God or chance to nudge them down some unforeseen trail.

40

Questions for Close Reading

1. What is the selection's thesis? Locate the sentence(s) in which Zinsser states his main idea. If he doesn't state the thesis explicitly, express it in your own words.
2. According to Zinsser, why are the pressures on college students today so harmful?
3. Zinsser says that some of the pressures are "intertwined." What does he mean? Give examples from the essay.
4. What actions or attitudes on the part of students can help free them from the pressures that Zinsser describes?
5. Refer to your dictionary as needed to define the following words used in the selection: *privy* (paragraph 3), *venerated* (6), *exhorted* (13), *tenacity* (15), *vacillates* (22), *furtively* (22), and *circuitous* (40).

Questions About the Writer's Craft

1. **The pattern.**   When analyzing a subject, writers usually try to identify divisions and classifications that are—within reason—mutually exclusive.

But Zinsser acknowledges that the four pressures he discusses can be seen as two distinct pairs, with each pair consisting of two "deeply intertwined" pressures. How does this overlapping of categories help Zinsser make his point?

2. **Other patterns.**   In addition to using classification in this essay, what other pattern of development does Zinsser use? How does this additional pattern help him make his point?

3. Why do you suppose Zinsser uses the notes to Carlos as his essay's introduction? What profile of college students does the reader get from these notes?

4. In paragraph 4, the author writes that students want a map "they can follow unswervingly to career security, financial security, Social Security and, presumably, a prepaid grave." What tone is Zinsser using here? Where else does he use this tone?

Questions for Further Thought

1. Zinsser was a college professor at Yale. Do you think he's well qualified to advise students about career choices? Do you think he knows enough about the real world to advise students to "relax" and take a wide range of courses, instead of focusing on a practical "pre-rich" major?

2. Is it possible both to major in something "safe" and practical and to take electives to become liberally educated? Is it desirable? Explain.

3. Zinsser states that today's students "engage in fewer extracurricular pursuits than their predecessors." Do you agree that students are focusing more on their majors? Are extracurricular activities at your college suffering from low membership and lack of interest?

4. What does Zinsser mean by saying that "One of the few rights that America does not proclaim is the right to fail"? Do you agree that students should take more risks? If so, what kinds of risks should they take?

Writing Assignments Using Division-Classification as a Pattern of Development

∞ 1. Zinsser writes as if all students are the same—panicky, overwrought, and materialistic. Take a position counter to his and write an essay explaining that campuses contain many students different from those Zinsser writes about. To support your point, categorize students into types, giving examples of what each type is like. Be sure that the categories you identify refute Zinsser's analysis of the typical student. The tone of your essay may be serious or playful. James Thurber's "University Days" (page 239) may give you some ideas for your essay, especially if you choose to approach your subject from a humorous or satiric perspective.

2. Is economic security the only kind of satisfaction that college students should pursue? Write an essay classifying the various kinds of satisfactions

that students could aim for. At the end of the paper, include brief recommendations about ways that students could best spend their time preparing for these different kinds of satisfactions.

Writing Assignments Using Other Patterns of Development

3. Using Zinsser's analysis of the pressures on college students, write an essay explaining how these pressures can be reduced or eliminated. Give practical suggestions showing how students can avoid or get around the pressures. Also, indicate what society, parents, and college staff can do to help ease students' anxieties.

4. Zinsser's essay indicates that today's students are "slotting" themselves into preordained careers and not leaving themselves open to later opportunities. Write an essay arguing that this tendency to specialize early in college is either beneficial or disastrous for students. Consider such issues as individual freedom, career confusion, changing job markets, changes in society, and the like.

Scott Russell Sanders

Scott Russell Sanders was born in 1945 to a farming family in Tennessee. After graduating from Brown University, where he studied physics and English, he began a writing career that has grown to include more than a dozen books. His work has been diverse, encompassing historical novels, children's stories, essays, and fiction. Two of Sanders's best-known works are the fictional *Fetching the Dead* (1984) and *The Engineer of Beasts* (1988), a science-fiction novel for young adults. His more recent books include a children's book on frontier life, *Warm as Wool* (1992), and a nonfiction work on nature, *Staying Put: Making a Home in a Restless World* (1993). The following essay is taken from *The Paradise of Bombs* (1987), an essay collection for which Sanders won the Associated Writing Programs Award for Creative Nonfiction.

The Men We Carry in Our Minds

How does each of us arrive at a personal understanding of what it means to be male or female? We gather some information from the schools we attend, the religious organizations we belong to, the books we read, the movies and television shows we watch. But the strongest influence is the adults we know and observe as we grow up. Scott Russell Sanders describes his early memories of the men around him and tells how those memories shaped his conception of manhood.

The first men, besides my father, I remember seeing were black   1
convicts and white guards, in the cotton field across the road from our farm on the outskirts of Memphis. I must have been three or four. The prisoners wore dingy gray-and-black zebra suits, heavy as canvas, sodden with sweat. Hatless, stooped, they chopped weeds in the fierce heat, row after row, breathing the acrid dust of boll-weevil poison. The overseers wore dazzling white shirts and broad shadowy hats. The oiled barrels of their shotguns flashed in the sunlight. Their faces in memory are utterly blank. Of course those men, white and black, have become for me an emblem of racial hatred. But they have

also come to stand for the twin poles of my early vision of man-hood—the brute toiling animal and the boss.

When I was a boy, the men I knew labored with their bodies. 2 They were marginal farmers, just scraping by, or welders, steelwork-ers, carpenters; they swept floors, dug ditches, mined coal, or drove trucks, their forearms ropy with muscle; they trained horses, stoked furnaces, built fires, stood on assembly lines wrestling parts onto cars and refrigerators. They got up before light, worked all day long what-ever the weather, and when they came home at night they looked as though somebody had been whipping them. In the evenings and on weekends they worked on their own places, tilling gardens that were lumpy with clay, fixing broken-down cars, hammering on houses that were always too drafty, too leaky, too small.

The bodies of the men I knew were twisted and maimed in ways 3 visible and invisible. The nails of their hands were black and split, the hands tattooed with scars. Some had lost fingers. Heavy lifting had given many of them finicky backs and guts weak from hernias. Racing against conveyor belts had given them ulcers. Their ankles and knees ached from years of standing on concrete. Anyone who had worked for long around machines was hard of hearing. They squinted, and the skin of their faces was creased like the leather of old work gloves. There were times, studying them, when I dreaded growing up. Most of them coughed, from dust or cigarettes, and most of them drank cheap wine or whisky, so their eyes looked bloodshot and bruised. The fathers of my friends always seemed older than the mothers. Men wore out sooner. Only women lived into old age.

As a boy I also knew another sort of men, who did not sweat and 4 break down like mules. They were soldiers, and so far as I could tell they scarcely worked at all. During my early school years we lived on a military base, an arsenal in Ohio, and every day I saw GIs in the guard shacks, on the stoops of barracks, at the wheels of olive drab Chevrolets. The chief fact of their lives was boredom. Long after I left the Arsenal I came to recognize the sour smell the soldiers gave off as that of souls in limbo. They were all waiting—for wars, for transfers, for leaves, for promotions, for the end of their hitch—like so many braves waiting for the hunt to begin. Unlike the warriors of older tribes, however, they would have no say about when the battle would start or how it would be waged. Their waiting was broken only when they practiced for war. They fired guns at targets, drove tanks across the churned-up fields of the military reservation, set off bombs in the wrecks of old fighter planes. I knew this was all play. But I also felt certain that when the hour for killing arrived, they would kill. When the real shooting started, many of them would die. This was what soldiers were *for*, just as a hammer was for driving nails.

Warriors and toilers: those seemed, in my boyhood vision, to be   5
the chief destinies for men. They weren't the only destinies, as I learned from having a few male teachers, from reading books, and from watching television. But the men on television—the politicians, the astronauts, the generals, the savvy lawyers, the philosophical doctors, the bosses who gave orders to both soldiers and laborers— seemed as removed and unreal to me as the figures in tapestries. I could no more imagine growing up to become one of these cool, potent creatures than I could imagine becoming a prince.

A nearer and more hopeful example was that of my father, who   6
had escaped from a red-dirt farm to a tire factory, and from the assembly line to the front office. Eventually he dressed in a white shirt and tie. He carried himself as if he had been born to work with his mind. But his body, remembering the earlier years of slogging work, began to give out on him in his fifties, and it quit on him entirely before he turned sixty-five. Even such a partial escape from man's fate as he had accomplished did not seem possible for most of the boys I knew. They joined the Army, stood in line for jobs in the smoky plants, helped build highways. They were bound to work as their fathers had worked, killing themselves or preparing to kill others.

A scholarship enabled me not only to attend college, a rare   7
enough feat in my circle, but even to study in a university meant for the children of the rich. Here I met for the first time young men who had assumed from birth that they would lead lives of comfort and power. And for the first time I met women who told me that men were guilty of having kept all the joys and privileges of the earth for themselves. I was baffled. What privileges? What joys? I thought about the maimed, dismal lives of most of the men back home. What had they stolen from their wives and daughters? The right to go five days a week, twelve months a year, for thirty or forty years to a steel mill or a coal mine? The right to drop bombs and die in war? The right to feel every leak in the roof, every gap in the fence, every cough in the engine, as a wound they must mend? The right to feel, when the lay-off comes or the plant shuts down, not only afraid but ashamed?

I was slow to understand the deep grievances of women. This   8
was because, as a boy, I had envied them. Before college, the only

people I had ever known who were interested in art or music or literature, the only ones who read books, the only ones who ever seemed to enjoy a sense of ease and grace were the mothers and daughters. Like the menfolk, they fretted about money, they scrimped and made-do. But, when the pay stopped coming in, they were not the ones who had failed. Nor did they have to go to war, and that seemed to me a blessed fact. By comparison with the narrow, ironclad days of fathers, there was an expansiveness, I thought, in the days of mothers. They went to see neighbors, to shop in town, to run errands at school, at the library, at church. No doubt, had I looked harder at their lives, I would have envied them less. It was not my fate to become a woman, so it was easier for me to see the graces. Few of them held jobs outside the home, and those who did filled thankless roles as clerks and waitresses. I didn't see, then, what a prison a house could be, since houses seemed to me brighter, handsomer places than any factory. I did not realize—because such things were never spoken of—how often women suffered from men's bullying. I did learn about the wretchedness of abandoned wives, single mothers, widows; but I also learned about the wretchedness of lone men. Even then I could see how exhausting it was for a mother to cater all day to the needs of young children. But if I had been asked, as a boy, to choose between tending a baby and tending a machine, I think I would have chosen the baby. (Having now tended both, I know I would choose the baby.)

So I was baffled when the women at college accused me and my 9
sex of having cornered the world's pleasures. I think something like my bafflement has been felt by other boys (and girls as well) who grew up in dirt-poor farm country, in mining country, in black ghettos, in Hispanic barrios, in the shadows of factories, in Third World nations—any place where the fate of men is as grim and bleak as the fate of women. Toilers and warriors. I realize now how ancient these identities are, how deep the tug they exert on men, the undertow of a thousand generations. The miseries I saw, as a boy, in the lives of nearly all men I continue to see in the lives of many—the body-breaking toil, the tedium, the call to be tough, the humiliating powerlessness, the battle for a living and for territory.

When the women I met at college thought about the joys and 10
privileges of men, they did not carry in their minds the sort of men I had known in my childhood. They thought of their fathers, who were bankers, physicians, architects, stockbrokers, the big wheels of

the big cities. These fathers rode the train to work or drove cars that cost more than any of my childhood houses. They were attended from morning to night by female helpers, wives and nurses and secretaries. They were never laid off, never short of cash at month's end, never lined up for welfare. These fathers made decisions that mattered. They ran the world.

The daughters of such men wanted to share in this power, this 11 glory. So did I. They yearned for a say over their future, for jobs worthy of their abilities, for the right to live at peace, unmolested, whole. Yes, I thought, yes yes. The difference between me and these daughters was that they saw me, because of my sex, as destined from birth to become like their fathers, and therefore as an enemy to their desires. I was an ally. If I had known, then, how to tell them so, would they have believed me? Would they now?

Questions for Close Reading

1. What is the selection's thesis? Locate the sentence(s) in which Sanders states his main idea. If he doesn't state the thesis explicitly, express it in your own words.
2. Who were the men Sanders knew most about in his childhood? What does Sanders mean when he says that these men were damaged "in ways both visible and invisible" (paragraph 3)?
3. How did Sanders learn that some men don't toil with their bodies? How did he feel about such men?
4. Why, according to Sanders, was he "slow to understand the deep grievances of women"(8)? Why did the women Sanders met at college consider men to be privileged? Why does Sanders feel he is "an ally" rather than "an enemy" of these women? What prevented the women from understanding how he felt?
5. Refer to your dictionary as needed to define the following words used in the selection: *sodden* (paragraph 1), *acrid* (1), *marginal* (2), *tapestries* (5), *potent* (5), *grievances* (8), *expansiveness* (8), and *tedium* (9).

Questions About the Writer's Craft

1. **The pattern.**   Sanders categorizes men into three types: toiling animals, warriors, and bosses. Of the three categories, which two does he describe most vividly? Why might he have chosen to describe these two in such detail?
2. In paragraphs 2 and 3, Sanders offers a vivid portrait of workingmen's lives. How does his word choice, as well as his use of parallel structure and repetition, lend power to this portrait?

3. **Other patterns.** In the second half of the essay, Sanders contrasts the lives of workingmen with those of women (paragraphs 7–8) and with those of professional men (10). What is the value of these contrasts?
4. From the middle of paragraph 7 to its end, Sanders frames his sentences as questions. Why might he have decided to pose all these questions? How do they help him achieve his purpose?

Questions for Further Thought

1. Sanders states that in his childhood experience, "Men wore out sooner. Only women lived into old age." Have you observed a similar pattern in your family? What might account for the statistical fact that men in our society die earlier than women?
2. In Sanders's childhood, the people of higher status "seemed as removed and unreal" as "the figures in tapestries." As you were growing up, what people did you look up to because of their high status? Why did you regard them so highly? Do you still look up to these people? Why or why not?
3. Sanders indicates that his peers didn't fare any better than their fathers. Will the young men and young women you knew growing up have a higher status than their parents? Explain. Do you feel children should expect to do better than their parents? Why or why not?
4. Do you believe that men can be allies of women in their fight for equality? Would some men find it difficult to support women's struggle "for a say over their future, for jobs worthy of their abilities, for the right to live at peace, unmolested, whole"? Explain.

Writing Assignments Using Division-Classification as a Pattern of Development

∞ 1. "Warriors and toilers," Sanders writes, "those seemed, in my boyhood vision, to be the chief destinies for men." Identify several men *or* women who helped create your "vision" of what it means to be male *or* female. (You may focus on your view of your own sex or your view of the opposite sex.) Group these individuals into types. Then write an essay describing these types and the people representing each type; your goal is to show whether these people enlarged or restricted your understanding of what it means to be male or female. Before writing your paper, you may want to read one or several of the essays in this book that deal with gender expectations: Judith Ortiz Cofer's "A Partial Remembrance of a Puerto Rican Childhood" (page 138), Alleen Pace Nilsen's "Sexism and Language" (page 229), Barbara Ehrenreich's "What I've Learned From Men" (page 261), Judy Brady's "Why I Want a Wife" (page 530), Camille Paglia's "Rape: A Bigger Danger Than Feminists Know" (page 638), and Susan Jacoby's "Common Decency" (page 645).

2. Sanders admits he was "slow to understand the deep grievances of women" against men. Consider another group that has grievances—for example, smokers and their disagreements with nonsmokers, parents and their complaints about teenagers, or vegetarians and their objections to meat eaters. Start by brainstorming with others to generate examples of the group's grievances; then write an essay in which you categorize the grievances by type, illustrating each with vivid examples. At the end, reach some conclusions about the validity of the group's complaints.

Writing Assignments Using Other Patterns of Development

3. Sanders's father transformed his life when he "escaped from a red-dirt farm...to the front office." Think about someone else who also made a positive life change. Perhaps you (or someone you know) stopped hanging out with a destructive crowd and became an academic star, or went back to school at age forty-something to prepare for a different career, or found the courage to end a painful marriage. Write an essay in which you describe the change that was made and explain the steps that the person took to make effective and lasting alterations in his or her life. To highlight the change the person made, start by showing what the person's life was like before it was turned around.

∞ 4. Since the time Sanders was in college, gender roles have become somewhat less rigid. For example, no one is surprised to see a man pushing a stroller or a woman delivering mail. What gender-role changes do you detect in such areas as dating, marriage, athletics, employment choices, or workplace conditions? Do you think the changes have been for the better? Select *one* such area and talk with people of varying ages about changes they have witnessed. Then write an essay showing that increased flexibility in sexual roles has affected men's or women's (or boys' or girls') lives in either a positive or a negative way. Provide persuasive examples that illustrate your attitude toward those changes. Alleen Pace Nilsen's "Sexism and Language" (page 229), Deborah Tannen's "Sex, Lies, and Conversation" (page 428), and Judy Brady's "Why I Want a Wife" (page 530) will offer some ideas worth exploring.

Ann McClintock

Ann McClintock (1946–   ) was educated at Temple University in Philadelphia and later earned an advanced degree from the University of Pennsylvania. Formerly Director of Occupational Therapy at Ancora State Hospital in New Jersey, she has also worked as a freelance editor and writer. A frequent speaker before community groups, McClintock is especially interested in the effects of advertising on American life. The following selection, revised for this text, is part of a work in progress on the way propaganda techniques are used to sell products and political candidates.

Propaganda Techniques in Today's Advertising

Propaganda is not just the tool of totalitarian governments and dictators. Rather, propaganda is all around us—in the form of commercials and advertisements. The author of this selection shows how Madison Avenue uses many of the techniques typical of political propaganda to convince us that we need certain products and services. After reading the essay, you may regard in a different light the jingles, endorsements, and slogans characteristic of today's commercials.

Americans, adults and children alike, are being seduced. They   1
are being brainwashed. And few of us protest. Why? Because the seducers and the brainwashers are the advertisers we willingly invite into our homes. We are victims, content—even eager—to be victimized. We read advertisers' propaganda messages in newspapers and magazines; we watch their alluring images on television. We absorb their messages and images into our subconscious. We all do it—even those of us who claim to see through advertisers' tricks and therefore feel immune to advertising's charm. Advertisers lean heavily on propaganda to sell products, whether the "products" are a brand of toothpaste, a candidate for office, or a particular political viewpoint.

Propaganda is a systematic effort to influence people's opinions,   2
to win them over to a certain view or side. Propaganda is not necessarily concerned with what is true or false, good or bad. Propagandists simply want people to believe the messages being sent. Often,
propagandists will use outright lies or more subtle deceptions to sway
people's opinions. In a propaganda war, any tactic is considered fair.

When we hear the word "propaganda," we usually think of a   3
foreign menace: anti-American radio programs broadcast by a totalitarian regime or brainwashing tactics practiced on hostages. Although propaganda may seem relevant only in the political arena, the
concept can be applied fruitfully to the way products and ideas are
sold in advertising. Indeed, the vast majority of us are targets in advertisers' propaganda war. Every day, we are bombarded with slogans, print ads, commercials, packaging claims, billboards,
trademarks, logos, and designer brands—all forms of propaganda.
One study reports that each of us, during an average day, is exposed
to over *five hundred* advertising claims of various types. This satura-
tion may even increase in the future since current trends include ads
on movie screens, shopping carts, videocassettes, even public television.

What kind of propaganda techniques do advertisers use? There   4
are seven basic types:

1. *Name Calling*   Name calling is a propaganda tactic in   5
which negatively charged names are hurled against the opposing side
or competitor. By using such names, propagandists try to arouse feelings of mistrust, fear, and hate in their audiences. For example, a political advertisement may label an opposing candidate a "loser,"
"fence-sitter," or "warmonger." Depending on the advertiser's target market, labels such as "a friend of big business" or "a dues-paying
member of the party in power" can be the epithets that damage an
opponent. Ads for products may also use name calling. An American
manufacturer may refer, for instance, to a "foreign car" in its commercial—not an "imported" one. The label of foreignness will have
unpleasant connotations in many people's minds. A childhood
rhyme claims that "names can never hurt me," but name calling is an
effective way to damage the opposition, whether it is another car
maker or a congressional candidate.

2. *Glittering Generalities*   Using glittering generalities is the   6
opposite of name calling. In this case, advertisers surround their

products with attractive—and slippery—words and phrases. They use vague terms that are difficult to define and that may have different meanings to different people: *freedom, democratic, all-American, progressive, Christian,* and *justice.* Many such words have strong, affirmative overtones. This kind of language stirs positive feelings in people, feelings that may spill over to the product or idea being pitched. As with name calling, the emotional response may overwhelm logic. Target audiences accept the product without thinking very much about what the glittering generalities mean—or whether they even apply to the product. After all, how can anyone oppose "truth, justice, and the American way"?

The ads for politicians and political causes often use glittering 7 generalities because such "buzz words" can influence votes. Election slogans include high-sounding but basically empty phrases like the following:

"He cares about people." (That's nice, but is he a better candidate than his opponent?)

"Vote for progress." (Progress by *whose* standards?)

"They'll make this country great again." (What does "great" mean? Does "great" mean the same thing to others as it does to me?)

"Vote for the future." (What kind of future?)

"If you love America, vote for Phyllis Smith." (If I don't vote for Smith, does that mean I don't love America?)

Ads for consumer goods are also sprinkled with glittering gen- 8 eralities. Product names, for instance, are supposed to evoke good feelings: *Luvs* diapers, *New Freedom* feminine hygiene products, *Joy* liquid detergent, *Loving Care* hair color, *Almost Home* cookies, *Yankee Doodle* pastries. Product slogans lean heavily on vague but comforting phrases: Kinney is "The Great American Shoe Store," General Electric "brings good things to life," and Dow Chemical "lets you do great things." Chevrolet, we are told, is the "heartbeat of America," and Chrysler boasts cars that are "built by Americans for Americans."

3. *Transfer* In transfer, advertisers try to improve the image of 9 a product by associating it with a symbol most people respect, like the American flag or Uncle Sam. The advertisers hope that the prestige attached to the symbol will carry over to the product. Many

companies use transfer devices to identify their products: Lincoln Insurance shows a profile of the president; Continental Insurance portrays a Revolutionary War minuteman; Amtrak's logo is red, white, and blue; Liberty Mutual's corporate symbol is the Statue of Liberty; Allstate's name is cradled by a pair of protective, fatherly hands.

Corporations also use the transfer technique when they sponsor   10
prestigious shows on radio and television. These shows function as symbols of dignity and class. Kraft Corporation, for instance, sponsored a "Leonard Bernstein Conducts Beethoven" concert, while Gulf Oil is the sponsor of *National Geographic* specials and Mobil supports public television's *Masterpiece Theater*. In this way, corporations can reach an educated, influential audience and, perhaps, improve their public image by associating themselves with quality programming.

Political ads, of course, practically wrap themselves in the flag.   11
Ads for a political candidate often show either the Washington Monument, a Fourth of July parade, the Stars and Stripes, a bald eagle soaring over the mountains, or a white-steepled church on the village green. The national anthem or "America the Beautiful" may play softly in the background. Such appeals to Americans' love of country can surround the candidate with an aura of patriotism and integrity.

4. *Testimonial*   The testimonial is one of advertisers' most-   12
loved and most-used propaganda techniques. Similar to the transfer device, the testimonial capitalizes on the admiration people have for a celebrity to make the product shine more brightly—even though the celebrity is not an expert on the product being sold.

Print and television ads offer a nonstop parade of testimonials: 13
here's Cher for Holiday Spas; here's basketball star Michael Jordan eating Wheaties; Michael Jackson sings about Pepsi; American Express features a slew of well-known people who assure us that they never go anywhere without their American Express card. Testimonials can sell movies, too; newspaper ads for films often feature favorable comments by well-known reviewers. And, in recent years, testimonials have played an important role in pitching books; the backs of paperbacks frequently list complimentary blurbs by celebrities.

Political candidates, as well as their ad agencies, know the value   14
of testimonials. Barbra Streisand lent her star appeal to the presidential campaign of Bill Clinton, while Arnold Schwarzenegger en-

dorsed George Bush. Even controversial social issues are debated by celebrities. The nuclear freeze, for instance, starred Paul Newman for the pro side and Charlton Heston for the con.

As illogical as testimonials sometimes are (Pepsi's Michael Jackson, for instance, is a health-food adherent who does not drink soft drinks), they are effective propaganda. We like the *person* so much that we like the *product* too.   15

5. *Plain Folks*   The plain folks approach says, in effect, "Buy me or vote for me. I'm just like you." Regular folks will surely like Bob Evans's Down on the Farm Country Sausage or good old-fashioned Countrytime Lemonade. Some ads emphasize the idea that "we're all in the same boat." We see people making long-distance calls for just the reasons we do—to put the baby on the phone to Grandma or to tell Mom we love her. And how do these folksy, warmhearted (usually saccharine) scenes affect us? They're supposed to make us feel that AT&T—the multinational corporate giant—has the same values we do. Similarly, we are introduced to the little people at Ford, the ordinary folks who work on the assembly line, not to bigwigs in their executive offices. What's the purpose of such an approach? To encourage us to buy a car built by these honest, hardworking "everyday Joes" who care about quality as much as we do.   16

Political advertisements make almost as much use of the "plain folks" appeal as they do of transfer devices. Candidates wear hard hats, farmers' caps, and assembly-line coveralls. They jog around the block and carry their own luggage through the airport. The idea is to convince voters that the candidates are average people, not the elite—not wealthy lawyers or executives but common citizens.   17

6. *Card Stacking*   When people say that "the cards were stacked against me," they mean that they were never given a fair chance. Applied to propaganda, card stacking means that one side may suppress or distort evidence, tell half-truths, oversimplify the facts, or set up a "straw man"—a false target—to divert attention from the issue at hand. Card stacking is a difficult form of propaganda both to detect and to combat. When a candidate claims that an opponent has "changed his mind five times on this important issue," we tend to accept the claim without investigating whether the candidate had good reasons for changing his mind. Many people are simply swayed by the distorted claim that the candidate is "waffling" on the issue.   18

Advertisers often stack the cards in favor of the products they are   19
pushing. They may, for instance, use what are called "weasel words."
These are small words that usually slip right past us, but that make
the difference between reality and illusion. The weasel words are underlined in the following claims:

> "<u>Helps control</u> dandruff symptoms." (The audience usually in-
> terprets this as *stops* dandruff.)
> "Most dentists <u>surveyed</u> recommend sugarless gum for their pa-
> tients <u>who chew gum</u>." (We hear the "most dentists" and
> "for their patients," but we don't think about how many
> were surveyed or whether the dentists first recommended
> that the patients not chew gum at all.)
> "Sticker price $1,000 lower than <u>most comparable</u> cars." (How
> many is "most"? What car does the advertiser consider
> "comparable"?)

Advertisers also use a card stacking trick when they make an un-   20
finished claim. For example, they will say that their product has
"twice as much pain reliever." We are left with a favorable impression. We don't usually ask, "Twice as much pain reliever as what?"
Or advertisers may make extremely vague claims that sound alluring
but have no substance: Toyota's "Oh, what a feeling!"; Vantage cigarettes' "The taste of success"; "The spirit of Marlboro"; Coke's
"the real thing." Another way to stack the cards in favor of a certain
product is to use scientific-sounding claims that are not supported by
sound research. When Ford claimed that its LTD model was "400%
quieter," many people assumed that the LTD must be quieter than
all other cars. When taken to court, however, Ford admitted that the
phrase referred to the difference between the noise level inside and
outside the LTD. Other scientific-sounding claims use mysterious
ingredients that are never explained as selling points: "Retsyn," "special whitening agents," "the ingredient doctors recommend."

7. *Bandwagon*   In the bandwagon technique, advertisers pres-   21
sure, "Everyone's doing it. Why don't you?" This kind of propaganda often succeeds because many people have a deep desire not to be
different. Political ads tell us to vote for the "winning candidate."
Advertisers know we tend to feel comfortable doing what others do;
we want to be on the winning team. Or ads show a series of people

proclaiming, "I'm voting for the Senator. I don't know why anyone wouldn't." Again, the audience feels under pressure to conform.

In the marketplace, the bandwagon approach lures buyers. Ads   22
tell us that "nobody doesn't like Sara Lee" (the message is that you must be weird if you don't). They tell us that "most people prefer Brand X two to one over other leading brands" (to be like the majority, we should buy Brand X). If we don't drink Pepsi, we're left out of "the Pepsi generation." To take part in "America's favorite health kick," the National Dairy Council urges us to drink milk. And Honda motorcycle ads, praising the virtues of being a follower, tell us, "Follow the leader. He's on a Honda."

Why do these propaganda techniques work? Why do so many of   23
us buy the products, viewpoints, and candidates urged on us by propaganda messages? They work because they appeal to our emotions, not to our minds. Often, in fact, they capitalize on our prejudices and biases. For example, if we are convinced that environmentalists are radicals who want to destroy America's record of industrial growth and progress, then we will applaud the candidate who refers to them as "treehuggers." Clear thinking requires hard work: analyzing a claim, researching the facts, examining both sides of an issue, using logic to see the flaws in an argument. Many of us would rather let the propagandists do our thinking for us.

Because propaganda is so effective, it is important to detect it   24
and understand how it is used. We may conclude, after close examination, that some propaganda sends a truthful, worthwhile message. Some advertising, for instance, urges us not to drive drunk, to become volunteers, to contribute to charity. Even so, we must be aware that propaganda is being used. Otherwise, we have consented to handing over to others our independence of thought and action.

Questions for Close Reading

1. What is the selection's thesis? Locate the sentence(s) in which McClintock states her main idea. If she doesn't state the thesis explicitly, express it in your own words.
2. What is *propaganda*? What mistaken associations do people often have with this term?
3. What are "weasel words"? How do they trick listeners?

4. Why does McClintock believe we should be better informed about propaganda techniques?
5. Refer to your dictionary as needed to define the following words used in the selection: *seduced* (paragraph 1), *warmonger* (5), and *elite* (17).

Questions About the Writer's Craft

1. **The pattern and other patterns.** Before explaining the categories into which propaganda techniques can be grouped, McClintock provides a definition of propaganda. Is the definition purely informative, or does it have a larger objective? If you think the latter, what is the definition's broader purpose?
2. In her introduction, McClintock uses loaded words like *seduced* and *brainwashed*. What effect do these words have on the reader?
3. Locate places in the essay where McClintock uses questions. Which are rhetorical and which are genuine queries?
4. What kind of conclusion does McClintock provide for the essay?

Questions for Further Thought

1. Do you agree with McClintock that we are subjected to commercial propaganda every day? Is *propaganda* the right term to use for today's advertising techniques? Explain.
2. Which of the advertising techniques described by McClintock are easiest to identify in an ad? Which are the least obvious? Can you recall examples of ads that make use of these techniques?
3. Do you think that you're relatively immune to advertising's ploys? What factors influence your decision to purchase a particular brand or product?
4. Since propaganda is so effective, is it ethical for advertisers and politicians to use it? Is awareness enough to protect us from the effects of such propaganda—or do we need stronger protection? What other means could we use to protect ourselves?

Writing Assignments Using Division-Classification as a Pattern of Development

1. McClintock cautions us to be sensitive to propaganda in advertising. Young children, however, aren't capable of this kind of awareness. With pen or pencil in hand, watch some commercials aimed at children, such as those for toys, cereals, and fast food. Then analyze the use of propaganda techniques in these commercials. Using division-classification, write an essay describing the main propaganda techniques you observed. Support your analysis with examples drawn from the commercials. Remember to provide a thesis that indicates your opinion of the advertising techniques.

2. Like advertising techniques, television shows can be classified. Avoiding the obvious system of classifying according to game shows, detective shows, and situation comedies, come up with your own original division-classification principle. Possibilities include how family life is depicted, the way work is presented, how male-female relationships are portrayed. Using one such principle, write an essay in which you categorize popular TV shows into three types. Refer to specific shows to support your classification system. Your attitude toward the shows being discussed should be made clear.

Writing Assignments Using Other Patterns of Development

∞ 3. McClintock says that card stacking "distort[s] evidence, tell[s] half-truths, oversimpli[fies] the facts" (18). Focusing on an editorial, a political campaign, a print ad, or a television commercial, analyze the extent to which card stacking is used as a persuasive strategy. Neil Postman's "Future Shlock" (page 248) will deepen your understanding of the extent to which the truth can be distorted.

4. To increase further your sensitivity to the moral dimensions of propaganda, write a proposal outlining an ad campaign for a real or imaginary product or elected official. The introduction to your proposal should identify who or what is to be promoted, and the thesis or plan of development should indicate the specific propaganda techniques you suggest. In the paper's supporting paragraphs, explain how these techniques would be used to promote your product or candidate.

Janet Mendell Goldstein

Born in Philadelphia in 1940, Janet Mendell Goldstein did her undergraduate work at Radcliffe College and earned advanced degrees at Harvard University and the University of Pennsylvania. An educator for thirty years, she now works as an editorial consultant, freelance writer, and textbook author. Coauthor of a college reading text, Goldstein is also an essayist and a poet. Her work has appeared in a variety of newspapers and magazines, including the *English Journal, Faith and Inspiration,* and the *Philadelphia Inquirer.* The following selection is drawn from a series of pieces Goldstein has written about contemporary life.

The Quick Fix Society

Not so long ago, we were told that if we worked hard and never gave up, we would eventually get what we wanted. These days, however, "eventually" isn't good enough for many people. Janet Mendell Goldstein urges us to consider where we are going in such a rush. And what, she asks, are we missing along the way?

My husband and I just got back from a week's vacation in West   1
Virginia. Of course, we couldn't wait to get there, so we took the Pennsylvania Turnpike and a couple of interstates. "Look at those gorgeous farms!" my husband exclaimed as pastoral scenery slid by us at 55 mph. "Did you see those cows?" But at 55 mph, it's difficult to see anything; the gorgeous farms look like moving green checkerboards, and the herd of cows is reduced to a sprinkling of dots in the rear-view mirror. For four hours, our only real amusement consisted of counting exit signs and wondering what it would feel like to hold still again. Getting there certainly didn't seem like half the fun; in fact, getting there wasn't any fun at all.

So, when it was time to return to our home outside of Philadel-   2
phia, I insisted that we take a different route. "Let's explore that

countryside," I suggested. The two days it took us to make the return trip were studded with new experiences. We toured a Civil War battlefield and stood on the little hill that fifteen thousand Confederate soldiers had tried to take on another hot July afternoon, one hundred and twenty-five years ago, not knowing that half of them would perish in the vain attempt. We meandered through main streets of sleepy Pennsylvania Dutch towns, slowing to twenty miles an hour so as not to crowd the horses and buggies on their way to market. We admired toy trains and antique cars in county museums and saved 70 percent in factory outlets. We stuffed ourselves with spicy salads and homemade bread pudding in an "all-you-can-eat" farmhouse restaurant, then wandered outside to enjoy the sunshine and the herds of cows—no little dots this time—basking in it. And we returned home refreshed, reeducated, revitalized. This time, getting there had *been* the fun.

Why is it that the featureless turnpikes and interstates are the routes of choice for so many of us? Why doesn't everybody try slowing down and exploring the countryside? But more and more, the fast lane seems to be the only way for us to go. In fact, most Americans are constantly in a hurry—and not just to get from Point A to Point B. Our country has become a nation in search of the quick fix—in more ways than one. 3

Now instead of later: Once upon a time, Americans understood the principle of deferred gratification. We put a little of each paycheck away "for a rainy day." If we wanted a new sofa or a week at a lakeside cabin, we saved up for it, and the banks helped us out by providing special Christmas Club and Vacation Club accounts. If we lived in the right part of the country, we planted corn and beans and waited patiently for the harvest. If we wanted to be thinner, we simply ate less of our favorite foods and waited patiently for the scale to drop, a pound at a time. But today we aren't so patient. We take out loans instead of making deposits, or we use our VISA or Mastercard to get that furniture or vacation trip—relax now, pay later. We buy our food, like our clothing, ready-made and off the rack. And if we're in a hurry to lose weight, we try the latest miracle diet, guaranteed to shed ten pounds in ten days...unless we're rich enough to afford liposuction. 4

Faster instead of slower: Not only do we want it now; we don't even want to be kept waiting for it. This pervasive impatience, the "I- 5 hate-to-wait" syndrome, has infected every level of our lives. Instead of standing in line at the bank, we withdraw twenty dollars in as many seconds from an automatic teller machine. Then we take our fast money to a fast convenience store (why wait in line at the supermarket?), where we buy a frozen dinner all wrapped up and ready to be popped into the microwave...unless we don't care to wait even that long and pick up some fast food instead. And if our fast meal doesn't agree with us, we hurry to the medicine cabinet for—you guessed it—some fast relief. We like fast pictures, so we buy Polaroid cameras. We like fast entertainment, so we record our favorite TV show on the VCR so we can "zap" each commercial, and stop watching if nothing exciting happens in the opening thirty seconds. We like our information fast, too: messages flashed on a computer screen, documents FAXed from your telephone to mine, current events in 90-second bursts on *Eyewitness News*, history reduced to "Bicentennial Minutes." Symbolically, the American eagle now flies for Express Mail. How dare anyone keep America waiting longer than overnight?

Superficially instead of thoroughly: What's more, we don't   6
even want *all* of it. Once, we lingered over every word of a classic novel or the latest best-seller. Today, since faster is better, we read the condensed version or pop an audiocassette of the book into our car's tape player to listen to on the way to work. Or we buy the *Cliff's Notes*, especially if we are students, so we don't have to deal with the book at all. Once, we listened to every note of Beethoven's Fifth Symphony. Today, we don't have the time; instead, we can enjoy 26 seconds of that famous "da-da-da-DUM" theme—and 99 other musical excerpts almost as famous—on our "Greatest Moments of the Classics" CD. After all, why waste 45 minutes listening to the whole thing when someone else has saved us the trouble of picking out the best parts? Our magazine articles come to us pre-digested in *Reader's Digest*. Our news briefings, thanks to *USA Today,* are more brief than ever. Even our personal relationships have become compressed. Instead of devoting large segments of our days to our loved ones—after all, we *are* busy people—we substitute something called "quality time," which, more often than not, is no time at all. As we rush from book to music to news item to relationship, we do not realize that we are living our lives by the iceberg principle—paying attention only to the top and ignoring the 8/9 that lies just below the surface.

When did it all begin, this urge to do it now, to get it over with,   7
to skim the surface of life? Why are we in such a hurry to save time?

And what, pray tell, are we going to do with all the time we save—besides, of course, rushing out to save some more? The sad truth is that we don't know how to use the time we save, because all we're good at is *saving* time...not *spending* time.

Don't get me wrong. I'm not saying we should go back to growing our own vegetables or knitting our own sweaters or putting our paychecks into piggy banks. I'm not even advocating a mass movement to cut all our credit cards into little pieces. But I am saying that all of us need to think more seriously about putting the brakes on our "we-want-it-all-and-we-want-it-now" lifestyle before we speed completely out of control. Let's take the time to read every word of that story, hear every note of that music, savor every nuance of that countryside—or that other person. Let's rediscover life in the slow lane.   8

Questions for Close Reading

1. What is the selection's thesis? Locate the sentence(s) in which Goldstein states her main idea. If she doesn't state the thesis explicitly, express it in your own words.
2. Goldstein and her husband enjoy looking at toy trains and antique cars, eating homemade pudding, and watching cows basking in sunshine. What do all of these pleasures have in common?
3. What evidence does Goldstein give to support her contention that in the past, Americans were willing to defer gratification?
4. In paragraph 6, Goldstein describes "the iceberg principle." What does she mean by this term? How, in Goldstein's view, does this principle apply to the way many people live their lives?
5. Refer to your dictionary as needed to define the following words used in the selection: *pastoral* (paragraph 1), *meander* (2), *bask* (2), *revitalized* (2), *pervasive* (5), *syndrome* (5), and *nuance* (8).

Questions About the Writer's Craft

1. **The pattern.**   The body of Goldstein's essay is divided into the three ways Americans seek a quick fix. Are the three subdivisions of the "quick fix" syndrome mutually exclusive? Explain.
2. **Other patterns.**   In addition to division-classification, Goldstein uses comparison-contrast to develop her essay. What are some contrasting images in the first and second paragraphs? Where else in the essay do you find similar juxtapositions? What purpose do these contrasts serve?

3. Goldstein often uses *rhetorical questions*—questions she doesn't expect her readers to answer—as when she asks "why wait in line at the supermarket?" (paragraph 5). Where else does she use rhetorical questions? What purposes do such questions serve?

4. Goldstein uses a number of contemporary expressions, abbreviations, and quoted clichés. What is the effect, for example, of "FAXed"? Why does she put "zap" and "quality time" in quotation marks?

Questions for Further Thought

1. According to Goldstein, Americans suffer from the "I-hate-to-wait" syndrome. In which aspects of your life are you willing to defer gratification; in which do you require immediate satisfaction?

2. Goldstein repeats the word *fast* throughout paragraph 5, always with negative implications. Think, however, of some modern convenience (a microwave oven, a word processor, a vacuum cleaner) that speeds up mundane chores. Discuss ways this device has freed you to spend more time in personally meaningful ways.

3. Goldstein's outgoing trip was planned to minimize travel time. The return trip, however, seems to have been more a matter of following impulse and finding surprises. What spontaneous thing have you ever done that led to some discovery or special pleasure? When have you acted on impulse and found the consequences to be disastrous?

4. Most Americans, Goldstein believes, don't know how to spend their time. If you were free of pressures and obligations, how would you spend your time? What would you do differently?

Writing Assignments Using Division-Classification as a Pattern of Development

1. Goldstein urges readers to slow down and appreciate life more fully. Consider the different activities of your everyday life. Write an essay classifying the activities according to those you like to give time to and those you like to speed through. Reach some conclusions about what is and is not important to you.

∞ 2. Goldstein laments the superficiality of many relationships. Consider those people with whom you spend time. Brainstorm and then categorize the characteristics these people do or do not have in common. Use your analysis to identify the qualities you value in others. Judith Viorst's "Friends, Good Friends—and Such Good Friends" (page 289) suggests some ideas worth exploring.

Writing Assignments Using Other Patterns of Development

3. Goldstein seems to find the natural and rural more appealing than the technological. Taking the opposite point of view, write a descriptive piece

conveying the beauty made possible by modern technology—an aerial view of a bayside city, the lit span of a suspension bridge, the graphics of your favorite computer program. Build your description around a dominant impression, selecting those details that best express your sense of wonder.

4. Although Goldstein writes that Americans like their clothing and food ready-made, many people take pleasure in a more leisurely approach to satisfying their basic needs. Think of something you enjoy cooking, building, or crafting. Or you might consider activities like planting a vegetable garden or going fishing. Write an essay guiding the reader, step by step, through the process you select. Your essay should capture the contentment and pride you experience in the process.

Additional Writing Topics

DIVISION-CLASSIFICATION

General Assignments

Choose one of the following subjects and write an essay developed wholly or in part through division-classification. Start by determining the purpose of the essay. Do you want to inform, compare and contrast, or persuade? Apply a single, significant principle of division or classification to your subject. Don't switch the principle midway through your analysis. Also, be sure that the types or categories you create are as complete and mutually exclusive as possible.

Division

1. A shopping mall
2. A video and/or stereo system
3. A fruit, such as a pineapple, an orange, or a banana
4. A tax dollar
5. A particular kind of team
6. A word-processing system
7. A human hand
8. A meal
9. A meeting
10. A favorite poem, story, or play
11. A favorite restaurant
12. A school library
13. A basement
14. A playground, gym, or other recreational area
15. A church service
16. A wedding or funeral
17. An eventful week in your life
18. A college campus
19. A television show or movie
20. A homecoming or other special weekend

Classification

1. People in a waiting room
2. Holidays
3. Closets
4. Roommates
5. Salad bars
6. Divorces

7. Beds
8. Students in a class
9. Shoes
10. Summer movies
11. Teachers
12. Neighbors
13. College courses
14. Bosses
15. TV watchers
16. Mothers or fathers
17. Commercials
18. Vacations
19. Trash
20. Relatives

Assignments With a Specific Purpose and Audience

1. You are a dorm counselor. During orientation week, you'll be talking to students on your floor about the different kinds of problems they may have with roommates. Write your talk, describing each kind of problem and explaining how to cope.

2. As a driving instructor, you decide to prepare a lecture on the types of drivers that your students are likely to encounter on the road. In your lecture, categorize drivers according to a specific principle and show the behaviors of each type.

3. You have been asked to write a pamphlet for "new recruits"—new workers on your job, new students in your college class, new members of your sports team, or the like. In the pamphlet, identify at least three general qualities needed for the recruits' success.

4. A seasoned camp counselor, you've been asked to prepare, for new counselors, an informational sheet on children's emotional needs. Categorizing those needs into types, explain what counselors can do to nurture youngsters emotionally.

5. As your college newspaper's TV critic, you plan to write a review of the fall shows, most of which—in your opinion—lack originality. To show how stereotypical the programs are, select one type (for example, situation comedies or crime dramas). Then use a specific division-classification principle to illustrate that the same stale formulas are trotted out from show to show.

6. Asked to write an editorial for the campus paper, you decide to do a half-serious piece on taking "mental health" days off from classes. Structure your essay around three kinds of occasions when "playing hooky" is essential for maintaining sanity.

8

PROCESS ANALYSIS

WHAT IS PROCESS ANALYSIS?

Perhaps you've noticed the dogged determination of small children when they learn how to do something new. Whether trying to tie their shoelaces or tell time, little children struggle along, creating knotted tangles, confusing the hour with the minute hand. But they don't give up. Mastering such basic skills makes them feel less dependent on the adults of the world—all of whom seem to know how to do everything. Actually, none of us is born knowing how to do very much. We spend a good deal of our lives learning—everything from speaking our first word to balancing our first bank statement. Indeed, the milestones in our lives are often linked to the processes we have mastered: how to cross the street alone; how to drive a car; how to make a speech without being paralyzed by fear.

Process analysis, a technique that explains the steps or sequence involved in doing something, satisfies our need to learn as well as our curiosity about how the world works. All the self-help books flooding the market today (*Managing Stress, How to Make a Million in Real Estate, Ten Days to a Perfect Body*) are examples of process analysis. The instructions on the federal tax form and the recipes in a cookbook are also process analyses. Several television classics, now seen in reruns, also capitalize on our desire to learn how things happen: *The Wild Kingdom* shows how animals survive in faraway lands, and *Mission: Impossible* has great fun detailing elaborate plans for preventing the triumph of evil. Process analysis can be more than merely interesting or entertaining, though; it can be of critical importance. Consider a waiter hurriedly skimming the "Choking Aid" instructions posted on a restaurant wall or an air-traffic controller following emergency procedures in an effort to prevent a midair collision. In these last examples, the consequences could be fatal if the process analyses were slipshod, inaccurate, or confusing.

Undoubtedly, all of us have experienced less dramatic effects of poorly written process analyses. Perhaps you've tried to assemble a bicycle and spent hours sorting through a stack of parts, only to end up with one or two extra pieces never mentioned in the instructions. Or maybe you were baffled when putting up a set of wall shelves because the instructions used unfamiliar terms like *mitered cleat, wing nut,* and *dowel pin*. No wonder many people stay clear of anything that actually admits "assembly required."

HOW PROCESS ANALYSIS FITS YOUR PURPOSE AND AUDIENCE

You will use process analysis in two types of writing situations: (1) when you want to give step-by-step instructions to readers showing how they can do something, or (2) when you want readers to understand how something happens even though they won't actually follow the steps outlined. The first kind of process analysis is *directional;* the second is *informational*.

When you look at the cooking instructions on a package of frozen vegetables or follow guidelines for completing a job application, you're reading directional process analysis. A serious essay explaining how to select a college and a humorous essay telling readers how to get on the good side of a professor are also examples of directional process analysis. Using a variety of tones, informational process analyses can range over equally diverse subjects; they can describe mechanical, scientific, historical, sociological, artistic, or psychological processes: for example, how the core of a nuclear reactor melts down; how television became so important in political campaigns; how abstract painters use color; how to survive a blind date.

Process analysis, both directional and informational, is often appropriate in *problem-solving situations.* In such cases, you say, "Here's the problem and here's what should be done to solve the problem." Indeed, college assignments frequently take the form of problem-solving process analyses. Consider these examples:

> Community officials have been accused of mismanaging recent unrest over the public housing ordinance. Describe the steps the officials took, indicating why you think their strategy was unwise. Then explain how you think the situation should have been handled.

> Over the years, there have been many reports citing the abuse of small children in day-care centers. What can parents do to guard against the mistreatment of their children?

> Because many colleges and universities have changed the eligibility requirements for financial aid, fewer students can depend on loans or scholarships. How can students cope with the increasing costs of obtaining a higher education?

Note that the first assignment asks students to explain what's wrong with the current approach before they present their own step-by-step solution. Problem-solving process analyses are often organized in this way. You may also have noted that none of the assignments explicitly requires an essay response using process analysis. However, the wording of the assignments—"*Describe* the steps," "*How* can students *cope,*" "*What* can parents *do*"—suggests that process analysis would be an appropriate strategy for developing the responses.

Assignments don't always signal the use of process analysis so clearly. But during the prewriting stage, as you generate material to support your thesis, you'll often realize that you can best achieve your purpose by developing the essay—or part of it—using process analysis.

Sometimes process analysis will be the primary strategy for organizing an essay; other times it will be used to help make a point in an essay organized according to another pattern of development. Let's take a look at process analysis as a supporting strategy.

Assume that you're writing a *causal analysis* examining the impact of television commercials on people's buying behavior. To help readers see that commercials create a need where none existed before, you might describe the various stages in an advertising campaign to pitch a new, completely frivolous product. In an essay *defining* a good boss, you could convey the point that effective managers must be skilled at settling disputes by explaining the steps your boss took to resolve a heated disagreement between two employees. If you write an *argumentation-persuasion* paper urging the funding of programs to ease the plight of the homeless, you would have to dramatize for readers the tragedy of these people's lives. To achieve your purpose, you could devote part of the paper to an explanation of how the typical street person goes about the desperate jobs of finding a place to sleep and getting food to eat.

SUGGESTIONS FOR USING PROCESS ANALYSIS IN AN ESSAY

The suggestions that follow will be helpful whether you use process analysis as a dominant or supportive pattern of development.

1. Identify the desired outcome of the process analysis. Many papers developed primarily through process analysis have a clear-cut purpose—simply to *inform* readers as objectively as possible about a process: "Here's a way of making french fries at home that will surpass the best served in your favorite fast-food restaurant." But a process analysis essay may also have a *persuasive* edge, with the writer advocating a point of view about the process, perhaps even urging a course of action: "If you don't want your arguments to deteriorate into ugly battles, you should follow a series of foolproof steps for having disagreements that leave friendships intact." Before starting to write, you need to decide if the essay is to be purely factual or if it will include this kind of persuasive dimension.

2. Formulate a thesis that clarifies your attitude toward the process. Like the thesis in any other paper, the thesis in a process analysis should do more than announce your subject. ("Here's how the college's work-study program operates.") It should also state or imply your attitude toward the process: "Enrolling in the college's work-study program has become unnecessarily complicated. The procedure could be simplified if the college adopted the helpful guidelines prepared by the Student Senate."

3. Keep your audience in mind.   Only when you gauge how much your readers already know (or don't know) about the process can you determine how much explanation you'll have to provide. Suppose you've been asked to write an article informing students of the best way to use the university computer center. The article will be published in a newsletter for computer science majors. You would seriously misjudge your audience—and probably put them to sleep—if you explained in detail how to transfer material from disk to disk or how to delete information from a file. However, an article on the same topic prepared for a general audience—your composition class, for instance—would probably require such detailed instructions.

To determine how much explanation is needed, put yourself in your readers' shoes. Don't assume readers will know something just because you do. Ask questions like these about your audience: "Will my readers need some background about the process before I describe it in depth?" "Are there technical terms I should define?" "If my essay is directional, should I specify near the beginning the ingredients, materials, and equipment needed to perform the process?" (For more help in analyzing your audience, see the checklist on page 18.)

4. Use prewriting to identify the steps in the process.   To explain a sequence to your readers, you need to think through the process thoroughly, identifying its major parts and subparts, locating possible missteps or trouble spots. With your purpose, thesis, and audience in mind, use the appropriate prewriting techniques (brainstorming and mapping should be especially helpful) to break down the process into its component parts. In prewriting, it's a good idea to start by generating more material than you expect to use. Then the raw material can be shaped and pruned to fit your purpose and the needs of your audience. The amount of work done during the prewriting stage will have a direct bearing on the clarity of your presentation.

5. Identify the directional and informational aspects of the process analysis. Directional and informational process analyses are not always distinct. In fact, they may be complementary. Your prewriting may reveal that you'll need to provide background information about a process before outlining its steps. For example, in a paper describing a step-by-step approach for losing weight, you might first need to explain how the body burns calories. Or, in a paper on gardening, you could provide some theory about the way organic fertilizers work before detailing a plan for growing vegetables. Although both approaches may be appropriate in a paper, one generally predominates.

The kind of process analysis chosen has implications for the way you will relate to your reader. When the process analysis is *directional,* the reader is addressed in the *second person:* "You should first rinse the residue from the radiator by...," or "Wrap the injured person in a blanket and then...." (In the second example, the pronoun *you* is implied.)

If the process analysis has an *informational* purpose, you won't address the reader directly but will choose from a number of other options. For example, you might use the *first-person* point of view. In a humorous essay explaining how not to prepare for finals, you could cite your own disastrous study habits: "Filled with good intentions, I sit on my bed, pick up a pencil, open my notebook, and promptly fall asleep." The *third-person singular or plural* can also be used in informational process essays: "The door-to-door salesperson walks up the front walk, heart pounding, more than a bit nervous, but also challenged by the prospect of striking a deal," or "The new recruits next underwent a series of important balance tests in what was called the 'horror chamber.'" Whether you use the first, second, or third person, avoid shifting point of view midstream.

You might have noticed that in the third-person examples, the present tense ("walks up") is used in one sentence, the past tense ("underwent") in the other. The past tense is appropriate for events already completed, whereas the present tense is used for habitual or ongoing actions. ("A dominant male goose usually flies at the head of the V-wedge during migration.") The present tense is also effective when you want to lend a sense of dramatic immediacy to a process, even if the steps were performed in the past. ("The surgeon gently separates the facial skin and muscle from the underlying bony skull.") As with point of view, be on guard against changing tenses in the middle of your explanation.

6. Explain the process, one step at a time. Prewriting helped you identify key stages and sort out the directional and informational aspects of the process. Now you're ready to organize your raw material into an easy-to-follow sequence. At times your purpose will be to explain a process with a *fairly fixed chronological sequence:* how to make pizza, how to pot a plant, how to change a tire. In such cases, you should include all necessary steps, in the correct chronological order. However, if a strict chronological ordering of steps means that a particularly important part of the sequence gets buried in the middle, the sequence probably should be juggled so that the crucial step receives the attention it deserves.

Other times your goal will be to describe a process having *no commonly accepted sequence*. For example, in an essay explaining how to discipline a child or how to pull yourself out of a blue mood, you will have to come up with your own definition of the key steps and then arrange those steps in some logical order. You may also use process analyses to *reject* or *reformulate* a traditional sequence. In this case, you would propose a more logical series of steps: "Our system for electing congressional representatives is inefficient and undemocratic; it should be reformed in the following ways."

Whether the essay describes a generally agreed-on process or one that is not commonly accepted, you must provide all the details needed to explain the process. Your readers should be able to understand, even visualize, the process. There should be no fuzzy patches or confusing cuts from one step to another. Don't, however, go into obsessive detail about minor stages or steps. If you dwell for several hundred words on how to butter the pan, your readers will never stay with you long enough to learn how to make the omelet.

It's not unusual, especially in less defined sequences, for some steps in a process to occur simultaneously and overlap. When this happens, you should present the steps in the most logical order, being sure to tell your readers that several steps are not perfectly distinct and may merge. For example, in an essay explaining how a species becomes extinct, you would have to indicate that overpopulation of hardy strains and destruction of endangered breeds are often simultaneous events. You would also need to clarify that the depletion of food sources both precedes and follows the demise of a species.

7. Provide readers with the help they need to follow the sequence. As you move through the steps of a process analysis, don't forget to *warn readers about difficulties* they might encounter. For example, when writing a paper on the artistry involved in butterflying a shrimp, you might say something like this:

> Next, make a shallow cut with your sharpened knife along the convex curve of the shrimp's intestinal tract. The tract, usually a faint black line along the outside curve of the shrimp, is faintly visible beneath the translucent flesh. But some shrimp have a thick orange, blue, or gray line instead of a thin black one. In all cases, be careful not to slice too deeply, or you will end up with two shrimp halves instead of one butterflied shrimp.

You have told readers what to look for, citing the exceptions, and have warned them against making too deep a cut. Anticipating spots where communication might break down is a key part of writing an effective process analysis.

Transitional words and phrases are also critical in helping readers understand the order of the steps being described. Time signals like *first, next, now, while, after, before,* and *finally* provide readers with a clear sense of the sequence. Entire sentences can also be used to link parts of the process, reminding your audience of what has already been discussed and indicating what will now be explained: "Once the panel of experts finishes its evaluation of the exam questions, randomly selected items are field-tested in schools throughout the country."

8. Maintain an appropriate tone.   When writing a process analysis essay, be sure your tone is consistent with your purpose, your attitude toward your subject, and the effect you want to have on the reader. When explaining how fraternities and sororities recruit new members, do you want to use an objective, nonjudgmental tone? To decide, take into account readers' attitudes toward your subject. Does your audience have a financial or emotional investment in the process being described? Does your own interest in the process coincide or conflict with that of your audience? Awareness of your readers' stance can be crucial. Consider another example: Assume you're writing a letter to the director of the student health center proposing a new system to replace the currently chaotic one. You'd do well to be tactful in your criticisms. Offend your reader, and your cause is lost. If, however, the letter is slated for the college newspaper and directed primarily to other students, you could adopt a more pointed, even sarcastic tone. Readers, you would assume, will probably share your view and favor change.

Once you settle on the essay's tone, maintain it throughout. If you're writing a light piece on the way computers are taking over our lives, you wouldn't include a grim step-by-step analysis of the way confidential computerized medical records may become public.

9. Open and close the process analysis effectively.   A paper developed primarily through process analysis should have a strong beginning. The introduction should state the process to be described and imply whether the essay has an informational or directional intent.

If you suspect readers are indifferent to your subject, use the introduction to motivate them, telling them how important the subject is:

> Do you enjoy the salad bars found in many restaurants? If you do, you probably have noticed that the vegetables are always crisp and fresh--no matter how many hours they have been exposed to the air. What are the restaurants doing to make the vegetables look so inviting? There's a simple answer. Many restaurants dip and spray the vegetables with potent chemicals to make them appetizing.

If you think your audience may be intimidated by your subject (perhaps because it's complex or relatively obscure), the introduction is the perfect spot to reassure them that the process being described is not beyond their grasp:

> Studies show that many people willingly accept a defective product just so they won't have to deal with the uncomfortable process of making a complaint. But once a few easy-to-learn basics are mastered, anyone can register a complaint that gets results.

Most process analysis essays don't end as soon as the last step in the sequence is explained. Instead, they usually include some brief final comments that round out the piece and bring it to a satisfying close. This final section of the essay may summarize the main steps in the process—not by repeating the steps verbatim but by rephrasing and condensing them in several concise sentences. The conclusion can also be an effective spot to underscore the significance of the process, recalling what may have been said in the introduction about the subject's importance. Or the essay can end by echoing the note of reassurance that may have been included at the start.

Despite the glut of how-to books on the market, effective process writing is not as easy to do as it might appear. Explaining how to do something is often as difficult as responding to the proverbial "How do I get there from here?" And explaining how something happened means re-creating often complex events so that logic and clarity take precedence over cloudiness and confusion. If, after reading your piece, the reader thinks or says, "I understand. I see what you mean," you can be confident that your process analysis has been successful. That's no small accomplishment.

STUDENT ESSAY

The following student essay was written by Robert Barry in response to this assignment:

> Stephen Leacock's "How to Live to Be 200" pokes fun at our obsessive concern with physical fitness. By observing people, identify another example of an obsessive behavior that borders on the addictive. Then write a light-spirited essay explaining the various stages in the addiction. Since your essay should be humorous in tone, be sure to describe an addiction that doesn't have serious consequences.

While reading Robert's paper, try to determine how effectively it applies the principles of process analysis. The annotations on Robert's paper and the commentary following it will help you look at the essay more closely.

Becoming a Videoholic
by Robert Barry

Introduction   In the last several years, videocassette recorders   1
(VCRs) have become popular additions in many American homes. A recent newspaper article notes

that one in three households has a VCR, with sales continuing to climb every day. VCRs seem to be the most popular technological breakthrough since television itself. No consumer warning labels are attached to these rapidly multiplying VCRs, but they should be. VCRs can be dangerous. Barely aware of what is happening, a person can turn into a compulsive videotaper. The descent from innocent hobby to full-blown addiction takes place in several stages.

Start of two-sentence thesis ——

Topic sentence ——▶ In the first innocent stage, the unsuspecting person buys a VCR for occasional use. I was at this stage when I asked my parents if they would buy me a VCR as a combined birthday and high school graduation gift. With the VCR, I could tape reruns of Star Trek and Miami Vice, shows I would otherwise miss on nights I was at work. The VCR was perfect. I hooked it up to the old TV in my bedroom, recorded the intergalactic adventures of Captain Kirk and the high-voltage escapades of Sonny Crockett, then watched the tapes the next day. Occasionally, I taped a movie which my friends and I watched over the weekend. I had just one cassette, but that was all I needed since I watched every show I recorded and simply taped over the preceding show when I recorded another. In these early days, my VCR was the equivalent of light social drinking.

First stage in process (VCR addiction)

Beginning of analogy to alcoholism ——

Topic sentence ——▶ In the second phase on the road to videoholism, an individual uses the VCR more frequently and begins to stockpile tapes rather than watch them. My troubles began in July when my family went to the shore for a week's vacation. I programmed the VCR to tape all five episodes of Star Trek while I was at the beach perfecting my tan. Since I used the VCR's long-play mode, I could get all five Star Treks on one cassette. But that ended up creating a problem. Even I, an avid Trekkie, didn't want to watch five shows in one sitting. I viewed two shows, but the three unwatched shows tied up my tape, making it impossible to record other shows. How did I resolve this dilemma? Very easily. I went out and bought several more cassettes. Once I had these additional tapes, I was free to record as many Star Treks as I wanted, plus I could tape reruns of classics like The Honeymooners and Mission: Impossible. Very quickly, I accumulated six Star Treks, four Honeymooners, and three Mission: Impossi-

Second stage in process

2

3

bles. Then a friend--who shall go nameless--told me that only eighty-two episodes of <u>Star Trek</u> were ever made. Excited by the thought that I could acquire as impressive a collection of tapes as a Hollywood executive, I continued recording <u>Star Trek</u>, even taping shows while I watched them. Clearly, my once innocent hobby was getting out of control. I was now using the VCR on a regular basis--the equivalent of several stiff drinks a day.

Continuation of analogy

Topic sentence

In the third stage of videoholism, the amount of taping increases significantly, leading to an even more irrational stockpiling of cassettes. The catalyst that propelled me into this third stage was my parents' decision to get cable TV. Selfless guy that I am, I volunteered to move my VCR and hook it up to the TV in the living room, where the cable outlet was located. Now I could tape all the most recent movies and cable specials. With that delightful possibility in mind, I went out and bought two six-packs of blank tapes. Then, in addition to my regulars, I began to record a couple of other shows every day. I taped <u>Rocky III</u>, <u>Magnum Force</u>, a James Bond movie, an HBO comedy special with Eddie Murphy, and an MTV concert featuring Mick Jagger. Where did I get time to watch all these tapes? I didn't. Taping at this point was more satisfying than watching. Reason and common sense were abandoned. Getting things on tape had become an obsession, and I was taping all the time.

Third stage in process

Continuation of analogy

Topic sentence

In the fourth stage, videoholism creeps into other parts of the addict's life, influencing behavior in strange ways. Secrecy becomes commonplace. One day, my mother came into my room and saw my bookcase filled with tapes--rather than with the paperbacks that used to be there. "Robert," she exclaimed, "isn't this getting a bit out of hand?" I assured her it was just a hobby, but I started hiding my tapes, putting them in a suitcase stored in my closet. I also taped at night, slipping downstairs to turn on the VCR after my parents had gone to bed and getting down first thing in the morning to turn off the VCR and remove the cassette before my parents noticed. Also, denial is not unusual during this stage of VCR addiction. At the dinner table, when

Fourth stage in process

Continuation of analogy

4

5

my younger sister commented, "Robert tapes all the time," I laughingly told everyone--including myself--that the taping was no big deal. I was getting bored with it and was going to stop any day, I assured my family. Obsessive behavior also charac- terizes the fourth stage of videoholism. Each week, I pulled out the TV magazine from the Sunday paper and went through it carefully, circling in red all the shows I wanted to tape. Another sign of addiction was my compulsive organization of all the tapes I had stockpiled. Working more diligently than I ever had for any term paper, I typed up labels and attached them to each cassette. I also created an elaborate list that showed my tapes broken down into categories such as Westerns, horror movies, and comedies.

Topic sentence ⟶   In the final stage of an addiction, the individual   6
either succumbs completely to the addiction or is
Continuation   able to break away from the habit. I broke my addic-
of analogy   tion, and I broke it cold turkey. This total withdrawal
occurred when I went off to college. There was no
Final stage in   point in taking my VCR to school because TVs were
process   not allowed in the freshman dorms. Even though there were many things to occupy my time during the school week, cold sweats overcame me whenever I thought about everything on TV I was not taping. I even considered calling home and asking members of my family to tape things for me, but I knew they would think I was crazy. At the beginning of the semester, I also had to resist the overwhelming desire to travel the three hours home every weekend so I could get my fix. But after a while, the urgent need to tape subsided. Now, months later, as I write this, I feel detached and sober.

Conclusion   I have no illusions, though. I know that once a   7
videoholic, always a videoholic. Soon I will return
home for the holidays, which, as everyone knows, can
be a time for excess eating--and taping. But I will
Final references   cope with the pressure. I will take each day one at a
to analogy   time. I will ask my little sister to hide my blank tapes. And if I feel myself succumbing to the temptations of taping, I will pick up the telephone and dial the video- holics' hotline: 1–800-VCR-TAPE. I will win the battle.

COMMENTARY

Purpose, thesis, and tone.   Robert's essay is an example of *informational process analysis;* his purpose is to describe—rather than teach—the process of becoming a "videoholic." The title, with its coined term *videoholic,* tips us off that the essay is going to be entertaining. And the introductory paragraph clearly establishes the essay's playful, mock-serious tone. The tone established, Robert briefly defines the term *videoholic* as a "compulsive videotaper" and then moves to the essay's *thesis:* "Barely aware of what is happening, a person can turn into a compulsive videotaper. The descent from innocent hobby to full-blown addiction takes place in several stages."

Throughout the essay, Robert sustains the introduction's humor by mocking his own motivations and poking fun at his quirks: "Selfless guy that I am, I volunteered to move my VCR" (paragraph 4), and "Working more diligently than I ever had for any term paper, I typed up labels" (5). Robert probably uses a bit of *dramatic license* when reporting some of his obsessive behavior, and we, as readers, understand that he's exaggerating for comic effect. Most likely he didn't break out in a cold sweat at the thought of the TV shows he was unable to tape, and he probably didn't hide his tapes in a suitcase. Nevertheless, this tinkering with the truth is legitimate because it allows Robert to create material that fits the essay's lightly satiric tone.

Organization and topic sentences.   To meet the requirements of the assignment, Robert needed to provide a *step-by-step* explanation of a process. And because he invented the term *videoholism,* Robert also needed to invent the stages in the progression of his addiction. During his prewriting, Robert discovered five stages in his videoholism: Presented *chronologically,* these stages provide the organizing focus for his paper. Specifically, each supporting paragraph is devoted to one stage, with the *topic sentence* for each paragraph indicating the stage's distinctive characteristics.

Transitions.   Although Robert's essay is playful, it is nonetheless a process analysis and so must have an easy-to-follow structure. Keeping this in mind, Robert wisely includes *transitions* to signal what happened at each stage of his videoholism: "*Once* I had these additional tapes, I was free to record" (paragraph 3); "*Then*, in addition to my regulars, I began to record" (4); "*One day*, my mother came into my room" (5); and "*But after a while*, the urgent need to tape subsided" (6). In addition to such transitions, Robert also uses crisp questions to move from idea to idea within a paragraph: "How did I resolve this dilemma? Very easily. I...bought several more cassettes" (3), and "Where did I get time to watch all these tapes? I didn't" (4).

Other patterns of development.   Even though Robert's essay is a process analysis, it contains elements of other patterns of development. For example, his paper is unified by an *analogy*—a sustained *comparison* between Robert's video addiction and the obviously more serious addiction to alcohol. Handled incorrectly, the analogy could have been offensive, but Robert makes the comparison work to his advantage. The analogy is stated specifically in several spots: "In these early days, my VCR was the equivalent of light social drinking" (paragraph 2); "I was now using the VCR on a regular basis—the equivalent of several stiff drinks a day" (3). Another place where Robert touches wittily on the analogy occurs in the middle of the fourth paragraph: "I went out and bought two six-packs of blank tapes." To illustrate his progression toward videoholism, Robert depicts the *effects* of his addiction. Finally, he generates numerous lively details or *examples* to illustrate the different stages in his addiction.

Two unnecessary sentences.   Perhaps you noticed that Robert runs into a minor problem at the end of the fourth paragraph. Starting with the sentence "Reason and common sense were abandoned," he begins to ramble and repeat himself. The paragraph's last two sentences fail to add anything substantial. Take a moment to read paragraph 4 aloud, omitting the last two sentences. Note how much sharper the new conclusion is: "Where did I get time to watch all these tapes? I didn't. Taping at this point was more satisfying than watching." This new ending says all that needs to be said.

Revising the first draft.   When it was time to revise, Robert—in spite of his apprehension—showed his paper to his roommate and asked him to read it out loud. Robert knew this strategy would provide a more objective point of view on his work. His roommate, at first an unwilling recruit, nonetheless laughed as he read the essay aloud. That was just the response Robert wanted. But when his roommate got to the conclusion, Robert heard that the closing paragraph was flat and anticlimactic. Here is Robert's original conclusion.

Original Version of the Conclusion

I have no illusions, though, that I am over my videoholism. Soon I will be returning home for the holidays, which can be a time for excess taping. All I can do is ask my little sister to hide my blank tapes. After that, I will hope for the best.

Robert and his roommate brainstormed ways to make the conclusion livelier and more in spirit with the rest of the essay. They decided that the best approach would be to continue the playful, mock-serious tone that characterized earlier parts of the essay. Robert thus made three major changes in the conclusion. First, he tightened the first sentence of the paragraph ("I have no illusions, though, that I am over my videoholism"), making it crisper and more dramatic: "I have no illusions, though." Second, he added a few sentences to sustain the light, self-deprecating tone he had used earlier: "I know that once a videoholic, always a videoholic"; "But I will cope with the pressure"; "I will win the battle." Third, and perhaps most important, he returned to the alcoholism analogy: "I will take each day one at a time....And if I feel myself succumbing to the temptations of taping, I will pick up the telephone and dial the videoholics' hotline...."

These weren't the only changes Robert made while reworking his paper, but they give you some sense of how sensitive he was to the effect he wanted to achieve. Certainly, the recasting of the conclusion was critical to the overall success of this amusing essay.

Process analysis is at the heart of each of the following selections. In "How to Live to Be 200," Stephen Leacock gives some light-hearted instructions for those who believe exercise is the key to immortality. Sue Hubbell's "The Beekeeper," part narration and part description, centers on the surprising technique that beekeepers use to develop resistance to bee venom. Jessica Mitford's "The

American Way of Death" looks at a process most of us will never perform but will, instead, have done *to* us. "How to Say Nothing in 500 Words," by Paul Roberts, shows students a way to write essays that will make their professors want to leave teaching. Last, Caroline Rego's "The Fine Art of Complaining" offers guidelines for registering complaints that get results.

Stephen Leacock

Stephen Leacock (1869–1944) was born in Great Britain but spent most of his life in Canada. Educated at the University of Toronto, Leacock became a professor of economics at McGill University. In later life, he wrote humorous essays that brought him great popularity. Leacock's work is collected in such books as *Literary Lapses* (1910) and *Winnowed Wisdom* (1926). The following essay is from *Literary Lapses*.

How to Live to Be 200

Are you tired of being urged to exercise by talk show hosts and sleek TV celebrities? Are you annoyed by friends who brag about how often they work out or how many miles they run? Do you enjoy a good fast-food meal packed with preservatives, salt, and calories? If so, you have an ally in Stephen Leacock, who many years ago chided the Health Maniacs of his day. Health fanaticism, you see, is not new; there were health nuts even in the early 1900s. But, as Leacock points out, they didn't live long enough to enjoy the current health craze.

Twenty years ago I knew a man called Jiggins, who had the 1
Health Habit.

He used to take a cold plunge every morning. He said it opened 2
his pores. After it he took a hot sponge. He said it closed the pores.
He got so that he could open and shut his pores at will.

Jiggins used to stand and breathe at an open window for half an 3
hour before dressing. He said it expanded his lungs. He might, of
course, have had it done in a shoe-store with a boot-stretcher, but
after all it cost him nothing this way, and what is half an hour?

After he had got his undershirt on, Jiggins used to hitch himself 4
up like a dog in harness and do Sandow exercises. He did them for-
wards, backwards, and hind-side up.

He could have got a job as a dog anywhere. He spent all his time   5
at this kind of thing. In his spare time at the office, he used to lie on
his stomach on the floor and see if he could lift himself up with his
knuckles. If he could, then he tried some other way until he found
one that he couldn't do. Then he would spend the rest of his lunch
hour on his stomach, perfectly happy.

In the evenings in his room he used to lift iron bars, cannon-   6
balls, heave dumb-bells, and haul himself up to the ceiling with his
teeth. You could hear the thumps half a mile.

He liked it.   7

He spent half the night slinging himself around his room. He   8
said it made his brain clear. When he got his brain perfectly clear, he
went to bed and slept. As soon as he woke, he began clearing it again.

Jiggins is dead. He was, of course, a pioneer, but the fact that he   9
dumb-belled himself to death at an early age does not prevent a
whole generation of young men from following in his path.

They are ridden by the Health Mania.   10

They make themselves a nuisance.   11

They get up at impossible hours. They go out in silly little suits   12
and run Marathon heats before breakfast. They chase around bare-
foot to get the dew on their feet. They hunt for ozone. They bother
about pepsin. They won't eat meat because it has too much nitrogen.
They won't eat fruit because it hasn't any. They prefer albumen and
starch and nitrogen to huckleberry pie and doughnuts. They won't
drink water out of a tap. They won't eat sardines out of a can. They
won't use oysters out of a pail. They won't drink milk out of a glass.
They are afraid of alcohol in any shape. Yes, sir, afraid. "Cowards."

And after all their fuss they presently incur some simple old-   13
fashioned illness and die like anybody else.

Now people of this sort have no chance to attain any great age.   14
They are on the wrong track.

Listen. Do you want to live to be really old, to enjoy a grand,   15
green, exuberant, boastful old age and to make yourself a nuisance
to your whole neighbourhood with your reminiscences?

Then cut out all this nonsense. Cut it out. Get up in the morn-   16
ing at a sensible hour. The time to get up is when you have to, not
before. If your office opens at eleven, get up at ten-thirty. Take your
chance on ozone. There isn't any such thing anyway. Or, if there is,
you can buy a thermos bottle full for five cents, and put it on a shelf

in your cupboard. If your work begins at seven in the morning, get up at ten minutes to, but don't be liar enough to say that you like it. It isn't exhilarating, and you know it.

Also, drop all that cold-bath nonsense. You never did it when you were a boy. Don't be a fool now. If you must take a bath (you don't really need to), take it warm. The pleasure of getting out of a cold bed and creeping into a hot bath beats a cold plunge to death. In any case, stop gassing about your tub and your "shower," as if you were the only man who ever washed.   17

So much for that point.   18

Next, take the question of germs and bacilli. Don't be scared of them. That's all. That's the whole thing, and if you once get on to that you never need to worry again.   19

If you see a bacilli, walk right up to it, and look it in the eye. If one flies into your room, strike at it with your hat or with a towel. Hit it as hard as you can between the neck and the thorax. It will soon get sick of that.   20

But as a matter of fact, a bacilli is perfectly quiet and harmless if you are not afraid of it. Speak to it. Call out to it to "lie down." It will understand. I had a bacilli once, called Fido, that would come and lie at my feet while I was working. I never knew a more affectionate companion, and when it was run over by an automobile, I buried it in the garden with genuine sorrow.   21

(I admit this is an exaggeration. I don't really remember its name; it may have been Robert.)   22

Understand that it is only a fad of modern medicine to say that cholera and typhoid and diphtheria are caused by bacilli and germs; nonsense. Cholera is caused by a frightful pain in the stomach, and diptheria is caused by trying to cure a sore throat.   23

Now take the question of food.   24

Eat what you want. Eat lots of it. Yes, eat too much of it. Eat till you can just stagger across the room with it and prop it up against a sofa cushion. Eat everything that you like until you can't eat any more. The only test is, can you pay for it? If you can't pay for it, don't eat it. And listen—don't worry as to whether your food contains starch, or albumen, or gluten, or nitrogen. If you are damn fool enough to want these things, go and buy them and eat all you want of them. Go to a laundry and get a bag of starch, and eat your fill of it. Eat it, and take a good long drink of glue after it, and a spoonful of Portland cement. That will gluten you, good and solid.   25

If you like nitrogen, go and get a druggist to give you a canful 26
of it at the soda counter, and let you sip it with a straw. Only don't
think that you can mix all these things up with your food. There isn't
any nitrogen or phosphorus or albumen in ordinary things to eat. In
any decent household all that sort of stuff is washed out in the kitch-
en sink before the food is put on the table.

And just one word about fresh air and exercise. Don't bother 27
with either of them. Get your room full of good air, then shut up the
windows and keep it. It will keep for years. Anyway, don't keep using
your lungs all the time. Let them rest. As for exercise, if you have to
take it, take it and put up with it. But as long as you have the price
of a hack and can hire other people to play baseball for you and run
races and do gymnastics when you sit in the shade and smoke and
watch them—great heavens, what more do you want?

Questions for Close Reading

1. What is the selection's thesis? Locate the sentence(s) in which Leacock
   states his main idea. If he doesn't state the thesis explicitly, express it in
   your own words.
2. What is the "Health Habit"? What does it include?
3. Why does Leacock call people who try to eat right "cowards"?
4. Instead of good health, what goals does the author imply should guide a
   person's daily behavior?
5. Refer to your dictionary as needed to define the following words used in
   the selection: *ozone* (paragraph 12), *pepsin* (12), and *cholera* (23).

Questions About the Writer's Craft

1. **The pattern.** What two processes does Leacock explain in this essay?
   How are the processes related?
2. Leacock uses the *imperative voice* ("Cut it out") from paragraph 15 on.
   What effect does the imperative have on the essay's tone?
3. Leacock uses exaggeration in his essay's title. Where else does he use exaggeration? Why do you suppose he uses this technique?
4. How would you characterize Leacock's sentence style? Why do you think
   Leacock frames his sentences in this way?

Questions for Further Thought

1. What kind of person does Leacock reveal himself to be? How seriously do
   you take his objections to health consciousness? Do you think he goes
   overboard?

2. Leacock describes a health maniac as an obsessed person. How do people become obsessed? Are obsessions always bad?
3. We're presently in the midst of a health and fitness boom. To what extent has this trend affected our culture in general and your life in particular?
4. Which is more important, to enjoy life's pleasures or to sacrifice some of them to keep physically fit? Are these two goals necessarily incompatible?

Writing Assignments Using Process Analysis as a Pattern of Development

∞ 1. Write a humorous essay showing how to conquer an addiction to some food, activity, or object that's not normally considered addictive. Since your paper will be light in tone, choose a topic that can be discussed in a playful manner. You might find it helpful to look at the student essay on page 342.
2. Imagine you're Jiggins and that Leacock has just "passed on" as a result of his Unhealthy Habit. Write an essay similar to Leacock's, deploring the daily habits of people like Leacock. Describe as specifically as you can how such people live, generating lively details to support your point. Then explain the steps these people should follow if they want to be healthy and live to be two hundred years old.

Writing Assignments Using Other Patterns of Development

3. Write an essay classifying one group's attitudes toward food. You might focus on junk-food addicts, food snobs, health-food fanatics, "chocoholics," finicky eaters, compulsive eaters, or dieters. Use specific facts and examples to convey how these people shop, cook, eat, and talk or think about food. Be sure to center your analysis on a single main point. Your tone may be serious or playful like Leacock's.
4. Leacock presents Jiggins, the health nut, as motivated by a concern for his health. In your experience, do people often have other, perhaps less legitimate motives for going to the gym or running? Write an essay about the "real" reasons people try to keep fit. Illustrate these reasons with specific examples of people you know.

Sue Hubbell

Sue Hubbell keeps bees on her ninety-acre farm in Missouri. Born and raised in Kalamazoo, Michigan, she holds a journalism degree from the University of Southern California and a library science degree from Drexel University in Philadelphia. Hubbell's freelance writing has appeared in such publications as *Time, Sports Illustrated, Country Journal,* and *Harper's.* Some of her works include *A Country Year: Living the Question* (1986), *A Book of Bees* (1988), *On This Hilltop* (1991), and *Broadsides From the Other Orders: A Book of Bugs* (1993). The following selection first appeared as a "Hers" column in the *New York Times* in 1984.

The Beekeeper

One of nature's miracles is the ability of bees to transform the nectar of flowers into honey. In the following essay, Sue Hubbell describes the removal of honey from the hives so it can be processed. Accomplishing this task means confronting thousands of angry bees. So Hubbell and her coworkers follow a series of unusual steps to protect themselves against the inevitable stings that await them. The process described by Hubbell implies something important about humans' tolerance of stressful situations.

For the past week I've been spending my afternoons out in the honey house getting things ready for the harvest. I'm making sure the screens are all tight because once I get started clouds of bees will surround the place and try to get in, lured by the scent of honey. I've been checking the machinery, repairing what isn't running properly, and I've been scrubbing everything down so that the health inspector will be proud. 1

My honey house contains a shiny array of stainless-steel tanks, a power uncapper for slicing honeycomb open, an extractor for spinning the honey out of the comb and a pump to move it—machinery 2 that whirs, whomps, hums and looks very special. My neighbors call it the honey factory, and I'm not above insinuating slyly that what I'm really running back here in the woods is a still.

The bees have been working since early spring, gathering nec-   3
tar, first from wild plum, peach, and cherry blossoms, later from blackberries, sweet clover, water willow and other wildflowers as they bloomed. As they have gathered it, their enzymes have changed the complex plant sugars in the nectar to the simple ones of honey. In the hive young bees have formed into work crews to fan the drop-lets of nectar with their wings, evaporating its water until it is thick and heavy. Summertime heat has helped them, and now the honey is ripe and finished. The bees have capped over each cell of honey-comb with snowy white wax from their bodies, so the honey is ready for my harvest.

The honey that I take from the bees is the extra that they will   4
not need for the winter; they store it above their hives in wooden boxes called supers. When I take it from them I stand behind the hives with a gasoline-powered machine called a bee blower and blow the bees out of the supers while the strong young men that I hire to help me carry the supers, weighing 60 pounds each, and stack them on pallets in the truck. There may be 30 to 50 supers in every one of my bee yards, and we have about half an hour to get them off the hives and stacked before the bees realize what we are up to and begin getting cross about it.

The time to harvest honey is summer's end, when it is hot. The   5
temper of the bees requires that we wear protective clothing: a full set of coveralls, a zippered bee veil and leather gloves. Even a very strong young man works up a sweat wrapped in a bee suit in the heat, hustling 60-pound supers while being harassed by angry bees. It is a hard job, harder even than haying, but jobs are scarce here and I've always been able to hire help.

This year David, the son of friends of mine, is working for me.   6
He is big and strong and used to labor, but he was nervous about bees. After we had made the job arrangement I set about desensitiz-ing him to bee stings. I put a piece of ice on his arm to numb it and then, holding a bee carefully by its head, I put it on the numbed spot and let it sting him. A bee stinger is barbed and stays in the flesh, pulling loose from the body of the bee as it struggles to free itself. The bulbous poison sac at the top of the stinger continues to pulsate

after the bee has left, pumping the venom and forcing the stinger deeper into the flesh.

That first day I wanted David to have only a partial dose of venom, so after a minute I scraped the stinger out. A few people are seriously sensitive to bee venom; each sting they receive can cause a more severe reaction than the one before—reactions ranging from hives, breathing difficulties, accelerated heart beat and choking to anaphylactic shock and death. I didn't think David would be allergic in that way, but I wanted to make sure.   7

We sat down and had a cup of coffee and I watched him. The spot where the stinger went in grew red and began to swell. That was a normal reaction, and so was the itching that he felt later on.   8

The next day I coaxed a bee into stinging him again, repeating the procedure, but I left the stinger in place for 10 minutes, until the venom sac was empty. Again the spot was red, swollen and itchy but had disappeared in 24 hours. By that time David was ready to catch a bee himself and administer his own sting. He also decided that the ice cube was a bother and gave it up. I told him to keep to one sting a day until he had no redness or swelling and then to increase to two stings. He was ready for them the next day. The greater amount of venom caused redness and swelling for a few days, but soon his body could tolerate it without reaction and he increased the number of stings once again.   9

Today he told me he was up to six stings. His arms look as though they have track marks on them, but the fresh stings are having little effect. I'll keep him at it until he can tolerate 10 a day with no reaction and then I'll not worry about taking him out to the bee yard.   10

I know what will happen to him there. For the first few days his movements will be nervous and quick and he will be stung without mercy. After that he will relax and the bees, in turn, will calm down.   11

The reason I am hiring David this year is that a young man I have used in the past has moved away. We worked well together and he liked bees though even he was stung royally at first. I admired his courage the first day we were out together, for he stood holding a super from which I was blowing bees while his arm was fast turning into a pin cushion from stings.   12

When we carried the stacked supers to the honey house's loading dock, he would scorn the hot bee veil as he wheeled the supers   13 on the handtruck despite the cross bees flying around the dock. One time, as I opened the door for him to bring in the load, I noticed that his face was contorted in what I took to be the effort of getting the handtruck down the ramp. We quickly wheeled the load of supers up to the scale, where we weigh each load. He was going too fast, so that when he stopped at the scale he fell backward and 350 pounds of supers dropped on him. Pinned down, he loyally balanced himself on one fist so that he didn't harm the honey pump against which he had fallen. The reason for his knotted face and his speed was obvious for the first time: He was being stung on the forehead by three bees.

Good boss that I am, I did not choose that moment to go to the   14
cabin and make myself a cup of coffee; I picked the supers off his chest, scraped off the stingers and helped him to his feet. It became one of our shared legends of working together. This year I miss him.

Now it is David, still shy about working for a friend of his par-   15
ents, still a little nervous about bees. He is 19 and eager to please. But he is going to be fine. In a month we will have finished and he will be easy and relaxed, and he and I will have our own set of shared legends.

Questions for Close Reading

1. What is the selection's thesis? Locate the sentence(s) in which Hubbell states her main idea. If she doesn't state the thesis explicitly, express it in your own words.
2. Why does the author hire David to harvest the honey? What qualities does David have that make him a good choice?
3. What is desensitization? What role does it play in the honey harvesting process?
4. What are the supers, and what role do they play in the harvesting process? How do the bees use them? How do the people use them?
5. Refer to your dictionary as needed to define the following words used in the selection: *enzymes* (paragraph 3), *desensitize* (6), *bulbous* (6), *pulsate* (6), and *anaphylactic* (7).

Questions About the Writer's Craft

1. **The pattern.**   How many steps are there in the process of making and gathering honey? Does Hubbell provide sufficient detail for you to understand this process?

2. What technical terms of the honey-making trade does the author take time to define? Where in the essay does she provide her definitions? What technical terms does she leave undefined? Why?

3. Where does Hubbell break out of the chronological sequence and present some additional information? Why do you think she includes this material in the essay? What does it add?

4. What is the author's attitude toward the essay's subject? Is the job of harvesting just another job, just in the day's work, or is it something more? Find places where this attitude is revealed.

Questions for Further Thought

1. Hubbell says that she has little trouble finding helpers because "jobs are scarce around here." Would you have to be desperate for a job to become a beekeeper's assistant? What other satisfactions might this job offer?

2. Is Hubbell a good boss? How would you describe her treatment of her employees?

3. Would you deliberately allow yourself to be stung by bees so you could work on a bee farm? Can you think of other jobs that require desensitization to pain? What are some of them? What kinds of pain are involved?

4. Is becoming "hardened" to physical or mental pain a good thing? A necessary thing? Explain.

Writing Assignments Using Process Analysis as a Pattern of Development

∞ 1. Write an essay about a personal experience that desensitized you to physical pain or to emotional distress. Describe the process of becoming used to the pain and growing able to perform without being physically harmed or unduly upset. Part of the essay should discuss the way the difficulties encountered helped you discover new things about yourself. Before writing the paper, you might want to read Richard Rodriguez's "Workers" (page 419) to see how one writer depicts his response to challenging work.

2. Write an essay describing a process that you know well, but that most people do not. You may have learned the process in school, on a job, from a relative or friend, or on your own. As Hubbell does, explain the steps clearly enough that a wide audience of people could understand the sequence. Make sure you define any special terms. Possible subjects could be making bread from scratch, moving a piano, carving a decoy, refinishing furniture. The essay should make clear the pleasure derived from mastering the process.

Writing Assignments Using Other Patterns of Development

3. Hubbell clearly finds pleasure and satisfaction in her work. Write an essay exploring the three most important satisfactions you hope for in your future career. Be specific about what you want and why you want it. As part of the paper, explain how you became interested in this kind of work.

∞ 4. Hubbell's essay concludes with a "shared legend"—a story of a crisis in which the author and her employee helped each other, survived, and became closer. Write an essay about an experience that became the basis for a shared legend between you and someone else. Explore what it was about the event that made it legendary, showing how your bond with the other person changed or deepened as a result of the experience. Before writing your paper, you might read Judith Ortiz Cofer's "A Partial Remembrance of a Puerto Rican Childhood" (page 138), an essay that evokes the richness of a shared family ritual.

Jessica Mitford

Dubbed "Queen of the Muckrakers" by *Time*, English-born Jessica Mitford (1917–   ) came to the United States in 1939 at the age of twenty-one. Mitford worked as a bartender and salesperson before becoming an investigator for the Office of Price Administration in Washington. She didn't begin her writing career until the age of thirty-eight. Her books include two autobiographies, *Daughters and Rebels* (1960) and *A Fine Old Conflict* (1976); an examination of the American penal system, *Kind and Usual Punishment* (1974); a collection of essays, *Poison Penmanship* (1979); a critique of the birthing business, *The American Way of Birth* (1993); and a novel about celebrities and the media, *Grace Had an English Heart* (1989). The following selection is from the book that earned Mitford a national reputation as an investigative writer, *The American Way of Death* (1963). A scathing attack on the American funeral industry, this book shocked readers and enraged morticians.

The American Way of Death

If you were in charge of the funeral arrangements for a loved one, would you ask to have that person's lips sewed, eyes glued, blood drained, and face painted? If you answered "No," you probably don't know much about the world of mortuary science. In this world, the appearance of death is to be avoided, and the goal is to make people look as if they are only asleep. In the following selection, Jessica Mitford parts the "formaldehyde curtain" to reveal our funeral practices. Such practices, she implies, reflect our deep-seated fear of death.

Embalming is indeed a most extraordinary procedure, and one must   1
wonder at the docility of Americans who each year pay hundreds of millions of dollars for its perpetuation, blissfully ignorant of what it is all about, what is done, how it is done. Not one in ten thousand has any idea of what actually takes place. Books on the subject are extremely hard to come by. They are not to be found in most libraries or bookshops.

In an era when huge television audiences watch surgical opera-   2
tions in the comfort of their living rooms, when, thanks to the ani-
mated cartoon, the geography of the digestive system has become
familiar territory even to the nursery school set, in a land where the
satisfaction of curiosity about almost all matters is a national pastime,
the secrecy surrounding embalming can, surely, hardly be attributed
to the inherent gruesomeness of the subject. Custom in this regard
has within this century suffered a complete reversal. In the early days
of American embalming, when it was performed in the home of the
deceased, it was almost mandatory for some relative to stay by the
embalmer's side and witness the procedure. Today, family members
who might wish to be in attendance would certainly be dissuaded by
the funeral director. All others, except apprentices, are excluded by
law from the preparation room.

A close look at what does actually take place may explain in large   3
measure the undertaker's intractable reticence concerning a procedure that has become his major *raison d'être*. Is it possible he fears
that public information about embalming might lead patrons to
wonder if they really want this service? If the funeral men are loath to
discuss the subject outside the trade, the reader may, understandably,
be equally loath to go on reading at this point. For those who have
the stomach for it, let us part the formaldehyde curtain. . . .

The body is first laid out in the undertaker's morgue—or rather,   4
Mr. Jones is reposing in the preparation room—to be readied to bid
the world farewell.

The preparation room in any of the better funeral establish-   5
ments has the tiled and sterile look of a surgery, and indeed the em-
balmer-restorative artist who does his chores there is beginning to
adopt the term "dermasurgeon" (appropriately corrupted by some
mortician-writers as "demisurgeon") to describe his calling. His
equipment, consisting of scalpels, scissors, augers, forceps, clamps,
needles, pumps, tubes, bowls and basins, is crudely imitative of the
surgeon's, as is his technique, acquired in a nine- or twelve-month
post-high-school course in an embalming school. He is supplied by
an advanced chemical industry with a bewildering array of fluids,
sprays, pastes, oils, powders, creams, to fix or soften tissue, shrink or
distend it as needed, dry it here, restore the moisture there. There are
cosmetics, waxes and paints to fill and cover features, even plaster of
Paris to replace entire limbs. There are ingenious aids to prop and
stabilize the cadaver: a Vari-Pose Head Rest, the Edwards Arm and

Hand Positioner, the Repose Block (to support the shoulders during the embalming), and the Throop Foot Positioner, which resembles an old-fashioned stocks.

Mr. John H. Eckles, president of the Eckles College of Mortuary Science, thus describes the first part of the embalming procedure: "In the hands of a skilled practitioner, this work may be done in a comparatively short time and without mutilating the body other than by slight incision—so slight that it scarcely would cause serious inconvenience if made upon a living person. It is necessary to remove the blood, and doing this not only helps in the disinfecting, but removes the principal cause of disfigurements due to discoloration." 6

Another textbook discusses the all-important time element: "The earlier this is done, the better, for every hour that elapses between death and embalming will add to the problems and complications encountered. . . ." Just how soon should one get going on the embalming? The author tells us, "On the basis of such scanty information made available to this profession through its rudimentary and haphazard system of technical research, we must conclude that the best results are to be obtained if the subject is embalmed before life is completely extinct—that is, before cellular death has occurred. In the average case, this would mean within an hour after somatic death." For those who feel that there is something a little rudimentary, not to say haphazard, about this advice, a comforting thought is offered by another writer. Speaking of fears entertained in early days of premature burial, he points out, "One of the effects of embalming by chemical injection, however, has been to dispel fears of live burial." How true; once the blood is removed, chances of live burial are indeed remote. 7

To return to Mr. Jones, the blood is drained out through the veins and replaced by embalming fluid pumped in through the arteries. As noted in *The Principles and Practices of Embalming,* "every operator has a favorite injection and drainage point—a fact which becomes a handicap only if he fails or refuses to forsake his favorites when conditions demand it." Typical favorites are the carotid artery, femoral artery, jugular vein, subclavian vein. There are various choices of embalming fluid. If Flextone is used, it will produce a "mild, flexible rigidity. The skin retains a velvety softness, the tissues are rubbery and pliable. Ideal for women and children." It may be blended with B. and G. Products Company's Lyf-Lyk tint, which is guaranteed to reproduce "nature's own skin texture...the velvety 8 appearance of living tissue." Suntone comes in three separate tints: Suntan; Special Cosmetic Tint, a pink shade "especially indicated for young female subjects"; and Regular Cosmetic Tint, moderately pink.

About three to six gallons of a dyed and perfumed solution of 9 formaldehyde, glycerin, borax, phenol, alcohol, and water is soon circulating through Mr. Jones, whose mouth has been sewn together with a "needle directed upward between the upper lip and gum and brought out through the left nostril," with the corners raised slightly "for a more pleasant expression." If he should be buck-toothed, his teeth are cleaned with Bon Ami and coated with color-less nail polish. His eyes, meanwhile, are closed with flesh-tinted eye caps and eye cement.

The next step is to have at Mr. Jones with a thing called a trocar. 10 This is a long, hollow needle attached to a tube. It is jabbed into the abdomen, poked around the entrails and chest cavity, the contents of which are pumped out and replaced with "cavity fluid." This done, and the hole in the abdomen sewn up, Mr. Jones's face is heavily creamed (to protect the skin from burns which may be caused by leakage of the chemicals), and he is covered with a sheet and left un-molested for a while. But not for long—there is more, much more, in store for him. He has been embalmed, but not yet restored, and the best time to start the restorative work is eight to ten hours after embalming, when the tissues have become firm and dry.

The object of all this attention to the corpse, it must be remem- 11 bered, is to make it presentable for viewing in an attitude of healthy repose. "Our customs require the presentation of our dead in the semblance of normality...unmarred by the ravages of illness, disease or mutilation," says Mr. J. Sheridan Mayer in his *Restorative Art*. This is rather a large order since few people die in the full bloom of health, unravaged by illness and unmarked by some disfigurement. The funeral industry is equal to the challenge: "In some cases the gruesome appearance of a mutilated or disease-ridden subject may be quite discouraging. The task of restoration may seem impossible and shake the confidence of the embalmer. This is the time for intestinal fortitude and determination. Once the formative work is begun and affected tissues are cleaned or removed, all doubts of success vanish. It is surprising and gratifying to discover the results which may be obtained."

The embalmer, having allowed an appropriate interval to elapse, 12 returns to the attack, but now he brings into play the skill and equipment of sculptor and cosmetician. Is a hand missing? Casting one in plaster of Paris is a simple matter. "For replacement purposes, only a cast of the back of the hand is necessary; this is within the ability of the average operator and is quite adequate." If a lip or two, a nose or an ear should be missing, the embalmer has at hand a variety of restorative waxes with which to model replacements. Pores and skin texture are simulated by stippling with a little brush, and over this cosmetics are laid on. Head off? Decapitation cases are rather routinely handled. Ragged edges are trimmed, and head joined to torso with a series of splints, wires and sutures. It is a good idea to have a little something at the neck—a scarf or high collar—when time for viewing comes. Swollen mouth? Cut out tissue as needed from inside the lips. If too much is removed, the surface contour can easily be restored by padding with cotton. Swollen necks and cheeks are reduced by removing tissue through vertical incisions made down each side of the neck. "When the deceased is casketed, the pillow will hide the suture incisions...as an extra precaution against leakage, the suture may be painted with liquid sealer."

The opposite condition is more likely to present itself—that of   13
emaciation. His hypodermic syringe now loaded with massage cream, the embalmer seeks out and fills the hollowed and sunken areas by injection. In this procedure the backs of the hands and fingers and the under-chin area should not be neglected.

Positioning the lips is a problem that recurrently challenges the   14
ingenuity of the embalmer. Closed too tightly they tend to give a stern, even disapproving expression. Ideally, embalmers feel, the lips should give the impression of being ever so slightly parted, the upper lip protruding slightly for a more youthful appearance. This takes some engineering, however, as the lips tend to drift apart. Lip drift can sometimes be remedied by pushing one or two straight pins through the inner margin of the lower lip and then inserting them between the two front upper teeth. If Mr. Jones happens to have no teeth, the pins can just as easily be anchored in his Armstrong Face Former and Denture Replacer. Another method to maintain lip closure is to dislocate the lower jaw, which is then held in its new position by a wire run through holes which have been drilled through the upper and lower jaws at the midline. As the French are fond of saying, *il faut souffrir pour être belle.*[1]

---

[1] One has to suffer to be beautiful.

If Mr. Jones has died of jaundice, the embalming fluid will very   15
likely turn him green. Does this deter the embalmer? Not if he has
intestinal fortitude. Masking pastes and cosmetics are heavily laid on,
burial garments and casket interiors are color-correlated with particular care, and Jones is displayed beneath rose-colored lights. Friends
will say, "How *well* he looks." Death by carbon monoxide, on the
other hand, can be rather a good thing from the embalmer's viewpoint: "One advantage is the fact that this type of discoloration is an
exaggerated form of a natural pink coloration." This is nice because
the healthy glow is already present and needs but little attention.

The patching and filling completed, Mr. Jones is now shaved,   16
washed and dressed. Cream-based cosmetic, available in pink, flesh,
suntan, brunette, and blond, is applied to his hands and face, his hair
is shampooed and combed (and, in the case of Mrs. Jones, set), his
hands manicured. For the horny-handed son of toil special care must
be taken; cream should be applied to remove ingrained grime, and
the nails cleaned. "If he were not in the habit of having them manicured in life, trimming and shaping is advised for better appearance—never questioned by kin."

Jones is now ready for casketing (this is the present participle of   17
the verb "to casket"). In this operation his right shoulder should be
depressed slightly "to turn the body a bit to the right and soften the
appearance of lying flat on the back." Positioning the hands is a matter of importance, and special rubber positioning blocks may be
used. The hands should be cupped slightly for a more lifelike, relaxed
appearance. Proper placement of the body requires a delicate sense
of balance. It should lie as high as possible in the casket, yet not so
high that the lid, when lowered, will hit the nose. On the other hand,
we are cautioned, placing the body too low "creates the impression
that the body is in a box."

Jones is next wheeled into the appointed slumber room where a   18
few last touches may be added—his favorite pipe placed in his hand
or, if he was a great reader, a book propped into position. (In the case
of little Master Jones a Teddy bear may be clutched.) Here he will
hold open house for a few days, visiting hours 10 A.M. to 9 P.M.

Questions for Close Reading

1. What is the selection's thesis? Locate the sentence(s) in which Mitford
   states her main idea. If she doesn't state the thesis explicitly, express it in
   your own words.

2. Why, according to Mitford, do Americans know so little about the embalming process?

3. Mitford quotes from a textbook on embalming practices (paragraph 11). What does the passage reveal about the goals of mortuary science?

4. In what ways is the body made to look even better than it did when alive?

5. Refer to your dictionary as needed to define the following words used in the selection: *docility* (paragraph 1), *intractable* (3), *raison d'être* (3), *augers* (5), *distend* (5), *stippling* (12), and *jaundice* (15).

Questions About the Writer's Craft

1. **The pattern.** What are the main stages of the mortician's craft? What happens in each step? What words and phrases does Mitford use to indicate that she's moving from one step to the next?

2. Why does Mitford refer to the body being embalmed as Mr. Jones? What effect does this naming have on the reader?

3. Mitford interweaves her description of the embalming and restoring process with many quotations from mortuary science texts. Why do you suppose she does this? What do you notice about the writing style of the authors of these texts?

4. What is Mitford's tone in this essay? Do you feel she is being objective in her description of the funeral industry? Explain.

Questions for Further Thought

1. Now that you know more about it, does embalming strike you as a worthwhile process? Do you feel it is appropriate? Explain.

2. One embalmers' manual states that cleaning and trimming the nails of a working man is "never questioned by kin." Are kin prevented from questioning embalmers' techniques? Do you think the funeral industry as a whole takes advantage of grief and disorientation?

3. How does Mitford's description of the preparation-for-burial process illustrate that funerals are for the living, not for the dead? What kinds of final rites would show more respect for the dead—and for the process of dying?

4. Once, Mitford says, relatives prepared a body for burial, and death was thus blended into ordinary life. Today, the process of burial is given over to specialists. Do you think this change has harmed the survivors? Have any other natural aspects of life been turned over to "specialists" and thus been separated from daily life?

Writing Assignments Using Process Analysis as a Pattern of Development

∞ 1. Many important events in our lives are marked by celebrations or rituals. Often, the basic outlines of these rituals are established by tradition, but we can always personalize these traditions in one way or another. Select an important event that you will celebrate in the future and explain how you would like to experience the event. Your choice could include any of the following: your marriage, the birth of a child, your graduation, your parent's retirement, or some other notable occurrence. Before writing, you may find it helpful to read Judith Ortiz Cofer's "A Partial Remembrance of a Puerto Rican Childhood" (page 138), an essay about a shared family ritual.

2. Write a paper telling your survivors how you wish to be treated after death. Explain how they should conduct your funeral, whether they should embalm you, where they should put your remains, and, most important, what you would like said in your eulogy. Be as specific as possible as you outline the steps to be taken.

Writing Assignments Using Other Patterns of Development

3. Write an essay describing a funeral or viewing that you attended. Focus on what seems to you the most important scene. Your thesis should express a dominant feeling about the scene: depression, grief, discomfort, fear, relief, or some other emotion. Alternatively, write an essay describing any other ceremony or ritual you have experienced (for example, a wedding, a bar or bat mitzvah, or a graduation). Your dominant feeling may be positive or negative.

4. Write an essay showing that Americans often pretend that death doesn't exist or isn't really happening. Give examples drawn from your own life, your family's life, or public events. You might consider the following: the expressions we use with children ("Grandpa's gone away"; "Kitty is sleeping"); the euphemistic language we have for death ("passed away"; "no longer with us"); our obsession with looking young and keeping fit; our beliefs about "eternal life"; people's resistance to making a will.

Paul Roberts

Paul Roberts (1917–1967) was a scholar of linguistics and a re-spected teacher whose textbooks helped scores of high school and college students become better writers. Roberts's works include *English Syntax* (1954) and *Patterns of English* (1956). The follow-ing selection is from his best-known book, *Understanding English* (1958).

How to Say Nothing in 500 Words

Student essays are written on the bus, in the cafeteria, during tele-vision shows, and after midnight. Not surprisingly, many are un-inspired last-ditch attempts to fulfill an assignment. Paul Roberts, who spent many bleary-eyed hours reading such papers, has great fun presenting a typical freshman essay for analysis. He then pro-vides students with lively and helpful advice on ways to write es-says that are worth something.

Nothing About Something

It's Friday afternoon, and you have almost survived another   1
week of classes. You are just looking forward dreamily to the week-end when the English instructor says: "For Monday you will turn in a five-hundred-word composition on college football."

Well, that puts a good big hole in the weekend. You don't have   2
any strong views on college football one way or the other. You get rather excited during the season and go to all the home games and find it rather more fun than not. On the other hand, the class has been reading Robert Hutchins in the anthology and perhaps Shaw's "Eighty-Yard Run," and from the class discussion you have got the idea that the instructor thinks college football is for the birds. You are no fool, you. You can figure out what side to take.

After dinner you get out the portable typewriter that you got for   3
high school graduation. You might as well get it over with and enjoy
Saturday and Sunday. Five hundred words is about two double-
spaced pages with normal margins. You put in a sheet of paper, think
up a title, and you're off:

Why College Football Should Be Abolished

College football should be abolished because it's bad   4
for the school and also bad for the players. The players are
so busy practicing that they don't have any time for their
studies.

This, you feel, is a mighty good start. The only trouble is that   5
it's only thirty-two words. You still have four hundred and sixty-
eight to go, and you've pretty well exhausted the subject. It comes
to you that you do your best thinking in the morning, so you put
away the typewriter and go to the movies. But the next morning you
have to do your washing and some math problems, and in the afternoon you go to the game. The English instructor turns up too, and
you wonder if you've taken the right side after all. Saturday night you
have a date, and Sunday morning you have to go to church. (You
shouldn't let English assignments interfere with your religion.) What
with one thing and another, it's ten o'clock Sunday night before you
get out the typewriter again. You make a pot of coffee and start to
fill out your views on college football. Put a little meat on the bones.

Why College Football Should Be Abolished

In my opinion, it seems to me that college football   6
should be abolished. The reason why I think this to be true
is because I feel that football is bad for the colleges in nearly
every respect. As Robert Hutchins says in his article in our
anthology in which he discusses college football, it would
be better if the colleges had race horses and had races with
one another, because then the horses would not have to attend classes. I firmly agree with Mr. Hutchins on this point,
and I am sure that many other students would agree too.

One reason why it seems to me that college football is   7
bad is that it has become too commercial. In the olden
times when people played football just for the fun of it,

maybe college football was all right, but they do not play football just for the fun of it now as they used to in the old days. Nowadays college football is what you might call a big business. Maybe this is not true at all schools, and I don't think it is especially true here at State, but certainly this is the case at most colleges and universities in America nowadays, as Mr. Hutchins points out in his very interesting article. Actually the coaches and alumni go around to the high schools and offer the high school stars large salaries to come to their colleges and play football for them. There was one case where a high school star was offered a convertible if he would play football for a certain college.

Another reason for abolishing college football is that it   8
is bad for the players. They do not have time to get a college education, because they are so busy playing football. A football player has to practice every afternoon from three to six, and then he is so tired that he can't concentrate on his studies. He just feels like dropping off to sleep after dinner, and then the next day he goes to his classes without having studied and maybe he fails the test.

(Good ripe stuff so far, but you're still a hundred and fifty-one words from home. One more push.)

Also I think college football is bad for the colleges and   9
the universities because not very many students get to participate in it. Out of a college of ten thousand students only seventy-five or a hundred play football, if that many. Football is what you might call a spectator sport. That means that most people go to watch it but do not play it themselves.

(Four hundred and fifteen. Well, you still have the conclusion, and when you retype it, you can make the margins a little wider.)

These are the reasons why I agree with Mr. Hutchins   10
that college football should be abolished in American colleges and universities.

On Monday you turn it in, moderately hopeful, and on Friday   11
it comes back marked "weak in content" and sporting a big "D."

This essay is exaggerated a little, not much. The English in-   12
structor will recognize it as reasonably typical of what an assignment
on college football will bring in. He knows that nearly half of the
class will contrive in five hundred words to say that college football
is too commercial and bad for the players. Most of the other half will
inform him that college football builds character and prepares one
for life and brings prestige to the school. As he reads paper after paper all saying the same thing in almost the same words, all bloodless,
five hundred words dripping out of nothing, he wonders how he allowed himself to get trapped into teaching English when he might
have had a happy and interesting life as an electrician or a confidence
man.

Well, you may ask, what can you do about it? The subject is one   13
on which you have few convictions and little information. Can you
be expected to make a dull subject interesting? As a matter of fact,
this is precisely what you are expected to do. This is the writer's essential task. All subjects, except sex, are dull until somebody makes
them interesting. The writer's job is to find the argument, the approach, the angle, the wording that will take the reader with him.
This is seldom easy, and it is particularly hard in subjects that have
been much discussed: College Football, Fraternities, Popular Music,
Is Chivalry Dead?, and the like. You will feel that there is nothing you
can do with such subjects except repeat the old bromides. But there
are some things you can do which will make your papers, if not
throbbingly alive, at least less insufferably tedious than they might
otherwise be.

Avoid the Obvious Content

Say the assignment is college football. Say that you've decided   14
to be against it. Begin by putting down the arguments that come to
your mind: it is too commercial, it takes the students' minds off their
studies, it is hard on the players, it makes the university a kind of cir-
cus instead of an intellectual center, for most schools it is financially
ruinous. Can you think of any more arguments just off hand? All
right. Now when you write your paper, *make sure that you don't use
any of the material on this list*. If these are the points that leap to your
mind, they will leap to everyone else's too, and whether you get a
"C" or a "D" may depend on whether the instructor reads your pa-

per early when he is fresh and tolerant or late, when the sentence "In my opinion, college football has become too commercial," inexorably repeated, has brought him to the brink of lunacy.

Be against college football for some reason or reasons of your   15
own. If they are keen and perceptive ones, that's splendid. But even
if they are trivial or foolish or indefensible, you are still ahead so long
as they are not everybody else's reasons too. Be against it because the
colleges don't spend enough money on it to make it worth while, because it is bad for the characters of the spectators, because the players
are forced to attend classes, because the football stars hog all the
beautiful women, because it competes with baseball and is therefore
un-American and possibly Communist inspired. There are lots of
more or less unused reasons for being against college football.

Sometimes it is a good idea to sum up and dispose of the trite   16
and conventional points before going on to your own. This has the
advantage of indicating to the reader that you are going to be neither
trite nor conventional. Something like this:

>   We are often told that college football should be abol-   17
>   ished because it has become too commercial or because it
>   is bad for the players. These arguments are no doubt very
>   cogent, but they don't really go to the heart of the matter.

Then you go to the heart of the matter.

Take the Less Usual Side

One rather simple way of getting interest into your paper is to   18
take the side of the argument that most of the citizens will want to
avoid. If the assignment is an essay on dogs, you can, if you choose,
explain that dogs are faithful and lovable companions, intelligent,
useful as guardians of the house and protectors of children, indispensable in police work—in short, when all is said and done, man's
best friends. Or you can suggest that those big brown eyes conceal,
more often than not, a vacuity of mind and an inconstancy of purpose; that the dogs you have known most intimately have been
mangy, ill-tempered brutes, incapable of instruction; and that only
your nobility of mind and fear of arrest prevent you from kicking the
flea-ridden animals when you pass them on the street.

Naturally, personal convictions will sometimes dictate your ap-   19
proach. If the assigned subject is "Is Methodism Rewarding to the
Individual?" and you are a pious Methodist, you have really no
choice. But few assigned subjects, if any, will fall in this category.
Most of them will lie in broad areas of discussion with much to be
said on both sides. They are intellectual exercises and it is legitimate
to argue now one way and now another, as debaters do in similar circumstances. Always take the side that looks to you hardest, least de-
fensible. It will almost always turn out to be easier to write
interestingly on that side.

This general advice applies where you have a choice of subjects.   20
If you are to choose among "The Value of Fraternities" and "My Favorite High School Teacher" and "What I Think About Beetles," by
all means plump for the beetles. By the time the instructor gets to
your paper, he will be up to his ears in tedious tales about the French
teacher at Bloombury High and assertions about how fraternities
build character and prepare one for life. Your views on beetles, whatever they are, are bound to be a refreshing change.

Don't worry too much about figuring out what the instructor   21
thinks about the subject so that you can cuddle up with him. Chances are his views are no stronger than yours. If he does have convictions and you oppose them, his problem is to keep from grading you
higher than you deserve in order to show he is not biased. This
doesn't mean that you should always cantankerously dissent from
what the instructor says; that gets tiresome too. And if the subject assigned is "My Pet Peeve," do not begin, "My pet peeve is the English
instructor who assigns papers on 'my pet peeve.'" This was still funny
during the War of 1812, but it has sort of lost its edge since then. It
is in general good manners to avoid personalities.

Slip out of Abstraction

If you will study the essay on college football...you will   22
perceive that one reason for its appalling dullness is that it never
gets down to particulars. It is just a series of not very glittering generalities: "football is bad for the colleges," "it has become too commercial," "football is a big business," "it is bad for the players,"
and so on. Such round phrases thudding against the reader's brain
are unlikely to convince him, though they may well render him
unconscious.

If you want the reader to believe that college football is bad for   23
the players, you have to do more than say so. You have to display the
evil. Take your roommate, Alfred Simkins, the second-string center.
Picture poor old Alfy coming home from football practice every
evening, bruised and aching, agonizingly tired, scarcely able to shovel the mashed potatoes into his mouth. Let us see him staggering up
to the room, getting out his econ textbook, peering desperately at it
with his good eye, falling asleep and failing the test in the morning.
Let us share his unbearable tension as Saturday draws near. Will he
fail, be demoted, lose his monthly allowance, be forced to return to
the coal mines? And if he succeeds, what will be his reward? Perhaps
a slight ripple of applause when the third-string center replaces him,
a moment of elation in the locker room if the team wins, of despair
if it loses. What will he look back on when he graduates from college?
Toil and torn ligaments. And what will be his future? He is not good
enough for pro football, and he is too obscure and weak in econ to
succeed in stocks and bonds. College football is tearing the heart
from Alfy Simkins and, when it finishes with him, will callously toss
aside the shattered hulk.

This is no doubt a weak enough argument for the abolition   24
of college football, but it is a sight better than saying, in three or
four variations, that college football (in your opinion) is bad for the
players.

Look at the work of any professional writer and notice how con-   25
stantly he is moving from the generality, the abstract statement, to
the concrete example, the facts and figures, the illustration. If he is
writing on juvenile delinquency, he does not just tell you that juveniles are (it seems to him) delinquent and that (in his opinion) something should be done about it. He shows you juveniles being
delinquent, tearing up movie theatres in Buffalo, stabbing high
school principals in Dallas, smoking marijuana in Palo Alto. And
more than likely he is moving toward some specific remedy, not just
a general wringing of the hands.

It is no doubt possible to be *too* concrete, too illustrative or an-   26
ecdotal, but few inexperienced writers err this way. For most the
soundest advice is to be seeking always for the picture, to be always
turning general remarks into seeable examples. Don't say, "Sororities
teach girls the social graces." Say "Sorority life teaches a girl how to
carry on a conversation while pouring tea, without sloshing the tea
into the saucer." Don't say, "I like certain kinds of popular music

very much." Say, "Whenever I hear Gerber Spinklittle play 'Mississippi Man' on the trombone, my socks creep up my ankles."

Get Rid of Obvious Padding

The student toiling away at his weekly English theme is too often tormented by a figure: five hundred words. How, he asks himself, is he to achieve this staggering total? Obviously by never using one word when he can somehow work in ten.   27

He is therefore seldom content with a plain statement like "Fast driving is dangerous." This has only four words in it. He takes thought, and the sentence becomes: 28

> In my opinion, fast driving is dangerous.

Better, but he can do better still:

> In my opinion, fast driving would seem to be rather dangerous.

If he is really adept, it may come out:

> In my humble opinion, though I do not claim to be an expert on this complicated subject, fast driving, in most circumstances, would seem to be rather dangerous in many respects, or at least so it would seem to me.

Thus four words have been turned into forty, and not an iota of content has been added.

Now this is a way to go about reaching five hundred words, and if you are content with a "D" grade, it is as good a way as any. But if you aim higher, you must work differently. Instead of stuffing your sentences with straw, you must try steadily to get rid of the padding, to make your sentences lean and tough. If you are really working at it, your first draft will greatly exceed the required total, and then you will work it down, thus: 29

> It is thought in some quarters that fraternities do not contribute as much as might be expected to campus life.

Some people think that fraternities contribute little to campus life.

The average doctor who practices in small towns or in the country must toil night and day to heal the sick.
Most country doctors work long hours.

When I was a little girl, I suffered from shyness and embarrassment in the presence of others.
I was a shy little girl.

It is absolutely necessary for the person employed as a marine fireman to give the matter of steam pressure his undivided attention at all times.
The fireman has to keep his eye on the steam gauge.

You may ask how you can arrive at five hundred words at this rate. Simply. You dig up more real content. Instead of taking a couple of obvious points off the surface of the topic and then circling warily around them for six paragraphs, you work in and explore, figure out the details. You illustrate. You say that fast driving is dangerous, and then you prove it. How long does it take to stop a car at forty and at eighty? How far can you see at night? What happens when a tire blows? What happens in a head-on collision at fifty miles an hour? Pretty soon your paper will be full of broken glass and blood and headless torsos, and reaching five hundred words will not really be a problem. 30

Call a Fool a Fool

Some of the padding in freshman themes is to be blamed not on anxiety about the word minimum but on excessive timidity. The student writes, "In my opinion, the principal of my high school acted in ways that I believe every unbiased person would have to call foolish." This isn't exactly what he means. What he means is, "My high school principal was a fool." If he was a fool, call him a fool. Hedging the thing about with "in-my-opinion's" and "it-seems-to-me's" and "as-I-see-it's" and "at-least-from-my-point-of-view's" gains you nothing. Delete these phrases whenever they creep into your paper. 31

The student's tendency to hedge stems from a modesty that in   32
other circumstances would be commendable. He is, he realizes,
young and inexperienced, and he half suspects that he is dopey and
fuzzy-minded beyond the average. Probably only too true. But it
doesn't help to announce your incompetence six times in every paragraph. Decide what you want to say and say it as vigorously as possible, without apology and in plain words.

Linguistic diffidence can take various forms. One is what we call   33
euphemism. This is the tendency to call a spade "a certain garden im-
plement" or women's underwear "unmentionables." It is stronger in
some eras than others and in some people than others but it always
operates more or less in subjects that are touchy or taboo: death, sex,
madness, and so on. Thus we shrink from saying "He died last night"
but say instead "passed away," "left us," "joined his Maker," "went
to his reward." Or we try to take off the tension with a lighter cliché:
"kicked the bucket," "cashed in his chips," "handed in his dinner
pail." We have found all sorts of ways to avoid saying *mad:* "mentally
ill," "touched," "not quite right upstairs," "feeble-minded," "innocent," "simple," "off his trolley," "not in his right mind." Even such
a now plain word as *insane* began as a euphemism with the meaning
"not healthy."

Modern science, particularly psychology, contributes many   34
polysyllables in which we can wrap our thoughts and blunt their
force. To many writers there is no such thing as a bad schoolboy.
Schoolboys are maladjusted or unoriented or misunderstood or in
need of guidance or lacking in continued success toward satisfactory
integration of the personality as a social unit, but they are never bad.
Psychology no doubt makes us better men or women, more sympathetic and tolerant, but it doesn't make writing any easier. Had
Shakespeare been confronted with psychology, "To be or not to be"
might have come out, "To continue as a social unit or not to do so.
That is the personality problem. Whether 'tis a better sign of integration at the conscious level to display a psychic tolerance toward the
maladjustments and repressions induced by one's lack of orientation
in one's environment or—" But Hamlet would never have finished
the soliloquy.

Writing in the modern world, you cannot altogether avoid mod-   35
ern jargon. Nor, in an effort to get away from euphemism, should

you salt your paper with four-letter words. But you can do much if you will mount guard against those roundabout phrases, those echoing polysyllables that tend to slip into your writing to rob it of its crispness and force.

Beware of the Pat Expression

Other things being equal, avoid phrases like "other things being   36
equal." Those sentences that come to you whole, or in two or three doughy lumps, are sure to be bad sentences. They are no creation of yours but pieces of common thought floating in the community soup.

Pat expressions are hard, often impossible, to avoid, because   37
they come too easily to be noticed and seem too necessary to be dispensed with. No writer avoids them altogether, but good writers avoid them more often than poor writers.

By "pat expressions" we mean such tags as "to all practical in-   38
tents and purposes," "the pure and simple truth," "from where I sit," "the time of his life," "to the ends of the earth," "in the twinkling of an eye," "as sure as you're born," "over my dead body," "under cover of darkness," "took the easy way out," "when all is said and done," "told him time and time again," "parted the best of friends," "stand up and be counted," "gave him the best years of her life," "worked her fingers to the bone." Like other clichés, these expressions were once forceful. Now we should use them only when we can't possibly think of anything else.

Some pat expressions stand like a wall between the writer and   39
thought. Such a one is "the American way of life." Many student writers feel that when they have said that something accords with the American way of life or does not they have exhausted the subject. Actually, they have stopped at the highest level of abstraction. The American way of life is the complicated set of bonds between a hundred and eighty million ways. All of us know this when we think about it, but the tag phrase too often keeps us from thinking about it.

So with many another phrase dear to the politician: "this great   40
land of ours," "the man in the street," "our national heritage." These may prove our patriotism or give a clue to our political beliefs, but otherwise they add nothing to the paper except words.

Colorful Words

The writer builds with words, and no builder uses a raw material   41
more slippery and elusive and treacherous. A writer's work is a constant struggle to get the right word in the right place, to find that particular word that will convey his meaning exactly, that will persuade
the reader or soothe him or startle or amuse him. He never succeeds
altogether—sometimes he feels that he scarcely succeeds at all—but
such successes as he has are what make the thing worth doing.

There is no book of rules for this game. One progresses through   42
everlasting experiment on the basis of ever-widening experience.
There are few useful generalizations that one can make about words
as words, but there are perhaps a few.

Some words are what we call "colorful." By this we mean that   43
they are calculated to produce a picture or induce an emotion. They
are dressy instead of plain, specific instead of general, loud instead of
soft. Thus, in place of "Her heart beat," we may write "Her heart
pounded, throbbed, fluttered, danced." Instead of "He sat in his
chair," we may say, "He *lounged, sprawled, coiled.*" Instead of "It was
hot," we may say, "It was *blistering, sultry, muggy, suffocating,
steamy, wilting.*"

However, it should not be supposed that the fancy word is al-   44
ways better. Often it is as well to write "Her heart beat" or "It was
hot" if that is all it did or all it was. Ages differ in how they like their
prose. The nineteenth century liked it rich and smoky. The twentieth
has usually preferred it lean and cool. The twentieth-century writer,
like all writers, is forever seeking the exact word, but he is wary of
sounding feverish. He tends to pitch it low, to understate it, to throw
it away. He knows that if he gets too colorful, the audience is likely
to giggle.

See how this strikes you: "As the rich, golden glow of the sunset   45
died away along the eternal western hills, Angela's limpid blue eyes
looked softly and trustingly into Montague's flashing brown ones,
and her heart pounded like a drum in time with the joyous song surg-
ing in her soul." Some people like that sort of thing, but most modern readers would say, "Good grief," and turn on the television.

Colored Words

Some words we would call not so much colorful as colored—   46
that is, loaded with associations, good or bad. All words—except per-

haps structure words—have associations of some sort. We have said that the meaning of a word is the sum of the contexts in which it occurs. When we hear a word, we hear with it an echo of all the situations in which we have heard it before.

In some words, these echoes are obvious and discussable. The word *mother*, for example, has, for most people, agreeable associations. When you hear *mother* you probably think of home, safety, love, food, and various other pleasant things. If one writes, "She was like a mother to me," he gets an effect which he would not get in "She was like an aunt to me." The advertiser makes use of the associations of *mother* by working it in when he talks about his product. The politician works it in when he talks about himself. 47

So also with such words as *home, liberty, fireside, contentment, patriot, tenderness, sacrifice, childlike, manly, bluff, limpid.* All of these words are loaded with favorable associations that would be rather hard to indicate in a straightforward definition. There is more than a literal difference between "They sat around the fireside" and "They sat around the stove." They might have been equally warm and happy around the stove, but *fireside* suggests leisure, grace, quiet tradition, congenial company, and *stove* does not. 48

Conversely, some words have bad associations. *Mother* suggests pleasant things, but *mother-in-law* does not. Many mothers-in-law are heroically lovable and some mothers drink gin all day and beat their children insensible, but these facts of life are beside the point. The thing is that *mother* sounds good and *mother-in-law* does not. 49

Or consider the word *intellectual.* This would seem to be a complimentary term, but in point of fact it is not, for it has picked up associations of impracticality and ineffectuality and general dopiness. So also with such words as *liberal, reactionary, Communist, socialist, capitalist, radical, schoolteacher, truck driver, undertaker, operator, salesman, huckster, speculator.* These convey meanings on the literal level, but beyond that—sometimes, in some places—they convey contempt on the part of the speaker. 50

The question of whether to use loaded words or not depends on what is being written. The scientist, the scholar, try to avoid them; for the poet, the advertising writer, the public speaker, they are standard equipment. But every writer should take care that they do not substitute for thought. If you write, "Anyone who thinks that is nothing but a Socialist (or Communist or capitalist)," you have said nothing except that you don't like people who think that, and such remarks are effective only with the most naïve readers. It is 51 always a bad mistake to think your readers more naïve than they really are.

Colorless Words

But probably most student writers come to grief not with words   52
that are colorful or those that are colored but with those that have no color at all. A pet example is *nice,* a word we would find it hard to dispense with in casual conversation but which is no longer capable of adding much to a description. Colorless words are those of such general meaning that in a particular sentence they mean nothing. Slang adjectives, like *cool* ("That's real cool") tend to explode all over the language. They are applied to everything, lose their original force, and quickly die.

Beware also of nouns of very general meaning, like *circumstances, cases, instances, aspects, factors, relationships, attitudes, eventualities,* etc. In most circumstances you will find that those cases of writing which contain too many instances of words like these will in this and other aspects have factors leading to unsatisfactory relationships with the reader resulting in unfavorable attitudes on his part and perhaps other eventualities, like a grade of "D." Notice also what "etc." means. It means "I'd like to make this list longer, but I can't think of any more examples."   53

Questions for Close Reading

1. What is the selection's thesis? Locate the sentence(s) in which Roberts states his main idea. If he doesn't state the thesis explicitly, express it in your own words.
2. According to Roberts, what do students assume they have to do to get a good grade on an English composition?
3. How do "colorful words," "colored words," and "colorless words" differ? Which should be used in essay writing? Why?
4. What are Roberts's most important pieces of advice for the student writer?
5. Refer to the dictionary as needed to define the following words used in the selection: *bromides* (paragraph 13), *insufferably* (13), *inexorably* (14), *dissent* (21), *abolition* (24), *adept* (28), *euphemism* (33), and *insensible* (49).

Questions About the Writer's Craft

1. **The pattern.**   What two processes does Roberts analyze in this essay? Is each process informational, directional, or a combination of the two?

2. Why do you think Roberts uses the second person "you" throughout the essay? How does this choice of point of view affect your response to the essay?

3. What is Roberts's tone in the essay? Find some typical examples of his tone. How does Roberts achieve this tone? Considering the author's intended audience, is this tone a good choice? Explain.

4. Does Roberts "practice what he preaches" about writing? Review the section headings of the essay and find examples of each piece of advice in the essay.

Questions for Further Thought

1. Roberts writes that making "a dull subject interesting...is precisely what you are expected to do" in college English. Do you agree that most writing subjects are dull? If so, do you think assignments could be made more interesting? And how could instructors get students to write honestly, instead of writing what they think the instructor wants to read?

2. Is Roberts's suggestion to write about the least obvious topic always appropriate? Would you follow this advice yourself? Explain why or why not.

3. In paragraph 14, Roberts says the difference between a "C" or a "D" may depend on when the teacher grades the paper. Do you think instructors' grades are usually fair, objective, and appropriate? Or do they often seem arbitrary and subjective?

4. Do you think most students are preoccupied with word-counting and guessing the instructor's opinion on a topic? Are you? Why do some students handle writing assignments this way? What could professors do to encourage students to focus more on the challenge of writing?

Writing Assignments Using Process Analysis as a Pattern of Development

1. Write a humorous essay showing how to avoid doing schoolwork, household chores, or anything else most people tend to put off. You may use the second person as Roberts does. Or you may use the first person and describe your typical method of avoidance.

∞ 2. Borrowing some of Roberts's lively techniques, make a routine, predictable process interesting to read about. You might choose an activity such as how to register to vote, apply for a driver's license, sign up for college courses, take care of laundry, play a simple game, study for an exam, or some other familiar process. Caroline Rego's "The Fine Art of Complaining" (page 385) may give you some ideas on how to explain a process in a helpful yet entertaining way.

Writing Assignments Using Other Patterns of Development

3. Should a composition course be required of all first-year college students? Write an essay arguing the value—or lack of value—of such a course. Follow Roberts's advice for writing a lively composition: avoid obvious padding, choose unusual points, avoid abstractions, go to the heart of the matter, use colorful words.

4. Write a paper detailing your experiences as a student in English classes—from elementary school up to now. Using several examples, describe how successfully or unsuccessfully English has been taught, and recommend any specific reforms or changes you feel are needed.

Caroline Rego

Caroline Rego was born in 1950 in Edmond, Oklahoma. A graduate of the University of Oklahoma, she began her journalistic career as a police reporter for a daily newspaper in Montana. Later, while filling in for a vacationing colleague in the features section of another newspaper, she found her true calling: writing consumer-affairs articles that teach readers how to protect themselves against shoddy service, dangerous products, and inefficiency. A sought-after public speaker, Rego talks frequently to students and community groups on strategies for becoming an informed consumer. The following selection is part of a work in progress on consumer empowerment.

The Fine Art of Complaining

How do you react when your "crisp" bacon is served rubbery, when your "waterproof" watch dies in the shower, or when your polite request for service elicits an insult from the store clerk? Do you meekly accept the situation, or do you explode in angry frustration? Perhaps you'll recognize yourself in the scenarios Caroline Rego describes.

You waited forty-five minutes for your dinner, and when it came 1
it was cold—and not what you ordered in the first place. You washed your supposedly machine-washable, preshrunk T-shirt (the one the catalogue claimed was "indestructible"), and now it's the size of a napkin. Your new car broke down a month after you bought it, and the dealer says the warranty doesn't apply.

Life's annoyances descend on all of us—some pattering down 2
like gentle raindrops, others striking with the bruising force of hailstones. We dodge the ones we can, but inevitably, plenty of them make contact. And when they do, we react fairly predictably. Many of us—most of us, probably—grumble to ourselves and take it. We scowl at our unappetizing food but choke it down. We stash the shrunken T-shirt in a drawer, vowing never again to order from a catalogue. We glare fiercely at our checkbooks as we pay for repairs that should have been free.

385

A few of us go to the other extreme. Taking our cue from the   3
crazed newscaster in the 1976 movie *Network,* we go through life
mad as hell and unwilling to take it anymore. In offices, we shout at
hapless receptionists when we're kept waiting for appointments. In
restaurants, we make scenes that have fellow patrons craning their
necks to get a look at us. In stores, we argue with salespeople for not
waiting on us. We may notice after a while that our friends seem reluctant to venture into public with us, but hey—we're just standing
up for our rights. Being a patsy doesn't get you anywhere in life.

It's true—milquetoasts live unsatisfying lives. However, people   4
who go through the day in an eye-popping, vein-throbbing state of
apoplectic rage don't win any prizes either. What persons at both
ends of the scale need—what could empower the silent sufferer and
civilize the Neanderthal—is a course in the gentle art of *effective*
complaining.

Effective complaining is not apologetic and half-hearted. It's   5
not making one awkward attempt at protest—"Uh, excuse me, I
don't think I ordered the squid and onions"—and then slinking away
in defeat. But neither is it roaring away indiscriminately, attempting
to get satisfaction through the sheer volume of our complaint.

Effective complainers are people who act businesslike and im-   6
portant. Acting important doesn't mean puffing up your chest and
saying, "Do you know who I am?"—an approach that would tempt
anyone to take you down a peg or two. It doesn't mean shouting
and threatening—techniques that will only antagonize the person
whose help you need. It *does* mean making it clear that you know
your request is reasonable and that you are confident it will be taken
care of. People are generally treated the way they expect to be treated. If you act like someone making a fair request, chances are that
request will be granted. Don't beg, don't explain. Just state your
name, the problem, and what you expect to have done. Remain polite. But be firm. "My car has been in your garage for three days, and
a mechanic hasn't even looked at it yet," you might say. "I want to
know when it is going to be worked on." Period. Now it is up to
them to give you a satisfactory response. Don't say, "Sorry to bother
you about this, but. . ." or "I, uh, was sort of expecting. . . ." You're
only asking people to remedy a problem, after all; that is not grounds
for apology.

If your problem requires an immediate response, try to make   7
your complaint in person; a real, live, in-the-flesh individual has to be

dealt with in some way. Complaining over the telephone, by contrast, is much less effective. When you speak to a disembodied voice, when the person at the other end of the line doesn't have to face you, you're more likely to get a runaround.

Most importantly, complain to the right person. One of the greatest frustrations in complaining is talking to a clerk or receptionist who cannot solve your problem and whose only purpose seems to be to drive you crazy. Getting mad doesn't help; the person you're mad at probably had nothing to do with your actual problem. And you'll have to repeat everything you've said to the clerk once you're passed along to the appropriate person. So make sure from the start that you're talking to someone who can help—a manager or supervisor.   8

If your problem doesn't require an immediate response, complaining by letter is probably the most effective way to get what you want. A letter of complaint should be brief, businesslike, and to the point. If you have a new vacuum cleaner that doesn't work, don't spend a paragraph describing how your Uncle Joe tried to fix the problem and couldn't. As when complaining in person, be sure you address someone in a position of real authority. Here's an example of an effective letter of complaint.   9

Ms. Anne Lublin   10
Manager
Mitchell Appliances
80 Front Street
Newton, MA 02159

Dear Ms. Lublin: 11

First section: Explain the problem. Include facts to back up your story.   12

On August 6, I purchased a new Perma-Kool freezer from your store (a copy of my sales receipt is enclosed). In the two weeks I have owned the freezer, I have had to call your repair department three times in an attempt to get it running properly. The freezer ran normally when it was installed, but since then it has repeatedly turned off, causing the food inside to spoil. My calls to your repair department have not been responded to promptly. After I called the first time, on August 10, I waited two days for the repair person to show up. It took three days to get a repair person here after my second call,   13

on August 15. The freezer stopped yet again on August 20. I called
to discuss this recent problem, but no one has responded to my call.

Second section: Tell how you trust the company and are confident that 14
your reader will fix the problem. This is to "soften up" the reader a bit.

I am surprised to receive such unprofessional service and poor qual- 15
ity from Mitchell Appliances since I have been one of your satisfied
customers for fifteen years. In the past, I have purchased a television, air conditioner, and washing machine from your company. I
know that you value good relations with your customers, and I'm
sure you want to see me pleased with my most recent purchase.

Third section: Explain exactly what you want to be done—repair, re- 16
placement, refund, etc.

Although your repair department initially thought that the freezer 17
needed only some minor adjustments, the fact that no one has been
able to permanently fix the problem convinces me that the freezer
has some serious defect. I am understandably unwilling to spend
any more time having repairs made. Therefore, I expect you to exchange the freezer for an identical model by the end of this week
(August 30). Please call me to arrange for the removal of the defective freezer and the delivery of the new one.

Sincerely, 18

Janice Becker

P.S. (Readers always notice a P.S.) State again when you expect the 19
problem to be taken care of, and what you will do if it isn't.

P.S. I am confident that we can resolve this problem by August 30. 20
If the defective freezer is not replaced by then, however, I will report
this incident to the Better Business Bureau.

Notice that the P.S. says what you'll do if your problem isn't 21
solved. In other words, you make a threat—a polite threat. Your
threat must be reasonable and believable. A threat to burn down the

store if your purchase price isn't refunded is neither reasonable nor believable—or if it *were* believed, you could end up in jail. A threat to report the store to a consumer-protection agency, such as the Better Business Bureau, however, is credible.

Don't be too quick to make one of the most common—and 22
commonly empty—threats: "I'll sue!" A full-blown lawsuit is more trouble, and more expensive, than most problems are worth. On the other hand, most areas have a small-claims court where suits involving modest amounts of money are heard. These courts don't use complex legal language or procedures, and you don't need a lawyer to use them. A store or company will often settle with you—if your claim is fair—rather than go to small-claims court.

Whether you complain over the phone, in person, or by letter, 23
be persistent. One complaint may not get results. In that case, keep on complaining, and make sure you keep complaining to the same person. Chances are he or she will get worn out and take care of the situation, if only to be rid of you.

Someday, perhaps, the world will be free of the petty annoyanc- 24
es that plague us all from time to time. Until then, however, toasters will break down, stores will refuse to honor rainchecks, and bills will include items that were never purchased. You can depend upon it—there will be grounds for complaint. You might as well learn to be good at it.

Questions for Close Reading

1. What is the selection's thesis? Locate the sentence(s) in which Rego states her main idea. If she doesn't state the thesis explicitly, express it in your own words.
2. In Rego's opinion, what types of actions and statements are *not* helpful when making a complaint?
3. What should be included in a letter of complaint? What should be omitted?
4. What does Rego suggest doing if a complaint is ignored?
5. Refer to your dictionary as needed to define the following words used in the selection: *hapless* (paragraph 3), *venture* (3), *patsy* (3), *milquetoasts* (4), *apoplectic* (4), *Neanderthal* (4), *indiscriminately* (5), *disembodied* (7), and *credible* (21).

Questions About the Writer's Craft

1. **The pattern.** Is Rego's process analysis primarily directional or primarily informational? Explain. To what extent does Rego try to persuade readers to follow her process?
2. **Other patterns.** Where does Rego include narrative elements in her essay? What do these brief narratives add to the piece?
3. **Other patterns.** Numerous oppositions occur throughout the essay. How do these contrasts enliven the essay and help Rego persuade readers to adopt her suggestions?
4. Reread the essay, noting where Rego shifts point of view. Where does she use the second-person (*you*), the first-person-plural (*we*), and the third-person-plural (*they*) points of view? How does her use of multiple points of view add to the essay's effectiveness?

Questions for Further Thought

1. Rego suggests that most people simply "grumble" and "take it" when they encounter poor service and shoddy merchandise. Do you agree that people tend to react this way? Explain. If you do agree, why do you think people have such "halfhearted" responses?
2. A character in the movie *Network* screams that he's mad as hell and won't "take it" anymore. What situations in life might prompt you to burst out in rage and indignation? Have you ever encountered a situation to which—in hindsight—you wished you had responded more assertively? Explain.
3. Rego offers guidelines for complaining effectively about flawed services and products. Do you think any of her suggestions are appropriate for making personal complaints to family or friends? Why or why not?
4. Rego remarks, "People are generally treated the way they expect to be treated." Do you agree? Give examples of experiences you've encountered or situations you've observed in which people were (or were not) treated according to their expectations. How did they react to the treatment they received?

Writing Assignments Using Process Analysis as a Pattern of Development

1. Write an essay explaining to college students how to register—with someone in a position of authority—an effective complaint about a campus problem. You could show, for example, how to complain to a professor about a course's grading policy, to the bookstore manager about the markup on textbooks, to security about the poorly maintained college parking lots. Feel free to adapt some of Rego's recommendations, but be

sure to invent several strategies of your own. In either case, provide—as Rego does—lively examples to illustrate the step-by-step procedure for registering an effective complaint with a specific authority figure on campus.

∞ 2. Rego argues that "people who go through the day in an eye-popping, vein-throbbing state of apoplectic rage don't win any prizes." But sometimes, getting mad can be appropriate—even productive. Write an essay explaining the best process for expressing anger effectively. Explain how to vent emotion safely, communicate the complaint in a nonthreatening way, encourage more honest interaction, and prompt change for the better. Illustrate the process by drawing upon your own experiences and observations. Barbara Ehrenreich's "What I've Learned From Men" (page 391) provides some insight into the dynamics of anger and resentment.

Writing Assignments Using Other Patterns of Development

3. Think about a service or product that failed to live up to your expectations. Perhaps you were disgruntled about your mechanic's car repair, a store's return policy, or a hotel's accommodations. Using Rego's suggestions, write a letter of complaint in which you describe the problem, convey confidence in the reader's ability to resolve the problem, and state your request for specific action. Remember that a firm but cordial tone will persuade your reader that you have legitimate grounds for seeking the resolution you propose.

4. Rego shows that events often don't turn out as we had hoped. In an essay, contrast how you thought a specific situation would be with the way it actually turned out. Was the unexpected outcome better or worse than what you had expected? Did you have trouble adjusting, or did you adapt with surprising ease? Provide vivid specifics about the unforeseen turn of events and your reaction to it.

Additional Writing Topics

PROCESS ANALYSIS

General Assignments

Develop one of the following topics through process analysis. Explain the process one step at a time, organizing the steps chronologically. If there's no agreed-upon sequence, design your own series of steps. Use transitions to ease the audience through the steps in the process. You may use any tone you wish, from serious to light.

Directional: How to Do Something

1. How to improve a course you have taken
2. How to drive defensively
3. How to get away with _____
4. How to succeed at a job interview
5. How to relax
6. How to show appreciation to others
7. How to get through school despite personal problems
8. How to be a responsible pet owner
9. How to conduct a garage or yard sale
10. How to look fashionable on a limited budget
11. How to protect a home from burglars
12. How to meet more people
13. How to improve the place where you work
14. How to gain or lose weight
15. How to get over a disappointment

Informational: How Something Happens

1. How a student becomes burned out
2. How a library's card catalog or computerized catalog organizes books
3. How a dead thing decays (or some other natural process works)
4. How the college registration process works
5. How *Homo sapiens* chooses a mate
6. How a VCR (or some other machine) works
7. How a bad habit develops
8. How people fall into debt

Assignments With a Specific Purpose and Audience

1. An author of books for elementary school children, you want to show children how to do something—take care of a pet, get along with siblings, keep a room clean. Explain the process in terms a child would understand yet not find condescending.

2. As a driver's education instructor in a high school, you decide to prepare a handout dealing with one of the following: making a three-point turn, parallel-parking, handling a skid, or executing any other driving maneuver. Explain the process one step at a time. Remember, your audience consists of teens who are just learning how to drive.

3. Write an article for *Consumer Reports* on how to shop for a certain product. Give specific steps explaining how to save money, buy a quality product, and the like.

4. Write a process analysis showing how to save a life by CPR, rescue breathing, the Heimlich maneuver, or some other method. Your audence will be average, everyday people who are taking a first-aid class.

5. Your closest friend plans to move into his or her own apartment but doesn't know the first thing about how to choose one. Explain the process of selecting an apartment—where to look, what to investigate, what questions to ask before signing a lease.

6. You write an "advice to the lovelorn" column for the campus newspaper. A correspondent asks for advice on how to break up with a steady boyfriend (or girlfriend) without hurting the person. Give the writer guidance on how to end a meaningful relationship with a minimal amount of pain.

9

COMPARISON-CONTRAST

WHAT IS COMPARISON-CONTRAST?

We frequently try to make sense of the world by finding similarities and differences in our experiences. Seeing how things are alike (comparing) and seeing how they are different (contrasting) helps us impose meaning on experiences that otherwise might remain fragmented and disconnected. Barely aware of the fact that we're comparing and contrasting, we may think to ourselves, "I woke up in a great mood this morning, but now I feel uneasy and anxious. I wonder why I feel so different." This inner questioning, which often occurs in a flash, is just one example of the way we use comparison and contrast to understand ourselves and our world.

Comparing and contrasting also helps us make choices. We compare and contrast everything—from two brands of soap we might buy to two colleges we might attend. We listen to a favorite radio station, watch a preferred nightly news show, select a particular dessert from a menu—all because we have done some degree of comparing and contrasting. We often weigh these alternatives in an unstudied, casual manner, as when we flip from one radio station to another. But when we have to make important decisions, we tend to think rigorously about how things are alike or different: Should I live in a dorm or rent an apartment? Should I accept the higher-paying job or the lower-paying one that offers more challenges? Such a deliberate approach to comparison-contrast may also provide us with needed insight into complex contemporary issues: Is television's coverage of political campaigns more or less objective than it used to be? What are the merits of the various positions on abortion?

HOW COMPARISON-CONTRAST FITS YOUR PURPOSE AND AUDIENCE

When is it appropriate in writing to use the comparison-contrast method of development? Often an assignment's wording signals clearly that comparison-contrast is called for:

> Compare the way male and female relationships are depicted in *Cosmopolitan, Ms., Playboy,* and *Esquire.* Which publication has the most limited view of men and women? Which has the broadest perspective?

> Many social commentators have observed that both college students and their parents feel that colleges should equip young people with immediately marketable skills. Indicate whether you think this is an accurate assessment by comparing your own beliefs about the purpose of a college degree with those of your parents.

> Football, basketball, and baseball differ in the ways they appeal to fans. Contrast the unique drawing power of each sport and arrive at some conclusions about the nature of each sport's following.

> The issue of prayer in public school continues to receive attention. Take a position on the controversy by contrasting the views of those who believe prayer should be allowed in public schools with those who believe it should be prohibited.

Other assignments will, in less obvious ways, lend themselves to comparison-contrast. For instance, although the words *compare* and *contrast* don't appear in the following assignments, essay responses to the assignments could be organized according to the comparison-contrast format:

> The emergence of the two-career family is one of the major phenomena of our culture. Discuss the advantages and disadvantages of having both parents work, showing how you feel about such two-career households.

> Some people believe that the 1950s, often called the golden age of television, produced several never-to-be-equaled comedy classics. Do you agree that such shows as *I Love Lucy* and *The Honeymooners* are superior to the situation comedies aired on television today?

> There has been considerable criticism recently of the news coverage by the city's two leading newspapers, the *Herald* and the *Beacon*. Indicate whether you think the criticism is valid by discussing the similarities and differences in the two papers' news coverage.

Note: The last assignment shows that a comparison-contrast essay may cover similarities *and* differences, not just one or the other.

As you have seen, comparison-contrast can be the key strategy for achieving an essay's purpose. But comparison-contrast can also be a supplemental method used to help make a point in an essay organized chiefly around another pattern of development. A serious, informative essay intended for laypeople might *define* clinical depression by contrasting that state of mind with ordinary run-of-the-mill blues. Writing humorously about the exhausting *effects* of trying to get in shape, you might dramatize your plight for readers by contrasting the leisurely way you used to spend your day with your current rigidly compulsive exercise regimen. Or, in an urgent *argumentation-persuasion* essay on the need for stricter controls over drug abuse in the workplace, you might provide readers with background by comparing several companies' approaches to the problem.

SUGGESTIONS FOR USING COMPARISON-CONTRAST IN AN ESSAY

The following suggestions will be helpful whether you use comparison-contrast as a dominant or supportive pattern of development.

1. Be sure your subjects are at least somewhat alike. Unless you plan to develop an *analogy* (see below), the subjects you choose to compare or contrast should share some obvious characteristics or qualities. It makes sense to compare different parts of the country, two comedians, or several college teachers. But a reasonable paper wouldn't result from, let's say, a comparison of a television game show with a soap opera. Your subjects must belong to the same general group so that your comparison-contrast stays within good logical bounds and doesn't veer off into pointlessness.

2. Stay focused on your purpose. When writing, remember that comparison-contrast isn't an end in itself. That is, your objective isn't to turn an essay into a mechanical list of "how A differs from B" or "how A is like B." Like the other patterns of development discussed in this book, comparison-contrast is a strategy for making a point or meeting a larger purpose.

Consider the assignment on page 397 about the two newspapers. Your purpose here might be simply to *inform*, to present information as objectively as possible: "This is what the *Herald*'s news coverage is like. This is what the *Beacon*'s news coverage is like."

More frequently, though, you'll use comparison-contrast to *evaluate* your subjects' pros and cons, your goal being to reach a conclusion or make a judgment: "Both the *Herald* and the *Beacon* spend too much time reporting local news," or "The *Herald*'s analysis of the recent hostage crisis was more insightful than the *Beacon*'s." Comparison-contrast can also be used to *persuade* readers to take action: "People interested in thorough coverage of international events should read the *Herald* rather than the *Beacon*." Persuasive essays may also propose a change, contrasting what now exists with a more ideal situation: "For the *Beacon* to compete with the *Herald*, it must assign more reporters to international stories."

Yet another purpose you might have in writing a comparison-contrast essay is to *clear up misconceptions* by revealing previously hidden similarities or differences. For example, perhaps your town's two newspapers are thought to be sharply different. However, a comparison-contrast analysis might reveal that—although one paper specializes in sensationalized stories while the other adopts a more muted approach—both resort to biased, emotionally charged analyses of local politics. Or the essay might illustrate that the tabloid's treatment of the local arts scene is surprisingly more comprehensive than that of its competitor.

Comparing and contrasting also make it possible to *draw an analogy* between two seemingly unrelated subjects. An analogy is an imaginative comparison that delves beneath the surface differences of subjects in order to expose their significant and often unsuspected similarities or differences. Your purpose may be to show that singles bars and zoos share a number of striking similarities. Or you may want to illustrate that wolves and humans raise their young in much the same way, but that wolves go about the process in a more civilized manner. The analogical approach can make a complex subject easier to understand—as when the national deficit is compared to a household budget gone awry. Analogies are often dramatic and instructive, challenging you and your audience to consider subjects in a new light. But analogies don't speak for themselves. You must make clear to the reader how the analogy demonstrates your purpose.

3. Formulate a strong thesis. An essay developed primarily through comparison-contrast should be focused by a solid thesis. Besides revealing your attitude, the thesis will often do the following:

- Name the subjects being compared and contrasted.
- Indicate whether the essay focuses on the subjects' similarities, differences, or both.
- State the essay's main point of comparison or contrast.

Not all comparison-contrast essays need thesis statements as structured as those that follow. Even so, these examples can serve as models of clarity. Note that the first thesis statement signals similarities, the second differences, and the last both similarities and differences:

Middle-aged parents are often in a good position to empathize with adolescent children because the emotional upheavals experienced by the two age groups are much the same.

The priorities of most retired people are more conducive to health and happiness than the priorities of most young professionals.

College students in their thirties and forties face many of the same pressures as younger students, but they are better equipped to withstand these pressures.

4. Select the points to be discussed. Once you have identified the essay's subjects, purpose, and thesis, you need to decide which aspects of the subjects to compare or contrast. College professors, for instance, could be compared and contrasted on the basis of their testing methods, ability to motivate students, confidence in front of a classroom, personalities, level of enthusiasm, and so forth.

Brainstorming, freewriting, and mapping are valuable for gathering possible points to cover. Whichever prewriting technique you use, try to produce more raw material than you'll need, so that you have the luxury of narrowing the material down to the most significant points.

When selecting points to cover, be sure to consider your audience. Ask yourself: "Will my readers be familiar with this item? Will I need it to get my message across? Will my audience find this item interesting or convincing?" What your readers know, what they don't know, and what you can project about their reactions should influence your choices. And, of course, you need to select points that support your thesis. If your essay explains the differences between healthy, sensible diets and dangerous crash diets, it wouldn't be appropriate to talk about aerobic exercise. Similarly, imagine you want to write an essay making the point that, despite their differences, hard rock of the 1960s and punk rock of the 1970s both reflected young people's disillusionment with society. It wouldn't make much sense to contrast the long uncombed hairstyle of the 1960s with the short spikey cuts of the 1970s. But contrasting song lyrics (protest versus nihilistic messages) would help support your thesis and lead to interesting insights.

5. Organize the points to be discussed. After deciding which points to include, you should use a systematic, logical plan for presenting those ideas. If the points aren't organized, your essay will be little more than a confusing jumble of ideas. There are two common ways to organize an essay developed wholly or in part by comparison-contrast: the one-side-at-a-time method and the point-by-point method. Although both strategies may be used in a paper, one method usually predominates.

In the *one-side-at-a-time method* of organization, you discuss everything relevant about one subject before moving to another subject. For example, responding to the earlier assignment that asked you to analyze the news coverage in two local papers, you might first talk about the *Herald's* coverage of international, national, and local news; then you would discuss the *Beacon's* coverage of the same categories. Note that the areas discussed should be the same for both newspapers. It wouldn't be logical to review the *Herald's* coverage of international, national, and local news and then to detail the *Beacon's* magazine supplements, modern living section, and comics page. Moreover, the areas compared and contrasted should be presented in the same order.

This is how you would organize the essay using the one-side-at-a-time method:

Everything about A	*Herald's* news coverage:
	• International
	• National
	• Local
Everything about B	*Beacon's* news coverage:
	• International
	• National
	• Local

In the *point-by-point method* of organization, you alternate from one aspect of the first subject to the same aspect of your other subject(s). For example, to use this method when comparing or contrasting the *Herald* and the *Beacon*, you would first discuss the *Herald's* international coverage, then the *Beacon's* international coverage; next the *Herald's* national coverage, then the *Beacon's*; and finally, the *Herald's* local coverage, then the *Beacon's*.

Using the point-by-point method, this is how the essay would be organized:

First aspect of A and B	*Beacon:* International coverage
	Herald: International coverage
Second aspect of A and B	*Beacon:* National coverage
	Herald: National coverage
Third aspect of A and B	*Beacon:* Local coverage
	Herald: Local coverage

Deciding which of these two methods of organization to use is largely a personal choice, though there are several factors to consider. The one-side-at-a-time method tends to convey a more unified feeling because it highlights broad similarities and differences. It is, therefore, an effective approach for subjects that are fairly uncomplicated. This strategy also works well when essays are brief; the reader won't find it difficult to remember what has been said about subject A when reading about subject B.

Because the point-by-point method permits more extensive coverage of similarities and differences, it is often a wise choice when subjects are complex. This pattern is also useful for lengthy essays since readers would probably find it difficult to remember, let's say, ten pages of information about subject A while reading the next ten pages about subject B. The point-by-point approach, however, may cause readers to lose sight of the broader picture, so remember to keep them focused on your central point.

6. Supply the reader with clear transitions.   Although a well-organized comparison-contrast format is important, it doesn't guarantee that readers will be able to follow your line of thought easily. *Transitions*—especially those signaling similarities or differences—are needed to show readers where they have been and where they are going. Such cues are essential in all writing, but they're especially crucial in a paper using comparison-contrast. By indicating clearly when subjects are being compared or contrasted, the transitions help weave the discussion into a coherent whole.

The transitions (in boldface) in the following examples could be used to *signal similarities* in an essay discussing the news coverage in the *Herald* and the *Beacon*:

- The *Beacon* **also** allots only a small portion of the front page to global news.
- **In the same way,** the *Herald* tries to include at least three local stories on the first page.
- **Likewise,** the *Beacon* emphasizes the importance of up-to-date reporting of town meetings.
- The *Herald* is **similarly** committed to extensive coverage of high school and college sports.

The transitions (in boldface) in these examples could be used to *signal differences*:

- **By way of contrast,** the *Herald's* editorial page deals with national matters on the average of three times a week.
- **On the other hand,** the *Beacon* does not share the *Herald's* enthusiasm for interviews with national figures.
- The *Beacon,* **however,** does not encourage its reporters to tackle national stories the way the *Herald* does.
- **But** the *Herald's* coverage of the Washington scene is much more comprehensive than its competitor's.

When using comparison-contrast, try not to pay obsessive attention to the mechanics of organizing your essay. Although the paper should have a logical structure, you don't want the essay to deteriorate into a rote listing of how things are alike or different. Nor do you want to become a slave to format, forcing points into an artificial or uncomfortable fit, rather like Cinderella's stepsisters hacking off their toes in order to squeeze into the glass slipper. Remember, comparison-contrast is a means to an end; that end is to open up a subject for exploration and provide new ways of thinking about a subject.

STUDENT ESSAY

The following student essay was written by Carol Siskin in response to this assignment:

In "That Lean and Hungry Look," Suzanne Britt contrasts two personality types, extolling the one normally considered less praiseworthy. In an essay of your own, contrast two personality types, life-styles, or stages of life, showing that the one most people consider inferior is actually superior.

While reading Carol's paper, try to determine how well it applies the principles of comparison-contrast. The annotations on Carol's paper and the commentary following it will help you look at the essay more closely.

The Virtues of Growing Older
by Carol Siskin

The first of a two-paragraph introduction → Our society worships youth. Advertisements convince us to buy Grecian Formula and Oil of Olay so we can hide the gray in our hair and smooth the lines on our face. Television shows feature attractive young stars with firm bodies, perfect complexions, and thick manes of hair. Middle-aged folks work out in gyms and jog down the street, trying to delay the effects of age. [1]

The second introductory paragraph →

Thesis → Wouldn't any person over thirty gladly sign with the devil just to be young again? Isn't aging an experience to be dreaded? Perhaps it is un-American to say so, but I believe the answer is "No." Being young is often pleasant, but being older has distinct advantages. [2]

First half of topic sentence for point 1: Appearance

Start of what it's like being young → When young, you are apt to be obsessed with your appearance. When my brother Dave and I were teens, we worked feverishly to perfect the bodies we had. Dave lifted weights, took megadoses of vitamins, and drank a half-dozen milk shakes a day in order to turn his wiry adolescent frame into some muscular ideal. And as a teenager, I dieted constantly. No matter what I weighed, though, I was never satisfied with the way I looked. My legs were too heavy, my shoulders too broad, my waist too big. When Dave and I were young, we begged and pleaded for the "right" clothes. If our parents didn't get them for us, we felt our world would fall apart. How could we go to school wearing loose-fitting blazers when everyone else would be wearing smartly [3]

Second half
of topic
sentence for
point 1

Start of what
it's like being
older

tailored leather jackets? We would be considered freaks. I often wonder how my parents, and parents in general, manage to tolerate their children during the adolescent years. Now, however, Dave and I are beyond such adolescent agonies. My rounded figure seems fine, and I don't deny myself a slice of pecan pie if I feel in the mood. Dave still works out, but he has actually become fond of his tall lanky frame. The two of us enjoy wearing fashionable clothes, but we are no longer slaves to style. And women, I'm embarrassed to admit, even more than men, have always seemed to be at the mercy of fashion. Now my clothes--and my brother's--are attractive yet easy to wear. We no longer feel anxious about what others will think. As long as we feel good about how we look, we are happy.

First half of
topic sentence
for point 2:
Life choices

Start of what
it's like being
older

Second half
of topic
sentence
for point 2

Start of what
it's like being
younger

Being older is preferable to being younger in another way. Obviously, I still have important choices to make about my life, but I have already made many of the critical decisions that confront those just starting out. I chose the man I wanted to marry. I decided to have children. I elected to return to college to complete my education. But when you are young, major decisions await you at every turn. "What college should I attend? What career should I pursue? Should I get married? Should I have children?" These are just a few of the issues facing young people. It's no wonder that, despite their carefree facade, they are often confused, uncertain, and troubled by all the unknowns in their future.

4

Topic sentence
for point 3:
Self-concept

Start of what
it's like being
younger

Start
of what it's
like being
older

But the greatest benefit of being forty is knowing who I am. The most unsettling aspect of youth is the uncertainty you feel about your values, goals, and dreams. Being young means wondering what is worth working for. Being young means feeling happy with yourself one day and wishing you were never born the next. It means trying on new selves by taking up with different crowds. It means resenting your parents and their way of life one minute and then feeling you will never be as good or as accomplished as they are. By way of contrast, forty is sanity. I have a surer self-concept now. I don't laugh at jokes I don't think are funny. I can make a speech in front

5

of a town meeting or complain in a store because I am no longer terrified that people will laugh at me; I am no longer anxious that everyone must like me. I no longer blame my parents for my every personality quirk or keep a running score of everything they did wrong raising me. Life has taught me that I, not they, am responsible for who I am. We are all human beings--neither saints nor devils.

Conclusion   Most Americans blindly accept the idea that   6 newer is automatically better. But a human life contradicts this premise. There is a great deal of happiness to be found as we grow older. My own parents, now in their sixties, recently told me that they are happier now than they have ever been. They would not want to be my age. Did this surprise me? At first, yes. Then it gladdened me. Their contentment holds out great promise for me as I move into the next--perhaps even better--phase of my life.

COMMENTARY

Purpose and thesis.   In her essay, Carol disproves the widespread belief that being young is preferable to being old. The *comparison-contrast* pattern allows her to analyze the drawbacks of one and the merits of the other, thus providing the essay with an *evaluative purpose*. Using the title to indicate her point of view, Carol places the *thesis* at the end of her two-paragraph introduction: "Being young is often pleasant, but being older has distinct advantages." Note that the thesis accomplishes several things. It names the two subjects to be discussed and clarifies Carol's point of view about her subjects. The thesis also implies that the essay will focus on the contrasts between these two periods of life.

Points of support and overall organization.   To   support   her assertion that older is better, Carol supplies examples from her own life and organizes the examples around three main points: attitudes about appearance, decisions about life choices, and questions of self-concept. Using the *point-by-point method* to organize the overall essay, she explores each of these key ideas in a separate paragraph. Each paragraph is further focused by one or two sentences that serve as a topic sentence.

Sequence of points, organizational cues, and paragraph development. Let's look more closely at the way Carol presents her three central points in the essay. She obviously considers appearance the least important of a person's worries, life choices more important, and self-concept the most critical. So she uses *emphatic order* to sequence the supporting paragraphs, with the phrase "But the greatest benefit" signaling the special significance of the last issue. Carol is also careful to use *transitions* to help readers follow her line of thinking: "*Now, however,* Dave and I are beyond such adolescent agonies" (3); "*But* when you are young, major decisions await you at every turn" (4); and "*By way of contrast,* forty is sanity" (5).

Although Carol has worked hard to write a well-organized paper—and has on the whole been successful—she doesn't feel compelled to make the paper fit a rigid format. As you've seen, the essay as a whole uses the point-by-point method, but each supporting paragraph uses the *one-side-at-a-time* method—that is, everything about one age group is discussed before there is a shift to the other age group. Notice too that the third and fifth paragraphs start with young people and then move to adults, whereas the fourth paragraph reverses the sequence by starting with older people.

Other patterns of development. Carol uses the comparison-contrast format to organize her ideas, but other patterns of development also come into play. To illustrate her points, she makes extensive use of *exemplification,* and her discussion also contains elements typical of *causal analysis.* Throughout the essay, for instance, she traces the effect of being a certain age on her brother, herself, and her parents.

A problem with unity. As you read the third paragraph, you might have noted that Carol's essay runs into a problem. Two sentences in the paragraph disrupt the *unity* of Carol's discussion: "I often wonder how my parents, and parents in general, manage to tolerate their children during the adolescent years," and "women, I'm embarrassed to admit...have always seemed to be at the mercy of fashion." These sentences should be deleted because they don't develop the idea that adolescents are overly concerned with appearance.

Conclusion. Carol's final paragraph brings the essay to a pleasing and interesting close. The conclusion recalls the point made in the introduction: Americans overvalue youth. Carol also uses the conclusion to broaden the scope of her discussion. Rather than continuing to focus on herself, she briefly mentions her parents and the pleasure they take in life. By bringing her parents into the essay, Carol is able to make a gently philosophical observation about the promise that awaits her as she grows older. The implication is that a similarly positive future awaits us, too.

Revising the first draft.   To help guide her revision, Carol asked her husband to read her first draft aloud. As he did, Carol took notes on what she sensed were the paper's strengths and weaknesses. She then jotted down her observations, as well as her husband's, on the draft. Keeping these comments in mind, Carol made a number of changes in her paper. You'll get a good sense of how she proceeded if you compare the original introduction reprinted here with the final version in the full essay.

Original Version of the Introduction

America is a land filled with people who worship youth. We admire dynamic young achievers; our middle-aged citizens work out in gyms; all of us wear tight tops and colorful sneakers--clothes that look fine on the young but ridiculous on aging bodies. Television shows revolve around perfect-looking young stars, while commercials entice us with products that will keep us young.

Wouldn't every older person want to be young again? Isn't aging to be avoided? It may be slightly unpatriotic to say so, but I believe the answer is "No." Being young may be pleasant at times, but I would rather be my forty-year-old self. I no longer have to agonize about my physical appearance, I have already made many of my crucial life decisions, and I am much less confused about who I am.

After hearing her original two-paragraph introduction read aloud, Carol was dissatisfied with what she had written. Although she wasn't quite sure how to proceed, she knew that the paragraphs were flat and that they failed to open the essay on a strong note. She decided to start by whittling down the opening sentence, making it crisper and more powerful: "Our society worships youth." That done, she eliminated two bland statements ("We admire dynamic young achievers" and "all of us wear tight tops and colorful sneakers") and made several vague references more concrete and interesting. For example, "Commercials entice us with products that will keep us young" became "Grecian Formula and Oil of Olay...hide the gray in our hair and smooth the lines on our face"; "perfect-looking young stars" became "attractive young stars with firm bodies, perfect complexions, and thick manes of hair." With the addition of these specifics, the first paragraph became more vigorous and interesting.

Carol next made some subtle changes in the two questions that opened the second paragraph of the original introduction. She replaced "Wouldn't every older person want to be young again?" and "Isn't aging to be avoided?" with two more emphatic questions: "Wouldn't any person over thirty gladly sign with the devil just to be young again?" and "Isn't aging an experience to be dreaded?" Carol also made some changes at the end of the original second paragraph. Because the paper is relatively short and the subject matter easy to understand, she decided to omit her somewhat awkward *plan of development* ("I no longer have to agonize about my physical appearance, I have already made many of my crucial life decisions, and I am much less confused about who I am"). This deletion made it possible to end the introduction with a strong statement of the essay's thesis.

Once these revisions were made, Carol was confident that her essay got off to a stronger start. Feeling reassured, she moved ahead and made changes in other sections of her paper. Such work enabled her to prepare a solid piece of writing that offers food for thought.

The selections in this chapter use comparison and contrast to explore a wide range of subjects. Ecologist Rachel Carson shows us two pictures in her "Fable for Tomorrow": one of a beautiful, environmentally healthy village, the other of the same village devastated by the irresponsible use of pesticides. With no pretense of objectivity, Suzanne Britt, in "That Lean and Hungry Look," contrasts fat and thin people and finds the latter an altogether inferior species. Richard Rodriguez's "Workers" is a highly personal account of different work situations. In "Sex, Lies, and Conversation," Deborah Tannen contrasts men's and women's different communication styles and explores the reasons behind those differences. Finally, Stephen Chapman's "The Prisoner's Dilemma" contrasts Islam's supposedly barbaric methods of punishment with the West's ostensibly more humane approach.

Rachel Carson

Once accused of being a fearmonger, biologist Rachel Carson (1907–64) is now recognized as one of the country's first environmentalists. She was the author of three popular books about the marine world: *The Sea Around Us* (1951), *Under the Sea Wind* (1952), and *The Edge of the Sea* (1955). But it was the publication of *Silent Spring* (1962), Carson's alarming study of the use of pesticides and herbicides, that brought her special attention and established her reputation as a passionate advocate for a clean environment. The following selection is taken from *Silent Spring*.

A Fable for Tomorrow

Fairy tales and fables often tell of people suffering under a wicked witch's curse. The evil spell robs life of its beauty and condemns people to a bleak existence until a clever hero or heroine finds a way to remove the curse and bring the story to a happy ending. But ecologist Rachel Carson's fable is different: the curse is one that we have brought upon ourselves and that we alone have the power to remove.

There was once a town in the heart of America where all life 1
seemed to live in harmony with its surroundings. The town lay in the midst of a checkerboard of prosperous farms, with fields of grain and hillsides of orchards where, in spring, white clouds of bloom drifted above the green fields. In autumn, oak and maple and birch set up a blaze of color that flamed and flickered across a backdrop of pines. Then foxes barked in the hills and deer silently crossed the fields, half hidden in the mists of the fall mornings.

Along the roads, laurel, viburnum and alder, great ferns and 2
wildflowers delighted the traveler's eye through much of the year. Even in winter the roadsides were places of beauty, where countless birds came to feed on the berries and on the seed heads of the dried weeds rising above the snow. The countryside was, in fact, famous

for the abundance and variety of its bird life, and when the flood of migrants was pouring through in spring and fall people traveled from great distances to observe them. Others came to fish the streams, which flowed clear and cold out of the hills and contained shady pools where trout lay. So it had been from the days many years ago when the first settlers raised their houses, sank their wells, and built their barns.

Then a strange blight crept over the area and everything began to change. Some evil spell had settled on the community: mysterious maladies swept the flocks of chickens; the cattle and sheep sickened and died. Everywhere was a shadow of death. The farmers spoke of much illness among their families. In the town the doctors had become more and more puzzled by new kinds of sickness appearing among their patients. There had been several sudden and unexplained deaths, not only among adults but even among children, who would be stricken suddenly while at play and die within a few hours.   3

There was a strange stillness. The birds, for example—where had they gone? Many people spoke of them, puzzled and disturbed. The feeding stations in the backyards were deserted. The few birds seen anywhere were moribund; they trembled violently and could not fly. It was a spring without voices. On the mornings that had once throbbed with the dawn chorus of robins, catbirds, doves, jays, wrens, and scores of other bird voices there was now no sound; only silence lay over the fields and woods and marsh.   4

On the farms the hens brooded, but no chicks hatched. The farmers complained that they were unable to raise any pigs—the litters were small and the young survived only a few days. The apple trees were coming into bloom but no bees droned among the blossoms, so there was no pollination and there would be no fruit.   5

The roadsides, once so attractive, were now lined with browned and withered vegetation as though swept by fire. These, too, were silent, deserted by all living things. Even the streams were now lifeless. Anglers no longer visited them, for all the fish had died.   6

In the gutters under the eaves and between the shingles of the roofs, a white granular powder still showed a few patches; some weeks before it had fallen like snow upon the roofs and the lawns, the fields and streams.   7

No witchcraft, no enemy action had silenced the rebirth of new life in this stricken world. The people had done it themselves.   8

This town does not actually exist, but it might easily have a thou-   9
sand counterparts in America or elsewhere in the world. I know of no
community that has experienced all the misfortunes I describe. Yet
every one of these disasters has actually happened somewhere, and
many real communities have already suffered a substantial number of
them. A grim specter has crept upon us almost unnoticed, and this
imagined tragedy may easily become a stark reality we all shall know.

Questions for Close Reading

1. What is the selection's thesis? Locate the sentence(s) in which Carson
   states her main idea. If she doesn't state the thesis explicitly, express it in
   your own words.
2. What are some of the delights of Carson's beautiful, healthy countryside?
3. When Carson writes of "a strange blight," an "evil spell" (paragraph 3),
   whose point of view is she adopting?
4. What are the effects of the blight?
5. Refer to your dictionary as needed to define the following words used in
   the selection: *viburnum* (paragraph 2), *alder* (2), *moribund* (4), and *specter* (9).

Questions About the Writer's Craft

1. **The pattern.**   To develop her essay, Carson uses the one-side-at-a-time
   method of comparison-contrast. What does this method enable her to do
   that the point-by-point approach would not?
2. **Other patterns.**   Throughout the essay, Carson appeals to the reader's
   senses of sight and hearing. Which paragraphs are developed primarily
   through visual or auditory description? How do the sensory images in
   these paragraphs reinforce Carson's thesis?
3. Carson's diction (word choice) and sentence rhythm often resemble
   those of the Bible. For example, we read, "So it had been from the days
   many years ago" (paragraph 2), "a strange blight crept over the area" (3),
   and "Everywhere was a shadow of death" (3). Why do you suppose Carson chose to echo the Bible in this way?
4. How does Carson's approach to her subject change in the last paragraph?
   What is the effect of this change?

Questions for Further Thought

1. What threat to the environment concerns you the most? Seepage from
   landfills? Disposal of nuclear wastes? Acid rain? Depletion of the ozone
   layer? What can the average person do to deal with this threat?

2. Environmentalists are sometimes referred to as "tree huggers." What attitude is suggested by this term? How do you feel about the term? About the attitude?

3. Do you think the concerns of environmentalists can be excessive and counterproductive? Explain.

4. Carson is concerned about the destruction of America's rural environment. Someone raised in a major city, however, may give little thought to flowing brooks, colorful orchards, and birdsongs. Why should someone accustomed to an urban environment care about what happens to forests, farmlands, or lakes?

Writing Assignments Using Comparison-Contrast as a Pattern of Development

1. Carson imagines a fictional town before and after a blight. Consider a place once special to you that has been changed for the worse by some external force. Perhaps the culprit was noise pollution, urban development, a tornado, or the like. Write an essay contrasting the place before and after the change. Reach some conclusion about the future of this formerly treasured place.

2. In her essay, Carson provides descriptive details unique to particular seasons. For example, she writes that "in autumn, oak and maple and birch set up a blaze of color that flamed and flickered across a backdrop of pines" (paragraph 1). Choosing a place you know well, contrast its sights, sounds, and smells during one season with those you've noticed during another time of year. Use rich sensory details to convey the differences between the two seasons.

Writing Assignments Using Other Patterns of Development

3. Carson cites "white granular powder" (paragraph 7) as the cause of the blight. Write an essay about a time you noticed a visible environmental problem—say, smog blurring a city skyline, soot coating a window, or medical syringes discarded on the beach. Use vivid narrative details to capture the effect of the experience on you.

∞ 4. Carson graphically shows the effects of herbicides and pesticides on the environment. Focus on some other less global environmental problem: graffiti on a public building; vandalized trees and shrubs; beer cans thrown in a neighborhood park, for example. Discuss the effects of this situation on the physical environment and on people's attitudes and actions. Conclude with suggestions about possible ways to remedy the problem. Gordon Parks's "Flavio's Home" (page 104) will help you appreciate the interaction between the environment and human behavior.

Suzanne Britt

Freelance writer and textbook author Suzanne Britt studied at Salem College and Washington University. Her work has been published in the *Baltimore Sun, Long Island Newsday,* the *Boston Globe,* and the *New York Times.* A regular columnist for *North Carolina Gardens and Homes* and for a newsletter devoted to the works of Charles Dickens, Britt contributes to Duke University's *Books and Religion,* a publication featuring religious and social commentary. Britt's first book, *Skinny People Are Dull and Crunchy Like Carrots* (1982), is an expansion of the following essay, which was first published in *Newsweek's* "My Turn" column. Her second book, *Show and Tell,* was published in 1983.

That Lean and Hungry Look[1]

When was the last time you saw a popular magazine that didn't advertise on its cover a new diet or exercise program? How many health clubs have sprung up in your town in recent years? Everywhere we look, we're bombarded by anti-fat propaganda. Essayist Suzanne Britt is fed up with it all. Here's her case for the idea that fat people have nothing to lose but skinnies have a lot to gain.

Caesar was right. Thin people need watching. I've been watching them for most of my adult life, and I don't like what I see. When these narrow fellows spring at me, I quiver to my toes. Thin people come in all personalities, most of them menacing. You've got your "together" thin person, your mechanical thin person, your condescending thin person, your tsk-tsk thin person, your efficiency-expert thin person. All of them are dangerous.   1

[1]Britt's title is a reference to a line from Shakespeare's *Julius Caesar.* In the play, Caesar says he distrusts Cassius because Cassius has "a lean and hungry look;...such men are dangerous." Later in the play, Cassius helps assassinate Caesar, proving Caesar's fears were justified.

In the first place, thin people aren't fun. They don't know how 2
to goof off, at least in the best, fat sense of the word. They've always
got to be adoing. Give them a coffee break, and they'll jog around
the block. Supply them with a quiet evening at home, and they'll fix
the screen door and lick S&H green stamps. They say things like
"there aren't enough hours in the day." Fat people never say that.
Fat people think the day is too damn long already.

Thin people make me tired. They've got speedy little metabo- 3
lisms that cause them to bustle briskly. They're forever rubbing their
bony hands together and eyeing new problems to "tackle." I like to
surround myself with sluggish, inert, easygoing fat people, the kind
who believe that if you clean it up today, it'll just get dirty again
tomorrow.

Some people say the business about the jolly fat person is a 4
myth, that all of us chubbies are neurotic, sick, sad people. I disagree.
Fat people may not be chortling all day long, but they're a hell of a
lot *nicer* than the wizened and shriveled. Thin people turn surly,
mean, and hard at a young age because they never learn the value of
a hot-fudge sundae for easing tension. Thin people don't like gooey
soft things because they themselves are neither gooey nor soft. They
are crunchy and dull, like carrots. They go straight to the heart of the
matter while fat people let things stay all blurry and hazy and vague,
the way things actually are. Thin people want to face the truth. Fat
people know there is no truth. One of my thin friends is always staring at complex, unsolvable problems and saying, "The key thing
is...." Fat people never say that. They know there isn't any such
thing as the key thing about anything.

Thin people believe in logic. Fat people see all sides. The sides 5
fat people see are rounded blobs, usually gray, always nebulous and
truly not worth worrying about. But the thin person persists. "If you
consume more calories than you burn," says one of my thin friends,
"you will gain weight. It's that simple." Fat people always grin when
they hear statements like that. They know better.

Fat people realize that life is illogical and unfair. They know very 6
well that God is not in his heaven and all is not right with the world.
If God is up there, fat people could have two doughnuts and a big
orange drink anytime they wanted it.

Thin people have a long list of logical things they are always 7
spouting off to me. They hold up one finger at a time as they reel off
these things, so I won't lose track. They speak slowly as if to a young

child. The list is long and full of holes. It contains tidbits like "get a grip on yourself," "cigarettes kill," "cholesterol clogs," "fit as a fiddle," "ducks in a row," "organize," and "sound fiscal management." Phrases like that.

They think these 2,000-point plans lead to happiness. Fat people know happiness is elusive at best and even if they could get the kind thin people talk about, they wouldn't want it. Wisely, fat people see that such programs are too dull, too hard, too off the mark. They are never better than a whole cheesecake.   8

Fat people know all about the mystery of life. They are the ones acquainted with the night, with luck, with fate, with playing it by ear. One thin person I know once suggested that we arrange all the parts of a jigsaw puzzle into groups according to size, shape, and color. He figured this would cut the time needed to complete the puzzle by at least 50 percent. I said I wouldn't do it. One, I like to muddle through. Two, what good would it do to finish early? Three, the jigsaw puzzle isn't the important thing. The important thing is the fun of four people (one thin person included) sitting around a card table, working a jigsaw puzzle. My thin friend had no use for my list. Instead of joining us, he went outside and mulched the boxwoods. The three remaining fat people finished the puzzle and made chocolate, double-fudged brownies to celebrate.   9

The main problem with thin people is they oppress. Their good intentions, bony torsos, tight ships, neat corners, cerebral machinations, and pat solutions loom like dark clouds over the loose, comfortable, spread-out, soft world of the fat. Long after fat people have removed their coats and shoes and put their feet up on the coffee table, thin people are still sitting on the edge of the sofa, looking neat as a pin, discussing rutabagas. Fat people are heavily into fits of laughter, slapping their thighs and whooping it up, while thin people are still politely waiting for the punch line.   10

Thin people are downers. They like math and morality and reasoned evaluation of the limitations of human beings. They have their skinny little acts together. They expound, prognose, probe, and prick.   11

Fat people are convivial. They will like you even if you're irregular and have acne. They will come up with a good reason why you never wrote the great American novel. They will cry in your beer with you. They will put your name in the pot. They will let you off the   12 hook. Fat people will gab, giggle, guffaw, galumph, gyrate, and gossip. They are generous, giving, and gallant. They are gluttonous and goodly and great. What you want when you're down is soft and jiggly, not muscled and stable. Fat people know this. Fat people have plenty of room. Fat people will take you in.

Questions for Close Reading

1. What is the selection's thesis? Locate the sentence(s) in which Britt states her main idea. If she doesn't state the thesis explicitly, express it in your own words.
2. Into what personality types does Britt categorize thin people? What do these personality types have in common?
3. Britt writes that thin people use their free time for such activities as jogging, fixing a screen door, and pasting in green stamps. How are these activities similar?
4. Why does Britt approve of fat people's tendency to "let things stay all blurry and hazy and vague"?
5. Refer to your dictionary as needed to define the following words used in the selection: *wizened* (paragraph 4), *nebulous* (5), *fiscal* (7), *mulch* (9), *machinations* (10), *expound* (11), and *convivial* (12).

Questions About the Writer's Craft

1. **The pattern.**   Which comparison-contrast format does Britt use to develop her essay? Why might she have chosen this format?
2. How does Britt's choice of words and sentence structure establish an informal, lighthearted tone?
3. Why is Britt's carrot simile especially apt?
4. Where in the last paragraph does Britt use *alliteration* (the repetition of initial consonant sounds)? What might have been her reason for using this technique?

Questions for Further Thought

1. Britt pokes fun at thin people who "always got to be adoing." Which do you value most—goal-oriented activity or the ability to relax and have a good time? Why?
2. Britt admires fat people's ability to recognize the limits of logic. How might this ability enrich life? How might it create problems?
3. Britt mocks those who are uncompromisingly principled. How might a person's overly scrupulous principles make life difficult for that individual and others?

4. According to Britt, people in need of reassurance prefer a "soft and jiggly" person to a "muscled and stable" one. Which kind of person comforts you more—someone who seems vulnerable or someone who seems more immune to distress? Why?

Writing Assignments Using Comparison-Contrast as a Pattern of Development

1. Write an essay contrasting two people who represent markedly dissimilar types. Perhaps one person is messy, the other neat. Or maybe one is worldly-wise while the other is unsophisticated. Or one might be punctual while the other is always late. Use the one-side-at-a-time or the point-by-point method to highlight the differences between the two people. Adopting a light, waggish tone, argue—as Britt does—that one type is superior to the other.

2. Britt scoffs at thin people who "believe in logic." Take two decisions you made recently—one fairly logical, the other more emotional. Contrast how you went about making the decisions, the outcomes of the decisions, and so on. Reach some conclusion about the value of logic and emotion in your life.

Writing Assignments Using Other Patterns of Development

∞ 3. Britt enjoys the pleasures of good food and company. In an essay, recall a gathering where the food and company were especially satisfying. Through sensory details, convey the aroma, taste, and appearance of the food, as well as the social atmosphere. For inspiration, you might read Judith Ortiz Cofer's "A Partial Remembrance of a Puerto Rican Childhood" (page 138), an essay that evokes the pleasures of shared family time.

4. Britt takes issue with the notion that thin is better than plump. What other prejudicial assumptions do you see at work in contemporary society? Select one and write an essay persuading readers that this idea is unfounded. Your tone may be serious or playful like Britt's.

Richard Rodriguez

In his autobiographical work *Hunger of Memory* (1981), from which the following selection is taken, Richard Rodriguez describes his experiences growing up in America as a first-generation Mexican-American. Born in 1944 in San Francisco, Rodriguez spoke only Spanish for the first six years of his life. After winning a scholarship to a private high school, Rodriguez attended Stanford, Columbia, and the University of California at Berkeley where he earned a Ph.D. in English literature. Rodriguez now writes for a variety of publications (*The American Scholar* and *Harper's,* to name just two) and serves as an editor at Pacific News Service in San Francisco. His book *Mexico's Children* (1991) examines the experience of Mexicans living in the United States, while *Days of Obligation: An Argument With My Mexican Father* (1992) is Rodriguez's second autobiographical book.

Workers

As a college student, you probably think about what you'll do after graduation. Perhaps you imagine finding work that offers respect and a sense of accomplishment. Richard Rodriguez discovered a very different world during a summer spent as a laborer, a world in which work meant survival and the boss was god. For such workers, there were no alternatives, no exits, no chances for fulfillment.

It was at Stanford, one day near the end of my senior year, that 1
a friend told me about a summer construction job he knew was available. I was quickly alert. Desire uncoiled within me. My friend said that he knew I had been looking for summer employment. He knew I needed some money. Almost apologetically he explained: It was something I probably wouldn't be interested in, but a friend of his, a contractor, needed someone for the summer to do menial jobs. There would be lots of shoveling and raking and sweeping. Nothing too hard. But nothing more interesting either. Still, the pay would be good. Did I want it? Or did I know someone who did?

I did. Yes, I said, surprised to hear myself say it. 2

In the weeks following, friends cautioned that I had no idea how   3
hard physical labor really is. ("You only *think* you know what it is like
to shovel for eight hours straight.") Their objections seemed to me
challenges. They resolved the issue. I became happy with my plan. I
decided, however, not to tell my parents. I wouldn't tell my mother
because I could guess her worried reaction. I would tell my father
only after the summer was over, when I could announce that, after
all, I did know what "real work" is like.

The day I met the contractor (a Princeton graduate, it turned   4
out), he asked me whether I had done any physical labor before. "In
high school, during the summer," I lied. And although he seemed to
regard me with skepticism, he decided to give me a try. Several days
later, expectant, I arrived at my first construction site. I would take
off my shirt to the sun. And at last grasp desired sensation. No longer
afraid. At last become like a *bracero*. "We need those tree stumps out
of here by tomorrow," the contractor said. I started to work.

I labored with excitement that first morning—and all the days   5
after. The work was harder than I could have expected. But it was
never as tedious as my friends had warned me it would be. There was
too much physical pleasure in the labor. Especially early in the day, I
would be most alert to the sensations of movement and straining.
Beginning around seven each morning (when the air was still damp
but the scent of weeds and dry earth anticipated the heat of the sun),
I would feel my body resist the first thrusts of the shovel. My arms,
tightened by sleep, would gradually loosen; after only several minutes, sweat would gather in beads on my forehead and then—a short
while later—I would feel my chest silky with sweat in the breeze. I
would return to my work. A nervous spark of pain would fly up my
arm and settle to burn like an ember in the thick of my shoulder. An
hour, two passed. Three. My whole body would assume regular
movements; my shoveling would be described by identical, even
movements. Even later in the day, my enthusiasm for primitive sensation would survive the heat and the dust and the insects pricking
my back. I would strain wildly for sensation as the day came to a
close. At three-thirty, quitting time, I would stand upright and slowly let my head fall back, luxuriating in the feeling of tightness relieved.

Some of the men working nearby would watch me and laugh.   6
Two or three of the older men took the trouble to teach me the right
way to use a pick, the correct way to shovel. "You're doing it wrong,
too fucking hard," one man scolded. Then proceeded to show me—

what persons who work with their bodies all their lives quickly learn—the most economical way to use one's body in labor.

"Don't make your back do so much work," he instructed. I 7
stood impatiently listening, half listening, vaguely watching, then noticed his work-thickened fingers clutching the shovel. I was annoyed. I wanted to tell him that I enjoyed shoveling the wrong way. And I didn't want to learn the right way. I wasn't afraid of back pain. I liked the way my body felt sore at the end of the day.

I was about to, but, as it turned out, I didn't say a thing. Rather 8
it was at that moment I realized that I was fooling myself if I expected a few weeks of labor to gain me admission to the world of the laborer. I would not learn in three months what my father had meant by "real work." I was not bound to this job; I could imagine its rapid conclusion. For me the sensations were to be feared. Fatigue took a different toll on their bodies—and minds.

It was, I know, a simple insight. But it was with this realization 9
that I took my first step that summer toward realizing something even more important about the "worker." In the company of carpenters, electricians, plumbers, and painters at lunch, I would often sit quietly, observant. I was not shy in such company. I felt easy, pleased by the knowledge that I was casually accepted, my presence taken for granted by men (exotics) who worked with their hands. Some days the younger men would talk and talk about sex, and they would howl at women who drove by in cars. Other days the talk at lunchtime was subdued; men gathered in separate groups. It depended on who was around. There were rough, good-natured workers. Others were quiet. The more I remember that summer, the more I realize that there was no single *type* of worker. I am embarrassed to say I had not expected such diversity. I certainly had not expected to meet, for example, a plumber who was an abstract painter in his off hours and admired the work of Mark Rothko. Nor did I expect to meet so many workers with college diplomas. (They were the ones who were not surprised that I intended to enter graduate school in the fall.) I suppose what I really want to say here is painfully obvious, but I must say it nevertheless: The men of that summer were middle-class Americans. They certainly didn't constitute an oppressed society. Carefully completing their work sheets; talking about the fortunes of local football teams; planning Las Vegas vacations; comparing the gas mileage of various makes of campers—they were not *los pobres* my mother had spoken about.

On two occasions, the contractor hired a group of Mexican   10
aliens. They were employed to cut down some trees and haul off debris. In all, there were six men of varying age. The youngest in his
late twenties; the oldest (his father?) perhaps sixty years old. They
came and they left in a single old truck. Anonymous men. They were
never introduced to the other men at the site. Immediately upon
their arrival, they would follow the contractor's directions, start
working—rarely resting—seemingly driven by a fatalistic sense that
work which had to be done was best done as quickly as possible.

I watched them sometimes. Perhaps they watched me. The only   11
time I saw them pay me much notice was one day at lunchtime when
I was laughing with the other men. The Mexicans sat apart when
they ate, just as they worked by themselves. Quiet. I rarely heard
them say much to each other. All I could hear were their voices calling out sharply to one another, giving directions. Otherwise, when
they stood briefly resting, they talked among themselves in voices
too hard to overhear.

The contractor knew enough Spanish, and the Mexicans—or at   12
least the oldest of them, their spokesman—seemed to know enough
English to communicate. But because I was around, the contractor
decided one day to make me his translator. (He assumed I could
speak Spanish.) I did what I was told. Shyly I went over to tell the
Mexicans that the *patrón* wanted them to do something else before
they left for the day. As I started to speak, I was afraid with my old
fear that I would be unable to pronounce the Spanish words. But it
was a simple instruction I had to convey. I could say it in phrases.

The dark sweating faces turned toward me as I spoke. They   13
stopped their work to hear me. Each nodded in response. I stood
there. I wanted to say something more. But what could I say in Spanish, even if I could have pronounced the words right? Perhaps I just
wanted to engage them in small talk, to be assured of their confidence, our familiarity. I thought for a moment to ask them where in
Mexico they were from. Something like that. And maybe I wanted
to tell them (a lie, if need be) that my parents were from the same
part of Mexico.

I stood there.   14

Their faces watched me. The eyes of the man directly in front of   15
me moved slowly over my shoulder, and I turned to follow his glance
toward *el patrón* some distance away. For a moment I felt swept up
by that glance into the Mexicans' company. But then I heard one of

them returning to work. And then the others went back to work. I left them without saying anything more.

When they had finished, the contractor went over to pay them in cash. (He later told me that he paid them collectively—"for the job," though he wouldn't tell me their wages. He said something quickly about the good rate of exchange "in their own country.") I can still hear the loudly confident voice he used with the Mexicans. It was the sound of the *gringo* I had heard as a very young boy. And I can still hear the quiet, indistinct sounds of the Mexican, the oldest, who replied. At hearing that voice I was sad for the Mexicans. Depressed by their vulnerability. Angry at myself. The adventure of the summer seemed suddenly ludicrous. I would not shorten the distance I felt from *los pobres* with a few weeks of physical labor. I would not become like them. They were different from me.

After that summer, a great deal—and not very much really— changed in my life. The curse of physical shame was broken by the sun; I was no longer ashamed of my body. No longer would I deny myself the pleasing sensations of my maleness. During those years when middle-class black Americans began to assert with pride, "Black is beautiful," I was able to regard my complexion without shame. I am today darker than I ever was as a boy. I have taken up the middle-class sport of long-distance running. Nearly every day now I run ten or fifteen miles, barely clothed, my skin exposed to the California winter rain and wind or the summer sun of late afternoon. The torso, the soccer player's calves and thighs, the arms of the twenty-year-old I never was, I possess now in my thirties. I study the youthful parody shape in the mirror: the stomach lipped tight by muscle; the shoulders rounded by chin-ups; the arms veined strong. This man. A man. I meet him. He laughs to see me, what I have become.

The dandy. I wear double-breasted Italian suits and custom-made English shoes. I resemble no one so much as my father—the man pictured in those honeymoon photos. At that point in life when he abandoned the dandy's posture, I assume it. At the point when my parents would not consider going on vacation, I register at the Hotel Carlyle in New York and the Plaza Athenée in Paris. I am as taken by the symbols of leisure and wealth as they were. For my parents, however, those symbols became taunts, reminders of all they could not achieve in one lifetime. For me those same symbols are reassuring reminders of public success. I tempt vulgarity to be reassured. I am filled with the gaudy delight, the monstrous grace of the nouveau riche.

    In recent years I have had occasion to lecture in ghetto high   19
schools. There I see students of remarkable style and physical grace.
(One can see more dandies in such schools than one ever will find in
middle-class high schools.) There is not the look of casual assurance
I saw students at Stanford display. Ghetto girls mimic high-fashion
models. Their dresses are of bold, forceful color; their figures elegant, long; the stance theatrical. Boys wear shirts that grip at their
overdeveloped muscular bodies. (Against a powerless future, they
engage images of strength.) Bad nutrition does not yet tell. Great
disappointment, fatal to youth, awaits them still. For the moment,
movements in school hallways are dancelike, a procession of postures
in a sexual masque. Watching them, I feel a kind of envy. I wonder
how different my adolescence would have been had I been
free....But no, it is my parents I see—their optimism during those
years when they were entertained by Italian grand opera.

    The registration clerk in London wonders if I have just been to   20
Switzerland. And the man who carries my luggage in New York
guesses the Caribbean. My complexion becomes a mark of my leisure. Yet no one would regard my complexion the same way if I entered such hotels through the service entrance. That is only to say
that my complexion assumes its significance from the context of my
life. My skin, in itself, means nothing. I stress the point because I
know there are people who would label me "disadvantaged" because
of my color. They make the same mistake I made as a boy, when I
thought a disadvantaged life was circumscribed by particular occupa-
tions. That summer I worked in the sun may have made me physically indistinguishable from the Mexicans working nearby. (My skin was
actually darker because, unlike them, I worked without wearing a
shirt. By late August my hands were probably as tough as theirs.) But
I was not one of *los pobres*. What made me different from them was
an attitude of *mind*, my imagination of myself.

    I do not blame my mother for warning me away from the sun   21
when I was young. In a world where her brother had become an old
man in his twenties because he was dark, my complexion was something to worry about. "Don't run in the sun," she warns me today.
I run. In the end, my father was right—though perhaps he did not
know how right or why—to say that I would never know what real
work is. I will never know what he felt at his last factory job. If to-

morrow I worked at some kind of factory, it would go differently for me. My long education would favor me. I could act as a public person—able to defend my interests, to unionize, to petition, to speak up—to challenge and demand. (I will never know what real work is.) I will never know what the Mexicans knew, gathering their shovels and ladders and saws.

Their silence stays with me now. The wages those Mexicans received for their labor were only a measure of their disadvantaged condition. Their silence is more telling. They lack a public identity. They remain profoundly alien. Persons apart. People lacking a union obviously, people without grounds. They depend upon the relative good will or fairness of their employers each day. For such people, lacking a better alternative, it is not such an unreasonable risk.   22

Their silence stays with me. I have taken these many words to describe its impact. Only: the quiet. Something uncanny about it. Its compliance. Vulnerability. Pathos. As I heard their truck rumbling away, I shuddered, my face mirrored with sweat. I had finally come face to face with *los pobres*.   23

Questions for Close Reading

1. What is the selection's thesis? Locate the sentence(s) in which Rodriguez states his main idea. If he doesn't state the thesis explicitly, express it in your own words.
2. What does Rodriguez find appealing about the construction job when his friend first offers it to him?
3. Once on the job, how long does it take Rodriguez to realize he will never be a "laborer"? Why does he feel this way?
4. According to Rodriguez, what makes him different from *los pobres*? Is poverty the only thing that makes them distinctive?
5. Refer to your dictionary as needed to define the following words used in the selection: *menial* (paragraph 1), *skepticism* (4), *luxuriating* (5), *diversity* (9), *ludicrous* (16), *nouveau riche* (18), and *pathos* (23).

Questions About the Writer's Craft

1. **The pattern.**   One way Rodriguez develops his essay is by comparing and contrasting himself to the two groups of workers. Which group is he more like? What specifics does Rodriguez provide to show his similarity to this group and his dissimilarity to the other?
2. **Other patterns.**   Rodriguez uses narration to develop his comparison-contrast of the two groups of workers. How many narrative segments

appear in the essay? Why do you think Rodriguez puts the story about the Mexican workers last?

3. **Other patterns.**   Rodriguez uses especially vivid language to describe the sun, his sweat, and the sensation of digging. Locate some examples of these descriptions. Which ones particularly stand out? Why?

4. Why does Rodriguez include some Spanish words in his essay? How is the use of these words related to the essay's overall theme?

Questions for Further Thought

1. Why does Rodriguez decide not to tell his parents about his summer job? What do you think his mother's fears would have been? How would your parents and friends react if you worked in construction (or in some other physically demanding job) after graduating from college?

2. Rodriguez discovers that "there is no single *type* of worker" on the construction job. What kind of preconceptions do you think he had about construction workers? What stereotypes do you, your family, and your friends have about other kinds of workers (teachers, lawyers, secretaries, bosses, and so forth)?

3. What does Rodriguez hope to gain from this job that he could not, presumably, learn at Stanford or in graduate school? Have you ever felt a similar need to learn outside the classroom?

4. How does Rodriguez characterize "real work" at the start of his summer? How would you say his definition of real work changes by the end of the job? Do you agree with his belief that a college-educated person can never know the meaning of real work?

Writing Assignments Using Comparison-Contrast as a Pattern of Development

1. Write an essay comparing and/or contrasting a part-time or summer job you've had with your (or someone else's) full-time or "real" job. Use examples, description, anecdotes, and illustrations to clarify the points of comparison or contrast.

2. Compare and/or contrast the job you hope to have after graduation with a job you now have or have had in the past. Your analysis should reach conclusions about your interests, skills, and values.

Writing Assignments Using Other Patterns of Development

∞ 3. In an essay, define what you mean by the term *real work*. Support your definition by citing experiences you have had and/or have heard about. Scott Russell Sanders's "The Men We Carry in Our Minds" (page 308), Sue Hubbell's "The Beekeeper" (page 355), and Virginia Woolf's "Professions for Women" (page 695) should prompt some interesting thoughts about work.

4. Talk show host Phil Donahue once did a show on people who had "terrible jobs." The guests included a garbage man, a toll collector, a car repossessor, an IRS auditor, and a diaper-service truck driver. Write an essay explaining what would be terrible work for you. It might be one or more of the jobs held by Donahue guests or some other type of job. Provide abundant reasons why you would never want to do such work and reach some conclusions about your priorities.

Deborah Tannen

The recipient of grants from the National Endowment for the Humanities, the Rockefeller Foundation, and the National Science Foundation, Deborah Tannen (1945–) is a linguistics professor at Georgetown University and has been a Distinguished McGraw Lecturer at Princeton University. She has shared her scholarly research with the general public through appearances on the *Today* show and CNN, through pieces in the *New York Times* and the *Washington Post,* and in popular books, including *That's Not What I Meant: How Conversational Style Makes or Breaks Relationships* (1987), her best-selling *You Just Don't Understand: Women and Men in Conversation* (1990), and *Talking From 9 to 5: How Women's and Men's Conversational Styles Affect Who Gets Ahead, Who Gets Credit, and What Gets Done at Work* (1994). The following selection, adapted from *You Just Don't Understand,* appeared in the *New York Times* in June 1990.

Sex, Lies, and Conversation

"She says I never talk to her, but I don't know what she wants to talk about!" "When I talk to him, it's like talking to a brick wall!" Men and women blame each other for the communication problems they invariably encounter. But linguist Deborah Tannen explains that neither sex deliberately chooses to sabotage communication. Males and females simply approach communication with divergent, often conflicting skills and expectations.

I was addressing a small gathering in a suburban Virginia living   1
room—a women's group that had invited men to join them. Throughout the evening, one man had been particularly talkative, frequently offering ideas and anecdotes, while his wife sat silently beside him on the couch. Toward the end of the evening, I commented that women frequently complain that their husbands don't talk to them. This man quickly concurred. He gestured toward his wife and said, "She's the talker in our family." The room burst into laughter; the man looked puzzled and hurt. "It's true," he explained. "When

I come home from work I have nothing to say. If she didn't keep the conversation going, we'd spend the whole evening in silence."

This episode crystallizes the irony that although American men 2 tend to talk more than women in public situations, they often talk less at home. And this pattern is wreaking havoc with marriage.

The pattern was observed by political scientist Andrew Hacker 3 in the late '70s. Sociologist Catherine Kohler Riessman reports in her new book *Divorce Talk* that most of the women she interviewed— but only a few of the men—gave lack of communication as the reason for their divorces. Given the current divorce rate of nearly 50 percent, that amounts to millions of cases in the United States every year—a virtual epidemic of failed conversation.

In my own research, complaints from women about their hus- 4 bands most often focused not on tangible inequities such as having given up the chance for a career to accompany a husband to his, or doing far more than their share of daily life-support work like cleaning, cooking, social arrangements and errands. Instead, they focused on communication: "He doesn't listen to me," "He doesn't talk to me." I found, as Hacker observed years before, that most wives want their husbands to be, first and foremost, conversational partners, but few husbands share this expectation of their wives.

In short, the image that best represents the current crisis is the 5 stereotypical cartoon scene of a man sitting at the breakfast table with a newspaper held up in front of his face, while a woman glares at the back of it, wanting to talk.

Linguistic Battle of the Sexes

How can women and men have such different impressions of 6 communication in marriage? Why the widespread imbalance in their interests and expectations?

In the April [1990] issue of *American Psychologist,* Stanford 7 University's Eleanor Maccoby reports the results of her own and others' research showing that children's development is most influenced by the social structure of peer interactions. Boys and girls tend to play with children of their own gender, and their sex-separate groups have different organizational structures and interactive norms.

I believe these systematic differences in childhood socialization 8 make talk between women and men like cross-cultural communication, heir to all the attraction and pitfalls of that enticing but difficult enterprise. My research on men's and women's conversations uncovered patterns similar to those described for children's groups.

For women, as for girls, intimacy is the fabric of relationships, and talk is the thread from which it is woven. Little girls create and maintain friendships by exchanging secrets; similarly, women regard conversation as the cornerstone of friendship. So a woman expects her husband to be a new and improved version of a best friend. What is important is not the individual subjects that are discussed but the sense of closeness, of a life shared, that emerges when people tell their thoughts, feelings, and impressions. 9

Bonds between boys can be as intense as girls', but they are based less on talking, more on doing things together. Since they don't assume talk is the cement that binds a relationship, men don't know what kind of talk women want, and they don't miss it when it isn't there. 10

Boys' groups are larger, more inclusive, and more hierarchical, so boys must struggle to avoid the subordinate position in the group. This may play a role in women's complaints that men don't listen to them. Some men really don't like to listen, because being the listener makes them feel one down, like a child listening to adults or an employee to a boss. 11

But often when women tell men, "You aren't listening," and the men protest, "I am," the men are right. The impression of not listening results from misalignment in the mechanics of conversation. The misalignment begins as soon as a man and a woman take physical positions. This became clear when I studied videotapes made by psychologist Paul Dorval of children and adults talking to their same-sex best friends. I found that at every age, the girls and women faced each other directly, their eyes anchored on each other's faces. At every age, the boys and men sat at angles to each other and looked elsewhere in the room, periodically glancing at each other. They were obviously attuned to each other, often mirroring each other's movements. But the tendency of men to face away can give women the impression they aren't listening even when they are. A young woman in college was frustrated: Whenever she told her boyfriend she wanted to talk to him, he would lie down on the floor, close his eyes, and put his arm over his face. This signaled to her, "He's taking a nap." But he insisted he was listening extra hard. Normally, he looks around the room, so he is easily distracted. Lying down and covering his eyes helped him concentrate on what she was saying. 12

Analogous to the physical alignment that women and men take 13
in conversation is their topical alignment. The girls in my study tended to talk at length about one topic, but the boys tended to jump
from topic to topic. The second-grade girls exchanged stories about
people they knew. The second-grade boys teased, told jokes, noticed
things in the room and talked about finding games to play. The
sixth-grade girls talked about problems with a mutual friend. The
sixth-grade boys talked about fifty-five different topics, none of
which extended over more than a few turns.

Listening to Body Language

Switching topics is another habit that gives women the impres- 14
sion men aren't listening, especially if they switch to a topic about
themselves. But the evidence of the tenth-grade boys in my study indicates otherwise. The tenth-grade boys sprawled across their chairs
with bodies parallel and eyes straight ahead, rarely looking at each
other. They looked as if they were riding in a car, staring out the
windshield. But they were talking about their feelings. One boy was
upset because a girl had told him he had a drinking problem, and the
other was feeling alienated from all his friends.

Now, when a girl told a friend about a problem, the friend re- 15
sponded by asking probing questions and expressing agreement and
understanding. But the boys dismissed each other's problems. Todd
assured Richard that his drinking was "no big problem" because
"sometimes you're funny when you're off your butt." And when
Todd said he felt left out, Richard responded, "Why should you? You
know more people than me."

Women perceive such responses as belittling and unsupportive. 16
But the boys seemed satisfied with them. Whereas women reassure
each other by implying, "You shouldn't feel bad because I've had
similar experiences," men do so by implying, "You shouldn't feel bad
because your problems aren't so bad."

There are even simpler reasons for women's impression that 17
men don't listen. Linguist Lynette Hirschman found that women
make more listener-noise, such as "mhm," "uhuh," and "yeah," to
show "I'm with you." Men, she found, more often give silent attention. Women who expect a stream of listener noise interpret silent attention as no attention at all.

Women's conversational habits are as frustrating to men as   18
men's are to women. Men who expect silent attention interpret a
stream of listener noise as overreaction or impatience. Also, when
women talk to each other in a close, comfortable setting, they often
overlap, finish each other's sentences and anticipate what the other is
about to say. This practice, which I call "participatory listenership,"
is often perceived by men as interruption, intrusion, and lack of
attention.

A parallel difference caused a man to complain about his wife,   19
"She just wants to talk about her own point of view. If I show her
another view, she gets mad at me." When most women talk to each
other, they assume a conversationalist's job is to express agreement
and support. But many men see their conversational duty as pointing
out the other side of an argument. This is heard as disloyalty by
women, and refusal to offer the requisite support. It is not that wom-
en don't want to see other points of view, but that they prefer them
phrased as suggestions and inquiries rather than as direct challenges.

In his book *Fighting for Life*, Walter Ong points out that men   20
use "agonistic" or warlike, oppositional formats to do almost anything; thus discussion becomes debate and conversation becomes a
competitive sport. In contrast, women see conversation as a ritual
means of establishing rapport. If Jane tells a problem and June says
she has a similar one, they walk away feeling closer to each other. But
this attempt at establishing rapport can backfire when used with
men. Men take too literally women's ritual "troubles talk," just as
women mistake men's ritual challenges for real attack.

The Sounds of Silence

These differences begin to clarify why women and men have   21
such different expectations about communication in marriage. For
women, talk creates intimacy. Marriage is an orgy of closeness: you
can tell your feelings and thoughts, and still be loved. Their greatest
fear is being pushed away. But men live in a hierarchical world, where
talk maintains independence and status. They are on guard to protect
themselves from being put down and pushed around.

This explains the paradox of the talkative man who said of his   22
silent wife, "She's the talker." In the public setting of a guest lecture,
he felt challenged to show his intelligence and display his understanding of the lecture. But at home, where he has nothing to prove

and no one to defend against, he is free to remain silent. For his wife, being home means she is free from the worry that something she says might offend someone, or spark disagreement, or appear to be showing off; at home she is free to talk.

The communication problems that endanger marriage can't be   23
fixed by mechanical engineering. They require a new conceptual framework about the role of talk in human relationships. Many of the psychological explanations that have become second nature may not be helpful, because they tend to blame either women (for not being assertive enough) or men (for not being in touch with their feelings). A sociolinguistic approach by which male-female conversation is seen as cross-cultural communication allows us to understand the problem and forge solutions without blaming either party.

Once the problem is understood, improvement comes naturally,   24
as it did to the young woman and her boyfriend who seemed to go to sleep when she wanted to talk. Previously, she had accused him of not listening, and he had refused to change his behavior, since that would be admitting fault. But then she learned about and explained to him the differences in women's and men's habitual ways of aligning themselves in conversation. The next time she told him she wanted to talk, he began, as usual, by lying down and covering his eyes. When the familiar negative reaction bubbled up, she reassured herself that he really was listening. But then he sat up and looked at her. Thrilled, she asked why. He said, "You like me to look at you when we talk, so I'll try to do it." Once he saw their differences as cross-cultural rather than right and wrong, he independently altered his behavior.

Women who feel abandoned and deprived when their husbands   25
won't listen to or report daily news may be happy to discover their husbands trying to adapt once they understand the place of small talk in women's relationships. But if their husbands don't adapt, the women may still be comforted that for men, this is not a failure of intimacy. Accepting the difference, the wives may look to their friends or family for that kind of talk. And husbands who can't provide it shouldn't feel their wives have made unreasonable demands. Some couples will still decide to divorce, but at least their decisions will be based on realistic expectations.

In these times of resurgent ethnic conflicts, the world desperate-   26
ly needs cross-cultural understanding. Like charity, successful cross-cultural communication should begin at home.

Questions for Close Reading

1. What is the selection's thesis? Locate the sentence(s) in which Tannen states her main idea. If she doesn't state the thesis explicitly, express it in your own words.
2. In paragraphs 8, 23, and 26, Tannen refers to "cross-cultural communication" and "cross-cultural understanding." What does she mean by the term *cross-cultural?* Why is this term central to an understanding of the selection?
3. According to Tannen, what aspects of communication are "misaligned" when males and females talk?
4. What evidence does Tannen provide to show that understanding males' and females' differing communication styles can improve the way the sexes relate to each other?
5. Refer to your dictionary as needed to define the following words used in the selection: *irony* (paragraph 2), *epidemic* (3), *inequities* (4), *socialization* (8), *hierarchical* (11), *misalignment* (12), *analogous* (13), *belittling* (16), *requisite* (19), *agonistic* (20), *sociolinguistic* (23), and *resurgent* (26).

Questions About the Writer's Craft

1. **The pattern.**   Which comparison-contrast method of organization (one-side-at-a-time or point-by-point) does Tannen use in the selection? Why might she have chosen this method?
2. **Other patterns.**   Tannen provides many brief examples to contrast male and female communication behaviors. Where in the selection does she introduce extended examples about two specific couples? Why do you think she returns to each of these examples later in the selection?
3. Look closely at paragraph 6. Besides its brevity, what else is distinctive about the paragraph? What purpose does the paragraph serve?
4. Do you think Tannen is addressing her ideas to an audience of men, of women, or of both sexes? How can you tell? What techniques does she use to establish her credibility with this audience?

Questions for Further Thought

1. From your own experience, do you think Tannen's characterization of male and female communication styles is accurate? Do you know males or females who don't fit her descriptions? How can you account for these people's communication patterns?
2. Think about arguments between the sexes that you have witnessed or participated in. To what extent did gender differences in communication style contribute to the argument? Would familiarity with the concepts that Tannen discusses help minimize or resolve such arguments? Why or why not?

3. Tannen states that "most wives want their husbands to be, first and foremost, conversational partners, but few husbands share this expectation of their wives." Do you agree that men and women have such different emotional needs and expectations? Explain.

4. Think about your childhood experiences playing with other children. Were your playgroups predominantly same-sex? If children were encouraged to play more often in mixed groups, would male-female communication improve later in life? Why or why not?

Writing Assignments Using Comparison-Contrast as a Pattern of Development

∞ 1. Tannen analyzes differences in male and female communication behaviors. Pick another area where you perceive significant gender differences. You might, for example, consider the way males and females act at parties, shop for clothes, watch television, or furnish their rooms. Focusing on a single area, write an essay comparing and contrasting what you observe about male and female attitudes and behavior. Your essay may be serious or lighthearted. In either case, reach some conclusions—as Tannen does—about the causes of the differences you perceive. For an additional perspective on gender differences and similarities, you might want to read Scott Russell Sanders's "The Men We Carry in Our Minds" (page 308).

∞ 2. Tannen points out that males and females often position their bodies differently when communicating. Spend some time on your college campus observing the body language of males and females as they walk, chat with friends, study at the library, congregate in the student center, raise their hands in class, listen to classroom discussion, and the like. See if you can detect any differences in the way that males and females use their bodies. Then write an essay comparing and contrasting the body language of college men and women. Barbara Ehrenreich's "What I've Learned From Men" (page 261) will provide additional perspectives on the nonverbal aspects of communication.

Writing Assignments Using Other Patterns of Development

∞ 3. Tannen attributes the rising divorce rate to a failure in communication between the sexes. In "The Faltering Family" (page 467), George Gallup, Jr., suggests other possible causes for divorce. Write an essay discussing the forces that you see operating to undermine couples, either married or dating. You'll probably want to refer in your essay to Tannen's and Gallup's ideas, but don't feel constrained by what they write. You may decide that a completely different set of causes is at work in breaking couples up.

4. In paragraphs 15 to 16, Tannen states that males and females react in very different ways when a friend confides a problem. Using Tannen's analysis as a point of departure, get together with others and discuss more fully possible ways to respond in such a situation. After reviewing the material gathered, write an essay explaining the specific steps you think someone should take when a friend wants to talk about a problem. Indicate whether you feel the steps should be modified depending on the sex of the people involved.

Stephen Chapman

Stephen Chapman was an associate editor for *The New Republic*, the publication for which he wrote "The Prisoner's Dilemma" in 1980. Since then, he has joined the staff of the *Chicago Tribune*, where his twice-weekly syndicated column on national and international affairs originates. Born in Texas in 1954, Chapman graduated *cum laude* from Harvard University in 1976 and did graduate work in business administration at the University of Chicago. He has contributed articles to national magazines including *Atlantic*, *Harper's*, *Reason*, and the *American Spectator*.

The Prisoner's Dilemma

How does society punish criminals? What does society hope to gain through such punishment? These are just two of the provocative questions that Stephen Chapman explores in his essay. By contrasting the traditional Islamic system of punishment—a system that strikes many Westerners as barbaric—with the West's own supposedly more civilized approach, Chapman helps readers view the "advanced" system of punishment with a clearer eye.

One of the amusements of life in the modern West is the oppor- 1
tunity to observe the barbaric rituals of countries that are attached to
the customs of the dark ages. Take Pakistan, for example, our newest
ally and client state in Asia. Last October President Zia, in harmony
with the Islamic fervor that is sweeping his part of the world, revived
the traditional Moslem practice of flogging lawbreakers in public. In
Pakistan, this qualified as mass entertainment, and no fewer than
10,000 law-abiding Pakistanis turned out to see justice done to 26
convicts. To Western sensibilities the spectacle seemed barbaric—
both in the sense of cruel and in the sense of pre-civilized. In keeping
with Islamic custom each of the unfortunates—who had been caught
in prostitution raids the previous night and summarily convicted and

sentenced—was stripped down to a pair of white shorts, which were painted with a red stripe across the buttocks (the target). Then he was shackled against an easel, with pads thoughtfully placed over the kidneys to prevent injury. The floggers were muscular, fierce-looking sorts—convicted murderers, as it happens—who paraded around the flogging platform in colorful loincloths. When the time for the ceremony began, one of the floggers took a running start and brought a five-foot stave down across the first victim's buttocks, eliciting screams from the convict and murmurs from the audience. Each of the 26 received from five to 15 lashes. One had to be carried from the stage unconscious.

Flogging is one of the punishments stipulated by Koranic law,   2
which has made it a popular penological device in several Moslem countries, including Pakistan, Saudi Arabia, and, most recently, the ayatollah's Iran. Flogging, or *ta'zir*, is the general punishment prescribed for offenses that don't carry an explicit Koranic penalty. Some crimes carry automatic *hadd* punishments—stoning or scourging (a severe whipping) for illicit sex, scourging for drinking alcoholic beverages, amputation of the hands for theft. Other crimes—as varied as murder and abandoning Islam—carry the death penalty (usually carried out in public). Colorful practices like these have given the Islamic world an image in the West, as described by historian G. H. Jansen, "of blood dripping from the stumps of amputated hands and from the striped backs of malefactors, and piles of stones barely concealing the battered bodies of adulterous couples." Jansen, whose book *Militant Islam* is generally effusive in its praise of Islamic practices, grows squeamish when considering devices like flogging, amputation, and stoning. But they are given enthusiastic endorsement by the Koran itself.

Such traditions, we all must agree, are no sign of an advanced   3
civilization. In the West, we have replaced these various punishments (including the death penalty in most cases) with a single device. Our custom is to confine criminals in prison for varying lengths of time. In Illinois, a reasonably typical state, grand theft carries a punishment of three to five years; armed robbery can get you from six to 30. The lowest form of felony theft is punishable by one to three years in prison. Most states impose longer sentences on habitual offenders. In Kentucky, for example, habitual offenders can be sentenced to life in prison. Other states are less brazen, preferring the more genteel sounding "indeterminate sentence," which allows parole boards to

keep inmates locked up for as long as life. It was under an indeterminate sentence of one to 14 years that George Jackson served 12 years in California prisons for committing a $70 armed robbery. Under a Texas law imposing an automatic life sentence for a third felony conviction, a man was sent to jail for life last year because of three thefts adding up to less than $300 in property value. Texas also is famous for occasionally imposing extravagantly long sentences, often running into hundreds or thousands of years. This gives Texas a leg up on Maryland, which used to sentence some criminals to life plus a day—a distinctive if superfluous flourish. . . .

What are the advantages of being a convicted criminal in an advanced culture? First there is the overcrowding in prisons. One Tennessee prison, for example, has a capacity of 806, according to accepted space standards, but it houses 2300 inmates. One Louisiana facility has confined four and five prisoners in a single six-foot-by-six-foot cell. Then there is the disease caused by overcrowding, unsanitary conditions, and poor or inadequate medical care. A federal appeals court noted that the Tennessee prison had suffered frequent outbreaks of infectious diseases like hepatitis and tuberculosis. But the most distinctive element of American prison life is its constant violence. In his book *Criminal Violence, Criminal Justice*, Charles Silberman noted that in one Louisiana prison, there were 211 stabbings in only three years, 11 of them fatal. There were 15 slayings in a prison in Massachusetts between 1972 and 1975. According to a federal court, in Alabama's penitentiaries (as in many others), "robbery, rape, extortion, theft and assault are everyday occurrences." 4

At least in regard to cruelty, it's not at all clear that the system of punishment that has evolved in the West is less barbaric than the grotesque practices of Islam. Skeptical? Ask yourself: would you rather be subjected to a few minutes of intense pain and considerable public humiliation, or be locked away for two or three years in a prison cell crowded with ill-tempered sociopaths? Would you rather lose a hand or spend 10 years or more in a typical state prison? I have taken my own survey on this matter. I have found no one who does not find the Islamic system hideous. And I have found no one who *given the choices* mentioned above, would not prefer its penalties to our own. . . . 5

Imprisonment is now the universal method of punishing criminals in the United States. It is thought to perform five functions, each of which has been given a label by criminologists. First, there is 6 simple *retribution:* punishing the lawbreaker to serve society's sense of justice and to satisfy the victims' desire for revenge. Second, there is *specific deterrence:* discouraging the offender from misbehaving in the future. Third, *general deterrence:* using the offender as an example to discourage others from turning to crime. Fourth, *prevention:* at least during the time he is kept off the streets, the criminal cannot victimize other members of society. Finally, and most important, there is *rehabilitation:* reforming the criminal so that when he returns to society he will be inclined to obey the laws and able to make an honest living.

How satisfactorily do American prisons perform by these criteria? Well, of course, they do punish. But on the other scores they don't do so well. Their effect in discouraging future criminality by the prisoner or others is the subject of much debate, but the soaring rates of the last 20 years suggest that prisons are not a dramatically effective deterrent to criminal behavior. Prisons do isolate convicted criminals, but only to divert crime from ordinary citizens to prison guards and fellow inmates. Almost no one contends any more that prisons rehabilitate their inmates. If anything, they probably impede rehabilitation by forcing inmates into prolonged and almost exclusive association with other criminals. And prisons cost a lot of money. Housing a typical prisoner in a typical prison costs far more than a stint at a top university. This cost would be justified if prisons did the job they were intended for. But it is clear to all that prisons fail on the very grounds—humanity and hope of rehabilitation—that caused them to replace earlier, cheaper forms of punishment. . . . 7

So the debate continues to rage in all the same old ruts. No one, of course, would think of copying the medieval practices of Islamic nations and experimenting with punishments such as flogging and amputation. But let us consider them anyway. How do they compare with our American prison system in achieving the ostensible objectives of punishment? First, do they punish? Obviously they do, and in a uniquely painful and memorable way. Of course any sensible person, given the choice, would prefer suffering these punishments to years of incarceration in a typical American prison. But presumably no Western penologist would criticize Islamic punishments on the grounds that they are not barbaric enough. Do they deter crime? Yes, and probably more effectively than sending convicts off to prison. Now we read about a prison sentence in the newspaper, then think no more about the criminal's payment for his crimes until, perhaps, years later we read a small item reporting his release. By contrast, one 8 can easily imagine the vivid impression it would leave to be wandering through a local shopping center and to stumble onto the scene of some poor wretch being lustily flogged. And the occasional sight of an habitual offender walking around with a bloody stump at the end of his arm no doubt also would serve as a forceful reminder that crime does not pay.

Do flogging and amputation discourage recidivism? No one   9
knows whether the scars on his back would dissuade a criminal from risking another crime, but it is hard to imagine that corporal measures could stimulate a higher rate of recidivism than already exists. Islamic forms of punishment do not serve the favorite new right goal of simply isolating criminals from the rest of society, but they may achieve the same purpose of making further crimes impossible. In the movie *Bonnie and Clyde,* Warren Beatty successfully robs a bank with his arm in a sling, but this must be dismissed as artistic license. It must be extraordinarily difficult, at the very least, to perform much violent crime with only one hand.

Do these medieval forms of punishment rehabilitate the crimi-   10
nal? Plainly not. But long prison terms do not rehabilitate either. And it is just as plain that typical Islamic punishments are no crueler to the convict than incarceration in the typical American state prison.

Of course there are other reasons besides its bizarre forms of   11
punishment that the Islamic system of justice seems uncivilized to the Western mind. One is the absence of due process. Another is the long list of offenses—such as drinking, adultery, blasphemy, "profiteering," and so on—that can bring on conviction and punishment. A third is all the ritualistic mumbo-jumbo in pronouncements of Islamic law. . . . Even in these matters, however, a little cultural modesty is called for. The vast majority of American criminals are convicted and sentenced as a result of plea bargaining, in which due process plays almost no role. It has been only half a century since a wave of religious fundamentalism stirred this country to outlaw the consumption of alcoholic beverages. Most states also still have laws imposing austere constraints on sexual conduct. Only two weeks ago the *Washington Post* reported that the FBI had spent two and a half years and untold amounts of money to break up a nationwide pornography ring. Flogging the clients of prostitutes, as the Pakistanis did, does seem silly. But only a few months ago Mayor Koch of New York was proposing that clients caught in his own city have their names broadcast by radio stations. We are not so far advanced on

such matters as we often like to think. Finally, my lawyer friends assure me that the rules of jurisdiction for American courts contain plenty of petty requirements and bizarre distinctions that would sound silly enough to foreign ears.

Perhaps it sounds barbaric to talk of flogging and amputation, 12 and perhaps it is. But our system of punishment also is barbaric, and probably more so. Only cultural smugness about their system and willful ignorance about our own make it easy to regard the one as cruel and the other as civilized. We inflict our cruelties away from public view, while nations like Pakistan stage them in front of 10,000 onlookers. Their outrages are visible; ours are not. Most Americans can live their lives for years without having their peace of mind disturbed by the knowledge of what goes on in our prisons. To choose imprisonment over flogging and amputation is not to choose human kindness over cruelty, but merely to prefer that our cruelties be kept out of sight, and out of mind.

Public flogging and amputation may be more barbaric forms of 13 punishment than imprisonment, even if they are not more cruel. Society may pay a higher price for them, even if the particular criminal does not. Revulsion against officially sanctioned violence and infliction of pain derives from something deeply ingrained in the Western conscience, and clearly it is something admirable. Grotesque displays of the sort that occur in Islamic countries probably breed a greater tolerance for physical cruelty, for example, which prisons do not do precisely because they conceal their cruelties. In fact it is our admirable intolerance for calculated violence that makes it necessary for us to conceal what we have not been able to do away with. In a way this is a good thing, since it holds out the hope that we may eventually find a way to do away with it. But in another way it is a bad thing, since it permits us to congratulate ourselves on our civilized humanitarianism while violating its norms in this one area of our national life.

Questions for Close Reading

1. What is the selection's thesis? Locate the sentence(s) in which Chapman states his main idea. If he doesn't state the thesis explicitly, express it in your own words.

2. Chapman calls Islamic punishment practices "barbaric." What are some of these practices? Why would they seem barbaric to most Americans?
3. According to our society's philosophy of punishment, what goals is imprisonment supposed to accomplish? How successful, in Chapman's view, are American prisons in meeting these goals?
4. For Chapman, what is the core difference between the American punishment system and that of Islamic nations like Pakistan? Which system does he find preferable? Why?
5. Refer to your dictionary as needed to define the following words used in the selection: *barbaric* (paragraph 1), *stipulated* (2), *penological* (2), *malefactors* (2), *effusive* (2), *brazen* (3), *genteel* (3), *indeterminate* (3), *superfluous* (3), *extortion* (4), *criteria* (7), *ostensible* (8), *recidivism* (9), *corporal* (9), *blasphemy* (11), and *sanctioned* (13).

Questions About the Writer's Craft

1. **The pattern.** In paragraphs 8 through 10, Chapman contrasts the success of the American and Islamic systems in meeting the five goals of punishment cited in paragraph 6. How does Chapman help readers keep those goals in mind as he develops his contrast?
2. **Other patterns.** In paragraphs 1, 2, and 6, Chapman provides a number of definitions. How do these definitions help him convince readers to accept key points in his argument?
3. **Other patterns.** Examine the examples that Chapman provides in paragraphs 3 and 4. Why do you think he sequences each set of examples as he does?
4. Examine Chapman's tone, especially in paragraphs 3, 4, 5, and 8 to 9. Where does he shift from a fairly neutral tone to a more sarcastic and mocking one? How does this change help Chapman convince readers of the seriousness of the problems in American justice?

Questions for Further Thought

1. In 1994, international controversy raged over the flogging of an American teenager convicted of vandalism in Singapore. Surveys conducted in this country at the time revealed that a majority of Americans supported the Singaporean sentence. Why do you think so many Americans felt this way? How do you feel about the sentence?
2. What means of punishing the guilty, other than imprisonment, do you think many Americans would be interested in seeing implemented?
3. Islamic countries, according to Chapman, make great use of public punishment. Do you consider this practice cruel and heartless, or do you think that public punishment serves an important purpose? Do you think,

for example, that executions (by injection or electrocution) should be televised? Explain.

4. Chapman catalogs many flaws not only in our prisons but in our justice system as well, finding our system as arbitrary and bizarre as any Islamic system. Do you agree that our system of justice is "uncivilized"? Why or why not?

Writing Assignments Using Comparison-Contrast as a Pattern of Development

1. Select one situation in which people are, in your opinion, ineffectively punished for violating a law or regulation. For example, you might focus on the punishment typically imposed for driving while intoxicated, plagiarizing a school paper, or habitually coming to work late. Write an essay describing the violation and its customary punishment. Then contrast this punishment with a more effective way of correcting the offending behavior. Whether you choose the one-side-at-a-time or the point-by-point method, be sure to provide clear signals, as Chapman does, to help readers follow your ideas.

2. Chapman contrasts two cultures' approaches to criminal punishment. Write an essay comparing and/or contrasting two cultures' approaches to another aspect of life. To structure your paper, use either the one-side-at-a-time or point-by-point method of development. The cultures you discuss need not be nationalities or ethnicities. You might, for example, focus on parents' and teenagers' preferences in music, male and female expectations in a relationship, or high school teachers' and college professors' attitudes toward student responsibility. If appropriate, consider using a humorous tone to make fun of both sides—or to convey which side's approach you find preferable.

Writing Assignments Using Other Patterns of Development

3. Chapman states that there is "universal acknowledgment that prisons do not rehabilitate." Conduct research on recent developments in criminal rehabilitation. Bibliographic sources like the *New York Times Index,* the *Social Sciences Index,* and *Criminal Justice Abstracts* will help you locate relevant information. Then write an essay refuting *or* defending the common view that the rehabilitation of prisoners is a futile goal. Start by acknowledging the opposing view, and then support your argument with convincing evidence drawn from your research.

4. Chapman describes people in Islamic cultures flocking to gawk at the misfortunes of others. People in our country are also fascinated, even entertained, by others' problems. They slow down to inspect traffic accidents, follow celebrities' troubles in tabloid publications, and glue themselves to the television when a natural disaster strikes. Write an essay

in which you account for the causes of our fascination with others' misfortunes. Begin with one or two dramatic examples of this phenomenon, and then explain why you think people are so attracted to the troubles of others. Mark Twain's "The Damned Human Race" (page 609) may provide some helpful insights.

Additional Writing Topics

COMPARISON-CONTRAST

General Assignments

Using comparison-contrast, write an essay on one of the following topics. Your thesis should indicate whether the two subjects are being compared, contrasted, or both. Organize the paper by arranging the details in a one-side-at-a-time or point-by-point pattern. Remember to use organizational cues to help the audience follow your analysis.

1. Two-career family versus one-career family
2. Two approaches for dealing with problems
3. Children's pastimes today and yesterday
4. Two rooms where you spend a good deal of time
5. Neighborhood stores versus shopping malls
6. Two characters in a novel or other literary work
7. Living at home versus living in an apartment or dorm
8. Two attitudes toward money
9. A sports team then and now
10. Watching a movie on television versus viewing it in a theater
11. Two attitudes about a controversial subject
12. Two approaches to parenting
13. Walking or biking versus driving a car
14. Marriage versus living together
15. The atmosphere in two classes
16. Two approaches to studying
17. The place where you live and the place where you would like to live
18. Two comedians
19. The coverage of an event on television versus the coverage in a newspaper
20. Significant trend versus passing fad
21. Two horror or adventure movies
22. Typewriter versus word processor
23. Two candidates for an office
24. Your attitude before and after getting to know someone
25. Two friends with different life-styles

Assignments With a Specific Purpose and Audience

1. You would like to change your campus living arrangements. Perhaps you want to move from a dormitory to an off-campus apartment or from home to a dorm. Before you do, though, you'll have to convince your parents (who are paying most of your college costs) that the move will be beneficial. Write out what you would say to your parents. Contrast your

current situation with your proposed one, explaining why the new arrangement would be better.

2. As store manager, you decide to write a memo to all sales personnel explaining how to keep customers happy. Compare and/or contrast the needs and shopping habits of several different consumer groups (by age, spending ability, or sex), and show how to make each comfortable in your store.

3. As a member of the College Orientation Committee, you volunteer to write a guide entitled "Passing Exams" for first-year college students. You decide to contrast the right and wrong ways to prepare for and take exams. Although your purpose is basically serious, leaven the section on how *not* to approach exams with some humor.

4. You work as a volunteer for a mental health hot line. Many people call simply because they feel "stressed out." Prepare a brochure for these people, recommending a Type B approach to stressful situations. Focus the brochure on the contrast between Type A and Type B personalities: the former is nervous, hard-driving, competitive; the latter is relaxed and noncompetitive. Give specific examples of how each type tends to act in stressful situations.

5. As president of your student senate, you're concerned about the way your school is dealing with a particular situation (for example, advisement, parking, financial assistance). Write a letter to your college president contrasting the way your school handles the situation with another school's approach. In your conclusion, point out the advantages of adopting the other college's strategy.

6. Your old high school has invited you back to make a speech before an audience of seniors. The topic will be "how to choose the college that is right for you." Write your speech in the form of a comparison-contrast analysis. Focus on the choices available (two-year versus four-year schools, large versus small, local versus faraway, and so on), showing the advantages and/or disadvantages of each.

10

CAUSE-EFFECT

WHAT IS CAUSE-EFFECT?

Superstition has it that curiosity killed the cat. Maybe so. Yet our science, technology, storytelling, and fascination with the past and future all spring from our determination to know "Why" and "What if." Seeking explanations, young children barrage adults with endless questions: "Why do trees grow tall?" "What would happen if the sun didn't shine?" But children aren't the only ones who wonder in this way. All of us think in terms of cause and effect, sometimes consciously, sometimes unconsciously: "Why did they give me such an odd look?" we wonder, or "How would I do at another college?" we speculate. This exploration of reasons and results is also at the heart of most professions: "What led to our involvement in Vietnam?" historians question; "What will happen if we administer this experimental drug?" scientists ask.

Cause-effect writing, often called *causal analysis,* is rooted in this elemental need to make connections. Because the drive to understand reasons and results is so fundamental, causal analysis is a common kind of writing. An article analyzing the unexpected out-come of an election, a report linking poor nutrition to low academic achievement, an editorial analyzing the impact of a proposed tax cut—all are examples of cause-effect writing.

Done well, cause-effect pieces can uncover the subtle and often surprising connections between events or phenomena. By rooting out causes and projecting effects, causal analysis enables us to make sense of our experiences, revealing a universe that is somewhat less arbitrary and chaotic.

HOW CAUSE-EFFECT FITS YOUR PURPOSE AND AUDIENCE

Many assignments and exam questions in college involve writing essays that analyze causes, effects, or both. Sometimes, as in the following examples, you'll be asked to write an essay developed primarily through the cause-effect pattern:

> Although divorces have leveled off in the last few years, the number of marriages ending in divorce is still greater than it was a generation ago. What do you think are the causes of this phenomenon?

> Political commentators were surprised that so few people voted in the last election. Discuss the probable causes of this weak voter turnout.

> Americans never seem to tire of gossip about the rich and famous. What effect has this fascination with celebrities had on American culture?

> The federal government is expected to pass legislation that will significantly reduce the funding of student loans. Analyze the possible effects of such a cutback.

Other assignments and exam questions may not explicitly ask you to address causes and effects, but they may use words that suggest causal analysis would be appropriate. Consider these examples, paying special attention to the words in boldface:

In contrast to the socially involved youth of the 1960s, many young people today tend to remove themselves from political issues. What do you think are the **sources** of the political apathy found among 18- to 25-year-olds? *(cause)*

A number of experts forecast that drug abuse will be the most significant factor affecting American productivity in the coming decade. Evaluate the validity of this observation by discussing the **impact** of drugs in the workplace. *(effect)*

According to school officials, a predictable percentage of entering students drop out of college at some point during their first year. What **motivates** students to drop out? What **happens** to them once they leave? *(cause and effect)*

In addition to serving as the primary strategy for achieving an essay's purpose, causal analysis can also be a supplemental method used to help make a point in an essay developed chiefly through another pattern of development. Assume, for example, that you want to write an essay *defining* the term *the homeless*. To help readers see that unfavorable circumstances can result in nearly anyone becoming homeless, you might discuss some of the unavoidable, everyday factors causing people to live on streets and in subway stations. Similarly, in a *persuasive* proposal urging your college administration to institute an honors program, you would probably spend some time analyzing the positive effect of such a program on students and faculty.

SUGGESTIONS FOR USING CAUSE-EFFECT IN AN ESSAY

The following suggestions will be helpful whether you use causal analysis as a dominant or supportive pattern of development.

1. Stay focused on the purpose of your analysis. When writing a causal analysis, don't lose sight of your overall purpose. Consider, for example, an essay on the causes of widespread child abuse. If you're concerned primarily with explaining the problem of child abuse to your readers, you might take a purely *informative* approach:

> Although parental stress is the immediate cause of child abuse, the more compelling reason for such behavior lies in the way parents were themselves mistreated in their own families.

Or you might want to *persuade* the audience about some point or idea concerning child abuse:

> The tragic consequences of child abuse provide strong support for more aggressive handling of such cases by social workers and judges.

Then again, you could choose a *speculative* approach, your main purpose being to suggest possibilities:

> Psychologists disagree about the potential effect on youngsters of all the media attention to child abuse. Will children exposed to this media coverage grow up assertive, self-confident, and able to protect themselves? Or will they become fearful and distrustful?

These examples illustrate that an essay's causal analysis may have more than one purpose. For instance, although the last example points to a paper with a primarily speculative purpose, the essay would probably start by informing readers of experts' conflicting views. The paper would also have a persuasive slant if it ended by urging readers to complain to the media about their sensationalized treatment of the child-abuse issue.

2. Adapt content and tone to your purpose and readers. Your purpose and audience determine what supporting material and what tone will be most effective in a cause-effect essay. Assume you want to direct your essay on child abuse to general readers who know little about the subject. To *inform* readers, you might use facts, statistics, and expert opinion to provide an objective discussion of the causes of child abuse. Your analysis might show the following: (1) adults who were themselves mistreated as children tend to abuse their own offspring; (2) marital stress contributes to the mistreatment of children; and (3) certain personality disorders increase the likelihood of child abuse. Sensitive to what your readers would and wouldn't understand, you would stay away from a technical or formal tone. Rather than writing "Pathological preabuse symptomatology predicts adult transference of high aggressivity," you would say "Psychologists can often predict, on the basis of family histories, who will abuse children."

Now imagine that your purpose is to *convince* future social workers that the failure of social service agencies to act authoritatively in child-abuse cases often has tragic consequences. Hoping to encourage more responsible behavior in the prospective social workers, you would adopt a more emotional tone in the essay, perhaps citing wrenching case histories that dramatize what happens when child abuse isn't taken seriously.

3. Think rigorously about causes and effects.   To write a meaningful causal analysis, you should do some careful thinking about the often complex relationship between causes and effects. Children tend to oversimplify causes and effects ("Mommy and Daddy are getting divorced because I was bad the other day"), and adults' arguments can be characterized by hasty, often slipshod thinking ("All these immigrants willing to work cheaply have made us lose our jobs"). But imprecise thinking has no place in essay writing. You should be willing to dig for causes, to think creatively about effects. You should examine your subject in depth, looking beyond the obvious and superficial.

Brainstorming, freewriting, and mapping will help you explore causes and effects thoroughly. No matter which prewriting technique you use, generate as many explanations as possible by asking yourself questions like these:

> *Causes:* What happened? What are the possible reasons? Which are most likely? Who was involved? Why?
>
> *Effects:* What happened? Who was involved? What were the observable results? What are some possible future consequences? Which consequences are negative? Which are positive?

If you remain open and look beyond the obvious, you'll discover that a cause may have many effects. Imagine that you're writing a paper on the effects of cigarette smoking. Prewriting would probably generate a number of consequences that could be discussed, some less obvious but perhaps more interesting than others: increased risk of lung cancer and heart disease, harm traced to secondhand smoke, legal battles regarding the rights of smokers and nonsmokers, lower birth weights in babies of mothers who smoke, and developmental problems experienced by such underweight infants.

In the same way, prewriting will help you see that an effect may have multiple causes. An essay analyzing the reasons for world hunger could discuss many causes, again some less evident but perhaps more thought-provoking than others: climatic changes, inefficient use of land, cultural predispositions for large families, and poor management of international relief funds.

Your analysis may also uncover a *causal chain* in which one cause (or effect) brings about another, which, in turn, brings about another, and so on. Here's an example of a causal chain: Prohibition went into effect; bootleggers and organized crime stepped in to supply public demand for alcoholic beverages; ordinary citizens began breaking the law by buying illegal alcohol and patronizing speakeasies; disrespect for legal authority became widespread and acceptable. As you can see, a causal chain often leads to interesting points. In this case, the subject of Prohibition leads not just to the obvious (illegal consumption of alcohol) but also to the more complex issue of society's decreasing respect for legal authority.

Don't grapple with so complex a chain, however, that you become hopelessly entangled. If your subject involves multiple causes and effects, limit what you'll discuss. Identify which causes and effects are *primary* and which are *secondary*. How extensively you cover secondary factors will depend on your purpose and audience. In an essay intended to inform a general audience about the harmful effects of pesticides, you would most likely focus on everyday dangers—polluted drinking water, residues in food, and the like. You probably wouldn't include a discussion of more long-range consequences (evolution of resistant insects, disruption of the soil's acid-alkaline balance).

Similarly, decide whether to focus on *immediate,* more obvious causes and effects, or on less obvious, more *remote* ones. Or perhaps you need to focus on both. In an essay about a faculty strike at your college, should you attribute the strike simply to the faculty's failure to receive a salary increase? Or should you also examine other factors: the union's failure to accept a salary package that satisfied most professors; the administration's inability to coordinate its negotiating efforts? It may be more difficult to explore more remote causes and effects, but it can also lead to more original and revealing essays. Thoughtful analyses take these less obvious considerations into account.

When developing a causal analysis, be careful to avoid the *post hoc fallacy*. Named after the Latin phrase *post hoc, ergo propter hoc,* meaning "after this, therefore because of this," this kind of faulty thinking occurs when you assume that simply because one event *followed* another, the first event *caused* the second. For example, if the Republicans win a majority of seats in Congress and, several months later, the economy collapses, can you conclude that the Republicans caused the collapse? A quick assumption of "Yes" fails the test of logic, for the timing of events could be coincidental and not indicative of any cause-effect relationship. The collapse may have been triggered by uncontrolled inflation that began well before the congressional elections. (For more information on the *post hoc* fallacy, see page 580.)

Also, be careful not to mistake *correlation* for *causation*. Two events correlate when they occur at about the same time. Such co-occurrence, however, doesn't guarantee a cause-effect relationship. For instance, while the number of ice cream cones eaten and the instances of heat prostration both increase during the summer months, this doesn't mean that eating ice cream causes heat prostration! A third factor—in this case, summer heat—is the actual cause. When writing causal analyses, then, use with caution words that imply a causal link (such as *therefore* and *because)*. Words that express simply time of occurrence (like *following* and *previously)* are safer and more objective.

Finally, keep in mind that a rigorous causal analysis involves more than loose generalizations about causes and effects. Creating plausible connections may require library research, interviewing, or both. Often you'll need to provide facts, statistics, details, personal observations, or other corroborative material if readers are going to accept the reasoning behind your analysis.

4. Write a thesis that focuses the paper on causes, effects, or both. The thesis in an essay developed through causal analysis often indicates whether the essay will deal mostly with causes, effects, or both. Here, for example, are three thesis statements for causal analyses dealing with the public school system. You'll see that each thesis signals that essay's particular emphasis:

> Our school system has been weakened by an overemphasis on trendy electives. *(causes)*

> An ineffectual school system has led to crippling teachers' strikes and widespread disrespect for the teaching profession. *(effects)*

> Bureaucratic inefficiency has created a school system unresponsive to children's emotional, physical, and intellectual needs. *(causes and effects)*

Note that the thesis statement—in addition to signaling whether the paper will discuss causes or effects or both—may also point to the essay's plan of development. Consider the last thesis statement; it makes clear that the paper will discuss children's emotional needs first, their physical needs second, and their intellectual needs last.

The thesis statement in a causal analysis doesn't have to specify whether the essay will discuss causes, effects, or both. Nor does the thesis have to be worded in such a way that the essay's plan of development is apparent. But when first writing cause-effect essays, you may find that a highly focused thesis will keep your analysis on track.

5. Choose an organizational pattern. There are two basic ways to organize the points in a cause-effect essay: you may use a chronological or an emphatic sequence. If you select a *chronological order,* you discuss causes and effects in the order in which they occur or will occur. Suppose you're writing an essay on the causes for the popularity of imported cars. These causes might be discussed in chronological sequence: American plant workers became frustrated and dissatisfied on the job; some workers got careless while others deliberately sabotaged the production of sound cars; a growing number of defective cars hit the market; consumers grew dissatisfied with American cars and switched to imports.

Chronology might also be used to organize a discussion about effects. Imagine you want to write an essay about the need to guard against disrupting delicate balances in the country's wildlife. You might start the essay by discussing what happened when the starling, a non-native bird, was introduced into the American environment. Because the starling had few natural predators, the starling population soared out of control; the starlings took over food sources and habitats of native species; the bluebird, a native species, declined and is now threatened with extinction.

Although a chronological pattern can be an effective way to organize material, a strict time sequence can present a problem if your primary cause or effect ends up buried in the middle of the sequence. In such a case, you might use *emphatic order,* reserving the most significant cause or effect for the end. For example, time order could be used to present the reasons behind a candidate's unexpected victory: Less than a month after the candidate's earlier defeat, a full-scale fund-raising campaign for the next election was started; the candidate spoke to many crucial power groups early in the campaign; the candidate did exceptionally well in the pre-election debates; good weather and large voter turnout on election day favored the candidate. However, if you believe that the candidate's appearance before influential groups was the key factor in the victory, it would be more effective to emphasize that point by saving it for the end. This is what is meant by emphatic order—saving the most important point for last.

Emphatic order is an especially effective way to sequence cause-effect points when readers hold what, in your opinion, are mistaken or narrow views about a subject. To encourage readers to look more closely at the issues, you present what you consider the erroneous or obvious views first, show why they are unsound or limited, then present what you feel to be the actual causes and effects. Such a sequence nudges the audience into giving further thought to the causes and effects you have discovered. Here are informal outlines for two causal analyses using this approach.

Subject: The causes of the riot at a rock concert

1. Some commentators blame the excessively hot weather.
2. Others cite drug use among the concertgoers.
3. Still others blame the liquor sold at the concessions.

4. But the real cause of the disaster was poor planning by the concert promoters.

Subject: The effects of campus crime

1. Immediate problems
   a. Students feel insecure and fearful.
   b. Many night-time campus activities have been curtailed.
2. More significant long-term problems
   a. Unfavorable publicity about campus crime will affect future student enrollments.
   b. Hiring faculty will become more difficult.

When using emphatic order in a causal analysis, you might want to word the thesis in such a way that it signals which point your essay will stress. Look at the following thesis statements:

Although many immigrants arrive in this country without marketable skills, their most pressing problem is learning how to make their way in a society whose language they don't know.

The space program has led to dramatic advances in computer technology and medical science. Even more important, though, the program has helped change many people's attitudes toward the planet we live on.

These thesis statements reflect an awareness of the complex nature of cause-effect relationships. While not dismissing secondary issues, the statements establish which points the writer considers most noteworthy. The second thesis, for instance, indicates that the paper will touch on the technological and medical advances made possible by the space program but will emphasize the way the program has changed people's attitudes toward the earth.

Whether you use a chronological or emphatic pattern to organize your essay, you'll need to provide clear *signals* to identify when you're discussing causes and when you're discussing effects. Expressions such as "Another reason" and "A final outcome" help readers follow your line of thought.

6. Use language that hints at the complexity of cause-effect relationships.   Because it's difficult—if not impossible—to identify causes and effects with certainty, you should avoid such absolutes as "It must be obvious" and "There is no doubt." Instead, try phrases like "Most likely" or "It's probable that." Using such language is not indecisive; rather, it reflects your understanding of the often tangled nature of causes and effects. Be careful, though, of going to the other extreme and being reluctant to take a stand on the issues. If you've thought carefully about causes and effects, you have a right to state your analysis with conviction. Don't undercut the hard work you've done by writing as if your ideas were unworthy of your reader's attention.

Cause-effect writing is gratifying for both writer and audience. As a writer, you experience the pleasure of stretching your mind, confident that your exploration of causes and effects has gone beyond the obvious. Readers feel a comparable satisfaction, knowing that they have a clearer understanding of an event or a phenomenon. Causal analysis also has the potential for generating vigorous discussion and honest disagreement about a variety of issues—from reasons for international terrorism to consequences of reducing support for school lunch programs. Cause-effect writing is certainly one of the most critical ways we have for thinking about matters that concern us.

STUDENT ESSAY

The following student essay was written by Carl Novack in response to this assignment:

> In "The Faltering Family," George Gallup, Jr., points to a number of factors that have caused the decline of the American family. Think of another institution, process, or practice that has changed recently and discuss several factors you believe are responsible for the change.

While reading Carl's paper, try to determine how well it applies the principles of causal analysis. The annotations on Carl's paper and the commentary following it will help you look at the essay more closely.

Americans and Food
by Carl Novack

Introduction   An offbeat but timely cartoon recently appeared   1
in the local newspaper. The single panel showed a
gravel-pit operation with piles of raw earth and large
cranes. Next to one of the cranes stood the owner of
the gravel pit--a grizzled, tough-looking character,
hammer in hand, pointing proudly to the new sign he
had just tacked up. The sign read, "Fred's Fill Dirt
and Croissants." The cartoon illustrates an interesting phenomenon: the changing food habits of Americans. Our meals used to consist of something like
home-cooked pot roast, mashed potatoes laced with
butter and salt, a thick slice of apple pie topped with
a healthy scoop of vanilla ice cream--plain, heavy

Thesis ——— meals, cooked from scratch, and eaten leisurely at
home. But America has changed, and as it has, so
have what we Americans eat and how we eat it.

We used to have simple, unsophisticated tastes   2
and looked with suspicion at anything more exotic
than hamburger. Admittedly, we did adopt some
foods from the various immigrant groups who flocked

Topic sentence: to our shores. We learned to eat Chinese food, pizza,
Background   and bagels. But in the last few years, the interna-
paragraph   tional character of our diet has grown tremendously.
We can walk into any mall in Middle America and
buy pita bread, quiche, and tacos. Such foods
are often changed on their journey from exotic
imports to ordinary "American" meals (no Pakistani,
for example, eats frozen-on-a-stick boysenberry-
flavored yogurt), but the imports are still a long way
from hamburger on a bun.

Topic sentence: ———→ Why have we become more worldly in our   3
Three causes   tastes? For one thing, television blankets the country
answer the   with information about new food products and
question   trends. Viewers in rural Montana know that the latest
craving in Washington, D.C., is Cajun cooking or that
First cause ——— something called tofu is now available in the local
supermarket. Another reason for the growing inter-
Second cause ——— national flavor of our food is that many young Americans have traveled abroad and gotten hooked on new
tastes and flavors. Backpacking students and young

professionals vacationing in Europe come home with cravings for authentic French bread or German beer.

Third cause ——▸ Finally, continuing waves of immigrants settle in the cities where many of us live, causing significant changes in what we eat. Vietnamese, Haitians, and Thais, for instance, bring their native foods and cooking styles with them and eventually open small markets or restaurants. In time, the new food will become Americanized enough to take its place in our national diet.

Topic sentence: ——▸ Our growing concern with health has also   4
Another cause   affected the way we eat. For the last few years, the media have warned us about the dangers of our traditional diet, high in salt and fat, low in fiber. The media also began to educate us about the dangers of processed foods pumped full of chemical additives.

Start of a ——▸ As a result, consumers began to demand healthier
causal chain   foods, and manufacturers started to change some of their products. Many foods, such as lunch meat, canned vegetables, and soups, were made available in low-fat, low-sodium versions. Whole-grain cereals and higher-fiber breads also began to appear on the grocery shelves. Moreover, the food industry started to produce all-natural products--everything from potato chips to ice cream--without additives and preservatives. Not surprisingly, the restaurant industry responded to this switch to healthier foods, luring customers with salad bars, broiled fish, and steamed vegetables.

Topic sentence: ——▸ Our food habits are being affected, too, by the   5
Another cause   rapid increase in the number of women working outside the home. Sociologists and other experts believe that two important factors triggered this phenomenon: the women's movement and a changing economic climate. Women were assured that it was acceptable, even rewarding, to work outside the home; many women also discovered that they had to work just to keep up with the cost of living. As the traditional role of homemaker changed, so did the way families ate. With Mom working, there wasn't time for her to prepare the traditional three square meals a day. Instead, families began looking for alter-

Start of a ——— natives to provide quick meals. What was the result?
causal chain

For one, thing, there was a boom in fast-food restaurants. The suburban or downtown strip that once contained a lone McDonald's now features Wendy's, Roy Rogers, Taco Bell, Burger King, and Pizza Hut. Families also began to depend on frozen foods as another time-saving alternative. Once again, though, demand changed the kind of frozen food available. Frozen foods no longer consist of foil trays divided into greasy fried chicken, watery corn niblets, and lumpy mashed potatoes. Supermarkets now stock a range of supposedly gourmet frozen dinners--from fettucini in cream sauce to braised beef en brochette.

Conclusion   It may not be possible to pick up a ton of fill dirt   6
and a half-dozen croissants at the same place, but America's food habits are definitely changing. If it is true that "you are what you eat," then America's identity is evolving along with its diet.

COMMENTARY

Title and introduction.   Asked to prepare a paper analyzing the reasons behind a change in our lives, Carl decided to write about a shift he had noticed in Americans' eating habits. The title of the essay, "Americans and Food," identifies Carl's subject but could be livelier and more interesting.

Despite his rather uninspired title, Carl starts his *causal analysis* in an engaging way—with the vivid description of a cartoon. He then connects the cartoon to his subject with the following sentence: "The cartoon illustrates an interesting phenomenon: the changing food habits of Americans." To back up his belief that there has been a revolution in our eating habits, Carl uses the first paragraph to summarize the kind of meal that people used to eat. He then moves into his *thesis:* "But America has changed, and as it has, so have what Americans eat and how we eat it." The thesis implies that Carl's paper will focus on both causes and effects.

Purpose.   Carl's *purpose* was to write an *informative* causal analysis. But before he could present the causes of the change in eating habits, he needed to show that such a change had, in fact, taken place. He therefore uses the second paragraph to document one aspect of this change—the internationalization of our eating habits.

Topic sentences.   At the beginning of the third paragraph, Carl uses a question—"Why have we become more worldly in our tastes?"—to signal that his discussion of causes is about to begin. This question also serves as the paragraph's *topic sentence,* indicating that the paragraph will focus on reasons for the increasingly international flavor of our food. The next two paragraphs, also focused by topic sentences, identify two other major reasons for the change in eating habits: "Our growing concern with health has also affected the way we eat" (paragraph 4), and "Our food habits are being affected, too, by the rapid increase in the number of women working outside the home" (5).

Other patterns of development.   Carl draws on two patterns— comparison-contrast and exemplification—to develop his causal analysis. At the heart of the essay is a basic *contrast* between the way we used to eat and the way we eat now. And throughout his essay, Carl provides convincing *examples* to demonstrate the validity of his points. Consider for a moment the third paragraph. Here Carl asserts that one reason for our new eating habits is our growing exposure to international foods. He then presents concrete evidence to show that we have indeed become more familiar with international cuisine: Television exposes rural Montana to Cajun cooking; students traveling abroad take a liking to French bread; urban dwellers enjoy the exotic fare served by numerous immigrant groups. The fourth and fifth paragraphs use similarly specific evidence (for example, "low-fat, low-sodium versions" of "lunch meat, canned vegetables, and soups") to illustrate the soundness of key ideas.

Causal chains.   Let's look more closely at the evidence in the essay. Not satisfied with obvious explanations, Carl thought through his ideas carefully and even brainstormed with friends to arrive at as comprehensive an analysis as possible. Not surprisingly, much of the evidence Carl uncovered took the form of *causal chains.* In the fourth paragraph, Carl writes, "The media also began to educate us about the dangers of processed foods pumped full of chemical additives. As a result, consumers began to demand healthier foods, and manufacturers started to change some of their products." And the next paragraph shows how the changing role of American women caused families to search for alternative ways of eating. This shift, in turn, caused the restaurant and food industries to respond with a wide range of food alternatives.

Making the paper easy to follow. Although Carl's analysis digs beneath the surface and reveals complex cause-effect relationships, he wisely limits his pursuit of causal chains to *primary causes and effects*. He doesn't let the complexities distract him from his main purpose: to show why and how the American diet is changing. Carl is also careful to provide his essay with abundant *connecting devices*, making it easy for readers to see the links between points. Consider the use of *transitions* (signaled by italics) in the following sentences: *"Another* reason for the growing international flavor of our food is that many young Americans have traveled abroad" (paragraph 3); *"As a result*, consumers began to demand healthier foods" (4); and *"As* the traditional role of homemaker changed, so did the way families ate" (5).

A problem with the essay's close. When reading the essay, you probably noticed that Carl's conclusion is a bit weak. Although his reference to the cartoon works well, the rest of the paragraph limps to a tired close. Ending an otherwise vigorous essay with such a slight conclusion undercuts the effectiveness of the whole paper. Carl spent so much energy developing the body of his essay that he ran out of the stamina needed to conclude the piece more forcefully. Careful budgeting of his time would have allowed him to prepare a stronger concluding paragraph.

Revising the first draft. When Carl was ready to revise, he showed the first draft of his essay to several classmates. Listening carefully to what they said, he jotted down their most helpful comments and eventually transferred them, numbered in order of importance, to his draft. Comparing Carl's original version of his fourth paragraph (shown here) with his final version in the essay will show you how he went about revising.

Original Version of the Fourth Paragraph

A growing concern with health has also affected the way we eat, especially because the media have sent us warnings the last few years about the dangers of salt, sugar, food additives, high-fat and low-fiber diets. We have started to worry that our traditional meals may have been shortening our lives. As a result, consumers demanded healthier foods and manufacturers started taking some of the salt and sugar out of canned foods. "All-natural" became an effective selling point, leading to many preservative-free products. Restaurants, too, adapted their menus, luring customers with light meals. Because we now know about the link between overweight and a variety of health problems, including heart attacks, we are counting calories. In turn, food companies made fortunes on diet beer and diet cola. Sometimes, though, we seem a bit confused about the health issue; we drink soda that is sugar-free but loaded with chemical sweeteners. Still, we believe we are lengthening our lives through changing our diets.

On the advice of his classmates, Carl decided to omit all references to the way our concern with weight has affected our eating habits. It's true, of course, that calorie-counting has changed how we eat. But as soon as Carl started to discuss this point, he got involved in a causal chain that undercut the paragraph's unity. He ended up describing the paradoxical situation in which we find ourselves. In an attempt to eat healthy, we stay away from sugar and use instead artificial sweeteners that probably aren't very good for us. This is an interesting issue, but it detracts from the point Carl wants to make: that our concern with health has affected our eating habits in a *positive* way.

Carl's editing team also pointed out that the fourth paragraph's first sentence contained too much material to be an effective topic sentence. Carl corrected the problem by breaking the overlong sentence into two short ones: "Our growing concern with health has also affected the way we eat. For the last few years, the media have warned us about the dangers of our traditional diet, high in salt and fat, low in fiber." The first of these sentences serves as a crisp topic sentence that focuses the rest of the paragraph.

Finally, Carl agreed with his classmates that the fourth paragraph lacked convincing specifics. When revising, he changed "manufacturers started taking some of the salt and sugar out of canned foods" to the more specific "Many foods, such as lunch meats, canned vegetables, and soups, were made available in low-fat, low-sodium versions." Similarly, generalizations about "light meals" and "all-natural products" gained life through the addition of concrete examples: restaurants lured "customers with salad bars, broiled fish, and steamed vegetables," and the food industry produced "everything from potato chips to ice cream— without additives and preservatives."

Carl did an equally good job revising other sections of his paper. With the exception of the weak spots already discussed, he made the changes needed to craft a well-reasoned essay, one that demonstrates his ability to analyze a complex phenomenon.

The selections in this chapter analyze a range of cause-effect relationships. In "The Faltering Family," George Gallup, Jr., studies why the American family is changing and makes some disturbing projections about future changes. Geoffrey Cowley's "Why a Disaster Brings Out the Best in People" tracks down explanations for human altruism. With poignancy, Alice Walker traces, in "Beauty: When the Other Dancer Is the Self," the impact on her life of a disfiguring eye injury. Lewis Thomas examines why "The Lie Detector" works as it does and comes away encouraged by what he learns about human nature. Finally, Jonathan Kozol asks the question "Are the Homeless Crazy?" and arrives at an answer that doesn't leave much room for optimism.

George Gallup, Jr.

Born in Illinois in 1930, George Gallup, Jr., is president of the Gallup Poll, the well-known research firm that measures public opinion. Gallup resides in Princeton, New Jersey, where he graduated from the University, and has served as executive director of the Princeton Religion Research Center. He has published articles about religion, politics, and other current issues. His books include *America's Search for Faith* (1980), with David Poling; *My Kid on Drugs?* (1981), with Art Linkletter; and *Adventures in Immortality* (1982) and *Forecast 2000* (1985), both with William Proctor. The following essay is from *Forecast 2000*.

The Faltering Family

For better or worse, the American family—one of the nation's fundamental cornerstones—has changed in response to a variety of cultural forces. Based on the results of several national opinion polls, the following selection presents George Gallup's conclusions about the future of the family. According to Gallup, if current trends continue, the traditional family will fade into a mere memory.

In a recent Sunday school class in a United Methodist Church   1
in the Northeast, a group of eight- to ten-year-olds were in a deep discussion with their two teachers. When asked to choose which of ten stated possibilities they most feared happening, their response was unanimous. All the children most dreaded a divorce between their parents.

Later, as the teachers, a man and a woman in their late thirties,   2
reflected on the lesson, they both agreed they'd been shocked at the response. When they were the same age as their students, they said, the possibility of their parents' being divorced never entered their heads. Yet in just one generation, children seemed to feel much less security in their family ties.

Nor is the experience of these two Sunday school teachers an   3
isolated one. Psychiatrists revealed in one recent newspaper investigation that the fears of children definitely do change in different periods; and in recent times, divorce has become one of the most
frequently mentioned anxieties. In one case, for example, a four-
year-old insisted that his father rather than his mother walk him to
nursery school each day. The reason? He said many of his friends had
"no daddy living at home, and I'm scared that will happen to me"
(New York Times, May 2, 1983).

In line with such reports, our opinion leaders expressed great   4
concern about the present and future status of the American family.
In the poll 33 percent of the responses listed decline in family structure, divorce, and other family-oriented concerns as one of the five
major problems facing the nation today. And 26 percent of the responses included such family difficulties as one of the five major
problems for the United States in the year 2000.

Historical and sociological trends add strong support to these   5
expressions of concern. For example, today about one marriage in
every two ends in divorce. Moreover, the situation seems to be getting worse, rather than better. In 1962, the number of divorces was
2.2 per 1,000 people, according to the National Center for Health
Statistics. By 1982, the figure had jumped to 5.1 divorces per 1,000
people—a rate that had more than doubled in two decades.

One common concern expressed about the rise in divorces and   6
decline in stability of the family is that the family unit has traditionally
been a key factor in transmitting stable cultural and moral values
from generation to generation. Various studies have shown that educational and religious institutions often can have only a limited impact on children without strong family support.

Even grandparents are contributing to the divorce statistics.   7
One recent study revealed that about 100,000 people over the age
of fifty-five get divorced in the United States each year. These divorces are usually initiated by men who face retirement, and the relationships being ended are those that have endured for thirty years
or more (*New York Times Magazine,* December 19, 1982).

What are the pressures that have emerged in the past twenty   8
years that cause long-standing family bonds to be broken?

Many now agree that the sexual revolution of the 1960s worked   9
a profound change on our society's family values and personal relationships. Certainly, the seeds of upheaval were present before that

critical decade. But a major change that occurred in the mid-sixties was an explicit widespread rejection of the common values about sexual and family relationships that most Americans in the past had held up as an ideal.

We're just beginning to sort through all the changes in social   10
standards that have occurred. Here are some of the major pressures that have contributed to those changes:

Pressure One: Alternative Lifestyles

Twenty years ago, the typical American family was depicted as a   11
man and woman who were married to each other and who produced children (usually two) and lived happily ever after. This was the pattern that young people expected to follow in order to become "full" or "normal" members of society. Of course, some people have always chosen a different route—remaining single, taking many partners, or living with a member of their own sex. But they were always considered somewhat odd, and outside the social order of the traditional family.

In the last two decades, this picture has changed dramatically.   12
In addition to the proliferation of single people through divorce, we also have these developments:

- Gay men and women have petitioned the courts for the right   13
  to marry each other and to adopt children. These demands
  are being given serious consideration, and there may even be
  a trend of sorts in this direction. For example, the National
  Association of Social Workers is increasingly supporting full
  adoption rights for gay people *(New York Times,* January 10,
  1983).
- Many heterosexual single adults have been permitted to   14
  adopt children and set up single-parent families. So being un-
  attached no longer excludes people from the joys of parenthood.
- Some women have deliberately chosen to bear children out of   15
  wedlock and raise them alone. In the past, many of these children would have been given up for adoption, but no longer.
      A most unusual case involved an unmarried psycholo-   16
  gist, Dr. Afton Blake, who recently gave birth after being artificially inseminated with sperm from a sperm bank to which

Nobel Prize winners had contributed *(New York Times,* September 6, 1983).

• In a recent Gallup Youth Poll, 64 percent of the teenagers   17
questioned said that they hoped their lives would be different
from those of their parents. This included having more money, pursuing a different kind of profession, living in a different
area, having more free time—and staying single longer.

   Most surveys show increasing numbers of unmarried   18
couples living together. Also, there are periodic reports of experiments in communal living, "open marriages," and other
such arrangements. Although the more radical approaches to
relationships tend to come and go and never seem to attract
large numbers of people, the practice of living together without getting married seems to be something that's here to
stay. The law is beginning to respond to these arrangements
with awards for "palimony"— compensation for long-term
unmarried partners in a relationship. But the legal and social
status of unmarried people who live together is still quite uncertain—especially as far as any children of the union are concerned.

• Increasing numbers of married couples are choosing to re-   19
main childless. Planned Parenthood has even established
workshops for couples to assist them in making this decision
(Los Angeles Herald-Examiner, November 27, 1979).

So clearly, a situation has arisen during the last twenty years in   20
which traditional values are no longer as important. Also, a wide variety of alternatives to the traditional family have arisen. Individuals
may feel that old-fashioned marriage is just one of many options.

Pressure Two: Sexual Morality

Attitudes toward sexual morality have changed as dramatically   21
in the last two decades as have the alternatives to traditional marriage. Hear what a widely used college textbook, published in 1953,
said about premarital sex:

The arguments against premarital coitus outweigh those in its   22
favor. Except for the matter of temporary physical pleasure, all
arguments about gains tend to be highly theoretical, while the

risks and unpleasant consequences tend to be in equal degree highly practical. . . .

The promiscuity of young men is certainly poor prepara-   23
tion for marital fidelity and successful family life. For girls it is certainly no better and sometimes leads still further to the physical and psychological shock of abortion or the more prolonged suffering of bearing an illegitimate child and giving it up to others. From the viewpoint of ethical and religious leaders, the spread of disease through unrestrained sex activities is far more than a health problem. They see it as undermining the dependable standards of character and the spiritual values that raise life to the level of the "good society."

(This comes from *Marriage and the Family* by Professor Ray E. Baber of Pomona College, California, which was part of the McGraw-Hill Series in Sociology and Anthropology and required reading for some college courses.)

Clearly, attitudes have changed a great deal in just three de-   24
cades. Teenagers have accepted the idea of premarital sex as the norm. In one recent national poll, 52 percent of girls and 66 percent of boys favored having sexual relations in their teens. Ironically, however, 46 percent of the teenagers thought that virginity in their future marital partner was fairly important. Youngsters, in other words, display some confusion about what they want to do sexually, and what they expect from a future mate.

But of course, only part of the problem of defining sexual stan-   25
dards lies with young people and premarital sex. The strong emphasis on achieving an active and rewarding sex life has probably played some role in encouraging many husbands and wives into rejecting monogamy. Here's some of the evidence that's been accumulating:

- Half of the men in a recent nationwide study admitted cheat-   26
  ing on their wives *(Pensacola Journal,* May 30, 1978).
- Psychiatrists today say they see more patients who are thinking   27
  about having an extramarital affair and who wonder if it would harm their marriage *(New York Post,* November 18, 1976).
- A psychiatrist at the Albert Einstein College of Medicine says,   28
  "In my practice I have been particularly struck by how many women have been able to use an affair to raise their consciousness and their confidence."

So the desire for unrestrained sex now tends to take a place   29
among other more traditional priorities, and this can be expected to
continue to exert strong pressure on marriage relationships.

Pressure Three: The Economy

The number of married women working outside the home has   30
been increasing steadily, and most of these women are working out
of economic necessity. As a result, neither spouse may have time
to concentrate on the nurturing of the children or of the marriage
relationship.

One mother we interviewed in New Jersey told us about her   31
feelings when she was forced to work full time in a library after her
husband lost his job.

"It's the idea that I have no choice that really bothers me," she   32
said. "I have to work, or we won't eat or have a roof over our heads.
I didn't mind working part-time just to have extra money. I suppose
that it's selfish, but I hate having to work every day and then to come
home, fix dinner, and have to start doing housework. Both my husband and I were raised in traditional families, where the father went
to work and the mother stayed home and took care of the house and
children. [My husband] would never think of cooking or doing
housework. I've raised my boys the same way, and now I'm paying
for it. Sometimes, I almost hate my husband, even though I know
it's not his fault."

Unfortunately, such pressures probably won't ease in the future.   33
Even if the economy improves and the number of unemployed workers decreases, few women are likely to give up their jobs. Economists
agree that working-class women who have become breadwinners
during a recession can be expected to remain in the work force. One
reason is that many unemployed men aren't going to get their old
jobs back, even when the economy improves.

"To the extent that [the men] may have to take lower-paying   34
service jobs, their families will need a second income," says Michelle
Brandman, associate economist at Chase Econometrics. "The trend
to two-paycheck families as a means of maintaining family income is
going to continue" *(Wall Street Journal,* December 8, 1982).

In addition to the pressures of unemployment, the cost of hav-   35
ing, rearing, and educating children is steadily going up. Researchers
have found that middle-class families with two children *think* they're

spending only about 15 percent of their income on their children. Usually, though, they *actually* spend about 40 percent of their money on them. To put the cost in dollars and cents, if you had a baby in 1977, the estimated cost of raising that child to the age of eighteen will be $85,000, and that figure has of course been on the rise for babies born since then *(New York Daily News,* July 24, 1977).

Another important factor that promises to keep both spouses   36
working full time in the future is the attitude of today's teenagers toward these issues. They're not so much concerned about global issues like overpopulation as they are about the high cost of living. Both boys and girls place a lot of emphasis on having enough money so that they can go out and do things. Consequently, most teenage girls surveyed say they expect to pursue careers, even after they get married.

So it would seem that by the year 2000 we can expect to see   37
more working mothers in the United States. The woman who doesn't hold down any sort of outside job but stays at home to care for her children represents a small percentage of wives today. By the end of the century, with a few exceptions here and there, she may well have become a part of America's quaint past.

As women have joined the work force in response to economic   38
needs, one result has been increased emotional strains on the marriage and family relationships. But there's another set of pressures that has encouraged women to pursue careers. That's the power of feminist philosophy to permeate attitudes in grassroots America during the past couple of decades.

Pressure Four: Grassroots Feminist Philosophy

Many women may not agree with the most radical expressions   39
of feminist philosophy that have arisen in the past decade or so. But most younger women—and indeed, a majority of women in the United States—tend to agree with most of the objectives that even the radical feminist groups have been trying to achieve. The basic feminist philosophy has filtered down to the grass roots, and young boys and girls are growing up with feminist assumptions that may have been foreign to their parents and grandparents.

For example, child care and housework are no longer regarded   40
strictly as "women's work" by the young people we've polled. Also, according to the Gallup Youth Poll, most teenage girls want to go to

college and pursue a career. Moreover, they expect to marry later in life and to continue working after they're married. Another poll, conducted by the *New York Times* and CBS News, revealed that only 2 percent of the youngest age group interviewed—that is, those eighteen to twenty-nine years old—preferred "traditional marriage." By this, they meant a marriage in which the husband is exclusively a provider and the wife is exclusively a homemaker and mother.

If these young people continue to hold views similar to these   41
into later life, it's likely that the changes that are occurring today in the traditional family structure will continue. For one thing, more day-care centers for children will have to be established. Consequently, the rearing of children will no longer be regarded as solely the responsibility of the family, but will become a community or institutional responsibility.

But while such developments may lessen the strain on mothers   42
and fathers, they may also weaken the bonds that hold families together. Among other things, it may become psychologically easier to get a divorce if a person is not getting along with a spouse, because the divorcing spouses will believe it's less likely that the lives of the children will be disrupted.

So the concept of broadening the rights of women vis-à-vis their   43
husbands and families has certainly encouraged women to enter the working world in greater numbers. They're also more inclined to seek a personal identity that isn't tied up so much in their homelife.

These grassroots feminist forces have brought greater benefits   44
to many, but at the same time they've often worked against traditional family ties, and we remain uncertain about what is going to replace them. Feminists may argue that the traditional family caused its own demise—or else why would supposedly content wives and daughters have worked so hard to transform it? Whatever its theories, though, feminism is still a factor that, in its present form, appears to exert a destabilizing influence on many traditional familial relationships among husbands, wives, and children.

As things stand now, our family lives are in a state of flux and   45
will probably continue to be out of balance until the year 2000. The pressures we've discussed will continue to have an impact on our family lives in future years. But at the same time, counterforces, which tend to drive families back together again, are also at work.

One of these factors is a traditionalist strain in the large majority   46
of American women. The vast majority of women in this country—
74 percent—continue to view marriage with children as the most interesting and satisfying life for them personally, according to a Gallup
Poll for the White House Conference on Families released in June,
1980.

Another force supporting family life is the attitude of American   47
teenagers toward divorce. According to a recent Gallup Youth Poll,
55 percent feel that divorces are too easy to get today. Also, they're
concerned about the high rate of divorce, and they want to have en-
during marriages themselves. But at the same time—in a response
that reflects the confusion of many adult Americans on this subject—
67 percent of the teens in this same poll say it's right to get a divorce
if a couple doesn't get along together. In other words, they place little importance on trying to improve or salvage a relationship that has
run into serious trouble.

There's a similar ambivalence in the experts we polled. As we've   48
seen, 33 percent of them consider family problems as a top concern
today, and 26 percent think these problems will be a big difficulty in
the year 2000. But ironically, less than 3 percent suggest that
strengthening family relationships is an important consideration in
planning for the future! It's obvious, then, that we're confused and
ambivalent in our feelings about marriage and the family. Most people know instinctively, without having to read a poll or a book, that
happiness and satisfaction in life are rooted largely in the quality of
our personal relationships. Furthermore, the most important of those
relationships usually begin at home. So one of the greatest challenges
we face before the year 2000, both as a nation and as individuals, is
how to make our all-important family ties strong and healthy. It's
only upon such a firm personal foundation that we can hope to venture forth and grapple effectively with more public problems.

Questions for Close Reading

1. What is the selection's thesis? Locate the sentence(s) in which Gallup
   states his main idea. If he doesn't state the thesis explicitly, express it in
   your own words.
2. According to Gallup, what are the major pressures that have caused the
   change in American attitudes toward marriage and family?

3. What new styles of pairing up and parenting have entered the American mainstream and now compete with traditional marriage?
4. Why are more and more women choosing to work outside the home? Why does the author believe that this is a permanent lifestyle change for American women?
5. Refer to your dictionary as needed to define the following words in the selection: *explicit* (paragraph 9), *proliferation* (12), *inseminated* (16), *salvage* (47), and *ambivalence* (48).

Questions About the Writer's Craft

1. **The pattern.** In this selection, Gallup tries to account for changes in the American ideals of marriage and family. Why do you think he uses the term *pressures* rather than *causes?*
2. What techniques does Gallup use to introduce the selection? What feeling toward marriage and family does this introduction create in you? How is the introduction related to the data presented in the selection?
3. Examine the supporting evidence for each "pressure." For which ones does Gallup provide facts or statistics? What kinds of evidence does he provide for the other pressures?
4. How does Gallup create a sense of objectivity? Which word choices suggest his personal opinions about the transformation in American family values?

Questions for Further Thought

1. Gallup believes that changing gender roles have helped undermine the traditional family structure. Do you think his assessment is fair? Why or why not?
2. Gallup's statement that "one marriage in two ends in divorce" suggests that 50 percent of the country's marriages dissolve. But the statistics mean that, in a given year, the number of divorces is equal to half the number of new marriages—*not* to the total number of marriages in the country. Can you find other places where Gallup's statistics are open to misinterpretation (for example, look closely at paragraph 4)? How do these instances affect your view of Gallup's causal analysis?
3. Does the media's depiction of family life reflect changes in American culture, or does the depiction help bring about those changes? Explain.
4. How widespread are the alternative lifestyles in the lives of people you know and go to school with?

Writing Assignments Using Cause-Effect as a Pattern of Development

1. Writing in 1985, Gallup places much of the blame for the family's decline on women. He ignores, however, a number of personal and social factors

that add stress to family life: Substance abuse, mental illness, homelessness, and industry's failure to provide day-care services to employees with young children are just some of the factors that come to mind. Select *one* of these factors, or another that seems important to you, and write an essay analyzing its effect on the family.

2. Write an essay explaining how people are affected when those close to them choose an alternative lifestyle. For example, think of someone you know who has chosen divorce, single parenthood, cohabitation, or some other nontraditional way of life. Decide what positive and/or negative effects resulted from this choice, and discuss these effects in your essay. You may wish to evaluate the choice on the basis of how it turned out, but avoid generalizing from one case to universal rules of behavior.

Writing Assignments Using Other Patterns of Development

3. When a family breaks apart, many lives are disrupted. Parents, children, grandparents, other relatives, friends, even neighbors must cope with disorder and confusion. Choose one of these groups and write an essay illustrating the kinds of turmoil that the group may face. Develop the paper by drawing on your own and/or other people's experience. Include some brief recommendations about how the group might cope with the situation.

4. To what extent, and in what light, do alternative lifestyles (extramarital affairs, divorce, single parenthood, and so on) appear in the plots of television sitcoms and dramas? To get some idea, watch TV for a week and take notes. Write up your findings in the form of a letter to *TV Guide*, either criticizing or praising the TV networks for the way they present one or two such life-styles. Support your argument with specific references to the shows you viewed.

Geoffrey Cowley

Following stints at the *Seattle Times* and the *Seattle Weekly,* Geoffrey Cowley joined *Newsweek* in 1988. His writings have focused on scientific and intellectual trends, leading to stories on cognition, evolutionary psychology, and animal rights. In 1990, Cowley was named *Newsweek's* editor for health and medicine, the position he holds today. Several of Cowley's medical reports for *Newsweek* have prompted action by the medical community and regulatory agencies. Cowley was born in 1955 and raised in Salt Lake City. A graduate of Lewis & Clark College in Portland, Oregon, he received a master's degree in English from the University of Washington in Seattle. Since the 1989 publication of the following piece in *Newsweek,* Cowley has continued his exploration of altruism. He is interested in research suggesting that morality is not a human cultural invention but part of our biological heritage as primates.

Why a Disaster Brings Out the Best in People

There have been well-publicized incidents in which bystanders refuse to assist someone in desperate need. Hearing of such incidents, we shake our heads and wonder at the selfishness of human beings. But there is another side to human nature. Friends, neighbors, and even strangers assist one another every day, usually without the prospect of a tangible reward. Under extraordinary circumstances, such altruistic behavior often reaches dramatic heights. In his essay, Geoffrey Cowley explores possible explanations for human behavior at its best.

When Dr. James Betts crawled into the smoking ruins of Oakland's collapsed Nimitz Freeway, he had no grounds for assuming he would come out alive. The Bay Area earthquake had slammed the upper span of the two-deck highway onto the lower one, crushing dozens of cars. What remained of the ruined structure was teetering in the aftershocks. Undeterred, Betts and several others inched through the narrow gap to reach 6-year-old Julio Berumen, who lay trapped by the corpse of his mother's friend. The rescue took several hours and involved not only dismembering the corpse with a chain saw but amputating the child's right leg at the knee. Yet Betts insists he never thought twice about going in or staying there.

Nor, it seems, did the scores of bystanders and uniformed rescue   2
workers who combed through collapsed structures seeking signs of life. Nor the Oakland residents who rushed to the freeway to prop it up with makeshift supports. Every human disaster seems to create heroes along with its victims. Their courage sometimes appears more glandular than intentional ("I just did what I had to do," 28-year-old Lenny Skutnik explained after diving into an ice-strewn Potomac River to rescue a drowning plane-crash victim in 1982). But even the most prolonged nightmares spawn astonishing acts of benevolence. A Dutch civilian named Miep Gies risked her life daily for more than two years to feed and shelter the Frank family[1] during the Nazi Holocaust. The 3,000 peasants of Le Chambon, a Huguenot[2] village in south-central France, took similar risks to help Jewish refugees flee the occupation.

Maybe Adam Smith[3] had it right when he remarked that "there   3
seem to be principles in man's nature which interest him in the fortunes of others, and render their happiness necessary to him." But what are those principles? What drives human beings to risk so much for one another? Social scientists think a lot about such questions. Their approaches to human altruism, even their definitions of it, are often disparate, and their findings sometimes raise more questions than they answer. No one can fully explain what propels individuals toward particular acts of bravery. But the research provides a broad framework within which an "interest in the fortunes of others" begins to make sense.

Samuel and Pearl Oliner are concerned specifically with the be-   4
neficence of gentiles who sheltered Jews in Nazi Europe. For their 1988 book *The Altruistic Personality*, the two social scientists in-

---

[1]Anne Frank, a young Jewish girl, kept a journal during the years she and her family hid in an attic to escape the Nazis. Years after she was killed in a Nazi death camp, her journal was published as *The Diary of a Young Girl.*

[2]French Protestant.

[3]Eighteenth-century British economist and author of *The Wealth of Nations.*

terviewed several hundred rescuers and compared their testimony to that of "nonrescuers." The rescuers, they found, were more likely to recall having Jewish co-workers, belonging to a Resistance group or having parents who stressed the value of caring for others. So the Oliners conclude that altruism is fueled by "empathy, allegiance to their group or institutional norms, or commitment to principle."

Fine, but what actually motivates people to act on their empathy   5
or allegiances or principles? Social psychologists have developed at least three competing hypotheses. According to the "empathy altruism" model, altruists have no motive beyond the welfare of the person in need. By contrast, the "negative-state relief" model holds that seeing someone in distress causes sadness. Getting involved serves to relieve the sadness, even if it does nothing for the recipient. Finally there's the "empathic joy" hypothesis. Like the sadness-relief model, it assumes that altruistic acts serve to enhance one's own state of mind. But according to this theory, the psychic payoff lies not in trying to help but in witnessing the effect.

Larger riddle: The third model got a boost recently, from an   6
experiment conducted at the University of Washington. Researchers had students watch a taped interview in which a freshman describes her trouble adjusting to college life. Each subject got a chance to tape some words of advice for the distraught student. But they tended to offer help only when assured that she would make another tape, describing the effect of the advice. (According to the other two theories, such feedback shouldn't have mattered.) So perhaps empathetic people act altruistically because they like to see the results. But that raises the question of why seeing the results is so gratifying.

Evolutionary biologists approach that larger riddle from the   7
premise that basic human preferences, like those of other animals, have been shaped over the centuries by the dictates of survival. Contrary to popular belief, Darwinian survival is not a purely competitive struggle among individuals. It consists of *genetic* survival, which can entail *individual* sacrifice. Evolutionary theory says nothing about why some people are more inclined to sacrifice than others. But it does help explain our shared capacity for moral heroism. To understand how, you have to start with what it says about cooperation generally.

From an evolutionary perspective, you would expect to find   8
people charitably inclined toward their kids and other genetic relatives: when kin tend to one another's survival, they tend to their own. Evolutionary theory predicts altruism among non-relatives,

too, as long as they have a fair expectation of being repaid. A monkey would further its own survival interest by picking ticks from a companion's back if the companion returned the favor.

Computer models can show how such reciprocal altruism might   9
arise within populations of genetically self-interested individuals. Game theorists start by placing imaginary characters in a situation known as a prisoner's dilemma. Suppose that Jack and Mack are hunter-gatherers. Jack picks berries and Mack kills rabbits. Obviously, both will eat a little better if they share their food. And one may win big if he takes from the other without giving in return. But if both try that trick, neither gains anything.

To see how creatures predisposed to cooperation (C) or defec-   10
tion (D) would fare in a given population, you simply program a computer to spit out strings of Cs and Ds on behalf of generations of Macks and Jacks. The indiscriminate altruists (all C) thrive as long as they're surrounded by others of their kind, but they make easy targets for defectors. Indeed, defectors spread like vermin in a population of these forgiving souls. But once the uncritical altruists are gone, the defectors die out themselves, for lack of anyone to prey on. The most stable strategy is that of the *reciprocal* altruists. Because they're never first to defect, they reap all the rewards of cooperation. But because they play tit-for-tat as soon as they're burned, they're well protected from defectors.

Reciprocity obviously permeates human relationships, bearing   11
on everything from wedding vows to arms control and dinner invitations. But does it shed any light on acts of moral heroism? Would natural selection preserve a tendency to risk one's life for strangers who are unlikely ever to return the favor? Yes and yes, according to Richard Alexander, an evolutionary biologist at the University of Michigan. Reciprocity can take many different forms, he notes in his book *The Biology of Moral Systems*. Helping a stranger might bring status, or even material rewards from others in society. Consider the case of Mark Smith, the Bay Area resident who won a $15,000 sports car in a radio contest but donated it to the Red Cross earthquake fund. Not only did he become an instant folk hero—the radio station matched his gift and gave him another car. Dead heroes don't drive sports cars. But as Alexander observes, their sacrifices can still pay off for their relatives. In many societies, there is a difference between being "a member of the family of a dead hero and being a member of the family of a living [or dead] coward."

Ancient impulses: John Tooby, an anthropologist at Stanford's   12
Center for Advanced Study in the Behavioral Sciences, places a
slightly different twist on the riddle of the hero. The question isn't
whether a heroic impulse pays off in a modern setting, he says, but
how it might have paid off in an ancestral one. Homo sapiens evolved
in small hunter-gatherer bands, not in anonymous cities. There was
no such thing as a stranger. Averting death by starvation, predation
and sickness was the business of daily life, and each group member
depended on the others. In evolutionary terms, individuals were under "selective pressure" to increase the likelihood of being rescued.
By the logic of reciprocal altruism, those perceived as the best and
most loyal rescuers would have stood the greatest chance.

It's only logical, by Tooby's analysis, that we should retain "a   13
spontaneous motivation to help people who are in deep trouble."
That the impulse evolved by the cold mechanics of natural selection
doesn't make it any less noble. Just ask Julio Berumen.

Questions for Close Reading

1. What is the selection's thesis? Locate the sentence(s) in which Cowley
   states his main idea. If he doesn't state the thesis explicitly, express it in
   your own words.
2. What theories have been offered as explanations of altruism? Which explanation, according to Cowley, seems the most likely?
3. How does Darwin's theory of evolution help explain human altruism?
4. In paragraphs 9 through 11, Cowley mentions a computer simulation.
   Why, according to the simulation, do reciprocal altruists form the most
   stable society?
5. Refer to your dictionary as needed to define the following words used in
   the selection: *undeterred* (paragraph 1), *spawn* (2), *altruism* (3), *disparate* (3), *beneficence* (4), *gentiles* (4), *empathy* (4), *allegiance* (4), *psychic*
   (5), *Darwinian* (7), *reciprocal* (9), *predisposed* (10), *defection* (10), *indiscriminate* (10), *averting* (12), and *predation* (12).

Questions About the Writer's Craft

1. **The pattern.**   In paragraph 3, Cowley asks, "What drives human beings
   to risk so much for one another?" He uses the rest of the essay to answer
   this question, showing that behind every answer lies another question.
   Trace the chain of questions and answers that Cowley uses to reveal the
   complex causes for the phenomenon of altruism.

2. Cowley presents a number of examples in the essay's first two paragraphs. Why do you suppose he presents so many examples from so many different locales? How do these examples help prepare the reader for what follows?

3. Throughout his essay, Cowley uses clear signaling devices to mark the progression of ideas. Consider paragraph 5, for example. What connecting devices there make the paragraph coherent and easy to follow?

4. In places, Cowley uses casual, colloquial phrasing—for example, he states in the third paragraph that "Adam Smith had it right." Find other examples in the essay of this conversational language. Why might he have chosen to use such a down-to-earth style when discussing complex theories about the sources of human heroism?

Questions for Further Thought

1. Have you ever been in an emergency situation requiring quick action? How did you react? If other people were involved, how did they react?

2. Think back to times you wanted to help someone but didn't. Consider, too, times you actually *did* intervene on someone else's behalf. In each case, what motivated your behavior?

3. Can you imagine a situation in which you would risk your life for someone else? Do you think you would put yourself at risk for a stranger? Explain.

4. Do you think most people are naturally helpful—or naturally selfish? Explain.

Writing Assignments Using Cause-Effect as a Pattern of Development

∞ 1. Think of an event that involved what Cowley calls "moral heroism." Perhaps someone put himself or herself in physical jeopardy, or bravely defied authority, or resisted conforming to group pressure. Write an essay in which you analyze the possible motives for the person's heroic action and describe the effect of the act on those involved. For insight into the more positive aspects of human nature, you might want to read Lewis Thomas's "The Lie Detector" (page 495) before preparing your paper.

∞ 2. Cowley describes times when people respond altruistically, but there are, of course, many situations when people do just the opposite. Brainstorm examples of such situations, both from your own experience and those you have heard about through the media, your reading, or friends and family. Then write an essay explaining why people avoid helping others; refer to specific situations to illustrate your points. George Orwell's "Shooting an Elephant" (page 172) and Mark Twain's "The Damned Human Race" (page 609) will provide some insight into this darker side of human nature.

Writing Assignments Using Other Patterns of Development

3. How could families, communities, schools, or religious organizations encourage altruism in children? Focus on *one* of these institutions, and talk to friends, classmates, and family members to gather insights and recommendations. Select the most compelling ideas, and write an essay explaining the steps that this particular institution could take to help develop children's more generous impulses. Develop your points with specific examples of what *could* be done and what *has* been done.

4. Some social critics argue that the anonymity of everyday American life has created a society of strangers—most of whom are unconcerned about others' well-being. Write an essay in which you argue against this view of America and show instead how kind and generous Americans can be. Acknowledge the opposing viewpoint near the beginning of the essay; then support your position with vivid examples drawn from your own and other people's experiences.

Alice Walker

The eighth child of Georgia sharecroppers, Alice Walker (1944–   ) has built a reputation as a sensitive chronicler of the black experience in America. After studying at Spelman College in Atlanta, Walker graduated from Sarah Lawrence College in New York. Soon after that, she worked in the civil rights movement helping to register black voters and teaching in Mississippi's Head Start program. The recipient of numerous writing fellowships and the founder of her own publishing company, Walker has written extensively: a biography, *Langston Hughes, American Poet* (1973); poetry, *Revolutionary Petunias and Other Poems* (1973); short stories, collected in *In Love & Trouble* (1973) and *You Can't Keep a Good Woman Down* (1981); essays, gathered in *Living by the Word* (1988); children's fiction, *To Hell with Dying* (1991); and novels for adults, including *Meridian* (1976), *The Color Purple* (1982), *The Temple of My Familiar* (1989), and *Possessing the Secret of Joy* (1992). *The Color Purple* won both the Pulitzer Prize and the American Book Award and was made into a feature film. The following selection comes from Walker's 1983 collection of essays, *In Search of Our Mothers' Gardens.*

Beauty: When the Other Dancer Is the Self

A disfiguring injury can seriously affect anyone's self-esteem. Alice Walker sustained such an injury as a child. In this essay, she describes what happened to her and provides glimpses of her Southern childhood and the people who changed her life for better or worse. Walker's experience is a commentary on the role of good looks in a young girl's life and on the importance of good sense in gaining self-acceptance and esteem as an adult.

It is a bright summer day in 1947. My father, a fat, funny man   1
with beautiful eyes and a subversive wit, is trying to decide which of
his eight children he will take with him to the county fair. My moth-

er, of course, will not go. She is knocked out from getting most of us ready: I hold my neck stiff against the pressure of her knuckles as she hastily completes the braiding and then beribboning of my hair.

My father is the driver for the rich old white lady up the road.   2
Her name is Miss Mey. She owns all the land for miles around, as well as the house in which we live. All I remember about her is that she once offered to pay my mother thirty-five cents for cleaning her house, raking up piles of her magnolia leaves, and washing her family's clothes, and that my mother—she of no money, eight children, and a chronic earache—refused it. But I do not think of this in 1947. I am two and a half years old. I want to go everywhere my daddy goes. I am excited at the prospect of riding in a car. Someone has told me fairs are fun. That there is room in the car for only three of us doesn't faze me at all. Whirling happily in my starchy frock, showing off my biscuit-polished patent-leather shoes and lavender socks, tossing my head in a way that makes my ribbons bounce, I stand, hands on hips, before my father. "Take me, Daddy," I say with assurance; "I'm the prettiest!"

Later, it does not surprise me to find myself in Miss Mey's shiny   3
black car, sharing the back seat with the other lucky ones. Does not surprise me that I thoroughly enjoy the fair. At home that night I tell the unlucky ones all I can remember about the merry-go-round, the man who eats live chickens, and the teddy bears, until they say: that's enough baby Alice. Shut up now, and go to sleep.

It is Easter Sunday, 1950. I am dressed in a green, flocked, scal-   4
loped-hem dress (handmade by my adoring sister, Ruth) that has its own smooth satin petticoat and tiny hot-pink roses tucked into each scallop. My shoes, new T-strap patent leather, again highly biscuit-polished. I am six years old and have learned one of the longest Easter speeches to be heard that day, totally unlike the speech I said when I was two: "Easter lilies / pure and white / blossom in / the morning light." When I rise to give my speech I do so on a great wave of love and pride and expectation. People in the church stop rustling their new crinolines. They seem to hold their breath. I can tell they admire my dress, but it is my spirit, bordering on sassiness (womanishness), they secretly applaud.

"That girl's a little *mess*," they whisper to each other, pleased.   5

Naturally I say my speech without stammer or pause, unlike   6
those who stutter, stammer, or, worst of all, forget. This is before the

word "beautiful" exists in people's vocabulary, but "Oh, isn't she the *cutest* thing?" frequently floats my way. "And got so much sense!" they gratefully add...for which thoughtful addition I thank them to this day.

It was great fun being cute. But then, one day, it ended.   7

I am eight years old and a tomboy. I have a cowboy hat, cowboy   8 boots, checkered shirt and pants, all red. My playmates are my brothers, two and four years older than I. Their colors are black and green, the only difference in the way we are dressed. On Saturday nights we all go to the picture show, even my mother; Westerns are her favorite kind of movie. Back home, "on the ranch," we pretend we are Tom Mix, Hopalong Cassidy, Lash LaRue (we've even named one of our dogs Lash LaRue); we chase each other for hours rustling cattle, being outlaws, delivering damsels from distress. Then my parents decide to buy my brothers guns. These are not "real" guns. They shoot "BBs," copper pellets my brothers say will kill birds. Because I am a girl, I do not get a gun. Instantly I am relegated to the position of Indian. Now there appears a great distance between us. They shoot and shoot at everything with their new guns. I try to keep up with my bow and arrows.

One day while I am standing on top of our makeshift "ga-   9 rage"—pieces of tin nailed across some poles—holding my bow and arrow and looking out toward the fields, I feel an incredible blow in my right eye. I look down just in time to see my brother lower his gun.

Both brothers rush to my side. My eye stings, and I cover it with   10 my hand. "If you tell," they say, "we will get a whipping. You don't want that to happen, do you?" I do not. "Here is a piece of wire," says the older brother, picking it up from the roof; "say you stepped on one end of it and the other flew up and hit you." The pain is beginning to start. "Yes," I say. "Yes, I will say that is what happened." If I do not say this is what happened, I know my brothers will find ways to make me wish I had. But now I will say anything that gets me to my mother.

Confronted by our parents we stick to the lie agreed upon. They   11 place me on a bench on the porch and I close my left eye while they examine the right. There is a tree growing from underneath the porch that climbs past the railing to the roof. It is the last thing my right eye sees. I watch as its trunk, its branches, and then its leaves are blotted out by the rising blood.

I am in shock. First there is intense fever, which my father tries   12
to break using lily leaves bound around my head. Then there are
chills: my mother tries to get me to eat soup. Eventually, I do not
know how, my parents learn what has happened. A week after the
"accident" they take me to see a doctor. "Why did you wait so long
to come?" he asks, looking into my eye and shaking his head. "Eyes
are sympathetic," he says. "If one is blind, the other will likely become blind too."

This comment of the doctor's terrifies me. But it is really how I   13
look that bothers me most. Where the BB pellet struck there is a glob
of whitish scar tissue, a hideous cataract, on my eye. Now when I
stare at people—a favorite pastime, up to now—they will stare back.
Not at the "cute" little girl, but at her scar. For six years I do not stare
at anyone, because I do not raise my head.

Years later, in the throes of a mid-life crisis, I ask my mother and   14
sister whether I changed after the "accident." "No," they say, puzzled. "What do you mean?"

What do I mean?   15

I am eight, and, for the first time, doing poorly in school, where   16
I have been something of a whiz since I was four. We have just
moved to the place where the "accident" occurred. We do not know
any of the people around us because this is a different county. The
only time I see the friends I knew is when we go back to our old
church. The new school is the former state penitentiary. It is a large
stone building, cold and drafty, crammed to overflowing with boisterous, ill-disciplined children. On the third floor there is a huge circular imprint of some partition that has been torn out.

"What used to be here?" I ask a sullen girl next to me on our   17
way past it to lunch.

"The electric chair," says she.   18

At night I have nightmares about the electric chair; and about   19
all the people reputedly "fried" in it. I am afraid of the school, where
all the students seem to be budding criminals.

"What's the matter with your eye?" they ask, critically.   20

When I don't answer (I cannot decide whether it was an "acci-   21
dent" or not), they shove me, insist on a fight.

My brother, the one who created the story about the wire,   22
comes to my rescue. But then brags so much about "protecting" me,
I become sick.

After months of torture at the school, my parents decide to send   23
me back to our old community, to my old school. I live with my
grandparents and the teacher they board. But there is no room for
Phoebe, my cat. By the time my grandparents decide there *is* room,
and I ask for my cat, she cannot be found. Miss Yarborough, the
boarding teacher, takes me under her wing, and begins to teach me
to play the piano. But soon she marries an African— a "prince," she
says—and is whisked away to his continent.

At my old school there is at least one teacher who loves me. She   24
is the teacher who "knew me before I was born" and bought my first
baby clothes. It is she who makes life bearable. It is her presence that
finally helps me turn on the one child at the school who continually
calls me "one-eyed bitch." One day I simply grab him by his coat and
beat him until I am satisfied. It is my teacher who tells me my mother
is ill.

My mother is lying in bed in the middle of the day, something   25
I have never seen. She is in too much pain to speak. She has an abscess in her ear. I stand looking down on her, knowing that if she
dies, I cannot live. She is being treated with warm oils and hot bricks
held against her cheeks. Finally a doctor comes. But I must go back
to my grandparents' house. The weeks pass but I am hardly aware of
it. All I know is that my mother might die, my father is not so jolly,
my brothers still have their guns, and I am the one sent away from
home.

"You did not change," they say.   26

Did I imagine the anguish of never looking up?   27

I am twelve. When relatives come to visit I hide in my room. My   28
cousin Brenda, just my age, whose father works in the post office and
whose mother is a nurse, comes to find me. "Hello," she says. And
then she asks, looking at my recent school picture, which I did not
want taken, and on which the "glob," as I think of it, is clearly visible,
"You still can't see out of that eye?"

"No," I say, and flop back on the bed over my book.   29

That night, as I do almost every night, I abuse my eye. I rant and   30
rave at it, in front of the mirror. I plead with it to clear up before
morning. I tell it I hate and despise it. I do not pray for sight. I pray
for beauty.

"You did not change," they say.   31

I am fourteen and baby-sitting for my brother Bill, who lives in   32
Boston. He is my favorite brother and there is a strong bond between
us. Understanding my feelings of shame and ugliness he and his wife
take me to a local hospital, where the "glob" is removed by a doctor
named O. Henry. There is still a small bluish crater where the scar
tissue was, but the ugly white stuff is gone. Almost immediately I become a different person from the girl who does not raise her head.
Or so I think. Now that I've raised my head I win the boyfriend of
my dreams. Now that I've raised my head I have plenty of friends.
Now that I've raised my head classwork comes from my lips as fault-
lessly as Easter speeches did, and I leave high school as valedictorian,
most popular student, and *queen,* hardly believing my luck. Ironically, the girl who was voted most beautiful in our class (and was) was
later shot twice through the chest by a male companion, using a
"real" gun, while she was pregnant. But that's another story in itself.
Or is it?

"You did not change," they say.   33

It is now thirty years since the "accident." A beautiful journalist   34
comes to visit and to interview me. She is going to write a cover story
for her magazine that focuses on my latest book. "Decide how you
want to look on the cover," she says. "Glamorous, or whatever."

Never mind "glamorous," it is the "whatever" that I hear. Sud-   35
denly all I can think of is whether I will get enough sleep the night
before the photography session: if I don't, my eye will be tired and
wander, as blind eyes will.

At night in bed with my lover I think up reasons why I should   36
not appear on the cover of a magazine. "My meanest critics will say
I've sold out," I say. "My family will now realize I write scandalous
books."

"But what's the real reason you don't want to do this?" he asks.   37

"Because in all probability," I say in a rush, "my eye won't be   38
straight."

"It will be straight enough," he says. Then, "Besides, I thought   39
you'd made your peace with that."

And I suddenly remember that I have.   40

I remember: 41

I am talking to my brother Jimmy, asking if he remembers any-   42
thing unusual about the day I was shot. He does not know I consider
that day the last time my father, with his sweet home remedy of cool
lily leaves, chose me, and that I suffered and raged inside because of

this. "Well," he says, "all I remember is standing by the side of the highway with Daddy, trying to flag down a car. A white man stopped, but when Daddy said he needed somebody to take his little girl to the doctor, he drove off."

I remember: 43

I am in the desert for the first time. I fall totally in love with it.   44
I am so overwhelmed by its beauty, I confront for the first time, consciously, the meaning of the doctor's words years ago: "Eyes are sympathetic. If one is blind, the other will likely become blind too." I realize I have dashed about the world madly, looking at this, looking at that, storing up images against the fading of the light. *But I might have missed seeing the desert!* The shock of that possibility—and gratitude for over twenty-five years of sight—sends me literally to my knees. Poem after poem comes—which is perhaps how poets pray.

On Sight   45

> *I am so thankful I have seen*
> *The Desert*
> *And the creatures in the desert*
> *And the desert Itself.*
>
> *The desert has its own moon*
> *Which I have seen*
> *With my own eye.*
> *There is no flag on it.*
>
> *Trees of the desert have arms*
> *All of which are always up*
> *That is because the moon is up*
> *The sun is up*
> *Also the sky*
> *The stars*
> *Clouds*
> *None with flags.*
>
> *If there* were *flags, I doubt*
> *the trees would point.*
> *Would you?*

But mostly, I remember this: 46
I am twenty-seven, and my baby daughter is almost three. Since   47
her birth I have worried about her discovery that her mother's eyes

are different from other people's. Will she be embarrassed? I think. What will she say? Every day she watches a television program called "Big Blue Marble." It begins with a picture of the earth as it appears from the moon. It is bluish, a little battered-looking, but full of light, with whitish clouds swirling around it. Every time I see it I weep with love, as if it is a picture of Grandma's house. One day when I am putting Rebecca down for her nap, she suddenly focuses on my eye. Something inside me cringes, gets ready to try to protect myself. All children are cruel about physical differences, I know from experience, and that they don't always mean to be is another matter. I assume Rebecca will be the same.

But no-o-o-o. She studies my face intently as we stand, her inside and me outside the crib. She even holds my face maternally between her dimpled little hands. Then, looking every bit as serious and lawyerlike as her father, she says, as if it may just possibly have slipped my attention: "Mommy, there's a *world* in your eye." (As in, "Don't be alarmed, or do anything crazy.") And then, gently, but with great interest: "Mommy, where did you *get* that world in your eye?"   48

For the most part, the pain left then. (So what, if my brothers grew up to buy even more powerful pellet guns for their sons and to carry real guns themselves. So what, if a young "Morehouse man" once nearly fell off the steps of Trevor Arnett Library because he thought my eyes were blue.) Crying and laughing I ran to the bathroom, while Rebecca mumbled and sang herself off to sleep. Yes indeed, I realized, looking into the mirror. There *was* a world in my eye. And I saw that it was possible to love it: that in fact, for all it had taught me of shame and anger and inner vision, I *did* love it. Even to see it drifting out of orbit in boredom, or rolling up out of fatigue, not to mention floating back at attention in excitement (bearing witness, a friend has called it), deeply suitable to my personality, and even characteristic of me.   49

That night I dream I am dancing to Stevie Wonder's song "Always" (the name of the song is really "As," but I hear it as "Always"). As I dance, whirling and joyous, happier than I've ever been in my life, another bright-faced dancer joins me. We dance and kiss each other and hold each other through the night. The other dancer has obviously come through all right, as I have done. She is beautiful, whole and free. And she is also me.   50

Questions for Close Reading

1. What is the selection's thesis? Locate the sentence(s) in which Walker states her main idea. If she doesn't state the thesis explicitly, express it in your own words.
2. How does Walker's injury affect her ability to express herself and relate to others?
3. What is the connection between the loss of young Alice's cat and her teacher's marriage (paragraph 23)?
4. How do you interpret the essay's title—"Beauty: When the Other Dancer Is the Self"? How does the title reinforce Walker's thesis?
5. Refer to your dictionary as needed to define the following words used in the selection: *subversive* (paragraph 1), *chronic* (2), *flocked* (4), *crinoline* (4), *cataract* (13), and *abscess* (25).

Questions About the Writer's Craft

1. **The pattern.**   Walker's essay is structured around a causal chain that shows the interaction between the external and the internal. Explain how Walker develops this chain throughout the essay.
2. **Other patterns.**   Although Walker narrates incidents occurring from infancy to midlife, she writes in the present tense. Why do you think she does this?
3. How does Walker signal the ages at which she experiences a crisis or some other major event? What technique does she use?
4. The refrain "You did not change" occurs in differing contexts throughout Walker's essay. What is the effect of this repetition?

Questions for Further Thought

1. Walker believes that her father's attitude toward her changed after her injury. Has someone's attitude toward you ever changed dramatically? What precipitated the change? What were its consequences?
2. Walker says that she lied about the cause of her injury partly to protect herself from her brothers' possible retaliation. If a person is bullied and intimidated, what is the best course of action—to comply with those more powerful, to go against their wishes secretly, or to defy them openly and face the consequences? Why?
3. Walker recalls being "relegated to the position of Indian." Think of a time when you were excluded from participation in some activity because of your age, sex, race, or economic status. How did you feel about being excluded?
4. Walker tells us that although she was the valedictorian and the "most popular student" in her high school class, another student was voted

most beautiful. If you could be academically outstanding, extremely well liked, or strikingly good-looking, which one would you choose? Why?

Writing Assignments Using Cause-Effect as a Pattern of Development

1. An event initially viewed as handicapping can prove, as Walker shows, to be a blessing. Write a paper showing the effect on your life of an experience that at first seemed negative but turned out for the best.

2. Walker expects her daughter to react with revulsion to her eye injury. To her surprise, her daughter's reaction is tender and gentle. Think of a time you expected someone to treat you with kindness, but instead you were treated harshly, or, conversely, you expected severity but were met with generosity. In an essay, trace the causes of your faulty expectation as well as the possible reasons for the other person's unexpected behavior. Draw some conclusions about human nature.

Writing Assignments Using Other Patterns of Development

3. Walker writes of an experience in which joyful, exuberant play turned—in an instant—to terror. Write about a time in your own or in someone else's life when there was a sudden reversal of events—a positive experience that became negative or vice versa. Use vivid images, varied sentence structure, and dialogue to capture what happened. Did the event leave a lasting impression? If so, end by writing briefly about this effect.

∞ 4. Walker mentions two elementary school teachers who responded to her in a loving, supportive way. Write a letter to beginning grade school teachers outlining the steps they should (and should not) take to make their students' school experience a positive one. Sophronia Liu's "So Tsi-Fai" (page 196) will help you appreciate the powerful influence that teachers can exert on children.

Lewis Thomas

Lewis Thomas (1913–94) earned a reputation as an outstanding scientist and physician. A graduate of Princeton University and Harvard Medical School, Thomas held both the deanship of Yale University's medical school and the presidency of Sloan-Kettering Memorial Cancer Center. But more remarkable than Thomas's professional accomplishments was his gift for communicating the wonder of medicine and biology to the average reader. His essays, many of which first appeared in the *New England Journal of Medicine,* are less about medicine than they are about what he called the "mystery of being." Thomas published many books: a memoir, *The Youngest Science* (1983); and five essay collections, *Lives of a Cell* (1974), which won a National Book Award; *The Medusa and the Snail* (1979); *Late Night Thoughts on Listening to Mahler's Ninth Symphony* (1984); *Etcetera, Etcetera* (1990); and *The Fragile Species* (1992). The following selection is from *Late Night Thoughts.*

The Lie Detector

The evidence against the innate goodness of the human race seems overwhelming at times. But writer-physician Lewis Thomas, expressing himself in typically plain-spoken but elegant prose, takes comfort in what a lie detector reveals about human impulses and instincts.

Every once in a while the reasons for discouragement about the human prospect pile up so high that it becomes difficult to see the way ahead, and it is then a great blessing to have one conspicuous and irrefutable good thing to think about ourselves, something solid enough to step onto and look beyond the pile.

Language is often useful for this, and music. A particular painting, if you have the right receptors, can lift the spirits and hold them high enough to see a whole future for the race. The sound of laughter in the distance in the dark can be a marvelous encouragement. But these are chancy stimuli, ready to work only if you happen to be ready to receive them, which takes a bit of luck.

I have been reading magazine stories about the technology of   3
lie detection lately, and it occurs to me that this may be the thing I've been looking for, an encouragement propped up by genuine, hard scientific data. It is promising enough that I've decided to take as given what the articles say, uncritically, and to look no further. For a while, anyway.

Lying Is a Strain

As I understand it, a human being cannot tell a lie, even a small   4
one, without setting off a kind of smoke alarm somewhere deep in a dark lobule of the brain, resulting in the sudden discharge of nerve impulses, or the sudden outpouring of neurohormones of some sort, or both. The outcome, recorded by the lie-detector gadgetry, is a highly reproducible cascade of changes in the electrical conductivity of the skin, the heart rate, and the manner of breathing, similar to the responses to various kinds of stress.

Lying, then, is stressful, even when we do it for protection, or   5
relief, or escape, or profit, or just for the pure pleasure of lying and getting away with it. It is a strain, distressing enough to cause the emission of signals to and from the central nervous system warning that something has gone wrong. It is, in a pure physiological sense, an unnatural act.

Now I regard this as a piece of extraordinarily good news, mean-   6
ing, unless I have it all balled up, that we are a moral species by compulsion, at least in the limited sense that we are biologically designed to be truthful to each other. Lying doesn't hurt, mind you, and perhaps you could tell lies all day and night for years on end without being damaged, but maybe not—maybe the lie detector informs us that repeated, inveterate untruthfulness will gradually undermine the peripheral vascular system, the sweat glands, the adrenals, and who knows what else. Perhaps we should be looking into the possibility of lying as an etiologic agent for some of the common human ailments still beyond explaining, recurrent head colds, for instance, or that most human of all unaccountable disorders, a sudden pain in the lower mid-back.

Truth: Genetically Required?

It makes a sort of shrewd biological sense, and might therefore 7
represent a biological trait built into our genes, a feature of humanity
as characteristic for us as feathers for birds or scales for fish, enabling
us to live, at our best, the kinds of lives we are designed to live. This
is, I suppose, the "sociobiological" view to take, with the obvious alternative being that we are brought up this way as children in response to the rules of our culture. But if the latter is the case, you
would expect to encounter, every once in a while, societies in which
the rule does not hold, and I have never heard of a culture in which
lying was done by everyone as a matter of course, all life through, nor
can I imagine such a group functioning successfully. Biologically
speaking, there is good reason for us to restrain ourselves from lying
outright to each other whenever possible. We are indeed a social species, more interdependent than the celebrated social insects; we can
no more live a solitary life than can a bee; we are obliged, as a species,
to rely on each other. Trust is a fundamental requirement for our
kind of existence, and without it all our linkages would begin to snap
loose.

The restraint is a mild one, so gentle as to be almost impercep- 8
tible. But it is there; we know about it from what we call guilt, and
now we have a neat machine to record it as well.

It seems a trivial thing to have this information, but perhaps it 9
tells us to look again, and look deeper. If we had better instruments,
designed for profounder probes, we might see needles flipping, lines
on charts recording quantitative degrees of meanness of spirit, or a
lack of love. I do not wish for such instruments, I hope they will never be constructed; they would somehow belittle the issues involved.
It is enough, quite enough, to know that we cannot even tell a plain
untruth, betray a trust, without scaring some part of our own brains.
I'd rather guess at the rest.

Questions for Close Reading

1. What is the selection's thesis? Locate the sentence(s) in which Thomas
   states his main idea. If he doesn't state the thesis explicitly, express it in
   your own words.
2. For what reasons does Thomas call lying an "unnatural act"? How does
   he feel about its being "unnatural"?

3. Thomas writes that receptivity to language, music, art, and laughter "takes a bit of luck" (paragraph 2). What do you think he means by this statement?

4. To his "sociobiological" view of truth telling, Thomas contrasts another viewpoint. What is this other interpretation? Does he give this other interpretation equal support? Why or why not?

5. Refer to your dictionary as needed to define the following words used in the selection: *irrefutable* (paragraph 1), *receptors* (2), *stimuli* (2), *lobule* (4), *neurohormones* (4), *inveterate* (6), and *etiologic* (6).

Questions About the Writer's Craft

1. **The pattern.**   At the heart of Thomas's essay is a causal chain consisting of a series of interwoven causes and effects. What is this causal chain?

2. Thomas mixes technical terms from neuroscience with a rather informal style, involving contractions, the first-person ("I") point of view, colloquial expressions ("unless I have it all balled up"), and sentence fragments. Why might he have chosen to blend two such contrasting styles?

3. When presenting his viewpoint, Thomas uses a number of qualifiers: "it occurs to me" (paragraph 3), "as I understand it" (4), "unless I have it all balled up" (6), and "I suppose" (7). What is the effect of these qualifiers? Do they contribute to or detract from his credibility?

4. Thomas's next-to-last paragraph is shorter than any other in the essay. What function does this brief paragraph serve?

Questions for Further Thought

1. Thomas opens his essay by saying that "reasons for discouragement about the human prospect" sometimes "pile up." But he doesn't go on to specify these reasons. What might these reasons be? What do you find most discouraging about our future?

2. Thomas doesn't differentiate between "white" lies and intentionally hurtful ones. For you, what situations might justify lying?

3. Thomas writes that he requires scientific evidence to support an optimistic outlook. Which is more important to you—concrete evidence or faith? Explain.

4. In nature, opossums "play dead," birds feign broken wings, and chimpanzees direct competitors away from a food source by falsely indicating that the food is located elsewhere. In what ways might humans' ability to deceive also serve an important function? Explain.

Writing Assignments Using Cause-Effect as a Pattern of Development

∞ 1. Reasons for lying, Thomas writes, include profit, protection, pleasure, and kindness. Write an essay tracing the reasons for a lie that you or someone else (a parent, friend, or public figure) once told. Also analyze the effect of the lie. Langston Hughes's "Salvation" (page 191) may provide some insight into the psychology of lying. End the paper with some conclusions about when lying is and is not acceptable.

2. Thomas welcomes the use of the lie detector but has qualms about the development of similar technologies. Focus on one technological breakthrough (word processors, videotape recorders, telephone answering machines) and discuss its negative and positive effects. Although your analysis may be serious or playful, it should have a basically persuasive intent.

Writing Assignments Using Other Patterns of Development

3. Thomas claims, "Trust is a fundamental requirement for our...existence." In an essay, define the word *trust*. Consider dramatic examples, brief anecdotes, a comparison of two people when developing the definition. Your essay should illustrate Thomas's point that without trust "all our linkages would...snap loose."

∞ 4. According to Thomas, "We are a moral species by compulsion." Write an essay in which you argue for or against this contention. Remembering to consider the opposing opinion, develop your argument by citing several examples of human behavior. Before writing the paper, you might want to read Geoffrey Cowley's "Why a Disaster Brings Out the Best in People" (page 478), an essay that takes a position similar to Thomas's, as well as Mark Twain's "The Damned Human Race" (page 609), an essay that presents a point of view very different from Thomas's.

Jonathan Kozol

Jonathan Kozol was born in 1936 and graduated from Harvard University in 1958. He has taught not only in prestigious universities such as Yale but also in several public schools nationwide. Kozol established his reputation as a passionate voice for educational reform with the 1967 publication of *Death at an Early Age: The Destruction of the Hearts and Minds of Negro Children in the Boston Public Schools,* for which he won a National Book Award. His later books, which continue to explore the devastating human cost of poverty, include *On Being a Teacher* (1981), *Illiterate America* (1985), *Rachel and Her Children: Homeless Families in America* (1986), and *Savage Inequalities: Children in America's Schools* (1991). The following selection first appeared in *Harper's* in September 1988.

Are the Homeless Crazy?

When faced with something we fear, we tend to push it away, to assume that it's foreign and strangely alien. That way we keep the situation at arm's length, where it can more easily be dismissed as beyond our comprehension. According to Jonathan Kozol, such a defense mechanism is at work when we assume that most homeless people are mentally ill. The truth about the homeless, though, is both simpler *and* more complex.

It is commonly believed by many journalists and politicians that the homeless of America are, in large part, former patients of large mental hospitals who were deinstitutionalized in the 1970s—the consequence, it is sometimes said, of misguided liberal opinion that favored the treatment of such persons in community-based centers. It is argued that this policy, and the subsequent failure of society to build such centers or to provide them in sufficient number, is the primary cause of homelessness in the United States.

Those who work among the homeless do not find that explanation satisfactory. While conceding that a certain number of the homeless are or have been mentally unwell, they believe that, in the case of most unsheltered people, the primary reason is economic rather than clinical. The cause of homelessness, they say with disarming logic, is the lack of homes and of income with which to rent or acquire them.

They point to the loss of traditional jobs in industry (two million every year since 1980) and to the fact that half of those who are laid off end up in work that pays a poverty-level wage. They point out that since 1968 the number of children living in poverty has grown by three million, while welfare benefits to families with children have declined by 35 percent.   3

And they note, too, that these developments have occurred during a time in which the shortage of low-income housing has intensified as the gentrification[1] of our major cities has accelerated. Half a million units of low-income housing are lost each year to condominium conversion as well as to arson, demolition, or abandonment. Between 1978 and 1980, median rents climbed 30 percent for people in the lowest income sector, driving many of these families into the streets. Since 1980, rents have risen at even faster rates.   4

Hard numbers, in this instance, would appear to be of greater help than psychiatric labels in telling us why so many people become homeless. Eight million American families now use half or more of their income to pay their rent or mortgage. At the same time, federal support for low-income housing dropped from $30 billion (1980) to $7.5 billion (1988). Under Presidents Ford and Carter, 500,000 subsidized private housing units were constructed. By President Reagan's second term, the number had dropped to 25,000.   5

In our rush to explain the homeless as a psychiatric problem even the words of medical practitioners who care for homeless people have been curiously ignored. A study published by the Massachusetts Medical Society, for instance, has noted that, with the exceptions of alcohol and drug use, the most frequent illnesses among a sample of the homeless population were trauma (31 percent), upper-respiratory disorders (28 percent), limb disorders (19 percent), mental illness (16 percent), skin diseases (15 percent), hypertension (14 percent),   6

---

[1]Gentrification occurs when members of the middle and upper-middle classes buy, improve, and move into low-income dwellings, thus strengthening the economic base of a neighborhood but also dislodging the less-well-off residents who previously lived there.

and neurological illnesses (12 percent). Why, we may ask, of all these calamities, does mental illness command so much political and press attention? The answer may be that the label of mental illness places the destitute outside the sphere of ordinary life. It personalizes an anguish that is public in its genesis; it individualizes a misery that is both general in cause and general in application.

There is another reason to assign labels to the destitute and single out mental illness from among their many afflictions. All these other problems—tuberculosis, asthma, scabies, diarrhea, bleeding gums, impacted teeth, etc.—bear no stigma, and mental illness does. It conveys a stigma in the United States. It conveys a stigma in the [former] Soviet Union as well. In both nations the label is used, whether as a matter of deliberate policy or not, to isolate and treat as special cases those who, by deed or word or by sheer presence, represent a threat to national complacence. The two situations are obviously not identical, but they are enough alike to give Americans reason for concern.   7

The notion that the homeless are largely psychotics who belong in institutions, rather than victims of displacement at the hands of enterprising realtors, spares us from the need to offer realistic solutions to the deep and widening extremes of wealth and poverty in the United States. It also enables us to tell ourselves that the despair of homeless people bears no intimate connection to the privileged existence we enjoy—when, for example, we rent or purchase one of those restored town houses that once provided shelter for people now huddled in the street.   8

What is to be made, then, of the supposition that the homeless are primarily the former residents of mental hospitals, persons who were carelessly released during the 1970s? Many of them are, to be sure. Among the older men and women in the streets and shelters, as many as one-third (some believe as many as one-half) may be chronically disturbed, and a number of these people were deinstitutionalized during the 1970s. But to operate on that assumption in a city such as New York—where nearly half the homeless are small children whose average age is six—makes no sense. Their parents, with an average age of twenty-seven, are not likely to have been hospitalized in the 1970s, either.   9

A frequently cited set of figures tells us that in 1955 the average daily census of non-federal psychiatric institutions was 677,000, and   10 that by 1984 the number had dropped to 151,000. But these people didn't go directly from a hospital room to the street. The bulk of those who had been psychiatric patients and were released from hospitals during the 1960s and early 1970s had been living in low-income housing, many in skid-row hotels or boardinghouses. Such housing—commonly known as SRO (single-room occupancy) units—was drastically diminished by the gentrification of our cities that began in the early '70s. Almost 50 percent of SRO housing was replaced by luxury apartments or office buildings between 1970 and 1980, and the remaining units have been disappearing even more rapidly.

Even for those persons who are ill and were deinstitutionalized 11 during the decades before 1980, the precipitating cause of homelessness in 1987 is not illness but loss of housing. SRO housing offered low-cost sanctuaries for the homeless, providing a degree of safety and mutual support for those who lived within them. They were a demeaning version of the community health centers that society had promised; they were the de facto "halfway houses" of the 1970s. For these people too—at most half of the homeless single persons in America—the cause of homelessness is lack of housing.

Even in those cases where mental instability is apparent, home- 12 lessness itself is often the precipitating factor. For example, many pregnant women without homes are denied prenatal care because they constantly travel from one shelter to another. Many are anemic. Many are denied essential dietary supplements by recent federal cuts. As a consequence, some of their children do not live to see their second year of life. Do these mothers sometimes show signs of stress? Do they appear disorganized, depressed, disordered? Frequently. They are immobilized by pain, traumatized by fear. So it is no surprise that when researchers enter the scene to ask them how they "feel," the resulting reports tell us that the homeless are emotionally unwell. The reports do not tell us that we have *made* these people ill. They do not tell us that illness is a natural response to intolerable conditions. Nor do they tell us of the strength and the resilience that so many of these people retain despite the miseries they must endure.

A writer in the *New York Times* describes a homeless woman 13 standing on a traffic island in Manhattan. "She was evicted from her small room in the hotel just across the street," and she is determined to get revenge. Until she does, "nothing will move her from that spot. . . . Her argumentativeness and her angry fixation on revenge, along with the apparent absence of hallucinations, mark her as a paranoid." Most physicians, I imagine, would be more reserved in passing judgment with so little evidence, but this reporter makes his diagnosis without hesitation. "The paranoids of the street," he says, "are among the most difficult to help."

Perhaps so. But does it depend on who is offering the help? Is anyone offering to help this woman get back her home? Is it crazy to seek vengeance for being thrown into the street? The absence of anger, some psychiatrists believe, might indicate much greater illness.   14

"No one will be turned away," says the mayor of New York City, as hundreds of young mothers with their infants are turned from the doors of shelters season after season. That may sound to some like a denial of reality. "Now you're hearing all kinds of horror stories," says the president of the United States as he denies that anyone is cold or hungry or unhoused. On another occasion he says that the unsheltered "are homeless, you might say, by choice." That sounds every bit as self-deceiving.   15

The woman standing on the traffic island screaming for revenge until her room has been restored to her sounds relatively healthy by comparison. If three million homeless people did the same, and all at the same time, we might finally be forced to listen.   16

Questions for Close Reading

1. What is the selection's thesis? Locate the sentence(s) in which Kozol states his main idea. If he doesn't state the thesis explicitly, express it in your own words.
2. What, in Kozol's opinion, is the connection between recent real estate policies and homelessness? What effect have the last few presidential administrations had on homelessness?
3. What changes in the U.S. economy have affected the homeless?
4. According to Kozol, why might the public prefer to hear that the homeless are mentally ill rather than learn about the real causes of homelessness?
5. Refer to your dictionary as needed to define the following words used in the selection: *deinstitutionalized* (paragraph 1), *disarming* (2), *condominium* (4), *subsidized* (5), *hypertension* (6), *psychotics* (8), *displacement* (8), *precipitating* (11), *sanctuaries* (11), *fixation* (13), and *paranoid* (13).

Questions About the Writer's Craft

1. **The pattern.**   What seems to be Kozol's purpose for pointing out the basic cause of homelessness? Is his purpose mainly informative, specula-

tive, or persuasive? How do you know? Where in the essay does Kozol imply his purpose?

2. **Other patterns.** Locate places where Kozol uses the argumentation technique of refutation to oppose those who believe that homelessness results from mental illness. What do these refutation passages suggest about the probable views of Kozol's audience?

3. Identify places in paragraph 12 where Kozol uses parallel structure and questions to express his points. Why do you think he chooses to use these two techniques? What effect do they have on his essay's tone?

4. Why do you suppose Kozol returns at the essay's end to the image (introduced in paragraph 13) of the homeless woman who won't leave the traffic island? How does the repetition of this image serve Kozol's purpose?

Questions for Further Thought

1. In paragraph 9, Kozol indicates that almost half of the homeless in Manhattan are young children "whose average age is six." The children's parents, in turn, are typically about twenty-seven years old. Does this information surprise you? Who do you usually picture when you think of the homeless? Do you view the situation differently now that you've read Kozol's analysis? Explain.

2. Do you agree, as Kozol asserts in paragraph 8, that most of us live with the belief that "the despair of homeless people bears no intimate connection to the privileged existence we enjoy"? Do you think that everyday people—you, your instructor, your friends and family—can be considered partially responsible for the problem of homelessness? If so, in what ways?

3. Do you know personally or have you heard or read about anyone who is helping the homeless? If so, who are they? Why did they get involved? What effects have their efforts had?

4. Who do you think should solve the problem of the homeless? Should it be the mayors and presidents that Kozol cites in paragraphs 5 and 14? Or the social workers and advocates that he refers to in paragraph 2? Should individuals and private citizens take action? Or can the homeless help themselves, as Kozol suggests in his conclusion? Determine who should be involved, and explain what these people should do.

Writing Assignments Using Cause-Effect as a Pattern of Development

1. Do you think it's a good idea to give money, blankets, clothes, or food to people sleeping on the street? Discuss with others the possible effects of such direct assistance, and consider other measures that might be as (or more) effective. Then write a paper analyzing the effects of various means

of helping the homeless. At the end, state your opinion about which approach or combination of approaches is most productive.

2. Homelessness isn't the only serious problem facing the country. Focus on another situation that strikes you as critical—perhaps drug addiction among pregnant women, sexual harassment, or the availability of semiautomatic weapons. Brainstorm with others to determine why the problem resists resolution, despite its obvious importance. Then write an essay discussing the causes for society's failure to take action on the situation. In your conclusion, describe steps that should be taken to remedy the problem. You may need to conduct some library research to develop your ideas.

Writing Assignments Using Other Patterns of Development

∞ 3. According to Kozol, labeling the homeless "mentally ill" obscures not only the basic cause of homelessness but also the true nature of the homeless individual. In an essay, narrate a time that you initially misjudged someone because of a label you attached to the person. Convey the individual's genuine character as well as your progressive discovery of the person behind the label. To get a better sense of the way prejudicial attitudes can distort the way we perceive others, you may want to read some of the following essays: Maya Angelou's "Grandmother's Victory" (page 161), Gloria Naylor's "Mommy, What Does 'Nigger' Mean?" (page 535), and William Raspberry's "The Handicap of Definition" (page 548).

4. Kozol criticizes former president Ronald Reagan and former New York City mayor Ed Koch for their callous stance toward the homeless. Examine the position of a campus, local, state, or national candidate or official on some important issue of your choice. Write an essay arguing that this person should or shouldn't hold a position of power.

Additional Writing Topics

CAUSE-EFFECT

General Assignments

Write an essay that analyzes the causes and/or effects of one of the following topics. Determine your purpose before beginning to write: Will the essay be informative, persuasive, or speculative? As you prewrite, think rigorously about causes and effects; try to identify causal chains. Provide solid evidence for the thesis and use either chronological or emphatic order to organize your supporting points.

1. Sleep deprivation
2. Having the parents you have
3. Lack of communication in a relationship
4. Overexercising or not exercising
5. A particular TV or rock star's popularity
6. Skill or ineptitude in sports
7. A major life decision
8. Stiffer legal penalties for drunken driving
9. Changing attitudes toward protecting the environment
10. A particular national crisis
11. The mass movement of women into the workforce
12. Choosing to attend this college
13. "Back to basics" movement in schools
14. Headaches
15. An act of violence
16. A natural event: leaves turning, birds migrating, animals hibernating, an eclipse occurring
17. Pesticide use
18. Use of computers in the classroom
19. Banning disposable cans and bottles
20. A bad habit
21. A fear of _____
22. Legalizing drugs
23. Abolishing the F grade
24. Joining a particular organization
25. Owning a pet

Assignments With a Specific Purpose and Audience

1. A debate about the prominence of athletics at colleges and universities is going to be broadcast on the local cable station. For this debate, prepare

a speech pointing out either the harmful or the beneficial effects of "big-time" college athletic programs.

2. Why do students "flunk out" of college? Write an article for the campus newspaper outlining the main causes of failure. Your goal is to steer students away from dangerous habits and situations that lead to poor grades or dropping out.

3. Write a letter to the editor of your favorite newspaper, analyzing the causes of the country's current "trash crisis." Be sure to mention the nationwide love affair with disposable items and the general disregard of the idea of thrift.

4. Employed by your college's work-study office, you've been asked to write a brief pamphlet: "Things to Keep in Mind If You Plan to Work While Attending College." The pamphlet will be given to your fellow students, and it will focus on the effects—both negative and positive—of combining a part-time job with college studies.

5. Why do you think teenage suicide is on the rise? Write a fact sheet for parents of teenagers and for high school guidance counselors, describing the factors that could make a young person desperate enough to attempt suicide. At the end, suggest what parents and counselors can do to help confused, unhappy young people.

6. Some communities have conducted campaigns encouraging residents to give up television for a fixed period of time. You feel your community should participate in such an experiment. Write a letter to your mayor encouraging a public relations effort in favor of "Turn Off the TV Month." Cite specifically the positive effects such a program would have on parents, children, and the community in general.

11
DEFINITION

WHAT IS DEFINITION?

In Lewis Carroll's wise and whimsical tale, *Through the Looking Glass*, Humpty Dumpty proclaims, "When *I* use a word…, it means just what I choose it to mean—neither more nor less." If the world were filled with characters like Humpty Dumpty, all of them bending words to their own purposes and accepting no challenges to their personal definitions, communication would be an exercise in frustration. You would say a word, and it would mean one thing to you but perhaps something completely different to a close friend. Without a common understanding, the two of you would talk at cross-purposes, missing each other's meanings as you blundered through a conversation.

For language to communicate, words must have accepted *definitions*. Dictionaries, the sourcebooks for accepted definitions, are compilations of current word-meanings, enabling speakers of a language to understand one another. But as you might suspect, things are not as simple as they first appear. We all know that a word like *discipline* has a standard dictionary definition. We also know, though, that parents argue over what constitutes "discipline" and that controversies about the meaning of "discipline" rage within school systems year after year. Moreover, many of the wrenching moral debates of our time also boil down to questions of definition. Much of the controversy over abortion, for instance, centers on what is meant by "life" and when it "begins."

Words can, in short, be slippery. Each of us has unique experiences, attitudes, and values that influence the way we use words and the way we interpret the words of others. Lewis Carroll may have been exaggerating, but Humpty Dumpty's attitude exists—in a very real way—in all of us.

In addition to the idiosyncratic interpretations that may attach to words, some words may shift in meaning over time. The word *pedagogue*, for instance, originally meant "a teacher or leader of children." However, with time, *pedagogue* has come to mean "a dogmatic, pedantic teacher." And, of course, we invent other words (*modem, byte*) as the need arises.

Writing a definition, then, is no simple task. Primarily, the writer tries to answer basic questions: "What does _____ mean?" and "What is the special or true nature of _____?" The word to be defined may be an object, a concept, a type of person, a place, or a phenomenon. Potential subjects might be the "user-friendly" computer, animal rights, a model teacher, cabin fever. As you will see, there are various strategies for expanding definitions far beyond the single-word synonyms or brief phrases that dictionaries provide.

HOW DEFINITION FITS YOUR PURPOSE AND AUDIENCE

Many times, short-answer exam questions call for definitions. Consider the following examples:

Define the term *mob psychology.*

What is the difference between a metaphor and a simile?

How would you explain what a religious cult is?

In such cases, a good response might involve a definition of several sentences or several paragraphs.

Other times, definition may be used in an essay organized mainly around another pattern of development. In this situation, all that's needed is a brief formal definition or a short definition given in your own words. For instance, a *process analysis* showing readers how computers have revolutionized the typical business office might start with a textbook definition of the term *artificial intelligence*. In an *argumentation-persuasion* paper urging students to support recent efforts to abolish fraternities and sororities, you could refer to the definitions of *blackballing* and *hazing* found in the university handbook. Or your personal definition of *hero* could be the starting point for a *causal analysis* that explains to readers why there are few real heroes in today's world.

But the most complex use of definition, and the one we are primarily concerned with in this chapter, involves exploring a subject through an *extended definition*. Extended definition allows you to apply a personal interpretation to a word, to make a case for a revisionist view of a commonly accepted meaning, to analyze words representing complex or controversial issues. "Pornography," "gun control," "secular humanism," and "right-to-life" would be excellent subjects for extended definition—each is multifaceted, often misunderstood, and fraught with emotional meaning. "Junk food," "anger," "leadership," "anxiety" could make interesting subjects, especially if the extended definition helped readers develop a new understanding of the word. You might, for example, define "anxiety" not as a negative state to be avoided but as a positive force that propels us to take action.

An extended definition could perhaps run several paragraphs or a few pages. Keep in mind, however, that an extended definition may require a chapter or even an entire book to develop. If this seems unlikely, remember that theologians, philosophers, and pop psychologists have devoted entire texts to such concepts as "evil" and "love."

SUGGESTIONS FOR USING DEFINITION IN AN ESSAY

The following suggestions will be helpful whether you use definition as a dominant or supportive pattern of development.

1. Stay focused on the essay's purpose, audience, and tone. Since your purpose for writing an extended definition shapes the entire paper, you need to keep that objective in mind when developing your definition. Suppose you decide to write an essay defining *jazz*. The essay could be purely *informative* and discuss the origins of jazz, its characteristic tonal patterns, and some of the great jazz musicians of the past. Or the essay could move beyond pure information and take on a *persuasive* edge. It might, for example, argue that jazz is the only contemporary form of music worth considering seriously.

Just as your purpose in writing will vary, so will your tone. A strictly informative definition will generally assume a detached, objective tone ("Apathy is an emotional state characterized by listlessness and indifference"). By way of contrast, a definition essay with a persuasive slant might be urgent in tone ("To combat student apathy, we must design programs that engage students in campus life"), or it might take a satiric approach ("An apathetic stance is a wise choice for any thinking student").

As you write, keep thinking about your audience as well. Not only do your readers determine what terms need to be defined (and in how much detail), but they also keep you focused on the essay's purpose and tone. For instance, you probably wouldn't write a serious, informative piece for the college newspaper about the "mystery meat" served in the campus cafeteria. Instead, you would adopt a light tone as you defined the culinary horror and might even make a persuasive pitch about improving the food prepared on campus.

2. Formulate an effective definition. A definition essay sometimes begins with a brief *formal definition*—the dictionary's, a textbook's, or the writer's—and then expands that initial definition with supporting details. Formal definitions are traditionally worded as three-part statements that consist of the following: the *term*, the *class* to which the term belongs, and the *characteristics* that distinguish the term from other members of its class.

Term	Class	Characteristics
The peregrine falcon,	an endangered bird,	is the world's fastest flyer.

Term	Class	Characteristics
A bodice-ripper	is a paperback book,	usually read by women, that deals with highly charged romance in exotic places and faraway times.
Back to basics	is a trend in education	that emphasizes skill mastery through rote learning.

A definition that meets these guidelines will clarify what your subject *is* and what it *is not*. These guidelines also establish the boundaries of your definition, removing unlike items from consideration in your (and your reader's) mind. For example, defining "back to basics" as a trend that emphasizes rote learning signals a certain boundary; it lets readers know that other educational trends, such as those that emphasize children's social or emotional development, will not be part of the essay's definition.

If you decide to include a formal definition, avoid tired openers like "the dictionary says" or "according to Webster." Such weak starts are just plain boring and often herald an unimaginative essay. You should also keep in mind that a strict dictionary definition may actually confuse readers. Suppose you're writing a paper on the way all of us absorb ideas and values from the media. Likening this automatic response to the process of osmosis, you decide to open the paper with a dictionary definition. If you write, "Osmosis is the tendency of a solvent to disperse through a semipermeable membrane into a more concentrated medium," readers are apt to be baffled, even hostile. Remember: The purpose of a definition is to clarify meaning, not obscure it.

You should also stay clear of ungrammatical "is when" definitions: "Blind ambition is when you want to get ahead, no matter how much other people are hurt." Instead, write "Blind ambition is wanting to get ahead, no matter how much other people are hurt." A final pitfall to avoid in writing formal definitions is *circularity*, saying the same thing twice and therefore defining nothing: "A campus tribunal is a tribunal composed of various members of the university community." Circular definitions like this often repeat the term being defined (*tribunal*) or use words having the same meaning (*campus; university community*). In this case, we learn nothing about what a campus tribunal is; the writer says only that "X is X."

3. Develop the extended definition. You can choose from a variety of patterns when formulating an extended definition. Description, narration, process analysis, and comparison-contrast can be used—alone or in combination. Imagine that you're planning to write an extended definition of "robotics." You might develop the term by providing *examples* of the ways robots are currently being used in scientific research; by *comparing* and *contrasting* human and robot capabilities; or by *classifying* robots, starting with the most basic and moving to the most advanced or futuristic models.

Which patterns of development to use will often become apparent during the prewriting stage. Here is a list of prewriting questions as well as the pattern of development implied by each question.

Question	Pattern of Development
How does X look, taste, smell, feel, and sound?	Description
What does X do? When? Where?	Narration
What are some typical instances of X?	Exemplification
What are X's component parts? What different forms can X take?	Division-classification
How does X work?	Process analysis
What is X like or unlike?	Comparison-contrast
What leads to X? What are X's consequences?	Cause-effect

Those questions yielding the most material often suggest the effective pattern(s) for developing an extended definition.

4. Organize the material that develops the definition.   If you use a single pattern to develop the extended definition, apply the principles of organization suited to that pattern, as described in the appropriate chapter of this book. Assume that you're defining "fad" by means of *process analysis*. You might organize your paragraphs according to the steps in the process: a fad's slow start as something avant-garde or eccentric; its wildfire acceptance by the general public; the fad's demise as it becomes familiar or tiresome. If you want to define "character" by means of a single *narration*, you would probably organize paragraphs chronologically.

In a definition essay using several methods of development, you should devote separate paragraphs to each pattern. A definition of "relaxation," for instance, might start with a paragraph that *narrates* a particularly relaxing day; then it might move to a paragraph that describes several *examples* of people who find it difficult to unwind; finally, it might end with a paragraph that explains a *process* for relaxing the mind and body.

5. Write an effective introduction.   It can be helpful to provide—near the beginning of a definition essay—a brief formal definition of the term you're going to develop in the rest of the paper. Beyond this basic element, the introduction may include a number of other features. You might explain the *origin* of the term being defined: "Acid rock is a term first coined in the 1960s to describe music that was written or listened to under the influence of the drug LSD." Similarly, you could explain the *etymology*, or linguistic origin, of the key word that focuses the paper. "The term *vigilantism* is derived from the Latin word meaning 'to watch and be awake.'"

You may also use the introduction to clarify what the subject is *not*. Such *definition by negation* can be an effective strategy at the beginning of a paper, especially if readers don't share your view of the subject. In such a case, you might write something like this: "The gorilla, far from being the vicious killer of jungle movies and popular imagination, is a sedentary, gentle creature living in a closely knit family group." Such a statement provides the special focus of your essay and signals some of the misconceptions or fallacies soon to be discussed.

In addition, you may include in the introduction a *stipulative definition*, one that puts special restrictions on a term: "Strictly defined, a mall refers to a one- or two-story enclosed building containing a variety of retail shops and at least two large anchor stores. Highway-strip shopping centers or downtown centers cannot be considered true malls." When a term has multiple meanings, or when its meaning has become fuzzy through misuse, a stipulative definition sets the record straight right at the start, so that readers know exactly what is, and is not, being defined.

Finally, the introduction may end with a *plan of development* that indicates how the definition essay will unfold. A student who returned to school after having raised a family decided to write a paper defining the *midlife crisis* that led to her enrollment in college. After providing a brief formal definition of "midlife crisis," the student rounded off her introduction with this sentence: "Such a midlife crisis starts with vague misgivings, turns into depression, and ends with a significant change in life-style."

Semanticists, those who study the nature of language, have noted that meaning lies in people, not in words. Because words are symbols—and therefore open to multiple interpretations—dictionaries can only be starting points, never ultimate authorities. The complex nature of language makes the formulation of definitions an important part of writing. Extended definitions are one way we can sort out for ourselves the confusing nature of a word or term. We see the importance of definition every day. The courts define "right to privacy"; the campus handbook explains what "plagiarism" is; international negotiators try to forge an agreement on the meaning of "arms parity." Because definition essays can be developed so many ways, they make demands quite different from most other assignments. Definition essays are, in short, a challenge worth mastering.

STUDENT ESSAY

The following student essay was written by Laura Chen in response to this assignment:

> In "Entropy," K. C. Cole takes a scientific term from physics and gives it a broader definition and a wider application. Choose another specialized term and define it in such a way that you reveal something significant about contemporary life.

While reading Laura's paper, try to determine how well it applies the principles of definition. The annotations on Laura's paper and the commentary following it will help you look at the essay more closely.

Physics in Everyday Life
by Laura Chen

Introduction

A boulder sits on a mountainside for a thousand 1 years. The boulder will remain there forever unless an outside force intervenes. Suppose a force does affect the boulder--an earthquake, for instance. Once the boulder begins to thunder down the mountain, it will remain in motion and head in one direction only-- downhill--until another force interrupts its progress. If the boulder tumbles into a gorge, it will finally come to rest as gravity anchors it to the earth once more. In

Formal definition

both cases, the boulder is exhibiting the physical principle of inertia: the tendency of matter to remain

Thesis

at rest or, if moving, to keep moving in one direction unless affected by an outside force. Inertia, an impor-

Plan of development

tant factor in the world of physics, also plays a crucial role in the human world. Inertia affects our individual lives as well as the direction taken by society as a whole.

Topic sentence

Inertia often influences our value systems and 2 personal growth. Inertia is at work, for example, when people cling to certain behaviors and views. Like the boulder firmly fixed to the mountain, most people are set in their ways. Without thinking, they vote Republican or Democratic because they have always voted that way. They regard with suspicion a couple having no children, simply because everyone

Start of a series of causes and effects

else in the neighborhood has a large family. It is only when an outside force--a jolt of some sort--occurs that people change their views. A white American couple may think little about racial discrimination, for instance, until they adopt an Asian child and must comfort her when classmates tease her because she looks different. Parents may consider promiscuous any unmarried teenage girl who has a baby until their seventeen-year-old honor student confesses that she is pregnant. Personal jolts like these force people to think, perhaps for the first time, about issues that now affect them directly.

Topic sentence ——————➤ To illustrate how inertia governs our lives, it is   3
helpful to compare the world of television with real life. On TV, inertia does not exist. Television shows

**Start of a series
of contrasts** and commercials show people making all kinds of drastic changes. They switch brands of coffee or try a new hair color with no hesitation. In one car commercial, an ambitious young accountant abandons her career with a flourish and is seen driving off into the sunset as she heads for a small cabin by the sea to write poetry. In a soap opera, a character may progress from homemaker to hooker to nun in a single year. But in real life, inertia rules. People tend to stay where they are, to keep their jobs, to be loyal to products. A second major difference between television and real life is that, on television, everyone takes prompt and dramatic action to solve problems. The construction worker with a thudding headache is pain-free at the end of the sixty-second commercial; the police catch the murderer within an hour; the family learns to cope with their son's life-threatening drug addiction by the time the made-for-TV movie ends at eleven. But in the real world, inertia persists, so that few problems are solved neatly or quickly. Illnesses drag on, few crimes are solved, and family conflicts last for years.

Topic sentence ——————➤ Inertia is, most importantly, a force at work in   4
the life of our nation. Again, inertia is two-sided. It keeps us from moving and, once we move, it keeps us pointed in one direction. We find ourselves mired in a certain path, accepting the inferior, even the dangerous. We settle for toys that break, winter coats

**Start of a series
of examples** with no warmth, and rivers clogged with pollution. Inertia also compels our nation to keep moving in one direction--despite the uncomfortable suspicion that it is the wrong direction. We are not sure if manipulating genes is a good idea, yet we continue to fund scientific projects in genetic engineering. More than fifty years ago, we were shaken when we saw the devastation caused by an atomic bomb. But we went on to develop weapons hundreds of times more

destructive. Although warned that excessive television viewing may be harmful, we continue to watch
hours of television each day.

Conclusion   We have learned to defy gravity, one of the basic   5
laws of physics; we fly high above the earth, even
float in outer space. But most of us have not learned
to defy inertia. Those special individuals who are
able to act when everyone else seems paralyzed are
rare. But the fact that such people do exist means
that inertia is not all-powerful. If we use our reasoning ability and our creativity, we can conquer inertia,
just as we have conquered gravity.

COMMENTARY

Introduction.   As the title of her essay suggests, Laura has taken a
scientific term (*inertia*) from a specialized field and drawn on the
term to help explain some everyday phenomena. Using the *simple-
to-complex* approach to structure the introduction, she opens with a
vivid *descriptive* example of inertia. This description is then followed
by a *formal definition* of inertia: "the tendency of matter to remain
at rest or, if moving, to keep moving in one direction unless affected
by an outside force." Laura wisely begins the paper with the easy-to-
understand description rather than with the more-difficult-to-grasp
scientific definition. Had the order been reversed, the essay would
not have gotten off to nearly as effective a start. She then ends her
introductory paragraph with a *thesis*, "Inertia, an important factor in
the world of physics, also plays a crucial role in the human world,"
and with a *plan of development*, "Inertia affects our individual lives
as well as the direction taken by society as a whole."

Organization.   To support her definition of inertia and her belief
that it can rule our lives, Laura generates a number of compelling
examples. She organizes these examples by grouping them into
three major points, each point signaled by a *topic sentence* that opens
each of the essay's three supporting paragraphs (2–4).

A definite organizational strategy determines the sequence of
Laura's three central points. The essay moves from the way inertia
affects the individual to the way it affects the nation. The phrase
"most importantly" at the beginning of the fourth paragraph shows

that Laura has arranged her points emphatically, believing that inertia's impact on society is most critical.

A weak example.   When reading the fourth paragraph, you might
have noticed that Laura's examples aren't sequenced as effectively as
they could be. To show that we, as a nation, tend to keep moving in
the same direction, Laura discusses our ongoing uneasiness about
genetic engineering, nuclear arms, and excessive television viewing.
The point about nuclear weapons is most significant, yet it gets lost
because it's sandwiched in the middle. The paragraph would be
stronger if it ended with the point about nuclear arms. Moreover,
the example about excessive television viewing doesn't belong in
this paragraph since, at best, it has limited bearing on the issue
being discussed.

Other patterns of development.   In addition to using numerous
examples to illustrate her points, Laura draws on several other patterns of development to show that inertia can be a powerful force.
In the second and fourth paragraphs, she uses *causal analysis* to
explain how inertia can paralyze people and nations. The second
paragraph indicates that only "an outside force—a jolt of some
sort—" can motivate inert people to change. To support this view,
Laura provides two examples of parents who experience such jolts.
Similarly, in the fourth paragraph, she contends that inertia causes
the persistence of specific national problems: shoddy consumer
goods and environmental pollution.

Another pattern, *comparison-contrast*, is used in the third paragraph to highlight the differences between television and real life:
on television, people zoom into action, but in everyday life, people
tend to stay put and muddle through. The essay also contains a distinct element of *argumentation-persuasion*, since Laura clearly wants
readers to accept her definition of inertia and her view that it often
governs human behavior.

Conclusion.   Laura's *conclusion* rounds off the essay nicely and
brings it to a satisfying close. Laura refers to another law of physics,
one with which we are all familiar—gravity. By creating an *analogy*
between gravity and inertia, she suggests that our ability to defy
gravity should encourage us to defy inertia. The analogy enlarges
the scope of the essay; it allows Laura to reach out to her readers by

challenging them to action. Such a challenge is, of course, appropriate in a definition essay having a persuasive bent.

Revising the first draft.   When it was time to rework her essay, Laura began by reading her paper aloud. She noted in the margin of her draft the problems she detected, numbering them in order of importance. After reviewing her notes, she started to revise in earnest, paying special attention to her third paragraph. The first draft of that paragraph is reprinted here:

Original Version of the Third Paragraph

The ordinary actions of daily life are, in part, determined by inertia. To understand this, it is helpful to compare the world of television with real life, for, in the TV-land of ads and entertainment, inertia does not exist. For example, on television, people are often shown making all kinds of drastic changes. They switch brands of coffee or try a new hair color with no hesitation. In one car commercial, a young accountant leaves her career and sets off for a cabin by the sea to write poetry. In a soap opera, a character may progress from homemaker to hooker to nun in a single year. In contrast, inertia rules in real life. People tend to stay where they are, to keep their jobs, to be loyal to products (wives get annoyed if a husband brings home the wrong brand or color of bathroom tissue from the market). Middle-aged people wear the hairstyles or makeup that suited them in high school. A second major difference between television and real life is that, on TV, everyone takes prompt and dramatic action to solve problems. A woman finds the solution to dull clothes at the end of a commercial; the police catch the murderer within an hour; the family learns to cope with a son's disturbing life-style by the time the movie is over. In contrast, the law of real-life inertia means that few problems are solved neatly or quickly. Things, once started, tend to stay as they are. Few crimes are actually solved. Medical problems are not easily diagnosed. Messy wars in foreign countries seem endless. National problems are identified, but Congress does not pass legislation to solve them.

After rereading what she had written, Laura realized that her third paragraph rambled. To give it more focus, she removed the last two sentences ("Messy wars in foreign countries seem endless" and "National problems are identified, but Congress does not pass legislation. . . .") because they referred to national affairs but were located in a section focusing on the individual. Then, she eliminated two flat, unconvincing examples: wives who get annoyed when their husbands bring home the wrong brand of bathroom tissue and middle-aged people whose hairstyles and makeup are outdated. Condensing the two disjointed sentences that originally opened the paragraph also helped tighten this section of the essay. Note how much crisper the revised sentences are: "To illustrate how inertia rules our lives, it is helpful to compare the world of television with real life. On TV, inertia does not exist."

Laura also worked to make the details and the language in the paragraph more specific and vigorous. The vague sentence "A woman finds the solution to dull clothes at the end of the commercial" is replaced by the more dramatic "The construction worker with a thudding headache is pain-free at the end of the sixty-second commercial." Similarly, Laura changed a "son's disturbing lifestyle" to a "son's life-threatening drug addiction"; "by the time the movie is over" became "by the time the made-for-TV movie ends at eleven"; and "a young accountant leaves her career and sets off for a cabin by the sea to write poetry" was changed to "an ambitious young accountant abandons her career with a flourish and is seen driving off into the sunset as she heads for a small cabin by the sea to write poetry."

Laura decided to round off the paragraph with a powerful summary statement highlighting how real life differs from television: "Illnesses drag on, few crimes are solved, and family conflicts last for years."

These third-paragraph revisions are similar to those that Laura made elsewhere in her first draft. Her astute changes enabled her to turn an already effective paper into an especially thoughtful analysis of human behavior.

As the selections in this chapter show, definition essays generally use a variety of patterns to develop the concept at the heart of the essay. K. C. Cole uses facts, examples, and anecdotes in the essay "Entropy" to show how a specialized concept applies to everyday life. In "Why I Want a Wife," Judy Brady generates examples to clarify her definition of a traditional wife. Gloria Naylor's "Mommy, What Does 'Nigger' Mean?" draws upon a childhood incident to explore the way context influences a word's meaning. Marie Winn draws a compelling analogy to clarify her definition of "TV Addiction." Finally, in "The Handicap of Definition," William Raspberry presents his understanding of the way that African-Americans define their "blackness."

K. C. Cole

K. C. Cole's writings about science, especially physics, have made a great deal of specialized knowledge available to the general public. A graduate of Barnard College, Cole has contributed numerous articles to such publications as the *New York Times*, the *Washington Post*, and *Long Island Newsday*, and writes a regular column for *Discover* magazine. Her work with the Exploratorium, a San Francisco science museum, led her to write several books on the exhibits there. In 1985, Cole published a collection of essays, *Sympathetic Vibrations: Reflections on Physics as a Way of Life*. The book *What Only a Mother Can Tell You About Having a Baby* appeared in 1986. The following selection was first published as a "Hers" column in the *New York Times* in 1982.

Entropy

Complex scientific principles often seem exotic—and intelligible only to those with specialized knowledge. But the natural laws at work in the universe control all creatures, not just a select few. In her essay, K. C. Cole takes a specialized concept from physics and shows how it is a factor in everyone's daily life.

It was about two months ago when I realized that entropy was getting the better of me. On the same day my car broke down (again), my refrigerator conked out and I learned that I needed root-canal work in my right rear tooth. The windows in the bedroom were still leaking every time it rained and my son's baby sitter was still failing to show up every time I really needed her. My hair was turning gray and my typewriter was wearing out. The house needed paint and I needed glasses. My son's sneakers were developing holes and I was developing a deep sense of futility.

After all, what was the point of spending half of Saturday at the Laundromat if the clothes were dirty all over again the following Friday?

Disorder, alas, is the natural order of things in the universe. There is even a precise measure of the amount of disorder, called entropy. Unlike almost every other physical property (motion, gravity, energy), entropy does not work both ways. It can only increase. Once it's created it can never be destroyed. The road to disorder is a one-way street.

Because of its unnerving irreversibility, entropy has been called   4
the arrow of time. We all understand this instinctively. Children's rooms, left on their own, tend to get messy, not neat. Wood rots, metal rusts, people wrinkle and flowers wither. Even mountains wear down; even the nuclei of atoms decay. In the city we see entropy in the rundown subways and worn-out sidewalks and torn-down buildings, in the increasing disorder of our lives. We know, without asking, what is old. If we were suddenly to see the paint jump back on an old building, we would know that something was wrong. If we saw an egg unscramble itself and jump back into its shell, we would laugh in the same way we laugh at a movie run backward.

Entropy is no laughing matter, however, because with every in-   5
crease in entropy energy is wasted and opportunity is lost. Water flowing down a mountainside can be made to do some useful work on its way. But once all the water is at the same level it can work no more. That is entropy. When my refrigerator was working, it kept all the cold air ordered in one part of the kitchen and warmer air in another. Once it broke down the warm and cold mixed into a lukewarm mess that allowed my butter to melt, my milk to rot and my frozen vegetables to decay.

Of course the energy is not really lost, but it has diffused and dis-   6
sipated into a chaotic caldron of randomness that can do us no possible good. Entropy is chaos. It is loss of purpose.

People are often upset by the entropy they seem to see in the   7
haphazardness of their own lives. Buffeted about like so many molecules in my tepid kitchen, they feel that they have lost their sense of direction, that they are wasting youth and opportunity at every turn. It is easy to see entropy in marriages, when the partners are too preoccupied to patch small things up, almost guaranteeing that they will fall apart. There is much entropy in the state of our country, in the relationships between nations—lost opportunities to stop the avalanche of disorders that seems ready to swallow us all.

Entropy is not inevitable everywhere, however. Crystals and   8
snowflakes and galaxies are islands of incredibly ordered beauty in the midst of random events. If it was not for exceptions to entropy, the sky would be black and we would be able to see where the stars

spend their days; it is only because air molecules in the atmosphere cluster in ordered groups that the sky is blue.

The most profound exception to entropy is the creation of life. A seed soaks up some soil and some carbon and some sunshine and some water and arranges it into a rose. A seed in the womb takes some oxygen and pizza and milk and transforms it into a baby.   9

The catch is that it takes a lot of energy to produce a baby. It also takes energy to make a tree. The road to disorder is all downhill but the road to creation takes work. Though combating entropy is possible, it also has its price. That's why it seems so hard to get ourselves together, so easy to let ourselves fall apart.   10

Worse, creating order in one corner of the universe always creates more disorder somewhere else. We create ordered energy from oil and coal at the price of the entropy of smog.   11

I recently took up playing the flute again after an absence of several months. As the uneven vibrations screeched through the house, my son covered his ears and said, "Mom, what's wrong with your flute?" Nothing was wrong with my flute, of course. It was my ability to play it that had atrophied, or entropied, as the case may be. The only way to stop that process was to practice every day, and sure enough my tone improved, though only at the price of constant work. Like anything else, abilities deteriorate when we stop applying our energies to them.   12

That's why entropy is depressing. It seems as if just breaking even is an uphill fight. There's a good reason that this should be so. The mechanics of entropy are a matter of chance. Take any ice-cold air molecule milling around my kitchen. The chances that it will wander in the direction of my refrigerator at any point are exactly 50-50. The chances that it will wander away from my refrigerator are also 50-50. But take billions of warm and cold molecules mixed together, and the chances that all the cold ones will wander toward the refrigerator and all the warm ones will wander away from it are virtually nil.   13

Entropy wins not because order is impossible but because there are always so many more paths toward disorder than toward order. There are so many more different ways to do a sloppy job than a good one, so many more ways to make a mess than to clean it up. The obstacles and accidents in our lives almost guarantee that constant collisions will bounce us on to random paths, get us off the track. Disorder is the path of least resistance, the easy but not the inevitable road.   14

Like so many others, I am distressed by the entropy I see around 15
me today. I am afraid of the randomness of international events, of
the lack of common purpose in the world; I am terrified that it will
lead into the ultimate entropy of nuclear war. I am upset that I could
not in the city where I live send my child to a public school; that people are unemployed and inflation is out of control; that tensions between sexes and races seem to be increasing again; that relationships
everywhere seem to be falling apart.

Social institutions—like atoms and stars—decay if energy is not 16
added to keep them ordered. Friendships and families and economies
all fall apart unless we constantly make an effort to keep them working and well oiled. And far too few people, it seems to me, are willing
to contribute consistently to those efforts.

Of course, the more complex things are, the harder it is. If there 17
were only a dozen or so air molecules in my kitchen, it would be likely—if I waited a year or so—that at some point the six coldest ones
would congregate inside the freezer. But the more factors in the
equation—the more players in the game—the less likely it is that
their paths will coincide in an orderly way. The more pieces in the
puzzle, the harder it is to put back together once order is disturbed.
"Irreversibility," said a physicist, "is the price we pay for complexity."

Questions for Close Reading

1. What is the selection's thesis? Locate the sentence(s) in which Cole states
   her main idea. If she doesn't state the thesis explicitly, express it in your
   own words.
2. How does entropy differ from the other properties of the physical world?
   Is the image "the arrow of time" helpful in establishing this difference?
3. Why is the creation of life an exception to entropy? What is the relationship between entropy and energy?
4. Why does Cole say that entropy "is no laughing matter"? What is so depressing about the entropy she describes?
5. Refer to your dictionary as needed to define the following words used in
   the selection: *futility* (paragraph 1), *dissipated* (6), *buffeted* (7), *tepid* (7),
   and *atrophied* (12).

Questions About the Writer's Craft

1. **The pattern.** What is Cole's underlying purpose in defining the scientific term *entropy*? What gives the essay its persuasive edge?

2. What tone does Cole adopt to make reading about a scientific concept more interesting? Identify places in the essay where her tone is especially prominent.

3. Cole uses such words as *futility*, *loss*, and *depressing*. How do these words affect you? Why do you suppose she chose such terms? Find similar words in the essay.

4. **Other Patterns.**   Many of Cole's sentences follow a two-part pattern involving a contrast: "The road to disorder is all downhill but the road to creation takes work" (paragraph 10). Find other examples of this pattern in the essay. Why do you think Cole uses it so often?

Questions for Further Thought

1. Besides the examples provided by Cole, what instances of entropy do you see around you?

2. Is entropy in nature the same as entropy in society? in a marriage? in a city? in international relations? Do you accept Cole's application of the term *entropy* to these various areas of life? Why or why not?

3. Entropy means that paint peels, "people wrinkle, flowers wither." How does our society respond to these phenomena?

4. Cole writes that it's "so hard to get ourselves together, so easy to let ourselves fall apart." If so, why do we bother? Overall, would you say the author is optimistic or pessimistic about humans getting themselves together?

Writing Assignments Using Definition as a Pattern of Development

1. Define *order* or *disorder* by applying the term to a system that you know well—for example, your school, dorm, family, or workplace. Develop your definition through any combination of writing patterns: by supplying examples, by showing contrasts, by analyzing the process underlying the system.

2. Choose, as Cole does, a technical term that you think will be unfamiliar to most readers. In a humorous or serious paper, define the term as it is used technically; then show how the term can shed light on some aspect of your life. For example, the concept in astronomy of a *supernova* could be used to explain your sudden emergence as a new star on the athletic field, in your schoolwork, or on the social scene. Here are a few suggested terms:

symbiosis	volatility	resonance
velocity	erosion	catalyst
neutralization	equilibrium	malleability

Writing Assignments Using Other Patterns of Development

3. Can one person make much difference in the amount of entropy—disorder and chaos—in the world? Share your view in an essay. Use examples of people who have tried to overcome the tendency of things to "fall apart." Make clear whether you think these people succeeded or failed in their attempts.

4. Cole claims that we humans are "buffeted about like so many molecules." Write an essay arguing that people either do or do not control their own fates. Support your point with a series of specific examples. For two quite different perspectives on the issue, you might want to read "So Tsi-Fai" (page 196) by Sophronia Liu and "The World House" (page 706) by Martin Luther King, Jr.

Judy Brady

Judy Brady was born in 1937 in San Francisco and was educated at the University of Iowa where she received her B.F.A. in 1962. She became a freelance writer during the 1960s and has written articles on such issues as abortion, education, and the labor and women's movements for a variety of publications. In 1991, she published a collection of essays, *1 in 3: Women With Cancer Confront an Epidemic*. The provocative essay reprinted here first appeared in *Ms.* magazine in 1971 and has become a classic of feminist satire.

Why I Want a Wife

According to the dictionary, a wife is a "woman married to a man." But, as many women know, a wife is much more: cook, housekeeper, nutritionist, chauffeur, friend, sex partner, valet, nurse, social secretary, ego-builder, and the list goes on. Rather than complain about all the responsibilities she and other women assume, Judy Brady explains why she herself would like to have a wife.

1 I belong to that classification of people known as wives. I am A Wife. And, not altogether incidentally, I am a mother.

2 Not too long ago a male friend of mine appeared on the scene from the Midwest fresh from a recent divorce. He had one child, who is, of course, with his ex-wife. He is obviously looking for another wife. As I thought about him while I was ironing one evening, it suddenly occurred to me that I, too, would like to have a wife. Why do I want a wife?

3 I would like to go back to school so that I can become economically independent, support myself, and, if need be, support those dependent upon me. I want a wife who will work and send me to school. And while I am going to school I want a wife to take care of my children. I want a wife to keep track of the children's doctor and

dentist appointments. And to keep track of mine, too. I want a wife to make sure my children eat properly and are kept clean. I want a wife who will wash the children's clothes and keep them mended. I want a wife who is a good nurturant attendant to my children, arranges for their schooling, makes sure that they have an adequate social life with their peers, takes them to the park, the zoo, etc. I want a wife who takes care of the children when they are sick, a wife who arranges to be around when the children need special care, because, of course, I cannot miss classes at school. My wife must arrange to lose time at work and not lose the job. It may mean a small cut in my wife's income from time to time, but I guess I can tolerate that. Needless to say, my wife will arrange and pay for the care of the children while my wife is working.

I want a wife who will take care of *my* physical needs. I want a   4 wife who will keep my house clean. A wife who will pick up after my children, a wife who will pick up after me. I want a wife who will keep my clothes clean, ironed, mended, replaced when need be, and who will see to it that my personal things are kept in their proper place so that I can find what I need the minute I need it. I want a wife who cooks the meals, a wife who is a *good* cook. I want a wife who will plan the menus, do the necessary grocery shopping, prepare the meals, serve them pleasantly, and then do the cleaning up while I do my studying. I want a wife who will care for me when I am sick and sympathize with my pain and loss of time from school. I want a wife to go along when our family takes a vacation so that someone can continue to care for me and my children when I need a rest and a change of scene.

I want a wife who will not bother me with rambling complaints   5 about a wife's duties. But I want a wife who will listen to me when I feel the need to explain a rather difficult point I have come across in my course of studies. And I want a wife who will type my papers for me when I have written them.

I want a wife who will take care of the details of my social life.   6 When my wife and I are invited out by my friends, I want a wife who will take care of the babysitting arrangements. When I meet people at school that I like and want to entertain, I want a wife who will have the house clean, will prepare a special meal, serve it to me and my friends, and not interrupt when I talk about the things that interest me and my friends. I want a wife who will have arranged that the children are fed and ready for bed before my guests arrive so that the children do not bother us. I want a wife who takes care of the needs of my guests so that they feel comfortable, who makes sure that they have an ashtray, that they are passed the hors d'oeuvres, that they are offered a second helping of the food, that their wine glasses are replenished when necessary, that their coffee is served to them as they like it. And I want a wife who knows that sometimes I need a night out by myself.

I want a wife who is sensitive to my sexual needs, a wife who   7
makes love passionately and eagerly when I feel like it, a wife who makes sure that I am satisfied. And, of course, I want a wife who will not demand sexual attention when I am not in the mood for it. I want a wife who assumes the complete responsibility for birth control, because I do not want more children. I want a wife who will remain sexually faithful to me so that I do not have to clutter up my intellectual life with jealousies. And I want a wife who understands that *my* sexual needs may entail more than strict adherence to monogamy. I must, after all, be able to relate to people as fully as possible.

If, by chance, I find another person more suitable as a wife than   8
the wife I already have, I want the liberty to replace my present wife with another one. Naturally, I will expect a fresh, new life; my wife will take the children and be solely responsible for them so that I am left free.

When I am through with school and have acquired a job, I want   9
my wife to quit working and remain at home so that my wife can more fully and completely take care of a wife's duties.

My God, who *wouldn't* want a wife?   10

Questions for Close Reading

1. What is the selection's thesis? Locate the sentence(s) in which Brady states her main idea. If she doesn't state the thesis explicitly, express it in your own words.
2. What event sparked Brady to think about why she would like to have a wife? How is this event related to her thesis?
3. What are the duties of a wife, according to Brady?
4. How are a wife's duties different from her spouse's? Which roles apply to the wife and not to her spouse?

5. Refer to your dictionary as needed to define the following words used in the selection: *nurturant* (paragraph 3), *replenished* (6), *entail* (7), and *adherence* (7).

Questions About the Writer's Craft

1. **The pattern.** How does Brady develop her definition of *wife*? Does she ever provide a direct summary statement of what a wife is? Explain.
2. What is Brady's tone in this essay? How does this tone help readers understand her definition of what it is to be a "wife"?
3. Why do you suppose the author repeats "I want a wife" over and over? How does this repetition add to the essay's effectiveness?
4. Are the reasons why Brady wants a wife listed in any particular order? Why do you think she saves for last sexual needs and the right to divorce?

Questions for Further Thought

1. This essay was first published in 1971, when the women's movement was still new. Have times changed? Or is Brady's message still relevant today?
2. Brady concludes, "My God, who *wouldn't* want a wife?" Would you? Why or why not?
3. Brady casts herself in the role of a certain kind of spouse. What's your opinion of this spouse? How do you think most husbands would react to this essay?
4. Do you know any married women who are the kind of "wife" that Brady describes? Are these people happy? Do you see any positive aspects to such a relationship?

Writing Assignments Using Definition as a Pattern of Development

1. Adopting either a positive or negative viewpoint, write an essay defining a husband. Use either "I want a husband" or "I don't want a husband" as your theme. Build your definition around numerous examples of the ways husbands behave.
∞ 2. Define what you mean by the phrase "a good marriage"—that is, the kind of marriage you would like to have. Develop your definition in an essay that explains what a couple should do to make a good marriage a reality. George Gallup's "The Faltering Family" (page 467) should spark some ideas worth exploring.

Writing Assignments Using Other Patterns of Development

3. Write an essay defending the life-style of a traditional homemaker. Remembering to take the opposing viewpoint into account, try to persuade

your audience that it is a worthy and fulfilling life-style. To support your point, provide plentiful reasons and examples of the life-style's benefits and advantages.

4. Brady claims that men and women experience marriage differently. Pick one other area that you think reflects sharp differences between the sexes. Possibilities include the following:

Friendships
Dating protocol
Academic achievement
Clothing worn
Language used

Using the comparison-contrast format to analyze the area selected, discuss what you observe about male and female attitudes and behavior. Part of your paper should deal with the extent to which societal expectations define these characteristic patterns. Alleen Pace Nilsen's "Sexism and Language" (page 290), Barbara Ehrenreich's "What I've Learned From Men" (page 261), Scott Russell Sanders's "The Men We Carry in Our Minds" (page 308), Deborah Tannen's "Sex, Lies, and Conversation" (page 428), Camille Paglia's "Rape: A Bigger Danger Than Feminists Know" (page 638), and Susan Jacoby's "Common Decency" (page 645) will provide insight into the complexities of male-female interaction and behavior.

Gloria Naylor

A native of New York City, Gloria Naylor (1950–   ) attended first Brooklyn College and then Yale University, where she earned a master's degree in African-American studies. Naylor is perhaps best known as the author of *The Women of Brewster Place* (1982), a novel made into a television drama starring Oprah Winfrey. *Brewster Place* was awarded the American Book Award for First Fiction in 1983. Naylor has also written the novels *Linden Hills* (1985) and *Mama Day* (1988). Her most recent work, *Bailey's Cafe,* was published in 1992. The following selection first appeared in the *New York Times* in 1986.

"Mommy, What Does 'Nigger' Mean?"

When a white classmate hissed the word "nigger" at her in the third grade, Gloria Naylor sensed its ugliness and meanness. Later, as an adult, thinking about the word's meaning and its power to wound, Naylor moves beyond that day's incident into an exploration of language, culture, and the bonds of kinship. The word, she concludes, takes on a different character depending upon its context.

Language is the subject. It is the written form with which I've managed to keep the wolf away from the door and, in diaries, to keep my sanity. In spite of this, I consider the written word inferior to the spoken, and much of the frustration experienced by novelists is the awareness that whatever we manage to capture in even the most transcendent passages falls far short of the richness of life. Dialogue achieves its power in the dynamics of a fleeting moment of sight, sound, smell and touch.

I'm not going to enter the debate here about whether it is language that shapes reality or vice versa. That battle is doomed to be waged whenever we seek intermittent reprieve from the chicken and

1

2

535

egg dispute. I will simply take the position that the spoken word, like the written word, amounts to a nonsensical arrangement of sounds or letters without a consensus that assigns "meaning." And building from the meanings of what we hear, we order reality. Words themselves are innocuous; it is the consensus that gives them true power.

I remember the first time I heard the word nigger. In my third-   3 grade class, our math tests were being passed down the rows, and as I handed the papers to a little boy in back of me, I remarked that once again he had received a much lower mark than I did. He snatched his test from me and spit out that word. Had he called me a nymphomaniac or a necrophiliac, I couldn't have been more puzzled. I didn't know what a nigger was, but I knew that whatever it meant, it was something he shouldn't have called me. This was verified when I raised my hand, and in a loud voice repeated what he had said and watched the teacher scold him for using a "bad" word. I was later to go home and ask the inevitable question that every black parent must face—"Mommy, what does 'nigger' mean?"

And what exactly did it mean? Thinking back, I realize that this   4 could not have been the first time the word was used in my presence. I was part of a large extended family that had migrated from the rural South after World War II and formed a close-knit network that gravitated around my maternal grandparents. Their ground-floor apartment in one of the buildings they owned in Harlem was a weekend mecca for my immediate family, along with countless aunts, uncles and cousins who brought along assorted friends. It was a bustling and open house with assorted neighbors and tenants popping in and out to exchange bits of gossip, pick up an old quarrel or referee the ongoing checkers game in which my grandmother cheated shamelessly. They were all there to let down their hair and put up their feet after a week of labor in the factories, laundries and shipyards of New York.

Amid the clamor, which could reach deafening proportions—   5 two or three conversations going on simultaneously, punctuated by the sound of a baby's crying somewhere in the back rooms or out on the street—there was still a rigid set of rules about what was said and how. Older children were sent out of the living room when it was time to get into the juicy details about "you-know-who" up on the third floor who had gone and gotten herself "p-r-e-g-n-a-n-t!" But my parents, knowing that I could spell well beyond my years, always demanded that I follow the others out to play. Beyond sexual misconduct and death, everything else was considered harmless for our young ears. And so among the anecdotes of the triumphs and disappointments in the various workings of their lives, the word nigger was used in my presence, but it was set within contexts and inflections that caused it to register in my mind as something else.

In the singular, the word was always applied to a man who had 6 distinguished himself in some situation that brought their approval for his strength, intelligence or drive:

"Did Johnny really do that?" 7

"I'm telling you, that nigger pulled in $6,000 of overtime last 8 year. Said he got enough for a down payment on a house."

When used with a possessive adjective by a woman—"my nig- 9 ger"—it became a term of endearment for husband or boyfriend. But it could be more than just a term applied to a man. In their mouths it became the pure essence of manhood—a disembodied force that channeled their past history of struggle and present survival against the odds into a victorious statement of being: "Yeah, that old foreman found out quick enough—you don't mess with a nigger."

In the plural, it became a description of some group within the 10 community that had overstepped the bounds of decency as my family defined it: Parents who neglected their children, a drunken couple who fought in public, people who simply refused to look for work, those with excessively dirty mouths or unkempt households were all "trifling niggers." This particular circle could forgive hard times, unemployment, the occasional bout of depression—they had gone through all of that themselves—but the unforgivable sin was lack of self-respect.

A woman could never be a "nigger" in the singular, with its con- 11 notation of confirming worth. The noun girl was its closest equivalent in that sense, but only when used in direct address and regardless of the gender doing the addressing. "Girl" was a token of respect for a woman. The one-syllable word was drawn out to sound like three in recognition of the extra ounce of wit, nerve or daring that the woman had shown in the situation under discussion.

"G-i-r-l, stop. You mean you said that to his face?" 12

But if the word was used in a third-person reference or short- 13 ened so that it almost snapped out of the mouth, it always involved some element of communal disapproval. And age became an important factor in these exchanges. It was only between individuals of the same generation, or from an older person to a younger (but never the other way around), that "girl" would be considered a compliment.

I don't agree with the argument that use of the word nigger at   14
this social stratum of the black community was an internalization of
racism. The dynamics were the exact opposite: the people in my
grandmother's living room took a word that whites used to signify
worthlessness or degradation and rendered it impotent. Gathering
there together, they transformed "nigger" to signify the varied and
complex human beings they knew themselves to be. If the word was
to disappear totally from the mouths of even the most racist of white
society, no one in that room was naïve enough to believe it would
disappear from white minds. Meeting the word head-on, they proved
it had absolutely nothing to do with the way they were determined
to live their lives.

So there must have been dozens of times that the word "nigger"   15
was spoken in front of me before I reached the third grade. But I
didn't "hear" it until it was said by a small pair of lips that had already
learned it could be a way to humiliate me. That was the word I went
home and asked my mother about. And since she knew that I had to
grow up in America, she took me in her lap and explained.

Questions for Close Reading

1. What is the selection's thesis? Locate the sentence(s) in which Naylor
   states her main idea. If she doesn't state the thesis explicitly, express it in
   your own words.
2. Why, when her classmate called her "nigger," did Naylor not understand
   the word's meaning?
3. What meanings of the word *girl* did Naylor pick up from her family? How
   did the context affect the word's meaning?
4. In paragraph 14, Naylor writes that she doesn't accept the view that the
   black community's use of the word *nigger* is an example of internalized
   racism. What evidence does she offer to disprove this theory?
5. Refer to your dictionary as needed to define the following words used in
   the selection: *transcendent* (paragraph 1), *dynamics* (1), *intermittent* (2),
   reprieve (2), *consensus* (2) *innocuous* (2), *nymphomaniac* (3), *necrophiliac*
   (3), *gravitated* (4), *mecca* (4), *anecdotes* (5), *inflections* (5), *disembodied*
   (9), *unkempt* (10), *trifling* (10), *connotation* (11), *communal* (13), *internalization* (14), *degradation* (14), and *impotent* (14).

Questions About the Writer's Craft

1. **The pattern.** Locate some of the contrasts that Naylor establishes to illustrate the various ways the word *nigger* is used. How do these contrasts

help her build her definition of "nigger"? How does this definition reinforce her thesis?

2. **Other patterns.** Throughout the essay, Naylor uses dialogue, a technique typically associated with narration. Identify several examples of dialogue, and explain why Naylor might have chosen to include direct quotations in each case.

3. Why do you think Naylor discusses at such length the "close-knit network" of family that surrounded her when she grew up? Why, for example, might she have mentioned that her grandparents owned the building where they lived, that the visiting adults worked in "factories, laundries, and shipyards," and that children were restricted from hearing certain conversations? How does Naylor's choice of details show her awareness of the reader?

4. Examine the essay's two concluding paragraphs. How does paragraph 14 enlarge the reader's understanding of the word *nigger?* What would have been lost if Naylor had ended the essay with paragraph 14?

Questions for Further Thought

1. "Words are innocuous," Naylor writes. "It is the consensus [of meaning] that gives them true power." Think of several words that have the power to evoke strong responses—either negative or positive—in you and in others. What makes these words so powerful?

2. Naylor depicts the confusion and pain that resulted from her classmate's use of a "bad" word. What words do you feel should be avoided because of their power to offend? What would you do if someone used one of these words in your presence?

3. Think of words that have different, perhaps opposite, meanings, depending upon who is using them and in what context. Have you or anyone you know ever been confused or upset when such words were used in an inappropriate context? Explain.

4. Naylor writes that the question about the meaning of the word *nigger* is an "inevitable" one "that every black parent must face." When you were a child, did you ask similar "inevitable" questions about ethnicity, culture, religion, or other aspects of your identity? How did the adults in your life help you answer these questions?

Writing Assignments Using Definition as a Pattern of Development

1. Naylor illustrates her attempt to arrive at a personally meaningful interpretation of an emotionally charged word. Choose a word, phrase, or expression whose meaning you have struggled to understand. Possible words or phrases include *loyalty, morality, family values,* or *sexual harassment*. Write an essay in which you present both your definition and the

personal experiences that led to your definition. You may provide the definition and then move to the personal examples, or you may begin with the examples and lead up to the definition. In either case, consider using dialogue—as Naylor does—to enliven and clarify your examples.

2. Choose a term or expression that you think is often misused or misunderstood. Possible examples include *feminism, adolescent, illiteracy, academic honesty, heavy metal, new age philosophy,* or *senior citizen.* Write an essay presenting what you believe to be the correct definition of this term. Begin with several illustrations showing how the word is commonly misused or misunderstood, and point out the errors in these interpretations. Then provide your own definition, using clear examples to convey why your understanding of the word is more accurate.

Writing Assignments Using Other Patterns of Development

∞ 3. The child who called the author "nigger" failed to recognize Naylor's individual worth. In an essay, tell about a time you had trouble viewing someone as an individual—either because of something about the person or because of something about you or the way you were raised. In an essay, explore what happened when you treated this person inappropriately or unjustly. How did you act? How did the other person respond? What did you learn from the experience? William Raspberry's "The Handicap of Definition" (page 548) provides insight into the way preconceptions influence behavior.

∞ 4. The boy who spit out the hateful term *nigger* undoubtedly acquired his prejudiced attitudes at home. Focus on one group that is often the object of prejudice (for example, the elderly, the physically handicapped, the overweight, or a particular ethnic or racial group), and write an essay illustrating the steps that parents *or* schools might take to develop children's appreciation of diversity in general and of that group in particular. To illustrate the need for such an approach, open with a dramatic example of children's prejudiced thinking about the group in question. Before writing the essay, brainstorm ideas with friends and classmates, and read Ji-Yeon Mary Yuhfill's "Let's Tell the Story of All America's Cultures" (page 630), an essay that pleads eloquently for the recognition of diversity. Also consider going to the library to read about programs that encourage children's tolerance. Bibliographic sources like the *New York Times Index*, the *Social Sciences Index*, and the *Education Index* will help you locate relevant information.

Marie Winn

Born in Czechoslovakia and brought by her family to New York, Marie Winn was educated at Radcliffe College. The author or editor of ten children's books, Winn developed a special interest in the effect of television on children. She has contributed numerous articles to such publications as the *New York Times* and *Village Voice*. Winn's provocative and influential study, *The Plug-In Drug: Television, Children and Family*, was originally published in 1977 and revised in 1985. The selection that follows is from that book. Other books by Winn include *Children Without Childhood* (1983) and *Unplugging the Plug-In Drug* (1987).

TV Addiction

You arrive home from work or school. Do you automatically flick on the TV—or is it already on, even though no one is watching? Television has become an overwhelming presence in our lives. In the following selection, Marie Winn suggests that television can be as addictive as alcohol and drugs. She warns that TV addiction, like other addictions, can cause people to lose their families, leave their jobs, and distort their perspective on life.

Cookies or Heroin?

The word "addiction" is often used loosely and wryly in conversation. People will refer to themselves as "mystery book addicts" or "cookie addicts." E. B. White wrote of his annual surge of interest in gardening: "We are hooked and are making an attempt to kick the habit." Yet nobody really believes that reading mysteries or ordering seeds by catalogue is serious enough to be compared with addictions to heroin or alcohol. The word "addiction" is here used jokingly to denote a tendency to overindulge in some pleasurable activity.

People often refer to being "hooked on TV." Does this, too, fall into the lighthearted category of cookie eating and other pleasures that people pursue with unusual intensity, or is there a kind of television viewing that falls into the more serious category of destructive addiction?

When we think about addiction to drugs or alcohol we fre-   3
quently focus on negative aspects, ignoring the pleasures that accompany drinking or drug-taking. And yet the essence of any serious
addiction is a pursuit of pleasure, a search for a "high" that normal
life does not supply. It is only the inability to function without the
addictive substance that is dismaying, the dependence of the organism upon a certain experience and an increasing inability to function
normally without it. Thus people will take two or three drinks at the
end of the day not merely for the pleasure drinking provides, but also
because they "don't feel normal" without them.

Real addicts do not merely pursue a pleasurable experience one   4
time in order to function normally. They need to *repeat* it again and
again. Something about that particular experience makes life without
it less than complete. Other potentially pleasurable experiences are
no longer possible, for under the spell of the addictive experience,
their lives are peculiarly distorted. The addict craves an experience
and yet is never really satisfied. The organism may be temporarily sated, but soon it begins to crave again.

Finally, a serious addiction is distinguished from a harmless pur-   5
suit of pleasure by its distinctly destructive elements. Heroin addicts,
for instance, lead a damaged life: their increasing need for heroin in
increasing doses prevents them from working, from maintaining relationships, from developing in human ways. Similarly alcoholics'
lives are narrowed and dehumanized by their dependence on alcohol.

Let us consider television viewing in the light of the conditions   6
that define serious addictions.

Not unlike drugs or alcohol, the television experience allows the   7
participant to blot out the real world and enter into a pleasurable and
passive mental state. The worries and anxieties of reality are as effectively deferred by becoming absorbed in a television program as by
going on a "trip" induced by drugs or alcohol. And just as alcoholics
are only vaguely aware of their addiction, feeling that they control
their drinking more than they really do ("I can cut it out any time I
want—I just like to have three or four drinks before dinner"), people
similarly overestimate their control over television watching. Even as
they put off other activities to spend hour after hour watching television, they feel they could easily resume living in a different, less passive
style. But somehow or other, while the television set is present in their
homes, the click doesn't sound. With television pleasures available,
those other experiences seem less attractive, more difficult somehow.

A heavy viewer (a college English instructor) observes: 8

"I find television almost irresistible. When the set is on, I cannot 9
ignore it. I can't turn it off. I feel sapped, will-less, enervated. As I
reach out to turn off the set, the strength goes out of my arms. So I
sit there for hours and hours."

Self-confessed television addicts often feel they "ought" to do 10
other things—but the fact that they don't read and don't plant their
garden or sew or crochet or play games or have conversations means
that those activities are no longer as desirable as television viewing. In
a way the lives of heavy viewers are as imbalanced by their television
"habit" as a drug addict's or an alcoholic's. They are living in a holding pattern, as it were, passing up the activities that lead to growth or
development or a sense of accomplishment. This is one reason people
talk about their television viewing so ruefully, so apologetically. They
are aware that it is an unproductive experience, that almost any other
endeavor is more worthwhile by any human measure.

Finally it is the adverse effect of television viewing on the lives 11
of so many people that defines it as a serious addiction. The television
habit distorts the sense of time. It renders other experiences vague
and curiously unreal while taking on a greater reality for itself. It
weakens relationships by reducing and sometimes eliminating normal opportunities for talking, for communicating.

And yet television does not satisfy, else why would the viewer 12
continue to watch hour after hour, day after day? "The measure of
health," writes Lawrence Kubie, "is flexibility...and especially the
freedom to cease when sated." But heavy television viewers can never
be sated with their television experiences—they do not provide the
true nourishment that satiation requires—and thus they find that
they cannot stop watching.

A former heavy watcher (filmmaker) describes such a syndrome: 13

"I remember when we first got the set I'd watch for hours and 14
hours, whenever I could, and I remember that feeling of tiredness
and anxiety that always followed those orgies, a sense of time terribly
wasted. It was like eating cotton candy; television promised so much
richness, I couldn't wait for it, and then it just evaporated into air. I
remember feeling terribly drained after watching for a long time."

Similarly a nursery school teacher remembers her own child- 15
hood television experience:

"I remember bingeing on television when I was a child and hav- 16
ing that vapid feeling after watching hours of TV. I'd look forward

to watching whenever I could, but it just didn't give back a real feeling of pleasure. It was like no orgasm, no catharsis, very frustrating. Television just wasn't giving me the promised satisfaction, and yet I kept on watching. It filled some sort of need, or had to do with an inability to get something started."

The testimonies of ex-television addicts often have the evangelistic overtones of stories heard at Alcoholics Anonymous meetings. 17

A handbag repair shop owner says: 18

"I'd get on the subway home from work with the newspaper 19 and immediately turn to the TV page to plan out my evening's watching. I'd come home, wash, change my clothes, and tell my wife to start the machine so it would be warmed up. (We had an old-fashioned set that took a few seconds before an image appeared.) And then we'd watch TV for the rest of the evening. We'd eat our dinner in the living room while watching, and we'd only talk every once in a while, during the ads, if at all. I'd watch anything, good, bad, or indifferent.

"All the while we were watching I'd feel terribly angry at myself 20 for wasting all that time watching junk. I could never go to sleep until at least the eleven o'clock news, and then sometimes I'd still stay up for the late-night talk show. I had a feeling that I *had* to watch the news programs, that I *had* to know what was happening, even though most of the time nothing much was happening and I could easily find out what was by reading the paper the next morning. Usually my wife would fall asleep on the couch while I was watching. I'd get angry at her for doing that. Actually, I was angry at myself. I had a collection of three years of back issues of different magazines that I planned to read sometime, but I never got around to reading them. I never got around to sorting or labeling my collection of slides I had made when traveling. I only had time for television. We'd take the telephone off the hook while watching so we wouldn't be interrupted! We like classical music, but we never listened to any, never!

"Then one day the set broke. I said to my wife, 'Let's not fix it. 21 Let's just see what happens.' Well, that was the smartest thing we ever did. We haven't had a TV in the house since then.

"Now I look back and I can hardly believe we could have lived 22 like that. I feel that my mind was completely mummified for all those years. I was glued to that machine and couldn't get loose, somehow. It really frightens me to think of it. Yes, I'm frightened of TV now.

I don't think I could control it if we had a set in the house again. I think it would take over no matter what I did."

A further sign of addiction is that "an exclusive craving for something is accompanied by a loss of discrimination towards the object which satisfies the craving...the alcoholic is not interested in the taste of liquor that is available; likewise the compulsive eater is not particular about what he eats when there is food around," write the authors of a book about the nature of addiction. And just so, for many viewers the process of *watching* television is far more important than the actual contents of the programs being watched. The knowledge that the act of watching is more important than *what* is being watched lies behind the practice of "roadblocking," invented by television advertisers and adopted by political candidates who purchase the same half-hour on all three channels in order to force-feed their message to the public. As one prominent candidate put it, "People will watch television no matter what is on, and if you allow them no other choice they will watch your show."

Questions for Close Reading

1. What is the selection's thesis? Locate the sentence(s) in which Winn states her main idea. If she doesn't state the thesis explicitly, express it in your own words.
2. Why, according to Winn, is a gardening addiction or a mystery book addiction a humorous kind of habit? What does she call "the essence of any serious addiction"?
3. In paragraph 7, the author says that television allows the viewer "to enter into a pleasurable...mental state," and later that "television does not satisfy." How does Winn prepare you earlier in the essay for this seeming contradiction?
4. Since television does "not provide the true nourishment that satiation requires," what activities does Winn suggest as truly nourishing alternatives?
5. Refer to your dictionary as needed to define the following words used in the selection: *wryly* (paragraph 1), *ruefully* (10), *adverse* (11), and *satiation* (12).

Questions About the Writer's Craft

1. **The pattern.**   At the beginning of the essay, Winn uses definition by negation to clarify her interpretation of the term *television addiction*. What kinds of things does Winn say are *not* the equivalents of TV addiction? Why does she use this strategy of definition by negation?

2. How does Winn organize the two extended definitions of addiction and TV addiction? How does this organizational pattern help Winn persuade readers to accept her point that TV is addicting?
3. What do the quotations from TV addicts add to Winn's argument? Why do you think Winn chooses quotations from these people?
4. How does the lengthy discussion of addiction (paragraphs 3–5) help Winn to convince readers that television is indeed addicting?

Questions for Further Thought

1. Do you agree with Winn that excess television viewing is as addictive as drug and alcohol abuse? Is using the medical idea of addiction a productive way for our society to go about understanding and solving the problem of "too much TV"?
2. Consider the characteristics of addiction as presented in paragraphs 3 through 5. Do you think all types of people are likely to become addicted to something? Are there any types of people who might be totally immune?
3. Do you or people you know watch too much television? Or do you find yourself addicted to some other electronic medium—or another nondrug activity? Is your addiction humorous or serious?
4. Reformed alcoholics and drug abusers are taught to avoid places where they might feel tempted. Few families would be willing to get rid of their televisions. What methods could parents or individuals use to prevent or lessen TV addiction?

Writing Assignments Using Definition as a Pattern of Development

1. In her introduction, Winn describes how people often use a very serious term—*addiction*—when referring to a light or harmless experience. Think of another term that you feel is serious, but that people use lightly and apply loosely. Your choice could be *friendship*, *love*, *hate*, or another word. Begin with an example that shows how the word is misused, and then provide an extended definition clarifying the proper use of the term.
2. TV addiction is only one of many forms of addiction. Others, such as addictions to gambling, baseball games, cars, bingo, chocolate, and the latest clothing styles, also exist. Write an essay on another addiction, using one of the addictions just listed or another of your own choice.

Writing Assignments Using Other Patterns of Development

∞ 3. Many kinds of television shows come in for criticism—"tabloid TV" talk shows, sitcoms, game shows, children's cartoons, news broadcasts, and so forth. Pick one kind of TV show and write an essay defending the genre. Or argue that this type of show has no merit. Your essay may be serious or playful. Neil Postman's view of television in "Future Shlock" (page 248) may spur you to imaginative thinking of your own.

4. You have probably heard from older relatives (or may yourself know) what life was like before TV. Write an essay for your future children or grandchildren describing what life was like before one or several of these new technologies: VCRs, cable TV, computers, microwave ovens, cash cards, and the like. Persuade your descendants that life was better *or* worse before these items were invented.

William Raspberry

Journalist William Raspberry was born in Okolona, Mississippi. From his mother, an English teacher and poet, Raspberry learned to care "about the rhythm and grace of words." His father, a shop teacher, taught him "that neither end tables nor arguments are worthwhile unless they stand solidly on all four legs." Raspberry graduated from Indiana Central College and later joined the staff of the Indianapolis *Recorder* as a reporter and editor. Following a two-year stint in the army, he was hired by the *Washington Post*, where his nationally syndicated column has originated since 1971. His coverage of the Watts race riots in 1965 won him the Capital Press Club Journalist of the Year award. Raspberry's views have been shaped by accidents of time and history: being born into a family of teachers, growing up as an African-American in segregated Mississippi, and coming of age in the era of the civil rights and women's movements. Raspberry's carefully reasoned arguments defy politics and place him in neither the liberal nor the conservative camp. He believes instead that both opportunity *and* self-motivation are essential if minorities are to move into mainstream American life. *Looking Backward at Us*, a collection of Raspberry's columns, was published in 1991. The following selection appeared in Raspberry's *Washington Post* column in 1982.

The Handicap of Definition

If youngsters are repeatedly told that they—indeed, the ethnic group to which they belong—are good at some things but not at others, eventually they'll internalize such assertions. Developing this point further, William Raspberry discusses the effect of such ingrained assumptions, asserting that ill-founded beliefs about what it means to be black have taken a tragic toll on his fellow African-Americans. Urging a reexamination of such limiting preconceptions, Raspberry advocates a more encompassing definition of black identity.

I know all about bad schools, mean politicians, economic deprivation and racism. Still, it occurs to me that one of the heaviest bur- 1 dens black Americans—and black children in particular—have to bear is the handicap of definition: the question of what it means to be black.

Let me explain quickly what I mean. If a basketball fan says that 2 the Boston Celtics' Larry Bird plays "black," the fan intends it—and Bird probably accepts it—as a compliment. Tell pop singer Tom Jones he moves "black" and he might grin in appreciation. Say to Teena Marie or the Average White Band that they sound "black" and they'll thank you.

But name one pursuit, aside from athletics, entertainment or 3 sexual performance, in which a white practitioner will feel complimented to be told he does it "black." Tell a white broadcaster he talks "black" and he'll sign up for diction lessons. Tell a white reporter he writes "black" and he'll take a writing course. Tell a white lawyer he reasons "black" and he might sue you for slander.

What we have here is a tragically limited definition of black- 4 ness, and it isn't only white people who buy it.

Think of all the ways black children can put one another down 5 with charges of "whiteness." For many of these children, hard study and hard work are "white." Trying to please a teacher might be criticized as acting "white." Speaking correct English is "white." Scrimping today in the interest of tomorrow's goals is "white." Educational toys and games are "white."

An incredible array of habits and attitudes that are conducive to 6 success in business, in academia, in the nonentertainment professions are likely to be thought of as somehow "white." Even economic success, unless it involves such "black" undertakings as numbers banking, is defined as "white."

And the results are devastating. I wouldn't deny that blacks of- 7 ten are better entertainers and athletes. My point is the harm that comes from too narrow a definition of what is black.

One reason black youngsters tend to do better at basketball, for 8 instance, is that they assume they can learn to do it well, and so they practice constantly to prove themselves right.

Wouldn't it be wonderful if we could infect black children with 9 the notion that excellence in math is "black" rather than white, or possibly Chinese? Wouldn't it be of enormous value if we could create the myth that morality, strong families, determination, courage and love of learning are traits brought by slaves from Mother Africa and therefore quintessentially black?

There is no doubt in my mind that most black youngsters could   10
develop their mathematical reasoning, their elocution and their attitudes the way they develop their jump shots and their dance steps: by
the combination of sustained, enthusiastic practice and the unques-
tioned belief that they can do it.

In one sense, what I am talking about is the importance of de-   11
veloping positive ethnic traditions. Maybe Jews have an innate talent
for communication; maybe the Chinese are born with a gift for mathematical reasoning; maybe blacks are naturally blessed with athletic
grace. I doubt it. What is at work, I suspect, is assumption, inculcated
early in their lives, that this is a thing our people do well.

Unfortunately, many of the things about which blacks make this   12
assumption are things that do not contribute to their career success—except for that handful of the truly gifted who can make it as
entertainers and athletes. And many of the things we concede to
whites are the things that are essential to economic security.

So it is with a number of assumptions black youngsters make   13
about what it is to be a "man": physical aggressiveness, sexual prow-
ess, the refusal to submit to authority. The prisons are full of people
who, by this perverted definition, are unmistakably men.

But the real problem is not so much that the things defined as   14
"black" are negative. The problem is that the definition is much too
narrow.

Somehow, we have to make our children understand that they   15
are intelligent, competent people, capable of doing whatever they
put their minds to and making it in the American mainstream, not
just in a black subculture.

What we seem to be doing, instead, is raising up yet another   16
generation of young blacks who will be failures—by definition.

Questions for Close Reading

1. What is the selection's thesis? Locate the sentence(s) in which Raspberry
   states his main idea. If he doesn't state the thesis explicitly, express it in
   your own words.
2. In paragraph 14, Raspberry emphasizes that the word *black* presents a
   problem not because it's negative but because it has become "much too
   narrow." According to Raspberry, what limitations have become associated with the term *black?* What negative consequences does he see resulting from these limitations?

3. In paragraph 11, Raspberry talks about "positive ethnic traditions." What does he mean by this term? What examples does he provide?
4. In Raspberry's opinion, what needs to be done to ensure the future success of African-American children?
5. Refer to your dictionary as needed to define the following words used in the selection: *diction* (paragraph 3), *scrimping* (5), *array* (6), *quintessentially* (9), *elocution* (10), *inculcated* (11), and *concede* (12).

Questions About the Writer's Craft

1. **The pattern.**   Raspberry is primarily concerned with showing how limited the definition of *black* has come to be in our society. In the course of the essay, though, he also defines three other terms. Locate these terms and their definitions. How do the definitions and the effects of the definitions help Raspberry make his point about the narrowness of the term *black*?

2. **Other patterns.**   In his opening paragraph, Raspberry uses the argumentation technique of refutation. What does he refute? What does he achieve by using this strategy at the very beginning of the essay?

3. A black journalist, Raspberry writes a nationally syndicated column that originates in the *Washington Post*, a major newspaper serving the nation's capital and the nation as a whole. Consider these facts when examining Raspberry's use of the pronouns *I*, *we*, and *our* in the essay. What do these pronouns seem to imply about Raspberry's intended audience? What is the effect of these pronouns?

4. Raspberry has chosen a relatively abstract topic to write about—the meaning of the term *black*. What techniques does he use to draw in readers and keep them engaged? Consider his overall tone, choice of examples, and use of balanced sentence structure.

Questions for Further Thought

1. Raspberry focuses on the limitations inherent in several terms. Can you think of other terms used to define a specific group of people? Do such terms ever have positive effects? If they do, in what circumstances?

2. Among your family and friends, do you detect any prejudice for or against the values Raspberry characterizes as "white"—for example, "hard study and hard work," "trying to please" a teacher, using "correct English," "scrimping," or buying "educational toys or games"? What does your response suggest about your family's or your friends' underlying assumptions?

3. Raspberry states that it isn't inherited talent that determines what a person accomplishes, but the person's belief that he or she can indeed achieve. Do you agree? In which situations might inherited or innate

talent be critical? In which situations might a person's self-confidence outweigh the genetic factor?

4. In paragraph 15, Raspberry explains that black children should be given a self-image that encourages them to succeed "in the American mainstream, not just in a black subculture." Do you agree that involvement in a subculture isn't as important as participation in the "American mainstream"? Do you have any criticisms of the "American mainstream" that make you less than enthusiastic about encouraging those outside it to join in?

Writing Assignments Using Definition as a Pattern of Development

∞ 1. Raspberry points out how restrictive the definitions of *black* and *white* can be. Do you think that the definitions of *male* and *female* can be equally restrictive? Focusing on the term *male* or *female*, write an essay showing how the term was defined as you were growing up. Considering the messages conveyed by your family, the educational system, and society at large, indicate whether you came to perceive the term as limiting or liberating. Before planning your paper, you may want to read one or more of the following essays, all of which deal with the way gender roles influence behavior: Scott Russell Sanders's "The Men We Carry in Our Minds" (page 308), Alleen Pace Nilsen's "Sexism and Language" (page 209), Barbara Ehrenreich's "What I've Learned From Men" (page 261), Deborah Tannen's "Sex, Lies, and Conversation" (page 428), Judy Brady's "Why I Want a Wife" (page 530), and Virginia Woolf's "Professions for Women" (page 695).

2. In paragraph 15, Raspberry seems to define *success* as "making it in the American mainstream," but not everyone would agree that this is what constitutes success. Write an essay in which you offer your personal definition of *success*. One way to proceed might be to contrast what you consider success with what you consider failure. Or you might narrate the success story of a person you respect highly. No matter how you proceed, be sure to provide telling specifics that support your definition.

Writing Assignments Using Other Patterns of Development

∞ 3. Like most people, you've probably had a "defining" term applied to you at one time or another. Perhaps you've been called "shy" or "stubborn" or "the class clown" or "the athlete in the family." Focusing on one such label that's been applied to you, write an essay showing the effect of this term on your life. Be sure to explain why you got the label and how you felt about it. The following essays will give you additional perspectives on the ways that labels and names affect people's lives and self-image: Alice Walker's "Beauty: When the Other Dancer Is the Self" (page 485), Gloria Naylor's "Mommy, What Does 'Nigger' Mean?" (page 535), and Joan Didion's "On Self-Respect" (page 715).

4. In his conclusion, Raspberry makes a plea for providing the younger generation with a more positive, more expansive definition of *black*. Consider the beliefs and principles that today's older generation seems to impart to the younger generation. Write an essay showing which aspects of this value system seem helpful and valid and which do not. Also explain what additional values and convictions the older generation should be passing on. How should parents, teachers, and others convey these precepts?

Additional Writing Topics

DEFINITION

General Assignments

Use definition to develop any of the following topics. Once you fix on a limited subject, decide if the essay has an informative or a persuasive purpose. The paper might begin with the etymology of the term, a stipulative definition, or a definition by negation. You may want to use a number of writing patterns—such as description, comparison, narration, process analysis—to develop the definition. Remember, too, that the paper doesn't have to be scholarly and serious. There is no reason it can't be a lighthearted discussion of the meaning of a term.

1. Fads
2. A family fight
3. Helplessness
4. An epiphany
5. A workaholic
6. A Pollyanna
7. A con artist
8. A stingy person
9. A team player
10. A Yiddish term like *mensch, klutz, chutzpah,* or *dreck,* or a term from some other ethnic group
11. Adolescence
12. Fast food
13. A perfect day
14. Hypocrisy
15. Inner peace
16. Obsession
17. Generosity
18. Exploitation
19. Depression
20. A double bind

Assignments With a Specific Purpose and Audience

1. *Newsweek* magazine runs a popular column called "My Turn," consisting of readers' opinions on subjects of general interest. Write a piece for this column defining *today's college students*. Use the piece to dispel some negative stereotypes (for example, that college students are apathetic, ill-informed, self-centered, and materialistic).

2. You're an attorney arguing a case of sexual harassment—a charge your client has leveled against her boss, a business executive. To win the case, you must present to the jury a clear definition of exactly what *sexual harassment* is and isn't. Write such a definition for your opening remarks in court.

3. You have been asked to write part of a pamphlet for students who come to the college health clinic. For this pamphlet, define *one* of the following conditions and its symptoms: *depression, stress, burnout, test anxiety, addiction* (to alcohol, drugs, or TV), *workaholism*. Part of the pamphlet should describe ways to cope with the condition described.

4. A new position has opened in your company. Write a job description to be sent to employment agencies that will screen candidates. Your description should define the job's purpose, state the duties involved, and outline essential qualifications.

5. Part of your job as peer counselor in your college's counseling center involves helping people communicate more effectively. To assist students, write a definition of some term that you think represents an essential component of a strong interpersonal relationship. You might, for example, define *respect, sharing, equality,* or *trust.* Part of the definition should employ definition by negation, a discussion of what the term is *not.*

6. Having waited on tables for several years at a resort hotel, you've been asked by the hotel manager to give some pointers to this year's new dining hall staff. Prepare a talk in which you define *courtesy,* the quality you consider most essential to the job. Use specific examples to illustrate your definition.

12
ARGUMENTATION-PERSUASION

WHAT IS
ARGUMENTATION-PERSUASION?

"You can't possibly believe what you're saying."
"Look, I know what I'm talking about, and that's that."

Does this heated exchange sound familiar? Probably. When we hear the word *argument,* most of us think of a verbal battle propelled by stubbornness and irrational thought, with one person pitted against the other.

    Argumentation in writing, though, is a different matter. Using clear thinking and logic, the writer tries to convince readers of the soundness of a particular opinion on a controversial issue. If, while trying to convince, the writer uses emotional language and dramatic appeals to readers' concerns, beliefs, and values, then the piece is called *persuasion.* Besides encouraging acceptance of an opinion, persuasion often encourages readers (or another group) to commit themselves to a course of action. Assume you're writing an essay protesting the federal government's policy of offering aid to those suffering from hunger in other countries while many Americans go hungry. If your purpose is to document, coolly and objectively, the presence of hunger in the United States, you would prepare an argumentation essay. Such an essay would be filled with statistics, report findings, and expert opinion to demonstrate how widespread hunger is nationwide. If, however, your purpose is to shake up readers, even motivate them to write letters to their congressional representatives and push for a change in policy, you would write a persuasive essay. In this case, your essay might contain emotional accounts of undernourished children, ill-fed pregnant women, and nearly starving elderly people.

Because people respond rationally *and* emotionally to situations, argumentation and persuasion are usually *combined*. Suppose you decide to write an article for the campus newspaper advocating a pre-Labor Day start for the school year. Your audience includes the college administration, students, and faculty. The article might begin by *arguing* that several schools starting the academic year earlier were able to close for the month of January and thus reduce heating and other maintenance expenses. Such an argument, supported by documented facts and figures, would help convince the administration. Realizing that you also have to gain student and faculty support for your idea, you might argue further that the proposed change would mean that students and faculty could leave for winter break with the semester behind them—papers written, exams taken, grades calculated and recorded. To make this part of your argument especially compelling, you could adopt a *persuasive* strategy by using emotional appeals and positively charged language: "Think how pleasant it would be to sleep late, spend time with family and friends, toast the New Year—without having to worry about work awaiting you back on campus."

When argumentation and persuasion blend in this way, emotion *supports* rather than *replaces* logic and sound reasoning. Although some writers resort to emotional appeals to the exclusion of rational thought, when you prepare argumentation-persuasion essays, you should advance your position through a balanced appeal to reason and emotion.

HOW ARGUMENTATION-PERSUASION FITS YOUR PURPOSE AND AUDIENCE

You probably realize that argumentation, persuasion, or a combination of the two is everywhere: an editorial urging the overhaul of an ill-managed literacy program; a commercial for a new shampoo; a scientific report advocating increased funding for AIDS research. Your own writing involves argumentation-persuasion as well. When you prepare a *causal analysis, descriptive piece, narrative,* or *definition essay,* you advance a specific point of view: MTV has a negative influence on teens' view of sex; Cape Cod in winter is imbued with a special kind of magic; a disillusioning experience can teach people much about themselves; *character* can be defined as the willingness to take unpopular positions on difficult issues. Indeed, an essay organized around any of the patterns of development described in this book may have a persuasive intent. You might, for example, encourage readers to try out a *process* you've explained, or to see one of the two movies you've *compared*.

Argumentation-persuasion, however, involves more than presenting a point of view and providing evidence. Unlike other forms of writing, it assumes controversy and addresses opposing viewpoints. Consider the following assignments, all of which require the writer to take a position on a controversial issue:

> In parts of the country, communities established for older citizens or childless couples have refused to rent to families with children. How do you feel about this situation? What do you think are the rights of the parties involved?

> Citing the fact that the highest percentage of automobile accidents involve young men, insurance companies consistently charge their highest rates to young males. Is this policy fair? Why or why not?

> Some colleges and universities have instituted a "no pass, no play" policy for athletes. Explain why this practice is or is not appropriate.

It's impossible to predict with absolute certainty what will make readers accept the view you advance or take the action you propose. But the ancient Greeks, who formulated our basic concepts of logic, isolated three factors crucial to the effectiveness of argumentation-persuasion: *logos, pathos,* and *ethos.*

Your main concern in an argumentation-persuasion essay should be with the *logos,* or soundness, of your argument: the facts, statistics, examples, and authoritative statements you gather to support your viewpoint. This supporting evidence must be unified, specific, sufficient, accurate, and representative (see pages 38–42). Imagine, for instance, you want to convince people that a popular charity misappropriates the money it receives from the public. Your readers, inclined to believe in the good works of the charity, will probably dismiss your argument unless you can substantiate your claim with valid, well-documented evidence that enhances the *logos* of your position.

Sensitivity to *pathos,* or the emotional power of language, is another key consideration for writers of argumentation-persuasion essays. *Pathos* appeals to readers' needs, values, and attitudes, encouraging them to commit themselves to a viewpoint or course of action. The *pathos* of a piece derives partly from the writer's language. *Connotative* language—words with strong emotional overtones—can move readers to accept a point of view and may even spur them to act.

Advertising and propaganda generally rely on *pathos* to the exclusion of logic, using emotion to influence and manipulate. Consider the following pitches for a man's cologne and a woman's perfume. The language—and the attitudes to which it appeals—is different in each case:

> Brawn: Experience the power. Bold. Yet subtle. Clean. Masculine. The scent for the man who's in charge.

> Black Lace is for you—the woman who dresses for success but who dares to be provocative, slightly naughty. Black Lace. Perfect with pearls by day and with diamonds by night.

The appeal to men plays on the impact that words like *Brawn, bold, power,* and *in charge* may have for some males. Similarly, the charged words *Black Lace, provocative, naughty,* and *diamonds* are intended to appeal to business women who—in the advertiser's mind, at least—may be looking for ways to reconcile sensuality and professionalism. (For more on slanted language, read Ann McClintock's "Propaganda Techniques in Today's Advertising," page 315.)

Like an advertising copywriter, you must select language that reinforces your message. In a paper supporting an expanded immigration policy, you might use evocative phrases like "land of liberty," "a nation of immigrants," and "America's open-door policy." However, if you were arguing for strict immigration quotas, you might use language like "save jobs for unemployed Americans," "flood of unskilled labor," and "illegal aliens." Remember, though: Such language should support, not supplant, clear thinking.

Finally, whenever you write an argumentation-persuasion essay, you should establish your *ethos*, or credibility and integrity. You cannot expect readers to accept or act on your viewpoint unless you convince them that you know what you're talking about and that you're worth listening to. Be sure, then, to tell readers about any experiences you've had that make you knowledgeable about the issue being discussed. You will also come across as knowledgeable and trustworthy if you present a logical, reasoned argument that takes opposing views into account. And make sure that your appeals to emotion aren't excessive. Overwrought emotionalism undercuts credibility. Remember, too, that *ethos* isn't constant. A writer may have credibility on one subject but not on another: An army general might be a reliable source for information on military preparedness but not for information on federal funding of day care.

Writing an effective argumentation-persuasion essay involves an interplay of *logos, pathos,* and *ethos.* The exact balance among these factors is determined by your audience and purpose (that is, whether you want the audience simply to agree with your view or whether you also want them to take action). More than any other kind of writing, argumentation-persuasion requires that you *analyze your readers* and tailor your approach to them. You need to determine how much they know about the issue, how they feel about you and your position, what their values and attitudes are, what motivates them.

In general, most readers will fall into one of three broad categories: supportive, wavering, or hostile. Each type of audience requires a different blend of *logos, pathos,* and *ethos* in an argumentation-persuasion essay.

1. A supportive audience. If your audience agrees with your position and trusts your credibility, you don't need a highly reasoned argument dense with facts, examples, and statistics. Although you may want to solidify support by providing additional information (*logos*), you can rely primarily on *pathos*—a strong emotional appeal—to reinforce readers' commitment to your shared viewpoint. Assume that you belong to a local fishing club and have volunteered to write an article encouraging members to support threatened fishing rights in state parks. You might begin by stating that fishing strengthens the fish population by thinning out overcrowded streams. Since your audience would certainly be familiar with this idea, you wouldn't need to devote much discussion to it. Instead, you would attempt to move them emotionally. You might evoke the camaraderie in the sport, the pleasure of a perfect cast, the beauty of the outdoors, and perhaps conclude with "If you want these enjoyments to continue, please make a generous contribution to our fund."

2. A wavering audience. At times, readers may be open to what you have to say but may not be committed fully to your viewpoint. Or perhaps they're not as informed about the subject as they should be. In either case, you don't want to risk alienating them with a heavy-handed emotional appeal. Concentrate instead on *ethos* and *logos,* bolstering your image as a reliable source and providing the evidence needed to advance your position. If you want to convince an audience of high school seniors to take a year off to work between high school and college, you might establish your credibility by recounting the year you spent working and by showing the positive effects it had on your life (*ethos*). In addition, you could cite studies indicating that delayed entry into college is related to higher grade point averages. A year's savings, you would explain, allows students to study when they might otherwise need to hold down a job to earn money for tuition (*logos*).

3. A hostile audience. An apathetic, skeptical, or hostile audience is obviously most difficult to convince. With such an audience, you should avoid emotional appeals because they might seem irrational, sentimental, or even comical. Instead, weigh the essay heavily in favor of logical reasoning and hard-to-dispute facts (*logos*). Assume your college administration is working to ban liquor from the student pub. You plan to submit to the campus newspaper an open letter supporting this generally unpopular effort. To sway other students, you cite the positive experiences of schools that have gone dry. Many colleges, you explain, have found their tavern revenues actually increase because all students—not just those of drinking age—can now support the pub. With the greater revenues, some schools have upgraded the food served in the pubs and have hired disc jockeys or musical groups to provide entertainment. Many schools have also seen a sharp reduction in alcohol-related vandalism. Readers may not be won over to your side, but your sound, logical argument may encourage them to be more tolerant of your viewpoint. Indeed, such increased receptivity may be all you can reasonably expect from a hostile audience. (For more help in analyzing your audience, see page 18.)

SUGGESTIONS FOR USING ARGUMENTATION-PERSUASION IN AN ESSAY

1. At the beginning of the paper, identify the controversy surrounding the issue and state your position in the thesis. Your introduction should clarify the controversy about the issue. In addition, it should provide as much background information as your readers are likely to need.

The thesis of an argumentation-persuasion paper is often called the *assertion* or *proposition*. Occasionally, the proposition appears at the paper's end, but it is usually stated at the beginning. If you state the thesis right away, your audience knows where you stand and is better able to evaluate the evidence presented.

Remember: Argumentation-persuasion assumes conflicting viewpoints. Be sure your proposition focuses on a controversial issue and indicates your view. Avoid a proposition that is merely factual; what is demonstrably true allows little room for debate. To see the difference between a factual statement and an effective thesis, examine the two statements that follow:

> *Fact:* In the past decade, the nation's small farmers have suffered financial hardships.

> *Thesis:* Inefficient management, rather than competition from agricultural conglomerates, is responsible for the financial plight of the nation's small farmers.

The first statement is certainly true. It would be difficult to find anyone who believes that these are easy times for small farmers. Because the statement invites little opposition, it can't serve as the focus of an argumentation-persuasion essay. The second statement, though, takes a controversial stance on a complex issue. Such a proposition is a valid starting point for a paper intended to argue and persuade. However, don't assume that such advice means that you should take a highly opinionated position in your thesis. A dogmatic, overstated proposition ("Campus security is staffed by overpaid, badge-flashing incompetents") is bound to alienate some readers.

Remember also to keep the proposition narrow and specific, so you can focus your thoughts in a purposeful way. Consider the following statements:

> *Broad thesis:* The welfare system has been abused over the years.

> *Narrow thesis:* Welfare payments should be denied to unmarried teenage girls who have more than one child out of wedlock.

If you tried to write a paper based on the first statement, you would face an unmanageable task—showing all the ways that welfare has been abused. Your readers would also be confused about what to expect in the paper: Will it discuss unscrupulous bureaucrats, fraudulent bookkeeping, dishonest recipients? In contrast, the revised thesis is limited and specific. It signals that the paper will propose severe restrictions on welfare payments. Such a proposal will surely have opponents and is thus appropriate for argumentation-persuasion.

The thesis in an argumentation-persuasion essay can simply state your opinion about an issue, or it can go a step further and call for some action:

> *Opinion:* The lack of affordable day-care centers discriminates against lower-income families.

Call for action: The federal government should support the creation of more day-care centers in low-income neighborhoods.

In either case, your stand on the issue must be clear to your readers.

2. Provide readers with strong support for the thesis. Finding evidence that relates to the readers' needs, values, and experience is a crucial part of writing an effective argumentation-persuasion essay. Readers will be responsive to evidence that is *unified, adequate, specific, accurate,* and *representative* (see pages 38–42). It might consist of personal experiences or observations. Or it could be gathered from outside sources—statistics; facts; examples; or expert authority taken from books, articles, reports, interviews, and documentaries. A paper arguing that elderly Americans are better off than they used to be might incorporate the following kinds of evidence:

- *Personal observation or experience:* A description of the writer's grandparents who are living comfortably on Social Security and pensions.
- *Statistics from a report:* A statement that the per capita after-tax income of older Americans is $335 greater than the national average.
- *Fact from a newspaper article:* The point that the majority of elderly Americans do not live in nursing homes or on the streets; rather, they have their own houses or apartments.
- *Examples from interviews:* Accounts of several elderly couples living comfortably in well-managed retirement villages in Florida.
- *Expert opinion cited in a documentary:* A statement by Dr. Marie Sanchez, a specialist in geriatrics: "An over-sixty-five American today is likely to be healthier, and have a longer life expectancy, than a fifty-year-old living only a decade ago."

As you seek outside evidence, you may—perhaps to your dismay—come across information that undercuts your argument. Resist the temptation to ignore such material; instead, use the evidence to arrive at a more balanced, perhaps somewhat qualified viewpoint. Conversely, don't blindly accept points made by sources agreeing with you. Retain a healthy skepticism, analyzing the material as rigorously as if it were advanced by the opposing side.

Also, keep in mind that outside sources aren't infallible. They may have biases that cause them to skew evidence. So be sure to evaluate your sources. If you're writing an essay supporting a woman's right to abortion, the National Abortion Rights Action League (NARAL) can supply abundant statistics, case studies, and reports. But realize that NARAL most likely won't give you the complete picture; it will probably present evidence that supports its "pro-choice" position only. To counteract such bias, you should review what those with differing opinions have to say. You should, for example, examine material published by such "pro-life" organizations as the National Right-to-Life Committee—keeping in mind, of course, that this material is also bound to present support for its viewpoint only. Remember, too, that there are more than two sides to a complex issue. To get as broad a perspective as possible, you should also track down sources that have no axe to grind—that is, sources that make a deliberate effort to examine all sides of the issue. For example, published proceedings from a debate on abortion or an in-depth article that aims to synthesize various views on abortion would broaden your understanding of this controversial subject.

Whatever sources you use, be sure to *document* (give credit to) that material. Otherwise, readers may dismiss your evidence as nothing more than your subjective opinion, or they may conclude that you have *plagiarized*—tried to pass off someone else's ideas as your own. (Documentation isn't necessary when material is commonly known or is a matter of historical or scientific record.) In brief informal papers, documentation may consist of simple citations like "Psychologist Aaron Beck believes depression is the result of distorted thoughts" or "*Newsweek* (May 1, 1989) reports that most college-admissions procedures are chaotic." In longer, more formal papers, documentation is more detailed (see Chapter 14). One additional point: Because documentation lends a note of objectivity to writing, it may not be appropriate in a paper that cites sources to use the first-person point of view ("I, like many college students, agree with the government report that. . ."). To be on the safe side, check with your instructor to see if you should use the third-person point of view ("Many college students agree with the government report that. . .") instead.

3. Seek to create goodwill. To avoid alienating readers with views different from your own, stay away from condescending expressions like "Anyone can see that..." or "It's obvious that..." Also, guard against personalizing the debate and being confrontational: "*My opponents* find the law ineffective" sounds adversarial, whereas "*Those opposed* to the law find it ineffective" or "*Opponents* of the law find it ineffective" is more evenhanded. The last two statements also focus—as they should—on the issue, not on the people involved in the debate.

Goodwill can also be established by finding a *common ground*—some points on which all sides can agree, despite their differences. Assume a township council has voted to raise property taxes. The additional revenues will be used to preserve, as parkland, a wooded area that would otherwise be sold to developers. Before introducing its tax-hike proposal, the council would do well to remind homeowners of everyone's shared goals: maintaining the town's beauty and preventing the community's overdevelopment. This reminder of the common values shared by the town council and homeowners will probably make residents more receptive to the tax hike. (For more on establishing common ground, see pages 568–70.)

4. Organize the supporting evidence. The support for an argumentation-persuasion paper can be organized in a variety of ways. Any of the patterns of development described in this book (description, narration, definition, causal analysis, and so on) may be used—singly or in combination—to develop the essay's proposition. Imagine you're writing a paper arguing that car racing should be banned from television. Your essay might contain a *description* of a horrifying accident that was televised in graphic detail; you might devote part of the paper to a *causal analysis* showing that the broadcast of such races encourages teens to drive carelessly; you could include a *process analysis* to explain how young drivers "soup up" their cars in a dangerous attempt to imitate the racers seen on television. If your essay includes several patterns, you may need a separate paragraph for each.

When presenting evidence, arrange it so you create the strongest possible effect. In general, you should end with your most compelling point, leaving readers with dramatic evidence that underscores your proposition's validity.

5. Use Rogerian strategy to acknowledge differing viewpoints. If your essay has a clear thesis and strong logical support, you've taken important steps toward winning readers over. However, because argumentation-persuasion focuses on controversial issues, you should also consider contrary points of view. A good argument seeks out and acknowledges conflicting viewpoints. Such a strategy strengthens your argument in several ways. It helps you anticipate objections, alerts you to flaws in your own position, and makes you more aware of the other sides' weaknesses. Further, by acknowledging dissenting views, you come across as reasonable and thorough—qualities that may disarm readers and leave them more receptive to your argument. You may not convince them to surrender their views, but you can enlarge their perspectives and encourage them to think about your position.

Psychologist Carl Rogers took the idea of acknowledging contrary viewpoints a step further. He believed that argumentation's goal should be to *reduce conflict,* rather than to produce a "winner" and a "loser." But he recognized that people identify so strongly with their opinions that they experience any challenge to those opinions as highly threatening. Such a challenge feels like an attack on their very identity. And what's the characteristic response to such a perceived attack? People become defensive; they dig in their heels and become more adamant than ever about their position. Indeed, when confronted with solid information that calls their opinion into question, they devalue that evidence rather than allow themselves to be persuaded. The old maxim about the power of first impressions demonstrates this point. Experiments show that after people form a first impression of another person, they are unlikely to let future conflicting information affect that impression. If, for example, they initially perceive someone to be unpleasant and disagreeable, they tend to reject subsequent evidence that casts the person in a more favorable light.

Taking into account this tendency to cling tenaciously to opinions in the face of a challenge, Rogerian strategy rejects the adversarial approach that often characterizes argumentation. It adopts, instead, a respectful, conciliatory posture—one that demonstrates a real understanding of opposing views, one that emphasizes shared interests and values. Such an approach makes it easier to negotiate differences and arrive at—ideally—a synthesis: a new position that both parties find at least as acceptable as their original positions.

How can you apply Rogerian strategy in your writing? Simply follow these steps:

- Begin by making a conscientious effort to *understand* the viewpoints of those with whom you disagree. As you listen to or read about their opinions, try to put yourself in their shoes; focus on *what they believe* and *why they believe* it, rather than on how you will challenge their beliefs.
- Open your essay with an unbiased, even-handed *restatement of opposing points of view.* Such an objective summary shows that you're fair and open-minded—and not so blinded by the righteousness of your own position that you can't consider any other. Typically, people respond to such a respectful approach by lowering their defenses. Because they appreciate your ability to understand what they have to say, they become more open to your point of view.
- When appropriate, *acknowledge the validity* of some of the arguments raised by those with differing views. What should you do if they make a well-founded point? You'll enhance your credibility if you concede that point while continuing to maintain that, overall, your position is stronger.
- Point out areas of *common ground* (see page 567) by focusing on interests, values, and beliefs that you and those with opposing views share. When you say to them, "Look at the beliefs we share. Look at our common concerns," you communicate that you're not as unlike them as they first believed.
- Finally, *present evidence* for your position. Since those not agreeing with you have been "softened up" by your noncombative stance and disarmed by the realization that you and they share some values and beliefs, they're more ready to consider your point of view.

Let's look at how you can draw upon essentially Rogerian strategy when writing an argumentation-persuasion essay. First, you can use a two-part proposition consisting of a subordinate clause followed by a main clause. The first part of the proposition (the subordinate clause) *acknowledges opposing opinions;* the second part (the main clause) *states your opinion* and implies that your view stands on more solid ground. (When using this kind of proposition, you may, but don't have to, discuss opposing opinions.) The following thesis statement illustrates this strategy (the opposing viewpoint is underlined once; the writer's position is underlined twice):

> <u>Although some instructors think that standardized finals restrict academic freedom, such exams are</u> <u><u>preferable to those prepared by individual professors.</u></u>

Second, you can take one or two paragraphs at the beginning of the essay to *summarize* arguments raised by *opposing viewpoints*, *grant* (when appropriate) the *validity* of some of those points, and then go on to *present evidence* for your position. Imagine you're preparing an editorial for your student newspaper arguing that fraternities and sororities on your campus should be banned. Realizing that many students don't agree with you, you "research" the opposing viewpoint by seeking out supporters of Greek organizations and listening respectfully to the points they raise. When it comes time to write the editorial, you decide not to begin with arguments for your position; instead, you start by summarizing the points made by those supporting fraternities and sororities. You might, for example, mention their argument that Greek organizations build college spirit, contribute to worthy community causes, and provide valuable contacts for entry into the business world. Following this summary of the opposing viewpoint, you might concede that the point about the Greeks' contributions to community causes is especially valid; you could then reinforce this conciliatory stance by stressing some common ground you share—perhaps you acknowledge that you share your detractors' belief that enjoyable social activities with like-minded people are an important part of campus life. Having done all that, you would be in a good position to present arguments for your viewpoint. Because you prepared readers to listen to your opinion, they would tend to be more receptive to your argument.

6. Refute differing viewpoints.   If you perceive weakness in dissenting views, you should try to refute as many of these flawed arguments as you can. *Refutation* means pointing out the *problems with dissenting views*, thereby highlighting your position's superiority. You may focus on the opposing sides' inaccurate evidence, or you may point to their faulty logic. (Some common types of illogical thinking are discussed on pages 573, 575–77, and 580–82.)

Let's consider how you could refute a competing position in an essay you're writing that supports sex education in public schools. Adapting the Rogerian approach to suit your purposes, you might start by acknowledging the opposing viewpoint's key argument: "Sex education should be the prerogative of parents." After granting the validity of this view in an ideal world, you might show that many parents don't provide such education. You could present statistics on the number of parents who avoid discussing sex with their children because the subject makes them uncomfortable; you could cite studies revealing that children in single-parent homes are apt to receive even less parental guidance about sex; and you could give examples of young people whose parents provided sketchy, even misleading information.

There are various ways to develop a paper's refutation section. The best method to use depends on the paper's length and the complexity of the issue. Two possible sequences are outlined here:

First Strategy

- State your proposition.
- Cite opposing viewpoints and the evidence for those views.
- Refute opposing viewpoints by presenting counterarguments.

Second Strategy

- State your proposition.
- Cite opposing viewpoints and the evidence for those views.
- Refute opposing viewpoints by presenting counterarguments.
- Present additional evidence for your proposition.

In the first strategy, you simply refute all or part of the opposing positions' arguments. The second strategy takes the first one a step further by presenting *additional evidence* to support your proposition. In such a case, the additional evidence *must be different* from the points made in the refutation. The additional evidence may appear at the essay's end (as in the preceding outline), or it may be given near the beginning (after the proposition); it may also be divided between the beginning and end.

No matter which strategy you select, you may refute opposing views one side at a time or one point at a time. (For more on comparing and contrasting the sides of an issue, see pages 400–02.) Throughout the essay, be sure to provide clear signals so that readers can distinguish your arguments from the other sides': "Despite the claims of those opposed to the plan, many think that..." and "Those not in agreement think that...."

7. Use induction or deduction to think logically about your argument. The line of reasoning used to develop an argument is the surest indicator of how rigorously you have thought through your position. There are two basic ways to think about a subject: *inductively* and *deductively*. Though the following discussion treats induction and deduction as separate processes, the two often overlap and complement each other.

Inductive reasoning involves examination of specific cases, facts, or examples. Based on these specifics, you then draw a conclusion or make a generalization. This is the kind of thinking scientists use when they examine evidence (the results of experiments, for example) and then draw a *conclusion:* "Smoking increases the risk of cancer." All of us use inductive reasoning in everyday life. We might think the following: "My head is aching" (evidence); "My nose is stuffy" (evidence); "I'm coming down with a cold" (conclusion). Based on the conclusion, we might go a step further and take some action: "I'll take an aspirin."

With inductive reasoning, the conclusion reached can serve as the proposition for an argumentation essay. (Of course, the essay will most likely include elements of persuasion since strict argumentation—with no appeal to emotions—is uncommon.) If the paper advances a course of action, the proposition often mentions the action, signaling an essay with a distinctly persuasive purpose.

Let's suppose that you're writing a paper about a crime wave in the small town where you live. You might use inductive thinking to structure the essay's argument:

Several people were mugged last month while shopping in the center of town. (*evidence*)

Several homes and apartments were burglarized in the past few weeks. (*evidence*)

Several cars were stolen from people's driveways over the weekend. (*evidence*)

The police force hasn't adequately protected town residents. (*conclusion, or proposition, for an argumentation essay with probable elements of persuasion*)

The police force should take steps to upgrade its protection of town residents. (*conclusion, or proposition, for an argumentation essay with a clearly persuasive intent*)

This inductive sequence highlights a possible structure for the essay. After providing a clear statement of your proposition, you might detail recent muggings, burglaries, and car thefts. Then you could move to the opposing viewpoint: a description of the steps the police say they have taken to protect town residents. At that point, you would refute the police's claim, citing additional evidence that shows the measures taken have not been sufficient. Finally, if you wanted your essay to have a decidedly persuasive purpose, you could end by recommending specific action the police should take to improve its protection of the community.

As in all essays, your evidence should be *specific, unified, sufficient*, and *representative* (see pages 38–42). These last two characteristics are critical when you think inductively; they guarantee that your conclusion would be equally valid even if other evidence were presented. Insufficient or atypical evidence often leads to *hasty generalizations* that mar the essay's logic. For example, you might think the following: "Some elderly people are very wealthy and do not need Social Security checks" (evidence), and "Some Social Security recipients illegally collect several checks" (evidence). If you then conclude, "Social Security is a waste of taxpayers' money," your conclusion is invalid and hasty because it's based on only a few atypical examples. Millions of Social Security recipients aren't wealthy and don't abuse the system. If you've failed to consider the full range of evidence, any action you propose ("The Social Security system should be disbanded") will probably be considered suspect by thoughtful readers. It's possible, of course, that Social Security should be disbanded, but the evidence leading to such a conclusion must be sufficient and representative.

When reasoning inductively, you should also be careful that the evidence you collect is both *recent* and *accurate*. No valid conclusion can result from dated or erroneous evidence. To ensure that your evidence is sound, you also need to evaluate the reliability of your sources. When a person who is legally drunk claims to have seen a flying saucer, the evidence is shaky, to say the least. But if two respected scientists, both with 20–20 vision, saw the saucer, their evidence is worth considering.

Finally, it's important to realize that there's always an element of uncertainty in inductive reasoning. The conclusion can never be more than an *inference*, involving what logicians call an *inductive leap*. There could be other explanations for the evidence cited and thus other positions to take and actions to advocate. For example, given a small town's crime wave, you might conclude not that the police force has been remiss but that residents are careless about protecting themselves and their property. In turn, you might call for a different kind of action—perhaps that the police conduct public workshops in self-defense and home security. In an inductive argument, your task is to weigh the evidence, consider alternative explanations, then choose the conclusion and course of action that seem most valid.

Unlike inductive reasoning, which starts with a specific case and moves toward a generalization or conclusion, *deductive reasoning* begins with a generalization that is then applied to a specific case. This movement from general to specific involves a three-step form of reasoning called a *syllogism*. The first part of a syllogism is called the *major premise*, a general statement about an entire group. The second part is the *minor premise*, a statement about an individual within that group. The syllogism ends with a *conclusion* about that individual.

Just as you use inductive thinking in everyday life, you use deductive thinking—often without being aware of it—to sort out your experiences. When trying to decide which car to buy, you might think as follows:

Major premise:	In an accident, large cars are safer than small cars.
Minor premise:	The Turbo Titan is a large car.
Conclusion:	In an accident, the Turbo Titan will be safer than a small car.

Based on your conclusion, you might decide to take a specific action, buying the Turbo Titan rather than the smaller car you had first considered.

To create a valid syllogism and thus arrive at a sound conclusion, you need to avoid two major pitfalls of deductive reasoning. First, be sure not to start with a *sweeping* or *hasty generalization* (see page 573) as your *major premise*. Second, don't accept as truth a *faulty conclusion*. Let's look at each problem.

Sweeping major premise.   Perhaps you're concerned about a trash-to-steam incinerator scheduled to open near your home. Your thinking about the situation might follow these lines:

Major premise:	Trash-to-steam incinerators have had serious problems and pose significant threats to the well-being of people living near the plants.
Minor premise:	The proposed incinerator in my neighborhood will be a trash-to-steam plant.
Conclusion:	The proposed trash-to-steam incinerator in my neighborhood will have serious problems and pose significant threats to the well-being of people living near the plant.

Having arrived at this conclusion, you might decide to join organized protests against the opening of the incinerator. But your thinking is somewhat illogical. Your *major premise* is a *sweeping* one because it indiscriminately groups all trash-to-steam plants into a single category. It's unlikely that you're familiar with the operations of all trash-to-steam incinerators in this country and abroad; it's probably not true that *all* such plants have had serious difficulties that endangered the public. For your argument to reach a valid conclusion, the major premise must be based on repeated observations or verifiable facts. You would have a better argument, and thus reach a more valid conclusion, if you restricted or qualified the major premise, applying it to some, not all, of the group:

Major premise:	A number of trash-to-steam incinerators have had serious problems and posed significant threats to the well-being of people living near the plants.
Minor premise:	The proposed incinerator in my neighborhood will be a trash-to-steam plant.
Conclusion:	It's possible that the proposed trash-to-steam incinerator in my neighborhood will run into

serious problems and pose significant threats to
the well-being of people living near the plant.

This new conclusion, the result of more careful reasoning, would
probably encourage you to learn more about trash-to-steam incinerators in general and about the proposed plant in particular. If further research still left you feeling uncomfortable about the plant,
you would probably decide to join the protest. On the other hand,
your research might convince you that the plant has incorporated
into its design a number of safeguards that have been successful at
other plants. This added information could reassure you that your
original fears were unfounded. In either case, the revised deductive
process would lead to a more informed conclusion and course of
action.

Faulty conclusion. Your syllogism—and thus your reasoning—
would also be invalid if your *conclusion reverses the "if...then" relationship implied in the major premise.* Assume you plan to write a letter to the college newspaper urging the resignation of the student
government president. Perhaps you pursue a line of reasoning that
goes like this:

Major premise:	Students who plagiarize papers must appear before the Faculty Committee on Academic Policies and Procedures.
Minor premise:	Yesterday, Jennifer Kramer, president of the student government, appeared before the Faculty Committee on Academic Policies and Procedures.
Conclusion:	Jennifer must have plagiarized a paper.
Action:	Jennifer should resign her position as president of the student government.

Such a chain of reasoning is illogical and unfair. Here's why. *If* students plagiarize their papers and are caught, *then* they must appear
before the committee. However, the converse isn't necessarily
true—that *if* students appear before the committee, *then* they must
have plagiarized. In other words, not *all* students appearing before
the committee have been called up on plagiarism charges. For
example, Jennifer could have been speaking on behalf of another

student; she could have been protesting some action taken by the committee; she could have been seeking the committee's help on an article she plans to write about academic honesty. The conclusion doesn't allow for these other possible explanations.

Now that you're aware of potential problems associated with deductive reasoning, let's look at the way you can use a syllogism to structure an argumentation-persuasion essay. Suppose you decide to write a paper advocating support for a projected space mission. You know that controversy surrounds the space program, especially since seven astronauts died in a 1986 launch. Confident that the tragedy has led to more rigorous controls, you want to argue that the benefits of an upcoming mission outweigh its risks. A deductive pattern could be used to develop your argument. In fact, outlining your thinking as a syllogism might help you formulate a proposition, organize your evidence, deal with opposing viewpoints, and—if appropriate—propose a course of action:

Major premise:	Space programs in the past have led to important developments in technology, especially in medical science.
Minor premise:	The Cosmos Mission is the newest space program.
Proposition (essay might be persuasive):	The Cosmos Mission will most likely lead to important developments in technology, especially in medical science.
Proposition (essay clearly is persuasive):	Congress should continue its funding of the Cosmos Mission.

Having outlined the deductive pattern of your thinking, you might begin by stating your proposition and then discuss some new procedures developed to protect the astronauts and the rocket system's structural integrity. With that background established, you could detail the opposing claim that little of value has been produced by the space program so far. You could then move to your refutation, citing significant medical advances derived from former space missions. Finally, the paper might conclude on a persuasive note, with a plea to Congress to continue funding the latest space mission.

8. Use Toulmin logic to establish a strong connection between your evidence and your thesis. Whether you use an essentially inductive or deductive approach, your argument depends on strong evidence. In *The Uses of Argument,* Stephen Toulmin describes a useful approach for strengthening the connection between evidence and thesis. Toulmin divides a typical argument into three parts:

- **Claim**—The thesis, proposition, or conclusion.
- **Data**—The evidence (facts, statistics, examples, observations, expert opinion) used to convince readers of the claim's validity.
- **Warrant**—The underlying assumption that justifies moving from evidence to claim.

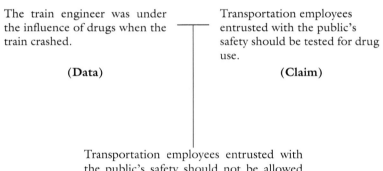

The train engineer was under the influence of drugs when the train crashed.

(Data)

Transportation employees entrusted with the public's safety should be tested for drug use.

(Claim)

Transportation employees entrusted with the public's safety should not be allowed on the job if they use drugs.

(Warrant)

As Toulmin explains in his book, readers are more apt to consider your argument valid if they know what your warrant is. Sometimes your warrant will be so obvious that you won't need to state it explicitly; an *implicit warrant* will be sufficient. Assume you want to argue that the use of live animals to test product toxicity should be outlawed. To support your claim, you cite the following evidence: first, current animal tests are painful and usually result in the animal's death; second, human cell cultures frequently offer more reliable information on how harmful a product may be to human tissue; and third, computer simulations often can more accurately rate a substance's toxicity. Your warrant, although not explicit, is nonetheless clear: "It is wrong to continue product testing on animals when more humane and valid test methods are available."

Other times, you'll do best to make your *warrant explicit.* Suppose you plan to argue that students should be involved in deciding which faculty members are granted tenure. To develop your claim, you present some evidence. You begin by noting that, currently, only faculty members and administrators review candidates for tenure. Next, you call attention to the controversy surrounding two professors, widely known by students to be poor teachers, who were nonetheless granted tenure. Finally, you cite a decision, made several years ago, to discontinue using student evaluations as part of the tenure process; you emphasize that since that time complaints about teachers' incompetence have risen dramatically. Some readers, though, still might wonder how you got from your evidence to your claim. In this case, your argument could be made stronger by stating your warrant explicitly: "Since students are as knowledgeable as the faculty and administrators about which professors are competent, they should be involved in the tenure process."

The more widely accepted your warrant, Toulmin explains, the more likely it is that readers will accept your argument. If there's no consensus about the warrant, you'll probably need to *back it up.* For the preceding example, you might mention several reports that found students evaluate faculty fairly (most students don't, for example, use the ratings to get back at professors against whom they have a personal grudge); further, students' ratings correlate strongly with those given by administrators and other faculty.

Toulmin describes another way to increase receptivity to an argument: *qualify the claim*—that is, explain under what circumstances it might be invalid or restricted. For instance, you might grant that most students know little about their instructors' research activities, scholarly publications, or participation in professional committees. You could, then, qualify your claim this way: "Because students don't have a comprehensive view of their instructors' professional activities, they should be involved in the tenure process but play a less prominent role than faculty and administrators."

As you can see, Toulmin's approach provides strategies for strengthening an argument. So, when prewriting or revising, take a few minutes to ask yourself the following questions:

- What data (*evidence*) should I provide to support my claim (*thesis*)?

- Is my warrant clear? Should I state it explicitly? What backup can I provide to justify my warrant?
- Would qualifying my claim make my argument more convincing?

Your responses to these questions will help you structure a convincing and logical argument.

9. Recognize logical fallacies.   When writing an argumentation-persuasion essay, you need to recognize *logical fallacies* both in your own argument and in points raised by opposing sides. Work to eliminate such gaps in logic from your own writing and, when they appear in opposing arguments, try to expose them in your refutation. Logicians have identified many logical fallacies —including the sweeping or hasty generalization and the faulty conclusion discussed on pages 575–77. Other logical fallacies are described in Ann McClintock's "Propaganda Techniques in Today's Advertising" (page 315) and in the paragraphs that follow.

The *post hoc fallacy* (short for a Latin phrase meaning "after this, therefore because of this") occurs when you conclude that a cause-effect relationship exists simply because one event preceded another. Let's say you note the growing number of immigrants settling in a nearby city, observe the city's economic decline, and conclude that the immigrants' arrival caused the decline. Such a chain of thinking is faulty because it assumes a cause-effect relationship based purely on co-occurrence. Perhaps the immigrants' arrival was a factor in the economic slump, but there could also be other reasons: the lack of financial incentives to attract business to the city, restrictions on the size of the city's manufacturing facilities, citywide labor disputes that make companies leery of settling in the area. Your argument should also consider these possibilities. (For more on the *post hoc* fallacy, see page 455.)

The *non sequitur fallacy* (Latin for "it does not follow") is an even more blatant muddying of cause-effect relationships. In this case, a conclusion is drawn that has no logical connection to the evidence cited: "Millions of Americans own cars, so there is no need to fund public transportation." The faulty conclusion disregards the millions of Americans who don't own cars; it also ignores pollution and road congestion, both of which could be reduced if people had access to safe, reliable public transportation.

An *ad hominem argument* (from the Latin meaning "to the man") occurs when someone attacks a person rather than a point of view. Suppose your college plans to sponsor a physicians' symposium on the abortion controversy. You decide to write a letter to the school paper opposing the symposium. Taking swipes at two of the invited doctors who disapprove of abortion, you mention that one was recently involved in a messy divorce and that the other is alleged to have a drinking problem. By hurling personal invective, you avoid discussing the issue. Mudslinging is a poor substitute for reasoned argument.

Appeals to questionable or faulty authority also weaken an argument. Most of us have developed a healthy suspicion of phrases like *sources close to, an unidentified spokesperson states, experts claim,* and *studies show.* If these people and reports are so reliable, they should be clearly identified.

Begging the question involves failure to establish proof for a debatable point. The writer expects readers to accept as given a premise that's actually controversial. For instance, you would have trouble convincing readers that prayer should be banned from public schools if you based your argument on the premise that school prayer violates the U.S. Constitution. If the Constitution does, either explicitly or implicitly, prohibit prayer in public education, your essay must demonstrate that fact. You can't build a strong argument if you pretend there's no controversy surrounding your premise.

A *false analogy* wrongly implies that because two things share *some* characteristics, they are therefore *alike in all respects.* You might, for example, compare nicotine and marijuana. Both, you could mention, involve health risks and have addictive properties. If, however, you go on to conclude, "Driving while smoking a cigarette isn't illegal, so driving while smoking marijuana shouldn't be illegal either," you're employing a false analogy. You've overlooked a major difference between tobacco and marijuana: Marijuana impairs perception and coordination—important aspects of driving—while there's no evidence that tobacco does the same.

The *either-or fallacy* occurs when you assume that a particular viewpoint or course of action can have only one of two diametrically opposed outcomes—either totally this or totally that. Say you argue as follows: "Unless colleges continue to offer scholarships based solely on financial need, no one who is underprivileged will be able to attend college." Such a statement ignores the fact that bright, underprivileged students could receive scholarships based on their potential or their demonstrated academic excellence.

Finally, a *red herring argument* is an intentional digression from the issue—a ploy to deflect attention from the matter being discussed. Imagine that you're arguing that condoms shouldn't be dispensed to high school students. You would introduce a red herring if you began to rail against parents who fail to provide their children with any information about sex. Most people would agree that parents *should* provide such information. However, the issue being discussed is not parents' irresponsibility but the pros and cons of schools' distributing condoms to students.

Few of today's critical problems—the battle against AIDS, unemployment, terrorism, care for the homeless—lend themselves to quick solutions. Overwhelmed by endless facts and speculations, many of us look to experts to help us arrive at meaningful positions on these complex issues. We may read one article and conclude, "Yes, this position makes sense," only to read another article that advances an opposing but equally compelling viewpoint. Perhaps the key to finding answers is to rely on ourselves—not on the experts—to sort out information and ideas. Writing an argumentation-persuasion essay helps us discover how we feel and what we think. Weighing fact against fact, stipulation against stipulation, we use reason to draw conclusions based on clear thinking. Argumentation-persuasion also gives us a chance to share such a well-reasoned point of view with others, perhaps even convincing readers of our position's soundness. Indeed, as average people with limited political clout or recognized expertise, we may find that argumentation-persuasion provides us with considerable power.

STUDENT ESSAY

The following student essay was written by Mark Simmons in response to this assignment:

> In "My Pistol-Packing Kids," Jean Marzollo invites controversy by attacking the popular notion that aggressive

toys and games encourage hostile behavior. Sel(
controversial issue, one that you feel strongly a
duct library research to gather evidence in sup;
position, and brainstorm with others to identify some
points that might be raised by those who oppose your
view. Then, using logic and formal, documented evidence,
convince readers that your viewpoint is valid.

Your instructor may not ask you to include research in your
essay. But, if you're asked—as Mark was—to research your paper
and to provide *formal documentation,* you'll want to pay special
attention to the way Mark credits his sources. (In *your* paper, the
Works Cited list should be double-spaced—along with the rest of
the paper—and placed at the end on a separate page.) You'll also
find it helpful to refer to Chapter 14, "A Concise Guide to Documentation" (page 721). If your instructor wants you to research
your paper but will accept *informal documentation,* the material on
page 566 should come in handy.

Whether or not you include research in your paper, the annotations on Mark's essay and the comments following it will help you
determine how well it applies the principles of argumentation-
persuasion.

Compulsory National Service
by Mark Simmons

Introduction   Our high school history class spent several   1
weeks studying the events of the 1960s. The most
interesting thing about that decade was the spirit
of service and social commitment among young
people. In the '60s, young people thought about
issues beyond themselves; they joined the Peace
Corps, worked in poverty-stricken Appalachian communities, and participated in freedom marches
against segregation. Most young people today,
despite their obvious concern with careers and getting ahead, would also like an opportunity to make a
Common   worthwhile contribution to society. Convinced that
knowledge: many young adults are indeed eager for such an
No need to   opportunity, the Clinton administration implemented
document   in 1994 a pilot program of voluntary national service.

Argumentation-Persuasion

Start of
two-sentence
thesis

The Clinton plan holds out so much promise that it seems only natural to go one step further and make participation for young people required. By instituting a program of compulsory national service, our country could tap youth's idealistic desire to contribute. Such a system would yield significant benefits.

Definition
paragraph

What exactly is meant by compulsory national service? Traditionally, it has tended to mean that everyone between the ages of seventeen and twenty-five would serve the country for two years. Young people could choose between two major options: military service or a public-service corps. They could serve their time at any point within the eight-year span. The unemployed or the uncertain could join immediately after high school; college-bound students could complete their education before joining the national service. More recently, Senator Sam Nunn and Representative Dave McCurdy gave a new twist to the definition of compulsory national service. They proposed a plan that would require all high school graduates applying for federal aid for college tuition to serve either in the military or in a Citizens Corps. Anyone in the Citizens Corps would be required to work full-time at public-service duties for one or two years. During that time, participants would receive a weekly stipend, and, at the end of the time, they would be given a voucher worth $10,000 for each year of civilian service. The voucher could then be applied toward college credit, employment training, or down payment on a house (Sudo 9).

Beginning of
summary of a
source's ideas

Parenthetic
citation—page
number *and*
author are
given since the
author is not
cited earlier in
the sentence

The traditional plan for compulsory national service and the one proposed by Nunn and McCurdy are just two of many variations that have been discussed over the years. While this country debates the concept, some nations such as France have gone ahead and accepted it enthusiastically. The idea could also be workable in this country. Unfortunately, opponents have prevented the idea from taking hold. They contend, first of all, that the program would cost too much; they argue that a great deal of money would have to be spent administering the program. In addition, young people would have to receive wages for

Common
knowledge isn't
documented

Topic sentence

Beginning of
summary of
three points
made by the
opposing
viewpoint

2

3

their work, and some of them would need housing--both expensive items. Another argument against compulsory national service is that it would demoralize young people; the plan would prevent the young from moving ahead with their careers and would make them feel as though they were engaged in work that had no personal reward. A final argument is that compulsory service would lay the groundwork for a military state. The picture is painted of an army of young robots totally at the mercy of the government, like the Hitler Youth of the Second World War.

Topic sentence: Refutation of first point

Despite opponents' claims that compulsory national service would involve exorbitant costs, the program would not have to be that expensive to run. To date, no definite figures have been established on the program's cost (Shapiro 32), but the program might use as a model the California Conservation Corps, which has achieved great benefits at reasonable expense (Moore 25). Also, the sums required for wages and housing could be reduced considerably through payments made by the towns, cities, and states using the corps' services. And the economic benefits of the program could be significant. As public-policy experts Richard Danzig and Peter Szanton argue, the service corps could perform a wide variety of tasks. It could repair highways, public buildings, and inner-city neighborhoods. The corps could organize recycling projects; it could staff public health clinics, day-care centers, legal aid centers, and homes for the disabled (296). The corps could also monitor pollution, clean up litter, provide day-care services, work with the homeless, and help care for the country's growing elderly population (Boldt 7). Corps members could also help rehabilitate run-down schools, tutor children, and organize activities that keep kids off the street and away from drugs and crime (Clinton 15). All these projects would help solve many of the problems that plague our nation, and they would probably cost less than if they were handled by traditional government bureaucracies or by private industry (Moore 25).

Attribution giving authors' full names and area of expertise

Just the page number is provided here because the authors' names are cited in the preceding attribution

Topic sentence: Refutation of second point

Also, rather than undermining the spirit of young people, as opponents contend, the program

4

5

Full-sentence quotation is preceded by a comma and begins with a capital letter

Where secondary source was quoted

Quotation with middle and final ellipses

Author and partial title are provided because the Works Cited page lists two works by this author

Quotation is blended into the sentence (no comma and the quotation begins with a lowercased word)

Only the authors' last names are given because their full names appear earlier, in an attribution

Topic sentence: Refutation of third point

would probably boost their morale. Many young people feel enormous pressure and uncertainty. They are not sure what they want to do, or they have trouble finding a way to begin their careers. Compulsory national service could give young people a much-needed breathing space. As Edward Lewis, president of St. Mary's College, says, "Many students are not ready for college at seventeen or eighteen and they need an extra year to mature. This kind of program responds to that need" (qtd. in Fowler 3). The executive director of the Coalition for National Service argues that a public-service stint enriches participants' lives in yet another way. When young people return to the academic world, the director contends, they find that their real-world experience adds "breadth to their grasp of... subject matter by exposing them to topics not covered in lectures..." (Eberly, *National Service* 86). And Joseph Duffey, chancellor of the University of Massachusetts, feels that such a program provides important "opportunities for knowledge and training" (29), especially for those not intending to further their formal education. Equally important, compulsory national service could provide an emotional boost for the young; all of them would experience the pride that comes from working hard, reaching goals, acquiring skills, and handling responsibilities (Levine 4). A positive mind-set would also result from the sense of community that would be created by serving in the national service. All young people--rich or poor, educated or not, regardless of sex and social class--would come together and perceive not their differences but their common interests and similarities (Wilkson 42). Each young person, as Danzig and Szanton state, would have the satisfaction of knowing that he or she has made a "worthwhile contribution, both as an individual and as part of a group" (205).

Finally, in contrast to what opponents claim, compulsory national service would not signal the start of a dictatorship. Although the service would be required, young people would have complete freedom to choose any two years between the ages of seventeen and twenty-five. They would also have

6

complete freedom to choose the branch of the military or public-service corps that suits them best. And the corps would not need to be outfitted in military uniforms or to live in barrack-like camps. It could be set up like a regular job, with young people living at home as much as possible, following a nine-to-five schedule, enjoying all the personal freedoms that would ordinarily be theirs. Also, a dictatorship would no more likely emerge from a program of compulsory national service than it has from our present military system. We would still have a series of checks and balances to prohibit the taking of power by one group or individual. We should also keep in mind that our system is different from that of Fascist regimes; our long tradition of personal liberty makes improbable the seizing of absolute power by one person or faction. A related but even more important point to remember is that freedom does not mean people are guaranteed the right to pursue only their individual needs. That is mistaking selfishness for freedom. And, as everyone knows, selfishness leads only to misery. The national service would not take away freedom. On the contrary, serving in the corps would help young people grasp this larger concept of freedom, a concept that is badly needed to counteract the deadly "look out for number one" attitude that is spreading like a poison across the nation.

Conclusion:
Echoes material
in the
introduction

Attribution
ending with a
colon leading to
a long quotation

Long quotation
is indented ten
spaces

Perhaps there will never be a time like the 1960s   7
when so many young people were concerned with remaking the world. Still, a good many of today's young people want meaningful work. They want to feel that what they do makes a difference. A program of compulsory national service would tap this willingness in young people, helping them realize the best in themselves. Such a program would also help us resolve some of the country's social problems. Eberly expresses with eloquence his belief in the power of such a program:

> The promise of national service can be manifested in many ways: in cleaner air and fewer forest fires; in well-cared-for infants and old folks; in a better-educated citizenry and better-satisfied work force;

For an indented quotation, the period is placed *before* the parenthetic citation

Partial title is provided here because two works by this author are listed in Works Cited

Newspaper article

Book with two authors

Section from a weekly publication

Book with one author

Second source by preceding author

Article from a bimonthly magazine

Article from a weekly magazine

perhaps in a more peaceful world. National service has a lot of promise. It's a promise well worth keeping. ("What the President Should Do" 651)

A pilot program of voluntary service has been 8 established. Now seems a perfect time to expand the concept and make compulsory national service a reality.

Works Cited

Boldt, David R.   "National Service: A Call to All Youth."   Philadelphia Inquirer 21 Apr. 1991, late ed., sec. 5: 7.

Clinton, Bill.   "National Service--Now."   New York Times 28 Feb. 1993, natl. ed., sec. 5: 15.

Danzig, Richard, and Peter Szanton.   National Service: What Would It Mean? Lexington, MA: Lexington, 1986.

Duffey, Joseph.   "Reconstituting America Through National Service."   Vital Speeches of the Day 5 Oct. 1989: 26–29.

Eberly, Donald.   National Service: A Promise to Keep.   Rochester, NY: Alden, 1988.

---.   "What the President Should Do About National Service."   Vital Speeches of the Day 15 Aug. 1989: 651–53.

Fowler, Margaret.   "New Interest in National Youth Corps."   New York Times 16 May 1989, natl. ed., sec. 2: 3.

Kelly, Dennis.   "Grants Go Out for National Service." New York Times 21 June 1994, natl. ed., sec. 1: 8.

Levine, Arthur.   "Toward a National Service Program."   Change Sept.–Oct. 1989: 4.

Moore, Thomas.   "For Whom the Corps Toils."   U.S. News & World Report 13 Feb. 1989: 24–25.

Shapiro, Walter.   "The Gap Between Will and Market."   Time 6 Feb. 1989: 32.

Sudo, Phil.   "Mandatory National Service?"   Scholastic Update 23 Feb. 1990: 9.

Wilkinson, Francis.   "Pork to the People."   Rolling Stone 22 Sept. 1994: 45.

COMMENTARY

Blend of argumentation and persuasion. In his essay, Mark tackles a controversial issue. He takes the position that compulsory national service would benefit both the country as a whole and its young people in particular. Mark's essay is a good example of the way argumentation and persuasion often mix: Although the paper presents Mark's position in a logical, well-reasoned manner (argumentation), it also appeals to readers' personal values and suggests a course of action (persuasion).

Audience analysis. When planning the essay, Mark realized that his audience—his composition class—would consist largely of two kinds of readers. Some, not sure of their views, would be inclined to agree with him if he presented his case well. Others would probably be reluctant to accept his view. Because of this mixed audience, Mark knew he couldn't depend on *pathos* (an appeal to emotion) to convince readers. Rather, his argument had to rely mainly on *logos* (reason) and *ethos* (credibility). So Mark organized his essay around a series of logical arguments—many of them backed by expert opinion—and he evoked his own authority by drawing on his knowledge of history and his "inside" knowledge of young people.

Introduction and thesis. Mark introduces his subject by discussing an earlier decade when large numbers of young people worked for social change. Mark's references to the Peace Corps, community work, and freedom marches reinforce his image as a knowledgeable source and establish a context for his position. These historical references, combined with the comments about President Clinton's program of voluntary national service, lead into the two-sentence thesis at the end of the introduction: "By instituting a system of compulsory national service, our country could tap youth's idealistic desire to contribute. Such a system would yield significant benefits."

Background paragraph and use of outside sources. The second paragraph provides a working *definition* of compulsory national service by presenting two common interpretations of the concept. Such background information guarantees that Mark's readers will share his understanding of the essay's central concept.

The second paragraph also illustrates Mark's first use of outside sources. Because the assignment called for research in support of an argument, Mark went to the library and identified sources that helped him defend his position. If Mark's instructor had required extensive investigation of an issue, Mark would have been obligated both to dig more deeply into his subject and to use more scholarly and specialized sources. But given the instructor's requirements, Mark proceeded just as he should have: He searched out expert opinion that supported his viewpoint; he presented that evidence clearly; he documented his sources carefully.

Acknowledging the opposing viewpoint.   Having explained the meaning of compulsory national service, Mark is now in a good position to launch his argument. Even though he wasn't required to research the opposing viewpoint, Mark wisely decided to get together with some friends to brainstorm some issues that might be raised by the dissenting view. He acknowledges this position in the *topic sentence* of the essay's third paragraph: "Unfortunately, opponents have prevented the idea from taking hold." Next he summarizes the main points the dissenting opinion might advance: compulsory national service would be expensive, demoralizing to young people, and dangerously authoritarian. Mark uses the rest of the essay to counter these criticisms.

Refutation.   The next three paragraphs (4–6) *refute* the opposing stance and present Mark's evidence for his position. Mark structures the essay so that readers can follow his *counterargument* with ease. Each paragraph argues against one opposing point and begins with a *topic sentence* that serves as Mark's response to the dissenting view. Note the way the italicized portion of each topic sentence recalls a dissenting point cited earlier: "Despite opponents' claims that *compulsory national service would involve exorbitant costs,* the program would not have to be that expensive to run" (paragraph 4); "Also, rather than *undermining the spirit of young people,* as opponents contend, the program would probably boost their morale" (5); "Finally, in contrast to what opponents claim, *compulsory national service would not signal the start of a dictatorship*" (6). Mark also guides the reader through the various points in the refutation by using *transitions* within paragraphs: "*And* the economic benefits...could be significant" (4); "*Equally important,* compulsory national service could provide an emotional boost…" (5); "*Also*, a dictatorship would no more likely emerge…" (6).

Throughout the three-paragraph refutation, Mark uses outside sources to lend power to his argument. If the assignment had called for in-depth research, he would have cited facts, statistics, and case studies to develop this section of his essay. Given the nature of the assignment, though, Mark's reliance on expert opinion is perfectly acceptable.

Mark successfully incorporates material from these outside sources into his refutation. He doesn't, for example, string one quotation numbingly after another; instead he usually develops his refutation by *summarizing* expert opinion and saves *direct quotations* for points that deserve emphasis. Moreover, whenever Mark quotes or summarizes a source, he provides clear signals to indicate that the material is indeed borrowed. (If you'd like some suggestions for citing outside sources in an essay of your own, see pages 566 and 722–26.)

Some problems with the refutation.   Overall, Mark's three-paragraph refutation is strong, but it would have been even more effective if the paragraphs had been resequenced. As it now stands, the last paragraph in the refutation (6) seems anticlimactic. Unlike the preceding two paragraphs, which are developed through fairly extensive reference to outside sources, paragraph 6 depends entirely on Mark's personal feelings and interpretations for its support. Of course, Mark was under no obligation to provide research in all sections of the paper. Even so, the refutation would have been more persuasive if Mark had placed the final paragraph in the refutation in a less emphatic position. He could, for example, have put it first or second in the sequence, saving for last either of the other two more convincing paragraphs.

You may also have felt that there's another problem with the third paragraph in the refutation. Here, Mark seems to lose control of his counterargument. Beginning with "And, as everyone knows…" Mark falls into the *logical fallacy* called *begging the question*. He shouldn't assume that everyone agrees that a selfish life inevitably brings misery. He also indulges in charged emotionalism when he refers—somewhat melodramatically—to the "deadly 'look out for number one' attitude that is spreading like a poison across the nation."

Inductive reasoning. In part, Mark arrived at his position *inductively,* through a series of *inferences* or *inductive leaps.* He started with some personal *observations* about the nation and its young people. Then, to support those observations, he added his friends' insights as well as information gathered through research. Combined, all this material led him to the general *conclusion* that compulsory national service would be both workable and beneficial.

Other patterns of development. To develop his argument, Mark draws on several patterns of development. The second paragraph relies on *definition* to clarify what is meant by compulsory national service. The introduction and conclusion *compare* and *contrast* young people of the 1960s with those of today. And, to support his position, Mark uses a kind of *causal analysis;* he both speculates on the likely consequences of compulsory national service and cites expert opinion to illustrate the validity of some of those speculations.

Conclusion. Despite some problems in the final section of his refutation, Mark comes up with an effective close for the essay. He starts by echoing the point made in the introduction about the 1960s and restates his thesis. Then he includes a dramatic quotation from a knowledgeable source; the quotation lends credibility to the crisp assertion and suggested course of action at the very end of the essay.

Revising the first draft. Given the complex nature of his argument, Mark found that he had to revise his essay several times. One way to illustrate some of the changes he made is to compare his final introduction with the original draft reprinted here:

Original Version of the Introduction

"There's no free lunch.""You can't get something for nothing." "You have to earn your way." In America, these sayings are not really true. In America, we gladly take but give back little. In America, we receive economic opportunity, legal protection, the right to vote, and, most of all, a personal freedom unequaled throughout the world. How do we repay our country for such gifts? In most cases, we don't. This unfair relationship must be changed. The best way to make a start is to institute a system of national compulsory service for young people. This system would be of real benefit to the country and its citizens.

When Mark met with a classmate for a feedback session, he found that his partner had a number of helpful suggestions for revising various sections of the essay. But Mark's partner focused most of her comments on the essay's introduction because she felt it needed special attention. Following his classmate's suggestion, Mark deleted the original introduction's references to Americans in general. He made this change because he wanted readers to know—from the very start of the essay—that the paper would focus not on all Americans but on American youth. To reinforce this emphasis, he also added the point about the social commitment characteristic of young people in the 1960s. Besides providing a logical lead-in to the thesis, this reference to an earlier period gave the discussion an important historical perspective and lent a note of authority to Mark's argument. Mark was also pleased to see that adding this new material helped unify and smooth out the paragraph.

These are just a few of the many changes Mark made while reworking his essay. Because he budgeted his time carefully, he was able to revise thoroughly. With the exception of some weak spots in the refutation, Mark's essay is well-reasoned and convincing.

The selections ahead demonstrate that argumentation-persuasion can stimulate thinking on numerous issues. Jean Marzollo, in "My Pistol-Packing Kids," contends that the violence in children's play doesn't lead to overall aggression. In "Let's Tell the Story of All America's Cultures," Ji-Yeon Mary Yuhfill argues that American history books tell a tale that is, at best, incomplete. Mark Twain's "The Damned Human Race" makes some compelling points about flaws in human nature. With scathing irony, Jonathan Swift advocates, in "A Modest Proposal," a solution to the agony of Ireland's poor. In "Free Speech on Campus," Nat Hentoff uses the power of the pen to assail campus liberals and leftists, arguing that their brand of censorship is as dangerous as any other. Camille Paglia, in "Rape: A Bigger Danger Than Feminists Know," argues that it's women who are responsible for preventing rape. Susan Jacoby rebuts Paglia, arguing that "Common Decency" is something women should be able to expect from men. Ron Kline, in "A Scientist: 'I Am the Enemy,'" and Patricia Curtis, in "The Argument Against Animal Experimentation," take opposing stands on the use of animals in medical research. Finally, Louis Nizer, in "Low-Cost Drugs for Addicts?" and Beth Johnson, in "Our Drug Problem," tackle different sides of the controversy surrounding the legalization of drugs.

Jean Marzollo

A Connecticut native, Jean Marzollo received her B.A. in English from the University of Connecticut and her M.A. from Harvard University. Before becoming a writer, Marzollo taught high school and directed educational programs for disadvantaged children. Her articles have appeared in many popular magazines, including *Redbook, Parents, Mademoiselle,* and *Working Mother.* The author of several books for children, including the popular *I Spy* series, Marzollo also writes for adults. Her most recent books are *Your Maternity Leave: How to Leave Work, Have a Baby, Go Back to Work Without Getting Lost, Trapped, or Sandbagged Along the Way* (1991) and *Fathers and Toddlers* (1994). The following selection was first published in *Parents* magazine (1977).

My Pistol-Packing Kids

Marbles, hopscotch, and hide-and-seek are all old, familiar childhood games. But the most favorite of all may be "Bang, bang, you're dead." All children seem to enjoy games of make-believe violence, played with sticks, pointed fingers, or toy weapons that shoot plastic darts, "laser" beams, or rubber projectiles. Parents debate whether such games are healthy or damaging to young minds. Drawing primarily on her observations of her own children, Jean Marzollo maintains that such shoot-'em-up games have valuable hidden dimensions that parents may not at first appreciate.

One day as I was loading the dishwasher, I glanced over at my two boys, Danny and David, ages seven and five, respectively, and thought how sweet and quiet they are. I wonder what they are drawing so intently; I think I'll go see. I went over to the kitchen table and found, rather to my dismay, two lurid pictures of outer space battles. Blood and destruction was everywhere. 1

These frail little babes I held in my arms, what made them grow up and want to create things like this? Repeatedly? Given clay, they 2 make monsters and destroy them limb by limb with home-made clay bombs. Given yarn, they devise tarantula traps behind the couch. Given board and blocks, they rig ramps to crash their cars into each other at high speed.

Outdoors, straight sticks are knives and bent ones are guns.   3
Danny and David stick them into their belts and swagger around on the grass like John Wayne and Burt Reynolds.

Oh, sure, they also like to roll out cookie dough, play the piano,   4
build sand castles, and pet cats, but nothing, I have noticed, quite catches their fancy as does violence.

With their friends they are superheroes or spacemen, and, as I   5
watch them run around shooting each other, I sometimes feel guilty that it was I who took them to (and enjoyed) the movies *Superman, Star Wars,* and *The Empire Strikes Back.* Adding to this guilt is the fact that my husband and I let them watch Saturday morning cartoons so we can sleep late.

On a slow, regular basis their innocent little minds have been   6
contaminated with kiddie media culture. It's excessively violent, which is why Danny and David, at the ripe old ages of five and seven, like it so much. They are at the ages when they know what they see on television is not real. Instead of worrying about reality as they did when they were three or four, they now spend their energy memorizing the exact order in which their favorite cartoons appear.

What About the Kids of Parents Who Say "No"?

Good and stalwart friends of ours, wishing to protect their chil-   7
dren's minds from nefarious influences, do not buy TVs, do not permit guns, and do not take their children to ungentle movies. But when their children come to visit, they dive into the box in the entryway that contains two squirt guns, a plastic laser gun, an orange pistol that shoots rubber darts (all of which have been lost), and a homemade wooden machine gun. Although these kids have never watched morning TV, they know exactly how to play with toy weapons, and they do so with the passion of converts.

Secretly, wickedly, I feel better. Why? Because I'm haunted by   8
the idea that our actions, or the lack of them, may be bringing out in our children a natural tendency toward aggressive violence that should be suppressed. In a time of assassinations, political terrorism,

nuclear buildup, and much publicized violence in people's daily lives, we desire more consciously than ever peace and safety in the world. It is out of this concern that we worry about the place and legitimacy of toy guns in the lives of our children.

What if, we wonder, all parents kept all children from toy weap- 9
ons and the media that glorifies them; wouldn't the world be better off? We could take the TV and the laser guns to the dump. But what about the sticks, yarns, and crayons? Should we take them, too?

We could also lay down the law: no more torpedoes in the bath- 10
tub. Play only with rubber ducks. No more bows and arrows may be made out of construction toys. Make houses instead. No more clay bombs. Make bowls. Our laws would require rigid surveillance and strict discipline, but the means (our dictatorship) would be justified by the end (their innocence). Childhood, after all, should be a time of kittens, mittens, gingerbread, and yo-yo's.

Think positive. Be happy. Play nice, our laws would say. 11

But our children don't want to play nice. They want to have fun. 12
And they have so much fun *pretending* to wipe each other out.

Kids Want Both Sides

It seems kids want to learn about *both* sides of childhood, not 13
just the mittens and kittens side, full of discovery and nurturing, but also the ghosts and ghouls side, full of dread and helplessness. Watching our children and their friends at play, it is clear to me that the mock violence in their play has a great deal to do with their need to *do* something about the underside of their lives. In order to fight back the witches, giants, and werewolves that menace them in the night, they run around in the daytime with toy pistols, toy knives, and toy swords. When I stop to think about their play in these terms, I find I can accept it.

I'm not talking about condoning real violence, nor am I sug- 14
gesting we avoid the responsibilities to teach morals and ethics to our children. As a matter of course, we teach them that no matter how mad they are at someone else, they must not hit, bite, pull hair, and pinch. We teach them to protest verbally, to negotiate a deal if they can, or simply to say, "I'm not going to play with you anymore if you do that." We teach them basically not to hurt others to get their own way. And just as we teach our children safety precautions about cars,

roads, matches, broken glass, and electrical outlets, we caution them about real knives and guns. We tell them how very dangerous these things are, how they must be used correctly, and that the use of guns is prohibited for young children.

"Your Thing, Not Mine"

Guns are a particularly sensitive topic for parents, and many of us feel uncomfortable when our children lust for plastic ones. Although I do not prohibit my children from playing with them, I try to make it clear that such activity is their thing, not mine. I say, "Don't point that rifle at me because it reminds me of a real gun and I don't like real guns." I also insist that gunplay take place outside.   15

Some friends of mine won't buy toy guns but permit their children to do so with their own money. Others will not allow any toy guns in their homes but do not interfere if their children play guns with sticks or their fingers. Still other parents own real guns, go hunting, and bring home carcasses on the top of the car. Their children, we hope, learn the ethic of the hunter: one must be a good shot, one must kill only for food.   16

But the use of real guns is not really the point here. Danny and David do not use real guns nor would they want to. *They are using toys and they are only pretending.* While I admit that it can be unsettling to see how truly inspired they can be at their games, I am impressed by their powers of invention and the fact that what they are doing is not only fun, but refined, effective, and safe.   17

It is refined in the sense that the children organize themselves to take the different parts involved. They also know how to act out all the parts and how to cooperate with each other to enhance the overall drama. They have a remarkable ability to improvise scenes and an almost professional attitude about giving and taking directions. Listening to them play with their little men dolls, it is almost as if I were listening to puppeteers or movie directors.   18

"All right," says Danny. "You land our guy behind the mountain, and I'll find him and blast him out of the water."   19

"Okay, here goes." (Realistic landing sounds.) "Let's set up camp here. Oh no! They found us. Watch out!" (Explosion sounds. Swimming sounds.) "Look, here's an underwater cave! Let's go in!" (Aside) "Let's pretend the cave is really a giant shark."   20

"Yeah, and I'll kill it and save you."   21

"Okay. Oh no! It's a giant shark! Look at those teeth!"   22

Their Own Play Therapy

It seems to me that fantasy play is effective in the sense that it   23
allows children to blow off a lot of steam. Let's face it, on some level
every child lives with tyrants (us) on whom he or she is absolutely dependent. We may be benevolent tyrants, but we are tyrants nonetheless, and the whole thrust of our children's growing up is to liberate
themselves from us.

By playing out fantasies, children release frustrations and expe-   24
rience illusory control over things, such as big people's power and
the threat of death, over which, in fact, they have no control at all.
Day after day, they take turns acting out scene after scene in which
they as good guys heroically defend themselves against horrible bad
guys. Every child I have watched can play both roles.

In a way children are their own play therapists, helping each oth-   25
er cope with pent-up rage. They seem to know how long each session
should last. The game is over when the kids are bored, or tired, or
someone thinks of something else to do and everyone agrees; in
short, when enough steam has been blown off.

As far as I can see, violent fantasies are safe precisely because   26
they're not real. They are thrilling for the same reason. Children
don't want to get hurt. From my observation, the kids who enjoy
playing with toy guns in the yard are those who have already learned
to be cautious around cars, ovens, and climbing equipment. *They
don't want to get hurt and they know how not to.* Just because they
crash toy cars now does not mean they will drive real ones over cliffs
when they are twenty. And just because they love to shoot each other
with imaginary guns now does not mean they will abuse guns when
they grow up.

It takes more than toy guns to make a killer. Conversely, many   27
peace-loving grown-ups I know tell me they played war with a vengeance when they were little.

No Winners, No Losers?

Another important point: Have you ever noticed that in mock   28
violent play no one ever wins or loses? You get shot, you fall down,
you get up, you shoot someone else. A five-year-old can play as skill-

fully as an eight-year-old. The weakest child is on a par with the strongest. The game is safe emotionally as well as physically.

Paradoxically, games that involve less violent imagination but more real jeopardy are harder for children to play, and one has to be mature enough to handle them. To play baseball, for example, you have to be able to strike out without bursting into tears. In Monopoly, you have to be able to land on Park Place when someone else owns it and lose all your money. In a class play you have to be able to keep going even though some kid in the back row whistles. 29

I don't want to see my kids strike out or forget their lines, but I know they may, that they have to, and that they will put up with such discomfort in order to participate in the next stage of life. On their own, I suspect, they will realize eventually that fantasy violence is for little kids. What's for big kids? Real violence? No, at least not for kids who have learned about love and respect for others. 30

Graduating into Life

For older kids there is a stage of activity that moves closer to real life. Sports, science projects, model making, music lessons, dancing, arts and crafts—all these activities help children sharpen their skills, develop their imagination, and explore their interests. The toy guns, toy dolls, and toy cars will be given away or collect dust on a shelf in the basement. Real tools and real equipment will have replaced them. 31

Eventually, Danny and David will move on to real life with its possibilities for real jeopardy, real success, real independence, and satisfaction. By then I hope they will have gained whatever skills and strength of character they need to play this last, and hardest, and most rewarding game of all. I trust that part of their maturity will be based upon the ability they gained at an early age to distinguish between fantasy and reality. 32

Questions for Close Reading

1. What is the selection's thesis? Locate the sentence(s) in which Marzollo states her main idea. If she doesn't state the thesis explicitly, express it in your own words.
2. Why, according to Marzollo, do kids want to play at violence?
3. Marzollo suggests children progress through different stages of maturity. What are these? In which stages do children focus on reality and in which on fantasy?

4. What does Marzollo mean by saying that play with toy guns is "refined"? How is it "effective" and safe?
5. Refer to your dictionary as needed to define the following words used in the selection: *stalwart* (paragraph 7), *legitimacy* (8), *condoning* (14), *improvise* (18), and *vengeance* (27).

Questions About the Writer's Craft

1. **The pattern.** Why do you think Marzollo chooses the first-person point of view to develop her argument? How do you suppose Marzollo hopes the first-person approach will affect her readers?
2. **Other patterns.** What contrast makes the introduction dramatic? How does this contrast underlie the theme of the essay?
3. Examine the places where Marzollo uses direct quotations rather than reporting conversation indirectly. What is gained by using exact words at these points?
4. Marzollo asks rhetorical questions at several points in the essay. How do these questions help focus her argument? How do these questions function as transitional devices?

Questions for Further Thought

1. What kinds of games involving pretended violence, destruction, and death did you play as a child? What was your parents' reaction?
2. From your experience, do you think all children (both male and female, from various ethnic groups and economic backgrounds) play games of pretended violence? Would you say such play is normal?
3. It has been said that play is "the child's work," meaning that through play children try on new behaviors and skills and test their abilities. Would Marzollo agree? What things specifically can children learn through play?
4. What might be some of the reasons that adults like violent action movies (such as the *Rambo* and *Dirty Harry* series)? Do you see any connection between children's fantasy play and the popularity of these films? Are these films beneficial, harmless, or dangerous for people to view?

Writing Assignments Using Argumentation-Persuasion as a Pattern of Development

1. In paragraphs 15 and 16, Marzollo mentions four different parental attitudes toward guns. Write an essay that makes a case for parents' adopting one of these attitudes. After citing possible counterarguments, support your proposition with a balanced appeal to reason and emotion. Draw on your own experiences as a child, babysitter, neighbor, parent, and so on.
2. One of Marzollo's points is that physical play and fantasy have important healing roles in children's lives. Write an essay defending the role of physical activity and/or fantasy in adults' lives as a way to release pent-up rage

about things that can't be controlled. Make your proposition as specific as possible, supporting it with examples from your own life and with references to films, TV programs, and books. At some point in the essay, you should acknowledge briefly the opposing view: that escaping from reality can have negative repercussions.

Writing Assignments Using Other Patterns of Development

3. Write an essay about the games (physical, fantasy, or other) that helped you grow up. These may have been games that taught you about yourself, others, feelings, or life in general. Describe the games that absorbed you and explain their benefits.

∞ 4. Marzollo contends that childhood play with weapons isn't a cause of violence among adults. What, then, do you think are the roots of such violence? Prepare an essay exploring the causes of *one* kind of violence that you find particularly distressing. If you decide to write about street crime, date rape, or racial assault, you'll find it helpful to read, respectively, Louis Nizer's "Low-Cost Drugs for Addicts?" (page 670) and Beth Johnson's "Our Drug Problem" (page 675); Camille Paglia's "Rape: A Bigger Danger Than Feminists Know" (page 638) and Susan Jacoby's "Common Decency" (page 645); and Maya Angelou's "Grandmother's Victory" (page 164) as well as Gloria Naylor's "Mommy, What Does 'Nigger' Mean?" (page 535). No matter which area you focus on, you'll probably need to conduct some library research to deepen your understanding of the issue.

Ji-Yeon Mary Yuhfill

In 1970, five years after Ji-Yeon Mary Yuhfill was born in Seoul, Korea, her family immigrated to the United States and settled in Chicago. By the time Yuhfill graduated from Stanford University in 1987, she had acquired an abiding love of writing. She has worked as an agricultural reporter for the *Omaha World-Herald* and a general assignment reporter for *Long Island Newsday.* Currently she is pursuing a doctorate at the University of Pennsylvania, where she is conducting in-depth research on the history of American immigration policy. Yuhfill's writing reflects the experience of nonwhite Americans and their lack of recognition—their marginalization—by mainstream culture. The following selection first appeared in the *Philadelphia Inquirer* in 1991.

Let's Tell the Story of All America's Cultures

Who are America's heroes? History books tell us, in often stirring detail, about Thomas Jefferson, Abraham Lincoln, John F. Kennedy, Neil Armstrong; the list goes on and on. But what of the country's women, African-Americans, Mexicans, and Asians? Did they merely sit on the sidelines as white men built the nation? Ji-Yeon Mary Yuhfill describes what it feels like to grow up Korean in an America that barely acknowledges her existence.

I grew up hearing, seeing and almost believing that America was 1
white—albeit with a little black tinge here and there—and that white was best.

The white people were everywhere in my 1970s Chicago child- 2
hood: Founding Fathers, Lewis and Clark, Lincoln, Daniel Boone, Carnegie, presidents, explorers and industrialists galore. The only black people were slaves. The only Indians were scalpers.

I never heard one word about how Benjamin Franklin was so 3
impressed by the Iroquois federation of nations that he adapted that

model into our system of state and federal government. Or that the Indian tribes were systematically betrayed and massacred by a greedy young nation that stole their land and called it the United States.

I never heard one word about how Asian immigrants were 4 among the first to turn California's desert into fields of plenty. Or about Chinese immigrant Ah Bing, who bred the cherry now on sale in groceries across the nation. Or that plantation owners in Hawaii imported labor from China, Japan, Korea and the Philippines to work the sugar cane fields. I never learned that Asian immigrants were the only immigrants denied U.S. citizenship, even though they served honorably in World War I. All the immigrants in my textbook were white.

I never learned about Frederick Douglass, the runaway slave 5 who became a leading abolitionist and statesman, or about black scholar W.E.B. Du Bois. I never learned that black people rose up in arms against slavery. Nat Turner wasn't one of the heroes in my childhood history class.

I never learned that the American Southwest and California 6 were already settled by Mexicans when they were annexed after the Mexican-American War. I never learned that Mexico once had a problem keeping land-hungry white men on the U.S. side of the border.

So when other children called me a slant-eyed chink and told me 7 to go back where I came from, I was ready to believe that I wasn't really an American because I wasn't white.

America's bittersweet legacy of struggling and failing and get- 8 ting another step closer to democratic ideals of liberty and equality and justice for all wasn't for the likes of me, an immigrant child from Korea. The history books said so.

Well, the history books were wrong. 9

Educators around the country are finally realizing what I real- 10 ized as a teenager in the library, looking up the history I wasn't get-ting in school. America is a multicultural nation, composed of many people with varying histories and varying traditions who have little in common except their humanity, a belief in democracy and a desire for freedom.

America changed them, but they changed America too. 11

A committee of scholars and teachers gathered by the New 12 York State Department of Education recognizes this in their recent report, "One Nation, Many Peoples: A Declaration of Cultural Interdependence."

They recommend that public schools provide a "multicultural 13
education, anchored to the shared principles of a liberal democracy."

What that means, according to the report, is recognizing that 14
America was shaped and continues to be shaped by people of diverse
backgrounds. It calls for students to be taught that history is a ongoing process of discovery and interpretation of the past, and that there
is more than one way of viewing the world.

Thus, the westward migration of white Americans is not just a 15
heroic settling of an untamed wild, but also the conquest of indigenous peoples. Immigrants were not just white, but Asian as well.
Blacks were not merely passive slaves freed by northern whites, but
active fighters for their own liberation.

In particular, according to the report, the curriculum should 16
help children "to assess critically the reasons for the inconsistencies
between the ideals of the U.S. and social realities. It should provide
information and intellectual tools that can permit them to contribute
to bringing reality closer to the ideals."

In other words, show children the good with the bad, and give 17
them the skills to help improve their country. What could be more
patriotic?

Several dissenting members of the New York committee public- 18
ly worry that America will splinter into ethnic fragments if this multicultural curriculum is adopted. They argue that the committee's
report puts the focus on ethnicity at the expense of national unity.

But downplaying ethnicity will not bolster national unity. The 19
history of America is the story of how and why people from all over
the world came to the United States, and how in struggling to make
a better life for themselves, they changed each other, they changed
the country, and they all came to call themselves Americans.

E pluribus unum. Out of many, one. 20

This is why I, with my Korean background, and my childhood 21
tormentors, with their lost-in-the-mist-of-time European backgrounds, are all Americans.

It is the unique beauty of this country. It is high time we let all 22
our children gaze upon it.

Questions for Close Reading

1. What is the selection's thesis? Locate the sentence(s) in which Yuhfill
   states her main idea. If she doesn't state the thesis explicitly, express it in
   your own words.

2. Yuhfill makes the rather shocking claim that "the history books were wrong" (paragraph 9). Why does she make this statement? What evidence does she offer to support it?
3. According to Yuhfill, what changes are needed in American history courses?
4. Why does Yuhfill feel it is critical that American students receive more than the traditional whites-only version of our nation's history? Who will be served by making history books more multicultural?
5. Refer to your dictionary as needed to define the following words used in the selection: *albeit* (paragraph 1), *tinged* (1), *galore (2)*, *multicultural* (10, 13, 18), *interdependence* (12), *indigenous* (15), *dissenting* (18), *ethnicity* (18), and *bolster* (19).

Questions About the Writer's Craft

1. **The pattern.**   Where in her argument does Yuhfill present the opposing viewpoint? Why do you suppose she waits so long to deal with the dissenting opinion? What effect does this delay have on her argument's effectiveness?
2. **Other patterns.**   Why might Yuhfill have decided to use so many examples in paragraphs 2 through 6? How do these examples contribute to the persuasiveness of her position? Why might she have placed these examples before her thesis statement?
3. Yuhfill mixes the subjective and the objective in her argument. Where does she use specifics from her own life? How do these personal details help persuade readers to accept her viewpoint?
4. Yuhfill often uses parallelism and repetition of phrases, particularly in paragraphs 1 through 6 and paragraph 15. What effect do you think she intended these two stylistic devices to have on her readers?

Questions for Further Thought

1. Were you surprised by any of the information that Yuhfill cites about nonwhite influences in our nation's history? How much did you already know?
2. Do you feel your schools did a good job acquainting you with the full range of contributors to American history? How else, besides school, might you have learned about various ethnic groups' contributions?
3. Yuhfill cites some decidedly nonheroic, even shameful, events in our country's history (paragraphs 3, 4, and 6). How does reading about these events make you feel? Do you believe that schoolchildren should be told all the truths about their country's history? Why or why not?
4. In an essay in *Time* (June 1991), historian Arthur Schlesinger argues that a multicultural curriculum could have "unhealthy consequences" since it

promotes separate ethnic identities rather than a common national identity. Do you agree that an emphasis on ethnicity could have a divisive, rather than a unifying, effect on the nation? Explain.

Writing Assignments Using Argumentation-Persuasion as a Pattern of Development

∞ 1. Using the resources of a library, read several articles about the ongoing debate over multiculturalism's role in contemporary education. You should find coverage of the 1991 New York State Department of Education Study (cited by Yuhfill in paragraph 12) and historian Arthur Schlesinger's *Time* essay "The Cult of Ethnicity: Good and Bad" (July 8, 1991) especially helpful. Review your research, and decide whether or not you support the idea of a multicultural curriculum. Then write an essay in which you argue your position, refuting as many of the opposing views as possible. Draw upon your own experiences as well as your research when developing your point of view. For additional insights into multicultural perspectives, you might read Judith Ortiz Cofer's "A Partial Remembrance of a Puerto Rican Childhood" (page 138), Maya Angelou's "Grandmother's Victory" (page 164), and Gloria Naylor's "Mommy, What Does 'Nigger' Mean?" (page 535).

∞ 2. Yuhfill cites a problem she encountered in her education. What problems or insufficiencies have you found in your own education? Perhaps you perceive an overemphasis on athletics, a reliance on rote memorization, a tendency to discourage female students from pursuing an interest in math and science. Select a single problem at one level of education, and brainstorm with others to gather material about the problem. Then write an essay directed at those who think all is well in our educational system. Be sure your argument illustrates the inaccuracy of these individuals' overly positive view. Before writing your paper, you may want to read William Zinsser's "College Pressures" (page 297) because it too offers a critique of education.

Writing Assignments Using Other Patterns of Development

3. Because the mainstream culture they lived in didn't recognize the presence of minorities, the author's classmates considered Yuhfill an outsider, almost a nonbeing. To what extent, in your opinion, does television contribute to the dehumanization of minorities? For several days, watch a variety of television shows, noting how a particular ethnic or minority group (such as African-Americans, Hispanic-Americans, or the elderly) is portrayed. Then write an essay showing that the depiction of this group on television is either accurate *or* distorted. Support your main idea with

plentiful references to specific television shows, including newscasts, situation comedies, talk shows, and so forth.

∞ 4. In her essay, Yuhfill refers to a report issued by the New York State Department of Education. The report argues that curriculum should encourage students to examine "the reasons for the inconsistencies between the ideals of the U.S. and social realities." Like most people, you probably detected such disparities when you were growing up. Perhaps as a ten-year-old, you heard an admired neighbor brag about padding an expense account. As an eighth-grader, you may have visited your state legislature, where you saw chaos and rudeness instead of order and respect. As a high school student, you might have learned that an esteemed coach took kickbacks from college recruiters. Focus on one such clash between the ethical ideal and the everyday reality, and write about the incident's effect on you. Provide dramatic details to show how you reacted, what you did to explain the discrepancy to yourself, and whether you asked adults to help you understand the situation. At the end, reach some conclusions about the way children can be helped to deal with such collisions between ideals and reality. Before writing your paper, you may want to read Langston Hughes's "Salvation" (page 191), a powerful essay that explores a child's disillusionment with adult realities.

Mark Twain

Mark Twain is a central figure in American literature. Published in 1884, *The Adventures of Huckleberry Finn,* Twain's finest work, recounts a journey down the Mississippi by two memorable figures: a white boy and a black slave. Twain was born Samuel Langhorne Clemens in 1835 and was raised in Hannibal, Missouri. During his early years, he worked as a riverboat pilot, newspaper reporter, printer, and gold prospector. Although his popular image is as the author of such comic works as *The Adventures of Tom Sawyer* (1876), *Life on the Mississippi* (1883), and *The Prince and the Pauper* (1882), Twain had a darker side that may have resulted from the bitter experiences of his life: financial failure and the deaths of his wife and daughter. His last writings are savage, satiric, and pessimistic. The following selection is taken from *Letters From the Earth,* one of Twain's later works.

The Damned Human Race

Does today's newspaper contain a headline about people fighting somewhere in the world? Most likely. In this selection, Mark Twain concludes that the combative and cruel nature of human beings makes them the lowest of creatures, not the highest. He concludes his scathing indictment by supplying a startling reason for humans' warlike nature.

I have been studying the traits and dispositions of the "lower animals" (so-called), and contrasting them with the traits and dispositions of man. I find the result humiliating to me. For it obliges me to renounce my allegiance to the Darwinian theory of the Ascent of Man from the Lower Animals; since it now seems plain to me that the theory ought to be vacated in favor of a new and truer one, this new and truer one to be named the *Descent* of Man from the Higher Animals. 1

In proceeding toward this unpleasant conclusion I have not guessed or speculated or conjectured, but have used what is commonly called the scientific method. That is to say, I have subjected 2 every postulate that presented itself to the crucial test of actual experiment, and have adopted it or rejected it according to the result. Thus I verified and established each step of my course in its turn before advancing to the next. These experiments were made in the London Zoological Gardens, and covered many months of painstaking and fatiguing work.

Before particularizing any of the experiments, I wish to state one 3 or two things which seem to more properly belong in this place than further along. This in the interest of clearness. The massed experiments established to my satisfaction certain generalizations, to wit:

1. That the human race is of one distinct species. It exhibits slight variations—in color, stature, mental caliber, and so on—due to climate, environment, and so forth; but it is a species by itself, and not to be confounded with any other.
2. That the quadrupeds are a distinct family, also. This family exhibits variations—in color, size, food preferences and so on; but it is a family by itself.
3. That the other families—the birds, the fishes, the insects, the reptiles, etc.—are more or less distinct, also. They are in the procession. They are links in the chain which stretches down from the higher animals to man at the bottom.

Some of my experiments were quite curious. In the course of my 4 reading I had come across a case where, many years ago, some hunters on our Great Plains organized a buffalo hunt for the entertainment of an English earl—that, and to provide some fresh meat for his larder. They had charming sport. They killed seventy-two of those great animals; and ate part of one of them and left the seventy-one to rot. In order to determine the difference between an anaconda and an earl—if any—I caused seven young calves to be turned into the anaconda's cage. The grateful reptile immediately crushed one of them and swallowed it, then lay back satisfied. It showed no further interest in the calves, and no disposition to harm them. I tried this experiment with other anacondas; always with the same result. The fact stood proven that the difference between an earl and an anaconda is that the earl is cruel and the anaconda isn't; and that the earl wantonly destroys what he has no use for, but the anaconda doesn't. This seemed to suggest that the anaconda was not descended from the earl. It also seemed to suggest that the earl was descended from the anaconda, and had lost a good deal in the transition.

I was aware that many men who have accumulated more millions of money than they can ever use have shown a rabid hunger for more, and have not scrupled to cheat the ignorant and the helpless out of their poor servings in order to partially appease that appetite. I furnished a hundred different kinds of wild and tame animals the opportunity to accumulate vast stores of food, but none of them would do it. The squirrels and bees and certain birds made accumulations, but stopped when they had gathered a winter's supply, and could not be persuaded to add to it either honestly or by chicanery. In order to bolster up a tottering reputation the ant pretended to store up supplies, but I was not deceived. I know the ant. These experiments convinced me that there is this difference between man and the higher animals: he is avaricious and miserly, they are not.

In the course of my experiments I convinced myself that among the animals man is the only one that harbors insults and injuries, broods over them, waits till a chance offers, then takes revenge. The passion of revenge is unknown to the higher animals.

Roosters keep harems, but it is by consent of their concubines; therefore no wrong is done. Men keep harems, but it is by brute force, privileged by atrocious laws which the other sex were allowed no hand in making. In this matter man occupies a far lower place than the rooster.

Cats are loose in their morals, but not consciously so. Man, in his descent from the cat, has brought the cat's looseness with him but has left the unconsciousness behind—the saving grace which excuses the cat. The cat is innocent, man is not.

Indecency, vulgarity, obscenity—these are strictly confined to man; he invented them. Among the higher animals there is no trace of them. They hide nothing; they are not ashamed. Man, with his soiled mind, covers himself. He will not even enter a drawing room with his breast and back naked, so alive are he and his mates to indecent suggestion. Man is "The Animal that Laughs." But so does the monkey, as Mr. Darwin pointed out; and so does the Australian bird that is called the laughing jackass. No—Man is the Animal that Blushes. He is the only one that does it—or has occasion to.

At the head of this article[1] we see how "three monks were burnt to death" a few days ago, and a prior "put to death with atrocious cruelty." Do we inquire into the details? No; or we should find out

5

6

7

8

9

10

---

[1]Twain originally began his article with newspaper clippings containing telegrams that reported atrocities in Crete.

that the prior was subjected to unprintable mutilations. Man—when he is a North American Indian—gouges out his prisoner's eyes; when he is King John, with a nephew to render untroublesome, he uses a red-hot iron; when he is a religious zealot dealing with heretics in the Middle Ages, he skins his captive alive and scatters salt on his back; in the first Richard's time he shuts up a multitude of Jew families in a tower and sets fire to it; in Columbus's time he captures a family of Spanish Jews and—but *that* is not printable; in our day in England a man is fined ten shillings for beating his mother nearly to death with a chair, and another man is fined forty shillings for having four pheasant eggs in his possession without being able to satisfactorily explain how he got them. Of all the animals, man is the only one that is cruel. He is the only one that inflicts pain for the pleasure of doing it. It is a trait that is not known to the higher animals. The cat plays with the frightened mouse; but she has this excuse, that she does not know that the mouse is suffering. The cat is moderate—unhumanly moderate: she only scares the mouse, she does not hurt it; she doesn't dig out its eyes, or tear off its skin, or drive splinters under its nails—man-fashion; when she is done playing with it she makes a sudden meal of it and puts it out of its trouble. Man is the Cruel Animal. He is alone in that distinction.

The higher animals engage in individual fights, but never in organized masses. Man is the only animal that deals in that atrocity of atrocities, War. He is the only one that gathers his brethren about him and goes forth in cold blood and with calm pulse to exterminate his kind. He is the only animal that for sordid wages will march out, as the Hessians did in our Revolution, and as the boyish Prince Napoleon did in the Zulu war, and help to slaughter strangers of his own species who have done him no harm and with whom he has no quarrel.   11

Man is the only animal that robs his helpless fellow of his country—takes possession of it and drives him out of it or destroys him. Man has done this in all the ages. There is not an acre of ground on the globe that is in possession of its rightful owner, or that has not been taken away from owner after owner, cycle after cycle, by force and bloodshed.   12

Man is the only Slave. And he is the only animal who enslaves. He has always been a slave in one form or another, and has always held other slaves in bondage under him in one way or another. In our day he is always some man's slave for wages, and does that man's work; and this slave has other slaves under him for minor wages, and   13 they do *his* work. The higher animals are the only ones who exclusively do their own work and provide their own living.

Man is the only Patriot. He sets himself apart in his own country, under his own flag, and sneers at the other nations, and keeps multitudinous uniformed assassins on hand at heavy expense to grab slices of other people's countries, and keep *them* from grabbing slices of *his.* And in the intervals between campaigns he washes the blood off his hands and works for "the universal brotherhood of man"—with his mouth.

14

Man is the Religious Animal. He is the only Religious Animal. He is the only animal that has the True Religion—several of them. He is the only animal that loves his neighbor as himself, and cuts his throat if his theology isn't straight. He has made a graveyard of the globe in trying his honest best to smooth his brother's path to happiness and heaven. He was at it in the time of the Caesars, he was at it in Mahomet's time, he was at it in the time of the Inquisition, he was at it in France a couple of centuries, he was at it in England in Mary's day, he has been at it ever since he first saw the light, he is at it today in Crete—as per the telegrams quoted above[2]—he will be at it somewhere else tomorrow. The higher animals have no religion. And we are told that they are going to be left out, in the Hereafter. I wonder why? It seems questionable taste.

15

Man is the Reasoning Animal. Such is the claim. I think it is open to dispute. Indeed, my experiments have proven to me that he is the Unreasoning Animal. Note his history, as sketched above. It seems plain to me that whatever he is he is *not* a reasoning animal. His record is the fantastic record of a maniac. I consider that the strongest count against his intelligence is the fact that with that record back of him he blandly sets himself up as the head animal of the lot: whereas by his own standards he is the bottom one.

16

In truth, man is incurably foolish. Simple things which the other animals easily learn, he is incapable of learning. Among my experiments was this. In an hour I taught a cat and a dog to be friends. I put them in a cage. In another hour I taught them to be friends with a rabbit. In the course of two days I was able to add a fox, a goose, a squirrel and some doves. Finally a monkey. They lived together in peace; even affectionately.

17

Next, in another cage I confined an Irish Catholic from Tipperary, and as soon as he seemed tame I added a Scotch Presbyterian from Aberdeen. Next a Turk from Constantinople; a Greek Christian

18

[2]See note, page 611

from Crete; an Armenian; a Methodist from the wilds of Arkansas; a Buddhist from China; a Brahman from Benares. Finally, a Salvation Army Colonel from Wapping. Then I stayed away two whole days. When I came back to note results, the cage of Higher Animals was all right, but in the other, there was but a chaos of gory odds and ends of turbans and fezzes and plaids and bones and flesh—not a specimen left alive. These Reasoning Animals had disagreed on a theological detail and carried the matter to a Higher Court.

One is obliged to concede that in true loftiness of character,   19 Man cannot claim to approach even the meanest of the Higher Animals. It is plain that he is constitutionally incapable of approaching that altitude; that he is constitutionally afflicted with a Defect which must make such approach forever impossible, for it is manifest that this defect is permanent in him, indestructible, ineradicable.

I find this Defect to be *the Moral Sense.* He is the only animal   20 that has it. It is the secret of his degradation. It is the quality *which enables him to do wrong.* It has no other office. It is incapable of performing any other function. It could never have been intended to perform any other. Without it, man could do no wrong. He would rise at once to the level of the Higher Animals.

Since the Moral Sense has but the one office, the one capacity—   21 to enable man to do wrong—it is plainly without value to him. It is as valueless to him as is disease. In fact, it manifestly *is* a disease. *Rabies* is bad, but it is not so bad as this disease. Rabies enables a man to do a thing which he could not do when in a healthy state: kill his neighbor with a poisonous bite. No one is the better man for having rabies: The Moral Sense enables a man to do wrong. It enables him to do wrong in a thousand ways. Rabies is an innocent disease, compared to the Moral Sense. No one, then, can be the better man for having the Moral Sense. What, now, do we find the Primal Curse to have been? Plainly what it was in the beginning: the infliction upon man of the Moral Sense; the ability to distinguish good from evil; and with it, necessarily, the ability to *do* evil; for there can be no evil act without the presence of consciousness of it in the doer of it.

And so I find that we have descended and degenerated, from   22 some far ancestor—some microscopic atom wandering at its pleasure between the mighty horizons of a drop of water perchance—insect by insect, animal by animal, reptile by reptile, down the long highway of smirchless innocence, till we have reached the bottom stage of development—namable as the Human Being. Below us—nothing.

Questions for Close Reading

1. What is the selection's thesis? Locate the sentence(s) in which Twain states his main idea. If he doesn't state the thesis explicitly, express it in your own words.
2. Because of their intelligence, humans are usually called the highest animal. What, according to Twain, are the specific traits that make humans the lowest animal?
3. How does the story of the earl who hunted down seventy-two buffalo show that an anaconda is superior to an earl?
4. What does Twain mean when he points out that humankind is the only animal that "has occasion to" blush? What are some of the occasions for blushing that he highlights in the essay?
5. Refer to your dictionary as needed to define the following words used in the selection: *confounded* (paragraph 3), *anaconda* (4), *wantonly* (4), *chicanery* (5), *heretics* (10), *constitutionally* (19), *ineradicable* (19), and *smirchless* (22).

Questions About the Writer's Craft

1. **The pattern.**   Most writers don't tell the reader outright the reasoning process they used to arrive at their essay's proposition. But Twain claims that he reached his conclusion about human beings inductively— through the use of the "scientific method." Why does Twain make this claim?
2. Where in the essay does Twain try to shock the audience? Why do you think he adopts this technique?
3. **Other patterns.**   In some paragraphs, Twain provides numerous examples of political and religious atrocities. Why do you suppose he supplies so many examples?
4. Black humor is defined as "the use of the morbid and the absurd for comic purposes." What elements of the morbid and the absurd do you find in Twain's essay? Would you say "The Damned Human Race" is an example of black humor? Explain.

Questions for Further Thought

1. Twain wrote this essay in the early 1900s. Is what he says about humans true today? If Twain were writing today, what events and situations would he include in this essay as proof of humanity's lowness?
2. Is Twain's indictment excessive? Has he gone overboard, or do we humans deserve his indictment? Explain.
3. If a person behaved like the cat with a mouse described in paragraph 10, would that person be evil—or innocent like the cat? Is it behavior that is the problem for Twain, or is it something else?

4. Twain's essay hinges on an idea most of us take for granted—that the human species tops a hierarchy of creatures. We are, we assume, the end result of a complex evolutionary process. What would happen if we became aware that we weren't the cleverest, most powerful creature in the universe? Which of our beliefs, habits, and actions might change as a result?

Writing Assignments Using Argumentation-Persuasion as a Pattern of Development

∞ 1. In an essay, argue that human beings are worthy of being considered the "highest animal." The paper should acknowledge and then refute Twain's charges that people are miserly, vengeful, foolish, and so on. To support your proposition, use specific examples of how human beings can be kind, caring, generous, and peace-loving. You might find it helpful to read Geoffrey Cowley's "Why a Disaster Brings Out the Best in People" (page 478) and Lewis Thomas's "The Lie Detector" (page 495), essays focusing on the more positive aspects of human nature.

∞ 2. Write an essay agreeing with Twain that it is our everyday meannesses, unkindness, and cruelties that make us the "lowest animal." Use compelling examples to support your argument, including description and dialogue whenever appropriate. You might focus on one of the following topics:

> Violence toward children
> Abuse of animals
> Hurtful sarcasm
> Insults of a racial, sexist, or religious nature
> Indifference to the unfortunate

Somewhere in the essay, you should acknowledge the view that humans are capable of considerable kindness and compassion. To gain some insight into this more optimistic perspective, you might want to read Geoffrey Cowley's "Why a Disaster Brings Out the Best in People" (page 478) and Lewis Thomas's "The Lie Detector" (page 495).

Writing Assignments Using Other Patterns of Development

∞ 3. What failings of human decency do you see around you every day in your town, on your campus, or at your job? Write an essay showing that inhumanity resides not just in atrocities but also in ordinary acts of indifference. Before planning the paper, you might want to see what Jonathan Kozol, in "Are the Homeless Crazy?" (page 500), has to say about people's often uncaring attitude—in this case, toward the homeless. In your essay, you may use Twain's kind of bitter sarcasm, or you may adopt a more objective, less vitriolic tone.

4. How could humans become less cruel? Write an essay outlining a new process for raising children or "re-civilizing" adults—a process that, if instituted, would improve human morality.

Jonathan Swift

The foremost satirist in the English language, Jonathan Swift (1667–1745) is most famous as the author of *Gulliver's Travels* (1726), an often scorching indictment of human conduct. Born in Ireland, Swift moved to London at a young age and in 1694 was ordained an Anglican priest. In 1714 he was appointed the dean of St. Patrick's Cathedral in Dublin, a minor post the ambitious Swift accepted with reluctance. For most of his life, Swift was an outspoken public figure, writing satiric poems, plays, and essays aimed at political and religious targets. His works include *A Tale of a Tub* and *The Battle of the Books,* both published in 1704. More than two decades later, outraged by the British government's treatment of the Irish people, Swift wrote "A Modest Proposal," the classic essay reprinted here.

A Modest Proposal

In 1729, Ireland was in tragic condition. Poverty was widespread, a devastating famine was in its third year, and people were starving. Moreover, the British government, which ruled Ireland, imposed high taxes on the already impoverished populace. Enraged by these injustices, Swift wrote a powerful satire attacking the English and wealthy Irish for ignoring the existence of the suffering masses. Speaking not as himself but in the guise of an impartial observer, Swift suggested an outrageous solution to Ireland's problems, a solution in keeping with the inhumanity he saw rampant in Ireland.

It is a melancholy object to those who walk through this great town[1] or travel in the country, when they see the streets, the roads, and cabin doors, crowded with beggars of the female sex, followed by three, four, or six children, all in rags and importuning every passenger for an alms. These mothers, instead of being able to work for their honest livelihood, are forced to employ all their time in strolling to beg

1

[1]Dublin.

sustenance for their helpless infants, who, as they grow up, either turn thieves for want of work, or leave their dear native country to fight for the Pretender in Spain, or sell themselves to the Barbadoes.[2]

I think it is agreed by all parties that this prodigious number of 2 children in the arms, or on the backs, or at the heels of their mothers, and frequently of their fathers, is in the present deplorable state of the kingdom a very great additional grievance; and therefore whoever could find out a fair, cheap, and easy method of making these children sound, useful members of the commonwealth would deserve so well of the public as to have his statue set up for a preserver of the nation.

But my intention is very far from being confined to provide only 3 for the children of professed beggars; it is of a much greater extent, and shall take in the whole number of infants at a certain age who are born of parents in effect as little able to support them as those who demand our charity in the streets.

As to my own part, having turned my thoughts for many years 4 upon this important subject, and maturely weighed the several schemes of other projectors, I have always found them grossly mistaken in their computation. It is true, a child just dropped from its dam may be supported by her milk for a solar year, with little other nourishment; at most not above the value of two shillings, which the mother may certainly get, or the value in scraps, by her lawful occupation of begging; and it is exactly at one year old that I propose to provide for them in such a manner as instead of being a charge upon their parents or the parish, or wanting food and raiment for the rest of their lives, they shall on the contrary contribute to the feeding, and partly to the clothing, of many thousands.

There is likewise another great advantage in my scheme, that it 5 will prevent those involuntary abortions, and that horrid practice of women murdering their bastard children, alas, too frequent among us, sacrificing the poor innocent babes, I doubt, more to avoid the expense than the shame, which would move tears and pity in the most savage and inhuman breast.

The number of souls in this kingdom being usually reckoned 6 one million and a half, of these I calculate there may be about two hundred thousand couples whose wives are breeders, from which

---

[2]Many poor Irish were leaving the country to try to find a living elsewhere.

number I subtract thirty thousand couples who are able to maintain their own children, although I apprehend there cannot be so many under the present distress of the kingdom; but this being granted, there will remain an hundred and seventy thousand breeders. I again subtract fifty thousand for those women who miscarry, or whose children die by accident or disease within the year. There only remain an hundred and twenty thousand children of poor parents annually born. The question therefore is, how this number shall be reared and provided for, which, as I have already said, under the present situation of affairs, is utterly impossible by all the methods hitherto proposed. For we can neither employ them in handicraft nor agriculture; we neither build houses (I mean in the country) nor cultivate land. They can very seldom pick up livelihood by stealing till they arrive at six years old, except where they are of towardly parts;[3] although I confess they learn the rudiments much earlier, during which time they can however be looked upon only as probationers, as I have been informed by a principal gentleman in the county of Cavan, who protested to me that he never knew above one or two instances under the age of six, even in a part of the kingdom so renowned for the quickest proficiency in that art.

I am assured by our merchants that a boy or a girl before twelve   7
years old is no salable commodity; and even when they come to this age, they will not yield above three pounds, or three pounds and half a crown at most on the Exchange; which cannot turn to account either to the parents or the kingdom, the charge of nutriment and rags having been at least four times that value.

I shall now therefore humbly propose my own thoughts, which   8
I hope will not be liable to the least objection.

I have been assured by a very knowing American of my acquain-   9
tance in London, that a young healthy child well nursed is at a year old a most delicious, nourishing, and wholesome food, whether stewed, roasted, baked, or boiled; and I make no doubt that it will equally serve in fricasee or a ragout.

I do therefore humbly offer it to public consideration that of the   10
hundred and twenty thousand children, already computed, twenty thousand may be reserved for breed, whereof only one fourth part to be males, which is more than we allow to sheep, black cattle, or swine; and my reason is that these children are seldom the fruits of

[3]Prematurely developed.

marriage, a circumstance not much regarded by our savages, therefore one male will be sufficient to serve four females. That the remaining hundred thousand may at a year old be offered in sale to the persons of quality and fortune through the kingdom, always advising the mother to let them suck plentifully in the last month, so as to render them plump and fat for a good table. A child will make two dishes at an entertainment for friends; and when the family dines alone, the fore or hind quarter will make a reasonable dish, and seasoned with a little pepper or salt will be very good boiled on the fourth day, especially in winter.

I have reckoned upon a medium that a child just born will weigh twelve pounds, and in a solar year if tolerably nursed increaseth to twenty-eight pounds.   11

I grant this food will be somewhat dear, and therefore very proper for landlords, who, as they have already devoured most of the parents, seem to have the best title to the children.   12

Infant's flesh will be in season throughout the year, but more plentiful in March, and a little before and after. For we are told by a grave author, an eminent French physician,[4] that fish being a prolific diet, there are more children born in Roman Catholic countries about nine months after Lent, than at any other season; therefore, reckoning a year after Lent, the markets will be more glutted than usual, because the number of popish infants is at least three to one in this kingdom; and therefore it will have one other collateral advantage, by lessening the number of Papists among us.   13

I have already computed the charge of nursing a beggar's child (in which list I reckon all cottagers, laborers, and four fifths of the farmers) to be about two shillings per annum, rags included; and I believe no gentleman would repine to give ten shillings for the carcass of a good fat child, which, as I have said, will make four dishes of excellent nutritive meat, when he hath only some particular friend or his own family to dine with him. Thus the squire will learn to be a good landlord, and grow popular among the tenants; the mother will have eight shillings net profit, and be fit for work till she produces another child.   14

Those who are more thrifty (as I must confess the times require) may flay the carcass; the skin of which artificially[5] dressed will make admirable gloves for ladies, and summer boots for fine gentlemen.   15

---

[4]François Rabelais, a sixteenth-century comic writer.
[5]Skillfully.

As to our city of Dublin, shambles[6] may be appointed for this   16
purpose in the most convenient parts of it, and butchers we may be
assured will not be wanting; although I rather recommend buying
the children alive, and dressing them hot from the knife as we do
roasting pigs.

A very worthy person, a true lover of his country, and whose vir-   17
tues I highly esteem, was lately pleased in discoursing on this matter
to offer a refinement upon my scheme. He said that many gentlemen
of his kingdom, having of late destroyed their deer, he conceived that
the want of venison might be well supplied by the bodies of young
lads and maidens, not exceeding fourteen years of age nor under
twelve, so great a number of both sexes in every county being now
ready to starve for want of work and service; and these to be disposed
of by their parents, if alive, or otherwise by their nearest relations.
But with due deference to so excellent a friend and so deserving a patriot, I cannot be altogether in his sentiments; for as to the males, my
American acquaintance assured me from frequent experience that
their flesh was generally tough and lean, like that of our schoolboys,
by continual exercise, and their taste disagreeable; and to fatten them
would not answer the charge. Then as to the females, it would, I
think with humble submission, be a loss to the public, because they
soon would become breeders themselves; and besides, it is not improbable that some scrupulous people might be apt to censure such
a practice (although indeed very unjustly) as a little bordering upon
cruelty; which, I confess, hath always been with me the strongest objection against any project, how well soever intended.

But in order to justify my friend, he confessed that this expedi-   18
ent was put into his head by the famous Psalmanazar,[7] a native of the
island Formosa, who came from thence to London above twenty
years ago, and in conversation told my friend that in his country
when any young person happened to be put to death, the execution-
er sold the carcass to the persons of quality as a prime dainty; and that
in his time the body of a plump girl of fifteen, who was crucified for
an attempt to poison the emperor, was sold to his Imperial Majesty's
prime minister of state, and other great mandarins of the court, in
joints from the gibbet, at four hundred crowns. Neither indeed can

---

[6]Slaughterhouses.

[7]A Frenchman, Georges Psalmanazar, who fooled London society into thinking he
was from the exotic land of Formosa.

I deny that if the same use were made of several plump young girls in this town, who without one single groat to their fortunes cannot stir abroad without a chair,[8] and appear at the playhouse and assemblies in foreign fineries which they never will pay for, the kingdom would not be the worse.

Some persons of a desponding spirit are in great concern about 19 that vast number of poor people who are aged, diseased, or maimed, and I have been desired to employ my thoughts what course may be taken to ease the nation of so grievous an encumbrance. But I am not in the least pain upon that matter, because it is very well known that they are every day dying and rotting by cold and famine, and filth and vermin, as fast as can be reasonably expected. And as to the younger laborers, they are now in almost as hopeful a condition. They cannot get work, and consequently pine away for want of nourishment to a degree that if any time they are accidentally hired to common labor, they have not strength to perform it; and thus the country and themselves are happily delivered from the evils to come.

I have too long digressed, and therefore shall return to my sub- 20 ject. I think the advantages by the proposal which I have made are obvious and many, as well as of the highest importance.

For first, as I have already observed, it would greatly lessen the 21 number of Papists, with whom we are yearly overrun, being the principal breeders of the nation as well as our most dangerous enemies; and who stay at home on purpose to deliver the kingdom to the Pretender, hoping to take their advantage by the absence of so many good Protestants, who have chosen rather to leave their country than to stay at home and pay tithes against their conscience to an Episcopal curate.

Secondly, the poorer tenants will have something valuable of 22 their own, which by law may be made liable to distress,[9] and help to pay their landlord's rent, their corn and cattle being already seized and money a thing unknown.

Thirdly, whereas the maintenance of an hundred thousand chil- 23 dren, from two years old and upwards, cannot be computed at less than ten shillings a piece per annum, the nation's stock will be thereby increased fifty thousand pounds per annum, besides the profit of

[8]A groat was a coin worth several pennies; a chair was a sedan chair in which a person was carried by servants.
[9]Seizure for the payment of debts.

a new dish introduced to the tables of all gentlemen of fortune in the kingdom who have any refinement in taste. And the money will circulate among ourselves, the goods being entirely of our own growth and manufacture.

Fourthly, the constant breeders, besides the gain of eight shillings sterling per annum by the sale of their children, will be rid of the charge for maintaining them after the first year. 24

Fifthly, this food would likewise bring great custom to taverns, where the vintners will certainly be so prudent as to procure the best receipts for dressing it to perfection, and consequently have their houses frequented by all the fine gentlemen, who justly value themselves upon their knowledge in good eating; and a skillful cook, who understands how to oblige his guests, will contrive to make it as expensive as they please. 25

Sixthly, this would be a great inducement to marriage, which all wise nations have either encouraged by rewards or enforced by laws and penalties. It would increase the care and tenderness of mothers toward their children, when they were sure of a settlement for life to the poor babes, provided in some sort by the public, to their annual profit instead of expense. We should see an honest emulation among the married women, which of them could bring the fattest child to the market. Men would become as fond of their wives during the time of pregnancy as they are now of their mares in foal, their cows in calf, or sows when they are ready to farrow; nor offer to beat or kick them (as is too frequent a practice) for fear of a miscarriage. 26

Many other advantages might be enumerated. For instance, the addition of some thousand carcasses in our exportation of barreled beef, the propagation of swine's flesh, and improvements in the art of making good bacon, so much wanted among us by the great destruction of pigs, too frequent at our tables, which are no way comparable in taste or magnificence to a well-grown, fat, yearling child, which roasted whole will make a considerable figure at a lord mayor's feast or any other public entertainment. But this and many others I omit, being studious of brevity. 27

Supposing that one thousand families in this city would be constant customers for infants' flesh, besides others who might have it at merry meetings, particularly weddings and christenings, I compute that Dublin would take off annually about twenty thousand carcasses, and the rest of the kingdom (where probably they will be sold somewhat cheaper) the remaining eighty thousand. 28

I can think of no one objection that will possibly be raised against   29
this proposal, unless it should be urged that the number of people will
be thereby much lessened in the kingdom. This I freely own, and it
was indeed one principal design in offering it to the world. I desire the
reader will observe; that I calculate my remedy for this one individual
kingdom of Ireland and for no other that ever was, is, or I think ever
can be upon earth. Therefore, let no man talk to me of other expedients: of taxing our absentees at five shillings a pound: of using neither
clothes nor household furniture except what is of our own growth and
manufacture: of utterly rejecting the materials and instruments that
promote foreign luxury: of curing the expensiveness of pride, vanity,
idleness, and gaming in our women: of introducing a vein of parsimo-
ny, prudence, and temperance: of learning to love our country, in the
want of which we differ even from Lowlanders and the inhabitants of
Topinamboo:[10] of quitting our animosities and factions, nor acting
any longer like the Jews,[11] who were murdering one another at the
very moment their city was taken: of being a little cautious not to sell
our country and conscience for nothing: of teaching landlords to have
at least one degree of mercy toward their tenants: lastly, of putting a
spirit of honesty, industry, and skill into our shopkeepers; who, if a
resolution could now be taken to buy only our native goods, would
immediately unite to cheat and exact upon us in the price, the measure, and the goodness, nor could ever yet be brought to make one
fair proposal of just dealing, though often and earnestly invited to it.

Therefore, I repeat, let no man talk to me of these and the like   30
expedients, till he hath at least some glimpse of hope that there will
ever be some hearty and sincere attempt to put them in practice.

But as to myself, having been wearied out for many years with   31
offering vain, idle, visionary thoughts, and at length utterly despair-
ing of success, I fortunately fell upon this proposal, which, as it is
wholly new, so it hath something solid and real, of no expense and
little trouble, full in our own power, and whereby we can incur no
danger in disobliging England. For this kind of commodity will not
bear exportation, the flesh being of too tender a consistence to admit
a long continuance in salt, although perhaps I could name a country
which would be glad to eat up our whole nation without it.

---

[10]A place in the Brazilian jungle.
[11]Rival factions were at war within Jerusalem when the city was seized by the Romans
in 70 A.D.

After all, I am not so violently bent upon my own opinion as to   32
reject any offer proposed by wise men, which shall be found equally
innocent, cheap, easy, and effectual. But before something of that
kind shall be advanced in contradiction to my scheme, and offering
a better, I desire the author or authors will be pleased maturely to
consider two points. First, as things now stand, how they will be able
to find food and raiment for an hundred thousand useless mouths
and backs. And secondly, there being a round million of creatures in
human figure throughout this kingdom, whose sole subsistence put
into a common stock would leave them in debt two millions of
pounds sterling, adding those who are beggars by profession to the
bulk of farmers, cottagers, and laborers, with their wives and children
who are beggars in effect; I desire those politicians who dislike my
overture, and may perhaps be so bold to attempt an answer, that they
will first ask the parents of these mortals whether they would not at
this day think it a great happiness to have been sold for food at a year
old in this manner I prescribe, and thereby have avoided such a perpetual scene of misfortunes as they have since gone through by the
oppression of landlords, the impossibility of paying rent without
money or trade, the want of common sustenance, with neither house
nor clothes to cover them from the inclemencies of the weather, and
the most inevitable prospect of entailing the like or greater miseries
upon their breed forever.

I profess, in the sincerity of my heart, that I have not the least   33
personal interest in endeavoring to promote this necessary work,
having no other motive than the public good of my country, by advancing our trade, providing for infants, relieving the poor, and giving some pleasure to the rich. I have no children by which I can
propose to get a single penny; the youngest being nine years old, and
my wife past childbearing.

Questions for Close Reading

1. What is the selection's thesis? Locate the sentence(s) in which Swift states
   his main idea. If he doesn't state the thesis explicitly, express it in your
   own words.
2. Swift mentions several economic, social, and political realities in Ireland
   that prompted him to write this essay. Identify a few of them.

3. What twisted reasoning does the speaker use to argue that his proposal will improve relationships between husbands and wives and between parents and children?

4. What problems does the speaker contend the British government will solve if it permits the butchering and sale of infants from impoverished families?

5. Refer to your dictionary as needed to define the following words used in the selection: *importuning* (paragraph 1), *alms* (1), *prodigious* (2), *raiment* (4), *prolific* (13), *repine* (14), *discoursing* (17), *encumbrance* (19), and *vintners* (25).

Questions About the Writer's Craft

1. **The pattern.** *Satire* uses humor to criticize a situation and create awareness of the need for change; *irony,* often used in satire, occurs when a writer or speaker implies—rather than explicitly states—a discrepancy or incongruity. (*Verbal irony* involves a discrepancy between literal words and what's actually meant. In *situational irony,* the circumstances are themselves incongruous.) How do satire and irony help Swift accomplish what a more conventional approach to persuasion would not?

2. Swift uses language laden with emotion to convey a sarcastic, downright bitter tone. Locate several examples of emotionally charged language. How does this language support Swift's real purpose for writing "A Modest Proposal"?

3. In paragraph 20, the speaker apologizes for having "digressed" in the last few paragraphs. Do paragraphs 17, 18, and 19 really represent a digression, or are they germane to the issue? Explain.

4. Writers of argumentation-persuasion essays often anticipate and then refute opposing opinions. In what paragraph does the speaker in "A Modest Proposal" refute the dissenting viewpoint? What is the real purpose of this refutation?

Questions for Further Thought

1. Are the causes of the poverty that Swift saw in eighteenth-century Ireland similar to some of the economic problems we experience in this country? Explain.

2. In paragraph 29, the speaker rejects several proposals that Swift actually believes would help alleviate poverty in Ireland. Which of these proposals might be used to address the problem of poverty in our nation?

3. Do the well-off, even the merely comfortable, have a responsibility to the poor? If so, what is the nature and extent of this responsibility?

4. Swift's epitaph reads, "He has gone where savage indignation can no longer lacerate his heart." About what do you feel "savage indignation"? What can you do about the situations that outrage you?

Writing Assignments Using Argumentation-Persuasion as a Pattern of Development

1. Select a subject that you feel strongly about—one that has an ethical or moral dimension to it. Then, like Swift, use an ironic approach to convince readers of your position. In other words, argue for one point of view while pretending to advance the other. For example, if you're concerned about some colleges' exemption of their star athletes from conventional academic requirements, you could write an essay arguing the "advantages" of letting student-athletes "coast" through college.

∞ 2. Read what Jonathan Kozol has to say in "Are the Homeless Crazy?" (page 500) about one segment of this country's poor—the homeless. Then write an essay advocating the steps that ordinary citizens can take to help alleviate the problem. As you draft your proposal, keep in mind what Kozol says about people's insensitivity and apathy. What persuasive strategies will you adopt to puncture this callous disregard?

Writing Assignments Using Other Patterns of Development

∞ 3. At the beginning of "A Modest Proposal," Swift describes briefly the poverty he witnessed in his native land. How would *you* describe the face of poverty? Write an essay describing an impoverished, blighted area. What are its streets, houses, stores, and people like? Organizing the essay around a dominant impression, depict what you see, smell, hear, and feel. Gordon Parks's "Flavio's Home" (page 104) will help you see how you might approach such an essay.

4. Seeking to improve the Irish economy, Swift advocates boycotting foreign-made products. Do you believe the United States should impose restrictive tariffs and import limits on goods manufactured abroad? Write a paper in which you identify the positive and negative consequences of such protective measures. Gather information by brainstorming with others and, if necessary, go to the library to locate several articles on this issue.

Nat Hentoff

Nat Hentoff was born in Boston in 1925. His writings for the *Village Voice* and the *New Yorker*, his columns for the *Washington Post*, and his more than twenty-five books of fiction and nonfiction have earned him the reputation as a respected voice of the political Left. Privacy, drug testing, racism, the draft, abortion, and educational reform have all come under Hentoff's keen observation. In 1987, Hentoff published his autobiography, *Boston Boy*, and 1989 saw the publication of his book *The First Freedom: The Tumultuous History of Free Speech in America*. *Free Speech for Me—But Not for Thee* (1993) and *Listen to the Stories* (1995) are his latest works. Despite his political stance as a leftist, Hentoff has criticized the zeal of the Left in suppressing speech it finds offensive. Such concerns led him to write the following essay, first published in the *Progressive* in May 1989.

Free Speech on Campus

Censorship, book-burning, imprisonment of political opponents—all are tools of ultra-Right, totalitarian governments bent on silencing the opposition. But what about attempts at colleges and universities to restrict racist, sexist, and otherwise bigoted speech? Should such efforts be condoned? "No," says Nat Hentoff. With characteristic fervor, Hentoff explains why he's concerned by the Left's adoption of rightist tactics to suppress campus views that aren't considered politically correct.

A flier distributed at the University of Michigan some months 1
ago proclaimed that blacks "don't belong in classrooms, they belong hanging from trees."

At other campuses around the country, manifestations of racism 2
are becoming commonplace. At Yale, a swastika and the words WHITE POWER! were painted on the building housing the University's Afro-American Cultural Center. At Temple University, a White Students Union has been formed with some 130 members.

Swastikas are not directed only at black students. The Nazi sym-   3
bol has been spray-painted on the Jewish Student Union at Memphis
State University. And on a number of campuses, women have been
singled out as targets of wounding and sometimes frightening
speech. At the law school of the State University of New York at Buffalo, several women students have received anonymous letters characterized by one professor as venomously sexist.

These and many more such signs of the resurgence of bigotry   4
and knownothingism throughout the society—as well as on campus—have to do solely with speech, including symbolic speech.
There have also been physical assaults on black students and on
black, white, and Asian women students, but the way to deal with
physical attacks is clear: call the police and file a criminal complaint.
What is to be done, however, about speech alone—however disgust-
ing, inflammatory, and rawly divisive that speech may be?

At more and more colleges, administrators—with the enthusias-   5
tic support of black students, women students, and liberal students—
have been answering that question by preventing or punishing
speech. In public universities, this is a clear violation of the First
Amendment. In private colleges and universities, suppression of
speech mocks the secular religion of academic freedom and free inquiry.

The Student Press Law Center in Washington, D.C.—a vital   6
source of legal support for student editors around the country—reports, for example, that at the University of Kansas, the student host
and producer of a radio news program was forbidden by school officials from interviewing a leader of the Ku Klux Klan. So much for free
inquiry on that campus.

In Madison, Wisconsin, the *Capital Times* ran a story in January   7
about Chancellor Sheila Kaplan of the University of Wisconsin
branch at Parkside, who ordered her campus to be scoured of "some
anonymously placed white supremacist hate literature." Sounding
like the legendary Mayor Frank ("I am the law") Hague of Jersey
City, who booted "bad speech" out of town, Chancellor Kaplan said,
"This institution is not a lamppost standing on the street corner. It
doesn't belong to everyone."

Who decides what speech can be heard or read by everyone?   8
Why, the Chancellor, of course. That's what George III[1] used to say,
too.

---

[1]King of England at the time of the American Revolution, George III reportedly lost
his sanity in his later years.

University of Wisconsin political science professor Carol   9
Tebben thinks otherwise. She believes university administrators "are
getting confused when they are acting as censors and trying to protect students from bad ideas. I don't think students need to be protected from bad ideas. I think they can determine for themselves
what ideas are bad."

After all, if students are to be "protected" from bad ideas, how   10
are they going to learn to identify and cope with them? Sending such
ideas underground simply makes them stronger and more dangerous.

Professor Tebben's conviction that free speech means just that   11
has become a decidedly minority view on many campuses. At the
University of Buffalo Law School, the faculty unanimously adopted
a "Statement Regarding Intellectual Freedom, Tolerance, and Political Harassment." Its title implies support of intellectual freedom,
but the statement warned students that once they enter "this legal
community," their right to free speech must become tempered "by
the responsibility to promote equality and justice."

Accordingly, swift condemnation will befall anyone who engag-   12
es in "remarks directed at another's race, sex, religion, national origin, age, or sex preference." Also forbidden are "other remarks based
on prejudice and group stereotype."

This ukase is so broad that enforcement has to be alarmingly   13
subjective. Yet the University of Buffalo Law School provides no
due-process procedures for a student booked for making any of these
prohibited remarks. Conceivably, a student caught playing a Lenny
Bruce, Richard Pryor, or Sam Kinison[2] album in his room could be
tried for aggravated insensitivity by association.

When I looked into this wholesale cleansing of bad speech at   14
Buffalo, I found it had encountered scant opposition. One protester
was David Gerald Jay, a graduate of the law school and a cooperating
attorney for the New York Civil Liberties Union. Said the appalled
graduate: "Content-based prohibitions constitute prior restraint and
should not be tolerated."

You would think that the law professors and administration at   15
this public university might have known that. But hardly any professors dissented, and among the students only members of the conser-

---

[2]Lenny Bruce was a stand-up comic popular in the 1950s and early 1960s. Bruce's
caustic social commentary and his use of language that many considered offensive
established the precedent for the confrontational style of many recent comedians,
including Richard Pryor and Sam Kinison.

vative Federalist Society spoke up for free speech. The fifty-strong chapter of the National Lawyers Guild was on the other side. After all, it was more important to go on record as vigorously opposing racism and sexism than to expose oneself to charges of insensitivity to these malignancies.

The pressures to have the "right" attitude—as proved by having   16
the "right" language in and out of class—can be stifling. A student who opposes affirmative action, for instance, can be branded a racist.

At the University of California at Los Angeles, the student   17
newspaper ran an editorial cartoon satirizing affirmative action. (A student stops a rooster on campus and asks how the rooster got into UCLA. "Affirmative action," is the answer.) After outraged complaints from various minority groups, the editor was suspended for violating a publication policy against running "articles that perpetuate derogatory or cultural stereotypes." The art director was also suspended.

When the opinion editor of the student newspaper at California   18
State University at Northridge wrote an article asserting that the sanctions against the editor and art director at UCLA amounted to censorship, he was suspended too.

At New York University Law School, a student was so disturbed   19
by the pall of orthodoxy at that prestigious institution that he wrote to the school newspaper even though, as he said, he expected his letter to make him a pariah among his fellow students.

Barry Endick described the atmosphere at NYU created by "a   20
host of watchdog committees and a generally hostile classroom reception regarding any student comment right of center." This "can be arguably viewed as symptomatic of a prevailing spirit of academic and social intolerance of...any idea which is not 'politically correct.'"

He went on to say something that might well be posted on cam-   21
pus bulletin boards around the country, though it would probably be torn down at many of them: "We ought to examine why students, so anxious to wield the Fourteenth Amendment, give short shrift to the First. Yes, Virginia, there are racist assholes. And you know what, the Constitution protects them, too."

Not when they engage in violence or vandalism. But when they   22
speak or write, racist assholes fall right into this Oliver Wendell Holmes[3] definition—highly unpopular among bigots, liberals, radicals, feminists, sexists, and college administrators: "If there is any

[3]Holmes was Associate Justice of the Supreme Court (1902–32).

principle of the Constitution that more imperatively calls for attachment than any other, it is the principle of free thought—not free only for those who agree with us, but freedom for the thought we hate."

The language sounds like a pietistic Sunday sermon, but if it 23 ever falls wholly into disuse, neither this publication nor any other journal of opinion—right or left—will survive.

Sometimes, college presidents and administrators sound as if 24 they fully understand what Holmes was saying. Last year, for example, when the *Daily Pennsylvanian*[4]—speaking for many at the University of Pennsylvania—urged that a speaking invitation to Louis Farrakhan[5] be withdrawn, University President Sheldon Hackney disagreed.

"Open expression," said Hackney, "is the fundamental principle 25 of a university." Yet consider what the same Sheldon Hackney did to the free-speech rights of a teacher at his own university. If any story distills the essence of the current decline of free speech on college campuses, it is the Ballad of Murray Dolfman.

For twenty-two years, Dolfman, a practicing lawyer in Philadel- 26 phia, had been a part-time lecturer in the Legal Studies Department of the University of Pennsylvania's Wharton School. For twenty-two years, no complaint had ever been made against him; indeed his student course evaluations had been outstanding. Each year students competed to get into his class.

On a November afternoon in 1984, Dolfman was lecturing 27 about personal-service contracts. His style somewhat resembles that of Professor Charles Kingsfield in *The Paper Chase*.[6] Dolfman insists that students he calls on be prepared—or suffer the consequences. He treats all students this way—regardless of race, creed, or sex.

This day, Dolfman was pointing out that no one can be forced 28 to work against his or her will—even if a contract has been signed. A court may prevent the resister from working for someone else so long as the contract is in effect but, Dolfman said, there can "be nothing that smacks of involuntary servitude."

[4]The student newspaper at the University of Pennsylvania.
[5]The leader of the Black Nation of Islam, Farrakhan holds controversial views that have been called anti-Semitic and racially inflammatory.
[6]Charles Kingsfield was the demanding law professor in the television show *The Paper Chase*. The series, popular in the 1970s, chronicled the struggles of first-year law students at a prestigious university.

Where does this concept come from? Dolfman looked around   29
the room. Finally, a cautious hand was raised: "The Constitution?"

"Where in the Constitution?" No hands. "The Thirteenth   30
Amendment," said the teacher. So, what does *it* say? The students
were looking everywhere but at Dolfman.

"We will lose our liberties," Dolfman often told his classes, "if   31
we don't know what they are."

On this occasion, he told them that he and other Jews, as ex-   32
slaves, spoke at Passover of the time when they were slaves under the
Pharaohs so that they would remember every year what it was like
not to be free.

"We have ex-slaves here," Dolfman continued, "who should   33
know about the Thirteenth Amendment." He asked black students
in the class if they could tell him what was in that amendment.

"I wanted them to really think about it," Dolfman told me re-   34
cently, "and know its history. You're better equipped to fight racism
if you know all about those post-Civil War amendments and civil
rights laws."

The Thirteenth Amendment provides that "neither slavery nor   35
involuntary servitude...shall exist within the United States."

The black students in his class did not know what was in that   36
amendment, and Dolfman had them read it aloud. Later, they complained to university officials that they had been hurt and humiliated
by having been referred to as ex-slaves. Moreover, they said, they had
no reason to be grateful for a constitutional amendment which gave
them rights which should never have been denied them—and gave
them precious little else. They had not made these points in class, although Dolfman—unlike Professor Kingsfield—encourages rebuttal.

Informed of the complaint, Dolfman told the black students he   37
had intended no offense, and he apologized if they had been offended.

That would not do—either for the black students or for the ad-   38
ministration. Furthermore, there were mounting black-Jewish tensions on campus, and someone had to be sacrificed. Who better than
a part-time Jewish teacher with no contract and no union? He was
sentenced by—George Orwell[7] would have loved this—the Committee on Academic Freedom and Responsibility.

---

[7]British essayist and novelist, George Orwell often wrote about the fragile line sepa-
rating democratic and despotic institutions. (For more information on Orwell, see
page 172.)

On his way to the stocks, Dolfman told President Sheldon 39
Hackney that if a part-time instructor "can be punished on this kind
of charge, a tenured professor can eventually be booted out, then a
dean, and then a president."

Hackney was unmoved. Dolfman was banished from the cam- 40
pus for what came to be a year. But first he was forced to make a public apology to the entire university and then he was compelled to
attend a "sensitivity and racial awareness" session. Sort of like a Vietnamese reeducation camp.

A few conservative professors objected to the stigmatization of 41
Murray Dolfman. I know of no student dissent. Indeed, those students most concerned with making the campus more "sensitive" to
diversity exulted in Dolfman's humiliation. So did most liberals on
the faculty.

If my children were still of college age and wanted to attend the 42
University of Pennsylvania, I would tell them this story. But where
else could I encourage them to go?

Questions for Close Reading

1. What is the selection's thesis? Locate the sentence(s) in which Hentoff
   states his main idea. If he doesn't state the thesis explicitly, express it in
   your own words.
2. What evidence does Hentoff present to support his statement that there's
   a "resurgence of bigotry and knownothingism throughout the society"?
3. According to Hentoff, how have officials on campuses at the University
   of Kansas, the University of Wisconsin, and the University of California
   at Los Angeles interfered with free inquiry and free speech? What reasons
   did university officials give for their actions?
4. Why, in Hentoff's opinion, should college campuses permit all types of
   speech? According to Hentoff, what problems arise when free speech is
   curtailed?
5. Refer to your dictionary as needed to define the following words used in
   the selection: *venomously* (paragraph 3), *knownothingism* (4), *ukase* (13),
   dissented (15), *malignancies* (15), *sanctions* (18), *pall* (19), *pariah* (19),
   pietistic (23), *distills* (25), *stocks* (39), and *stigmatization* (41).

Questions About the Writer's Craft

1. **The pattern.** Writing on a complex and controversial issue, Hentoff
   wisely confronts the opposing viewpoint—in this case, the position that
   the free speech of extremists should be suppressed. What strategies does
   Hentoff use to deal with this view?

2. **Other patterns.** Where in the selection does Hentoff use examples and a narrative account to support his argument? How do the examples and the narrative help him support his case?
3. What tone does Hentoff employ when describing those who believe that sometimes it is necessary to limit free speech? How do Hentoff's sentence structure and word choice help create this tone?
4. Examine the quotations in paragraphs 20 through 22. Why do you think Hentoff chooses to quote these two particular individuals—law student Barry Endick and Supreme Court Justice Oliver Wendell Holmes? What does he achieve by juxtaposing Endick's words with those of Holmes?

Questions for Further Thought

1. Hentoff states that violent action motivated by bigotry should be handled by calling the police and filing a criminal complaint. But he believes that offensive speech motivated by bigotry is a different issue and doesn't call for suppression. Do you agree that these two situations should be handled differently? Do you think that the difference between a bigoted action and bigoted speech is always apparent? Explain.
2. Reread Hentoff's description of the incident that occurred in instructor Murray Dolfman's class at the University of Pennsylvania Law School (paragraphs 26–37). Do you feel, as Hentoff does, that Dolfman was incorrectly punished? Why or why not?
3. Is it necessary for students to be exposed to "bad ideas" during their education, as Hentoff indicates in paragraph 10? Do you find that there's intolerance of "bad" or out-of-favor ideas at your college? Does your school have any guidelines that limit the expression of such ideas? How do you feel about the guidelines?
4. How far should society go in protecting what law student Barry Endick calls "racist assholes" and in guarding the rights of extremists' free speech? Are there ideas and political positions that you would prefer to see suppressed? Which ones? How comfortable are you with ideas that are opposed to your own?

Writing Assignments Using Argumentation-Persuasion as a Pattern of Development

1. Consider the stereotyping, the economic deprivations, and the personal slurs that many members of minority groups continue to suffer. Then decide which you believe is more important: totally free speech or the protection of the rights, feelings, and status of groups that have been discriminated against. Write an essay in which you argue that on college campuses protecting "equality and justice" either is or isn't more important than protecting freedom of speech. Provide specific examples to defend your position, and don't forget to deal with opposing viewpoints.

2. Hentoff mentions that on one campus student journalists were punished for publishing a satirical cartoon that proved offensive to several minority groups. But satire and comedy, especially when they have some bite, often offend one group or another. Carefully consider the comedy and satire currently in vogue. Do they provide harmless entertainment? Do they perpetuate negative stereotypes? Do they open up helpful discussion and debate? Prepare an essay in which you argue your position, supporting it with a number of persuasive examples. And don't forget to acknowledge (and, if possible, to refute) opposing viewpoints at some point in your paper.

Writing Assignments Using Other Patterns of Development

3. What procedures has your college or university established so that people on campus—faculty, staff, and/or students—can file grievances if they feel they have been discriminated against in some way? In an essay, describe this process and indicate whether you feel it's adequate. If it isn't, explain what steps need to be taken to improve the procedures.

∞ 4. Stereotyping isn't restricted to minorities. Most of us have felt unfairly stereotyped at some time or another, perhaps because of gender, physical or intellectual abilities, even a hobby or interest. Write an essay about a time you were treated unfairly or cruelly because of some personal characteristic. Be sure to show how the event affected you. The following essays will provide insight into the potentially corrosive effect of labels and stereotypes: Alice Walker's "Beauty: When the Other Dancer Is the Self" (page 485), Jonathan Kozol's "Are the Homeless Crazy?" (page 500), Gloria Naylor's "Mommy, What Does 'Nigger' Mean?" (page 535), and William Raspberry's "The Handicap of Definition" (page 548).

Camille Paglia

Before 1991, Camille Paglia, Professor of Humanities at Philadelphia's University of the Arts, was known primarily for her electrifying performance in the classroom. Then came the publication of Paglia's *Sexual Personae: Art and Decadence From Nefertiti to Emily Dickinson,* a sweeping book that moves with dizzying speed from the days of cave art to the nineteenth century. *Sexual Personae* makes the case that man creates art as a defensive response to woman's terrifying cosmic power—specifically, her sexual and procreative force. Suddenly Paglia became an international celebrity and had many opportunities to express her controversial views. She has been both revered and reviled for making statements like these: "Male aggression and lust are the energizing factors in culture" and "If I ever got into a dating situation where I was raped and overwhelmed, I would say, 'Oh well, I misread the signals.'" Born in 1947, Paglia earned her doctorate from Yale University, where her Ph.D. thesis was an early version of *Sexual Personae. Sex, Art, and American Culture: Essays* (1992) and *Vamps and Tramps: New Essays* (1994) are Paglia's latest works. The following selection, written in Paglia's characteristically provocative style, first appeared in *Long Island Newsday* in 1988.

Rape: A Bigger Danger
Than Feminists Know

Are there fundamental obstacles that prevent men and women from ever truly understanding one another? Will the sexes be forever at war? Is there "only one thing" men want from women, and is it women's responsibility to foil men's efforts to get it? In this essay, Camille Paglia advances answers to these and other questions.

Rape is an outrage that cannot be tolerated in civilized society.   1
Yet feminism, which has waged a crusade for rape to be taken more seriously, has put young women in danger by hiding the truth about sex from them.

In dramatizing the pervasiveness of rape, feminists have told   2
young women that before they have sex with a man, they must give
consent as explicit as a legal contract's. In this way, young women
have been convinced that they have been the victims of rape. On elite
campuses in the Northeast and on the West Coast, they have held
consciousness-raising sessions, petitioned administrations, demanded inquests. At Brown University, outraged, panicky "victims" have
scrawled the names of alleged attackers on the walls of women's rest
rooms. What marital rape was to the '70s, "date rape" is to the '90s.

The incidence and seriousness of rape do not require this kind   3
of exaggeration. Real acquaintance rape is nothing new. It has been
a horrible problem for women for all of recorded history. Once, father and brothers protected women from rape. Once, the penalty for
rape was death. I come from a fierce Italian tradition where, not so
long ago in the motherland, a rapist would end up knifed, castrated,
and hung out to dry.

But the old clans and small rural communities have broken   4
down. In our cities, on our campuses far from home, young women
are vulnerable and defenseless. Feminism has not prepared them for
this. Feminism keeps saying the sexes are the same. It keeps telling
women they can do anything, go anywhere, say anything, wear anything. No, they can't. Women will always be in sexual danger.

One of my male students recently slept overnight with a friend   5
in a passageway of the Great Pyramid in Egypt. He described the
moon and sand, the ancient silence and eerie echoes. I am a woman.
I will never experience that. I am not stupid enough to believe I
could ever be safe there. There is a world of solitary adventure I will
never have. Women have always known these somber truths. But
feminism, with its pie-in-the-sky fantasies about the perfect world,
keeps young women from seeing life as it is.

We must remedy social injustice whenever we can. But there are   6
some things we cannot change. There are sexual differences that are
based in biology. Academic feminism is lost in a fog of social con-
structionism. It believes we are totally the product of our environment. This idea was invented by Rousseau.[1] He was wrong.
Emboldened by dumb French language theory, academic feminists
repeat the same hollow slogans over and over to each other. Their

[1]A French political writer and philosopher (1712–78).

view of sex is naive and prudish. Leaving sex to the feminists is like letting your dog vacation at the taxidermist's.

The sexes are at war. Men must struggle for identity against the overwhelming power of their mothers. Women have menstruation to tell them they are women. Men must do or risk something to be men. Men become masculine only when other men say they are. Having sex with a woman is one way a boy becomes a man. 7

College men are at their hormonal peak. They have just left their mothers and are questing for their male identity. In groups, they are dangerous. A woman going to a fraternity party is walking into Testosterone Flats, full of prickly cacti and blazing guns. If she goes, she should be armed with resolute alertness. She should arrive with girlfriends and leave with them. A girl who lets herself get dead drunk at a fraternity party is a fool. A girl who goes upstairs alone with a brother at a fraternity party is an idiot. Feminists call this "blaming the victim." I call it common sense. 8

For a decade, feminists have drilled their disciples to say, "Rape is a crime of violence but not of sex." This sugar-coated Shirley Temple nonsense has exposed young women to disaster. Misled by feminism, they do not expect rape from the nice boys from good homes who sit next to them in class. 9

Aggression and eroticism, in fact, are deeply intertwined. Hunt, pursuit and capture are biologically programmed into male sexuality. Generation after generation, men must be educated, refined, and ethically persuaded away from their tendency toward anarchy and brutishness. Society is not the enemy, as feminism ignorantly claims. Society is woman's protection against rape. Feminism, with its solemn Carry Nation[2] repressiveness, does not see what is for men the eroticism or fun element in rape, especially the wild, infectious delirium of gang rape. Women who do not understand rape cannot defend themselves against it. 10

The date-rape controversy shows feminism hitting the wall of its own broken promises. The women of my '60s generation were the first respectable girls in history to swear like sailors, get drunk, stay out all night—in short, to act like men. We sought total sexual freedom and equality. But as time passed, we woke up to cold reality. The old double standard protected women. When anything goes, it's women who lose. 11

---

[2]A nineteenth-century reformer who advocated the abolition of alcohol.

Today's young women don't know what they want. They see   12
that feminism has not brought sexual happiness. The theatrics of public rage over date rape are their way of restoring the old sexual rules
that were shattered by my generation. Yet nothing about the sexes has
really changed. The comic film *Where the Boys Are* (1960), the ultimate expression of '50s man-chasing, still speaks directly to our time.
It shows smart, lively women skillfully anticipating and fending off the
dozens of strategies with which horny men try to get them into bed.
The agonizing date-rape subplot and climax are brilliantly done. The
victim, Yvette Mimieux, makes mistake after mistake, obvious to the
other girls. She allows herself to be lured away from her girlfriends
and into isolation with boys whose character and intentions she mis-
reads. *Where the Boys Are* tells the truth. It shows courtship as a dangerous game in which the signals are not verbal but subliminal.

Neither militant feminism, which is obsessed with politically   13
correct language, nor academic feminism, which believes that knowledge and experience are "constituted by" language, can understand
preverbal or nonverbal communication. Feminism, focusing on sexual politics, cannot see that sex exists in and through the body. Sexual desire and arousal cannot be fully translated into verbal terms.
This is why men and women misunderstand each other.

Trying to remake the future, feminism cut itself off from sexual   14
history. It discarded and suppressed the sexual myths of literature, art
and religion. Those myths show us the turbulence, the mysteries and
passions of sex. In mythology we see men's sexual anxiety, their fear
of woman's dominance. Much sexual violence is rooted in men's
sense of psychological weakness toward women. It takes many men
to deal with one woman. Woman's voracity is a persistent motif.
Clara Bow,[3] it was rumored, took on the USC[4] football team on
weekends. Marilyn Monroe, singing "Diamonds Are a Girl's Best
Friend," rules a conga line of men in tuxes. Half-clad Cher, in the
video for "If I Could Turn Back Time," deranges a battleship of
screaming sailors and straddles a pink-lit cannon. Feminism, coveting
social power, is blind to woman's cosmic sexual power.

To understand rape, you must study the past. There never was   15
and never will be sexual harmony. Every woman must be prudent
and cautious about where she goes and with whom. When she makes
a mistake, she must accept the consequences and, through self-

---

[3]A movie star from the Roaring Twenties era.
[4]University of Southern California.

criticism, resolve never to make that mistake again. Running to mommy and daddy on the campus grievance committee is unworthy of strong women. Posting lists of guilty men in the toilet is cowardly, infantile stuff.

The Italian philosophy of life espouses high-energy confronta-   16
tion. A male student makes a vulgar remark about your breasts? Don't slink off to whimper with the campus shrinking violets. Deal with it. On the spot. Say, "Shut up, you jerk! And crawl back to the barnyard where you belong!" In general, women who project this take-charge attitude toward life get harassed less often. I see too many dopey, immature, self-pitying women walking around like melting sticks of butter. It's the Yvette Mimieux syndrome: make me happy. And listen to me weep when I'm not.

The date-rape debate is already smothering in propaganda   17
churned out by the expensive Northeastern colleges and universities, with their overconcentration of boring, uptight academic feminists and spoiled, affluent students. Beware of the deep manipulativeness of rich students who were neglected by their parents. They love to turn the campus into hysterical psychodramas of sexual transgression, followed by assertions of parental authority and concern. And don't look for sexual enlightenment from academe, which spews out mountains of books but never looks at life directly.

As a fan of football and rock music, I see in the simple, swagger-   18
ing masculinity of the jock and in the noisy posturing of the heavy-metal guitarist certain fundamental, unchanging truths about sex. Masculinity is aggressive, unstable, combustible. It is also the most creative cultural force in history. Women must reorient themselves toward the elemental powers of sex, which can strengthen or destroy.

The only solution to date rape is female self-awareness and self-   19
control. A woman's number-one line of defense against rape is herself. When a real rape occurs, she should report it to the police. Complaining to college committees because the courts "take too long" is ridiculous. College administrations are not a branch of the judiciary. They are not equipped or trained for legal inquiry. Colleges must alert incoming students to the problems and dangers of adulthood. Then colleges must stand back and get out of the sex game.

Questions for Close Reading

1. What is the selection's thesis? Locate the sentence(s) in which Paglia states her main idea. If she doesn't state the thesis explicitly, express it in your own words.

2. In Paglia's opinion, why are women more "vulnerable and defenseless" now than in the past?
3. According to Paglia, what "truths about sex" has feminism hidden from young women?
4. What does Paglia believe is "the only solution to date rape"?
5. Refer to your dictionary as needed to define the following words used in the selection: *inquests* (paragraph 2), *testosterone* (8), *constituted* (13), *grievance* (15), and *judiciary* (19).

Questions About the Writer's Craft

1. **The pattern.**   Examine the way Paglia develops her argument in paragraphs 6 and 8. Which of her assertions in these paragraphs can be assumed to be true without further proof? Why do you think Paglia includes these essentially incontestable statements? Conversely, which of her assertions in paragraphs 6 and 8 require further proof before their truth can be demonstrated? Does Paglia provide such support? Explain.
2. **Other patterns.**   How does Paglia use the comparison-contrast pattern to develop her argument?
3. Paglia's style is frequently characterized by short sentences strung together with few transitions. Locate some examples of this style. Why might Paglia have chosen this style? What is its effect?
4. Where does Paglia use emotional, highly connotative language? Where does she employ strongly worded absolute statements? Do you think that this use of *pathos* makes Paglia's argument more or less convincing? Explain.

Questions for Further Thought

1. Do young women today believe that "they can [safely] do anything, go anywhere, say anything, wear anything," as Paglia claims in paragraph 4? Or do the young women you know behave more moderately and cautiously? Explain.
2. In paragraph 16, Paglia advocates that women adopt an assertive, even combative response to men who harass them. Do you agree that such an approach works? If not, how do you think women should handle harassment? What do you think constitutes harassment?
3. Assume a young woman who had been drinking heavily is raped at a party. Should she, as Paglia says in paragraph 15, "accept the consequences and...resolve never to make that mistake again"? Should she, as students at Brown University and elsewhere have done, write the name of the attacker on the walls of women's rest rooms? Should she report what happened to the campus grievance committee and file charges with the police? Or should she deal with the offense and offender in yet another way? How?
4. Do you think that men who commit date rape believe they have done wrong? Or do they believe they engaged in a permissible expression of their masculinity? Do men in general think that "no" means "yes"? Explain.

Writing Assignments Using Argumentation-Persuasion as a Pattern of Development

∞ 1. Read Susan Jacoby's "Common Decency" (page 645), an essay that takes exception to Paglia's view of date rape. Decide which writer presents her case more convincingly. Then write an essay arguing that the *other writer* has trouble making a strong case for her position. Consider the merits and flaws (including any logical fallacies) in the argument, plus such issues as the writer's credibility, strategies for dealing with the opposing view, and use of emotional appeals. Throughout, support your opinion with specific examples drawn from the selection. Keep in mind that you're critiquing the effectiveness of the writer's argument. It's not appropriate, then, simply to explain why you agree or disagree with the writer's position or merely to summarize what the writer says.

∞ 2. Paglia criticizes those who claim that the environment, or social climate, is primarily responsible for shaping gender differences. She believes that such differences "are based in biology." Write an essay arguing your own position about the role that environment and biology play in determining sex-role attitudes and behavior. Remembering to acknowledge opposing views, defend your own viewpoint with plentiful examples based on your experiences and observations. You may also need to conduct some library research to gather support for your position. The following essays will provide insights that you may want to draw upon in your paper: Alleen Pace Nilsen's "Sexism and Language" (page 229), Barbara Ehrenreich's "What I've Learned From Men" (page 261), Deborah Tannen's "Sex, Lies, and Conversation" (page 428), Scott Russell Sanders's "The Men We Carry in Our Minds" (page 308), and Judy Brady's "Why I Want a Wife" (page 530).

Writing Assignments Using Other Patterns of Development

3. Paglia writes in paragraph 8 that "men become masculine only when other men say they are. Having sex with a woman is one way a boy becomes a man." Write an essay constructing your own definition of masculinity. Comment on the extent to which you feel being sexually active is an important criterion, but also include other hallmarks of masculinity.

4. Date rape seems to be on the rise. Brainstorm with others to identify what may be leading to its growing occurrence. Focusing on several related factors, write an essay showing how these factors contribute to the problem. Possible factors include the following: the way males and females are depicted in the media (advertisements, movies, television, rock videos); young people's use of alcohol; the emergence of co-ed college dorms. At the end of the essay, offer some recommendations about what can be done to create a safer climate for dating.

Susan Jacoby

In her first job as a newspaper reporter, Susan Jacoby (1947–   ) carefully avoided doing "women's stories," believing that such features weren't worthy of a serious journalist. However, Jacoby's opinion changed with the times, especially as women's issues began to gain increasing attention. Indeed, many of her essays—including those in the *New York Times* and *McCall's*—have dealt with women's concerns. A good number of Jacoby's essays have been collected in *The Possible She* (1979) and *Money, Manners, and Morals* (1993). In 1994, she coauthored the biography *A Black Russian American Family 1865–1992*. The following selection, published in the *New York Times* in April 1991, was written in response to the book *Sexual Personae* by Camille Paglia (see page 638).

Common Decency

In the last several years, debate has raged over the complex issues surrounding date rape. Some claim that saying "no" should be enough to protect a woman from sexual assault by a male acquaintance. Others contend that women are naive if they don't recognize that men are ruled by ungovernable sexual passions. This second point of view is one that Susan Jacoby finds depressing. Why? According to Jacoby, it assumes that the world is inhabited by hostile brutes rather than by civilized human beings.

She was deeply in love with a man who was treating her badly.   1
To assuage her wounded ego (and to prove to herself that she could get along nicely without him), she invited another man, an old boyfriend, to a dinner *à deux* in her apartment. They were on their way to the bedroom when, having realized that she wanted only the man who wasn't there, she changed her mind. Her ex-boyfriend was understandably angry. He left her apartment with a not-so-politely phrased request that she leave him out of any future plans.

And that is the end of the story—except for the fact that he was   2
eventually kind enough to accept her apology for what was surely a
classic case of "mixed signals."

I often recall this incident, in which I was the embarrassed fe-   3
male participant, as the controversy over "date rape"—intensified by
the assault that William Kennedy Smith[1] has been accused of—heats
up across the nation. What seems clear to me is that those who place
acquaintance rape in a different category from "stranger rape"—
those who excuse friendly social rapists on grounds that they are too
dumb to understand when "no" means no—are being even more insulting to men than to women.

These apologists for date rape—and some of them are women—   4
are really saying that the average man cannot be trusted to exercise
any impulse control. Men are nasty and men are brutes—and a woman must be constantly on her guard to avoid giving a man any excuse
to give way to his baser instincts.

If this view were accurate, few women would manage to get   5
through life without being raped, and few men would fail to commit
rape. For the reality is that all of us, men as well as women, send and
receive innumerable mixed signals in the course of our sexual lives—
and that is as true in marital beds at age fifty as in the back seats of
cars at age fifteen.

Most men somehow manage to decode these signals without   6
using superior physical strength to force themselves on their partners. And most women manage to handle conflicting male signals
without, say, picking up carving knives to demonstrate their displea-
sure at sexual rejection. This is called civilization.

Civilized is exactly what my old boyfriend was being when he   7
didn't use my muddleheaded emotional distress as an excuse to rape
me. But I don't owe him excessive gratitude for his decent behavior—any more than he would have owed me special thanks for not
stabbing him through the heart if our situations had been reversed.
Most date rapes do not happen because a man honestly mistakes a
woman's "no" for a "yes" or a "maybe." They occur because a minority of men—an ugly minority, to be sure—can't stand to take
"no" for an answer.

[1]William Kennedy Smith, the nephew of John, Robert and Edward Kennedy, was
accused of raping a woman in 1991. Kennedy was acquitted, but the trial, broadcast
on television, created a national furor and generated heated debate on the issue of
date rape.

This minority behavior—and a culture that excuses it on grounds that boys will be boys—is the target of the movement against date rape that has surfaced on many campuses during the past year.

It's not surprising that date rape is an issue of particular importance to college-age women. The campus concentration of large numbers of young people, in an unsupervised environment that encourages drinking and partying, tends to promote sexual aggression and discourage inhibition. Drunken young men who rape a woman at a party can always claim they didn't know what they were doing—and a great many people will blame the victim for having been there in the first place.

That is the line adopted by antifeminists like Camille Paglia,[2] author of the controversial *Sexual Personae: Art and Decadence From Nefertiti to Emily Dickinson.* Paglia, whose views strongly resemble those expounded twenty years ago by Norman Mailer[3] in *The Prisoner of Sex,* argues that feminists have deluded women by telling them they can go anywhere and do anything without fear of rape. Feminism, in this view, is both naïve and antisexual because it ignores the power of women to incite uncontrollable male passions.

Just to make sure there is no doubt about a woman's place, Paglia also links the male sexual aggression that leads to rape with the creative energy of art. "There is no female Mozart," she has declared, "because there is no female Jack the Ripper." According to this "logic," one might expect to discover the next generation of composers in fraternity houses and dorms that have been singled out as sites of brutal gang rapes.

This type of unsubtle analysis makes no distinction between sex as an expression of the will to power and sex as a source of pleasure. When domination is seen as an inevitable component of sex, the act of rape is defined not by a man's actions but by a woman's signals.

It is true, of course, that some women (especially the young) initially resist sex not out of real conviction but as part of the elaborate persuasion and seduction rituals accompanying what was once called courtship. And it is true that many men (again, especially the young) take pride in the ability to coax a woman a step further than she intended to go.

8

9

10

11

12

13

---

[2]For information on Camille Paglia, see page 638.
[3]An American essayist and novelist.

But these mating rituals do not justify or even explain date rape. 14
Even the most callow youth is capable of understanding the difference between resistance and genuine fear; between a halfhearted
"no, we shouldn't" and tears or screams; between a woman who is
physically free to leave a room and one who is being physically
restrained.

The immorality and absurdity of using mixed signals as an ex- 15
cuse for rape is cast in high relief when the assault involves one woman and a group of men. In cases of gang rape in a social setting
(usually during or after a party), the defendants and their lawyers frequently claim that group sex took place but no force was involved.
These upright young men, so the defense invariably contends, were
confused because the girl had voluntarily gone to a party with them.
Why, she may have even displayed sexual interest in *one* of them.
How could they have been expected to understand that she didn't
wish to have sex with the whole group?

The very existence of the term "date rape" attests to a slow 16
change in women's consciousness that began with the feminist
movement of the late 1960s. Implicit in this consciousness is
the conviction that a woman has the right to say no at any point
in the process leading to sexual intercourse—and that a man who
fails to respect her wishes should incur serious legal and social
consequences.

The other, equally important half of the equation is respect for 17
men. If mixed signals are the real cause of sexual assault, it behooves
every woman to regard every man as a potential rapist.

In such a benighted universe, it would be impossible for a 18
woman (and, let us not forget, for a man) to engage in the tentative
emotional and physical exploration that eventually produces a mature erotic life. She would have to make up her mind right from the
start in order to prevent a rampaging male from misreading her
intentions.

Fortunately for everyone, neither the character of men nor the 19
general quality of relations between the sexes is that crude. By cen-
suring the minority of men who use ordinary socializing as an excuse
for rape, feminists insist on sex as a source of pure pleasure rather
than as a means of social control. Real men want an eager sexual partner—not a woman who is quaking with fear or even one who is ambivalent. Real men don't rape.

Questions for Close Reading

1. What is the selection's thesis? Locate the sentence(s) in which Jacoby states her main idea. If she doesn't state the thesis explicitly, express it in your own words.

2. Why does Jacoby feel that she doesn't owe her old boyfriend a great deal of gratitude, even though she sent mixed signals about what type of relationship she wanted?

3. What does Jacoby mean in paragraph 6 by her comment, "This is called civilization"? How does this comment support her thesis?

4. Why does Jacoby think that it's insulting to men to accept Paglia's notion that men are ruled by uncontrollable passions?

5. Refer to your dictionary as needed to define the following words used in the selection: *apologists* (paragraph 4), *deluded* (10), *unsubtle* (12), *implicit* (16), *benighted* (18), *erotic* (18), *rampaging* (18), and *ambivalent* (19).

Questions About the Writer's Craft

1. **The pattern.** One way to refute an idea is to carry it to its logical extreme, thus revealing its inherent falsity or absurdity. This technique is called *reductio ad absurdum*. Examine paragraphs 4–5 and 15 and explain how Jacoby uses this technique to refute Paglia's position on date rape.

2. **Other patterns.** Locate places in the essay where Jacoby compares and contrasts male and female behavior or the behavior of rapists and non-rapists. How does her use of comparison-contrast help her build her argument?

3. What introduction technique (see pages 60–62) does Jacoby use to begin the essay? How does this type of introduction help her achieve her persuasive goal?

4. How would you characterize Jacoby's tone? Identify specific sentences and words that convey this tone. What effect might Jacoby have hoped this tone would have on readers?

Questions for Further Thought

1. Do you agree with Jacoby that the cause of date rape is the failure to "take 'no' for an answer"? How difficult or easy is it to take "no" for an answer in any circumstances? Explain.

2. Do you accept Jacoby's statement that courtship rituals "do not justify or even explain date rape"? Or do you agree with Camille Paglia (page 638) that dating is inherently a "dangerous game"? Explain.

3. The phrase "Boys will be boys," used by Jacoby in paragraph 8, is often cited to explain certain types of male behavior. What kinds of actions typically fall in this category? Do you feel that date rape is one of them? Do you feel it's all right for boys or men to "be boys"? If not, how might they

be persuaded to be "real men"—the kind who, according to Jacoby, "don't rape"?

4. In your relations, sexual or not, with the opposite sex, have you found there to be conflict and "the will to power," as Jacoby puts it in paragraph 12? Or have you experienced equality and mutual respect? Which do you feel is typical of your generation? Which do you feel might prevail in future generations?

Writing Assignments Using Argumentation-Persuasion as a Pattern of Development

∞ 1. Jacoby feels that Camille Paglia and others "excuse rapists." If you haven't already done so, read "Rape: A Bigger Danger Than Feminists Know" (page 638) to see what Paglia says about who bears primary responsibility for preventing rape. Then decide to what degree you feel men who commit date rape should be held accountable for their actions. Argue your position in an essay, making reference to both Jacoby's and Paglia's ideas to support your case. Also include reasons and evidence of your own.

2. Determine what your campus is doing about date rape. Does it have a formal policy defining date rape, a hearing process, ongoing workshops, discussions during orientation for incoming students? Write a paper explaining how your college deals with date rape. Then argue either that more attention should be devoted to this issue or that your college has adopted fair and comprehensive measures to deal with the problem. If you feel the college should do more, indicate what additional steps should be taken.

Writing Assignments Using Other Patterns of Development

∞ 3. Jacoby acknowledges that males and females often send "mixed signals" and cause each other confusion. Select one time that you found "mixed signals" with a person of the opposite sex to be a problem. For example, you might have conflicted because of different ways of expressing anger or because of dissimilar styles in asking for support. Describe what happened and explain why you think such mixed signals occurred. Before writing the paper, you may want to read "Sex, Lies, and Conversation" (page 428) to see what Deborah Tannen has to say about some basic differences between men and women.

4. Interview some people, both males and females, to determine their definition of date rape. In an essay, discuss any differences between the two sexes' perspectives. That done, present your own definition of date rape, explaining what it is and what it isn't.

Ron Kline

A graduate of the University of California at Los Angeles Medical School, Ron Kline (1961–) is a pediatrician involved in immunology research. Most of his writings are intended for other physicians; for example, several medical journals have published papers he has written on bone marrow transplants. The following essay, however, written for the general public, was published in *Newsweek* magazine in 1989. Soon thereafter, Kline appeared on educational television as a member of a panel debating the complex issues regarding animal experimentation.

A Scientist: "I Am the Enemy"

The use of animals for medical research is a highly emotional topic for many people. Animal-rights activists decry research on animals, claiming that many medical experiments are not only inhumane but actually unnecessary. Alternatives to animal experimentation exist, they argue, if only medical researchers were willing to make use of them. A physician and medical researcher, Ron Kline addresses the claims of the activists and, in the process, makes some compelling claims of his own.

I am the enemy! One of those vilified, inhumane physician-scientists involved in animal research. How strange, for I have never thought of myself as an evil person. I became a pediatrician because of my love for children and my desire to keep them healthy. During medical school and residency, however, I saw many children die of leukemia, prematurity and traumatic injury—circumstances against which medicine has made tremendous progress, but still has far to go. More important, I also saw children, alive and healthy, thanks to advances in medical science such as infant respirators, potent antibiotics, new surgical techniques and the entire field of organ transplantation. My desire to tip the scales in favor of the healthy, happy children drew me to medical research.

1

My accusers claim that I inflict torture on animals for the sole 2
purpose of career advancement. My experiments supposedly have no
relevance to medicine and are easily replaced by computer simulation. Meanwhile, an apathetic public barely watches, convinced that
the issue has no significance, and publicity-conscious politicians increasingly give way to the demands of the activists.

We in medical research have also been unconscionably apathet- 3
ic. We have allowed the most extreme animal-rights protesters to
seize the initiative and frame the issue as one of "animal fraud." We
have been complacent in our belief that a knowledgeable public
would sense the importance of animal research to the public health.
Perhaps we have been mistaken in not responding to the emotional
tone of the argument created by those sad posters of animals by waving equally sad posters of children dying of leukemia or cystic fibrosis.

Much is made of the pain inflicted on these animals in the name 4
of medical science. The animal-rights activists contend that this is evidence of our malevolent and sadistic nature. A more reasonable argument, however, can be advanced in our defense. Life is often cruel,
both to animals and human beings. Teenagers get thrown from the
back of a pickup truck and suffer severe head injuries. Toddlers, barely able to walk, find themselves at the bottom of a swimming pool
while a parent checks the mail. Physicians hoping to alleviate the pain
and suffering these tragedies cause have but three choices: create an
animal model of the injury or disease and use that model to understand the process and test new therapies; experiment on human beings—some experiments will succeed, most will fail—or finally, leave
medical knowledge static, hoping that accidental discoveries will lead
us to the advances.

Some animal-rights activists would suggest a fourth choice, 5
claiming that computer models can simulate animal experiments,
thus making the actual experiments unnecessary. Computers can
simulate, reasonably well, the effects of well-understood principles
on complex systems, as in the application of the laws of physics to air-
plane and automobile design. However, when the principles themselves are in question, as is the case with the complex biological
systems under study, computer modeling alone is of little value.

One of the terrifying effects of the effort to restrict the use of an- 6
imals in medical research is that the impact will not be felt for years
and decades: drugs that might have been discovered will not be; surgical techniques that might have been developed will not be, and
fundamental biological processes that might have been understood

will remain mysteries. There is the danger that politically expedient solutions will be found to placate a vocal minority, while the consequences of those decisions will not be apparent until long after the decisions are made and the decision makers forgotten.

Fortunately, most of us enjoy good health, and the trauma of 7 watching one's child die has become a rare experience. Yet our good fortune should not make us unappreciative of the health we enjoy or the advances that make it possible. Vaccines, antibiotics, insulin and drugs to treat heart disease, hypertension and stroke are all based on animal research. Most complex surgical procedures, such as coronary-artery bypass and organ transplantation, are initially developed in animals. Presently undergoing animal studies are techniques to insert genes in humans in order to replace the defective ones found to be the cause of so much disease. These studies will effectively end if animal research is severely restricted.

In America today, death has become an event isolated from our 8 daily existence—out of the sight and thoughts of most of us. As a doctor who has watched many children die, and their parents grieve, I am particularly angered by people capable of so much compassion for a dog or a cat, but with seemingly so little for a dying human being. These people seem so insulated from the reality of human life and death and what it means.

Make no mistake, however: I am not advocating the needlessly 9 cruel treatment of animals. To the extent that the animal-rights movement has made us more aware of the needs of these animals and made us search harder for suitable alternatives, they have made a significant contribution. But if the more radical members of this movement are successful in limiting further research, their efforts will bring about a tragedy that will cost many lives. The real question is whether an apathetic majority can be aroused to protect its future against a vocal, but misdirected, minority.

Questions for Close Reading

1. What is the selection's thesis? Locate the sentence(s) in which Kline states his main idea. If he doesn't state the thesis explicitly, express it in your own words.
2. What does Kline mean when he writes that he is the "enemy"? Whose "enemy" is he? Of what does he stand accused?
3. How does Kline justify experimentation on animals? Why, in his opinion, are many people unaware of the need for such experiments?

4. What does Kline predict will eventually happen if scientists remain apathetic and if animal rights activists have their way?
5. Refer to your dictionary as needed to define the following words used in the selection: *vilified* (paragraph 1), *apathetic* (2), *unconscionably* (3), *complacent* (3), *leukemia* (3), *cystic fibrosis* (3), *malevolent* (4), *alleviate* (4), *expedient* (6), *placate* (6), and *misdirected* (9).

Questions About the Writer's Craft

1. **The pattern.** What position on his topic do you think Kline expects his *Newsweek* readers to hold? How do you know? How does Kline's awareness of these readers influence his choice of appeals—in particular, the way he blends *pathos, logos,* and *ethos*?
2. Rogerian argument (see pages 568–70) stresses the importance of acknowledging—early on—any valid points raised by the opposing opinion. But Kline doesn't grant anything to the opposing view until paragraphs 5 and 9. Where specifically in these two paragraphs does Kline make some concessions? Why do you suppose he waits so long?
3. **Other patterns.** Examine the comparison Kline sets up in paragraphs 2 through 3 as well as the contrasts he establishes in paragraphs 1, 2, 3, 4, 5, and 8. How does Kline's use of comparison and contrast reinforce his viewpoint?
4. What tone does Kline use at the beginning of the essay? Where else in the piece does he use this tone? Where does he shift the tone? Why do you think Kline varies the tone in this manner?

Questions for Further Thought

1. Kline indicates that most people are apathetic about the issue of animal research. Do you agree? Explain.
2. Animal-rights protesters have used emotionally laden images to influence the public. Would you advise medical researchers to do likewise, as Kline ironically suggests in paragraph 3? Do you think such an appeal might work? Why or why not?
3. Some of the more militant animal-rights protesters have broken into medical laboratories, destroyed equipment, and freed the animals used in research. Do you consider such tactics legitimate? Explain.
4. Kline frames the animal experimentation question as a life-or-death issue—not for us immediately but for people in the future. Do you think that individuals focus too much on the present to appreciate this aspect of Kline's argument? Explain.

Writing Assignments Using Argumentation-Persuasion as a Pattern of Development

∞ 1. Kline bases his argument for using animals in medical research on several important points, including the following:

There is no viable alternative to medical experimentation on animals.
Restricting the use of animals in medical research will lead in the
   future to life-threatening gaps in medical knowledge.
Preventing the suffering and death of humans is more important than
   preventing the suffering and death of animals.

Write an essay defending or challenging any *one* of these points. No matter which position you take, one section of your paper should recognize and, if possible, refute opposing viewpoints. If you haven't already done so, be sure to read Patricia Curtis's "The Argument Against Animal Experimentation" (page 657) before planning your paper.

∞ 2. Many animal-rights activists cite other instances of animal abuse. For example, they protest hunting, the eating of meat, the method used to slaughter livestock, the establishment of zoos, the wearing of fur, and the use of animals in circuses. Select *one* such issue, read about it in the library, and discuss it with people who hold varying viewpoints. Evaluate all the material you gather so you can determine your personal position on the issue. Then write an essay supporting that point of view. Like Kline, direct your essay to apathetic readers, drawing upon whatever logical and emotional appeals you think will pierce their indifference. T. H. Watkins's "Little Deaths" (page 181) will help sensitize you to some of the complexities of the animal-rights issue.

Writing Assignments Using Other Patterns of Development

3. In recent years, many Americans have become concerned about another animal-related issue: the overpopulation of both domestic pets (dogs and cats) and certain strains of wildlife (for example, deer and coyote). Select *one* such animal, and do some research both on the extent of its overpopulation and on existing controls to regulate its growth. Bibliographies like the *New York Times Index* and the *General Science Index* as well as computer databases like the National Newspaper Index, Newsbank, CD News, Periodical Abstracts Ondisc, Infotrac, and LEXIS (an on-line database covering federal and state laws) will help you locate relevant information. Drawing upon your research, write an essay that begins by describing the effects of such overpopulation. Then show why current regulations fail to solve the problem. At the end of the paper, explain what additional controls are needed.

∞ 4. According to animal activists, many of us push animals' suffering out of our minds so that we don't have to deal with it. Write an essay telling the story of a single representative of another group whose suffering tends to be ignored or disregarded. You might, for example, write about someone who is homeless, illiterate, emotionally ill, or physically disabled. Using vivid narrative details that dramatize what this person's life is like, make a strong case for treating the whole group more sympathetically. Maya Angelou's "Grandmother's Victory" (page 164) and George Orwell's "Shooting an Elephant" (page 172) will provide insight into the tendency people have to distance themselves from others' pain.

Patricia Curtis

The welfare of animals is a passionate concern for Patricia Curtis (1924–), author of many books on the subject. Her works, the majority written for children and young adults, include *Animal Rights: Stories of People Who Defend the Rights of Animals* (1980) and *The Animal Shelter* (1984). A few of her most recent works are *Urban Dog: How to Understand, Enjoy, and Care for a Dog in the City* (1990), *Animals and the New Zoos* (1991), and *Aquatic Animals in the Wild and in Captivity* (1992). In all her books, Curtis assumes the stance of an advocate for the rights of the non-human species with whom we share the planet. "The Argument Against Animal Experimentation" was originally published in the *New York Times* in 1978.

The Argument Against Animal Experimentation

People seem to accept animal experimentation because of the benefits it yields—an acceptance made easier because they don't witness the suffering endured by animals in the course of those experiments. Patricia Curtis doesn't allow the luxury of such ignorance. She takes readers inside the medical labs, cosmetic firms, and drug companies to show exactly what's being done to animals in the name of research. Are the discoveries made so valuable that we can disregard the pain inflicted on animals in the process? That is the basic question that Curtis poses.

The professor was late leaving the medical school because he'd   1
had to review papers by his third-year students in experimental surgery. It was well after 11 when he wearily drove his car into the garage. The house was dark except for a hall light left on for him. His wife and youngsters were already asleep, he realized, and the professor suddenly felt lonely as he fit his key in the lock. But even as he pushed open the door, Sabrina was there to welcome him. She was always waiting for him, lying on the rug just inside the door.

The little dog leaped up ecstatically, wagging her tail and licking 2
the professor's hand. The professor stroked her affectionately. She
flopped on her back and grinned at him as he tickled her chest and
belly; then she jumped to her feet and danced around his legs as he
walked into the kitchen to get something to eat. Sabrina's exuberant
joy at his return never failed to cheer him.

Early next morning, the professor drove back to the medical 3
school and entered the laboratory. He noticed that a dog on which
one of his students had operated the previous afternoon still had an en-
dotracheal tube in its throat and obviously had not received pain med-
ication. He must be more strict in his orders, he thought to himself.
Another dog had bled through its bandages and lay silently in a pool
of blood. Sloppy work, the professor thought—must speak to that student. None of the dogs made any sounds, because new arrivals at the
laboratory were always subjected to an operation called a ventriculo-
cordectomy that destroyed their vocal cords so that no barks or howls
disturbed people in the medical school and surrounding buildings.

The professor looked over the animals that would be used that 4
day by his surgery students. He came across a new female dog that
had just been delivered by the dealer. Badly frightened, she whined
and wagged her tail ingratiatingly as he paused in front of her cage.
The professor felt a stab. The small dog bore an amazing resem-
blance to Sabrina. Quickly he walked away. Nevertheless, he made a
note to remind himself to give orders for her vocal cords to be destroyed and for her to be conditioned for experimental surgery.

American researchers sacrifice approximately 64 million animals 5
annually. Some 400,000 dogs, 200,000 cats, 33,000 apes and monkeys, thousands of horses, ponies, calves, sheep, goats and pigs, and
millions of rabbits, hamsters, guinea pigs, birds, rats and mice are
used every year in experiments that often involve intense suffering.
The research establishment has generally insisted that live animals
provide the only reliable tests for drugs, chemicals and cosmetics that
will be used by people. Researchers also believe that animal experiments are necessary in the search for cures for human illnesses and
defects. There is no question that many important medical discoveries, from polio vaccine to the physiology of the stress response, have
indeed been made through the use of animals. Thus universities,
medical and scientific institutions, pharmaceutical companies, cosmetics manufacturers and the military have always taken for granted
their right to use animals in almost any way they see fit.

But increasing numbers of scientists are beginning to ask them-   6
selves some hard ethical questions and to re-evaluate their routine
use of painful testing tools such as electric shock, stomach tubes, hot
plates, restraining boxes and radiation devices. A new debate has aris-
en over whether all such experiments are worth the suffering they
entail.

Strongly opposing curtailment of animal experimentation are   7
groups such as the National Society for Medical Research, which insists that any such reduction would jeopardize public safety and scientific progress. The N.S.M.R. was formed to resist what it considers
the threat of Government regulation of animal research and to refute
the charges of humane societies. Many scientists, however, although
they firmly believe that some animal research is necessary, no longer
endorse such an absolutist approach to the issue.

"Some knowledge can be obtained at too high a price," writes   8
British physiologist Dr. D. H. Smyth in his recent book *Alternatives
to Animal Experiments.*

"The lives and suffering of animals must surely count for some-   9
thing," says Jeremy J. Stone, director of the Washington-based Federation of American Scientists, which has devoted an entire
newsletter to a discussion of the rights of animals.

According to physiologist Dr. F. Barbara Orlans of the National   10
Institutes of Health, "Within the scientific community there's a growing concern for animals that has not yet had a forum." Dr. Orlans is
president of the newly formed Scientists' Center for Animal Welfare,
which hopes to raise the level of awareness on the part of fellow scientists and the public about avoidable suffering inflicted on lab animals, wildlife, and animals raised for meat. "We will try to be a voice
of reason. We can perhaps be a link between scientists and the humane organizations," Dr. Orlans explains. "We hope also to provide
solid factual data on which animal-protection decisions can be based."

Another link between researchers and humane organizations is   11
a new committee comprising more than 400 doctors and scientists
that has been formed by Friends of Animals, a national animal-welfare
group. Headed by eight M.D.'s, the committee is making a survey of
Federally funded animal-research projects. Friends of Animals hopes
that the study will expose not only needless atrocities performed on
animals, but also boondoggles involving taxpayers' money.

One reason scientists are no longer so indifferent to the suffer-   12
ing they inflict on animals is the discoveries that science itself has

made. We now know that many animals feel, think, reason, communicate, have sophisticated social systems, and even, on occasion, behave altruistically toward each other. Communication by sign language with higher primates, demonstrations of the intelligence of dolphins and whales, observations of the complex societies of wolves and other animals, and many other investigations have narrowed the gap between ourselves and the rest of the animal kingdom, making it more difficult to rationalize inhumane experiments. Dr. Dallas Pratt, author of *Painful Experiments on Animals,* points out that "among the rats and mice, the computers and oscilloscopes, there is Koko"—referring to the young gorilla whom a California primatologist has taught a working vocabulary of 375 words and concepts in sign language and who has even learned to take snapshots with a Polaroid camera. It's hard not to feel squeamish about subjecting animals to inhumane experiments when they possess almost-human intelligence.

The thinking of researchers is also beginning to be affected by   13
the growing movement for animal rights. The rising concern for the welfare of animals is seen by some people as a natural extension of contemporary movements promoting civil rights, women's rights, homosexual rights, human rights, and children's rights. Public interest in preserving endangered species is based first on an increasing awareness of the complexity and fragility of ecosystems, and second on the notion, still much debated, that any species of plant or animal, from the lowly snail darter to the blue whale, has the right to continue to exist. From here it is only a short logical step to the belief that animals have the right to exist without suffering unnecessarily.

Near the top of the list of animal-welfare activists' causes is put-   14
ting an end to inhumane experiments on laboratory animals. In Great Britain, where a vigorous antivivisection movement has existed for more than a century, a clandestine group called the Animal Liberation Front conducts commando-style raids on laboratories, liberating animals and sabotaging research equipment. A.L.F. members have also been known to slash tires and pour sugar in the gas tanks of trucks used by animal dealers who supply labs. To be sure, this group of zealots hasn't made much of a dent in England's vast research community, but it does appeal to a gut reaction on the part of many Britons against animal research.

Animal-rights activists are not merely sentimental do-gooders   15
and pet-lovers. They have mounted a philosophical attack on the traditional Western attitude toward animals, branding it as "species-

ist" (like racist or sexist), a term derived from the word "speciesism," coined by psychologist and author Dr. Richard Ryder. The Australian philosopher Peter Singer, in his influential 1975 book *Animal Liberation,* argued that the "speciesist" rationalization, "Human beings come first," is usually used by people who do nothing for either human or nonhuman animals. And he pointed out the parallels between the oppression of blacks, women, and animals: Such oppression is usually rationalized on the grounds that the oppressed group is inferior.

In 1977, when outraged antivivisectionists heard about some   16
highly unpleasant electric-shock and burn experiments conducted on young pigs in Denmark, they wasted no time in pointing out the irony that the tests were being conducted by Amnesty International, the human-rights organization. Amnesty International was attempting to prove that human prisoners could be tortured without leaving any marks, and pigs were used because of the similarity of their skin to ours. (The test were subsequently discontinued.)

Paradoxically, the public tends to be "speciesist" in its reaction   17
to animal experimentation: For many people, a test is permissible when it inflicts pain on a "lower" animal like a hamster, but not when the victim is a dog. When it was discovered in the summer of 1976 that the American Museum of Natural History was damaging the brains of cats and running painful sex experiments on them, hundreds of people picketed in protest. The museum's Animal Behavior Department defended itself on the grounds that the research was intended to gain a better understanding of human sexual responses. Animal-rights groups, scientists among them, were not convinced of the necessity of the tests, which came to an end only when the chief researcher retired. But the protesters made no stir about the pigeons, doves, and rats that suffered in the same laboratory.

If United States Army researchers had used guinea pigs instead   18
of beagles when they tried out a poison gas, they probably would not have provoked the public outcry that resulted in the curtailment of their funding in 1974. When a few Avon saleswomen quit their jobs last spring after reading about painful eye-makeup tests the company conducts on rabbits, they did not complain about the thousands of guinea pigs and rats Avon routinely puts to death in acute-toxicity tests.

It is not known whether any single vertebrate species is more or   19
less immune to pain than another. A neat line cannot be drawn across the evolutionary scale dividing the sensitive from the insensitive. Yet

the suffering of laboratory rats and mice is regarded as trivial by scientists and the public alike. These rodents have the dubious honor of being our No. 1 experimental animals, composing possibly 75 percent of America's total lab-animal population. As Russell Baker once wrote, "This is no time to be a mouse."

Rats and mice are specifically excluded from a Federal law designed to give some protection to laboratory animals. The Animal Welfare Act, passed in 1966 and amended in 1970, is administered by the Department of Agriculture and covers only about 4 percent of laboratory animals. Animal advocates worked hard for the bill, which sets some standards for the housing of animals in laboratories and at the dealers' facilities from which many of them are obtained. But the law places no restrictions on the kinds of experiments to which animals may be subjected. It does indicate that pain-relieving drugs should be used on the few types of animals it covers—but it includes a loophole so as not to inhibit researchers unduly. If a scientist claims that pain is a necessary part of an experiment, anesthetics or analgesics may be withheld. 20

One standard test conducted on rats by drug companies is called the "writhing test" because of the agonized way the animals react to irritants injected into their abdomens. Paradoxically, this test assesses the efficacy of pain-killers, which are administered only after the rats show signs of acute suffering. 21

Equally common are psychological experiments in "learned helplessness" that have been conducted on rats, dogs, and other kinds of animals. In some of these tests, caged animals are given painful electric shocks until they learn certain maneuvers to obtain their food. As they become adept at avoiding the shocks, the researchers keep changing the rules so that the animals have to keep learning more and more ways to avoid shocks. Ultimately no way remains to escape, and the animals simply give up and lie on the floors of their cages, passively receiving shock after shock. Researchers have attempted to draw parallels between "learned helplessness" and depression in human beings, but some critics have difficulty perceiving their necessity. "What more are we going to learn about human depression by continuing to produce immobility in animals?" asks former animal experimenter Dr. Roger Ulrich, now a research professor of psychology at Western Michigan University. 22

Electric shock is widely used on many different kinds of animals   23
in various types of research. In one experiment typical of a series that
has been under way since 1966 at the Armed Forces Radiobiology
Research Institute in Bethesda, Md., 10 rhesus monkeys were starved
for 18 hours and then "encouraged" with electric prods to run rapidly on treadmills. This went on for several weeks before the monkeys
were subjected to 4,600 rads of gamma-neutron radiation. Then
they were retested on the treadmills for six hours, and subsequently
for two hours each day until they died. Mean survival time for the
vomiting, incapacitated monkeys was recorded in A.F.R.R.I.'s report
as 37 hours. Dogs have been used in similar experiments, whose purpose is to get an idea of the effects of radiation on human endurance.

Now A.F.R.R.I. and other American research facilities are hav-   24
ing to look for new sources of monkeys. In March 1978, the Government of India banned further export of rhesus monkeys to the
United States. The native population was dwindling and Prime Minister Morarji R. Desai cited violations of a previous agreement that
restricted the use of rhesus monkeys to medical research under humane conditions. "There is no difference between cruelty to animals
and cruelty to human beings," the ascetic Prime Minister stated. The
International Primate Protection League, a four-year-old watchdog
group whose members include many scientists and especially prima-
tologists (Jane Goodall, for one), had spread word in the Indian press
that American scientists were using rhesus monkeys in grisly trauma
experiments. According to the Primate Protection League, these
tests included dipping monkeys in boiling water at the University of
Kansas, shooting them in the face with high-powered rifles at the
University of Chicago, and slamming them in the stomach with a
cannon-impactor traveling at a speed of 70 miles per hour at the University of Michigan.

"I feel justified in stating that fully 80 percent of the experi-   25
ments involving rhesus monkeys are either unnecessary, represent
useless duplication of previous work, or could utilize nonanimal alternatives," wrote Illinois Wesleyan University biologist Dr. John E.
McArdle, a specialist in primate functional anatomy, in a letter to
Prime Minister Desai, who so far has held firm despite pressure from
the American scientific community to rescind the ban. In the meantime, researchers are making do with non-Indian rhesus monkeys
and a close relative, the crab-eating macaque.

One of the arguments in favor of animal tests is that under the   26
controlled circumstances of the experimental laboratory they are
likely to be objective and consistent. But the results of the same tests
conducted on the same kinds of animals often differ from one laboratory to the next. When 25 cooperating companies, including Avon,
Revlon, and American Cyanamid, conducted a comprehensive study
of eye- and skin-irritation tests using rabbits, the results varied widely. The study concluded that these tests "should not be recommend-
ed as standard procedures in any new regulations" because they
yielded "unreliable results."

One of these tests, the Draize Ophthalmic Irritancy Test,[1] is   27
used to evaluate the effect upon the eyes of household and aerosol
products, shampoos, and eye makeup. Rabbits are used because their
eyes do not have effective tear glands and thus cannot easily flush
away or dissolve irritants. The animals are pinioned in stocks and
their eyes are exposed to a substance until inflammation, ulceration,
or gross damage occurs.

Many investigators concede that the data provided by such ex-   28
periments are often inconsistent and that the stresses caused by
crowded cages, callous treatment, pain, and fear can affect animals'
metabolisms and thus confuse test results. "Since there is hardly a
single organ or biochemical system in the body that is not affected
by stress," says Dr. Harold Hillman, a British physiologist, "it is almost certainly the main reason for the wide variation reported
among animals on whom painful experiments have been done."

Very often, different species respond differently to substances or   29
situations. The rationale for many animal tests is that they predict human reactions, but thalidomide, for example, did not produce defor-
mities in the fetuses of dogs, cats, monkeys, and hamsters. On the
other hand, insulin has been proved harmful to rabbits and mice although it saves human lives.

Researchers are becoming increasingly dubious about the ef-   30
ficacy of the LD/50, a test for acute toxicity that consists of force-
feeding a group of animals a specific substance until half of them die,
ostensibly providing a quantitative measure of how poisonous the
substance is. In *Painful Experiments on Animals,* Dr. Pratt asks what

---

[1]Since the time Curtis wrote her essay, legislation has been passed prohibiting the
Draize Test as well as several other procedures mentioned in the selection. A number
of companies in the cosmetics and toiletries industry have also voluntarily suspended
testing of their products on animals.

we learn from forcing hair dye or face powder into a dog or rat through a stomach tube until its internal organs rupture.

One small victory for animal-welfare activists that was hailed by   31 many American scientists was the 1975 Canadian ban on the use of vertebrate animals by students participating in science fairs. Children had been awarded prizes for attempting heart-transplant surgery on unanesthetized rabbits, amputating the feet of lizards, performing Caesarean operations on pregnant mice, bleeding dogs into a state of shock and blinding pigeons. Remarking that such "experiments" were a distortion of the spirit of research, science fair officials ruled out all such projects except observations of the normal living patterns of wild or domestic animals.

In this country, the search for adequate substitutes for laboratory   32 animals was officially launched last summer when the year-old American Fund for Alternatives to Animal Research made its first grant— $12,500 to a biology professor at Whitman College in Walla Walla, Wash. The award to Dr. Earl William Fleck will help finance his development of a test substituting one-celled organisms called tetrahymena for animals in screening substances for teratogens, agents that can cause birth defects. It is expected that the test, if and when perfected, will be cheaper, quicker, more accurate, and certainly more humane than putting thousands of pregnant animals to death.

According to veterinarian Thurman Grafton, executive director   33 of the National Society for Medical Research, people who talk about alternatives to animals are creating false hopes. "These new technologies can only be adjuncts to the use of animals," he claims. "While they serve a purpose in furnishing clues as to what direction a type of research might take, you will always ultimately need an intact animal with all its living complications and interchanging biochemical functions to properly assay a drug."

"Not so," says Ethel Thurston, administrator of the American   34 Fund for Alternatives. "Enough progress has already been made to indicate that certain techniques can completely replace animals."

Several of these techniques have been developed over the last   35 five years in Great Britain, where the Lord Dowding Fund for Humane Research has given grants totaling more than $400,000 to dozens of scientists engaged in research aimed at finding experimental substitutes for animals. Dowding is currently financing several developmental studies of the Ames Test, a promising technique invented by a Berkeley biochemistry professor, Dr. Bruce Ames, that uses salmonella bacteria rather than animals to determine the carcinogenic properties of chemicals. (It was the Ames Test that recently revealed the possible carcinogenic dangers of certain hair dyes.) Another Dowding Fund recipient, research physician Dr. John C. Petricciani, now with the Food and Drug Administration, has devised a method of assessing how tumors grow by inoculating the tumor cells into skin from 9-day-old chicken embryos instead of into living animals.

Animal tests are frequently replaced by other methods discov-   36
ered and developed by scientists like Dr. Ames who are not trying to avoid the use of animals per se but are simply searching for simpler and more cost-efficient ways to achieve their goals. Dr. Hans Stich, a Canadian cancer researcher, for example, has devised a new test for detecting carcinogenicity in chemicals; it uses human cells, takes one week and costs only about $260. The traditional method, using rats and mice, takes three years and costs approximately $150,000.

In addition to egg embryos, bacteria, and simple organisms,   37
possible substitutes for animals include tissue cultures, human and other mammal cells grown in test tubes, and organ banks. Preserved human corneas, for instance, might be used to spare rabbits the agony of the Draize test. Computers could also play a role if researchers used them fully to analyze experimental data, predict the properties of new drugs, and test theoretical data. Computers can even be programmed to simulate living processes. Mechanical models and audio-visual aids can and do substitute for animals as teaching instruments. Simulated human models could provide valid information in car-crash tests.

Last winter, Representative Robert F. Drinan, Democrat of   38
Massachusetts, introduced a bill authorizing the Department of Health, Education and Welfare to fund projects aimed at discovering research methods that would reduce both the numbers of animals used in laboratories and the suffering to which they are subjected.

Meanwhile, medical and military research and an unending   39
stream of new pharmaceutical, cosmetic, and household products are resulting in an ever-increasing use of animals in the laboratory.

The most recent and thorough exploration of alternatives is Dr.   40
D. H. Smyth's book *Alternatives to Animal Experiments,* which examines every option and weighs its pros and cons. He concludes that there is certainly reason to hope that the numbers of laboratory animals can be drastically reduced, but also warns that it is unlikely a complete phasing out of animal experimentation will happen soon.

"By the time we can produce complete alternatives to living tissue," Dr. Smyth writes, "we will not need those alternatives because we will already understand how living tissues work."

Still, Dr. Smyth asks, "Does this mean we can perpetrate any cruelty on animals to satisfy scientific curiosity in the hope that it will one day be useful? To me it certainly does not.... Everyone has a right to decide that certain procedures are unacceptable." 41

Richard Ryder calls animal experimenters to task for trying to have it both ways: Researchers defend their work scientifically on the basis of the *similarities* between human beings and animals, but defend it morally on the basis of the *differences.* 42

And there's the rub: The differences aren't as reassuringly clearcut as they once were. We now know that some animals have a more highly developed intelligence than some human beings—infants, for example, or the retarded and the senile. Dr. Ryder asks, "If we were to be discovered by some more intelligent creatures in the universe, would they be justified in experimenting on us?" 43

Questions for Close Reading

1. What is the selection's thesis? Locate the sentence(s) in which Curtis states her main idea. If she doesn't state the thesis explicitly, express it in your own words.
2. What is Curtis's main reason for opposing the use of animals in medical research?
3. What does Curtis mean by "speciesist"?
4. What alternatives to animal experimentation does Curtis advocate?
5. Refer to your dictionary as needed to define the following words used in the selection: *exuberant* (paragraph 2), *ingratiatingly* (4), *curtailment* (7), *jeopardize* (7), *absolutist* (7), *boondoggles* (11), *altruistically* (12), *primates* (12), *ecosystems* (13), *antivivisection* (14), *clandestine* (14), *commando* (14), *zealots* (14), *rationalized* (15), *analgesics* (20), *rescind* (25), *pinioned* (27), *assay* (33), and *carcinogenicity* (36).

Questions About the Writer's Craft

1. **The pattern.** Because Curtis is a layperson, she can't rely upon her own credibility (*ethos*) as an expert to build her case against animal experimentation. How, then, does she create credibility for her position?
2. **Other patterns.** Why might Curtis have decided to open her essay with the four-paragraph narrative about the medical school professor? What would have been lost if she had begun the piece with paragraph 5 instead?

3. **Other patterns.** After providing brief details about animal abuse in paragraphs 3 and 4, Curtis doesn't mention other instances of abuse until paragraphs 16 through 18. And she doesn't discuss any examples in depth until the essay's midpoint (paragraphs 21, 24–27, and 30–31). Why do you think she waited until the midpoint to provide these additional in-depth examples? What purpose, in other words, do paragraphs 5–15 and 19–20 serve?

4. Examine Curtis's language in paragraphs 1 through 5. What tone does this language convey? How does her tone here differ from the tone she projects later in the essay—for example, in paragraphs 16 and 22 through 23? Why do you think she varies her tone in this manner?

Questions for Further Thought

1. In paragraph 14, a former prime minister of India is quoted as saying, "There is no difference between cruelty to animals and cruelty to human beings." Do you agree? Why or why not?

2. In Curtis's opinion, differentiating between "higher" and "lower" animals is a rationalization that permits the suffering of rodents, birds, and other small animals. Would you protest the mistreatment of a mouse as strongly as you would protest cruelty to horses, cats, and dogs? Why or why not?

3. Curtis quotes British physiologist Dr. D. H. Smyth who asserts, "Some knowledge can be obtained at too high a price." What do you feel is the "highest price" that should be paid for a new discovery—in any field? For example, is the knowledge gained from manned space flight worth the lives of several humans? Explain.

4. How would you answer the question posed by Dr. Richard Ryder: "If we were to be discovered by some more intelligent creatures in the universe, would they be justified in experimenting on us?"

Writing Assignments Using Argumentation-Persuasion as a Pattern of Development

∞ 1. New regulations governing animal use in medical research have eliminated some of the abuses Curtis cites. Conduct some research to determine what regulations regarding the use of animals in medical research are currently in effect. Bibliographies like the *New York Times Index* and the *General Science Index* as well as computer databases like the National Newspaper Index, Newsbank, CD News, Periodical Abstracts, Ondisc, Infotrac, and LEXIS (an on-line database covering federal and state laws) will help you locate relevant information. Review your research, and decide whether existing restrictions are sufficient or whether additional ones are needed. Argue your position in an essay. Remember to acknowledge and, where possible, to refute the opposing point of view. If you haven't already done so, read Ron Kline's "A Scientist: 'I Am the Enemy'" (page 651) for another point of view on the animal-experimentation issue.

∞ 2. Recently, a group called the Animal Liberation Front (referred to in paragraph 14) has become active in this country. To call attention to the abuses they perceive, the ALF adopts essentially illegal tactics—breaking into medical labs, destroying equipment, and releasing the animals. Read in the library about the ALF or some other radical group that uses illegal means to combat a perceived injustice. You might, for example, focus on groups protesting abortion, nuclear power, or the "bussing" of children to achieve racial integration in schools. Do you agree with the group's strategies? Write an essay in which you argue your position, remembering to acknowledge the opposing viewpoint. No matter which position you take, make sure you indicate whether you believe illegal actions are justified in the fight against a perceived unjust or immoral practice. Nat Hentoff's "Free Speech on Campus" (page 629) provides an interesting perspective on protest and the law.

Writing Assignments Using Other Patterns of Development

∞ 3. Curtis's opening anecdote describes a man with a sharp discrepancy in his life: he responds one way to his pet dog and a distinctly different way to a similar dog in his laboratory. Most of us have observed similar contradictions in our own or in someone else's life. For instance, you may believe in honesty but didn't protest a friend's shoplifting, or perhaps a male relative preaches respect for women but treats his dates with a swaggering disregard. Write an essay about *one* such discrepancy, using vivid details to tell about its appearance in your life or in someone else's. Indicate whether the person was aware of the contradiction and whether it was resolved. Be sure, too, to state or imply your feelings about the discrepancy. Before writing, you might want to read T. H. Watkins's "Little Deaths" (page 181) and Langston Hughes's "Salvation" (page 191), essays that focus on the clash between values and behavior.

4. Curtis obviously feels that experimenting on animals is wrong, no matter what good might come of it. Think of a situation that you feel is morally wrong. You might believe, for example, that an advertising campaign defending cigarette smoking is morally unsupportable, that the nation's high rate of illiteracy is unacceptable, or that the violent content of today's movies is indefensible. Write an essay in which you present compelling examples showing why this situation is so objectionable.

Louis Nizer

One of this country's best-known attorneys, Louis Nizer (1902–94) shared his legal expertise and courtroom experiences in such best-sellers as *My Life in Court* (1961), *The Jury Returns* (1966), and *Reflections Without Mirrors* (1978). Portions of his books have been adapted for the theater, cinema, and television. Respected for his lucid prose style, Nizer wrote for such diverse publications as the *New York Times, Reader's Digest, McCall's,* and numerous scholarly legal journals. In addition to being a skilled attorney, author, and lecturer, Nizer was an accomplished painter and composer. The following essay was first published in the *New York Times* in 1986.

Low-Cost Drugs for Addicts?

Drug addiction and drug-related crimes cost the nation millions of dollars and thousands of lives each year. Louis Nizer argues that many of the ills associated with drug use exist only because narcotics are illegal. Legalizing drugs, he contends, would sharply reduce what many believe is the number one problem facing our nation today.

We are losing the war against drug addiction. Our strategy is wrong. I propose a different approach. 1

The Government should create clinics, manned by psychiatrists, 2 that would provide drugs for nominal charges or even free to addicts under controlled regulations. It would cost the Government only 20 cents for a heroin shot, for which the addicts must now pay the mob more than $100, and there are similar price discrepancies in cocaine, crack and other such substances.

Such a service, which would also include the staff support of psy- 3 chiatrists and doctors, would cost a fraction of what the nation now spends to maintain the land, sea and air apparatus necessary to interdict illegal imports of drugs. There would also be a savings of hundreds of millions of dollars from the elimination of the prosecutorial procedures that stifle our courts and overcrowd our prisons.

We see in our newspapers the triumphant announcements by Government agents that they have intercepted huge caches of cocaine, the street prices of which are in the tens of millions of dollars. Should we be gratified? Will this achievement reduce the number of addicts by one? All it will do is increase the cost to the addict of his illegal supply.

Many addicts who are caught committing a crime admit that they have mugged or stolen as many as six or seven times a day to accumulate the $100 needed for a fix. Since many of them need two or three fixes a day, particularly for crack, one can understand the terror in our streets and homes. It is estimated that there are in New York City alone 200,000 addicts, and this is typical of cities across the nation. Even if we were to assume that only a modest percentage of a city's addicts engage in criminal conduct to obtain the money for the habit, requiring multiple muggings and thefts each day, we could nevertheless account for many of the tens of thousands of crimes each day in New York City alone.

Not long ago, a Justice Department division issued a report stating that more than half the perpetrators of murder and other serious crimes were under the influence of drugs. This symbolizes the new domestic terror in our nation. This is why our citizens are unsafe in broad daylight on the most traveled thoroughfares. This is why typewriters and television sets are stolen from offices and homes and sold for a pittance. This is why parks are closed to the public and why murders are committed. This is why homes need multiple locks, and burglary systems, and why store windows, even in the most fashionable areas, require iron gates.

The benefits of the new strategy to control this terrorism would be immediate and profound.

First, the mob would lose the main source of its income. It could not compete against a free supply for which previously it exacted tribute estimated to be hundreds of millions of dollars, perhaps billions, from hopeless victims.

Second, pushers would be put out of business. There would be no purpose in creating addicts who would be driven by desperate compulsion to steal and kill for the money necessary to maintain their habit. Children would not be enticed. The mob's macabre public-relations program is to tempt children with free drugs in order to create customers for the future. The wave of street crimes in broad daylight would diminish to a trickle. Homes and stores would not have to be fortresses. Our recreational areas could again be used. Neighborhoods would not be scandalized by sordid street centers where addicts gather to obtain their supply from slimy merchants.

Third, police and other law-enforcement authorities, domestic or foreign, would be freed to deal with traditional nondrug crimes.   10

There are several objections that might be raised against such a salutary solution.   11

First, it could be argued that by providing free drugs to the addict we would consign him to permanent addiction. The answer is that medical and psychiatric help at the source would be more effective in controlling the addict's descent than the extremely limited remedies available to the victim today. I am not arguing that the new strategy will cure everything. But I do not see many addicts being freed from their bonds under the present system.   12

In addition, as between the addict's predicament and the safety of our innocent citizens, which deserves our primary concern? Drug-induced crime has become so common that almost every citizen knows someone in his immediate family or among his friends who has been mugged. It is these citizens who should be our chief concern.   13

Another possible objection is that addicts will cheat the system by obtaining more than the allowable free shot. Without discounting the resourcefulness of the bedeviled addict, it should be possible to have Government cards issued that would be punched so as to limit the free supply in accord with medical authorization.   14

Yet all objections become trivial when matched against the crisis itself. What we are witnessing is the demoralization of a great society: the ruination of its school children, athletes and executives, the corrosion of the workforce in general.   15

Many thoughtful sociologists consider the rapidly spreading drug use the greatest problem that our nation faces—greater and more real and urgent than nuclear bombs or economic reversal. In China, a similar crisis drove the authorities to apply capital punishment to those who trafficked in opium—an extreme solution that arose from the deepest reaches of frustration.   16

Free drugs will win the war against the domestic terrorism caused by illicit drugs. As a strategy, it is at once resourceful, sensible and simple. We are getting nowhere in our efforts to hold back the ocean of supply. The answer is to dry up demand.   17

Questions for Close Reading

1. What is the selection's thesis? Locate the sentence(s) in which Nizer states his main idea. If he doesn't state the thesis explicitly, express it in your own words.
2. Nizer believes his plan would yield numerous benefits. What are they?
3. Nizer acknowledges some possible objections to his plan. What are they? How does he refute these arguments?
4. How much concern does Nizer have for those addicted to drugs? How do you know?
5. Refer to your dictionary as needed to define the following words used in the selection: *nominal* (paragraph 2), *interdict* (3), *cache* (4), *macabre* (9), *salutary* (11), *consign* (12), and *illicit* (17).

Questions About the Writer's Craft

1. **The pattern.**   Which of the two possible strategies for organizing a refutation (see page 571) does Nizer use in this essay?
2. Nizer's essay starts with a brief introductory paragraph consisting of three crisp, almost clipped sentences. What is the effect of this unusually brief introduction?
3. What words with militaristic connotations does Nizer use in his essay? What might have been Nizer's reason for using such language?
4. To what audience does Nizer seem to be addressing his proposal? How do you know?

Questions for Further Thought

1. Besides those Nizer mentions, what additional objections might people have to legalizing drugs? How valid are these objections?
2. Nizer holds drug users accountable for their acts. Do you think that courts should take into account the environmental and psychological factors that may have precipitated a crime? Explain.
3. Can any of Nizer's ideas be used to argue that other "vices" should be legalized? Consider, for example, gambling or prostitution.
4. Nizer suggests that organized crime is most responsible for the country's drug problem. Can you identify other players in this tragedy?

Writing Assignments Using Argumentation-Persuasion as a Pattern of Development

∞ 1. Nizer argues that legalizing drugs would not necessarily increase the number of addicts and that it would definitely reduce crime. Write an essay supporting or challenging *one* of these conclusions. No matter which side you take, assume that some readers are opposed to your point of view. Acknowledge and try to dismantle as many of their objections as you can. Beth Johnson's "Our Drug Problem" (page 675) will familiarize you with some of the counterarguments to Nizer's position.

2. Propose measures that *one* of the following groups might take to educate people about the effects of drug addiction: parent groups; public schools; colleges or universities; the local, state, or federal government. Put your proposal in the form of a letter to the appropriate person (a high school principal, college president, and so on). Try to anticipate and rebut possible objections to your proposal.

Writing Assignments Using Other Patterns of Development

∞ 3. According to psychologists, many individuals have an "addictive personality." Referring to people you know well, write an essay defining this term. However, instead of focusing on addiction to a substance, illustrate the "addictive personality" by writing about the excessive need for approval, danger, competition, and the like. Marie Winn's "TV Addiction" (page 541) may spark some thoughts worth exploring.

4. Assume that the Dean of Students has asked you to write an open letter to be published in next year's orientation brochure for first-year students. Your assignment is to warn incoming students about the long-term effects of drug abuse, or too much partying, or excessive procrastination—anything that might affect their well-being and success in college. Develop your letter by drawing on your own and other people's experiences. You might, in addition, use a source like the *Readers' Guide to Periodical Literature* to track down helpful articles, so that you can include relevant facts, statistics, or expert opinion in your letter.

Beth Johnson

A journalist and freelance writer, Beth Johnson received an advanced degree in literacy education from Syracuse University. Johnson's crisp, no-nonsense prose style has served her well in the public relations writing she has done for a college news bureau and a community mental health center. Formerly on the faculties of Goshen College and New England College, Johnson has also written for a number of publications, among them the *Starke County Ledger* and the *New Hampshire Business Review*. Revised for this text, the following selection is taken from a collection of Johnson's essays dealing with the impact of drugs on society.

Our Drug Problem

Nearly everyone agrees that drug abuse is an overwhelming national problem. But a solution to that problem finds far less consensus. Some advocate such drastic measures as the automatic execution of drug dealers. Others favor the legalization of narcotics, believing that the illicit nature of the drug trade is largely responsible for our predicament. Beth Johnson argues in this selection that the removal of legal restraints would be the beginning of a drug-induced nightmare from which America might never awaken.

Imagine, if you will, the final reel of a trashy "B" movie based on the Biblical story of Sodom and Gomorrah. You remember the tale of two cities so given over to evil practices, immorality, and mindless self-indulgence that God finally destroyed them by raining down fire and brimstone.

What sort of activity do you suppose a filmmaker would choose in order to portray, in an updated fashion, the wickedness of Sodom and Gomorrah? The perfect choice, in my mind, would be unrestricted drug use. Think of the potential for destructive behavior: self-annihilation through drug overdose; sexual excesses with no concern for consequences; reckless acts leading to crippling or fatal accidents; obsession with narcotics to the point of ignoring family needs...the possibilities go on and on. Unlimited access to drugs would provide the perfect metaphor for the legendary evil that was Sodom and Gomorrah.

Incredibly, in America today, supposedly responsible and intel-   3
ligent people are recommending the legalization of narcotics. The war on drugs has been lost, they say; it's time to stop pouring enormous resources into a futile battle. Let's change strategies, they argue, and try attacking the problem by removing all legal restrictions on drug use.

Has a more ludicrous proposal ever been seriously introduced   4
for public discussion? Are we honestly being asked to consider raising our children in a society that says, "Yes, we know that these substances will ruin your and your family's lives and will kill you sooner or later. We'd really rather you didn't use drugs, but it's just too difficult to try to enforce the law"?

Apparently we are. Conservative columnist William F. Buckley,   5
Jr., Nobel Prize-winning economist Milton Friedman, Mayor Kurt Schmoke of Baltimore, and U.S. Reps. Fortney Stark of California and Steny Hoyer of Maryland have been among the respected—and presumably not drug-addled—folks who have suggested that legalization of drugs is an idea whose time may have come.

Let's look at their arguments one by one. But be forewarned;   6
dismantling them will not take too much time or effort.

"Legalizing drugs would mean the end of drug-related crime."   7
Presumably it's true that if narcotics were legalized, drug lords, pushers, and drug gangs would no longer reap enormous profits. It does not follow, however, that the addicted would be any less driven to desperate measures to obtain a fix. To feed their habit, many would obtain money by resorting to robbery and prostitution. Indeed, as the number of addicts continued to grow, so would the number of drug-related crimes.

"The government could tax drug sales and regulate the purity   8
of narcotics if they were sold legally." The advocates of legalization point out that two other addictive substances—alcohol and tobacco—are legal and subject to government regulation. True. But with what results? Alcohol and tobacco combined kill more than half a million people each year. Illegal drugs leave an even more deadly leg-

acy. Drug abuse has been linked to many devastating diseases and medical conditions; 55 percent of pediatric AIDS cases and 36 percent of hepatitis C cases are tied to intravenous drug use. And when substance abusers are hospitalized for almost any ailment—burns, pneumonia, and blood poisoning, for example—they recuperate more slowly, remaining in the hospital up to twice as long as non-abusers for the same conditions. In 1991, substance abuse was linked to 2.3 million days Americans spent in the hospital, with one-third of those days involving infants born with complications due to their mothers' drug abuse during pregnancy. Would we consider it progress to have more people seriously ill or dying, more infants suffering, more patients unable to heal because they had injected, inhaled, or consumed purer forms of poison?

"The war on drugs is simply too expensive and too ineffective. 9 The country can't afford to continue spending money at this rate." No doubt about it, the price tag attached to fighting drug abuse is phenomenal. It's estimated that federal, state, and local governments spend over $8 billion a year on drug enforcement. Add to that the uncounted billions spent on feeding and housing those imprisoned for drug-related crimes (more than a third of all federal prisoners fall into this category), and you end up with some breathtaking sums.

True, the war on drugs is not being won. The courts are over- 10 flowing with cases waiting to be tried. Huge seizures of narcotics stop only a small fraction of the drugs coming into the country. Countless dragnets snare only the small-time pusher, not the drug kingpin. Clearly, as it is being waged now, the national fight against drug abuse is futile.

The only thing more costly than continuing the current war on 11 drugs would be the legalization of narcotics; such a measure would claim innumerable human lives. Government figures estimate that crimes involving drug use cost society more than $58 billion a year. Substance abuse is linked with 52 percent of rapes committed; 49 percent of murders; 62 percent of assaults; and 50 percent of traffic fatalities and incidents of spousal abuse. The legalization of narcotics could only push those figures higher.

Currently, drug abuse costs American industry as much as $100 12 billion per year in lost productivity, liability for errors committed by substance-abusing employees, and drug-related injuries. Imagine how that figure would soar if legal restraints were removed. If people didn't have to drive into a seedy neighborhood...if they didn't risk arrest and disgrace...if they could justify their actions as legal...how many could resist trying drugs "just once"? And how many addicts started out by experimenting with drugs "just once"? Every one of them, that's how many. Moreover, what would be the fate of addicts if narcotics were available legally? In the words of one cocaine addict, "I'd be dead....I'd just sit down with a big pile of the stuff and snort it until I dropped."

One more number to consider: Today, the health costs of treat-   13
ing drug abuse are estimated at $65 billion per year. Care to guess what that figure might become if drugs were made legal?

Aren't these facts enough to dissuade anyone from believing   14
that the legalization of narcotics has anything to recommend it? Why, then, would anyone recommend legalization? The answer has to do with racism, elitism, and sheer indifference to the suffering of others. "These people are going to kill themselves anyway," many middle-class Americans reason. "I'm not going to have my tax dollars used to try to save them. Besides, what does it matter if drugs wipe out a generation—as long as it's a generation of black and Hispanic kids?"

If you doubt that this kind of thinking is pervasive, consider the   15
public indifference to the last decade's gutting of education and job-training programs. Such programs address the major causes of drug abuse: poverty and despair. When the number of families living beneath the poverty level increased more than sixfold between 1979 and 1993, did more fortunate Americans protest? Who objected when federal funds for low-income housing dropped from $32 billion to $7 billion between 1981 and 1993? There was little public protest when federal aid for public education decreased by nearly $6 billion in the 1980s. Nor did the average American complain when funding of job-training programs dropped by $42 billion from 1981 to 1993. And the minimum wage, despite a recent increase, has fallen to its lowest level in terms of buying power since 1955. Is it any wonder that poor teenagers choose the lucrative jobs offered by drug lords over the chance to flip hamburgers at a fast-food restaurant? Given the harshness of their lives, it's not surprising that the underprivileged have turned to drugs in such massive numbers.

The nation's devastating drug problem illustrates that our coun-   16
try is reaping what it has sowed: a harvest of poverty, violence, and despair. That the problem has grown to this extent is immoral in

itself; to encourage it further through the legalization of narcotics would be not only impractical but also unethical. Unless this once-great country acts quickly to address the drug problem in the only way that can work—through providing real education, more affordable housing, and greater employment opportunities—it will truly deserve comparison with cities that suffered the fate of fire and brimstone.

Questions for Close Reading

1. What is the selection's thesis? Locate the sentence(s) in which Johnson states her main idea. If she doesn't state the thesis explicitly, express it in your own words.
2. According to Johnson, for what reasons do "supposedly responsible and intelligent people" advocate the legalization of narcotics?
3. How does the number of deaths from illegal drug abuse compare with the number of deaths from the abuse of alcohol and tobacco? In what ways does this information strengthen Johnson's argument?
4. Johnson admits that, as it is currently being fought, the war on drugs is ineffectual and costly. Why, then, is she against legalizing narcotics? What does she advocate instead?
5. Refer to your dictionary as needed to define the following words used in the selection: *ludicrous* (paragraph 4), *addled* (5), *forewarned* (6), *dismantling* (6), *dissuade* (14), and *elitism* (14).

Questions About the Writer's Craft

1. **The pattern.**   Johnson often employs provocative, even inflammatory language, as when she refers to the idea of legalizing narcotics as "ludicrous." Find additional examples of such language. What assumptions about her audience might have motivated Johnson to adopt this style?
2. Johnson also draws on facts, statistics, illustrations, and expert testimony to support her argument. Identify examples in the essay of each kind of evidence. What is the effect of this evidence?
3. Johnson creates an interesting *analogy* when she compares the consequences of legalizing narcotics to the fate of Sodom and Gomorrah. What purpose does this analogy serve? Where else does the author use *figurative language?*
4. Although Johnson works to refute the arguments of her opponents, she also concedes points to the opposing view. In paragraph 9, for example, she admits, "No doubt about it, the price tag attached to fighting drug abuse is phenomenal." Why does she make such concessions?

Questions for Further Thought

1. In paragraph 12, Johnson argues that narcotics abuse would soar if there were no risk attached to buying drugs. Is this a fair conclusion? Do you know people who would begin using or would increase their consumption of drugs if legal restraints were removed?
2. Johnson claims that the real causes of most drug abuse are poverty and despair. What, then, accounts for the abuse of illegal substances like cocaine and marijuana among the middle class and the rich?
3. Some people believe that drug addicts are criminals and should, if convicted, suffer stiff prison sentences. Others consider drug abuse a disease that can be corrected only through careful, compassionate medical attention. What's your opinion? Explain.
4. For Johnson, "real education, more affordable housing, and greater employment opportunities" are the only genuine solutions for the drug problem. What specific measures do you think should be taken to help stem the tide of drug abuse in this country?

Writing Assignments Using Argumentation-Persuasion as a Pattern of Development

∞ 1. Johnson contends that "racism and elitism and sheer indifference to the suffering of others" are behind the proposal to legalize drugs. Write an essay in which you defend or challenge Johnson's charge. Remember to mention and, when possible, refute opposing arguments. Louis Nizer's "Low-Cost Drugs for Addicts?" (page 670) will familiarize you with a viewpoint sharply different from Johnson's.
2. Assume that your college's Office of Student Life has just hired you as a peer counselor whose job it is to reach out to students in distress. Your first task is to write a letter to students with drug and/or alcohol problems, persuading them to seek help through the college's professional and peer counseling services. The letter will be posted on campus bulletin boards and will appear in the student newspaper. As you write the letter, keep in mind that people in difficulty often resist offers of help. What persuasive strategies can you use to overcome this resistance?

Writing Assignments Using Other Patterns of Development

3. In an essay, examine the possible effects of mandatory drug testing on a specific group of people (for example, public school students, college athletes, airline employees). Be sure your paper expresses a clear attitude toward such a program. Brainstorm with others and conduct library research to gather material for your essay.

4. Assume that you're a student member of your college's Disciplinary Action Committee. On this week's agenda is the case of a student who has been caught selling drugs on campus. Write a brief report detailing the step-by-step procedure you think your college should follow with this and similar cases.

Additional Writing Topics

ARGUMENTATION-PERSUASION

General Assignments

Using argumentation-persuasion, develop one of the topics below in an essay. After choosing a topic, think about your purpose and audience. Remember that the paper's thesis should state the issue under discussion as well as your position on the issue. As you work on developing evidence, you might want to do some outside research. Keep in mind that effective argumentation-persuasion usually means that some time should be spent acknowledging and perhaps refuting opposing points of view. Be careful not to sabotage your argument by basing your case on a logical fallacy.

1. Mercy killing
2. Hiring quotas
3. Giving birth-control devices to teenagers
4. Prayer in the schools
5. Living off campus
6. The drinking age
7. Spouses sharing housework equally
8. Smoking in public places
9. Big-time sports in college
10. Music videos
11. Working mothers with young children
12. Acid rain
13. Drugs on campus
14. Political campaigns
15. Requiring college students to pass a comprehensive exam in their majors before graduating
16. Fifty-five-mile-per-hour speed limit
17. Putting elderly parents in nursing homes
18. An optional pass-fail system for courses
19. The homeless
20. Nonconformity in a neighborhood: allowing a lawn to go wild, keeping many pets, painting a house an odd color, or some other atypical behavior

Assignments With a Specific Purpose and Audience

1. A college has rejected your or your child's application on the basis of low SAT scores. Write to the college admissions director, arguing that SAT scores are not a fair indicator of your or your child's abilities and potential.

2. As a staff writer for the college opinion magazine, you've been asked to nominate the "Outstanding Man or Woman on Campus," to be featured on the magazine's cover. Write a letter to your supervising editor in support of your nominee.

3. You and your parents don't agree on some aspect of your romantic life (you want to live with your partner and they don't approve; you want to get married and they want you to wait; they simply don't like your partner). Write your parents a letter explaining why your preference is reasonable. Try hard to win them over to your side, and remember not to be antagonistic.

4. As a high school teacher, you support some additional restriction on students. The restriction might be "no radios in school," "no T-shirts," "no food in class," "no smoking on school grounds." Write an article for the school newspaper, justifying this new rule to the student body.

5. Someone you know is convinced that the music you listen to is trashy or boring. Write a letter to the person arguing that your music has value. Support your contention with specific references to lyrics, musical structure, and performers' talent.

6. Assume you're a member of a racial, ethnic, religious, or social minority. You might, for example, be a Native American, an elderly person, a female executive. On a recent television show or in a TV commercial, you saw something that depicts your group in an offensive way. Write a letter (to the network or the advertiser) expressing your feelings and explaining why you feel the material should be taken off the air.

13

FOR FURTHER READING

Throughout this book, you've studied the patterns of development—narration, process analysis, definition, and so on—in depth. You've seen how the patterns are used as strategies for generating, developing, and organizing ideas for essays. You've also learned that, in practice, most types of writing combine two or more patterns. The two sections that follow provide additional information about these important points. The rest of the chapter then gives you an opportunity to look more closely at the way several writers use the patterns of development in their work.

THE PATTERNS IN ACTION: DURING THE WRITING PROCESS

The patterns of development come into play throughout the composing process. In the prewriting stage, awareness of the patterns encourages you to think about your subject in fresh, new ways. Assume, for example, that you've been asked to write an essay about the way children are disciplined in school. However, you draw a blank as soon as you try to limit this general subject. To break the logjam, you could apply one or more patterns of development to your subject. *Comparison-contrast* might prompt you to write an essay investigating the differences between your parents' and your own feelings about school discipline. *Division-classification* might lead you to another paper—one that categorizes the kinds of discipline used in school. And *cause-effect* might point to still another essay—one that explores the way students react to being suspended.

Further along in the writing process—after you've identified your limited subject and your thesis—the patterns of development can help you generate your paper's evidence. Imagine that your thesis is "Teachers shouldn't discipline students publicly just to make an example of them." You're not sure, though, how to develop this thesis. Calling upon the patterns might spark some promising possibilities. *Narration* might encourage you to recount the disastrous time you were singled out and punished for the misdeeds of an entire class. Using *definition*, you might explain what is meant by an *autocratic* disciplinary style. *Argumentation-persuasion* might prompt you to advocate a new plan for disciplining students fairly and effectively.

The patterns of development also help you organize your ideas by pointing the way to an appropriate framework for a paper. Suppose you plan to write an essay for the campus newspaper about the disturbingly high incidence of shoplifting among college students; your purpose is to warn young people away from this tempting, supposedly victimless crime. You believe that many readers will be deterred from shoplifting if you tell them about the harrowing *process* set in motion once a shoplifter is detected. With this step-by-step explanation in mind, you can now map out the essay's content: what happens when a shoplifter is detained by a salesperson, questioned by store security personnel, led to a police car, booked at the police station, and tried in a courtroom.

THE PATTERNS IN ACTION: IN AN ESSAY

Although this book devotes a separate chapter to each of the nine patterns of development, all chapters emphasize the same important point: Most writing consists of several patterns, with the dominant

pattern providing the piece's organizational framework. To reinforce this point, each chapter contains a section, "How [the Pat-
tern] Fits Your Purpose and Audience," that shows how a writer's
purpose often leads to a blending of patterns. You might also have
noticed that one of the "Questions About the Writer's Craft" following each professional selection asks you to analyze the piece's
combination of patterns. Further, the "Writing Assignments Using
Other Patterns of Development" encourage you to discover for
yourself which mix of patterns would work best in a given piece of
writing. In short, all through *The Macmillan Reader* we emphasize
that the patterns of development are far from being mechanical formulas. On the contrary: They are practical strategies that open up
options in every stage of the composing process.

In this section of the book, you'll have a chance to focus on the
way writers combine patterns in their essays. The following six selections are by three writers whose styles and subjects differ sharply.
(Before reading the selections, you'll probably find it helpful to
glance back at pages 25–26 so you can review the broad purpose of
each pattern of development.) As you read each selection, ask yourself these questions:

1. What is the writer's *purpose* and *thesis?*
2. What *pattern of development dominates* the essay? How does
   this pattern help the writer support the essay's thesis and
   fulfill the essay's purpose?
3. What *other patterns appear* in the essay? How do these secondary patterns help the writer support the essay's thesis
   and fulfill the essay's purpose?

Your responses to these three questions will reward you with a
richer understanding of the way writers work and with a deeper
appreciation of three skilled prose stylists. To give you an even
clearer sense of how writers mix patterns, we have annotated Virginia Woolf's "The Death of the Moth" (page 688), using the preceding three questions as a guide. By making your own annotations
on Woolf's essay and then comparing them to ours, you can measure your ability to analyze Woolf's use of the patterns. You can further evaluate your analysis of the piece by answering the three
questions on your own and then comparing your responses to ours
on pages 692–94.

Virginia Woolf

Virginia Woolf is considered one of the most innovative writers of the twentieth century. Born in 1882 in London, Woolf was educated at home by her father, a well-known biographer, critic, and scholar. Along with her sister, Woolf became a key member of the Bloomsbury Group, a circle of writers and artists committed to the highest standards in art and literature. Woolf married a fellow Bloomsbury member, author and publisher Leonard Woolf. Together, they established Hogarth Press, which went on to publish Woolf's ground-breaking writings, including the novels *Mrs. Dalloway* (1923) and *To the Lighthouse* (1927), as well as the collection of essays *A Room of One's Own* (1920). Woolf's experimentation with point of view and her use of stream of consciousness earned her a place as a pivotal figure in English literature. Although Woolf's work met with critical acclaim and her collaboration with her husband was productive, Woolf was troubled all her life by severe depression. She committed suicide in 1941. The first of the following two selections by Woolf, "The Death of the Moth," appeared in the volume *The Death of the Moth and Other Essays* (1948); the second, "Professions for Women," was delivered as a speech to the Women's Service League in 1931.

The Death of the Moth

A moth dying on the windowsill is hardly an unusual sight and generally won't excite much emotion. But Virginia Woolf, with characteristic depth of perception, sees the moth as an emblem of the eternal battle between life and death.

Description of the moth

Definition (by negation): How this moth differs from the usual kind

Moths that fly by day are not properly to be   1
called moths; they do not excite that pleasant sense
of dark autumn nights and ivy-blossom which the
commonest yellow-underwing asleep in the shadow
of the curtain never fails to rouse in us. They are hy-
brid creatures, neither gay like butterflies nor som-
bre like their own species. Nevertheless the present

specimen, with his narrow hay-coloured wings, fringed with a tassel of the same colour, seemed to be content with life. It was a pleasant morning, mid-September, mild, benignant, yet with a keener breath than that of the summer months. The plough was already scoring the field opposite the window, and where the share had been, the earth was pressed flat and gleamed with moisture. Such vigour came rolling in from the fields and the down beyond that it was difficult to keep the eyes strictly turned upon the book. The rooks too were keeping one of their annual festivities; soaring round the tree tops until it looked as if a vast net with thousands of black knots in it had been cast up into the air; which, after a few moments, sank slowly down upon the trees until every twig seemed to have a knot at the end of it. Then, suddenly, the net would be thrown into the air again in a wider circle this time, with the utmost clamour and vociferation, as though to be thrown into the air and settle slowly down upon the tree tops were a tremendously exciting experience.

The same energy which inspired the rooks, the ploughmen, the horses, and even, it seemed, the lean bare-backed downs, sent the moth fluttering from side to side of his square of the windowpane. One could not help watching him. One was, indeed, conscious of a queer feeling of pity for him. The possibilities of pleasure seemed that morning so enormous and so various that to have only a moth's part in life, and a day moth's at that, appeared a hard fate, and his zest in enjoying his meagre opportunities to the full, pathetic. He flew vigorously to one corner of his compartment, and, after waiting there a second, flew across to the other. What remained for him but to fly to a third corner and then to a fourth? That was all he could do, in spite of the size of the downs, the width of the sky, the far-off smoke of houses, and the romantic

---

Margin annotations:

Part of implied purpose/thesis: Nature's energy

Description of nature's energy here *contrasts* with *description* of nature in ¶5 (part of purpose/thesis)

Comparison between nature's energy and the moth's strong life force (part of purpose/thesis)

Start of *narrative* (main pattern) about the moth's plight

Start of *narrative* about Woolf's reaction to the moth's plight

Description of moth's strong life force—despite its small size (these two

(paragraph number) 2

contrasting qualities are part of purpose/thesis)

Part of purpose/thesis: The moth represents life

Narrative about Woolf's reaction continues

Restatement of part of purpose/thesis: The moth's two contrasting qualities

Restatement of part of purpose/thesis: The moth represents life

Narrative about the moth's plight continues; tension builds

Narrative about Woolf's reaction continues

voice, now and then, of a steamer out at sea. What he could do he did. Watching him, it seemed as if a fibre, very thin but pure, of the enormous energy of the world had been thrust into his frail and diminutive body. As often as he crossed the pane, I could fancy that a thread of vital light became visible. He was little or nothing but life.

Yet, because he was so small, and so simple a 3 form of the energy that was rolling in at the open window and driving its way through so many narrow and intricate corridors in my own brain and in those of other human beings, there was something marvellous as well as pathetic about him. It was as if someone had taken a tiny bead of pure life and decking it as lightly as possible with down and feathers, had set it dancing and zigzagging to show us the true nature of life. Thus displayed one could not get over the strangeness of it. One is apt to forget all about life, seeing it humped and bossed and garnished and cumbered so that it has to move with the greatest circumspection and dignity. Again, the thought of all that life might have been had he been born in any other shape caused one to view his simple activities with a kind of pity.

After a time, tired by his dancing apparently, 4 he settled on the window ledge in the sun, and, the queer spectacle being at an end, I forgot about him. Then, looking up, my eye was caught by him. He was trying to resume his dancing, but seemed either so stiff or so awkward that he could only flutter to the bottom of the window-pane; and when he tried to fly across it he failed. Being intent on other matters I watched these futile attempts for a time without thinking, unconsciously waiting for him to resume his flight, as one waits for a machine, that has stopped momentarily, to start again without considering the reason of its failure. After perhaps a seventh attempt he slipped from the wooden ledge and fell, fluttering his wings, on to his back on the window sill. The helplessness of his attitude roused

Hint of the resolution of the *narrative* about the moth ——

Narrative about Woolf's reaction ——

Description of nature's indifference here *contrasts* with *description* of nature in ¶1 (part of purpose/thesis)

Restatement of part of purpose/thesis: The strength of the moth's life force—despite small size

Part of purpose/thesis: Death's inevitability

Narrative about—moth continues

Narrative about—Woolf's reaction continues

Restatement of part of purpose/thesis: The strength of the moth's life force—despite its size

Resolution of—the *narrative* about the moth

me. It flashed upon me that he was in difficulties; he could no longer raise himself; his legs struggled vainly. But, as I stretched out a pencil, meaning to help him to right himself, it came over me that the failure and awkwardness were the approach of death. I laid the pencil down again.

The legs agitated themselves once more. I looked as if for the enemy against which he struggled. I looked out of doors. What had happened there? Presumably it was midday, and work in the fields had stopped. Stillness and quiet had replaced the previous animation. The birds had taken themselves off to feed in the brooks. The horses stood still. Yet the power was there all the same, massed outside, indifferent, impersonal, not attending to anything in particular. Somehow it was opposed to the little hay-coloured moth. It was useless to try to do anything. One could only watch the extraordinary efforts made by those tiny legs against an oncoming doom which could, had it chosen, have submerged an entire city, not merely a city, but masses of human beings; nothing, I knew, had any chance against death. Nevertheless after a pause of exhaustion the legs fluttered again. It was superb, this last protest, and so frantic that he succeeded at last in righting himself. One's sympathies, of course, were all on the side of life. Also, when there was nobody to care or to know, this gigantic effort on the part of an insignificant little moth, against a power of such magnitude, to retain what no one else valued or desired to keep, moved one strangely. Again, somehow, one saw life, a pure bead. I lifted the pencil again, useless though I knew it to be. But even as I did so, the unmistakable tokens of death showed themselves. The body relaxed, and instantly grew stiff. The struggle was over. The insignificant little creature now knew death. As I looked at the dead moth, this minute wayside triumph of so great a force over so mean an antagonist filled me with wonder. Just as life had been strange a few minutes

5

Restatement of part of purpose/ thesis: Death's inevitability	before, so death was now as strange. The moth having righted himself now lay most decently and uncomplainingly composed. O yes, he seemed to say, death is stronger than I am.

The following answers to the questions on page 687 will help you analyze Virginia Woolf's use of the patterns of development in the essay "The Death of the Moth."

1. *What is the writer's purpose and thesis?*

Woolf's *purpose* is to show that the tiny moth's courageous but ultimately futile battle to cling to life embodies the struggle at the very heart of all existence. Woolf achieves her purpose by relating the story of the moth's efforts to resist death. Her *thesis* might be expressed this way: Although living creatures may make "extraordinary efforts" (paragraph 5) to hold onto life, these attempts aren't strong enough to defy death. Nothing, Woolf writes, has "any chance against death" (5).

Woolf's purpose and thesis first become apparent at the end of paragraph 2. There she shows that the moth, with his "frail and diminutive body," represents "nothing but life." Although "small...and simple" (3), the moth is suffused with the same extraordinary energy that is evident in the natural world beyond Woolf's window. This energy, combined with the moth's tiny size, makes the creature both "marvellous" and "pathetic" (3)—two qualities that are particularly apparent during the moth's final struggles. During those moments, the moth makes a final "superb" (5) protest against death, but ultimately the "insignificant" (5) creature—like all forms of life—must cease his valiant struggle and die.

2. *What pattern of development dominates the essay? How does this pattern help the writer support the essay's thesis and fulfill the essay's purpose?*

Although the essay's first paragraph is largely descriptive, it becomes clear by paragraph 2 that the description is in service of a larger *narrative* about the moth's struggles. It's this narrative that dominates the essay.

At the beginning, the moth is imbued with vitality, as he flies "vigorously" (paragraph 2) and with "zest" (2) from one side of the window to the other. But narrative tension begins to build in paragraph 4. There Woolf writes that the moth tries once again to cross the windowpane, fails repeatedly, and slips "onto his back," seemingly defeated. However, even then, the moth doesn't abandon his hold on life, for—as Woolf relates in paragraph 5—he tries, despite exhaustion, to right himself. Against all odds, he finally succeeds, but his frantic struggle to hold onto life takes its toll, and the tiny creature soon dies. This detailed story of the moth's futile battle against death is presented as an emblem of the fate of all life. Through this narrative, Woolf achieves her purpose and thesis: to convey the power of nature and the inability of living creatures—despite heroic efforts—to defy this power.

Paralleling the tale of the moth's struggle is another *narrative:* the story of Woolf's changing understanding of the event that unfolds before her. When the moth is "dancing" (3), energetic, and vital, Woolf "can't help watching him" (2) and feels a kind of wonderment at this "tiny bead of pure life" (3). Then in paragraph 4, Woolf writes that she forgets about the moth for a while until she happens to look up and see his "futile attempts" to "resume dancing." For a few moments, she watches the moth's "stiff" and "awkward" efforts to fly, expecting him to demonstrate the same vitality as before. Suddenly, she understands that the moth is "in difficulties" and can no longer lift himself up. She tries to help but abandons her efforts when she realizes that the moth's labored efforts signify the "approach of death." Paragraph 5 presents the final stage of Woolf's interior narrative. She looks outside her window for an explanation of the moth's plight. But now she finds that the forces of nature—earlier so exuberant and vibrant—are, if anything, "opposed to the little hay-colored moth." With that, her attention is once again drawn to the moth and the fluttering of his legs. Although drained, the tiny creature makes one last effort to resist death—and, improbably enough, picks himself up one more time. Struck by the sheer power of the moth's life force, Woolf is prompted, as before, to help the creature, even though she recognizes the futility. But then the "unmistakable" tokens of death appear, and the moth gives up his struggle, succumbing—as all forms of life must—to the forces of nature. With the moth lying "uncomplainingly composed," Woolf comes to accept that "death is stronger than life."

3. *What other patterns appear in the essay? How do these secondary patterns help the writer support the essay's thesis and fulfill the essay's purpose?*

Although the essay is predominantly a narrative, it also contains other patterns. The *descriptive* passage at the beginning of the essay includes a brief *definition by negation* in which Woolf explains how the creature she is observing differs from the usual, more colorful night moth. The rest of paragraph 1 draws upon description to evoke the sense of early autumn and nature's extraordinary energy. This description of the natural world's vibrancy and abundance, exemplified by the rooks and plowed earth, *contrasts* with Woolf's later characterization of the natural world in paragraph 5. There she writes, "Stillness and quiet. . .replaced the previous animation," and she senses not that nature fosters vitality, but that it is "indifferent, impersonal, not attending to anything in particular."

Shifting her focus in paragraph 2 from the natural world to the moth, Woolf exercises her *descriptive* powers to convey the moth's extraordinary zest as he flies across the windowpane. In this paragraph, Woolf also draws upon *comparison-contrast* to show that despite *differences* in their sizes, the tiny moth and the vast natural world embody the *same* primal energy. Woolf's consideration of this elemental similarity leads her to the basic *contrast* at the heart of the essay: While the moth's tiny size makes him "pathetic," his formidable life spirit makes him "marvellous." He may be small and lightweight, but he is abuzz with vitality. When contrasted to the enormous power of nature, the moth—like all forms of life—may be puny, but his impulse to defy such power inspires awe and reverence.

Virginia Woolf

Professions for Women

In the following speech given to the Women's Service League in 1931, Virginia Woolf uses her experience as a writer to describe the obstacles standing between women and accomplishment in their chosen fields. Those barriers, she points out, don't necessarily assume an outwardly malevolent form; often they appear in the guise of an angel.

When your secretary invited me to come here, she told me that   1
your Society is concerned with the employment of women and she suggested that I might tell you something about my own professional experiences. It is true I am a woman; it is true I am employed; but what professional experiences have I had? It is difficult to say. My profession is literature; and in that profession there are fewer experiences for women than in any other, with the exception of the stage—fewer, I mean, that are peculiar to women. For the road was cut many years ago—by Fanny Burney, by Aphra Behn, by Harriet Martineau, by Jane Austen, by George Eliot[1]—many famous women, and many more unknown and forgotten, have been before me, making the path smooth, and regulating my steps. Thus, when I came to write, there were very few material obstacles in my way. Writing was a reputable and harmless occupation. The family peace was not broken by the scratching of a pen. No demand was made upon the family purse. For ten and sixpence one can buy paper enough to write all the plays of Shakespeare—if one has a mind that way. Pianos and models, Paris, Vienna and Berlin, masters and mistresses, are not needed by a writer. The cheapness of writing paper is, of course, the reason why women have succeeded as writers before they have succeeded in the other professions.

[1]Fanny Burney (1752–1840), Aphra Behn (1640–89), Harriet Martineau (1802–76), Jane Austen (1775–1817), and Marian Evans (1819–80), whose pen name was George Eliot, were all English women of letters.

But to tell you my story—it is a simple one. You have only got   2
to figure to yourselves a girl in a bedroom with a pen in her hand.
She had only to move that pen from left to right—from ten o'clock
to one. Then it occurred to her to do what is simple and cheap
enough after all—to slip a few of those pages into an envelope, fix a
penny stamp in the corner, and drop the envelope into the red box
at the corner. It was thus that I became a journalist; and my effort
was rewarded on the first day of the following month—a very glorious day it was for me—by a letter from an editor containing a cheque
for one pound ten shillings and sixpence. But to show you how little
I deserve to be called a professional woman, how little I know of the
struggles and difficulties of such lives, I have to admit that instead of
spending that sum upon bread and butter, rent, shoes and stockings,
or butcher's bills, I went out and bought a cat—a beautiful cat, a Persian cat, which very soon involved me in bitter disputes with my
neighbors.

What could be easier than to write articles and to buy Persian   3
cats with the profits? But wait a moment. Articles have to be about
something. Mine, I seem to remember, was about a novel by a famous man. And while I was writing this review, I discovered that if I
were going to review books I should need to do battle with a certain
phantom. And the phantom was a woman, and when I came to know
her better I called her after the heroine of a famous poem, "The Angel in the House." It was she who used to come between me and my
paper when I was writing reviews. It was she who bothered me and
wasted my time and so tormented me that at last I killed her. You
who come of a younger and happier generation may not have heard
of her—you may not know what I mean by the Angel in the House.
I will describe her as shortly as I can. She was intensely sympathetic.
She was immensely charming. She was utterly unselfish. She excelled
in the difficult arts of family life. She sacrificed herself daily. If there
was chicken, she took the leg; if there was a draught she sat in it—in
short she was so constituted that she never had a mind or a wish of
her own, but preferred to sympathize always with the minds and
wishes of others. Above all—I need not say it—she was pure. Her purity was supposed to be her chief beauty—her blushes, her great
grace. In those days—the last of Queen Victoria—every house had
its Angel. And when I came to write I encountered her with the very
first words. The shadow of her wings fell on my page; I heard the rustling of her skirts in the room. Directly, that is to say, I took my pen

in hand to review that novel by a famous man, she slipped behind me and whispered: "My dear, you are a young woman. You are writing about a book that has been written by a man. Be sympathetic; be tender; flatter; deceive; use all the arts and wiles of our sex. Never let anybody guess that you have a mind of your own. Above all, be pure." And she made as if to guide my pen. I now record the one act for which I take some credit to myself, though the credit rightly belongs to some excellent ancestors of mine who left me a certain sum of money—shall we say five hundred pounds a year?—so that it was not necessary for me to depend solely on charm for my living. I turned upon her and caught her by the throat. I did my best to kill her. My excuse, if I were to be had up in a court of law, would be that I acted in self-defence. Had I not killed her she would have killed me. She would have plucked the heart out of my writing. For, as I found, directly I put pen to paper, you cannot review even a novel without having a mind of your own, without expressing what you think to be the truth about human relations, morality, sex. And all these questions, according to the Angel in the House, cannot be dealt with freely and openly by women; they must charm, they must conciliate, they must—to put it bluntly—tell lies if they are to succeed. Thus, whenever I felt the shadow of her wing or the radiance of her halo upon my page, I took up the inkpot and flung it at her. She died hard. Her fictitious nature was of great assistance to her. It is far harder to kill a phantom than a reality. She was always creeping back when I thought I had despatched her. Though I flatter myself that I killed her in the end, the struggle was severe; it took much time that had better have been spent upon learning Greek grammar; or in roaming the world in search of adventures. But it was a real experience; it was an experience that was bound to befall all women writers at that time. Killing the Angel in the House was part of the occupation of a woman writer.

But to continue my story. The Angel was dead; what then remained? You may say that what remained was a simple and common object—a young woman in a bedroom with an inkpot. In other words, now that she had rid herself of falsehood, that young woman had only to be herself. Ah, but what is "herself"? I mean, what is a woman? I assure you, I do not know. I do not believe that you know. I do not believe that anybody can know until she has expressed herself in all the arts and professions open to human skill. That indeed is one of the reasons why I have come here—out of respect for you, who are in process of showing us by your experiments what a woman is, who are in process of providing us, by your failures and successes, with that extremely important piece of information.

But to continue the story of my professional experiences. I 5 made one pound ten and six by my first review; and I bought a Persian cat with the proceeds. Then I grew ambitious. A Persian cat is all very well, I said; but a Persian cat is not enough. I must have a motor car. And it was thus that I became a novelist—for it is a very strange thing that people will give you a motor car if you will tell them a story. It is a still stranger thing that there is nothing so delightful in the world as telling stories. It is far pleasanter than writing reviews of famous novels. And yet, if I am to obey your secretary and tell you my professional experiences as a novelist, I must tell you about a very strange experience that befell me as a novelist. And to understand it you must try first to imagine a novelist's state of mind. I hope I am not giving away professional secrets if I say that a novelist's chief desire is to be as unconscious as possible. He has to induce in himself a state of perpetual lethargy. He wants life to proceed with the utmost quiet and regularity. He wants to see the same faces, to read the same books, to do the same things day after day, month after month, while he is writing, so that nothing may break the illusion in which he is living—so that nothing may disturb or disquiet the mysterious nosings about, feelings round, darts, dashes and sudden discoveries of that very shy and illusive spirit, the imagination. I suspect that this state is the same both for men and women. Be that as it may, I want you to imagine me writing a novel in a state of trance. I want you to figure to yourself a girl sitting with a pen in her hand, which for minutes, and indeed for hours, she never dips into the inkpot. The image that comes to my mind when I think of this girl is the image of a fisherman lying sunk in dreams on the verge of a deep lake with a rod held out over the water. She was letting her imagination sweep unchecked round every rock and cranny of the world that lies submerged in the depths of our unconscious being. Now came the experience, the experience that I believe to be far commoner with women writers than with men. The line raced through the girl's fingers. Her imagination had rushed away. It had sought the pools, the depths, the dark places where the largest fish slumber. And then there was a smash. There was an explosion. There was foam and confusion. The imagination had dashed itself against something hard.

The girl was roused from her dream. She was indeed in a state of the most acute and difficult distress. To speak without figure she had thought of something, something about the body, about the passions which it was unfitting for her as a woman to say. Men, her reason told her, would be shocked. The consciousness of what men will say of a woman who speaks the truth about her passions had roused her from her artist's state of unconsciousness. She could write no more. The trance was over. Her imagination could work no longer. This I believe to be a very common experience with women writers— they are impeded by the extreme conventionality of the other sex. For though men sensibly allow themselves great freedom in these respects, I doubt that they realize or can control the extreme severity with which they condemn such freedom in women.

These then were two very genuine experiences of my own. 6 These were two of the adventures of my professional life. The first— killing the Angel in the House—I think I solved. She died. But the second, telling the truth about my own experiences as a body, I do not think I solved. I doubt that any woman has solved it yet. The obstacles against her are still immensely powerful—and yet they are very difficult to define. Outwardly, what is simpler than to write books? Outwardly, what obstacles are there for a woman rather than for a man? Inwardly, I think, the case is very different: she has still many ghosts to fight, many prejudices to overcome. Indeed it will be a long time still, I think, before a woman can sit down to write a book without finding a phantom to be slain, a rock to be dashed against. And if this is so in literature, the freest of all professions for women, how is it in the new professions which you are now for the first time entering?

Those are the questions that I should like, had I time, to ask 7 you. And indeed, if I have laid stress upon these professional experiences of mine, it is because I believe that they are, though in different forms, yours also. Even when the path is nominally open—when there is nothing to prevent a woman from being a doctor, a lawyer, a civil servant—there are many phantoms and obstacles, as I believe, looming in her way. To discuss and define them is, I think, of great value and importance; for thus only can the labour be shared, the difficulties be solved. But besides this, it is necessary also to discuss the ends and the aims for which we are fighting, for which we are doing battle with these formidable obstacles. Those aims cannot be taken for granted; they must be perpetually questioned and examined. The whole position, as I see it—here in this hall surrounded by women practicing for the first time in history I know not how many different professions—is one of extraordinary interest and importance. You have won rooms of your own in the house hitherto exclusively owned by men. You are able, though not without great labor and effort, to pay the rent. You are earning your five hundred pounds a year. But this freedom is only a beginning; the room is your own, but it is still bare. It has to be furnished; it has to be decorated; it has to be shared. How are you going to furnish it, how are you going to decorate it? With whom are you going to share it, and upon what terms? These, I think, are questions of the utmost importance and interest. For the first time in history you are able to ask them; for the first time you are able to decide for yourselves what the answers should be. Willingly would I stay and discuss those questions and answers—but not tonight. My time is up; and I must cease.

Martin Luther King, Jr.

More than a quarter of a century after his assassination, Martin Luther King, Jr. (1929–68), is still recognized as the towering figure in the struggle for civil rights in America. Born in Atlanta, Georgia, King earned doctorates from Boston University and Chicago Theological Seminary and served as pastor of a Baptist congregation in Montgomery, Alabama. Advocating a philosophy of nonviolent resistance to racial injustice, he led bus boycotts, marches, and sit-ins that brought about passage of the 1964 Civil Rights Act and the Voting Rights Act of 1965. Dr. King was awarded the Nobel Peace Prize in 1964. The following two selections by King are taken from *Where Do We Go From Here: Community or Chaos?* (1967).

Where Do We Go From Here: Community or Chaos?

Political leaders present convincing arguments for military aggression. They advocate supplying weapons to countries that are fighting communism; they urge the stockpiling of deadly warheads as a defense strategy; they argue for the funding of nuclear missiles euphemistically called "peace-keepers." But to Dr. King the belief that war can lead to peace is absurd. In this essay, he maintains that only nonviolent methods can bring stability and peace to a troubled world.

A final problem that mankind must solve in order to survive in the world house that we have inherited is finding an alternative to war and human destruction. Recent events have vividly reminded us that nations are not reducing but rather increasing their arsenals of weapons of mass destruction. The best brains in the highly developed nations of the world are devoted to military technology. The proliferation of nuclear weapons has not been halted, in spite of the limited-test-ban treaty.

1

In this day of man's highest technical achievement, in this day   2
of dazzling discovery, of novel opportunities, loftier dignities and
fuller freedoms for all, there is no excuse for the kind of blind craving
for power and resources that provoked the wars of previous generations. There is no need to fight for food and land. Science has provided us with adequate means of survival and transportation, which
make it possible to enjoy the fullness of this great earth. The question
now is, do we have the morality and courage required to live together as brothers and not be afraid?

One of the most persistent ambiguities we face is that everybody   3
talks about peace as a goal, but among the wielders of power peace
is practically nobody's business. Many men cry "Peace! Peace!" but
they refuse to do the things that make for peace.

The large power blocs talk passionately of pursuing peace while   4
expanding defense budgets that already bulge, enlarging already
awesome armies and devising ever more devastating weapons. Call
the roll of those who sing the glad tidings of peace and one's ears will
be surprised by the responding sounds. The heads of all the nations
issue clarion calls for peace, yet they come to the peace table accompanied by bands of brigands each bearing unsheathed swords.

The stages of history are replete with the chants and choruses of   5
the conquerors of old who came killing in pursuit of peace. Alexander, Genghis Khan, Julius Caesar, Charlemagne and Napoleon
were akin in seeking a peaceful world order, a world fashioned after
their selfish conceptions of an ideal existence. Each sought a world at
peace which would personify his egotistic dreams. Even within the
life span of most of us, another megalomaniac strode across the
world stage. He sent his blitzkrieg-bent legions blazing across Europe, bringing havoc and holocaust in his wake. There is grave irony
in the fact that Hitler could come forth, following nakedly aggressive
expansionist theories, and do it all in the name of peace.

So when in this day I see the leaders of nations again talking   6
peace while preparing for war, I take fearful pause. When I see our
country today intervening in what is basically a civil war, mutilating
hundreds of thousands of Vietnamese children with napalm, burning
villages and rice fields at random, painting the valleys of that small
Asian country red with human blood, leaving broken bodies in
countless ditches and sending home half-men, mutilated mentally
and physically; when I see the unwillingness of our government to

create the atmosphere for a negotiated settlement of this awful conflict by halting bombings in the North and agreeing unequivocally to talk with the Vietcong—and all this in the name of pursuing the goal of peace—I tremble for our world.[1] I do so not only from dire recall of the nightmares wreaked in the wars of yesterday, but also from dreadful realization of today's possible nuclear destructiveness and tomorrow's even more calamitous prospects.

Before it is too late, we must narrow the gaping chasm between   7
our proclamations of peace and our lowly deeds which precipitate and perpetuate war. We are called upon to look up from the quagmire of military programs and defense commitments and read the warnings on history's signposts.

One day we must come to see that peace is not merely a distant   8
goal that we seek but a means by which we arrive at that goal. We must pursue peaceful ends through peaceful means. How much longer must we play at deadly war games before we heed the plaintive pleas of the unnumbered dead and maimed of past wars?

President John F. Kennedy said on one occasion, "Mankind   9
must put an end to war or war will put an end to mankind." Wisdom born of experience should tell us that war is obsolete. There may have been a time when war served as a negative good by preventing the spread and growth of an evil force, but the destructive power of modern weapons eliminates even the possibility that war may serve any good at all. If we assume that life is worth living and that man has a right to survive, then we must find an alternative to war. In a day when vehicles hurtle through outer space and guided ballistic missiles carve highways of death through the stratosphere, no nation can claim victory in war. A so-called limited war will leave little more than a calamitous legacy of human suffering, political turmoil and spiritual disillusionment. A world war will leave only smoldering ashes as mute testimony of a human race whose folly led inexorably to ultimate death. If modern man continues to flirt unhesitatingly with war, he will transform his earthly habitat into an inferno such as even the mind of Dante[2] could not imagine.

---

[1] Only after more than 58,000 Americans had been killed did the United States withdraw from Vietnam. The war then continued until the North Vietnamese, aided by the Vietcong, took over all of Vietnam.

[2] In *The Divine Comedy* (1321), Italian poet Dante depicts the burning torments of hell endured by a lost soul before it can attain salvation.

Therefore I suggest that the philosophy and strategy of non-   10
violence become immediately a subject for study and for serious experimentation in every field of human conflict, by no means exclud-
ing the relations between nations. It is, after all, nation-states which
make war, which have produced the weapons that threaten the
survival of mankind and which are both genocidal and suicidal in
character.

We have ancient habits to deal with, vast structures of power, in-   11
describably complicated problems to solve. But unless we abdicate
our humanity altogether and succumb to fear and impotence in the
presence of the weapons we have ourselves created, it is as possible
and as urgent to put an end to war and violence between nations as
it is to put an end to poverty and racial injustice.

The United Nations is a gesture in the direction of nonviolence   12
on a world scale. There, at least, states that oppose one another have
sought to do so with words instead of with weapons. But true nonviolence is more than the absence of violence. It is the persistent and
determined application of peaceable power to offenses against the
community—in this case the world community. As the United Nations moves ahead with the giant tasks confronting it, I would hope
that it would earnestly examine the uses of nonviolent direct action.

I do not minimize the complexity of the problems that need to   13
be faced in achieving disarmament and peace. But I am convinced
that we shall not have the will, the courage and the insight to deal
with such matters unless in this field we are prepared to undergo a
mental and spiritual re-evaluation, a change of focus which will enable us to see that the things that seem most real and powerful are
indeed now unreal and have come under sentence of death. We need
to make a supreme effort to generate the readiness, indeed the eager-
ness, to enter into the new world which is now possible, "the city
which hath foundation, whose Building and Maker is God."

It is not enough to say, "We must not wage war." It is necessary   14
to love peace and sacrifice for it. We must concentrate not merely on
the eradication of war but on the affirmation of peace. A fascinating
story about Ulysses and the Sirens[3] is preserved for us in Greek literature. The Sirens had the ability to sing so sweetly that sailors could

---

[3]Ulysses and the Sirens, as well as Orpheus (mentioned later in the paragraph), are all
figures in Greek mythology.

not resist steering toward their island. Many ships were lured upon the rocks, and men forgot home, duty and honor as they flung themselves into the sea to be embraced by arms that drew them down to death. Ulysses, determined not to succumb to the Sirens, first decided to tie himself tightly to the mast of his boat and his crew stuffed their ears with wax. But finally he and his crew learned a better way to save themselves: They took on board the beautiful singer Orpheus, whose melodies were sweeter than the music of the Sirens. When Orpheus sang, who would bother to listen to the Sirens?

So we must see that peace represents a sweeter music, a cosmic 15 melody that is far superior to the discords of war. Somehow we must transform the dynamics of the world power struggle from the nuclear arms race, which no one can win, to a creative contest to harness man's genius for the purpose of making peace and prosperity a reality for all the nations of the world. In short, we must shift the arms race into a "peace race." If we have the will and determination to mount such a peace offensive, we will unlock hitherto tightly sealed doors of hope and bring new light into the dark chambers of pessimism.

Martin Luther King, Jr.

The World House

We live in an age of technological marvels. We travel from continent to continent at unheard-of speed; we communicate instantaneously with one another across thousands of miles; we can barely remember the names of now-conquered diseases that once devastated entire communities. But what of our moral development? Has our tolerance for diversity, our love for fellow human beings, our concern for the welfare of others kept pace with our scientific progress? We have much work still to do, as Martin Luther King, Jr., explains with stirring eloquence.

Some years ago a famous novelist died. Among his papers was 1 found a list of suggested plots for future stories, the most prominently underscored being this one: "A widely separated family inherits a house in which they have to live together." This is the great new problem of mankind. We have inherited a large house, a great "world house" in which we have to live together—black and white, Easterner and Westerner, Gentile and Jew, Catholic and Protestant, Moslem and Hindu—a family unduly separated in ideas, culture and interest, who, because we can never again live apart, must learn somehow to live with each other in peace.

However deeply American Negroes are caught in the struggle to 2 be at last at home in our homeland of the United States, we cannot ignore the larger world house in which we are also dwellers. Equality with whites will not solve the problems of either whites or Negroes if it means equality in a world society stricken by poverty and in a universe doomed to extinction by war.

All inhabitants of the globe are now neighbors. This worldwide 3 neighborhood has been brought into being largely as a result of the modern scientific and technological revolutions. The world of today is vastly different from the world of just one hundred years ago. A century ago Thomas Edison had not yet invented the incandescent lamp to bring light to many dark places of the earth. The Wright brothers had not yet invented that fascinating mechanical bird that would spread its gigantic wings across the skies and soon dwarf distance and place time in the service of man. Einstein had not yet challenged an axiom and the theory of relativity had not yet been posited.

Human beings, searching a century ago as now for better understanding, had no television, no radios, no telephones and no motion pictures through which to communicate. Medical science had not yet discovered the wonder drugs to end many dread plagues and diseases. One hundred years ago military men had not yet developed the terrifying weapons of warfare that we know today—not the bomber, an airborne fortress raining down death; nor napalm, that burner of all things and flesh in its path. A century ago there were no skyscraping buildings to kiss the stars and no gargantuan bridges to span the waters. Science had not yet peered into the unfathomable ranges of interstellar space, nor had it penetrated oceanic depths. All these new inventions, these new ideas, these sometimes fascinating and sometimes frightening developments came later. Most of them have come within the past sixty years, sometimes with agonizing slowness, more characteristically with bewildering speed, but always with enormous significance for our future.

The years ahead will see a continuation of the same dramatic developments. Physical science will carve new highways through the stratosphere. In a few years astronauts and cosmonauts will probably walk comfortably across the uncertain pathways of the moon. In two or three years it will be possible, because of the new supersonic jets, to fly from New York to London in two and one-half hours. In the years ahead medical science will greatly prolong the lives of men by finding a cure for cancer and deadly heart ailments. Automation and cybernation will make it possible for working people to have undreamed-of amounts of leisure time. All this is a dazzling picture of the furniture, the workshop, the spacious rooms, the new decorations and the architectural pattern of the large world house in which we are living.

Along with the scientific and technological revolution, we have also witnessed a worldwide freedom revolution over the last few decades. The present upsurge of the Negro people of the United States grows out of a deep and passionate determination to make freedom and equality a reality "here" and "now." In one sense the civil rights movement in the United States is a special American phenomenon which must be understood in the light of American history and dealt with in terms of the American situation. But on another and more important level, what is happening in the United States today is a significant part of a world development.

We live in a day, said the philosopher Alfred North Whitehead, 7 "when civilization is shifting its basic outlook; a major turning point in history where the presuppositions on which society is structured are being analyzed, sharply challenged, and profoundly changed." What we are seeing now is a freedom explosion, the realization of "an idea whose time has come," to use Victor Hugo's[1] phrase. The deep rumbling of discontent that we hear today is the thunder of disinherited masses, rising from dungeons of oppression to the bright hills of freedom. In one majestic chorus the rising masses are singing, in the words of our freedom song, "Ain't gonna let nobody turn us around." All over the world like a fever, freedom is spreading in the widest liberation movement in history. The great masses of people are determined to end the exploitation of their races and lands. They are awake and moving toward their goal like a tidal wave. You can hear them rumbling in every village street, on the docks, in the houses, among the students, in the churches and at political meetings. For several centuries the direction of history flowed from the nations and societies of Western Europe out into the rest of the world in "conquests" of various sorts. That period, the era of colonialism, is at an end. East is moving West. The earth is being redistributed. Yes, we are "shifting our basic outlooks."

These developments should not surprise any student of history. 8 Oppressed people cannot remain oppressed forever. The yearning for freedom eventually manifests itself. The Bible tells the thrilling story of how Moses stood in Pharaoh's court centuries ago and cried, "Let my people go." This was an opening chapter in a continuing story. The present struggle in the United States is a later chapter in the same story. Something within has reminded the Negro of his birthright of freedom, and something without has reminded him that it can be gained. Consciously or unconsciously, he has been caught up by the spirit of the times, and with his black brothers of Africa and his brown and yellow brothers in Asia, South America and the Caribbean, the United States Negro is moving with a sense of great urgency toward the promised land of racial justice.

[1]French poet, dramatist, and novelist (1802–85).

Nothing could be more tragic than for men to live in these rev-   9
olutionary times and fail to achieve the new attitudes and the new
mental outlooks that the new situation demands. In Washington Irv-
ing's familiar story of Rip Van Winkle, the one thing that we usually
remember is that Rip slept twenty years. There is another important
point, however, that is almost always overlooked. It was the sign on
the inn in the little town on the Hudson from which Rip departed
and scaled the mountain for his long sleep. When he went up, the
sign had a picture of King George III of England. When he came
down, twenty years later, the sign had a picture of George Washington. As he looked at the picture of the first President of the United
States, Rip was confused, flustered and lost. He knew not who Washington was. The most striking thing about this story is not that Rip
slept twenty years, but that he slept through a revolution that would
alter the course of human history.

One of the great liabilities of history is that all too many people   10
fail to remain awake through great periods of social change. Every society has its protectors of the status quo and its fraternities of the indifferent who are notorious for sleeping through revolutions. But
today our very survival depends on our ability to stay awake, to adjust
to new ideas, to remain vigilant and to face the challenge of change.
The large house in which we live demands that we transform this
worldwide neighborhood into a worldwide brotherhood. Together
we must learn to live as brothers or together we will be forced to perish as fools.

We must work passionately and indefatigably to bridge the gulf   11
between our scientific progress and our moral progress. One of the
great problems of mankind is that we suffer from a poverty of the
spirit which stands in glaring contrast to our scientific and technological abundance. The richer we have become materially, the poorer
we have become morally and spiritually.

Every man lives in two realms, the internal and the external. The   12
internal is that realm of spiritual ends expressed in art, literature,
morals, and religion. The external is that complex of devices, techniques, mechanisms, and instrumentalities by means of which we
live. Our problem today is that we have allowed the internal to become lost in the external. We have allowed the means by which we
live to outdistance the ends for which we live. So much of modern
life can be summarized in that suggestive phrase of Thoreau[2]: "Im-

[2]American philosopher and essayist (1817–62).

proved means to an unimproved end." This is the serious predicament, the deep and haunting problem, confronting modern man. Enlarged material powers spell enlarged peril if there is not proportionate growth of the soul. When the external of man's nature subjugates the internal, dark storm clouds begin to form.

Western civilization is particularly vulnerable at this moment, 13
for our material abundance has brought us neither peace of mind nor serenity of spirit. An Asian writer has portrayed our dilemma in candid terms:

> You call your thousand material devices "labor-saving machinery," yet you are forever "busy." With the multiplying of your machinery you grow increasingly fatigued, anxious, nervous, dissatisfied. Whatever you have, you want more; and wherever you are you want to go somewhere else...your devices are neither time-saving nor soul-saving machinery. They are so many sharp spurs which urge you on to invent more machinery and to do more business.

This tells us something about our civilization that cannot be cast 14
aside as a prejudiced charge by an Eastern thinker who is jealous of Western prosperity. We cannot escape the indictment.

This does not mean that we must turn back the clock of scien- 15
tific progress. No one can overlook the wonders that science has wrought for our lives. The automobile will not abdicate in favor of the horse and buggy, or the train in favor of the stagecoach, or the tractor in favor of the hand plow, or the scientific method in favor of ignorance and superstition. But our moral and spiritual "lag" must be redeemed. When scientific power outruns moral power, we end up with guided missiles and misguided men. When we foolishly minimize the internal of our lives and maximize the external, we sign the warrant for our own day of doom.

Our hope for creative living in this world house that we have in- 16
herited lies in our ability to reestablish the moral ends of our lives in personal character and social justice. Without this spiritual and moral reawakening we shall destroy ourselves in the misuse of our own instruments.

Joan Didion

Known for her taut prose style and sharp social commentary, Joan Didion (1934–   ) graduated from the University of California at Berkeley. Her essays have appeared in the *Saturday Evening Post,* the *American Scholar,* and the *National Review,* as well as in three collections: *Slouching Towards Bethlehem* (1969), *The White Album* (1979), and *After Henry* (1992). *Salvador* (1983) is a book-length essay about a 1982 visit to Central America. The coauthor of several screenplays, Didion has also written novels, including *Run River* (1963), *Play It as It Lays* (1971), *A Book of Common Prayer* (1977), and *Democracy* (1984). The two selections that follow are from *The White Album.*

In Bed

Perhaps you're skeptical of people who take to bed with a bad headache, or maybe you use the term *migraine* to describe your own occasional discomfort. If so, reading this essay will probably put you in your place. A chronic migraine sufferer since childhood, Joan Didion frequently falls victim to bouts of debilitating pain. Brace yourself for some excruciating details; you'll never use the word *migraine* loosely again.

Three, four, sometimes five times a month, I spend the day in   1
bed with a migraine headache, insensible to the world around me. Almost every day of every month, between these attacks, I feel the sudden irrational irritation and flush of blood into the cerebral arteries which tell me that migraine is on its way, and I take certain drugs to avert its arrival. If I did not take the drugs, I would be able to function perhaps one day in four. The physiological error called migraine is, in brief, central to the given of my life. When I was fifteen, sixteen, even twenty-five, I used to think that I could rid myself of this error by simply denying it, character over chemistry. "Do you have headaches *sometimes? frequently? never?*" the application forms would

demand. "Check one." Wary of the trap, wanting whatever it was that the successful circumnavigation of that particular form could bring (a job, a scholarship, the respect of mankind and the grace of God), I would check one. *"Sometimes,"* I would lie. That in fact I spent one or two days a week almost unconscious with pain seemed a shameful secret, evidence not merely of some chemical inferiority but of all my bad attitudes, unpleasant tempers, wrongthink.

For I had no brain tumor, no eyestrain, no high blood pressure, nothing wrong with me at all: I simply had migraine headaches, and migraine headaches were, as everyone who did not have them knew, imaginary. I fought migraine then, ignored the warnings it sent, went to school and later to work in spite of it, sat through lectures in Middle English and presentations to advertisers with involuntary tears running down the right side of my face, threw up in washrooms, stumbled home by instinct, emptied ice trays onto my bed and tried to freeze the pain in my right temple, wished only for a neurosurgeon who would do a lobotomy on house call, and cursed my imagination.

It was a long time before I began thinking mechanistically enough to accept migraine for what it was: something with which I would be living, the way some people live with diabetes. Migraine is something more than the fancy of a neurotic imagination. It is an essentially hereditary complex of symptoms, the most frequently noted but by no means the most unpleasant of which is a vascular headache of blinding severity, suffered by a surprising number of women, a fair number of men (Thomas Jefferson had migraine, and so did Ulysses S. Grant, the day he accepted Lee's surrender), and by some unfortunate children as young as two years old. (I had my first when I was eight. It came on during a fire drill at the Columbia School in Colorado Springs, Colorado. I was taken first home and then to the infirmary at Peterson Field, where my father was stationed. The Air Corps doctor prescribed an enema.) Almost anything can trigger a specific attack of migraine: stress, allergy, fatigue, an abrupt change in barometric pressure, a contretemps over a parking ticket. A flashing light. A fire drill. One inherits, of course, only the predisposition. In other words I spent yesterday in bed with a headache not merely because of my bad attitudes, unpleasant tempers, and wrongthink, but because both my grandmothers had migraine, my father has migraine, and my mother has migraine.

No one knows precisely what it is that is inherited. The chemistry of migraine, however, seems to have some connection with the nerve hormone named serotonin, which is naturally present in the brain. The amount of serotonin in the blood falls sharply at the onset of migraine, and one migraine drug, methysergide, or Sansert, seems to have some effect on serotonin. Methysergide is a derivative of lysergic acid (in fact Sandoz Pharmaceuticals first synthesized LSD-25 while looking for a migraine cure), and its use is hemmed about with so many contraindications and side effects that most doctors prescribe it only in the most incapacitating cases. Methysergide, when it is prescribed, is taken daily, as a preventive; another preventive which works for some people is old-fashioned ergotamine tartrate, which helps to constrict the swelling blood vessels during the "aura," the period which in most cases precedes the actual headache.

Once an attack is under way, however, no drug touches it. Migraine gives some people mild hallucinations, temporarily blinds others, shows up not only as a headache but as a gastrointestinal disturbance, a painful sensitivity to all sensory stimuli, an abrupt overpowering fatigue, a strokelike aphasia, and a crippling inability to make even the most routine connections. When I am in a migraine aura (for some people the aura lasts fifteen minutes, for others several hours), I will drive through red lights, lose the house keys, spill whatever I am holding, lose the ability to focus my eyes or frame coherent sentences, and generally give the appearance of being on drugs, or drunk. The actual headache, when it comes, brings with it chills, sweating, nausea, a debility that seems to stretch the very limits of endurance. That no one dies of migraine seems, to someone deep into an attack, an ambiguous blessing.

My husband also has migraine, which is unfortunate for him but fortunate for me: perhaps nothing so tends to prolong an attack as the accusing eye of someone who has never had a headache. "Why not take a couple of aspirin," the unafflicted will say from the doorway, or "I'd have a headache, too, spending a beautiful day like this inside with all the shades drawn." All of us who have migraine suffer not only from the attacks themselves but from this common conviction that we are perversely refusing to cure ourselves by taking a couple of aspirin, that we are making ourselves sick, that we "bring it on ourselves." And in the most immediate sense, the sense of why we have a headache this Tuesday and not last Thursday, of course we often do. There certainly is what doctors call a "migraine personality," and that personality tends to be ambitious, inward, intolerant of error, rather rigidly organized, perfectionist. "You don't look like a migraine personality," a doctor once said to me. "Your hair's messy. But I suppose you're a compulsive housekeeper." Actually my house is kept even more negligently than my hair, but the doctor was right nonetheless: perfectionism can also take the form of spending most of a week writing and rewriting and not writing a single paragraph.

But not all perfectionists have migraine, and not all migrainous people have migraine personalities. We do not escape heredity. I have tried in most of the available ways to escape my own migrainous heredity (at one point I learned to give myself two daily injections of histamine with a hypodermic needle, even though the needle so frightened me that I had to close my eyes when I did it), but I still have migraine. And I have learned now to live with it, learned when to expect it, how to outwit it, even how to regard it, when it does come, as more friend than lodger. We have reached a certain understanding, my migraine and I. It never comes when I am in real trouble. Tell me that my house is burned down, my husband has left me, that there is gunfighting in the streets and panic in the banks, and I will not respond by getting a headache. It comes instead when I am fighting not an open but a guerrilla war with my own life, during weeks of small household confusions, lost laundry, unhappy help, canceled appointments, on days when the telephone rings too much and I get no work done and the wind is coming up. On days like that my friend comes uninvited. 7

And once it comes, now that I am wise in its ways, I no longer fight it. I lie down and let it happen. At first every small apprehension is magnified, every anxiety a pounding terror. Then the pain comes, and I concentrate only on that. Right there is the usefulness of migraine, there in that imposed yoga, the concentration on the pain. For when the pain recedes, ten or twelve hours later, everything goes with it, all the hidden resentments, all the vain anxieties. The migraine has acted as a circuit breaker, and the fuses have emerged intact. There is a pleasant convalescent euphoria. I open the windows and feel the air, eat gratefully, sleep well. I notice the particular nature of a flower in a glass on the stair landing. I count my blessings. 8

Joan Didion

On Self-Respect

What determines how we feel about ourselves? Is it our ability to land the right job, achieve the right look, be accepted by the right people? For Joan Didion, self-respect is none of these things. It's what happens in the still hours of the morning when we lie alone in bed with no one but ourselves for company. Then, during those moments of self-reckoning, we discover whether we have the "toughness and...moral nerve" that's at the heart of self-respect.

Once, in a dry season, I wrote in large letters across two pages of a notebook that innocence ends when one is stripped of the delusion that one likes oneself. Although now, some years later, I marvel that a mind on the outs with itself should have nonetheless made painstaking record of its every tremor, I recall with embarrassing clarity the flavor of those particular ashes. It was a matter of misplaced self-respect.

I had not been elected to Phi Beta Kappa.[1] This failure could scarcely have been more predictable or less ambiguous (I simply did not have the grades), but I was unnerved by it; I had somehow thought myself a kind of academic Raskolnikov,[2] curiously exempt from the cause-effect relationships which hampered others. Although even the humorless nineteen-year-old that I was must have recognized that the situation lacked real tragic stature, the day that I did not make Phi Beta Kappa nonetheless marked the end of something, and innocence may well be the word for it. I lost the conviction that lights would always turn green for me, the pleasant certainty that those rather passive virtues which had won me approval as a child automatically guaranteed me not only Phi Beta Kappa keys but happiness, honor, and the love of a good man; lost a certain touching

---

[1] An honorary society of college students with records of high academic achievement.

[2] In Dostoyevsky's *Crime and Punishment* (1866), Raskolnikov deliberately sets out to commit murder to show that he is exempt from conventional moral codes. However, he is subsequently plagued by guilt and remorse.

faith in the totem power of good manners, clean hair, and proven competence on the Stanford-Binet scale.[3] To such doubtful amulets had my self-respect been pinned, and I faced myself that day with the nonplused apprehension of someone who has come across a vampire and has no crucifix at hand.

Although to be driven back upon oneself is an uneasy affair at best, rather like trying to cross a border with borrowed credentials, it seems to me now the one condition necessary to the beginnings of real self-respect. Most of our platitudes notwithstanding, self-deception remains the most difficult deception. The tricks that work on others count for nothing in that very well-lit back alley where one keeps assignations with oneself: no winning smiles will do here, no prettily drawn lists of good intentions. One shuffles flashily but in vain through one's marked cards—the kindness done for the wrong reason, the apparent triumph which involved no real effort, the seemingly heroic act into which one had been shamed. The dismal fact is that self-respect has nothing to do with the approval of others—who are, after all, deceived easily enough; has nothing to do with reputation, which, as Rhett Butler told Scarlett O'Hara, is something people with courage can do without.   3

To do without self-respect, on the other hand, is to be an unwilling audience of one to an interminable documentary that details one's failings, both real and imagined, with fresh footage spliced in for every screening. *There's the glass you broke in anger, there's the hurt on X's face; watch now, this next scene, the night Y came back from Houston, see how you muff this one.* To live without self-respect is to lie awake some night, beyond the reach of warm milk, phenobarbital, and the sleeping hand on the coverlet, counting up the sins of commission and omission, the trusts betrayed, the promises subtly broken, the gifts irrevocably wasted through sloth or cowardice or carelessness. However long we postpone it, we eventually lie down alone in that notoriously uncomfortable bed, the one we make ourselves. Whether or not we sleep in it depends, of course, on whether or not we respect ourselves.   4

To protest that some fairly improbable people, some people who *could not possibly respect themselves,* seem to sleep easily enough is to miss the point entirely, as surely as those people miss it who think   5

---

[3]A test designed to measure intelligence.

that self-respect has necessarily to do with not having safety pins in one's underwear. There is a common superstition that "self-respect" is a kind of charm against snakes, something that keeps those who have it locked in some unblighted Eden, out of strange beds, ambivalent conversations, and trouble in general. It does not at all. It has nothing to do with the face of things, but concerns instead a separate peace, a private reconciliation. Although the careless, suicidal Julian English in *Appointment in Samarra*[4] and the careless, incurably dishonest Jordan Baker in *The Great Gatsby*[5] seem equally improbable candidates for self-respect, Jordan Baker had it, Julian English did not. With that genius for accommodation more often seen in women than in men, Jordan took her own measure, made her own peace, avoided threats to that peace: "I hate careless people," she told Nick Carraway.[6] "It takes two to make an accident."

Like Jordan Baker, people with self-respect have the courage of their mistakes. They know the price of things. If they choose to commit adultery, they do not then go running, in an excess of bad conscience, to receive absolution from the wronged parties; nor do they complain unduly of the unfairness, the undeserved embarrassment, of being named corespondent. In brief, people with self-respect exhibit a certain toughness, a kind of moral nerve; they display what was once called *character*, a quality which, although approved in the abstract, sometimes loses ground to other, more instantly negotiable virtues. The measure of its slipping prestige is that one tends to think of it only in connection with homely children and United States senators who have been defeated, preferably in the primary, for reelection. Nonetheless, character—the willingness to accept responsibility for one's own life—is the source from which self-respect springs.

Self-respect is something that our grandparents, whether or not they had it, knew all about. They had instilled in them, young, a certain discipline, the sense that one lives by doing things one does not particularly want to do, by putting fears and doubts to one side, by weighing immediate comforts against the ability of larger, even intangible, comforts. It seemed to the nineteenth century admirable,

6

7

[4]A novel by American writer John O'Hara.
[5]A novel by American writer F. Scott Fitzgerald.
[6]A character in *The Great Gatsby*.

but not remarkable, that Chinese Gordon put on a clean white suit and held Khartoum against the Mahdi; it did not seem unjust that the way to free land in California involved death and difficulty and dirt. In a diary kept during the winter of 1846, an emigrating twelve-year-old named Narcissa Cornwall noted coolly: "Father was busy reading and did not notice that the house was being filled with strange Indians until Mother spoke about it." Even lacking any clue as to what Mother said, one can scarcely fail to be impressed by the entire incident: the father reading, the Indians filing in, the mother choosing the words that would not alarm, the child duly recording the event and noting further that those particular Indians were not, "fortunately for us," hostile. Indians were simply part of the *donnée.*[7]

In one guise or another, Indians always are. Again, it is a question of recognizing that anything worth having has its price. People who respect themselves are willing to accept the risk that the Indians will be hostile, that the venture will go bankrupt, that the liaison may not turn out to be one in which *every day is a holiday because you're married to me.* They are willing to invest something of themselves; they may not play at all, but when they do play, they know the odds.   8

That kind of self-respect is a discipline, a habit of mind that can never be faked but can be developed, trained, coaxed forth. It was once suggested to me that, as an antidote to crying, I put my head in a paper bag. As it happens, there is a sound physiological reason, something to do with oxygen, for doing exactly that, but the psychological effect alone is incalculable: it is difficult in the extreme to continue fancying oneself Cathy in *Wuthering Heights*[8] with one's head in a Food Fair bag. There is a similar case for all the small disciplines, unimportant in themselves; imagine maintaining any kind of swoon, commiserative or carnal, in a cold shower.   9

But those small disciplines are available only insofar as they represent larger ones. To say that Waterloo[9] was won on the playing fields of Eton[10] is not to say that Napoleon might have been saved by   10

---

[7]From the French, meaning "given"—that is, the raid was an accepted fact and life went on despite it.

[8]A reference to Catherine Earnshaw in Emily Bronte's *Wuthering Heights* (1848). In the novel, Cathy and the wild Heathcliff love each other with a passionate—and tragic—intensity.

[9]The scene of Napoleon's final defeat.

[10]A private preparatory school for British boys.

a crash program in cricket; to give formal dinners in the rain forest would be pointless did not the candlelight flickering on the liana call forth deeper, stronger disciplines, values instilled long before. It is a kind of ritual, helping us to remember who and what we are. In order to remember it, one must have known it.

To have that sense of one's intrinsic worth which constitutes 11
self-respect is potentially to have everything: the ability to discriminate, to love and to remain indifferent. To lack it is to be locked within oneself, paradoxically incapable of either love or indifference. If we do not respect ourselves, we are on the one hand forced to despise those who have so few resources as to consort with us, so little perception as to remain blind to our fatal weaknesses. On the other, we are peculiarly in thrall to everyone we see, curiously determined to live out—since our self-image is untenable—their false notions of us. We flatter ourselves by thinking this compulsion to please others an attractive trait: a gist for imaginative empathy, evidence of our willingness to give. Of *course* I will play Francesca[11] to your Paolo, Helen Keller[12] to anyone's Annie Sullivan: no expectation is too misplaced, no role too ludicrous. At the mercy of those we cannot but hold in contempt, we play roles doomed to failure before they are begun, each defeat generating fresh despair at the urgency of divining and meeting the next demand made upon us.

It is the phenomenon sometimes called "alienation from self." 12
In its advanced stages, we no longer answer the telephone, because someone might want something; that we could say *no* without drowning in self-reproach is an idea alien to this game. Every encounter demands too much, tears the nerves, drains the will, and the specter of something as small as an unanswered letter arouses such disproportionate guilt that answering it becomes out of the question. To assign unanswered letters their proper weight, to free us from the expectations of others, to give us back to ourselves—there lies the great, the singular power of self-respect. Without it, one eventually discovers the final turn of the screw: one runs away to find oneself, and finds no one at home.

[11]A thirteenth-century Italian woman seduced into an affair by her brother-in-law, Paolo.

[12]An American writer and lecturer, blind and deaf from infancy, who was taught to speak and read by her teacher, Annie Sullivan.

14

A CONCISE
GUIDE TO
DOCUMENTATION

In Chapter 12, you learned the importance of *documentation*—giving credit to the sources whose words and ideas you borrow in an essay (see page 566). That earlier discussion showed you how to document sources in informal papers. This chapter will show you how to use the documentation system of the Modern Language Association (MLA)[1] when citing sources in more formal papers.

The following discussion covers key features of the MLA system. For more detailed coverage, you may want to consult a recent composition handbook or the latest edition of the *MLA Handbook for Writers of Research Papers*. For a sample paper that uses MLA documentation, turn to the student essay on pages 583–88.

---

[1]MLA documentation is appropriate in papers written for humanities courses, such as your composition class. If you're writing a paper for a course in the social sciences (for example, psychology, economics, or sociology), your professor will probably expect you to use the citation format developed by the American Psychological Association (APA). For information about APA documentation, consult a composition handbook or the most recent edition of the *Publication Manual of the American Psychological Association.*

WHAT TO DOCUMENT

You may inadvertently fall into the trap of *plagiarizing*—passing off someone else's ideas as your own—if you're not sure when you need to acknowledge outside sources in an essay. To avoid plagiarism, you must provide documentation in the following situations:

- When you include a *word-for-word quotation* from a source.
- When you *summarize or restate in your own words* ideas or information from a source, unless that material is *commonly known* or is a *matter of historical or scientific record.*
- When you *combine a summary and a quotation.*

An important note: On the whole, you should try to state borrowed material in your own words. A string of quotations signals that you haven't sufficiently evaluated and distilled your sources. Use quotations sparingly; draw upon them only when they dramatically illustrate key points you want to make. Also, keep in mind that quotations won't, by themselves, make your case for you. You need to interpret and comment on them, showing how they support your points.

HOW TO DOCUMENT

The MLA documentation system uses the *parenthetic reference,* a brief note in parentheses inserted into the text after borrowed material. The parenthetic reference doesn't provide full bibliographic information, but it presents enough so that readers can turn to the Works Cited list (see page 726) at the end of the paper for complete information. If the method of documentation you learned in high school involved footnotes or endnotes, you will be happy to know that parenthetic documentation—currently the preferred method—is much easier to use. While it is now accepted by most college professors, be sure to check with your professors to determine their documentation preferences.

Whenever you quote or summarize material from an outside source, you must do two things: (1) *identify the author* and (2) *specify the page(s)* in your source on which the material appears. The author's name may be given *either* in a lead-in sentence (often called the *attribution) or* in the parentheses following the borrowed material. The page number *always* appears in parentheses. The examples that follow, using material from George Gallup's "The Faltering Family" (see page 467), illustrate the MLA documentation style. (If you like, turn to Gallup's piece and compare the documentation with the original.)

Using Parentheses Only

Nowadays, several alternative family lifestyles are common, but a generation ago, most families consisted of "a man and a woman who were married to each other and who produced children (usually two) and lived happily ever after" (Gallup 469).

It's clear that "we're confused...in our feelings about marriage and the family" (Gallup 475).

In the early 1980s, most women believed that being married and having children would offer them the best prospect of a satisfying life (Gallup 475).

Using Parentheses and Attributions

The pollster George Gallup, Jr., argues, "The basic feminist philosophy has filtered down to the grass roots..." (473).

Gallup believes that another factor contributing to change in the family has been the "power of feminist philosophy to permeate..." attitudes (473) and modify behavior.

Gallup states that most families find they need dual incomes to meet the escalating costs of raising children--expenses that are, in practice, almost three times greater than parents imagine (472–473).

Key Points to Remember

Take a moment to look again at the preceding examples and note the following points:

- The parenthetic reference is placed *immediately after* the borrowed material, at a natural pause in the sentence or at the end of the sentence.

- The parenthetic reference is placed *before* any *internal punctuation* (a comma or semicolon) as well as *before* any *terminal punctuation* (a period or question mark).
- When the author's name is provided in the attribution, the name is *not* repeated in the parentheses.
- The first time an author is referred to in an attribution, the author's *full name* is given; afterwards, only the *last name* is provided.
- Sometimes, to inform readers of an author's area of expertise, the person may be identified by profession *("pollster* George Gallup, Jr.,..."*)*, title, or affiliation.
- When the author's name is provided in the parentheses, only the last name is given.
- The page number comes directly after the author's name. (If the source is only one page long, only the author's name is needed.)
- There is no punctuation between the author's name and the page number.
- There is no *p.* or *page* preceding the page number.
- Words may be deleted from a quotation as long as the author's original meaning isn't changed. In such a case, three spaced periods—called an *ellipsis* (. . .)—are inserted in place of the deleted words. An ellipsis is not needed, however, when material is omitted from the start of a quotation.

Three Other Important Points

Here are three additional situations you may encounter when documenting sources.

1. More than one source by the same author.   When your paper includes references to more than one work by the same author, you must specify—either in the parentheses or in the attribution—the particular work being cited. You do this by providing the *title,* as well as the author's name and the page(s). As with the author's name, the title may be given in *either* the attribution *or* the parenthetic citation. Here are some examples:

In The Language and Thought of the Child, Jean Piaget states that "discussion forms the basis for a logical point of view" (240).

Piaget considers dialogue essential to the development of logical thinking (Language and Thought 240).

The Child's Conception of the World shows that young children think that the name of something can never change (Piaget 81).

Young children assume that everything has only one name and that no others are possible (Piaget, Child's Conception 81).

Notice that when a work is named in the attribution, the full title appears; when a title is given in the parenthetic citation, though, only the first few significant words appear. (However, don't use the ellipsis to indicate that some words have been omitted from the title; the ellipsis is used only when quoting a source.)

2. Long quotations. A quotation extending beyond four typed lines starts on a new line and is indented ten spaces from the left margin throughout. Since this so-called *block format* already indicates a quotation, quotation marks are unnecessary. Double-space the block quotation, as you do the rest of your paper. Don't leave space above or below the quotation. Long quotations, which should be used sparingly, require a lead-in. A lead-in that *isn't* a full sentence is followed by a comma, while a lead-in that *is* a full sentence (as in the accompanying example) is followed by a colon:

Gallup cites changed sexual mores as one reason for the decline of marriage:

> Clearly, attitudes have changed a great deal in just three decades. Teenagers have accepted the idea of premarital sex as the norm. In one recent national poll, 52 percent of girls and 66 percent of boys favored having sexual relations in their teens. Ironically, however, 46 percent of the teenagers thought that virginity in their future marital partner was fairly important. (471)

Notice that the page number appears in parentheses, just as in a short quotation. But in a long quotation, the parenthetic citation is placed two spaces *after* the period that ends the quotation.

3. Quoting or summarizing a source within a source. If you quote or summarize a *secondhand source* (someone whose ideas come to you only through another source), you need to make this clear. The parenthetic documentation should indicate "as quoted in" with the abbreviation *qtd. in:*

According to Sherman, "Recycling has, in several communities, created unanticipated expenses" (qtd. in Pratt 3–4).

Sherman explains that recycling can be surprisingly costly (qtd. in Pratt 3–4).

Your Works Cited list would include the source you actually read (Pratt), rather than the source you refer to secondhand (Sherman).

LIST OF WORKS CITED

A documented paper ends with a list of Works Cited, which includes only those sources you actually acknowledge in the paper. Placed on its own page, the Works Cited list provides the reader with full bibliographic information about the sources cited in the parenthetic references (see page 723). By referring to the Works Cited list that appears at the end of the student essay on page 588, you will notice the following:

- The list is organized alphabetically by authors' last names. Entries without an author are alphabetized by the first major word in the title (that is, not *A, An,* or *The*).
- Entries are not numbered.
- If an entry runs longer than one line, each additional line is indented five spaces. Entries are double-spaced with no extra space between entries.

Note: In *your* paper, the Works Cited list should be double-spaced— along with the rest of the paper—and placed at the end on a separate page.

Sample Works Cited Entries

Listed here are sample Works Cited entries for the most commonly used kinds of sources. Refer to these samples when you prepare your own Works Cited list, taking special care to reproduce the punctuation and spacing exactly. If you don't spot an entry for the kind of source you need to document, consult the *MLA Handbook* for more comprehensive examples.

Book With One Author

Yesley, Marjorie G. <u>Political Campaigns: A Retrospec-</u>
   <u>tive</u>. New York: Vintage, 1989.

Several Works by the Same Author

Reedy, George E. <u>The Presidency in Flux</u>. New York:
   Columbia UP, 1973.

---. <u>The Twilight of the Presidency</u>. New York: World,
   1970.

   If you use more than one work by the same author, list each book separately. Give the author's name in the first entry only; begin the entries for other books by that author with three hyphens followed by a period. Arrange the works alphabetically by title.

Book With Two or Three Authors

Beddoes, Richard, Stan Fischler, and Ira Gitler. <u>Hockey!</u>
   <u>The Story of the World's Fastest Sport</u>. Toronto:
   Collier-Macmillan, 1969.

Book With Four or More Authors

Dansker, Isadora, et al. <u>Geological Formations in New</u>
   <u>England</u>. Boston: Newtown, 1990.

   For a work with four or more authors, give only the first author's name followed by a comma and *et al.* (Latin for "and others").

Revised Edition of a Book

Fiedler, Leslie A. <u>Love and Death in the American Novel</u>.
   2nd ed. New York: Dell, 1966.

Book With an Editor or Translator

Jonson, Ben. <u>Epicoene</u>. Ed. L. A. Beaurline. Lincoln: U
   of Nebraska, 1966.

An Anthology or Compilation of Several Authors

Ghiselin, Brewster, ed. The Creative Process: A Sympo-
    sium. Berkeley: U of California P, 1952.

Section of an Anthology or Compilation of Several Authors

Shapero, Harold. "The Musical Mind." The Creative Pro-
    cess: A Symposium. Ed. Brewster Ghiselin. Berke-
    ley: U of California P, 1952. 49-53.

Use *UP,* as in *Columbia UP* and *U of California P,* to abbrevi-
ate the names of university presses.

Section or Chapter in a Book by One Author

Canin, Ethan. "The Year of Getting to Know Us." Emperor
    of the Air. New York: Harper, 1988. 21-43.

Book by an Institution or Corporation

Commission on Higher Education. Characteristics of
    Excellence in Higher Education: Standards for
    Accreditation. Philadelphia: Commission on Higher
    Education of the Middle States Association of Col-
    leges and Schools, 1982.

Article From a Weekly or Biweekly Magazine

"Short Takes." Publishers Weekly 22 Aug. 1986: 20.

Strobe, Talbot. "Why Kohl Is Right." Time 15 May 1989:
    26.

Article From a Monthly or Bimonthly Magazine

Steele, Shelby. "The Recoloring of Campus Life: Student
    Racism, Academic Pluralism, and the End of a Dream."
    Harper's Feb. 1989: 47-55.

Article From a Daily Newspaper

Bartlett, Sarah. "Why Wall Street's So Topsy-Turvy."
    New York Times 7 May 1989, natl. ed., sec. 4:1.

Editorial, Letter to the Editor, or Reply to a Letter

"Patience on Panama." Editorial. Philadelphia Inquirer
    12 May 1989, late ed., sec. 1: 22.

Article From a Scholarly Journal

Connors, Robert J. "Personal Writing Assignment." <u>College Composition and Communication</u> 38 (1987): 166–83.

Juneja, Renu. "The Trinidad Carnival: Ritual, Performance, Spectacle, and Symbol." <u>Journal of Popular Culture</u> 21.4 (1988): 87–90.

Some journals are paged continuously (the first example); the first issue of each year starts with page one, and each subsequent issue picks up where the previous one left off. For such journals, use numerals to indicate the volume number after the title, and then indicate the year in parentheses. Note that neither *volume* nor *vol.* is used. The article's page(s) appear at the end, separated from the year by a colon.

For a journal that pages each issue separately (the second example), use numerals to indicate the *volume and issue numbers;* separate the two with a period but leave no space after the period.

Television or Radio Program

"Colonial Days." <u>The United States and the Philippines: In Our Image</u>. Narr. Stanley Karnow. Part 1 of 3. PBS. WHYY-TV. Philadelphia. 8 May 1989.

Movie, Record, Videotape, Filmstrip, or Slide Program

<u>Field of Dreams</u>. Dir. Phil Alden Robinson. With Kevin Costner. Universal, 1989.

Personal Interview

Harrow, Morgan. Personal interview. 5 Aug. 1989.

Lecture

Kahn, Linda. "Resolving Family Conflicts." Lecture. Sociology 202, William Patterson College. Wayne, New Jersey. 10 Oct. 1989.

GLOSSARY

Abstract and concrete language refers to two different qualities of words. Abstract words and phrases convey concepts, qualities, emotions, and ideas that we can think and talk about but not actually see or experience directly. Examples of abstract words are *conservatism, courage, avarice, joy,* and *hatred.* Words or phrases whose meanings are directly seen or experienced by the senses are concrete terms. Examples of phrases using concrete words are *split-level house, waddling penguin,* and *short pink waitress uniform.*

Adequate—see *Evidence.*

Ad hominem **argument**—see *Logical fallacies.*

Analogy refers to an imaginative comparison between two subjects that seem to have little in common. Often a complex idea or topic can be made understandable by comparing it to a more familiar subject, and such an analogy can be developed over several paragraphs or even an entire essay. For example, to explain how the economic difficulties of farmers weaken an entire nation, a writer might create an analogy between failing farms and a cancer that slowly destroys a person's life.

Argumentation-persuasion tries to encourage readers to accept a writer's point of view on some controversial issue. In *argumentation,* a writer uses objective reasoning, facts, and hard evidence to demonstrate the soundness of a position. In *persuasion,* the writer uses appeals to the readers' emotions and value systems, often in the hope of encouraging them to take a specific action. Argumentation and persuasion are frequently used together in an essay. For example, a writer might argue for the construction of a highway through town by pointing out that the road would bring new business, create new jobs, and lighten traffic. The writer also might try to persuade readers to vote for a highway appropriations bill by appealing to their emotions, claiming that the highway would allow people to get home faster, thus giving them more time for family life and leisure activities. A whole essay can be organized around argumentation-persuasion, or an essay developed chiefly through another pattern may contain elements of argumentation-persuasion.

Assertion refers to the *thesis* of an *argumentation-persuasion* essay. The assertion, or *proposition,* is a point of view or opinion on a controversial issue or topic. The assertion cannot be merely a statement of a fact. Such statements as "Women still experience discrimination in the job market," "General Rabb would make an ideal mayor for our town," and "This university should devote more funds to raising the quality of the food services" are examples of assertions that could serve as theses for argumentation-persuasion essays.

Audience refers to a writer's intended readers. In planning the content and tone of an essay, you should identify your audience and consider its needs. How similar are the members of your audience to you in knowledge and point of view? What will they need to know for you to achieve your *purpose?* What *tone* will make them open to receiving your message? For example, if you were to write a description of a trip to Disney World, you would have to explain a lot more to an eighty-year-old grandmother who had never seen a theme park than to a young parent who has probably visited several. If you wrote about the high cost of clothing for an economics professor, you would choose a serious, analytic tone and supply statistical evidence for your points. If you write about the same topic for the college newspaper, you might use a tone tinged with humor and provide helpful hints on finding bargain clothing.

Begging the question—see *Logical fallacies.*

Brainstorming is a technique used in the *prewriting* stage. It helps you discover the limited subject you can successfully write about and also generates raw material—ideas and details—to develop that subject. In brainstorming, you allow your mind to play freely with the subject. You try to capture fleeting thoughts about it, no matter how random, minor, or tangential, and jot them down rapidly before they disappear from your mind.

Causal analysis—see *Cause-effect.*

Causal chain refers to a series of causes and effects, in which the result or effect of a cause becomes itself the cause of a further effect, and so on. For example, a person's alarm clock failing to buzz might begin a causal chain by causing the person to oversleep. Oversleeping then causes the person to miss the bus, and missing the bus causes the person to arrive late to work. Arriving late causes the person to miss an important phone call, which causes the person to lose a chance at a lucrative contract.

Cause-effect, sometimes called *causal analysis,* involves analyzing the reasons for or results of an event, action, decision, or phenomenon. Writers develop an essay through an analysis of causes whenever they attempt to answer such questions as "Why has this happened?" or "Why does this exist?" When writers explore such questions as "What happens or would happen if a certain change occurs?" or "What will happen if a condition continues?" their essays involve a discussion of effects. Some cause-effect essays concentrate on the causes of a situation, some focus on the effects, and others present both causes and effects. Causal analysis can be an essay's central pattern, or it can be used to help support a point in an essay developed primarily through another pattern.

Characteristics—see *Formal definition.*

Chronological sequence—see *Narrative sequence* and *Organization.*

Circularity is an error in *formal definition* resulting from using variations of the to-be-defined word in the definition. For example, "A scientific hypothesis is a hypothesis made by a scientist about the results of an experiment" is circular because the unknown term is used to explain itself.

Class—see *Formal definition.*

Coherence refers to the clear connection among the various parts of an essay. As a writer, you can draw upon two key strategies to make writing coherent. You can use a clear *organizational format* (for example, a chronological, spatial, emphatic, or simple-to-complex sequence). You can also provide *appropriate signaling* or *connecting devices* (transitions, bridging sentences, repeated words, synonyms, and pronouns).

Comparison-contrast means explaining the similarities and/or differences between events, objects, people, ideas, and so on. The comparison-contrast format can be used to meet a purely factual purpose ("This is how A and B are alike or different"). But usually writers use comparison-contrast to make a judgment about the relative merits of the subjects under discussion. Sometimes a writer will concentrate solely on similarities *or* differences. For instance, when writing about married versus single life, you would probably devote most of your time to discussing the differences between these lifestyles. Other times, comparison and contrast are found together. In an essay analyzing two approaches to U.S. foreign policy, you would probably discuss the similarities *and* the differences in the goals and methods characteristic of each approach. Comparison-contrast can be the dominant pattern in an essay, or it can help support a point in an essay developed chiefly through another pattern.

Conclusion refers to the one or more paragraphs that bring an essay to an end. Effective conclusions give the reader a sense of completeness and finality. Writers often use the conclusion as a place to reaffirm the *thesis* and to express a final thought about the subject. Methods of conclusion include summarizing main points, using a quotation, predicting an outcome, and recommending an action.

Conflict creates tension in the readers of a *narration*. It is produced by the opposition of characters or other forces in a story. Conflict can occur between individuals, between a person and society or nature, or within a person. Readers wonder how a conflict will be resolved and read on to find out.

Connecting devices signal the relationships among ideas in an essay. They help the reader follow the train of thought from sentence to sentence and from paragraph to paragraph. There are three types of connectives. *Transitions* are words that clarify flow of meaning. They can signal an additional or contrasting point, an enumeration of ideas, the use of an example, or other movement of ideas. *Linking sentences* summarize a point just made and then introduce a follow-up point. *Repeated words, synonyms,* and *pronouns* create a sense of flow by keeping important concepts in the mind of the reader.

Connotative and denotative language describe the ability of language to emphasize one or another aspect of a word's range of meaning. *Denotative language* stresses the dictionary meaning of words. *Connotative language* emphasizes the echoes of feeling that cluster around some words. For example, the terms *weep, bawl, break down,* and *sob* all denote the same thing: to cry. But they have different associations and call up different images. A writer employing the connotative resources of language would choose the term among these that suggested the appropriate image.

Controlling idea—see *Thesis.*

Deductive reasoning is a form of logical thinking in which general statements believed to be true are applied to specific situations or cases. The result of deduction is a conclusion or prediction about the specific situation. Deduction is often expressed in a three-step pattern called a *syllogism.* The first part of the syllogism is a general statement about a large class of items or situations, the *major premise.* The second part is the *minor premise,* a more limited statement about a specific item or case. The third part is the *conclusion,* drawn from the major premise, about that specific case or item. Deductive reasoning is very common in everyday thinking. For example, you might use deduction when car shopping:

In an accident, large cars are safer than small cars. (*major premise*)

The Turbo Titan is a large car. (*minor premise*)

In an accident, the Turbo Titan will be safer than a small car. (*conclusion*)

Definition explains the meaning of a word or concept. The brief formal definitions found in the dictionary can be useful if you need to clarify or restrict the meaning of a term used in an essay. In such cases, the definition is short and to the point. But you may also use an *extended definition* in an essay, taking several paragraphs, even the entire piece, to develop the meaning of a term. You may use extended definition to convey a personal slant on a well-known term, to refute a commonly held interpretation of a word, or to dissect a complex or controversial issue. Definition can be the chief method of development in an essay, or it can help support a point in an essay organized around another pattern.

Definition by negation is a method of defining a term by first explaining what the term is *not,* and then going on to explain what it is. For example, you might begin a critical essay about television with a definition by negation: "Television, far from being a medium that dispenses only light, insubstantial fare, actually disseminates a dangerously distorted view of family life." Definition by negation can provide a stimulating introduction to an essay.

Denotative language—see *Connotative and denotative language.*

Description involves the use of vivid word pictures to express what the five senses have experienced. The subject of a descriptive essay can be a person, a place, an object, or an event. Description can be the dominant pattern in an essay, or it can be used as a supplemental method in an essay developed chiefly through another pattern.

There are two main types of description. In an *objective description,* a writer provides details about a subject without conveying the emotions the subject arouses. For example, if you were involved in a traffic accident, your insurance agent might ask you to write an objective description of the events leading up to and during the crash. But in a *subjective description,* the writer's goal is to evoke in the reader the emotions felt during the experience. For example, in a cautionary letter to a friend who has a habit of driving dangerously, you might write a subjective description of your horrifyingly close call with death during a car accident.

Development—see *Evidence.*

Dialogue is the writer's way of directly presenting the exact words spoken by characters in a *narration.* By using dialogue, writers can convey people's individuality and also add drama and immediacy to an essay.

Directional process analysis—see *Process analysis.*

Division-classification refers to a logical method for analyzing a single subject or several related subjects. Though often used together in an essay, division and classification are separate processes. *Division* involves breaking a subject or idea into its component parts. For instance, the concept "an ideal vacation" could be divided according to its destination, accommodations, or cost. *Classification* involves organizing a number of related items into categories. For example, in an essay about the overwhelming flow of paper in our everyday lives, you might classify the typical kinds of mail most people receive: personal mail (letters, birthday cards, party invitations), business mail (bills, bank statements, charge-card receipts), and junk mail (flyers about bargain sales, solicitations to donate, contest announcements). Division-classification can be the dominant pattern in a paper, or it may be used to support a point in an essay organized chiefly around another pattern of development.

Dominant impression refers to the purpose of a descriptive essay. While some descriptive essays have a thesis, others do not; instead, they convey a dominant impression or main point. For example, one person writing a descriptive essay about New York City might use its architectural diversity as a focal point. Another person writing a description of Manhattan might concentrate on the overpowering sense of hustle and speed about everyone and everything in the city. Both writers would select only those details that supported their dominant impressions.

Dramatic license refers to the writer's privilege, when writing a narrative, to alter facts or details to strengthen the support of the *thesis* or *narrative point.* For example, a writer is free to flesh out the description of an event whose specific details may be partially forgotten or to modify or omit details of a narrative that do not contribute to the meaning the writer wishes to convey.

Either-or fallacy—see *Logical fallacies.*

Emphatic sequence—see *Organization.*

Ethos refers to a writer's reliability or credibility. Such an image of trustworthiness is particularly important to readers of an *argumentation-persuasion* essay or piece. Writers establish their *ethos* by using reason and logic, by being moderate in their appeals to emotions, by avoiding a hostile tone, and by demonstrating overall knowledgeability of the subject. The most effective argumentation-persuasion involves an interplay of *ethos, logos,* and *pathos.*

Etymology refers to the history of a word or term. All English words have their origins in other, often ancient, languages. Giving a brief etymology of a word can help a writer establish the context for developing an *extended definition* of the word. For example, the word *criminal* is derived from a Latin word meaning "accusation" or "accused." Today, our word *criminal* goes beyond the concept of "accused" to mean "guilty."

Evidence lends substance to a writer's main ideas and thus helps the reader to accept the writer's viewpoint. Evidence should meet several criteria. First of all, it should be *unified,* in the sense that all supporting ideas and details should relate directly to the key point the writer is making. Second, evidence should be *adequate;* there should be enough evidence to convince the reader to agree with the thesis. Third, evidence should be *specific;* that is, vivid and detailed rather than vague and general. Fourth, evidence must be *accurate* and not overstate or understate information. Fifth, evidence should be *representative,* relying on the typical rather than the atypical to make a point. The bulk of an essay is devoted to supplying evidence. Supporting the thesis with solid evidence is the third stage in the writing process.

Exemplification, at the heart of all effective writing, involves using concrete specifics to support generalizations. In exemplification, writers provide examples or instances that support or clarify broader statements. You might support the thesis statement "I have a close-knit family" by using such examples as the following: "We have a regular Sunday dinner at my grandmother's house with at least ten family members present"; "My sisters and brothers visit my parents every week"; "I spend so much time on the phone talking with my sisters that sometimes I have trouble finding time for my new college friends." Exemplification may be an essay's central pattern, or it may supplement an essay developed mainly around another pattern.

Extended definition—see *Definition.*

Fallacies—see *Logical fallacies.*

False analogy—see *Logical fallacies.*

Figures of speech are imaginative comparisons between two things usually thought of as dissimilar. Some major figures of speech are *simile, metaphor,* and *personification. Similes* are comparisons that use the signal words *like* or *as:* "Superman was as powerful as a locomotive." *Metaphors,* which do not use signal words, directly equate unlike things: "The boss is a tiger when it comes to landing a contract." "The high-powered pistons of the boxer's arms pummeled his opponent." *Personification* attributes human characteristics to inanimate things or nonhuman beings: "The angry clouds unleashed their fury on the town"; "The turtle shyly poked his head out of his shell."

First draft refers to the writer's first try at producing a basic, unpolished version of the whole essay. It is often referred to as the "rough" draft, and nothing about it is final or unchangeable. The process of writing the first draft often brings up new ideas or details. Writers sometimes break off writing the draft to *brainstorm* or *freewrite* as new ideas occur to them and then return to the draft with new inspiration. You shouldn't worry about spelling, grammar, or style in the first-draft stage; instead, you should keep focused on casting your ideas into sentence and paragraph form. Writing the first draft is the fifth stage in the writing process.

Flashback—see *Narrative sequence.*

Flashforward—see *Narrative sequence.*

Formal definition involves stating a definition in a three-part pattern of about one sentence in length. In presenting a formal definition, a writer puts the *term* in a *class* and then lists the *characteristics* that separate the term from other members of its class. For example, a formal definition of a word processor might be, "A word processor (term) is an electronic machine (class) that is used to write, edit, store, and produce typewritten documents (characteristics)." Writers often use a formal definition to prepare a reader for an extended definition that follows.

Freewriting is most often used during the *prewriting* stage to help writers generate ideas about a limited topic. To use this method, write nonstop for five or ten minutes about everything your topic brings to mind. Disregard grammar, spelling, and organization as you keep your pen and mind moving. Freewriting is similar to *brainstorming,* except that the result is a rambling, detail-filled paragraph rather than a list. Freewriting can also be used to generate ideas during later stages of the writing process.

Gender-biased language gives the impression that one sex is more important, powerful, or valuable than the other. When writing, you should work to replace such sexist language with *gender-neutral* or *nonsexist* terms that convey no sexual prejudice. First of all, try to avoid *sexist vocabulary* that demeans or excludes one of the sexes: *stud, jock, chick, fox,* and so on. Also, just as adult males should be called *men,* adult females should be referred to as *women,* not *girls.* And men shouldn't be empowered with professional and honorary titles (*President* Clinton) while professional women—such as congressional representatives—are assigned only personal titles (*Mrs.* Shroeder). Here are some examples of the way you can avoid words that exclude women: Change "chairman" to *chairperson*, "layman" to *layperson*, "congressman" to *congressional representative*, "workmen" to *workers*, the "average guy" to the *average person*. Second, be aware of the fact that indefinite singular nouns—those representing a general group of people consisting of both genders—can lead to *sexist pronoun use:* for example, "On *his* first day of school, a young child often experiences separation anxiety." This sentence excludes female children from consideration, although the situation being described applies equally to them. Third, recognize that indefinite pronouns like *anyone, each,* and *everybody* may also pave the way to sexist pronoun use. Although such pronouns often refer to a number of individuals, they're considered singular. So, wanting to be grammatically correct, you may write a sentence like the following: "Everybody wants *his* favorite candidate to win." The sentence, however, is sexist because *everybody* is certainly not restricted to men. One way to avoid this type of sexist construction is to use both male and female pronouns: "Everybody wants *his* or *her* favorite candidate to win." Another approach is to use *s/he* in place of *he*. A third possibility is to use the gender-neutral pronouns *they, their,* or *themselves:* "Everybody wants *their* favorite candidate to win." Be warned, though. Some people object to using these plural pronouns with singular indefinite pronouns, even though the practice is common in everyday speech. Two alternative strategies enable you to eliminate the need for *any* gender-marked singular pronouns. First, you can change singular general nouns or indefinite pronouns to their plural equivalents and then use nonsexist plural pronouns. For example, you may change "A *workaholic* feels anxious when *he* isn't busy" to "*Workaholics* feel anxious when *they're* not busy" and "*Everyone* in the room expressed *his* opinion freely" to "*Those* in the room expressed *their* opinions freely." Second, you can recast the sentence to omit the singular pronoun: For instance, you may change "A *manager* usually spends part of each day settling squabbles among *his* staff" to "A manager usually spends part of each day settling *staff squabbles*" and "No *one* wants *his* taxes raised" to "No one wants *to pay more taxes.*"

Hasty generalization—see *Logical fallacies.*

Inductive reasoning is a form of logical thinking in which specific cases and facts are examined to draw a wider-ranging conclusion. The result of inductive reasoning is a generalization that is applied to situations or cases similar to the ones examined. Induction is typical of scientific investigation and of everyday thinking. For example, on the basis of specific experiences, you may have concluded that when you feel chilly in a room where everyone else is comfortable, you are likely to develop a cold and fever in the next day or two. In an *argumentation-persuasion* essay, the conclusion reached by induction would be your *assertion* or *thesis*.

Inference is the term for a conclusion based on *inductive reasoning*. Because the reasoning behind specific cases may not be simple, there is usually an element of uncertainty in an inductive conclusion. Choosing the correct explanation for specific cases is a matter of carefully weighing and selecting alternative conclusions.

Informational process analysis—see *Process analysis*.

Introduction refers to the first paragraph or several paragraphs of an essay. The introduction serves three purposes. It informs readers of the general subject of the essay, it catches their attention, and it presents the controlling idea or thesis. The methods of introducing an essay include the use of an anecdote, a quotation or surprising statistic or fact, and questions. Or you may narrow your discussion down from a broad subject to a more limited one.

Irony occurs when a writer or speaker implies (rather than states directly) a discrepancy or incongruity of some kind. *Verbal irony,* which is often tongue-in-cheek, involves a discrepancy between the literal words and what's actually meant ("I know you must be unhappy about receiving the highest grade in the course"). If the ironic comment is designed to be hurtful or insulting, it qualifies as *sarcasm* ("Congratulations! You failed the final exam"). In *situational irony,* the circumstances are themselves incongruous. For example, although their constitutional rights were violated when the federal government detained them in internment camps, Japanese-Americans nevertheless played American football, sang American songs, and saluted the American flag during their imprisonment.

Journal writing is a form of prewriting in which writers make daily entries in a private journal, much as they would in a diary. Whether they focus on one topic or wander freely, journal writers jot down striking incidents, images, and ideas encountered in the course of a day. Such journal material can produce ideas for future essays.

Logical fallacies are easily committed mistakes in reasoning that writers must avoid, especially when writing *argumentation-persuasion* essays. There are many kinds of logical fallacies. Here are several:

    Ad hominem argument occurs when someone attacks another person's point of view by criticizing that person, not the issue. Often called "mudslinging," *ad hominem* arguments try to invalidate a person's ideas by revealing unrelated, past or present, personal or ethical flaws. For example, to claim a person cannot govern the country well because it can be proven he or she has little sense of humor is to use an *ad hominem* argument.

Begging the question is a fallacy in which the writer assumes the truth of something that needs to be proven. Imagine a writer argues the following: "A law should be passed requiring dangerous pets like German shepherds and Doberman pinschers to be restrained by fences, leashes, and muzzles." Such an argument begs the question since it assumes readers will automatically accept the view that such dogs are indeed dangerous.

Either-or fallacies occur when it's argued that a complex situation can be resolved in only one of two possible ways. Here's an example: "If the administration doesn't grant striking professors more money, the college will never be able to attract outstanding teachers in years ahead." Such an argument oversimplifies matters. Excellent teachers might be attracted to a college for a variety of reasons, not just because of good salaries: the school's location, research facilities, reputation for scholarship, hardworking students, and so on.

False analogy erroneously suggests that because two things are alike in some regards, they are similar in all ways. In the process, significant differences between the two are disregarded. If you argue that a woman prosecuting a rapist is subjected to a second rape in court, you're guilty of a false analogy. As embarrassing, painful, and hurtful as the court proceedings may be, the woman is not physically assaulted, as she was when she was raped. Also, as difficult as her decision to seek justice might be, she's in court by choice and not against her will.

Hasty generalizations are unsound *inductive inferences* based on too few instances of a behavior, situation, or process. For example, it would be a hasty generalization to conclude that you're allergic to a food such as curry because you once ate it and became ill. There are several other possible explanations for your illness, and only repetitions of this experience or a lab test could prove conclusively that you're allergic to this spice.

Non sequiturs are faulty conclusions about cause and effect. Here's an example: "Throughout this country's history, most physicians have been male. Women apparently have little interest in becoming doctors." The faulty conclusion accords one factor—the possible vocational preferences of women—the status of sole cause. The conclusion fails to consider pressures on women to devote themselves to homemaking and to avoid an occupation sexually stereotyped as "masculine."

Post hoc thinking results when it's presumed that one event caused another just because it occurred first. For instance, if your car broke down the day after you lent it to your brother, you would be committing the *post hoc* fallacy if you blamed him, unless you knew he did something to your car's engine.

Questionable authority, revealed by such phrases as "studies show" and "experts claim," undercuts a writer's credibility. Readers become suspicious of such vague and unsubstantial appeals to authority. Writers should demonstrate the reliability of their sources by citing them specifically.

Red herring arguments are deliberate attempts to focus attention on a peripheral matter rather than examine the merits of the issue under discussion. Imagine that a local environmental group advocates stricter controls for employees at a nearby chemical plant. The group points out that plant employees are repeatedly exposed to high levels of toxic chemicals. If you respond, "Many of the employees are illegal aliens and shouldn't be allowed to take jobs from native-born townspeople," you're throwing in a red herring. By bringing in immigration policies, you sidetrack attention from the matter at hand: the toxic level to which plant employees—illegal aliens or not—are exposed.

Logos is a major factor in creating an effective argument. It refers to the soundness of *argumentation,* as created by the use of facts, statistics, information, and commentary by authoritative sources. The most effective arguments involve an interplay among *logos, pathos,* and *ethos.*

Major premise—see *Deductive reasoning.*

Minor premise—see *Deductive reasoning.*

MLA documentation is the system developed by the Modern Language Association for citing sources in a paper. When you quote or summarize source material, you must do two things within your paper's text: (1) identify the author and (2) specify the pages on which the material appears. You may provide the author's name in a lead-in sentence or within parentheses following the borrowed material; the page number always appears in parentheses, inserted in the text after the borrowed material. The material in the parentheses is called a *parenthetic reference.* A paper using MLA documentation ends with a *Works Cited* list, which includes only those sources actually acknowledged in the paper. Entries are organized alphabetically by authors' last names. Entries without an author are alphabetized by the first major word in the title.

Narration means recounting an event or a series of related events to make a point. Narration can be an essay's principal pattern of development, or it can be used to supplement a paper organized primarily around another pattern. For instance, to persuade readers to avoid drug use, a writer might use the narrative pattern by recounting the story of an abuser's addiction and recovery.

Narrative point refers to the meaning the writer intends to convey to a reader by telling a certain story. This narrative point might be a specific message, or it might be a feeling about the situation, people, or place of the story. This underlying meaning is achieved by presenting details that support it and eliminating any that are nonessential. For example, in an essay about friendship, a writer's point might be that friendships change when one of the friends acquires a significant partner of the opposite sex. The writer would focus on the details of how her close female friend had less time for her, changed their usual times of getting together, and confided in her less. The writer would omit judgments of the friend's choice of boyfriend and her friend's declining grades because these details, while real for the writer, would distract the reader from the essay's narrative point.

Narrative sequence refers to the order in which a writer recounts events. When you follow the order of the events as they happened, you're using *chronological sequence*. This sequence, in which you begin at the beginning and end with the last event, is the most basic and commonly used narrative sequence. If you interrupt this flow to present an event that happened before the beginning of the narrative sequence, you're employing a *flashback*. If you skip ahead to an event later than the one that comes next in your narrative, you're using the *flashforward* technique.

Non sequiturs—see *Logical fallacies.*

Objective description—see *Description.*

One-side-at-a-time method refers to one of the two techniques for organizing a *comparison-contrast* essay. In using this method, a writer discusses all the points about one of the compared and contrasted subjects before going on to the other. For example, in an essay titled "Single or Married?" a writer might first discuss single life in terms of amount of independence, freedom of career choice, and companionship. Then the writer would, within reason, discuss married life in terms of these same three subtopics. The issues the writer discusses in each half of the essay would be identical and presented in the same order. See also *Point-by-point method.*

Organization refers to the process of arranging evidence to support a thesis in the most effective way. When organizing, a writer decides what ideas come first, next, and last. In *chronological* sequence, details are arranged according to occurrence in time. In *spatial* sequence, details appear in the order in which they occur in space. In *emphatic* order, ideas are sequenced according to importance, with the most significant, outstanding, or convincing evidence being reserved for last. In *simple-to-complex* order, easy-to-grasp material is presented before more-difficult-to-comprehend information. Organizing is the fourth stage of the writing process.

Outlining involves making a formal plan before writing a *first draft*. Writing an outline helps you determine whether your supporting evidence is logical and adequate. As you write, you can use the outline to keep yourself on track. Many writers use the indentation system of Roman numerals, letters, and Arabic numbers to outline; sometimes writers use a less formal system.

Paradox refers to a statement that seems impossible, contrary to common sense, or self-contradictory, yet that can—after consideration—be seen to be plausible or true. For example, Oscar Wilde produced a paradox when he wrote "When the gods wish to punish us, they answer our prayers." The statement doesn't contradict itself because often, Wilde believes, that which we wish for turns out to be the very thing that will bring us the most pain.

Parenthetic reference—see *MLA documentation.*

Pathos refers to the emotional power of an *argumentation-persuasion* essay. By appealing to the needs, values, and attitudes of readers and by using *connotative language,* writers can increase the chances that readers will come to agree with the ideas in an essay. Although *pathos* is an important element of persuasion, such emotional appeals should reinforce rather than replace reason. The most effective argumentation-persuasion involves an interplay among *pathos, logos,* and *ethos.*

Plan of development refers to a technique whereby the writer supplies the reader with a brief map of the main points to be covered in an essay. If used, the plan of development occurs as part of the *thesis* or in a sentence following the thesis. In it, the main ideas are mentioned in the order in which they'll appear in the supporting paragraphs. Longer essays and term papers usually need a plan of development to maintain unity, but shorter papers may do without one.

Point-by-point method refers to one of the two techniques for organizing a *comparison-contrast* essay. A writer using this method moves from one aspect of one subject to the same aspect of another subject before going on to the second aspect of each subject. For example, in an essay titled "Single or Married?" a writer might first discuss the amount of independence a person has when single and when married. Then, the writer might go on to discuss how much freedom of career choice a person has when single and when married. Finally, the writer might discuss, in turn, the amount of companionship available in each of the two life-styles. See also *One-side-at-a-time method.*

Point of view refers to the perspective a writer chooses when writing about a subject. If you narrate events as you experience them, you're using the *first-person* point of view. You might say, for example, "*I* noticed jam on the child's collar and holes in her shirt." If you relate the events from a distance—as if you observed them but did not experience them personally—you're using the *third-person* point of view, for instance, "Jam splotched the child's collar, and her shirt had several holes in it." The point of view should be consistent throughout an essay.

Post hoc thinking—see *Logical fallacies.*

Prewriting is the first stage of the writing process. During prewriting, you jot down rough ideas about your subject without yet moving to writing a draft of your essay. Your goals at this stage are to (1) understand the boundaries of the assignment, (2) discover the limited subject you could write about, (3) generate raw material about the limited subject, and (4) organize the raw material into a very rough *scratch outline*. If you keep in mind that prewriting is "unofficial," it can be a low-pressure, even enjoyable activity.

Process analysis refers to writing that explains the steps involved in doing something or the sequence of stages in an event or behavior. There are two types of process analysis. In *directional process analysis*, readers are shown how to do something step by step. Cookbook recipes, tax form instructions, and how-to books are some typical uses of directional process analysis. In *informational process analysis*, the writer explains how something is done or occurs, without expecting the reader to attempt the process. "A Senator's Road to Political Power," "How a Bee Makes Honey," and "How a Convict Gets Paroled" would be titles of essays developed through informational process analysis. Process analysis can be the dominant mode in an essay, as in these examples, or it may help make a point in an essay developed chiefly through another pattern. For example, in a cause-effect essay that explores the impact of the two-career family, process analysis might be used to explain how parents arrange for day care.

Proofreading involves rereading a final draft carefully to catch any errors in spelling, grammar, punctuation, or typing that have slipped by. While such errors are minor, a significant number of them can seriously weaken the effectiveness of an essay. Proofreading is the last stage in the writing process.

Proposition—see *Assertion.*

Purpose is the reason a writer has for preparing a particular essay. Usually, writers frame their purposes in terms of the effect they wish to have on their *audience*. They may wish to explore the personal meaning of a subject or experience, explain an idea or process, provide information, influence opinion, or entertain. Many essays combine purposes, with one purpose predominating and providing the essay's focus.

Red herring argument—see *Logical fallacies.*

Refutation is an important strategy in *argumentation-persuasion*. In refutation, writers acknowledge that there are opposing views on the subject under discussion and then go on to do one of two things. Sometimes they may admit that the opposing views are somewhat valid but assert that their own position has more merit and devote their essay to demonstrating that merit. For example, a writer might assert, "Business majors often find interesting and lucrative jobs. However, in the long run, liberal arts graduates have many more advantages in the job market because the breadth of their background helps them think better, learn faster, and communicate more effectively." This writer would concentrate on proving the advantages that liberal arts graduates have. At other times, writers may choose to argue actively against an opposing position by dismantling that view point by point. Such refutation of opposing views can strengthen the writer's own arguments.

Repeated words, synonyms, and pronouns—see *Connecting devices.*

Revision means, literally, "reseeing" a *first draft* with a fresh eye, as if the writer had not actually prepared the draft. When revising, you move from more global issues (like clarifying meaning and organization) to more specific matters (like fine-tuning sentences and word choice). While revising, you make whatever changes are necessary to increase the essay's effectiveness. You might strengthen your thesis, resequence paragraph order, or add more transitions. Such changes often make the difference between mediocre and superior writing. Revision, itself a multi-stage process, is the last stage of the writing process.

Satire is a humorous form of social criticism usually aimed at society's institutions or human behavior. Often irreverent as well as witty, satire is serious in purpose: to point out evil, injustice, and absurdity and bring about change through an increase in awareness. Satire ranges widely in tone: it may be gentle or biting; it may sarcastically describe a real situation or use fictional characters and events to spoof reality. Satire often makes use of *irony.* Examples of essays using satire in this book include Stephen Leacock's "How to Live to Be 200" and Jonathan Swift's "A Modest Proposal."

Scratch outline refers to your first informal plan for an essay, devised at the end of the *prewriting* stage. In making a scratch outline, you select ideas and details from your raw material for inclusion in your essay and discard the rest. You also arrange these ideas in an order that makes sense and that will help you achieve your *purpose.* A scratch outline is tentative and flexible, and can be reshaped as needed.

Sensory description vividly evokes the sights, smells, taste, sounds, and physical feelings of a scene or event. For example, if a writer carefully chooses words and images, readers can see the vibrant reds and oranges of falling leaves, taste the sourness of an underripe grapefruit, hear the growling of motorcycles as a gang sweeps through a town, smell the spicy aroma of a grandmother's homemade tomato soup, and feel the pulsing pain of a jaw after Novocain wears off. Sensory description is particularly important in writing *description* or *narration.*

Sentence variety adds interest to the style of an essay or paragraph. In creating sentence variety, writers mix different kinds of sentences and sentence patterns. For example, you might vary the way your sentences open or intersperse short sentences with long ones, simple sentences with complex ones. Repetitive sentence patterns tend to make readers lose interest.

Spatial sequence—see *Organization.*

Specific—see *Evidence.*

Stipulative definition is a way of restricting a term for the purposes of discussion. Many words have multiple meanings that can get in the way of clarity when a writer is creating an *extended definition.* For example, you might stipulate the following definition of *foreign car:* "While many American automobiles use parts or even whole engines made by foreign car manufacturers, for the purposes of discussion, 'foreign car' refers only to those automobiles designed and manufactured wholly by a company based in another country. By this definition, a European vehicle made in Pennsylvania is *not* a foreign car."

Subjective description—see *Description.*

Support—see *Evidence.*

Syllogism—see *Deductive reasoning.*

Term—see *Formal definition.*

Thesis is the central idea in any essay, usually expressed in a one- or two-sentence *thesis statement.* Writers accomplish two things by providing a thesis statement in an essay: they indicate the essay's limited subject and express an attitude about that subject. Also called the *controlling idea,* the thesis statement consists of a particular slant, angle, or point of view about the limited subject. Stating the thesis is the second stage of the writing process.

Tone conveys your attitude toward yourself, your purpose, your topic, and your readers. As in speaking, tone in writing may be serious, playful, sarcastic, and so on. Generally, readers detect tone more by how you say something (that is, through your sentence structure and word choice) than by what you say.

Topic sentence is the term for the sentence(s) that convey the main idea of a paragraph. Such sentences are often, but not always, found at the start of a paragraph. They provide a statement of the subject to be discussed and an indication of the writer's attitude toward that subject. Writers usually concern themselves with topic sentences during the writing of the first draft, the fifth stage of the writing process.

Transitions—see *Connecting devices.*

Unified—see *Evidence.*

Works Cited—see *MLA documentation.*

ACKNOWLEDGMENTS

Cofer, Judith Ortiz, "A Partial Remembrance of a Puerto Rican Childhood." Reprinted with permission from the publisher of *Silent Dancing: A Partial Remembrance of a Puerto Rican Childhood,* Houston: Arte Publico Press-University of Houston, 1990.

Cole, K. C., "Entropy." From *The New York Times,* March 18, 1982. Copyright © 1982 by The New York Times Company. Reprinted by permission.

Cowley, Geoffrey, "Why a Disaster Brings Out the Best in People." From *Newsweek,* November 6, 1989 and © 1989, Newsweek, Inc. All rights reserved. Reprinted by permission.

Curtis, Patricia, "The Argument Against Animal Experimentation." From *The New York Times,* December 31, 1978. Copyright © 1978 by The New York Times Company. Reprinted by permission.

Didion, Joan, "In Bed." From *The White Album* by Joan Didion. Copyright © 1979 by Joan Didion. Reprinted by permission of Farrar, Straus & Giroux, Inc. "On Self-Respect" from *Slouching Towards Bethlehem* by Joan Didion. Copyright © 1961, 1968 by Joan Didion. Reprinted by permission of Farrar, Straus & Giroux, Inc.

Dillard, Annie, "In the Jungle." From *Teaching a Stone to Talk* by Annie Dillard. Copyright © 1982 by Annie Dillard. Reprinted by permission of HarperCollins Publishers, Inc.

Ehrenreich, Barbara, "What I've Learned From Men." Reprinted by permission of *Ms. Magazine,* © 1985.

Gallup, George, Jr., "The Faltering Family." Pages 113–123 from *Forecast 2000* by George Gallup, Jr., with William Proctor. Copyright © 1984 by George Gallup, Jr. Reprinted by permission of William Morrow & Company, Inc.

Goldstein, Janet Mendell, "The Quick Fix Society." Reprinted by permission of the author.

Hentoff, Nat, "Free Speech on Campus." Reprinted by permission of the author.

Hubbell, Sue, "The Beekeeper." From the *New York Times,* August 2, 1984. Copyright © 1984 by The New York Times Company. Reprinted by permission.

Hughes, Langston, "Salvation." From *The Big Sea* by Langston Hughes. Copyright © 1940 by Langston Hughes. Renewal copyright © 1968 by Arna Bontemps and George Houston Bass. Reprinted by permission of Hill and Wang, a division of Farrar, Straus & Giroux, Inc.

Jacoby, Susan, "Common Decency." From the *New York Times,* May 19, 1991. Copyright © 1991 by The New York Times Company. Reprinted by permission.

Johnson, Beth, "Our Drug Problem." Reprinted by permission of Trend Publications, 31 Price's Lane, Moylan, PA 19065.

King, Martin Luther, Jr., "Where Do We Go From Here: Community or Chaos?" and "The World House." Reprinted by arrangement with The Heirs to the Estate of Martin Luther King, Jr., c/o Joan Dave Agency as agent for the proprietor. Copyright 1967 by Martin Luther King, Jr.

Kline, Ron, "A Scientist: 'I Am the Enemy.'" Reprinted with permission of the author.

Kozol, Jonathan, "Are the Homeless Crazy?" From *Rachel and Her Children: Homeless Families in America,* by Jonathan Kozol. Copyright © 1991 by Jonathan Kozol. Reprinted by permission of Crown Publishers, Inc.

Liu, Sophronia, "So Tsi-Fai." Reprinted by permission of the author.

Marzollo, Jean, "My Pistol-Packing Kids." From *Parents Magazine,* January 1983. Copyright © 1983 by Jean Marzollo. Reprinted by permission of Jean Marzollo.

McClintock, Ann, "Propaganda Techniques in Today's Advertising." Reprinted by permission of the author.

Mitford, Jessica, "The American Way of Death." Reprinted by permission of Jessica Mitford. All rights reserved. Copyright © 1963, 1978 by Jessica Mitford.

Naylor, Gloria, "Mommy, What Does 'Nigger' Mean?" From the *New York Times,* February 20, 1986. Copyright © 1986 by The New York Times Company. Reprinted by permission.

Nilsen, Alleen Pace, "Sexism and Language." From "Sexism as Shown Through the English Vocabulary," from *Sexism and Language* by Alleen Pace Nilsen, Haig Bosmajian, H. Lee Gershuny, and Julia P. Stanley. Copyright 1977 by the National Council of Teachers of English. Reprinted with permission.

Nizer, Louis, "Low-Cost Drugs for Addicts?" From *The New York Times,* June 8, 1986. Copyright © 1986 by The New York Times Company. Reprinted by permission.

Orwell, George, "Shooting an Elephant." From *Shooting an Elephant and Other Essays* by George Orwell. Copyright 1950 by Sonia Brownell Orwell and renewed 1978 by Sonia Pitt-Rivers. Reprinted by permission of Harcourt Brace & Company.

Paglia, Camille, "Rape: A Bigger Danger Than Feminists Know." Reprinted by permission of the author.

Parks, Gordon, "Flavio's Home." From *Voices in the Mirror* by Gordon Parks. Copyright © 1990 by Gordon Parks. Used by permission of Doubleday, a division of Bantam Doubleday Dell Publishing Group, Inc.

Postman, Neil, "Future Shlock." From *Conscientious Objections* by Neil Postman. Copyright © 1988 by Neil Postman. Reprinted by permission of Alfred A. Knopf, Inc.

Raspberry, William, "The Handicap of Definition." © 1982, Washington Post Writers Group. Reprinted with permission.

Rego, Caroline, "The Fine Art of Complaining." Reprinted with permission of the author.

Roberts, Paul, "How to Say Nothing in 500 Words." From *Understanding English* by Paul Roberts. Copyright © 1958 by Paul Roberts. Copyright renewed. Reprinted by permission of HarperCollins Publishers, Inc.

Rodriguez, Richard, "Workers." From *Hunger of Memory* by Richard Rodriguez. Copyright © 1982 by Richard Rodriguez. Reprinted by permission of David R. Godine, Publisher.

Sanders, Scott Russell, "The Men We Carry in Our Minds." Copyright © 1984 by Scott Russell Sanders; first appeared in *Milkweed* Chronicle; reprinted by permission of the author and Virginia Kidd, Literary Agent.

Tannen, Deborah, "Sex, Lies, and Conversation." From *You Just Don't Understand* by Deborah Tannen, Ph.D. Copyright © 1990 by Deborah Tannen, Ph.D. By permission of William Morrow & Company, Inc.

Theroux, Phyllis, "The Worry Factor." Copyright © 1981 by Phyllis Theroux, from *Night Lights* by Phyllis Theroux. Used by permission of Viking Penguin, a division of Penguin Books USA Inc.

Thomas, Lewis, "The Lie Detector." Copyright © 1980 by Lewis Thomas, from *Late Night Thoughts on Listening to Mahler's Ninth* by Lewis Thomas. Used by permission of Viking Penguin, a division of Penguin Books USA Inc.

Thurber, James, "University Days." Copyright © 1933, 1961 by James Thurber. From *My Life and Hard Times,* published by HarperCollins.

Twain, Mark, "The Damned Human Race." From *Letters from the Earth by Mark Twain,* edited by Bernard DeVoto. Copyright © 1938, 1944, 1946, 1959, 1962 by The Mark Twain Company. Copyright renewed. Reprinted by permission of HarperCollins Publishers, Inc.

INDEX

To the Student
From the Authors

By now, you realize that almost all writing goes through a series of revisions. The same was true for this book. *The Macmillan Reader*, fourth edition, has been reworked a number of times, with each revision taking into account students' and instructors' reactions to drafts of material.

Before we prepare the fifth edition of *The Macmillan Reader*, we'd like to know how you, the student, feel about the book. We hope you'll spend a few minutes completing this brief questionnaire. You can be sure that your responses will help shape subsequent editions. Please send your completed survey to the College English Editor, Allyn and Bacon Publishing Company, 866 Third Avenue, New York, NY 10022.

Thanks for your time.

College _____ City and state _____

Course title_____ Instructor _____

DESCRIPTION	I really liked it.	It was okay.	I didn't like it.	I didn't read it.
Parks, *Flavio's Home*	____	____	____	____
Baker, *In My Day*	____	____	____	____
Dillard, *In the Jungle*	____	____	____	____
White, *Once More to the Lake*	____	____	____	____
Cofer, *A Partial Remembrance of a Puerto Rican Childhood*	____	____	____	____

NARRATION

Angelou, *Grandmother's Victory*	____	____	____	____
Orwell, *Shooting an Elephant*	____	____	____	____

	I really liked it.	It was okay.	I didn't like it.	I didn't read it.
Watkins, *Little Deaths*	____	____	____	____
Hughes, *Salvation*	____	____	____	____
Liu, *So Tsi-Fai*	____	____	____	____

EXEMPLIFICATION

Carey, *Things Fall Apart*	____	____	____	____
Nilsen, *Sexism and Language*	____	____	____	____
Thurber, *University Days*	____	____	____	____
Postman, *Future Shlock*	____	____	____	____
Ehrenreich, *What I've Learned From Men*	____	____	____	____

DIVISION-CLASSIFICATION

Viorst, *Friends, Good Friends—and Such Good Friends*	____	____	____	____
Zinsser, *College Pressures*	____	____	____	____
Sanders, *The Men We Carry in Our Minds*	____	____	____	____
McClintock, *Propaganda Techniques in Today's Advertising*	____	____	____	____
Goldstein, *The Quick Fix Society*	____	____	____	____

PROCESS ANALYSIS

Leacock, *How to Live to Be 200*	____	____	____	____
Hubbell, *The Beekeeper*	____	____	____	____
Mitford, *The American Way of Death*	____	____	____	____
Roberts, *How to Say Nothing in 500 Words*	____	____	____	____
Rego, *The Fine Art of Complaining*	____	____	____	____

COMPARISON-CONTRAST	I really liked it.	It was okay.	I didn't like it.	I didn't read it.
Carson, *A Fable for Tomorrow*	___	___	___	___
Britt, *That Lean and Hungry Look*	___	___	___	___
Rodriguez, *Workers*	___	___	___	___
Tannen, *Sex, Lies, and Conversation*	___	___	___	___
Chapman, *The Prisoner's Dilemma*	___	___	___	___

CAUSE-EFFECT

Gallup, *The Faltering Family*	___	___	___	___
Cowley, *Why a Disaster Brings Out the Best in People*	___	___	___	___
Walker, *Beauty: When the Other Dancer Is the Self*	___	___	___	___
Thomas, *The Lie Detector*	___	___	___	___
Kozol, *Are the Homeless Crazy?*	___	___	___	___

DEFINITION

Cole, *Entropy*	___	___	___	___
Brady, *Why I Want a Wife*	___	___	___	___
Naylor, *"Mommy, What Does 'Nigger' Mean?"*	___	___	___	___
Winn, *TV Addiction*	___	___	___	___
Raspberry, *The Handicap of Definition*	___	___	___	___

ARGUMENTATION-PERSUASION

Marzollo, *My Pistol-Packing Kids*	___	___	___	___
Yuhfill, *Let's Tell the Story of All America's Cultures*	___	___	___	___
Twain, *The Damned Human Race*	___	___	___	___
Swift, *A Modest Proposal*	___	___	___	___

	I really liked it.	It was okay.	I didn't like it.	I didn't read it.
Hentoff, *Free Speech on Campus*	___	___	___	___
Paglia, *Rape: A Bigger Danger Than Feminists Know*	___	___	___	___
Jacoby, *Common Decency*	___	___	___	___
Kline, *A Scientist: "I Am the Enemy"*	___	___	___	___
Curtis, *The Argument Against Animal Experimentation*	___	___	___	___
Nizer, *Low-Cost Drugs for Addicts?*	___	___	___	___
Johnson, *Our Drug Problem*	___	___	___	___

FOR FURTHER READING

Woolf, *The Death of the Moth*	___	___	___	___
Woolf, *Professions for Women*	___	___	___	___
King, *Where Do We Go From Here: Community or Chaos?*	___	___	___	___
King, *The World House*	___	___	___	___
Didion, *In Bed*	___	___	___	___
Didion, *On Self-Respect*	___	___	___	___

Any general comments or suggestions?

Name_____ Date_____

Address_____

THANKS AGAIN!